Jan '11

HANDBOOK OF TECHNOLOGY AND INNOVATION MANAGEMENT

HANDBOOK OF TECHNOLOGY AND INNOVATION MANAGEMENT

Edited by

SCOTT SHANE
Case Western Reserve University

A John Wiley and Sons, Ltd., Publication

Other Wiley Editorial Offices

John Wiley & Sons Inc., 111 River Street, Hoboken, NJ 07030, USA

Jossey-Bass, 989 Market Street, San Francisco, CA 94103-1741, USA

Wiley-VCH Verlag GmbH, Boschstr. 12, D-69469 Weinheim, Germany

John Wiley & Sons Australia Ltd, 42 McDougall Street, Milton, Queensland 4064, Australia

John Wiley & Sons (Asia) Pte Ltd, 2 Clementi Loop #02-01, Jin Xing Distripark, Singapore 129809

John Wiley & Sons Canada Ltd, 6045 Freemont Blvd, Mississauga, Ontario, L5R 4J3, Canada

Wiley also publishes its books in a variety of electronic formats. Some content that appears
in print may not be available in electronic books.

Library of Congress Cataloging-in-Publication Data

Handbook of technology and innovation management / edited by Scott Shane.
    p. cm.
  Includes bibliographical references and index.
  ISBN 978-1-4051-2791-2 (cloth : alk. paper)
1. Technological innovations – Management. 2. Knowledge management. I.
Shane, Scott Andrew, 1964-
    HD45.H295 2008
    658.4'062 – dc22
            2008022824

British Library Cataloguing in Publication Data

A catalogue record for this book is available from the British Library

ISBN 978-1-4051-2791-2 (H/B)

Typeset in 10/12 Baskerville by Laserwords Private Limited, Chennai, India
Printed and bound in Great Britain by CPI Antony Rowe, Chippenham, Wiltshire

Contents

Preface

When Rosemary Nixon, an editor for Blackwell Publishing, now part of John Wiley & Sons, approached me in 2003 to edit a *Handbook on the Management of Technological Innovation*, I quickly agreed. The field of management of technology had undergone major changes in the previous two decades, with an increased focus on technology strategy, entrepreneurship, and product development, and I thought that the time was right for a handbook that provided some order to the plethora of new arguments and findings. Moreover, many of the names associated with cutting edge research in this area were not leading scholars two decades earlier – frankly, many of them were not even scholars 20, or even 10, years before. And I thought that a book that collected their views and summaries of the field would be extremely useful to current scholars and Ph.D. students. Finally, I thought that it would be easy to put together this handbook and that it would be published within a year.

Maybe I should have thought a little more about this undertaking before agreeing to do it. Instead of taking one year, it has taken closer to five years. Unfortunately, we lost several authors due to personal issues and had to replace them with others, which upturned all plans to get the handbook out quickly. However, with the manuscript now complete, I can reflect upon the effort and conclude that I was right about the idea behind the book. The changes in the field demand this handbook, and bringing together the work of the giants in the field will prove to be of value to both current and future scholars – even if agreeing to edit this handbook was probably a bad idea personally.

I need to offer my thanks to the authors of the chapters of this handbook and to my editor, Rosemary Nixon, and the staff at Blackwell Publishing and John Wiley & Sons for their extraordinary patience and flexibility. You are all better people than me. I probably would not have tolerated the delays in the development of this book with the grace that all of you showed.

I would also like to offer my thanks to A. Malachi Mixon III and the AT&T Foundation (formerly the SBC Foundation) for their financial support of my scholarly efforts since arriving at Case Western Reserve University. Without their generosity this book would not have occurred.

Lastly, I would like to thank my wife Lynne, daughter Hannah, and son Ryan. Each of them helped me in their own ways. Hannah and Ryan helped by being excellent playmates when I needed breaks from this project, and Lynne helped me by encouraging and supporting my efforts to create this book.

Scott Shane

List of Contributors

Rajshree Agarwal
College of Business
University of Illinois at Urbana-Champaign
Champaign, IL 61820
agarwalr@uiuc.edu

Paul Almeida
McDonough School of Business
Georgetown University
Washington, DC 20057
almeidap@msb.edu

David Audretsch
Institute for Development Strategies
Indiana University
Bloomington, IN 47405
daudrets@indiana.edu

Barry L. Bayus
Kenan-Flagler Business School
University of North Carolina
Chapel Hill, NC 27599
Barry_Bayus@UNC.edu

David Brunner
Harvard Business School
Harvard University
Boston, MA 02163
dbrunner@hbs.edu

Eric L. Chen
Department of Management Science and Engineering
Stanford University
Stanford, CA 94305
elchen@stanford.edu

Henry Chesbrough
Haas School of Business
University of California at Berkeley
Berkeley, CA 94720
chesbrou@haas.berkeley.edu

Deborah Dougherty
Rutgers Business School
Rutgers University
Newark, NJ 07102
doughert@rbsmail.rutgers.edu

Maryann P. Feldman
Department of Public Policy
UNC Chapel Hill
Chapel Hill, NC 27599
maryann.feldman@unc.edu

Lee Fleming
Harvard Business School
Harvard University
Boston, MA 02163
lfleming@hbs.edu

Shane Greenstein
Kellogg School of Management
Northwestern University
Evanston, IL 60208
Greenstein@kellogg.northwestern.edu

Bronwyn Hall
Department of Economics
University of California at Berkeley
Berkeley, CA 94720-3880
bhhall@econ.berkeley.edu

Jan Hohberger
Department of Business Policy
ESADE Business School
08034 Barcelona, Spain
Jan.hohberger@esade.edu

David Hsu
Wharton School of Business
University of Pennsylvania
Philadelphia, PA 19104
dhsu@wharton.upenn.edu

Riitta Katila
Department of Management Science and Engineering
Stanford University
Stanford, CA 94305-4026
rkatila@stanford.edu

Ralph Katz
College of Business Administration
Northeastern University
Boston, MA 02115
r.katz@neu.edu

Dieter Kogler
Department of Geography
University of Toronto
Toronto, ON M5S 3G3
dieter.kogler@utoronto.ca

Alan MacCormack
Harvard Business School
Harvard University
Boston, MA 02163
amaccormack@hbs.edu

Pedro Parada
Department of Business Policy
ESADE Business School
08034 Barcelona, Spain
Pedro.parada@esade.edu

Scott Shane
Weatherhead School of Management
Case Western Reserve University
Cleveland, OH 44106
Scott.shane@case.edu

Venkatesh Shankar
Mays Business School
Texas A&M University
College Station, TX 77843
vshankar@mays.tamu.edu

Victor Stango
Tuck School of Business
Dartmouth College
Hanover, NH 03755
vstango@ucdavis.edu

Christian Terwiesch
Wharton School of Business
University of Pennsylvania
Philadelphia, PA 19104
terwiesch@wharton.upenn.edu

Mary Tripsas
Harvard Business School
Harvard University
Boston, MA 02163
mtripsas@hbs.edu

Rosemarie Ziedonis
Stephen M. Ross School of Business
University of Michigan
Ann Arbor, MI 48109
rzied@umich.edu

Darren Zinner
Harvard Business School
Harvard University
Boston, MA 02163
dzinner@brandeis.edu

Editor's Introduction

SCOTT SHANE

For thousands of years, technological innovation – the application of knowledge about tools, materials, processes, and techniques to problem solving (Afuah, 2003) – has had a profound effect on our lives as people, sometimes positively, and other times negatively, as any user of electronic mail can attest. Perhaps more importantly for the scholarly study of business, technological innovation has been a central component of the way in which new economic value is created by permitting people and companies to use existing resources more efficiently, as well as to come up with products and services that meet people's needs in ways that were not met before (Mokyr, 1990).

Because technological innovation creates economic value, it also affects the growth and decline in shareholder wealth. This effect on shareholder wealth impacts all shareholders, regardless of whether they are founding entrepreneurs, employees, or investors in companies, and regardless of whether they are shareholders in the innovating company or the company that competes with innovators.

The importance of technological innovation to economic value creation and shareholder wealth has made the management of it a central part of business activity. Although technological innovation can be accidental as well as planned, many firms seek to manage it in the hopes of making innovation more profitable to the firm. This effort to manage technological innovation is important because, as the chapters in this handbook point out, the management of technological innovation differs from the management of other aspects of business. Thus, an understanding of the management of technological innovation requires the development and testing of novel theories.

Moreover, these theories do not just cover a narrow slice of business activity, but instead, need to explain a wide variety of business activities at a number of different levels of analysis. For instance, technological innovation affects the process through which firms come up with novel products, and the products that they create. It affects the speed and cost of their ongoing operations. It influences the adoption and diffusion of new products and the methods that firms use for forecasting sales. Technological innovation also affects marketing strategy including pricing, timing of entry, and marketing mix decisions. The way in which companies learn about customer needs is affected by technological innovation, as is the management of organizations and the people in those organizations. In addition, firm strategy depends a great deal on technological innovation, as evolutionary patterns of development, the presence or absence of standards, and the strength of intellectual property all affect what are effective strategic decisions for managers. Finally, technological innovation affects who undertakes different business activities and how those activities are financed.

In some industries the management of technological innovation is very important because those industries are very reliant on new technology. In these industries, technological innovation has become a fundamental part of the process through which companies create competitive advantages, and is a central focus of managers. Figure 1 identifies many of these industries.

Developing accurate explanations for the management of technological innovation is subject to an additional complexity. The theories that scholars use to explain and predict need to hold regardless of the form that technological innovation takes. This makes the development of well supported theory difficult because technological innovation comes from many different sources of technical knowledge – from computer science to biology to materials science – and technological innovation takes a variety of different forms – from new microorganisms to mechanical devices to new materials to drugs.

Why Publish a Handbook?

This handbook is necessary because the focus of technology and innovation management research has changed in several important ways in recent years. In particular, four changes necessitate a new book to summarize the field and make suggestions for future research directions. First, research has confirmed several important empirical regularities that scholars need to understand to develop accurate theories.For instance, as Chapter 2 points out, the evidence is clear that most industries evolve through periods of growth, shakeout, and decline, and that these stages in industry evolution are associated with both certain characteristics of firms and certain attributes of products. Similarly, as Chapter 3 points out, numerous studies show that new product adoption tends to follow an S-shaped pattern of development rather than a straight line of growth.

Second, certain aspects of the management of technological innovation have taken on greater importance in recent years than they had in the past. Scholars need to be aware of these developments to keep abreast of the state of the art of the field. As Chapters 2 and 3 of the handbook show, the two most noticeable aspects of the management of technological innovation that have grown in importance over the past two decades are technology strategy and technology entrepreneurship. The creation of this handbook, and the inclusion of the chapters on these topics, allows attention to be drawn to areas of growing scholarly attention.

Third, new theories have been written that better answer questions about the management of technological innovation than did previous theories. For instance, in recent years, scholars have begun to look at product development through the

Industry
Aerospace product and parts manufacturing
Agriculture, construction, and mining machinery manufacturing
All other electrical equipment and component manufacturing
Architectural, engineering, and related services
Audio and video equipment manufacturing
Basic chemical manufacturing
Commercial and service industry machinery manufacturing
Communications equipment manufacturing
Computer and office machine repair and maintenance
Computer and peripheral equipment manufacturing
Computer systems design and related services
Data processing services
Educational support services
Electrical equipment manufacturing
Engine, turbine, and power transmission equipment manufacturing
Industrial machinery manufacturing
Management, scientific, and technical consulting services
Manufacturing and reproducing magnetic and optical media
Medical equipment and supplies manufacturing
Motor vehicle body and trailer manufacturing
Motor vehicle manufacturing
Motor vehicle parts manufacturing
Navigational, measuring, electromedical, and control instrument manufacturing
Online information services
Ordnance and accessories manufacturing – ammunition (except small arms) manufacturing
Ordnance and accessories manufacturing – other ordnance and accessories manufacturing
Ordnance and accessories manufacturing – small arms ammunition manufacturing
Ordnance and accessories manufacturing – small arms manufacturing
Other chemical product and preparation manufacturing
Other general purpose machinery manufacturing
Paint, coating, and adhesive manufacturing
Pesticide, fertilizer, and other agricultural chemical manufacturing
Petroleum refineries
Pharmaceutical and medicine manufacturing
Resin, synthetic rubber, and artificial and synthetic fiber and filament manufacturing
Scientific research and development services
Semiconductor and other electronic component manufacturing
Soap, cleaning compound, and toilet preparation manufacturing
Software publishers

(*Source*: Adapted from Science and Engineering Indicators, 2006. Downloaded from http://www.nsf.gov/statistics/seind06/)

FIGURE 1 Technology intensive industries.

lens of problem solving, which has led to new and different insights into the product development process. By presenting these theories to scholars in the field, this handbook helps researchers to understand the new answers provided to previously unresolved questions.

Fourth, several tools to manage technological innovation have been developed, and they do not all work equally well. To develop the next generation of tools, scholars need to understand why some tools work better than others. For instance, as Chapter 7 shows, many project selection and portfolio management tools do not work very well, despite theory holding that they should. This chapter helps scholars to understand how to develop better tools for an important part of the innovation management process by providing an analysis of what works and what does not work, and why.

THE FOCUS OF THE HANDBOOK

Technology and innovation management is an inherently interdisciplinary topic. Although many of the important research questions of the field are not central to particular social science disciplines, such as economics or sociology, they are of primary importance to the practice of management. Because of their lack of centrality to core disciplines these topics would not be addressed, or would be addressed poorly, if approached from a purely disciplinary perspective. Therefore, this handbook takes an interdisciplinary approach to the management of technological innovation. The chapters in this handbook are written by scholars who themselves are interdisciplinary or who hail from a variety of fields, including economics, organizational behavior, strategic management, marketing, operations management, and public policy. Moreover, they review research conducted by scholars from an even wider array of fields, including sociology, psychology, political science, finance, and engineering design.

The handbook takes a very broad and eclectic approach to the collection of the empirical evidence used to support theories about the management of technological innovation. The studies reviewed in the handbook vary greatly in approach; some are theoretical and others are empirical. The theoretical papers include both formal, mathematical models and more verbal approaches. The empirical papers discussed by the authors of the different chapters include simulations, case studies, experiments, and regression analysis of cross-sectional and longitudinal survey and archival data collected from a wide variety of sources.

A handbook on any topic is not a random selection of papers but an effort by an editor to identify the key topics, and therefore it is only fair to identify the set of research questions that motivated the selection of authors and the chapter topics. Rightly or wrongly, they represent my interpretation of what constitutes the central questions of the field, as follows:

- How does technological change affect industry evolution?
- Why do industries experience high rates of firm entry followed by a shakeout?
- How should firms manage product adoption and diffusion?
- Why does the shape and timing of adoption and diffusion vary across products and services?
- How do firms assess customer needs for new technology products?
- Why do some tools predict customer needs more efficiently than others?
- How do firms develop new products and services?
- Why are some approaches to product development more effective than others?
- How should companies manage new product introduction?
- Why do firms perform so poorly at new product introduction?

- How should firms balance exploration and exploitation in innovation?
- Why do sequential approaches sometimes perform better than simultaneous approaches and sometimes perform worse?
- How should firms manage R&D projects and portfolios of projects?
- Why do the models for the management of projects and portfolios not work well in practice?
- How is the management of technical professionals different from the management of other employees?
- Why do technical professionals engage in innovation?
- How does strategy in industries based on technical standards differ from strategy in other industries?
- What strategic actions improve firm performance in industries based on technical standards?
- How do firms capture the financial returns to their investments in innovative activity?
- How has the role of intellectual property in firm strategy changed over time?
- Why has there been an increased focus on intellectual property?
- How do firms enhance their abilities to appropriate the returns to their investments in innovation?
- Why do some firms profit from innovation whereas others do not?
- How does individual level collaboration affect firms in knowledge-intensive industries?
- Why do firms have both individual and firm level collaboration across firm boundaries?
- How do entrepreneurs develop new businesses in technology intensive industries?
- Why do some technology entrepreneurs perform better than others?
- Where do entrepreneurial opportunities come from?
- How do entrepreneurial opportunities get exploited in technology-intensive industries?
- Why does the market fail to finance innovation effectively?
- How can market failures in the market for innovation finance be overcome?
- How do governments, universities, and nonprofit organizations contribute to innovation?
- Why is the involvement of nonfirms in the innovation process necessary?

THE CHAPTERS

This handbook is divided into five parts. Part I includes chapters devoted to the evolution of technologies, markets, and industries. One of the defining features of the literature on the management of technological innovation has been its reliance on evolutionary models to explain key phenomena. The evidence for evolutionary patterns is now so robust that the core assumption that technologies, markets, and industries follow standard evolutionary patterns of development is taken as given. The focus of research in this area now lies in fleshing out the basic model.

Chapter 1, entitled 'Technology and Industry Evolution' by Rajshree Agarwal and Mary Tripsas, identifies key stylized facts in the empirical literature on industry evolution and contrasts three theoretical perspectives coming from technology management, organizational ecology, and evolutionary economics, which are used to explain these facts. The chapter summarizes four key empirical regularities:

♦ Most industries go through systematic phases. They initially display a wide variety of technological approaches and products, and firms focus on product innovation. This can eventually lead to the emergence of a dominant design, after which innovation becomes incremental and more focused on process improvements.

♦ Both the number of companies operating in an industry and aggregate sales display an inverted U-shape pattern over time, while prices tend to decline as the industry becomes more mature.

♦ Most technological discontinuities are brought to the market by new companies or companies moving into the industry from other industries, and the performance of incumbent firms in response to this change depends on the degree to which the technology undermines the value of their existing assets, their relationships to other firms, and the timing of the change.

♦ Firm survival is a function of the number of existing firms in the industry, firm age, firm size, access to resources, prior experience, timing of entry, and institutional ties.

Agarwal and Tripsas also identify four outstanding questions about technology and industry evolution for which different theoretical explanations have been proposed, but for which more research needs to be done to reconcile conflicting perspectives.

♦ 'Why is there a flurry of entry early on?' They explain that a lack of scale economies, an absence of learning curve advantages, and social processes of legitimization have been offered as possible explanations.

♦ 'What drives dominant designs?' They contrast the multitude of explanations offered including bandwagon effects; network externalities; the characteristics of the technology itself; economies of scale; and social, political, institutional, economic, and cognitive factors.

♦ 'What drives shakeouts?' They discuss the alternative explanations offered, including the development of a dominant design, a shift in competition towards efficiency and scale, and the increase in the importance of competition rather than legitimization.

♦ 'What firms have a higher probability of survival and why?' They explain that two categories of explanations have been offered: conditions at the time of entry and firm-specific adaptation to environmental conditions.

In Chapter 2, 'The Evolution of Markets: Innovation Adoption, Diffusion, Market Growth, New Product Entry, and Competitor Responses', Venkatesh Shankar reviews research on the evolution of product markets, focusing on two key aspects of this evolution: the nature of patterns of adoption and diffusion of products, and firm strategy for new product introduction. For the first of these topics, Shankar identifies the different stages of the product life cycle, and explains how the diffusion of new products is affected by the characteristics of the adopter of the product, the innovation itself, the innovator that provides the product, and the external environment. He describes both the qualitative and quantitative approaches for forecasting sales of new products, and reviews the empirical evidence that has been gathered to test the validity of different diffusion models, including the Bass model, the repeat purchase diffusion model, and the product cycle model. Shankar also identifies the effect of different marketing mix variables on the diffusion process, discusses the variation in the usefulness of these models across different geographic locations, and identifies the methodological issues present in explaining new product diffusion.

On the topic of new product entry strategy, Shankar discusses the empirical support for different game theoretic models of new product introduction that focus on the optimal price for new products, the right timing of market entry, and the appropriate competitive response for incumbent firms. He also discusses the implications of new product entry strategy for different aspects of new product management, including forecasting sales, making marketing mix decisions, managing innovation over the product cycle, developing a geographic marketing strategy, and responding to competitive dynamics. He concludes with a discussion of the important open research questions on the nature of the adoption and diffusion of products and new product entry strategy.

Part II of this handbook addresses the issue of new product development. The field of technology and innovation management has had a long history of interest in this question, approaching it from a variety of different points of view, including marketing, operations management and engineering design, and management. The handbook includes chapters that discuss new product development from each of these perspectives. In Chapter 3, entitled, 'Understanding Customer Needs', Barry Bayus looks at the development of new products from the perspective of marketing, focusing on the central question of how companies understand customers' needs for new products. Bayus recounts the stylized fact that 90 % of new product introductions fail, and explains that a good portion of these failures result from a lack of understanding of customer needs. The chapter defines what the literature means by customer needs, and why understanding customer needs is important to developing innovative new products. It then moves on to explain how companies identify customer needs, reviewing the advantages and disadvantages of different approaches and tools recommended by the literature, such as the Kano method, market research surveys, focus groups, and observational methods. The chapter also considers the issues that companies face in interpreting information from customers when they design new products. The chapter ends by identifying the key unresolved issues for researchers, asking:

- How valuable are the recently developed tools for understanding customer needs, such as web based methodologies, virtual communities, and advances in conjoint analysis?
- How can companies develop and use decision-making models that use customer information in ways not so distorted by biases as to be useless?
- How can companies develop road maps of what customer needs will be in the future and how technological alternatives map to those needs?

In Chapter 4, entitled 'Product Development as a Problem-Solving Process', Christian Terwiesch provides a problem-solving framework to understand product design and development. The chapter begins by putting product development research in historical perspective, and by reviewing prior work in product design and development. It then moves to a discussion of the value of viewing product design and development through the lens of problem solving. Terwiesch identifies generic processes that designers use in problem solving, and offers a four-part taxonomy: the stage gate process, the iterative process, parallel prototyping, and Darwinian selection.

Because product development does not occur in a vacuum, but, rather, occurs inside of organizations, the chapter also discusses several important organizational issues in product development, including fitting the right product development processes to the right product development problems; overcoming the obstacles created by organizational structure for the management of product development projects; and ensuring coordination and knowledge management.

The chapter concludes by asking whether recent advances in the field will come to an end because the field has become too large and specialized. Terwiesch highlights the tension that the growth of the field has created as increasingly focused scholars seek to explain this inherently interdisciplinary phenomenon through the lens of particular disciplines or perspectives.

In Chapter 5, 'Managing the "Unmanageables" For Sustained Product Innovation', Deborah Dougherty examines the very basic question of how companies should structure the work of product innovation. She points out that although thousands of books and articles have been written on the subject, many organizations still cannot generate streams of new products over time. She argues that one major reason is that managers structure their organizations according to bureaucratic principles, which produce three 'unmanageables' that preclude the work of innovation. *Segmentalism* chops up innovation work into separate bits, *rigidity* prevents necessary creative problem solving, and *coercive control* de-motivates people from taking on the complex work of innovation. These unmanageables are not the inevitable outcomes of large size and old age as some people believe, but in fact are created by this misguided approach to structuring. Of course structuring is necessary for complex work such as innovation, but it need not follow the taken-for-granted bureaucratic views.

This chapter develops ways to replace the unmanageables with alternate approaches that accomplish the same structuring need but also accommodate innovation. Instead of breaking complex work up by function or business, Dougherty recommends breaking it up by core problems of innovation management, each to be set and solved by horizontal communities of practice. Rather than stabilizing work with rigid jobs and routines, she recommends using reflective practice, and rather than controlling work coercively, she recommends resourcing everyday social action in three specific ways. These alternate structures highlight socially constructed frames for the everyday collective actions of innovation, and the need to deliberately manage these actions.

Part III looks at the management and organization of innovation. This is probably the oldest stream of research in the management of technological innovation area, dating back to early work on managing innovative individuals and designing organization structures for innovation. However, it is also a stream of research for which major unresolved questions still remain. The authors of the chapters in this section address several of the major issues. For instance, should firms emphasize exploration or exploitation of new technology? How should firms select innovation projects and manage their portfolio of these projects? And how should firms manage their technical professionals?

In Chapter 6, 'Rival Interpretations of Balancing Exploration and Exploitation: Simultaneous or Sequential?', Eric Chen and Riitta Katila examine the age-old question of achieving a balance between exploration and exploitation in the management of technological innovation. However, rather than focusing on the question of whether firms should focus more on exploration or exploitation in the innovation process, Chen and Katila assume that the two are complementary and examine how to manage them collectively. The authors summarize two different approaches to managing this balance – engaging in simultaneous and sequential exploration and exploitation – and develop a framework for choosing between the two approaches as a function of external environment. In more dynamic environments, the authors explain, the simultaneous approach is superior; whereas in more stable environments, the sequential approach dominates. The authors conclude by suggesting two important areas for future research. One is to consider whether too much exploration is a problem for firms; another is to consider the way in which simultaneous and sequential approaches are related to each other.

In Chapter 7, 'R&D Project Selection and Portfolio Management: A Review of the Past, a Description of the Present, and a Sketch of the Future', David Brunner, Lee Fleming, Alan MacCormack, and Darren Zinner examine the selection of research and development projects, a topic that has concerned academics and managers since the 1950s. The authors review the existing literature, focusing on two aspects of the project selection problem: figuring out what individual projects are worth; and selecting the right combination of projects for a firm's portfolio. The authors review a wide range of different types of selection models, beginning with relative value models, and including both comparative models and scoring models. Then they turn their attention to economic value models, examining cost benefit models; decision tree models; Monte Carlo simulations; and real options.

The second half of Chapter 7 examines portfolio selection. It reviews three types of portfolio selection models: mathematical programming models, portfolio diagrams, and strategic approaches. The chapter then discusses the effectiveness of these models, explaining that they tend to work poorly in industries in which projects tend to be uncertain, and in industries in which firms rely on external resources to innovate. The authors conclude by arguing that the field should do a better job bringing together theory and practice in this area.

In Chapter 8, entitled 'Managing the Innovative Performance of Technical Professionals', Ralph Katz looks at the micro level issues involved in encouraging innovation by an organization's technical professionals. Katz explains that although a great deal has been written about the management and organization of technological innovation, very little of this scholarly work actually looks at the management of technical professionals. The chapter reviews the scholarly work on this topic, beginning with a review and discussion of the important role that intrinsic as opposed to extrinsic motivation plays in encouraging innovative activity. Focusing on these types of motivators, rather than the external motivators, such as compensation, Katz explains that psychological need-based models are usually offered as the best predictors of the motivation to innovate. Among the need-based models on which he focuses are Maslow's hierarchy of needs, Herzberg's two-factor theory of motivation, McClelland's theory of needs, and Schein's career anchor model.

Katz also explains that technical professionals' perception of the task dimensions of their work, in particular those dimensions that have something in common with what the technical professional sees as fun, is another important part of explaining the motivation to innovate. Jobs can, Katz explains, be evaluated on whether their task dimensions motivate innovation – both from the organization's perspective as well as the professional's point of view. Therefore, an important issue for managing technical professionals is designing jobs so that technical professionals perceive them as enjoyable within organizational demands and practices.

Chapter 8 also deals with three other important aspects of managing technical professionals: the effect of job tenure stages on innovation, the need to manage human resources for both current activity and innovation, and the disagreements between parts of the organization on the allocation of resources to different activities. Katz explains that these issues need to be managed effectively or organizations will fail to have innovative technical professionals.

Part IV focuses on technology strategy. This has been the area with the richest growth in research in recent years. Whereas earlier work on the management of technological innovation focused a great deal on the management of technical professionals and the management organization of innovation, the dramatic growth of technology-intensive industries in recent years has led to an interest in explaining the aspects of firm strategy that are unique to high technology settings, or, if not unique to those settings, at least more likely to be found in them. Among the areas of intense scrutiny have been intellectual property, technical standards and network externalities, and contractual organizational arrangements, such as licensing, joint ventures, and strategic alliances. The four chapters in this part all deal, in one way or another, with these three issues.

In Chapter 9, entitled 'The Economics and Strategy of Standards and Standardization', Shane Greenstein and Victor Stango examine technology strategy in industries that revolve around technical standards. The authors explain that standards-based industries are an important subset of technology-intensive industries and are ones that involve a number of unique strategic issues. After defining technical standards and network effects, Greenstein and Stango move on to describe the different ways that standards emerge, and offer an analysis of the issues involved in standards battles. The authors discuss both short and long-term issues in the strategic management of businesses based on technical standards. They examine such questions as: When is coordination on a common standard valuable? Do markets choose the 'right' standards? When and how do firms use standards as strategic (anticompetitive) weapons? Does open cooperation among firms in the form of joint ventures and alliances improve matters? When might nonmarket institutions such as standards bodies improve upon market-mediated outcomes? And how do property rights for standards affect the efficiency of their adoption?

In Chapter 10, 'Intellectual Property and Innovation', Rosemarie Ziedonis explores the recent contributions to the scholarly literature on intellectual property – the legal rights to protect innovation – that have been published in leading management and economics journals from 1986 to 2006. She finds that the growth in the scholarly literature on intellectual property in the past decade has been quite rapid, and seeks to explain why scholars have turned so much attention to this area. Her first explanation is methodological. The rise in patent databases, search tools, and computing power, have made it much easier to conduct research on innovation using patents. Thus scholars are paying more attention to patents than they used to because patents are now easier to study. Her second explanation is more interesting. The shift towards a knowledge economy and the greater focus on the creation of intellectual property at companies has led to a greater use of intellectual property-focused firm strategy. Academics have devoted more attention to explaining the role of intellectual property in firm strategy because this activity is more important to companies than it used to be. Her third explanation is also interesting. Ziedonis explains that changes in the legal environment have led policy makers and firm strategists to pay more attention to intellectual property. Academics have responded to these shifts in the legal environment by seeking to examine how they have affected the actions taken by firm strategists and policy makers.

Ziedonis focuses on the most highly cited of these papers to identify the themes in this burgeoning literature. The first theme that she explores is the use of patents to examine firm capabilities. She explains that many scholars have sought to examine patents to explain how firms exploit technical capabilities, develop competitive advantage, and source and transfer knowledge because patents are an observable output of innovation. The second theme that she identifies is the use of intellectual property as a strategic asset that is accumulated and managed by firms. In this stream of research, scholars have examined intellectual property to see how firms use it to deter competition, to design effective strategies, and to identify the right organizational form to pursue innovation. The third theme that Ziedonis explores is the effect of laws and policies toward intellectual property on the incentive to innovate and the tendency to patent.

Ziedonis concludes by asking about the value of the recent scholarly focus on intellectual property. She notes that the use of patent data has probably reached a point of diminishing marginal returns, and that the use of patents to study innovation per se is probably not going to yield a great deal of value. The value of additional research on intellectual property will come, she argues, from studies that examine how firms use patents, copyrights, and other pieces of intellectual property as strategic assets to derive competitive advantage, and from studies that look at how public policy in this area affects firm and managerial behavior.

In Chapter 11, entitled 'Orchestrating Appropriability: Towards an endogenous view of capturing value from innovation investments', Hank Chesbrough re-examines the core research question behind Teece's (1986) paper: why do some firms profit from innovation while others do not? Teece's answer focused on the appropriability regime of the industry, identifying the strength of intellectual property protection, and the importance of complementary assets as the central elements in determining the appropriability of investments in innovation. In this chapter, Chesbrough reframes Teece's explanation by relaxing the assumption that the appropriability regime is an exogenously determined industry characteristic, and replacing it with the argument that appropriability is an endogenously determined result of firm strategy. After reviewing the prior empirical literature on this question and identifying studies that illustrate the endogenous nature of complementary assets, Chesbrough argues that firms can take strategic actions, such as countersuits, cross-licensing, divestiture of downstream operations, providing safe harbor, and pre-emptive publishing to increase their ability to appropriate the returns to their investments in innovation. Their different abilities to carry out these strategic actions means that firms within the same industry can vary in the appropriability of their innovations, explaining why some firms that possess the appropriate complementary assets fail to appropriate the returns to their investments in innovation.

In Chapter 12, 'Individual Collaborations, Strategic Alliances, and Innovation: Insights from the Biotechnology Industry', Paul Almeida, Jan Hohberger, and Pedro Parada examine a frequently discussed aspect of knowledge intensive industry: the use of cooperative behavior. However, instead of focusing on the standard firm level cooperative activities, such as strategic alliances and licensing, the authors push the examination of cooperative behavior down to the individual level of analysis. In doing so, they focus on two key questions: First, do firms gain when individual scientists and engineers collaborate with colleagues outside of the firm? Second, how does this individual level of collaboration relate to the firm-level collaboration discussed in the literature on strategic alliances, joint ventures, and licensing? Using qualitative evidence from the biotechnology industry to flesh out their arguments, the authors propose that firms derive similar benefits from individual cooperation between scientists and engineers as they do from firm-level cooperation. Almeida, Hohberger, and Parada then suggest two hypotheses that are worthy of future scholarly investigation. The first is that the two forms of collaboration are complementary, accessing different types of knowledge assets, and following a pattern in which individual level collaboration leads to firm-level cooperation. The second is that the two forms of collaboration operate through different mechanisms, with the individual level collaboration being less formal and planned than the firm-level collaboration.

The final part of this book examines the issue of who innovates. In recent years, scholars have made major advances in understanding the role of public sector entities and new companies in the national innovation system. In particular, this stream of research has pointed out that many aspects of the management of technological innovation are different for new firms, small firms, and public sector entities, than they are for the large, established companies that have historically been studied. In Chapter 13, 'Technology-Based Entrepreneurship', David Hsu reviews many of the important issues involved in understanding the creation of technology start-ups, and highlights the key research questions that emerge from these issues. He focuses first on the origins of new ventures and asks why new firms are more likely to 'spin-off' from some companies than from others, and why some spin-offs perform better than others. He then turns to an examination of the role of search processes, prior (technical and market) knowledge, and employment experience in the identification of new business opportunities. Third, he turns to issues of resource assembly and identifies the key factors affecting the acquisition of human and financial resources. Fourth, he looks at new firm strategy, focusing on niche entry, organizational flexibility, strategic differentiation, and cooperative approaches to incumbent firms. Finally, he examines issues of organizational growth, concentrating on the topics of organizational governance and leadership development. He concludes by identifying some of the methodological issues that make good research on technology entrepreneurship difficult to undertake, and offers some recommendations for improving this research.

In Chapter 14, 'Knowledge Spillover Entrepreneurship and Innovation in Large and Small Firms', David Audretsch asks the fundamental question, 'from where do entrepreneurial opportunities emerge and what do people do in response to those opportunities?' He argues that entrepreneurship is an endogenous function of the investments that existing firms make in the creation of knowledge, but do not fully appropriate. Audretsch argues that individuals recognize entrepreneurial opportunities during the course of their employment at existing firms and make decisions about whether or not they want to exploit them. Because of the uncertainty, information asymmetry, and transactions costs associated with the exploitation of knowledge-based entrepreneurial opportunities, the management of existing organizations may choose not to pursue the very opportunities that entrepreneurs or teams of entrepreneurs view as worth pursuing. When this divergence of views occurs, the employee will quit employment and start a new firm. Thus, technology entrepreneurship results from a failure of existing firms to appropriate completely the value of the knowledge that they have created. Audrestch also points out that this mechanism has an important implication for economic geography: certain places will have more entrepreneurial opportunities, and thus more new firms created, because more existing firms have created knowledge, some portion of which they cannot appropriate.

In Chapter 15, entitled 'The Financing of Innovation', Bronwyn Hall addresses the central research questions in the financing of innovation. Building off a line of reasoning that began with Schumpeter (1942) and was laid out by Arrow (1962), Hall explains that it may be difficult for new companies to obtain external financing for innovation because of a gap between the entrepreneur's rate of return and the investors cost of capital. This gap means that some innovative new businesses will fail to get funded simply because their cost of capital is too high.

Hall outlines the three major explanations that researchers have provided for why this gap between the internal and external cost of capital exists: information asymmetry between investors and entrepreneurs; moral hazard by the entrepreneur; and the effects of taxes on retained and distributed earnings. After reviewing the empirical evidence on this question, Hall concludes that new and small firms, indeed, face a shortage of capital and that venture capital is only a partial solution to this problem. Because venture capital is focused only on certain industries, can only be offered in chunks that are too large for many start-ups, and only works in places where IPO markets are well developed, it cannot provide a complete solution to the financing needs of new technology companies. As a result, a market failure exists, which demands government intervention. Hall concludes by suggesting that researchers should consider the value of different policy solutions to this problem, including incubators, loan guarantees, and subsidies for seed funding of start-ups.

In the final chapter, entitled 'The Contribution of Public Entities to Innovation and Technical Change', Maryann Feldman and Dieter Kogler discuss the role of universities, government agencies, nonprofit organizations, and other public entities in the management of technological innovation. The authors discuss why these supporting institutions are an intricate part of the national innovation system, and they explain why government involvement in the innovation process is important, and how governments influence technological innovation. Furthermore, the authors carefully examine the debate found in the scholarly literature concerning the amount that government should be involved in the innovation process and the form that such involvement should take. They also discuss the contributions that nonprofit organizations, universities, and government laboratories make to the innovation process. The authors conclude with a discussion of why it is difficult to evaluate the role of these public entities in the innovation process, and how researchers might overcome some of the difficulties in their empirical research.

REFERENCES

Afuah, A. (2003). *Innovation management*. New York: Oxford University Press.

Arrow, K. (1962). Economic welfare and the allocation of resources for invention. In R. Nelson (ed.), *The Rate and Direction of Inventive Activity*, Princeton, NJ: Princeton University Press.

Mokyr, J. (1990). *The lever of riches*. New York: Oxford University Press.

Schumpeter, J. (1942). *Capitalism, socialism, and democracy*. New York: Harper and Row (reprinted 1960).

Teece, D. (1986). Profiting from technological innovation: Implications for integration, collaboration, licensing and public policy. *Research Policy* 15, (December): 285–305.

Part I

THE EVOLUTION OF TECHNOLOGY, MARKETS, AND INDUSTRY

1

Technology and Industry Evolution

RAJSHREE AGARWAL AND MARY TRIPSAS

We would like to thank Barry Bayus, Martin Ganco, Scott Shane, and Mike Tushman for their helpful comments on this manuscript. We would also like to thank Tal Levy for research assistance.

THE LIFE CYCLE PHENOMENON

Scholars across a range of disciplines have found the life cycle metaphor useful in describing the evolution of industries. Subsequent to the first commercialization of a product, industries are seen to go through a progression that has substantial regularities in the time trends of key variables, such as number of firms, sales, price, and innovation patterns. Although life cycle models apply to a broad range of settings, our focus in this chapter is on the relationship between technological and industry evolution, two processes that we posit are inextricably linked. We begin by developing stylized observations about technology and industry development – that is, a generic industry life cycle model, building on empirical work from three areas of the literature: technology management, evolutionary economics, and organizational ecology. We then compare and contrast these literatures and finally propose a future research agenda motivated by this comparison.

For purposes of exposition, we distinguish three stages of evolution – emergence/ growth, shakeout, and maturity[1] – to describe the basic model put forth in the literature (Table 1.1). In the initial stage, high levels of uncertainty permeate every aspect of an industry. Firms experiment with a variety of technologies, since the performance trajectory of different technologies is unclear. Customers have undeveloped preferences and explore a range of product uses. The market is small and production processes are not specialized, so manufacturing is inefficient. Some industries never progress beyond emergence, but those that do generally experience

---

[1]These three stages are roughly equivalent to what evolutionary theorists label 'variation, selection, and retention'; what Utterback and Abernathy (1975) label 'fluid, transitional, and specific'; and what Klepper and Graddy (1990) call 'growth, shakeout, and stabilization'.

Handbook of Technology and Innovation Management. Edited by Scott Shane
© 2008 John Wiley & Sons, Ltd

TABLE 1.1 Stylized facts related to the stages in the industry life cycle.

Emergence/growth stage	Shakeout stage	Mature stage
Inception of industry due to initial commercialization of an invention. Other words used to describe this stage, such as *fragmentation, fluid phase, variation, era of ferment, and entrepreneurial regime* reflect that this stage is characterized by	Transition occurs due to establishment of efficiencies in production, dominant design, and ensuing competitive pressures. Other words used to describe this stage include *selection and transitional phase*. This stage is characterized by	Transition occurs when an 'equilibrium' number of firms has been reached. Other words used to describe this stage include *retention, specific phase, era of incremental change, and routinized regime*. This stage is characterized by
◆ very few firms initially, followed by rapid entry by firms, both entrepreneurial and diversifying entrants with pre-entry capabilities;	◆ rapid decline in the number of firms from the peak, as inefficient firms exit due to increased competitive pressures;	◆ stable number of firms, with low levels of both entry and exit rates relative to the other stages of the life cycle;
◆ high technology and demand uncertainty;	◆ establishment of a dominant design;	◆ reduction in overall innovation rates relative to the earlier stages, with most innovations being incremental in nature;
◆ experimentation with different approaches and product design;	◆ increasing emphasis on process relative to product innovation;	◆ innovation conducted by large, established firms, which focus on economies of scale;
◆ emphasis on both product and process innovation, with the relative ratio of product to process innovation decreasing over the stage;	◆ innovation conducted by large, established firms, which focus on economies of scale;	◆ leveling off in the growth rate of sales, as industry reaches high penetration rates;
	◆ decrease in the growth rate of sales;	

- very low levels of initial sales, and sustained growth in output over the entire period;
- decrease in price, particularly when adjusted for quality;
- gradual development of complementary assets (e.g., distribution channels, supply chain relationships, related infrastructure).

There is wide variation across industries in the number of years that is characterized as the emergence/growth stage, with some products never progressing beyond the emergence stage.

- continuing decline in prices, particularly when adjusted for quality.

There is wide variation in industries in the number of years and severity of shakeout in the number of firms.

- stable price levels;
- well-established complementary assets.

There is wide variation in industries in the number of years and the 'equilibrium' number of firms that exist in the mature stage. Transition to a decline or a cycle back to the Emergence Stage may occur due to new (radical) innovations being introduced rapid growth as the new technology diffuses across a set of consumers. The growth in the industry manifests itself in the form of increasing sales, an increasing number of firms, and declining price, particularly when price is adjusted for quality improvements. Quite salient is the entry by all types of firms, including entrepreneurial start-ups and entrants diversifying from related industries. In addition, high levels of product innovation characterize this stage, although the relative rate of process innovation increases over time.

The transition to the shakeout stage occurs because of the establishment of production efficiencies and the standardization of product designs, a process that leads to a dominant model. On the demand side, as users become more familiar with the industry's products, their preferences stabilize, and product variety decreases. Thus, this stage is characterized by an increasing emphasis on process innovation relative to product innovation, and an increasing share of the innovation stems from large, established firms that focus on efficient mass production. The competitive pressures unleashed in consequence of economies of scale, and specialized manufacturing processes that increase efficiency, result in a rapid decline in the number of firms. The rate of change in sales and price begins to decline towards the end of this stage, though output generally increases, and prices continue to fall, particularly when adjusted for quality.

During the mature phase of the industry, growth slows, and the technological and competitive environments are relatively stable. This stage is characterized by a stable number of firms. Although entry and exit of firms occur and are positively correlated, these rates are lower than they are in the other stages of the industry life cycle. Similarly, although some product and process innovation takes place, most of the innovations are incremental. The industry exhibits stable prices, level sales growth, and a well-established infrastructure supporting its activities.

Finally, industries in periods of stability may either transition into decline or spiral back into emergence as the result of disruptions by discontinuous technological change. This cycle may repeat multiple times as waves of discontinuous technological change invade an industry over time.

Underlying this stylized description is a wealth of empirical research that has documented a broad range of empirical regularities. We review the findings of three distinct literatures that have addressed technology and industry evolution: technology management, evolutionary economics, and organization ecology. We then explore the differing explanations for the observed regularities, comparing and contrasting these three literatures. Finally, we conclude with a discussion of outstanding research questions in this line of inquiry.

EMPIRICAL REGULARITIES

Empirical regularities in the technology management literature: patterns of technological and industry evolution

The technology life cycle literature is motivated by the premise that evolutionary changes in technology underlie the development of many new industries. Understanding patterns of technological change over time is therefore an important component of understanding competition. Empirical studies in this domain tend to be longitudinal, tracking the technological and competitive progress of a single industry or of a small set of industries over extended time periods. Empirical regularities become evident when we examine the patterns of technological change that accompany the stages of industry evolution; Table 1.2 summarizes these change patterns.

Innovative activity. In the nascent stage of most industries, technical variety is high, with a diverse set of innovations embodied in a range of competing products. Product artifacts look different, incorporate fundamentally different core technologies, emphasize different functions, and offer different features. This phenomenon is well documented. In early automobiles, steam and electric engines, along with the eventually dominant internal combustion engine, were present; the now ubiquitous round steering wheel competed with a joystick-type tiller for controlling the direction of a vehicle; and some cars had three wheels instead of four (Abernathy, 1978; Basalla, 1988). In another example, early radio transmitters used alternator, arc, and vacuum tube technologies before vacuum tubes became dominant (Aitken, 1985; Rosenkopf and Tushman, 1994). In typesetters, over 170 diverse designs were originally developed, including 'cold metal' machines that used pre-cast letters and 'hot metal' machines that cast entire lines of text as an operator typed (Tripsas, 1997b). Airplane landing gear between 1928 and 1933 included not only retractable designs, which eventually dominated, but also many types of fixed landing gear, including unstreamlined versions and 'trouser' streamlined versions with casings that covered the wheels for better aerodynamics (Vincenti, 1994). In many cases, different firms, or communities of firms, proactively introduce and push the adoption of particular technical variants. Examples of this type of competition include AC versus DC power distribution systems (David, 1992), full flight versus flight training device flight simulators (Rosenkopf and Tushman, 1998) and VHS versus beta video standards (Cusumano, Mylonadis, and Rosenbloom, 1992).

Two key studies have explicitly measured technical variety across stages of the technology life cycle. Anderson and Tushman (1990) analyzed technological change in the portland cement, minicomputer, and glass-manufacturing industries, identifying technological discontinuities, periods of ferment, dominant designs, and periods of incremental change. Within each industry, they then compared the number of new designs introduced during periods of ferment as opposed to eras of incremental change, finding that in three of four comparisons significantly more designs were introduced during the period of ferment. Second, in their longitudinal study of the development of cochlear implants, Van de Ven and Garud (1993) developed a chronological list of 771 significant events, covering the history of the industry from 1955 to 1989. They classified these events into three categories:

♦ variation events, which created technical novelty;
♦ selection events, which created or modified institutional rules (rules that narrowed the range of technical solutions considered);
♦ retention events, which followed existing rules.

TABLE 1.2 Technology management: empirical regularities in patterns of technological evolution.

Key studies	Sample	Innovative activity over the life cycle	Does a dominant design emerge?	Are there subsequent technological discontinuities	Number of firms, entry and exit over the life cycle
Utterback and Abernathy (1975)	567 commercially successful innovations from 5 industries	Product innovation starts high and decreases; process innovation increases over time	n/a	n/a	n/a
Abernathy (1978) Abernathy and Clark (1985)	Automobile industry 1900–1970s	High level of product variety early, decreasing over time; process innovation increases over time	Yes; the internal combustion engine, closed body vehicle	n/a	An inverted U-shaped curve for the number of firms in the industry over time
Aitken (1985)	History of radio transmission	Early competition among alternator, arc, and vacuum-tube transmitters	Yes; vacuum tube transmitters	Yes: transistor	n/a

Tushman and Anderson (1986) Anderson and Tushman (1990)	Minicomputer, cement, airline, and glass industries from birth through 1980.	New product designs are more prevalent during an era of ferment than an era of incremental change	Yes; dominant designs observed in all three industries	Yes: a series of discontinuities, characterized as competence-enhancing or competence-destroying	Initially entry exceeds exit; after competence-enhancing change, exits exceed entry, except for minicomputers
Van de Ven and Garud (1993, 1994) Garud and Rappa (1994)	Cochlear implants 1955–1989	Early competition between single and multi-channel devices; technical variation events occurred early in the life cycle	Yes; multi-channel cochlear implants	n/a	n/a
Vincenti (1994)	Airplane landing gear in the first half of the 1930s	Early variety including retractable and fixed (unstreamlined, pants, and trouser) landing gear	Yes; retractable landing gear	n/a	n/a

(continued overleaf)

TABLE 1.2 (continued)

Key studies	Sample	Innovative activity over the life cycle	Does a dominant design emerge?	Are there subsequent technological discontinuities	Number of firms, entry and exit over the life cycle
Rosenkopf and Tushman (1998)	Flight simulators	Early competition between variants; community network structure varies across technology life cycle	Yes: full flight simulation standard	Yes	n/a
Murmann (2003)	Synthetic dyes		Yes		An inverted U-shaped curve for the number of firms over time, but the timing varies by country
Tripsas (2008)	Typesetter industry 1886–1990	Highest technological variation during eras of ferment	Yes: hot metal linecaster	Yes: three subsequent waves of technology, driven by preference discontinuities	An inverted U-shaped curve for the number of firms over time, with a new curve for each technological generation

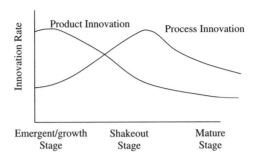

FIGURE 1.1 Relative importance of product as opposed to process innovation over the course of the industry life cycle.
Source: Adapted from Abernathy and Utterback (1978)

The distribution of these events over time showed that technical variation events occurred earliest and exceeded the other two categories until 1983, when the industry began to expand; furthermore, the establishment and reinforcement of institutional rules and routines supported that expansion.

Studies have also documented the relative importance of product as opposed to process innovation over the course of the industry life cycle and found a pattern similar to the stylized depiction of Figure 1.1. Utterback and Abernathy (1975) used Myers and Marquis's (1969) cross-section of 567 innovations from 120 firms in five industries to analyze the nature of innovation by industry stage. They classified each firm into one of three stages, roughly equivalent to the three industry stages we delineated above, and found that product innovation counts started high and decreased, while process innovation counts started low and increased. Abernathy (1978) found a similar pattern in his in-depth study of the automobile industry. In addition, Abernathy, Clark, and Kantrow (1983) categorized 631 automobile innovations from 1893 to 1981 as product or process innovations, and Klepper (1997) analyzed time trends in these data. This analysis showed that although initially process innovations increased and product innovations decreased, the trend was eventually reversed as the industry experienced new upheaval owing to internationalization and shifts in demand. The importance of demand in driving patterns of innovative activity is also highlighted through simulation by Adner and Levinthal, (2001), who show that demand heterogeneity can explain the transition from product to process innovation in an industry.

One significant exception to this finding is McGahan and Silverman's (2001) study of patenting patterns across a broad range of industries from 1981–1997. Defining industries at the SIC code level, they found that even in the subset of technologically-oriented industries, patents did not reflect a shift from product to process innovation as industries matured (McGahan and Silverman, 2001).

Emergence of a dominant design. A key turning point in the evolution of many industries is the emergence of a dominant design, a generally accepted product architecture with standardized modules and interfaces, which incorporates a particular set of features. A dominant design codifies corresponding movements down two hierarchies, the design and need hierarchies, as technological choices are matched with articulations of preferences (Clark, 1985). Empirical work has identified dominant designs in a range of industries. Utterback and Suarez (Utterback and Suarez, 1993; Suarez and Utterback, 1995) identified dominant designs in the automobile, transistor, typewriter, TV picture tube, TV, and electronic calculator industries. They did not identify a dominant design in the supercomputer industry but postulated that one would emerge soon. Utterback and Suarez used interviews with industry experts to identify retrospectively the occurrence of a dominant design and the introduction date of the first product that incorporated those design parameters. Anderson and Tushman (1990) defined dominant design emergence as having occurred once a particular technology controlled over 50 % of a market. Using data from the cement, minicomputers, and glass industries, they found that in 12 of 14 cases where they hypothesized a dominant design should emerge, one did, and in the two exceptions, new technological discontinuities disrupted the industry before a dominant design had a chance to take hold. Other studies have identified dominant designs in the cochlear implant (Van de Ven and Garud, 1993), typesetter (Tripsas, 1997a), flight simulation (Rosenkopf and Tushman, 1998), synthetic dye (Murmann, 2003), and personal computer (Teagarden, Echols, and Hatfield, 2000; Bayus and Agarwal, 2007) industries.

Once a particular design emerges as dominant, firms focus their attention on improving and extending it. Periods of incremental technological change following the emergence of dominant designs have been documented in the cement, minicomputer, and glass (Anderson and Tushman, 1990), synthetic dye (Murmann, 2003), and machine tool (Noble, 1984) industries, among others. Stuart and Podolny (1996) used patent data to track technological distance, measuring a firm's technological niche as the extent to which the firm's patents built upon the same technology as other firms. Using data from the semiconductor industry from 1978 to 1992, they showed that, with the exception of one firm, the technological niche changed very little over that time period.

The progress made through these incremental improvements, however, can be significant. In the typesetter industry, once the hot metal linecaster architecture emerged as dominant around 1911, incremental innovations over a 50-year period resulted in hundredfold increases in speed (Tripsas, 2008). While a dominant architecture prevails, significant innovation can also occur in modular subsystems. New product generations in the mainframe computer, personal computer, and automobile industries incorporated improvements to subsystems that had major impacts on performance (Abernathy and Clark, 1985; Baldwin and Clark, 2000; Iansiti and Khanna, 1995; Bayus and Agarwal, 2007).

Emergence of a dominant design also accelerates diffusion of a technology across the heterogeneous set of potential adopters. An extensive marketing literature on the diffusion of innovations (e.g., Bass, 1969; Rogers, 1995) documented an S-shaped diffusion curve for most products and identified different segments of adopters over the lives of industries. Early adopters were willing to experiment and were often technically sophisticated users. Later adopters, however, preferred the comfort of a dominant design with clearly specified features and evaluation metrics.

Subsequent technological discontinuities. Much of the technology management literature has focused on technological discontinuities that disrupt the mature stage of an industry, creating a new period of turbulence akin to the first stage of the industry life cycle. These multiple cycles of discontinuous and incremental change are well documented. In the photography industry, collodion plates, gelatin plates, and roll film all sparked significant technological turmoil (Jenkins, 1975). Similarly, Cooper and Schendel (1976) document technological disruptions in many established industries, including conflicts between diesel locomotives (versus steam), ball point pens (versus fountain pens), nuclear power plants (versus fossil fuel plants), electric razors (versus safety blades), and jet engines (versus propellers). This type of discontinuous technological change has been shown to result in high levels of new entry into an industry after a period of relative stability as documented in the photolithography (Henderson, 1993) and typesetter (Tripsas, 1997b) industries.

Number of firms, entry, and exit. Although the technology life cycle literature defines stages by shifts in technology, and not shifts in numbers of firms, many studies have documented how the number of firms in an industry and entry/exit patterns relate to changes in technology. The basic pattern is highly consistent: early on there are high levels of entry with little exit, and later there is a shakeout, with high levels of exit and relatively little entry; the result is an inverted U-shaped pattern of the number of firms in an industry over time. As noted above, this pattern has been documented in the automobile, transistor, typewriter, TV tube, TV, electronic calculator, and supercomputer industries, with the shakeout coinciding with the introduction of the technology that eventually became the dominant design (Utterback and Suarez, 1993).

Empirical regularities in the technology management literature: firm performance

Much empirical work in the technology management tradition has focused on understanding the competitive implications of technological discontinuities – that is, what firms introduce new technologies, what characterizes firms that succeed technologically and commercially, and what firms are more likely to survive? (see Table 1.3 for a summary).

Where do technological discontinuities originate? Most studies show that new entrants – either start-ups or diversifiers – introduce radically new technologies into industries. In four of the seven industries Cooper and Schendel (1976) studied, the first commercial introduction of a product with radically new technology came from outside the industries. Tushman and Anderson (1986) classified innovations by how they affect the competencies of incumbent firms and showed that competence-enhancing discontinuities were more likely to originate with incumbent firms, and competence-destroying discontinuities, with new entrants.

TABLE 1.3 Technology management: empirical regularities in firm performance.

Key studies	Sample and methods	Who develops the new technology?	Technical and commercial performance in the new technology	Survival
Cooper and Schendel (1976)	Cross-section of industries: steam locomotives to safety razors and covering much of the 1800s and 1900s	New entrants were first in 4 of 7 industries		n/a
Henderson and Clark (1990) Henderson (1993)	Photolithography industry 1962–1986	New entrants	Incumbents underperform new entrants technologically and commercially in architectural innovations	n/a
Utterback and Suarez (1993)	8 industries: typewriters, TV, electronic calculators spanning 1874–1990	n/a	n/a	Pre-dominant design entrants have an increased likelihood of survival
Christensen and Bower (1996) Christensen, Suarez, and Utterback (1998)	Disk drives 1975–1990	Both incumbents and new entrants	Incumbents initially match new entrants technologically, but withdraw investment, and so underperform commercially	Entrants in a brief pre-dominant design window have a higher likelihood of survival

Mitchell (1989, 1991)	Medical Diagnostic imaging 1952–1989	Incumbents with specialized assets are more likely to enter	Incumbents with specialized assets that retain value perform well	Incumbents with specialized assets that retain value are more likely to survive
Tripsas (1997b)	Typesetter industry 1886–1990	Both incumbents and new entrants	Incumbents underperform new entrants technologically, but outperform them commercially due to possession of specialized complementary assets	n/a
King and Tucci (2002)	Disk drives	Both incumbents and new entrants	Incumbents with more experience in a prior generation are more likely to enter the new generation	n/a
Benner and Tushman (2003)	Paint and photography industries 1980–1999	n/a	Incumbents that invest heavily in process innovation (ISO 9000) underperform those that don't	n/a

(continued overleaf)

TABLE 1.3 (continued)

Key studies	Sample and methods	Who develops the new technology?	Technical and commercial performance in the new technology	Survival
Rothaermel and Hill (2005)	The computer industry, the steel industry, and the pharmaceutical industry 1972–1997	Both incumbents and new entrants	A competence destroying technological discontinuity decreases incumbent firm performance if the complementary assets of the new technology are generic, but increases it if they are specialized	n/a
Bayus and Agarwal (2007)	PC Industry, 1974–1994	Both incumbents (diversifying firms) and new entrants	Diversifying entrants are better able to migrate to the dominant design relative to entrepreneurial startups. However, entrepreneurial startups are more likely to introduce products with the latest technology	Diversifying entrants that enter early have a survival advantage over start-ups that enter early, but the reverse is true for late entrants

In some cases, what appears to be a technological discontinuity in a particular industry is actually the application of an incrementally developing technology from a different market. For instance, Levinthal (1998) traced the development of wireless communication as it sequentially revolutionized multiple new application domains and Tripsas (2008) extended this work, examining what sparked the movement of new technology between industries. She showed that major shifts in user preferences – preference discontinuities – could precipitate technological discontinuities as firms in an industry imported what was for them radically new technology from another industry.

Which firms succeed?   Many studies have compared incumbents and new entrants and examined how the type of technological discontinuity influences which type of firm performs well, without distinguishing firm-specific strategies or behaviors. These studies have shown that for most types of technological discontinuities, incumbents underperform new entrants. This pattern was found when the new technology was competence destroying (Tushman and Anderson, 1986), architectural (Henderson and Clark, 1990), disruptive (Christensen and Bower, 1996), or destructive to the value of complementary assets (Tripsas, 1997b).

Several scholars have also examined the main and moderating effect of entry timing vis-à-vis the establishment of a dominant design in an industry (Suarez and Utterback, 1995; Christensen *et al.* 1998; Bayus and Agarwal, 2007). Suarez and Utterback (1995) and Christensen *et al.* (1998) examined how entry timing, as it related to the introduction of a dominant design, affected survival chances. Both studies defined the date of a dominant design as the year in which the first product with a design that eventually became dominant was introduced. Suarez and Utterback (1995) found that firms entering before a dominant design had a greater chance of survival than those entering after the dominant design. This effect was stronger the more distant a firm was from the date of the dominant design. In other words, firms that entered long after a dominant design was introduced were much worse off than those that entered immediately afterwards. Christensen *et al.* (1998), who used data from the disk drive industry, found that firms were still better off entering before the dominant design date, but the benefit was limited to a short window of three years beforehand. Bayus and Agarwal (2007) found evidence consistent with these studies on the main effect of entering before or after the dominant design, and additionally examined how entry timing, product technology strategy, and entrant capabilities may interact to explain performance differentials. They found that the survival advantage of diversifying entrants over entrepreneurial startups in the pre-dominant design stage is reversed in the post-dominant design stage. They explained this result by demonstrating that the product technology strategies related to higher survival rates differed by entry time and pre-entry experience.

Finally, there is extensive literature examining how specific firm-level change mechanisms, including shifts in organizational structure, external relationships, and investments in innovative activity affect firm performance. Reviewing this literature in depth is beyond the scope of this paper; however, we have highlighted significant mechanisms. First, organizational structure appears to play a significant role, with completely separate organizations (Gilbert, 2005) and ambidextrous organizations (O'Reilly and Tushman, 2008) achieving superior results when simultaneously managing old and new technologies. Second, external knowledge transfer from acquisitions (Ahuja and Katila, 2001), formal alliances (Rothaermel, 2001), and informal infrastructures (Tripsas, 1997a) is beneficial in transforming the organization's knowledge base. Finally, managing the tension between investments in exploitation and exploration is also critical (Katila, 2002; Taylor and Greve, 2006), with excess investment in activities such as Total Quality Management (TQM) limiting a firm's ability to explore (Benner and Tushman, 2002).

Empirical regularities in the evolutionary economics literature

Research in evolutionary economics has linked systematic changes in the technological characteristics and sources of innovations to the various stages in the evolution of an industry. In Table 1.4, we provide the main empirical findings of key studies in evolutionary economics, and below we summarize the robust patterns that can be seen in that research for number of firms, entry and exit rates, output, price, and firm performance.

Number of firms, entry, and exit. Perhaps the most robust empirical regularity documented in the evolutionary economics literature is the pattern exhibited in the numbers of firms in industries over time. Starting with Gort and Klepper (1982), evolutionary economists have studied multiple industries by using panel data that allow them to track the time trends in number of firms, entry, and exit. Gort and Klepper (1982), in a study of the diffusion of 45 product innovations, identified five distinct industry life cycle stages (see Figure 1.2). Klepper and Graddy (1990) grouped some of these stages to highlight growth, shakeout, and maturity. In particular, these studies show that 83 % of the industries in their samples conform to the stylized patterns for number of firms depicted in Figure 1.2. Tracking the (relatively young) industries that did not conform to the pattern, Agarwal (1998) extended the time series and found that the numbers of firms in several of these industries also conformed to the stylized pattern.[2] Particularly noteworthy in these studies was the severity of the shakeouts and the subsequent stability in number of firms; on average, the industries exhibited a 40 % decline in number of firms from their peaks, with several industries experiencing a more than 70 % decline. Furthermore, the industry life cycle may be contracting over chronological time; preliminary evidence provided in Gort and Klepper (1982) and systematic investigation of the issue by Agarwal and Gort (2001) revealed that the time until competitive entry into an industry occurs has decreased. For instance, it took 33 years for competitive entry to occur in the phonograph industry in the early 20th century, and only three years for the same to occur in the CD player industry in the late 20th century.

Klepper and Miller (1995) and Agarwal and Gort (1996) examined the gross entry and exit trends that underlay trends in number of firms and found that

---

[2]Rather than using stages in the life cycle, Agarwal (1998) regressed number of firms on industry age for 33 industries and found a quadratic functional form to be the best fit for the data for 26 of these industries.

TABLE 1.4 Evolutionary economics: empirical regularities in industry patterns.

Key studies	Sample	Number of firms, entry and exit	Innovative/technological activity	Output, sales, and market share	Prices
Gort and Klepper (1982)	46 industries spanning 1887–1960	An inverted U-shaped curve for the number of firms over the industry life cycle – decomposed into five stages	Major innovations occur early, and minor innovations occur later in the industry life cycle. Increase rate of patenting activity over the five stages of the life cycle	Output increases over the life cycle, but the rate in growth of output steadily declines over the consecutive stages	Greatest percentage decreases in the early stages of development, with a decreasing rate of decline thereafter
Klepper and Graddy (1990)	46 industries 1887–1960	The inverted U-shaped curve for number of firms is used to characterize the three stages in the life cycle: growth, shakeout, and mature stage	Major innovations, particularly from small entrants and entrants from related fields occur early in the life cycle. Later innovations are incremental in nature	The average percentage change in output is greatest in the first five-year interval, and subsequently declines over the next five five-year intervals	The annual percentage decline in price is greatest in the first five-year interval, and monotonically declines in absolute value over all the next five-year intervals

(continued overleaf)

TABLE 1.4 (continued)

Key studies	Sample	Number of firms, entry and exit	Innovative/technological activity	Output, sales, and market share	Prices
Lieberman (1990)	30 chemical industries spanning 1961–1987	There was a 32 % decline in the number of firms in the sample of declining industries		Output in the sample of declining industries decreased by an average of 42 %	
Jovanovic and Mac-Donald (1994a,b)	Automobile tire industry 1906–1973; diesel locomotive engines 1925–1966; semiconductor industry 1978–1986	An inverted U-shape in number of firms	Innovation opportunities fuel entry, and relative failure to innovate results in exit. Diffusion of technology over time due to spillovers of technology and increased imitation effort by 'laggard' firms	Output increases, but at a decreasing rate. Stock market share prices indicate rising value in the growth period of automobile tires, and drops in value during the shakeout period	Price declines exponentially in the initial years of the industry

Audretsch (1995)	Small Business Database (almost every manufacturing firm) from 1976–1986	Entry rates are higher in periods of high ratios of small firm innovation to total innovation	There are systematic differences over time in small firm innovation rates; the entrepreneurial regime is characterized by a higher level of small firm innovation relative to the total innovation rate		
Agarwal and Gort (1996)	25 industries spanning 1908–1991	An inverted U shaped curve in the number of firms; gross entry rates peak early in Stage 2, while gross exit rates peak early in Stage 4 (see Figure 1.1)			
Agarwal (1998)	33 industries spanning 1908–1991	The number of firms in the industry has a quadratic relation to industry age	The number of patents has a quadratic relation (inverted U shape) to industry age, with the peak in patenting activity occurring after the peak in the number of firms	Output increases at a decreasing rate over industry age	Price declines at a decreasing rate over industry age

(continued overleaf)

TABLE 1.4 (continued)

Key studies	Sample	Number of firms, entry and exit	Innovative/technological activity	Output, sales, and market share	Prices
Klepper and Simons (2000a)	Television receiver industry 1947–1989	A confirmation of the above empirical regularities; diversifying entrants from related industries enter earlier than other types of entrants	Diversifying entrants from radio (a related industry) had higher product and process innovation rates than other entrants	Output increases at a decreasing rate over industry age	Price declines at a decreasing rate over industry age
Filson (2001)	Automobiles, personal computers, rigid disk drives, computer monitors, and computer printers	An inverted U-shaped pattern in the number of firms	No evidence in support of the notion that new industries experience quality innovation early on and cost innovation later on. In the microelectronics industries the rate of quality improvement does not diminish over time. In the automobile industry, even though the rate of quality improvement is highest early on, the profitability of quality advantages is highest later on	Output increases at a decreasing rate over industry age	Price declines are most rapid early in the industry's history, and slow down later in the life cycle

Agarwal and Bayus (2002)	30 industries spanning 1849–1991.	Early period of the industry is characterized by a hockey stick pattern in the number of firms – a sharp takeoff in number of firms characterizes the onset of the growth stage	Early period of the industry is characterized by a hockey stick pattern in the industry output – but the sharp takeoff in output is preceded by the takeoff in the number of firms	Prices are generally declining in the early period of the industry
Klepper and Simons (2000a)	Automobiles 1895–1966; Automobile tires 1905–1981; Televisions 1946–1989; Penicillin 1943–1992.	Number of firms follows an inverted U shaped pattern. Initially, a surge in entrants causes the number of firms to rise dramatically. Entry then slows markedly and coupled with relatively steady exit rates causes a severe shakeout of firms	All four industries became oligopolies with several firms commanding much of the market; output continued to grow after the shakeout	

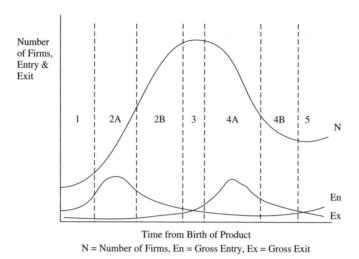

Time from Birth of Product

N = Number of Firms, En = Gross Entry, Ex = Gross Exit

FIGURE 1.2 Entry, exit, and number of firms across stages.

the trend in gross entry peaked early in the growth stage while the trend in gross exit peaked in shakeout stage 4 (see Table 1.5). Several studies replicated these findings for other industries, depicting the robustness of these patterns across consumer/industrial and technologically intensive and nonintensive industries alike (Lieberman, 1990; Audretsch, 1995; Klepper and Simons, 2000b; Filson, 2001; Agarwal and Bayus, 2002).

Innovative and technological activity.   Many of the evolutionary economics studies identify innovation and technological change as a key driver for industry evolution, and as a result, several scholars have examined technological activity for distinctive empirical regularities. Gort and Klepper (1982) examined the timing of major and minor innovations, and found that major innovations were typically introduced early in the industry life cycle. Jovanovic and Macdonald (1994a, b) modeled innovative activity as the causal driver of the patterns observed for key industry variables over the life cycle. In Jovanovic and MacDonald (1994a) for instance, the competitive diffusion was a result of innovation by the technological leaders, and imitation activity by the laggards in the firm. In Jovanovic and MacDonald (1994b), entry was initially fueled by innovative opportunities and shakeout occurred due to failure of firms to innovate in the later stages. Audretsch (1995) identified systematic differences over time between the innovation rate in small manufacturing firms and the total innovation rate, which he interpreted as indicative of the growth stages or 'entrepreneurial regimes' in manufacturing industries. Thus, in keeping with the technology studies discussed above, evolutionary economists identify the bulk of the innovations introduced later in the industry life cycle as minor or incremental.

Although patenting activity may not capture all innovation, Agarwal (1998) examined patent trends across 33 industries and found that the number of patents increased initially, but then fell over time. This effect was most profound in the

TABLE 1.5 Standardized annual entry, exit, and number of firms by stages for 25 product markets.*

	Stage						
	1	*2A*	*2B*	*3*	*4A*	*4B*	*5* *(to 1991)*
Number of years							
Mean	9.76	13.68	5.77	6.38	10.05	7.06	15.00
Median	7.00	10.00	3.50	5.00	9.00	7.00	10.00
Average entry							
Mean	0.59	1.77	1.50	0.91	0.51	0.53	1.03
Median	0.44	1.50	1.33	0.90	0.47	0.51	0.93
Average exit							
Mean	0.15	0.58	0.94	1.45	2.06	1.10	0.99
Median	0.02	0.46	0.81	1.35	2.03	0.99	0.92
Average number of firms							
Mean	0.20	0.95	1.39	1.58	1.24	0.91	1.07
Median	0.41	0.87	1.37	1.51	1.22	0.89	1.08

*All statistics except number of years were standardized by taking the ratio for each product of the average value of the relevant statistic (entry, exit and number of firms) per year in each stage to its average value per year across all stages experienced by the product.

Source: Reproduced from Agarwal and Gort (1996)

high-technology context, where 75 % of industries exhibited this pattern, as opposed to 55 % in other settings. Interestingly, a comparison of the peaks in patents and in numbers of firms revealed that, particularly for technologically intensive industries, the peak in patenting activity occurred after the peak in the number of firms.

Although evolutionary economists have not studied the rates of product versus process innovation in depth, a few studies address whether there are systematic differences in the rates of product and process innovation in the industry life cycle. Klepper and Simons (1997) examined the automobile industry and found that product innovation owing to commercialization had peaked by the first decade of the 20th century, whereas process innovation was very low during this period. The rate of process innovation increased subsequently, with the most dramatic improvements in manufacturing occurring when Ford pioneered the moving assembly line (1913–14). However, Filson (2001) found evidence to the contrary; in his examination of five technologically intensive industries, he obtained no support for the notion that new industries experience product innovation early on and cost (process) innovation later in the life cycle. In particular, his study showed that the rate of quality improvements did not, in general, diminish over time. In addition, even in the automobile industry, where there was evidence of product innovations being highest early on, Filson (2001) found that the profitability of quality advantages was greatest during the later stages.

Furthermore, Klepper and Simons (2000a) examined the source of the innovative activity and found that firms with pre-entry capabilities had superior technological and experiential resources. Examining entry into the television receiver industry, they found that radio producers had higher product and process innovation rates than did other entrants, and their early entry into the industry had a significant impact on the industry evolution.

Industry output, sales, and market share. Evolutionary economics studies also demonstrate a consistent pattern in industry output or sales. Gort and Klepper (1982) and later researchers documented systematic increases in industry sales followed by steady decline in the growth of output (Klepper and Graddy, 1990; Jovanovic and MacDonald, 1994a, b; Klepper, 1997; Agarwal 1998; Filson, 2001; Agarwal and Bayus, 2002). Together, these studies examined over 50 industries to find remarkable consistency across these markets.

The evolutionary economics studies are also corroborated by marketing research investigating the evolution in the sales of successful consumer and industrial product innovations (e.g., Mahajan, Muller, and Bass, 1990; Moore, 1991; Rogers, 1995; Golder and Tellis, 1997). In most new industries, there is evidence of a 'takeoff' point, the first distinct, large increase in sales. The time between industry inception and sales takeoff varies significantly across industries; some products achieve sales takeoff within five years of their commercial introduction, but others have low sales for more than 20 years after their inception (Mahajan, Muller, and Bass, 1990; Golder and Tellis, 1997; Agarwal and Bayus, 2002).

An interesting question arises about the interplay of number of firms and sales takeoff. Examining the emergence stages of 30 new industries more closely, Agarwal and Bayus (2002) found a distinct hockey-stick pattern in the time trend for both number of firms and sales, highlighting a discontinuous takeoff point in each of these industry variables. Furthermore, they found that the takeoff in the number of firms ('firm takeoff') systematically preceded the takeoff in sales. Although there was significant variation across industries, the average time between commercialization and firm takeoff was six years, and the time between firm and sales takeoff was eight years. Approximately 13% of all potential competitors entered before firm takeoff and, interestingly, another 30% of all potential competitors entered in the period between firm and sales takeoff. Thus, by the time that significant sales occurred, almost 44% of all potential competitors had already entered the market.

At the other end, Lieberman (1990) examined the decline of 30 chemical industries and found that their output decreased by an average of 42%. His study also provides evidence of the interplay between firms and output. He found evidence for both 'stake-out' and shakeout in this sample: the decline in output was systematically related to small firm exits, and also to plant closures and decreases in capacity for the larger firms in the sample.

Prices. Studies examining price trends in evolutionary economics once again show remarkable consistency. Gort and Klepper (1982) and Klepper and Graddy (1990) documented that the average annual percentage decline in price was highest in the first five years of an industry and then declined steadily over subsequent five-year intervals or stages in the life cycle. Other studies corroborate the finding that prices decline, but at a declining rate (Jovanovic and MacDonald, 1994a, b; Agarwal, 1998;

Klepper and Simons, 2000b; Agarwal and Bayus, 2002; Filson, 2001). Once again, marketing studies support these findings, showing an exponential time trend ($\lambda e^{\theta t}$) to be the best fit for the trend in prices observed in industry life cycles (Bayus, 1992; Bass, 1995).

The overall declining trend in prices is observed in almost all industries, yet there is nonetheless considerable variation in the rate of decline, with some industries taking longer to exhibit price declines than others. Agarwal and Bayus (2002) found the declines in price trends to be systematically correlated with the technology intensiveness of the industries; in markets that exhibited high R&D costs, the price declines were much smaller than in industries with lower R&D costs.

Firm performance.   The last ten years have seen an increasing focus on the determinants of firm survival in the context of industry life cycles, in addition to other measures of firm performance. Although several of the evolutionary economics studies emphasize environmental selection mechanisms, recent research has also begun to examine empirical regularities related to firm-specific characteristics. Table 1.6 highlights some of the key findings related to firm performance.

Research on evolutionary economics is related to the literature on first mover advantages and order of entry, but its focus is more on systematic variations in firms' performance that arise from the life cycle stage at which firms enter an industry. Almost all the empirical studies show that entering early in the industry life cycle bestows survival advantages (Agarwal and Gort, 1996; Klepper and Simons, 2000a; Agarwal, Sarkar, and Echambadi, 2002; Klepper 2002b). In addition, studies have also examined how the timing of entry and life cycle stage may condition important relationships between firm and industry characteristics and firm performance. We turn to these aspects below.

The relationship between firm survival and age has been documented with the use of hazard rate analysis. Some evolutionary studies confirm that hazard rates decline monotonically with age (Klepper and Simons, 2000a; Klepper, 2002a,b) in a manner similar to other studies based on longitudinal, but not industry evolution data (see the review by Sutton, 1997). However, other studies indicate that the industry life cycle may affect this relationship. Agarwal and Gort (1996) found that the hazard rates of early entrants exhibit nonmonotonicity – the hazard rates of early-stage entrants exhibited an initial increase, a period of decline, and a subsequent increase, which the authors attributed to 'senility'. In contrast, later-stage entrants exhibited the highest hazard rates immediately after entry, and their hazard rates declined as they aged, though these rates also began to increase after a certain point.

Similarly, in studying the relationship between firm performance and firm size in the context of industry evolution, researchers find broad support for the positive relationship between firm size and survival or market share, a relationship captured in our initial description of industry development (Klepper and Simons, 2000b; Agarwal, Sarkar, and Echambadi, 2002; Sarkar *et al.*, 2006; Bayus and Agarwal, 2007). However, disadvantages related to size may differ over the course of the industry life cycle, and based on the technological intensity of the industry. Lieberman (1990), focusing on the declining stage only, found that small firms

TABLE 1.6 Evolutionary economics: empirical regularities in drivers of firm performance.

Key studies	Sample	Timing of entry	Age of firm	Size of firm	Pre-entry experience	Technology and other variables
Lieberman (1990)	30 chemical industries spanning 1961–1987			In industries facing decline, small firms exited at a disproportion-ately higher rate than large firms		In industries facing decline, single product firms are less likely to exit the market than diversified firms
Audretsch (1991)	11 000 firms in 295 4-digit SIC industries.					Survival is promoted by small-firm innovative activity, but is lower in industries with economies of scale, and high capital-labor ratio

Agarwal and Gort (1996)	25 industries spanning 1908–1991	Entrants in earlier stages have higher survival rates relative to entrants in later stages	Hazard rates of early entrants have an inverted-U shaped relationship with firm age, while hazard rates of late entrants generally decrease monotonically with age		High technology intensity industries have higher ratios of entrant to incumbent survival rates
Klepper and Simons (2000a)	Television receiver industry 1947–1989	Pre-entry experienced firms enter earlier than other firms, and survival is positively related to timing of entry	Larger diversifying entrants (radio producers) entered earlier, and had higher survival rates and market shares relative to all other types of firms	Diversifying entrants (radio producers) survived longer and had larger market shares relative to other entrants	Firm level innovation is positively related to survival rates

(continued overleaf)

TABLE 1.6 (continued)

Key studies	Sample	Timing of entry	Age of firm	Size of firm	Pre-entry experience	Technology and other variables
Klepper (2002a,b); Klepper and Simons (2005)	Automobiles 1895–1966; Automobile tires 1905–1981; Televisions 1946–1989; Penicillin 1943–1992	Early entrants have higher survival rates than late entrants. Early entrants are by far the dominant source of innovation	Hazard rates decline with age of the firm		Inexperienced firms have a higher hazard than experienced firms at all ages and in all entry cohorts.	Higher rates of innovation caused the longer survival of early entrants and affected the survival of all market entrants.
Agarwal, Sarkar, and Echambadi (2002)	33 industries spanning 1908–1991	Entrants in the growth phase have higher survival rates than entrants in the mature phase	Liability of newness is observed for firms entering in the mature phase, but not in the growth phase	Liability of smallness is higher in the growth phase relative to the mature phase		There is a U-shaped relationship between failure rates and density for firms existing in the growth phase, or for firms that enter in the mature phase, but no relationship between density and mortality for growth entrants that transition to mature phase

Agarwal and Bayus (2004)	22 industries spanning 1887–1991	Controlling for industry age effects, early entry cohorts have higher survival rates, but do not have higher market share or percentage of new model offerings	The probability of survival *decreases* with firm age	Size of the firm is positively related to both survival rates and the percentage of new model offerings	The interaction of pre-entry experience and industry age is negative; the advantages of pre-entry experience in terms of survival and market share dissipate (and even reverse) over time	New model offerings by entrepreneurial start-ups increase over the industry life cycle
Cefis and Marsili (2005)	Broad cross-sectional survey of businesses in the Netherlands 1996–2003		Older firms are less likely to fail	Larger firms are less likely to fail		Firms that have higher rates of process innovation are more likely to survive. Effect is most pronounced in high technology sector

(*continued overleaf*)

TABLE 1.6 (continued)

Key studies	Sample	Timing of entry	Age of firm	Size of firm	Pre-entry experience	Technology and other variables
Sarkar, Echambadi, Agarwal, and Sen (2006)	33 industries spanning 1908–1991	Firms that enter in the growth stage (entrepreneurial regime) have higher survival probabilities relative to firms that enter in the mature stage (routinized regime)		Liability of smallness is observed only in the 'non-aligned' innovative environments		The innovative environment (two-dimensional measure based on industry life cycle and technological intensity) increases survival rate, and disproportionately benefits small firms relative to large firms

are disproportionately more likely to exit than large firms; however, a comparison of survival rates over life cycle stages indicates that the liability of smallness may be higher in the growth phase than in the mature phase (Agarwal, Sarkar, and Echambadi, 2002). A recent study by Sarkar *et al.* (2006) found that aligned innovative environments – defined two dimensionally as the growth stage of technologically intensive industries – mitigated the liability that small firms experienced in partially aligned or nonaligned environments that arose in mature stages, low technology industries, or both.

Heterogeneity in pre-entry and subsequent capabilities is another important factor examined in evolutionary economics studies. Although we present a brief synopsis of the main findings here, we refer interested readers to the in-depth review by Helfat and Lieberman (2002), and the identification of stylized facts in Bayus and Agarwal (2007). Researchers have distinguished between entrepreneurial start-ups and diversifying firms from related industries (Klepper and Simons, 2000a; Klepper, 2002a; Bayus and Agarwal, 2007). Klepper and Simons (2000a) showed that radio producers tended to enter the television receiver industry earlier than other entrants and also experienced higher market shares and survival rates. Furthermore, these diversifying entrants had higher rates of innovation, and they dominated over the other firms for much of the industry life cycle.

Pre-entry experience also matters at the more micro level of analysis. Klepper (2002a) and Agarwal *et al.* (2004) further identified the distinct class of entrepreneurial start-ups whose founders had pre-entry experience in a focal industry and found that such spinouts had lower failure rates relative to every other type of entrant. There is. however, some evidence that the industry life cycle may condition the pre-entry experience–firm performance relationship. Bayus and Agarwal (2007) showed that the performance advantages of diversifying entrants, which accrued due to differences in product technology strategies, dissipated over time.

Finally, industry-level characteristics such as technological intensity have also been shown to affect firm performance. Corroborating findings about firm-level innovation and technology strategy (Klepper and Simons, 2000a; Bayus and Agarwal, 2007), scholars have shown that at the industry level too, technological intensity can have a positive effect on overall survival rates, particularly for entrants (Agarwal and Gort, 1996; Sarkar *et al.* 2006).

Empirical regularities in the organization ecology literature

Organizational ecologists have sought to explain how social environments shape the evolution of industries, in particular changes in organizational populations over time. Although technological change has not been the explicit focus of research in this tradition, many of the patterns studied in this literature inform our understanding of technology and industry evolution. Two aspects are particularly relevant – the determinants of the number of organizations/entry rates in an industry over time, and the determinants of organizational survival. For our purposes we focus on ecological studies set in technology-based industries (see Singh and Lumsden (1990) and Baum and Amburgey (2002) for more comprehensive reviews).

Number of organizations (population density) and entry (founding). Empirical studies in organizational ecology have traced the number of organizations in an industry from its inception through maturity, documenting the same highly robust pattern found in the technology management and evolutionary economics literature: the number of organizations (population density) starts low, increases rapidly, peaks, and then begins to decline (see Table 1.7). This pattern was initially documented in a range of settings including American labor unions (Hannan and Freeman 1987, 1988) newspapers (Carroll and Delacroix, 1982), and microbreweries (Carroll and Swaminathan, 2000), but it has also been documented in technology-based industries including telephones (Barnett, 1990), fax machines (Baum, Korn, and Kotha, 1995), disk arrays (McKendrick and Carroll, 2001) and microprocessors (Wade, 1995).

In addition to noting patterns in the overall number of organizations, organizational ecologists have focused on the drivers of gross entry into an industry. The dominant finding – density dependence – is an inverted U-shaped relationship between entry rates and population density. Increases in the population of organizations initially drives increased levels of entry due to legitimization, but eventually competition associated with high levels of density discourages entry. This pattern also holds for technology-based industries. Wade (1995, 1996) studied entry patterns in the microprocessor industry. Instead of looking at aggregate industry density, he split the industry into technical communities, each comprised of a leading firm that sponsored one or more designs, and second source firms that followed. Wade found that sponsor entry had an inverted U relationship with the number of technical communities, and second source entry had an inverted U-shaped relationship with both the density of communities within the industry, and with the density of second source firms within each community.

Baum, Korn, and Kotha (1995) examined facsimile transmission service organizations in the context of the establishment of a dominant design. They documented the growth in the number of facsimile producers from the inception of the industry in the late 1960s through the 1980s, with the establishment of the dominant design occurring in 1980. Their findings for Manhattan area organizations showed an important interplay between the setting of the dominant design and ecological processes of entry and exit. Entry rates increased over time during the pre-dominant-design period but were suppressed immediately after the establishment of a dominant design. However, the effect of the dominant design on both entry and exit rates attenuated over time, disappearing altogether from four to six years after the dominant design standard was set.

Organizational mortality. In addition to relating founding rates to population density, a key area of interest in organization ecology relates to the determinants of organizational mortality. Table 1.8 lists key studies in technology-based industries that have examined the relationship between firm mortality and environmental and firm characteristics. A key empirical regularity in the organizational ecology literature relates to the mortality–density relationship. Researchers have consistently found that failures initially tend to decrease with increases in density, and then increase (e.g., Hannan and Freeman, 1988; Carroll and Hannan, 1989; Baum and Oliver 1991; Carroll *et al.*, 1996). An integrative study by Agarwal, Sarkar, and

TABLE 1.7 Organizational ecology studies: empirical regularities in industry patterns for technology-based industries.

Key studies	Sample	Number of firms (density)	Entry (founding) rates as a function of density
Baum, Korn, and Kotha (1995)	Facsimile transmission service organizations 1965–1992	Number of firms is relatively flat, and then increases dramatically once a dominant design emerges	Entry rates increased over time during the pre-dominant design period, were suppressed immediately after the setting of dominant design, but the suppression effect attenuated over time. Entry rates had an inverse U shaped relationship with the focal firm's cohort density
Barnett (1990)	Telephone companies in Pennsylvania 1877–1934 and telephone companies in Southeast Iowa 1900–1930	Number of firms first increases, and then decreases, although decrease is substantially more pronounced in Pennsylvania	There is a surge of firms entering in the first seven years after two Bell Telephone Companies' patents expired
Wade (1995)	Microprocessor industry 1971–1989	n/a	Second source entry has an inverted U shape relationship with density of communities and density within community
Wade (1996)	Microprocessor industry 1971–1989	During most of the time period, density of sponsor firms increases, but at a decreasing rate. There is a slight decrease in density at the very end of the time period	Sponsor entry has an inverted U shape relationship with density of communities. Sponsor entry has a negative relationship with the density of second source firms

TABLE 1.8 Empirical regularities in firm survival from organizational ecology studies.

Key studies	Sample	Number of firms (density)	Age of firm	Size of firm	Pre-entry experience and other variables
Freeman, Carroll, and Hannan (1983)	US semiconductors 1951–1979, local newspapers 1800–1975, and American National Labor Unions 1860–1980	n/a	Failure rates decrease monotonically with age, with the initial failure rate being almost five times higher than the asymptote rate	Size increases the likelihood of failure	n/a
Barnett (1990)	Telephone companies in Pennsylvania 1877–1934 and telephone companies in Southeast Iowa 1900–1930	Failure rates increase with density of firms using the same technology, but can actually decrease with density of firms using a different but complementary technology	In the Pennsylvania sample, failure rates increase with firm age; failure rates were not affected by firm age in the Iowa sample	Size of firm was not found to be significant	Failure rates decreased with market size

Baum, Korn, and Kotha (1995)	Facsimile transmission service organizations 1965–1992	Failure rates for pre-dominant design cohort firms increase with own cohort density Failure rates for post-dominant design cohort firms increase with pre-dominant design cohort density, but have a U-shaped relationship with own cohort density	Failure rates for pre-dominant design cohort firms increase with firm age; failure rates of post-dominant design cohort firms were not affected by firm age	Failure rates for the pre-dominant design cohort increase with analog sales but decrease with digital sales; reverse is true for the post-dominant design cohort	Diversified entrants had lower failure rates than firms offering only facsimile services; the establishment of the dominant design decreased (increased) failure rates of the pre-dominant design (post-dominant design) cohorts, but this effect attenuates over time; the failure rates for firms in the pre-dominant design cohorts decrease with number of firms founded and number of firms failed in the same cohort
Carroll, Bigelow, Seidel, and Tsai (1996)	US automobile industry 1885–1981	Failure rates have a U-shaped relationship with density	Failure rates decrease with firm age	Failure rates decrease with size	Entrepreneurial start-ups (*de novo* entrants) have higher failure rates than diversifying entrants (*de alio* entrants); this effect attenuates over firm age

(continued overleaf)

TABLE 1.8 (continued)

Key studies	Sample	Number of firms (density)	Age of firm	Size of firm	Pre-entry experience and other variables
Dobrev, Kim, and Carroll (2003)	US automobile industry 1885–1981	Failure rates increase with density of firms whose niche overlaps focal firms' niche	n/a	Larger firms are less likely to initiate a change. The risk of failure for a firm changing market niches has an inverted U shaped relationship with size	Failure rates have inverse relationship with tenure in industry. Experience with change makes a firm more likely to survive subsequent change
Dowell, and Swami-nathan (2006)	US bicycle manufac-turers (1880–1918)	Failure rates have a U-shaped relationship with density	Failure rates decrease with firm age	Failure rates decreases with firm size	Failure rates are lower for firms that entered the industry earlier, but the effect only lasts until the establishment of a dominant design. After the establishment of the dominant design, failure rates are higher for firms that were founded with technology that is distant from dominant design. Failure rates are higher for firms that enter with the dominant design

Echambadi (2002) showed that the stage of industry life cycle conditions the density-mortality relationship. They found evidence for a U-shaped relationship between failure rates and number of firms in an industry's growth stage and for firms that enter in its mature stage, but they found no relationship between competitive density and mortality for growth-stage entrants that transitioned into the mature phase.

Among firm-specific characteristics, organizational ecologists have studied the effects of age and size on firm survival. Although early organizational ecology studies (e.g., Carroll and Delacroix, 1982; Freeman, Carroll, and Hannan, 1983) generally found evidence for a 'liability of newness', i.e., young organizations are more likely to die than older organizations, more recent studies have documented both 'liability of adolescence' (Bruderl and Schussler, 1990; Fichman and Levinthal, 1991) and 'liability of senescence' (Barron, West, and Hannan, 1994; Khessina, 2003). Similarly, studies document a 'liability of smallness', a remarkably consistent finding that size is negatively related to firm failure (Freeman, Carroll, and Hannan, 1983; Hannan and Freeman, 1988; Baum and Oliver, 1991; Carroll *et al.*, 1996).

Although density, age, and size are relevant in technology-based industries, most studies also examined other firm characteristics. Carroll *et al.* (1996) found that diversifying entrants in the automobile industry, particularly from related industries, had a significantly lower failure rate than entrepreneurial start-ups.

In his 1990 study of telephone companies, Barnett split the industry along technological lines, between magneto and the more advanced common battery firms. He then also split the common battery firms into single exchange and multi-exchange firms and found that common battery firms only competed with common battery firms with the same type of exchange. In addition, increased density of multi-exchange firms actually decreased the failure rate of single exchange firms, and vice versa. Thus, Barnett (1990) argued that populations of firms with complementary technologies could have a mutual relationship. Finally, in her dissertation work, Khessina (2003) linked pre-entry experience with innovative behavior in the optical disk drive industry. She found that whereas startups innovated at a higher rate than diversifying entrants, the more developed competencies of diversifying entrants resulted in longer market life spans for their products.

THEORETICAL PERSPECTIVES

The earlier section highlights the impressive regularities in the evolutionary trajectories that have been observed in diverse product innovations and industries; however, it has been removed from the underlying theoretical perspectives with which the evolution of the industries have been examined. In this section, we compare and contrast the theoretical perspectives of the three main bodies of literature reviewed above: technology management, organizational ecology, and evolutionary economics, focusing on the complementary or contradictory explanations of key questions that the three streams offer (see Table 1.9).

Why is there a flurry of entry early on? Although all three of these research streams document high levels of entry early in an industry, the underlying drivers that

TABLE 1.9 Theoretical underpinnings of key stylized facts in the industry evolution literature.

	Why do we see 'herds' of entrants?	What drives convergence on a dominant design	What drives the shakeout?	Who has a higher probability of survival and why
Technology management	R&D is on a small scale enabling new entrants to compete effectively (Mueller and Tilton, 1969)	Interactions among institutional arrangements, resource endowments, and technical economic activities (Van de Ven and Garud, 1993; Tushman and Rosenkopf, 1992)	The dominant design enables standardization and investments in process innovation to increase minimum efficient scale (Abernathy and Utterback, 1978)	Pre-dominant design entrants have a higher survival probability. These firms accumulate collateral assets, benefit from experimentation, and benefit from economies of scale and increasing barriers to entry/mobility (Suarez and Utterback, 1995)
	Technical variety of entrants enables industry-wide experimentation (Utterback and Abernathy, 1975)	Interactions among beliefs, artifacts, and routines (Garud and Rappa, 1994)	Dominant design causes increase in competitive pressures resulting in exit of inefficient firms and mergers of small and specialized firms with the dominant firms (Utterback and Suarez, 1993)	
		Consensus building in community networks (Rosenkopf and Tushman, 1998)		
		The interaction of firm-level and environmental factors (Suarez, 2004)		

Evolutionary economics	Differences in information conditions by life cycle stage (Gort and Klepper, 1982; Winter, 1984)	Decreased variety resulting from the shakeout causes convergence on a dominant design (Klepper, 1996)	Rise in innovation that increases barriers to entry (Gort and Klepper, 1982)	Emergence/growth stage entrants have a high survival probability. These firms are the source of innovation, and also benefit from a growth in demand (Agarwal and Gort, 1996)
		Increasing returns to scale due to network externalities result in tipping towards a single technology	Firm growth results in higher incentives for process innovation and economies of scale that drives shakeout (Klepper, 1996)	Diversifying entrants from related industries have a higher survival probability. These firms enter earlier, have the most relevant knowledge for the focal industry, and innovate at higher rates than other firms (Klepper and Simons, 2000a)
			Increasing adoption of external innovation that increases barriers to entry (Jovanovic and MacDonald, 1994a,b)	Stage of life cycle conditions the relationships of key firm/industry variables with survival. Structural changes in the competitive conditions cause and the intensification of survival barriers interact with firm heterogeneity to cause differential effects on survival (Agarwal, Sarkar, and Echambadi, 2002)

(continued overleaf)

TABLE 1.9 (*continued*)

	Why do we see 'herds' of entrants?	*What drives convergence on a dominant design*	*What drives the shakeout?*	*Who has a higher probability of survival and why*
Organization ecology	Increased social and political legitimacy that accompanies initial increases in density	Not addressed	Overcrowding. High contemporaneous density, causes competitive pressures to overshadow legitimization effects causing a negative effect on founding rates, along with an increase in exit (failure) rates (Hannan and Carroll, 1992; Hannan and Freeman, 1989 Founding density create *liability of resource scarcity* and force firms with inferior resources to exit (Carroll and Hannan, 1989)	Early entrants have a higher survival probability. Firms that enter in periods of resource munificence perform better than firms that enter in periods of resource scarcity (Hannan and Freeman, 1989; Hannan and Carroll, 1992) 'Specialist' firms in the initial period have a higher survival probability since they are better able to withstand environment fluctuations and uncertainty; 'generalist' firms perform better when economies of scale and mass production efficiencies dominate; though resource-partitioning may imply that there is a rise in the failure rates of generalist firms relative to specialist firms (Hannan and Freeman, 1977; Brittain and Freeman, 1980; Carroll, 1985, 1987)

are posited differ substantially. Early theoretical work in this area (Mueller and Tilton, 1969) proposed that high technical uncertainty early in an industry's history make R&D efforts experimental and on a small scale. Small firms are thus able to enter and compete technologically, since large firms do not hold a scale advantage. The expectation of positive profits from successful innovation spurs entry. The technology management literature makes similar arguments, focusing on the need for small-scale experimentation to uncover user preferences (e.g., Utterback and Abernathy, 1975; Abernathy and Utterback, 1978).

Evolutionary economists attribute entry to favorable information conditions early on. Gort and Klepper (1982) distinguish between 'type 1 information' – the knowledge of an industry's incumbents – and 'type 2 information', which emanates from sources external to an industry. They propose that in the initial stages of an industry's evolution, external type 2 information exceeds type 1 information, encouraging entry that exploits the external information sources. In later stages, when innovations stem from type 1 sources, incumbents have the advantage of learning by doing and established, familiar routines. Similarly, Winter (1984) identifies two regimes in an industry's evolution. Conditions under the 'entrepreneurial regime' are favorable to innovative entry, since the sources of knowledge critical to generating radical innovations lie outside established routines. In contrast, under the 'routinized regime', conditions favor incumbent innovation over innovative entry, because knowledge has accumulated in firm routines and a pattern of innovation has deepened. Shane (2001) documents the importance of technological regime empirically, in his analysis of whether a university licenses a new technology to a start-up rather than to an established firm for commercialization

Finally, from the perspective of organization ecology, social processes explain entry. Initially the increasing number of firms in an industry (density) enhances the social and political legitimacy of the population, enabling an inflow of resources that further increases new entries (foundings; see Hannan and Freeman, 1987). Different types of legitimization processes have been emphasized in the literature, including the effects of regulation (Dobbin and Dowd, 1997; Wade, Swaminathan, and Saxon, 1998), labor unions (Haveman and Cohen, 1994), resource availability (Carroll and Delacroix, 1982), social processes (Carroll and Swaminathan, 2000), and cultural images and frames (Hannan et al., 1995).

What drives shakeouts? In addition to the wave of entry, the shakeout in the number of firms is a consistent observation in all three literature streams. However, there is little consensus on what causal factors underlie this empirical regularity. Technology management scholars, notably Utterback and colleagues, attribute shakeouts to the establishment of dominant designs (Abernathy and Utterback, 1978, Utterback and Suarez, 1993). A dominant design enables standardization of product design in an industry and marks the end of experimentation. A reinforcing loop relationship between a dominant design and the development of collateral assets implies that firms have an incentive to achieve economies of scale and to invest in process innovation and process integration, and that the minimum efficient scale of production increases as a result (Utterback and Suarez, 1993). Thus, these scholars theorize that firms that are unable to transition to the dominant design in their industry or are unable to change their structures and practices to fit the new evolutionary stage will either exit or merge with the dominant firms in the industry; industry shakeout is the outcome (Utterback and Abernathy, 1975; Abernathy and Utterback, 1978; Suarez and Utterback, 1995).

Evolutionary economists have invoked formal models to explain shakeout, but they are split as to whether dominant designs are the cause or the effect of shakeouts (Jovanovic and MacDonald, 1994a, b; Klepper, 1996). Jovanovic and MacDonald (1994b), for instance, assume an industry has one basic innovation and one refinement of the initial innovation and that a new firm's ability or inability to implement the superior technology causes a shakeout. Their model implicitly invokes the idea of a dominant design: firms that are unable to transition to an industry's dominant design end up exiting the industry because of inefficiencies in production and inability to lower their price.

In contrast, Klepper (1996) develops a model showing that the dominant design can be the outcome of the shakeout process. He assumes that firms with different technologies enter an industry and initially compete on the basis of both product and process innovation. Product innovation, which occurs through R&D, is subject to increasing returns, so larger firms are more efficient at it. Early stages of the industry life cycle are characterized by low start-up costs, thus enabling entry, particularly for firms armed with product innovations. However, the advantage of incumbents over entrants increases over time, given incumbent efforts to grow and their investments in R&D activities related to process innovations. The downward pressure on price that these competitive forces place causes both an increase in the threshold level of product innovation expertise for profitable entry and a shakeout survived by only the more efficient firms (Klepper, 1996). Thus, an important implication of Klepper's model is that an increase in entry barriers during shakeouts decreases variation in product design, and hence a dominant design emerges.

Other evolutionary economics models are noncommittal regarding whether shakeouts and dominant designs are causes or effects, and instead focus on underlying changes in industries' technological regimes (Winter, 1984) and on selection processes as causes of shakeouts. Drawing on Schumpeter's distinction between 'Mark I' (Schumpeter, 1911) and 'Mark II' (Schumpeter, 1950) periods of innovation, Nelson and Winter (1982) and Winter (1984) contend that as a technological regime changes from entrepreneurial to routinized, industry, conditions favor incumbent innovation over entrants (this distinction is similar in spirit to Gort and Klepper's (1982) distinction between sources of innovation and information). The resulting accumulation of knowledge in firm routines and a deepening pattern of innovation favors larger firms that emphasize process innovation and economies of scale, thus causing the selection of the more efficient firms and the exit of firms that are unable to withstand the competitive pressures (Breschi, Malerba, and Orsenigo, 2000).

Finally, organization ecologists attribute shakeouts to a shifting balance between the forces of legitimization and competition (Hannan, 1986; Hannan and Freeman, 1989; Carroll and Hannah, 1989). The intensity of competition increases at an increasing rate with population density, and the effects of competition soon overshadow the effects of legitimacy. The competitive pressures of an increasing population of firms causes resource scarcity, so that as population density increases beyond a certain level, a shakeout occurs because of the simultaneous decrease in foundings and increase in exits. In addition to the effects of contemporaneous density highlighted by the early ecology models, the effects of founding density are highlighted in subsequent models as explanations for decline in numbers of firms and increases in market concentration. Based on the notion of imprinting (Stinchcombe, 1965), these models propose that a firm's probability of failure is affected not only by contemporaneous density, but also by density at the time of its founding (Carroll and Hannan, 1989). Since organizations are shaped by the environment at their times of entry, 'founding density' is positively related to failure rates, and shakeouts occur because firms that entered during times of resource scarcity exit.

What drives a dominant design? Since the emergence of a dominant design is not a key part of the explanation for patterns of entry and exit for organizational ecologists, these scholars do not address the forces that drive convergence on a dominant design. Scholars in the technology management and evolutionary economics literatures, however, agree that a dominant design is not necessarily the technologically best solution. Utterback and Suarez (1993) describe it as the synthesis of features and innovations from prior product variants, and Anderson and Tushman (1990) specifically hypothesize that a dominant design is not the most technologically advanced variant. But if technical superiority does not drive outcomes, what does? By what selection process does a particular dominant design emerge?

Van de Ven and Garud (1993) propose a social system framework for understanding the emergence of technology. They identify three broad domains that interact to guide technological selection:

♦ institutional factors, such as standards, rules, and regulations;
♦ resource endowments, including financing and labor for research along a particular technological path;
♦ technical economic activities, primarily firm activities such as applied research, manufacturing, and sales.

In related work, Garud and Rappa (1994) focus on how the evaluation routines applied to new technologies will select out specific variants. They propose that the interaction among beliefs about a technology, evaluation routines, and technological artifacts, or products, drive technological evolution. One important element of an institutional environment is the set of technical communities that develop around different technologies. Rosenkopf and Tushman (1998) show how the co-evolution of technology and associated community networks resulted in the eventual dominance of one type of flight simulator – flight training devices – over the alternative, full flight simulators. Finally, Kaplan and Tripsas (2008) propose that along with the social, political, institutional, and economic factors considered by others, cognitive forces also drive an industry towards a dominant design. Producers, users, and other stakeholders interact to develop a common set of beliefs about what the product is and how it will be used.

As discussed above, evolutionary economists have developed models that show a dominant design is either the cause of a shakeout (Jovanovic and MacDonald, 1994b) or the outcome of a shakeout (Klepper, 1996). Other economists focus on the role of increasing returns to scale resulting from network externalities in driving markets to tip towards one dominant standard (e.g., Farrell and Saloner, 1986; Arthur, 1989). Although related to the literature on the technology life cycle, the standards literature is not reviewed here in depth. Excellent reviews include David and Steinmueller (1994) and Matutes and Regibeau (1989).

Who has a higher probability of survival and why?   Although technology management scholars have not invested a great deal of effort in investigating the determinants of firm survival, this is a subject of intense interest to organizational ecologists and evolutionary economists. Once again, though, attributions of the causes of differences in firm survival diverge significantly.

Continuing the emphasis placed on dominant designs, technology management scholars attribute survival probabilities to the timing of firm entry relative to the establishment of a dominant design. Suarez and Utterback (1995) hypothesize that firms entering before that point have better chances of survival, because their early entry lets them accumulate collateral assets and benefit from experimentation. These pre-dominant-design entrants can shape the development of the dominant design and also profit from economies of scale and the creation of barriers to entry/mobility. Suarez and Utterback (1995) propose that the earlier firms enter relative to the onset of a dominant design, the higher are their probabilities of survival.

Evolutionary economists who examine the determinants of firm survival emphasize forces related to the underlying innovative activity and the source of information, consistent with their causal attribution for other empirical regularities. Like technology management and organizational ecology, this literature stream also theorizes timing of entry as an important determinant of survival; furthermore, it theorizes that emergence/growth stage entrants have a higher probability of survival than later entrants. Agarwal and Gort (1996) hypothesize that early entrants have the advantage of being the source of innovation in an industry and that they also benefit from a growth in demand. Developing this theory further, Klepper and Simons (2000a) discuss the role of superior capabilities possessed by diversifying entrants from industries related to the one they are entering. Since firms that operate in related industries have knowledge that is relevant for a focal industry, they enter earlier and harness their pre-existing resources for a survival (and market share) advantage. In addition, they innovate at higher rates than other firms, causing them to have a 'dominance by birthright' (Klepper and Simons, 2000a).

Importantly, although evolutionary economics studies show that firm and industry attributes that are found to affect probabilities of survival in cross-sectional studies also matter in evolutionary studies, they also indicate that life cycle stage conditions these relationships. This theory is based on the idea that entry barriers may also be survival barriers and that structural changes in competitive conditions interact with firm heterogeneity to differentiate survival probabilities (Agarwal, Sarkar, and Echambadi, 2002).

As with the other empirical regularities, organizational ecologists continue to emphasize the role of density dependence in determining firm survival. In keeping with the change role of legitimization and competition, these researchers theorize that firms that enter an industry in periods of resource munificence perform better than firms that enter in periods of resource scarcity (Hannan and Freeman, 1989; Hannan and Carroll, 1992). Thus, firms that enter or compete in periods of low competitive density have a higher survival probability than firms that enter or compete when the number of firms in the industry is high.

Finally, organizational ecologists also advance the resource-partitioning theory to explain differences in the probability of survival in the mature stages of an industry (Carroll, 1985). According to this theory, in environments characterized by a few generalist firms competing directly with each other in the 'center of the market', freed-up peripheral resources enable specialist firms to occupy niches. As a result of this resource partitioning, the theory predicts, more generalists and fewer specialists will fail (Carroll, 1985, 1987). A study by Khessina and Carroll (2002) examined how firms with different capabilities compete across different technological niches in the optical disk drive industry. They found that startups competed in the latest technological areas, while diversifying firms and incumbents are more evenly spread out, a result consistent with findings by Bayus and Agarwal (2007) in the personal computer industry.

DIRECTIONS FOR FUTURE RESEARCH

Combining these perspectives raises interesting research questions going forward. In some cases, these perspectives offer complementary explanations that enhance our understanding of the phenomena of interest here. In other cases, additional work is needed to tease out the contingencies that might reconcile conflicting perspectives.

One common theme in all three streams of literature, but particularly in the organization ecology and evolutionary economics perspectives, is the primacy of selection over adaptation. Organizational ecology originated because researchers wanted to identify environmental conditions rather than factors related to adaptation in determining failure rates (Hannan and Freeman, 1987, 1988). Ironically, although many evolutionary economists have implicitly moved away from the traditional structure-conduct-performance paradigm and the hypothesis of equilibrium when describing industry-level phenomena, they have done the opposite when theorizing about firm performance; their models of firm survival all focus on implications of life cycle stage conditions for firm advantages and performance. To be fair, each literature stream does attribute overall industry trends to the underlying firm conduct in terms of entry and exit from a focal industry, but there is scant attention to the conduct of firms while they are still in existence. Interestingly, several scholars examine firm evolution in parallel, with several of these studies using Nelson and Winter (1982) as a base. For example, Helfat and Peteraf (2003) examine the capability life cycle of firms. An important area of future research will be to look at firm and industry evolution together and examine how one may affect the other. Several industry evolution studies have highlighted the role of diversifying entrants, and therefore potentially fruitful research avenues relate to linking firm strategic renewal efforts with entrepreneurial entry and creation of new industries and markets.

Another important question going forward is how life cycle dynamics differ by geographic region. How can studies of national innovation systems (e.g., Nelson, 1993) inform our understanding of industry-level phenomena? With the exception of Chesbrough (1999) and Murmann (2003), very little comparative work exists in this field. Chesbrough (1999) finds that, in contrast to Christensen and Bower's (1996) analysis of US disk drive firms, Japanese disk drive firms were not displaced by new entrants, despite successive waves of disruptive technological change. Chesbrough attributes these differing fates to variations in institutional factors – in particular, labor mobility, access to venture capital, and particular buyer-supplier relationships. Murmann's (2003) detailed analysis of the synthetic dye industry in several nations shows significant differences in institutional contexts, entry and exit patterns, and innovation patterns. Although all the countries display an inverted U-shaped curve for the number of firms over time, the timing and magnitude of the peaks differ. These results raise a number of interesting questions. Do industry life cycle patterns generally differ across countries? What are the contingencies? In what situations do specific institutional factors matter more or less? How can firms take advantage of country differences in managing innovation portfolios?

Another area for future inquiry relates to level of analysis. Although much of the technology life cycle work has defined dominant designs at the system level, standardization of subsystems is also crucial. In fact, Tushman and Murmann (1998) propose that the concept of a dominant design may be more appropriately applied at the subsystem level. Relating the work on dominant designs to the literature on modularity (e.g., Baldwin and Clark, 2000) is therefore an important future step. For instance, interdependencies among system modules can affect the attractiveness of different technological alternatives as well as their evolutionary paths. Fixed landing gear for airplanes had worse aerodynamic performance than retractable gear, but Northrop created an innovative wing structure whose performance was compromised by retractable gear. Northrop therefore continued to experiment with fixed landing gear even after much of the industry had moved away from it (Vincenti, 1994). In this example, Northrop controlled both the wing and landing gear design choices. In many cases, however, different firms control different modules (Staudenmayer, Tripsas, and Tucci, 2005), raising a number of questions. Does the level of product modularity shift over the industry life cycle? Specifically, how does the level of inter-firm modularity change over time? Related questions address the level of vertical integration. How does vertical integration change over the industry life cycle? Are vertically integrated firms at an advantage during any particular stage?

Similarly, whereas in the past industry evolution studies have primarily focused on firms or industries as their units of analysis, future research could examine the role of *people*, particularly entrepreneurial founders, in greater depth. There have been some recent studies (Klepper 2002a, b, 2007; Agarwal et al., 2004) on the issue, but much work still needs to be done on how people may be the fountainheads of innovation and may bring about both the emergence of new industries and their subsequent growth.

References

Abernathy, W.J. (1978). *The productivity dilemma*. Baltimore, MA: Johns Hopkins University Press.

Abernathy, W.J., and Clark, K.B. (1985). Innovation: mapping the winds of creative destruction. *Research Policy*, 14, 3–22.

Abernathy, W.J., Clark, K.B., and Kantrow, A.M. (1983). *Industrial renaissance: producing a competitive future for America*. New York: Basic Books.

Abernathy, W.J., and Utterback, J.M. (1978). Patterns of industrial innovation. *Technology Review*, 80(7), 40–7.

Adner, R., and Levinthal, D. (2001). Demand heterogeneity and technology evolution: implications for product and process innovation. *Management Science*, 47(5), 611–28.

Agarwal, A. (1998). Small firm survival and technological activity. *Small Business Economics*, 11(3), 215–24.

Agarwal, A., and Bayus, B. (2002). The market evolution and take-off of new product innovations. *Management Science*, 48(8), 1024–41.

Agarwal, A., and Bayus, B. (2004). Creating and surviving in new industries. In J.A.C. Baum and A.M. McGahan (eds), *Business Strategy over the Industry Life Cycle*, Volume 21, Oxford UK: JAI/Elsevier, 107–130.

Agarwal, A., Echambadi, R., Franco, A., and Sarkar, M. (2004). Knowledge transfer through inheritance: spin-out generation, development and survival. *Academy of Management Journal*, 47(4), 501–23.

Agarwal, A., and Gort, M. (1996). The evolution of markets and entry, exit and survival of firms. *Review of Economics and Statistics*, 78(3), 489–98.

Agarwal, A., and Gort, M. (2001). First mover advantage and the speed of competitive entry: 1887–1986. *Journal of Law and Economics*, 44(1), 161–78.

Agarwal, R., Sarkar, M., and Echambadi, R. (2002). The conditioning effect of time on firm survival: an industry life cycle approach. *Academy of Management Journal*, 45(5), 971–94.

Ahuja, G., and Katila, R. (2001). Technological acquisitions and the innovation performance of acquiring firms: a longitudinal study. *Strategic Management Journal*, 22(3), 197–220.

Aitken, H.G.J. (1985). *The continuous wave: technology and American radio, 1900–1932*. Princeton, NJ: Princeton University Press.

Anderson, P.C., and Tushman, M. (1990). Technological discontinuities and dominant designs: a cyclical model of technological change. *Administrative Science Quarterly*, 35(4), 604–33.

Arthur, W.B. (1989). Competing technologies, increasing returns, and lock-in by historical events. *The Economic Journal*, 99, 116–31.

Audretsch, D.B. (1991). New-firm survival and the technological regime. *The Review of Economics and Statistics*, 73(3), 441–50.

Audretsch, D.B. (1995). *Innovation and industry evolution*. Cambridge, MA: MIT Press.

Baldwin, C., and Clark, K.B. (2000). *Design rules: the power of modularity*. Boston, MA: Harvard Business School Press.

Barnett, W.P. (1990). The organizational ecology of a technological system. *Administrative Science Quarterly*, 35(1), 31–60.

Barron, D.N., West, E., and Hannan, M.T. (1994). A time to grow and a time to die: growth and mortality of credit unions in New York City, 1914–1990. *American Journal of Sociology*, 100, 196–241.

Basalla, G. (1988). *The evolution of technology*. New York: Cambridge University Press.

Bass, F. (1969). A new product growth model for consumer durables. *Management Science*, 15(5), 215–27.

Bass, F.M. (1995). Empirical generalizations and marketing science – a personal view. *Marketing Science*, 14(3), G6–G19.

Baum, J.A.C., and Amburgey, T.L. (2002). Organizational ecology. In J.A.C. Baum (ed.), *The Blackwell Companion to Organizations*: Malden, MA: Blackwell, 304–26.

Baum, J.A.C., Korn, H.J., and Kotha, S. (1995). Dominant designs and population dynamics in telecommunications services: founding and failure of facsimile transmission service organizations, 1965–1992. *Social Science Research*, 24(2), 97–135.

Baum, J.A.C., and Oliver, C. (1991). Institutional linkages and organizational mortality. *Administrative Science Quarterly*, 36(2), 187–218.

Bayus, B.L. (1992). The dynamic pricing of next generation consumer durables. *Marketing Science*, 11(3), 251–65.

Bayus, B.L., and Agarwal, R. (2007). The role of pre-entry experience, entry timing and product technology strategies in explaining firm survival. *Management Science*, 53, 1887–1902.

Benner, M.J., and Tushman, M. (2002). Process management and technological innovation: a longitudinal study of the photography and paint industries. *Administrative Science Quarterly*, 47(4), 676–706.

Benner, M.J., and Tushman, M.L. (2003). Exploitation, exploration, and process management: The productivity dilemma revisited. *Academy of Management Review*, 28(2), 238–56.

Breschi, S., Malerba, F., and Orsenigo, L. (2000). Technological regimes and Schumpeterian patterns of innovation. *The Economic Journal*, 110(463), 388–410.

Brittain, J.W., and Freeman, J. (1980). Organizational proliferation and density dependent selection. In R.M.J. Kimberly & Associates (ed.), *The Organizational Life Cycle*. San Francisco: Jossey-Bass, 291–338.

Bruderl, J., and Schussler, R. (1990). Organizational mortality: the liability of newness and adolescence. *Administrative Science Quarterly*, 35, 530–47.

Carroll, G.R. (1985). Concentration and specialization: dynamics of niche width in populations of organizations. *American Journal of Sociology*, 90(6), 1262–83.

Carroll, G.R. (1987). Organizational approaches to strategy – an introduction and overview. *California Management Review*, 30(1), 8–10.

Carroll, G.R., Bigelow, L.S., Seidel, M-D.L., and Tsai, L.B. (1996). The fates of De Novo and De Alio producers in the American automobile industry 1885–1981. *Strategic Management Journal*, 17, 117–37.

Carroll, G. and Delacroix, J. (1982). Organizational mortality in the newspaper industries of Argentina and Ireland: an ecological approach. *Administrative Science Quarterly*, 27(2), 169–98

Carroll, G.R., and Hannan, M.T. (1989). Density delay in the evolution of organizational population. *Administrative Science Quarterly*, 34(3), 411–30.

Carroll, G.R., and Swaminathan, A. (2000). Why the microbrewery movement? Organizational dynamics of resource partitioning in the U.S. brewing industry. *The American Journal of Sociology*, 106(3), 715–62.

Cefis, E., and Marsili, O. (2005). A matter of life and death: innovation and firm survival. *Industrial and Corporate Change*, 14(6), 1167–92.

Chesbrough, H. (1999). *Assembling the elephant: a review of empirical studies on the impact of technical change upon competing firms*. In R. Burgleman and H.W. Chesbrough (eds), *Comparative Technological Evolution: Towards a Global Understanding of Innovation*, Volume 7, Amsterdam: Elsevier.

Christensen, C.M., and Bower, J.L. (1996). Customer power, strategic investment, and the failure of leading firms. *Strategic Management Journal*, 17, 197–218.

Christensen, C.M., Suarez F.F., and Utterback, J.M. (1998). Strategies for survival in fast-changing industries. *Management Science*, 44(12), S207–S221.

Clark, K.B. (1985). The interaction of design hierarchies and market concepts in technological evolution. *Research Policy*, 14(12), 235–51.

Cooper, A., and Schendel, D. (1976). Strategic responses to technological threats. *Business Horizons*, 19, 61–9.

Cusumano, M.A., Mylonadis, Y., and Rosenbloom, R.S. (1992). Strategic maneuvering and mass-market dynamics: the triumph of VHS over Beta. *Business History Review*, 66(1), 51–94.

David, P.A. (1992). Heroes, herds and hysteresis in technological history: Thomas Edison and 'The Battle of the Systems' reconsidered. *Industrial and Corporate Change*, (1), 129–80.

David, P.A., and Steinmueller, W.E. (1994). Economics of compatibility standards and competition in telecommunication networks. *Information Economics and Policy*, 6(3–4), 217–41.

Dobbin, F.J.R, and Dowd, T. (1997). How policy shapes competition: early railroad foundings in Massachusetts. *Administrative Science Quarterly*, 42(3), 501–29.

Dobrev, S.D., Kim, T-Y., and Carroll, G.R. (2003. Shifting gears, shifting niches: organizational inertia and change in the evolution of the U.S. automobile industry, 1885–1981. *Organization Science*, 14(3), 264–82.

Dowell, G., and Swaminathan, A. (2006). Entry timing, exploration, and firm survival in the early U.S. bicycle industry. *Strategic Management Journal*, 27(12), 1159–82.

Farrell, J., and Saloner, G. (1986). Installed base and compatibility: innovation, product preannouncements, and predation. *The American Economic Review*, 76(5), 940–55.

Fichman, M., and Levinthal, D.A. (1991). Honeymoons and the liability of adolescence: a new perspective on duration dependence in social and organizational relationships *Academy of Management Review*, 16, 442–68.

Filson, D. (2001). The nature and effects of technological change over the industry life cycle. *Review of Economic Dynamics*, 4, 460–94.

Freeman, J., Carroll, G.R., and Hannan, M.T. (1983). The liability of newness: age dependence in organizational death rates. *American Sociological Review*, 48(5), 692–710.

Garud, R., and Rappa, M.A. (1994). A socio-cognitive model of technology evolution: the case of cochlear implants. *Organizational Science*, 5(3), 344–62.

Gilbert, C. (2005). Unbundling the structure of inertia: resource versus routine rigidity. *Academy of Management Journal*, 48(5), 741–63.

Golder, P.N., and Tellis, G.J. (1997). Will it every fly? modeling the takeoff of really new consumer durables. *Marketing Science*, 16(3), 256–70.

Gort, M., and Klepper, S. (1982). Time paths in the diffusion of product innovations. *The Economic Journal*, 92(367), 630–53.

Hannan, M.T. (1986). Competitive and institutional process in organizational ecology. In M.T. Hannan (ed.). Technical report, Department of Sociology, Cornell University: Ithaca, NY.

Hannan, M.T., and Carroll, G.R. (1992). *Dynamics of organizational populations: density, competition, and legitimation*. New York: Oxford University Press.

Hannan, M.T., Carroll, G.R., Dundon, E.A., and Torres, J.C. (1995). Organizational evolution in a multinational context: entries of automobile manufacturers in Belgium, Britain, France, Germany, and Italy – comment/reply. *American Sociological Review*, 60(4), 509–28.

Hannan, M., and Freeman, J. (1977). The population ecology of organizations. *American Journal of Sociology*, 82, 929–64.

Hannan, M.T., and Freeman, J. (1987). The ecology of organizational founding – American Labor Unions, 1836–1985. *American Journal of Sociology*, 92(4), 910–43.

Hannan, M.T., and Freeman, J. (1988). Density dependence in the growth of organizational populations. In G. Carroll (ed.), *Ecological Models of Organizations*, Cambridge, MA: Ballinger Books, 7–32.

Hannan, M., and Freeman, J. (1989). *Organizational ecology*. Cambridge, MA: Harvard University Press.

Haveman, H.A., and Cohen, L.E. (1994). The ecological dynamics of careers: the impact of organizational founding, dissolution, and merger on job mobility. *The American Journal of Sociology*, 100(1), 104–52.

Helfat, C.E., and Lieberman, M.B. (2002). The birth of capabilities: market entry and the importance of pre-history. *Industrial and Corporate Change*, 11(4), 725–60.

Helfat C.E., and Peteraf, M.A. (2003). The dynamic resource-based view: capability lifecycles. *Strategic Management Journal*, 24(10), 997–1010.

Henderson, R., and Clark, K.B. (1990). Architectural innovation: the reconfiguration of existing product technologies and the failure of established firms. *Administrative Science Quarterly*, 35(1), 9–30.

Henderson, R.M. (1993). Underinvestment and incompetence as responses to radical innovation: evidence from the photolithographic alignment equipment industry. *The Rand Journal of Economics*, 24(2), 248–70.

Iansiti, M., and Khanna, T. (1995). Technological evolution, system architecture and the obsolescence of firm capabilities. *Industrial and Corporate Change*, 4(2), 333–61.

Jenkins, R. (1975). *Images and enterprise*. Cambridge, MA: Harvard University Press.

Jovanovic, B., and MacDonald, G.M. (1994a). Competitive diffusion. *The Journal of Political Economy*, 102(1), 24–52.

Jovanovic, B., and MacDonald, G.M. (1994b). The life cycle of a competitive industry. *The Journal of Political Economy*, 102(2), 322–47.

Kaplan, S., and Tripsas, M. (2008). Thinking about technology: applying a cognitive lens to technical change. *Research Policy*, 37(5), 790–805.

Katila, R. (2002). New product search over time: past ideas in their prime? *Academy of Management Journal*, 45(5), 995–1010.

Khessina, O.M. (2003). Entry mode, technological innovation and firm survival in the worldwide optical diskdrive industry, 1983–1999. Ph.D. Thesis, University of California at Berkeley, Berkeley, CA.

Khessina, O.M., and Carroll, G.R. (2002). Product dynamics of denovo and dealio firms in the worldwide optical disk drive industry, 1983–1999. *Paper presented at the Academy of Management Meetings*: Denver, CO.

King, A.A., and Tucci, C.L. (2002). Incumbent entry into new market niches: the role of experience and managerial choice in the creation of dynamic capabilities. *Management Science*, 48(2), 171–86.

Klepper, S. (1996). Entry, exit, growth, and innovation over the product life cycle. *The American Economic Review*, 86(3), 562–83.

Klepper, S. (1997). Industry life cycles. *Industrial and Corporate Change*, 6(1), 145–81.

Klepper, S. (2002a). The capabilities of new firms and the evolution of the US automobile industry. *Industrial and Corporate Change*, 11(4), 645–66.

Klepper, S. (2002b). Firm survival and the evolution of oligopoly. *RAND Journal of Economics*, 33(1), 37–61.

Klepper, S., and Graddy, E. (1990). The evolution of new industries and determinants of market structure. *RAND Journal of Economics*, 21(1), 27–44.

Klepper, S., and Miller, J.H. (1995). Entry, exit, and shakeouts in the United States in new manufactured products. *International Journal of Industrial Organization*, 13(4), 567–91.

Klepper, S., and Simons, K.L. (1997). Technological extinctions of industrial firms: an inquiry into their nature and causes. *Industrial and Corporate Change*, 6(2), 1–82.

Klepper, S., and Simons, K.L. (2000a) Dominance by birthright: entry of prior radio producers and competitive ramifications in the U.S. television receiver industry. *Strategic Management Journal*, 21(10/11), 997–1016.

Klepper, S., and Simons, K.L. (2000b). The making of an oligopoly: firm survival and technological change in the evolution of the U.S. tire industry. *The Journal of Political Economy*, 108(4), 728–60.

Klepper, S., and Simons, K.L. (2005). Industry shakeouts and technological change. *International Journal of Industrial Organization*, 23, 23–43.

Klepper, S. (2007). Disagreements, spinoffs, and the evolution of Detroit as the capital of the U.S. automobile industry. *Management Science*, 53(4), 616–31.

Levinthal, D. (1998). The slow pace of rapid technological change: gradualism and punctuation in technological change. *Industrial and Corporate Change*, 7(2), 217–47.

Lieberman, M.B. (1990). Exit from declining industries: 'Shakeout' or 'Stakeout'? *RAND Journal of Economics*, 21(4), 538–54.

Mahajan, V., Muller, E., and Bass, F.M. (1990). New product diffusion models in Marketing: a review and directions for research. *Journal of Marketing*, 54(1), 1–26.

Matutes, C., and Regibeau, P. (1989). Standardization across markets and entry. *The Journal of Industrial Economics*, 37(4), 359–71.

McGahan, A.M., and Silverman, B.S. (2001). How does innovative activity change as industries mature? *International Journal of Industrial Organization*, 19(7), 1141–60.

McKendrick, D.G., and Carroll, G.R. (2001). On the genesis of organizational forms: evidence from the market for disk arrays. *Organization Science*, 12(6), 661–82.

Mitchell, W. (1989). Whether and when? Probability and timing of incumbents' entry into emerging industrial subfields. *Administrative Science Quarterly*, 34, 208–30.

Mitchell, W. (1991). Dual clocks: entry order influences on incumbent and newcomer market share and survival when specialized assets retain their value. *Strategic Management Journal*, 12, 85–100.

Moore, G. (1991). *Crossing the chasm*. New York: Harper Collins.

Mueller, D.C., and Tilton, J.E. (1969). Research and development costs as a barrier to entry. *The Canadian Journal of Economics*, 2(4), 570–79.

Murmann, J.P. (2003). *Knowledge and competitive advantage: the coevolution of firms, technology, and national institutions*. New York: Cambridge University Press.

Myers, S., and Marquis, D.G. (1969). *Successful industrial innovations: a study of factors underlying innovation in selected firms*. Washington DC: National Science Foundation.

Nelson, R.R. (1993). *National innovation systems: a comparative analysis*. New York: Oxford University Press.

Nelson, R.R., and Winter, S. (1982). *An evolutionary theory of economic change*. Cambridge, MA: Harvard University Press.

Noble, D. (1984). *Forces of production*. New York: Knopf.

O'Reilly, C. and Tushman, M.L. (2008). Ambidexterity as a dynamic capability: resolving the innovator's dilemma. *Research in Organizational Behavior*, 28, 185–206.

Rogers, E.M. (1995). *Diffusion of innovations*. New York: Free Press.

Rosenkopf, L., and Tushman, M. (1994). The coevolution of technology and organization. In J.A.C. Baum and J. Singh (eds), *Evolutionary Dynamics of Organizations*. New York: Oxford University Press.

Rosenkopf, L., and Tushman, M.L. (1998). The coevolution of community networks and technology: lessons from the flight simulation industry. *Industrial and Corporate Change*, 7(2), 311–46.

Rothaermel, F.T. (2001). Incumbent's advantage through exploiting complementary assets via interfirm cooperation. *Strategic Management Journal*, 22(6/7), 687–99.

Rothaermel, F.T., and Hill, C.W.L. (2005). Technological discontinuities and complementary assets: a longitudinal study of industry and firm performance. *Organization Science*, 16(1), 52–70.

Sarkar, M.B., Echambadi, R., Agarwal, R., and Sen, B. (2006). The effect of the innovative environment on exit of entrepreneurial firms. *Strategic Management Journal*, 27, 519–39.

Schumpeter, J. (1911) (1934). *The theory of economic development*. Harvard University Press: Cambridge, MA.

Schumpeter, J.A. (1950). *Capitalism, Socialism and Democracy*. New York: Harper & Row.

Shane, S. (2001). Technology regimes and new firm formation. *Management Science*, 47(9), 1173–90.

Singh, J.V., and Lumsden, C.J. (1990). Theory and research in organizational ecology. *Annual Review of Sociology*, 16, 161–95.

Staudenmayer, N., Tripsas, M., and Tucci, C. (2005). Interfirm modularity and the implications for product development. *Jounal of Product Innovation Management*, 22, 303–21.

Stinchcombe, A.L. (1965). Social structure and organizations. In J.G. March (ed.), *Handbook of Organizations*. Chicago, IL: Rand-McNally.

Stuart, T.E., and Podolny, J.M. (1996). Local search and the evolution of technological capabilities. *Strategic Management Journal* 17, (Special Issue: Evolutionary Perspectives on Strategy), 21–38.

Suarez, F. (2004). Battles for technological dominance: an integrative framework. *Research Policy*, 33(2), 271–86.

Suarez, F.F., and Utterback, J.M. (1995). Dominant designs and the survival of firms. *Strategic Management Journal*, 16(6), 415–30.

Sutton, J. (1997). Gibrat's legacy. *Journal of Economic Literature*, 35(1), 40–59.

Taylor, A., and Greve, H. (2006). Superman or the Fantastic Four? Knowledge combination and experience in innovative teams. *Academy of Management Journal*, 49(4), 723–40.

Teagarden, L., Echols, A., and Hatfield, D. (2000). The value of patience and start-up firms: a re-examination of entry timing for emerging markets. *Entrepreneurship Theory and Practice*, 24(4), 41–8.

Tripsas, M. (1997a). Surviving radical technological change through dynamic capability: evidence from the typesetter industry. *Industrial and Corporate Change*, 6(2), 341–77.

Tripsas, M. (1997b). Unraveling the process of creative destruction: complementary assets and incumbent survival in the typesetter industry. *Strategic Management Journal*, 18, 119–142.

Tripsas, M. (2008). Customer preference discontinuities: a trigger for radical technological change. *Managerial and Decision Economics*, 29, 79–97.

Tushman, M.L., and Anderson, P.C. (1986). Technological discontinuities and organizational environments. *Administrative Science Quarterly*, 31(3), 439–65.

Tushman, M., and Murmann, J.P. (1998). Dominant designs, technology cycles, and organizational outcomes. *Research in Organizational Behavior*, 20, 231–66.

Tushman, M.L., and Rosenkopf, L. (1992). On the organizational determinants of technological change: towards a sociology of technological evolution. In L. Cummings and B. Staw (eds), *Research in Organizational Behavior*, Vol. 14. Greenwich, CT: JAI Press, 311–47.

Utterback, J.M., and Abernathy, W.J. (1975). A dynamic model of process and product innovation. *Omega*, 3(6), 639–56.

Utterback, J.M., and Suarez, F.F. (1993). Innovation, competition, and industry structure. *Research Policy*, 22(1), 1–21.

Van de Ven, A.H., and Garud, R. (1993). Innovation and industry development: the case of cochlear implants. *Research on Technological Innovation, Management, and Policy*, 5, 1–46.

Van de Ven, A.H., and Garud, R. (1994). The coevolution of technical and institutional events in the development of an innovation. In J.A.C. Baum and J.V. Singh (eds), *Evolutionary Dynamics of Organizations*, New York: Oxford University Press, 425–43.

Vincenti, W.G. (1994). Variation-selection in the innovation of the retractable airplane landing gear: the Northrop 'anomaly'. *Research Policy*, 23(5), 575–82.

Wade, J. (1995). Dynamics of organizational communities and technological bandwagons: an empirical investigation of community evolution in the microprocessor market. *Strategic Management Journal (1986–1998)*, 16(Special Issue), 111–33.

Wade, J.B. (1996). A community-level analysis of sources and rates of technological variation in the microprocessor market. *Academy of Management Journal*, 39(5), 1218–44.

Wade, J.B., Swaminathan, A., and Saxon, M.S. (1998). Normative and resource flow consequences of local regulations in the American brewing industry, 1845–1918. *Administrative Science Quarterly*, 43(4), 905–35.

Winter, S.G. (1984). Schumpeterian competition in alternative technological regimes. *Journal of Economic Behavior & Organization*, 5(3–4), 287–320.

2

The Evolution of Markets: Innovation Adoption, Diffusion, Market Growth, New Product Entry, and Competitor Responses

VENKATESH SHANKAR

I thank Thomas Dotzel and Sujan Dan for research assistance.

INTRODUCTION

The success or failure of an innovation or a new product[1] in the marketplace is determined by how well it is accepted by customers, how fast it diffuses among the adopter population, and how large a market it creates over a period of time. New product entry strategy and competitor responses to the entry also play important roles in the success or failure of the innovation. Thus, customer adoption, diffusion, market growth, product life cycle, new product entry strategy, and competitor responses all help to shape the market evolution process for an innovation. Therefore, managers and researchers need a better understanding of the market evolution process for innovations.

The purpose of this chapter is to review existing research on market evolution for new products, focusing on the adoption pattern, diffusion process, market growth, product life cycle, new product entry strategy, and competitive responses to innovations. The review will summarize existing theories, frameworks, and results from the relevant literature and provide insights into the market evolution of innovations, while highlighting the implications for new product management and identifying fruitful opportunities for future research.

---

[1]We use the term 'product' to denote a good, service, or solution, or more generally, any offering.

Handbook of Technology and Innovation Management. Edited by Scott Shane
© 2008 John Wiley & Sons, Ltd

Researchers have examined the market evolution process for innovations by focusing on different aspects of evolution. Two streams of research are relevant. The first stream is on innovation adoption, diffusion, market growth, and product life cycle. The second one is on new product entry strategy and competitor response to new product entries. These two streams of research are interrelated and some studies address issues that span both research streams.

We first discuss the literature on innovation adoption and diffusion. In particular, we examine the growth of a new product as it moves through its product life cycle. A typical life cycle of a product is marked by four major stages in the life cycle as shown in Figure 2.1. The four stages are: introduction, growth (comprising takeoff, early growth, and late growth), maturity, and decline. Although these stages reflect the sales revenue path, the profit path is also important to study. Profits typically lag sales revenues and unlike sales revenues, they may not have a prolonged peak period in the life cycle. The exact shape and duration of each stage in the life cycle differs across product categories and geographies.

We next discuss new product entry strategy and competitor response. We focus on the marketing strategies of products at the time of entering the market and the resulting responses from incumbent competitors. We examine these issues through an organizing framework developed from prior research[2].

This chapter is organized as follows. First, we discuss the literature on diffusion of innovations, market growth, and product life cycle. Then, we discuss existing and emerging research on new product entry and competitive response to new product entry, before discussing the implications for managing and marketing new product innovations. We conclude by identifying the opportunities for future research.

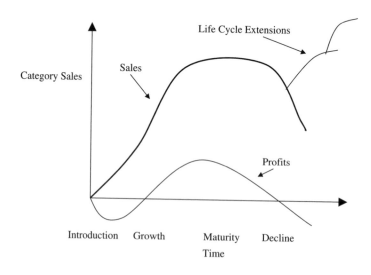

FIGURE 2.1 A typical product life cycle curve.

[2]We do not explicitly address topics such as consumer innovativeness, technological evolution and rivalry. For a review of these topics, see Hauser, Tellis, and Griffin (2006).

DIFFUSION OF INNOVATION/MARKET GROWTH

A conceptual framework that captures the factors influencing the diffusion of new products is shown in Figure 2.2. Four major groups of factors affect both the first and repeat purchases of a new product by customers. These factors are: adopter characteristics, innovation characteristics, firm characteristics, and environment characteristics. The adopter characteristics that affect the purchase of a new product include adopter class, risk disposition, geodemographics, economic value need, and word of mouth behavior. The innovation characteristics include relative advantage, relative cost price, perceived usefulness, ease of use, and network externality. The firm characteristics comprise firm size, firm marketing efforts, and firm reputation. The environment characteristics that drive new product trials and repeat purchases include infrastructure, availability and demand for related products, and market conditions. In addition, first purchases influence repeat purchases, sales revenues, and profits of a new product and firm value (e.g., Sorescu, Chandy, and Prabhu, 2003). Toward the end of the life cycle of an innovation, replacement product or technology takes over. The adoption of the replacement product is driven by the same set of factors that determine the original product's purchases.

Five classes of adopters comprise a population: innovators, early adopters, early majority, late majority, and laggards (Rogers, 2003). Adopters differ in their risk disposition. For example, innovators are very risk-taking, whereas laggards are very risk averse. Adopters are also heterogeneous with regard to geodemographic variables such as location, age, income, gender, and education. The economic value of an innovation may differ across adopters. These adopter characteristics along with word of mouth from previous adopters influence the purchases of an innovation.

Among innovation characteristics, relative advantage refers to the functional superiority of the innovation over other alternatives. Rogers (2003) proposes that relative advantage and relative cost (price to the adopter) determine the success of an innovation. Furthermore, according to the technology acceptance model (TAM), perceived usefulness and ease of use are two dominant factors influencing the adoption of technological innovations (Davis, 1989). Network externality, the property of an innovation by which the utility to an adopter increases with the number of adopters (e.g., telephones, automated teller machines, videogames), also influences the innovation's sales (e.g., Katz and Shapiro, 1985; Shankar and Bayus, 2003).

With regard to firm characteristics, size and reputation of the firm introducing a new product influence its adoption. Large firms can induce trial by deploying superior resources. Potential adopters are likely to try a new product from a reputed firm. The firm's marketing mix efforts such as advertising, sales force, and distribution significantly influence both trial and repeat purchases for a new product.

Environmental factors also contribute toward the purchases of a new product. Presence of the right technological and economic infrastructures is important for the adoption of innovations. The availability and demand for related products such as complements and accessories also determine the rate and level of adoption of a new product. The market conditions at the time of new product introduction also

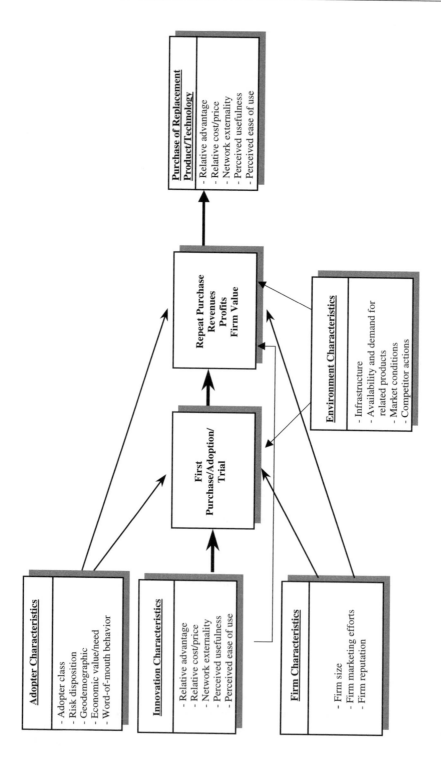

FIGURE 2.2 Determinants of customer response to an innovation.

influence first and repeat purchases. Competitor (re)actions to the introduction of the new product innovation are also likely to affect a new product's purchases.

Several models have been developed to capture the diffusion process of new product innovations.[3] Some models (e.g., Bass, 1969) are at the product category (e.g., washers) level, whereas a few models (e.g., Parker and Gatignon, 1994, 1996; Shankar, Carpenter, and Krishnamurthi, 1998) are at the brand (e.g., Whirlpool washer) level. Most models consider only first purchases (e.g., Bass, 1969; Mahajan, Muller, and Srivastava, 1990), although a few models incorporate repeat purchases as well (Lilien, Rao, and Kalish, 1981; Shankar, Carpenter, and Krishnamurthi, 1998). Some diffusion models examine the effects of marketing variables such as price and advertising, and a few diffusion models capture market evolution across countries. Many models are primarily used for forecasting purposes. We discuss each of these issues in the following sections.

First purchase diffusion model

The seminal first purchase model is the Bass (1969) model of the timing of first purchase of new products, especially consumer durables. The Bass model is based on the assumption that the timing of a consumer's initial purchase of a new product is related to the number of its previous buyers. The behavioral rationale for the model is rooted in two types of customer behavior: innovative and imitative. The model is given by

$$S_t = (a + bCS_t)(M - CS_t) + \varepsilon_t \tag{1}$$

where S_t is first purchases of a product category at time t, CS_t is the cumulative first purchases of the product category at the beginning of t, a and b are parameters representing the coefficients of external influence (innovation) and internal influence (imitation or word of mouth), M is the product category's market potential parameter, and ε is an error term. Bass empirically tested the model using data from 11 consumer durables. The model predicts the sales peak and the timing of peak well on these historical data.

Several models have tested or applied the Bass model. For example, Dodds (1973) tested long-term sales forecasts of cable television from the Bass model using data from *Television Digest* during 1963–1966. He found that the Bass model offered a very good description of the adoption pattern for cable television. Tigert and Farivar (1981) assessed the performance of the Bass model using quarterly and annual sales data. In particular, they addressed the question of how many monthly or quarterly periods are required for the diffusion model to show stability and robustness for data on scanning equipment. They found that the Bass model and a modified analog of the Bass model produced robust results in the estimation period. However, the models failed to predict sales levels accurately in subsequent time periods. They concluded that no forecasting model should be a substitute for other elements in the strategic planning process and that an in-depth analysis of

---

[3]Most models in the literature have been developed for goods, not services. Although many factors that drive the adoption and success of service innovations are the same as those for goods, some are unique to services (see Berry *et al.*, 2005 for a detailed review).

product/market structure is required to justify the choices relating to the adopting unit, initial estimates of market potential, level of temporal aggregation of the data, and the starting period for the analysis.

Mahajan, Muller, and Srivastava (1990) use the Bass model to develop adopter categories for a product innovation. By estimating the Bass model over data on 11 consumer durable products, they found that their diffusion model of adopter classification has several advantages over the classical categorization scheme of Rogers:

◆ It yields a category structure in which the size of adopter categories is not assumed to be identical for all innovations.
◆ Interstudy comparisons across the various products can be based on the basic parameters of the diffusion models.
◆ Unlike Rogers' classification, it does not assume a normal distribution for adoptors.

Easingwood, Mahajan, and Muller (1983) extend the Bass model through a Nonuniform Influence (NUI) diffusion model, which relaxes three assumptions of the Bass model:

◆ word of mouth effect is constant;
◆ an innovation attains its maximum penetration rate before capturing a pre-specified level of potential market (i.e., the location of the inflection point for the diffusion curves is restricted);
◆ the diffusion curve is symmetric (adoption pattern before and after the location of maximum penetration are different).

By empirically testing their model using data on five consumer durables, Easingwood, Mahajan, and Muller (1983) find that the coefficient of imitation varies systematically over time. This variation enables the model to accommodate different diffusion patterns. Furthermore, the diffusion curve can be symmetric or asymmetric and the word of mouth effects are also varying.

Jain, Mahajan, and Muller (1991) propose a parsimonious diffusion model that integrates demand side dynamics with supply side restrictions. They examine the sensitivity of innovation diffusion patterns in the presence of supply restrictions and test the model on data from new telephones in Israel. They find that supply restrictions can generate diffusion patterns that are negatively skewed.

The diffusion of technology products with multiple generations has been modeled using extensions of the Bass model. Norton and Bass (1987) develop a multi-generation diffusion model that encompasses both diffusion and substitution. The model captures substitution effects of multiple generations of a new product on one another's sales in a relatively accurate, yet parsimonious form. Norton and Bass (1987) tested their model with data from the semiconductor industry. The model forecasts overall industry demand as well as the market shares of the various generations of the new product. Kim, Chang, and Shocker (2000) propose a diffusion model that captures both interproduct category and technology substitution effects simultaneously. They show that other categories or generations and the overall structure of the geographic market significantly affect the market potential and sales growth of one category or generation. Their model offers good predictions of the sales of multiple categories and generations of wireless telecommunication services in Hong Kong and Korea.

Bayus (1987) proposes a modeling framework to estimate the sales of new contingent product categories by drawing on existing product diffusion models. Contingent product categories are categories whose sales mutually depend on one another (e.g., software and hardware). Bayus proposes a practical method for estimating hardware and software sales at the product category level and illustrates the model on compact disc market data. The model assumes that hardware purchases have long inter-purchase times, whereas software purchases have shorter purchase intervals. It includes the effects due to market segments, pricing, awareness levels, and purchase intentions and expresses software sales as a multiplicative function of the hardware sales.

Gatignon and Robertson (1989) build an empirical foundation for understanding organizational adoption of innovation, test the role of supply side (innovation developer) and competitive (adopting industry) factors in explaining adoption, and examine innovation rejection behavior. The authors use survey data of technological innovations adopted at the organizational level by a key decision maker whose position in the organization could be identified in advance. They find that supply-side factors and information processing characteristics are particularly important in explaining adoption. Firms most receptive to innovation are in concentrated industries with limited price intensity. Supplier incentives and vertical links to buyers are important in achieving adoption. Adopters can be separated from nonadopters by their information-processing characteristics. Finally, rejection is not a mirror image of adoption but a different form of behavior.

Sinha and Chandrasekharan (1992) propose and evaluate a split hazard model that allows simultaneous modeling of observed heterogeneity with respect to two conceptually different but related aspects of innovativeness, namely, the probability and timing of eventual adoption. They estimate and validate their model using data on ATMs of 3689 banks. If the goal of a marketing strategy is to increase the size of the market, the appropriate segmentation variables are those that have an impact on the overall probability of adoption. However, if a firm wants to use a market penetration strategy and increase its share of the current market, it should segment according to the variables that have the effect of hastening the adoption decision.

Chatterjee and Eliashberg (1990) develop a model of the innovation diffusion process using a micromodeling approach that explicitly considers the determinants of adoption at the individual level in a decision analytic framework. The model incorporates heterogeneity in the population with respect to initial perceptions, preference characteristics, and responsiveness to information. The individual-level characteristics, combined with the true performance and price of the innovation, can be parsimoniously described by two composite parameters. One parameter describes how far the consumer is from adoption prior to product launch, while the other parameter measures the price hurdle and is conceptually equivalent to the consumer's reservation price for the product under full information. The micromodeling framework model is flexible and, given its conceptualization of the adoption process, provides a behavioral basis for explaining a variety of diffusion patterns.

From a consumer behavioral standpoint, many studies have addressed the adoption of new products. Addressing this literature is beyond the scope of this chapter. However, to provide a flavor for this research stream, we summarize two studies. Based on experiments, Moreau, Lehmann, and Markman (2001) analyze prior product knowledge and its influence on consumers' perceptions of both continuous and discontinuous innovations. They suggest that relationships between expertise and adoption are relatively complex. Compared with novices, experts report higher comprehension, more net benefits, and therefore higher preferences for continuous innovations. For discontinuous innovations, experts' entrenched knowledge is related to lower comprehension, fewer perceived net benefits, and lower preferences compared with that of novices. Only when entrenched knowledge is accompanied by relevant information from a supplementary knowledge base are experts able to understand and appreciate discontinuous innovations.

Ziamou (2002) uses an experimental approach to examine factors that influence consumers' judgments of uncertainty about the performance of a new interface and consumers' adoption intentions. The authors find that consumers perceive lower uncertainty about the performance of a new interface and higher intentions to adopt a new product when the new interface is introduced with a new (versus pre-existing) functionality. When a new interface is introduced with a new functionality, imagining the product in use increases consumers' uncertainty about the performance of the new interface and decreases their intention to adopt the new product. In contrast, when a new interface is introduced with pre-existing functionality, imagining the product in use decreases consumers' uncertainty about the performance of the new interface and increases their intention to adopt the new product.

Repeat purchase diffusion model

A few models capture both the first and repeat purchases of a new product in its diffusion process. Lilien, Rao, and Kalish (1981) propose a repeat purchase diffusion model (the LRK model) that uses Bayesian estimation with priors to incorporate the effect of marketing variables such as detailing and word of mouth effects. The Bayesian procedure, developed on other, similar products, to permit parameter estimates earlier in the life of the product, differs from judgmental methods in that it

- specifically and systematically accounts for information available in similar product areas;
- allows for updating of parameter estimates for purposes of forecasting and control, gradually improving the parameter estimates as new data come in;
- allows for calculation and dynamic updating of optimal marketing policies at a point in a product's life when sufficient historical data are not available to make clear classic inferences.

Based on the LRK model, Rao and Yamada (1988) develop a methodology for forecasting the sales of an ethical drug as a function of marketing efforts before any sales data are available. The model conceptualizes the drug adoption process as a repeat purchase diffusion model. Sales are expressed as a function of a drug's own and competitive marketing efforts and word of mouth. The authors test the model on data from 19 drugs prescribed by three types of physicians. Physicians' perceptions of the drug on a number of attributes (e.g., effectiveness, range of ailments for which appropriate) are used to estimate the parameters of the LRK model. The authors find that the model results are encouraging, but inconclusive. The identification of the market potential parameter in their model is also somewhat problematic.

Hahn *et al.* (1994) develop a four-segment repeat purchase diffusion model. Their model includes marketing mix effects and assumes a constant repeat purchase rate. They estimate their model using pharmaceutical data. However, their model does not include competitor diffusion effects. Parker and Gatignon (1994, 1996) estimate diffusion models with competitor diffusion effects, but their model does not include repeat purchases.

Shankar, Carpenter, and Krishnamurthi (1998) extend Hahn *et al.* (1994) by developing a brand level repeat purchase diffusion model with competitor diffusion effects. They estimate the model using data on 13 brands from two ethical drug categories. Their results show that innovative late entrant brands can surmount pioneering advantage by enjoying a higher market potential and a higher repeat rate than the pioneer or noninnovative late movers, growing faster than the pioneer, slowing the growth of the pioneer, and reducing the pioneer's marketing mix effectiveness.

Product Life Cycle (PLC)

The sales of new product categories grow over time, resulting in different stages of the product life cycle as discussed earlier. Many studies have examined different aspects of the PLC (e.g., Lilien and Weinstein 1981; Lambkin and Day 1989; Bayus 1998; Agarwal and Bayus 2002; Tellis, Stremersch, and Yin 2003; Lam and Shankar 2008; Shankar 2008).[4]

In a longitudinal study, Redmond (1989) collected data on market concentration at four points in the PLC for a mix of manufactured products. He examined the influence of pioneer firms' price on the evolution of market structure during the early stages of market development. His findings suggest that markets pioneered by skim pricers tend to have lower levels of concentration during the growth stage, but rise to levels comparable to penetration markets by the onset of market maturity. Furthermore, structural effects resulting from initial price policy are bounded by the onset of maturity and do not have a further impact on concentration.

Golder and Tellis (1997) suggest that price is a key variable determining the sales takeoff of a new product. In contrast, Agarwal and Bayus (2002) suggest that outward shifting supply and demand curves actually lead to sales takeoff. Using Cox's proportional hazards regression model applied on secondary data, they find that

♦ sales and the number of competing firms for consumer and industrial product innovations exhibit an initial period of slow growth that is eventually followed by sharp takeoff

[4]Product life cycle is different from technology life cycle (see Shane, 2001, for details on technology life cycle).

- the time between firm and sales takeoff varies considerably across products, and firm takeoff systematically occurs before the sales takeoff
- firm factors dominate price reductions in explaining takeoff times.

The findings suggest that the market entry decisions of early entrants are based on expected sales rather than actual realized sales and that demand shifts during the early evolution of a new market due to nonprice factors is the key driver of sales takeoff.

Tellis, Stremersch, and Yin (2003) model the diffusion of 10 consumer durable categories across 16 European countries. They find that sales takeoff occurs at an average of six years after launch and the time to takeoff is four times shorter for entertainment products than kitchen and laundry appliances; it is almost half as long in Scandinavian countries as in Mediterranean countries.

Marketing spending over the PLC influences the market outcomes for products. If a firm allocates more (less) of its expenditures to advertising over the PLC, then it would be moving more toward a 'pull' ('push') marketing strategy.

The results of prior research on the main effect (due to changes in market growth) of the PLC on advertising expenditures are inconclusive. Lilien and Weinstein (1981) and Parsons (1975) suggest that advertising expenditures should decline over the life cycle. In contrast, Winer (1979) indicates that advertising spending should increase over the life cycle. Furthermore, Farris and Buzzell (1979) found no significant effect of the PLC on advertising expenditures. These studies, however, did not consider any interaction or moderating effects of the PLC. Tellis and Fornell (1988) examine the interaction effect of product quality and the PLC on advertising and find that the positive effect of product quality on advertising is stronger in the later stages rather than the earlier stages of the PLC; that is, as a brand's product quality increases, a firm advertises more in the mature stage than it does during the growth stage.

Shankar (2008) shows that the effects of variables such as market concentration and firm size on advertising and sales force expenditures are moderated by the stage in the PLC. Dominant brands significantly shift their allocation toward sales force between the growth and mature stages of the PLC. Weak brands, on the other hand, shift their allocation toward advertising from the growth to the mature stages. He also finds that the impact of marketing spending of dominant and weak brands on each other is asymmetric – dominant brands have a significant effect on weak brand spending, but weak brands have no effect on dominant brand spending. Furthermore, the effect of dominant brands on weak brand spending is different in the early and the late stages of the PLC.

Lam and Shankar (2008) investigate the differences between early and late adopters of an innovation on the relationships among customer value, trust, satisfaction, and loyalty. They define early adopters of technological innovations as different from late adopters in their knowledge about technology and motivation to learn how technology works. Using latent class structural equation models of survey data on cellular phone brands of two technology generations, they show that customer trust of a cellular phone brand critically affects loyalty for both early and late adopters. However, brand satisfaction is a key determinant of both attitudinal and behavioral loyalty for late adopters, but not for early adopters. Furthermore, the effect of attitudinal loyalty on behavioral loyalty is also larger for late adopters than it is for early adopters. In contrast, the effect of customer trust on attitudinal loyalty is larger for early adopters.

The role of marketing variables in diffusion

The role of marketing mix variables such as price and advertising on a new product's diffusion has been extensively studied. Although the Bass model fits reasonably well without marketing decision variables (Bass, Krishnan, and Jain, 1994), by explicitly incorporating marketing mix variables, many studies have been able to come up with useful managerial insights and guidelines. Horsky (1990) uses a variant of the Bass model to study the diffusion of consumer durables as a function of consumer income, price, and information. He finds that utility maximizing individuals have a reservation price for a durable, which is a function of the product benefits and the individual's wage rate. In his model, the income-price process and the awareness-uncertainty-expectations process can jointly or separately explain the PLC phenomenon. However, the dependence on the awareness-uncertainty-expectations delay process is only present in certain product categories and is relatively weak. Horsky suggests that if word of mouth effects are weak, a price skimming strategy is optimal for a monopolist and is likely to be implemented by oligopolists as well.

Kalish (1985) offers optimal pricing and advertising paths for a new durable monopoly based on a two-stage diffusion model of awareness and adoption. He shows that under certain conditions, the optimal price and advertising are monotonically decreasing over time.

Narasimhan (1989) uses game theory to examine the sensitivity of the optimal price path of a new durable product to the price expectations of consumers. He finds that in the absence of expectations and diffusion, price will decline monotonically due to heterogeneity in reservation prices; in the presence of expectations and no diffusion, price can still decline over time except that the expectations impose restrictions on how fast prices can decline; if there is no expectation, and if consumers enter the market according to diffusion process, we know from prior research that the price initially will be low, will increase, and then will fall off unless the diffusion effect is very small; in the presence of expectations, and if consumers enter the market according to diffusion process, prices cycle up and down. The impact of consumer expectations on the price path is to place restrictions on how fast a monopolist can reduce its price to clear the market periodically of consumers with low reservation price. The price path will decline monotonically from period one and there will be no cycling if consumers who place a high valuation on the product enter first and only then do all consumers enter who place lower valuation on the product.

Jain and Rao (1990) propose a modified Bass model that incorporates the effect of price and estimate it on four consumer durable products. They find that price influences consumers' decisions on whether or not to buy and that the diffusion process governs the timing of purchase given the decision to buy. They also find that the estimated coefficient of imitation in the Bass model is understated if price is inappropriately modeled.

Horsky and Simon (1983) examine the effects of advertising on sales growth of new, infrequently purchased products by developing a diffusion model and testing it on banking innovation data. The authors find that using advertising, a firm could control the distribution of sales over time. Furthermore, they argue that the optimal advertising strategy for a firm is to advertise heavily in the initial periods, informing all innovators early about the existence of the new product. As these innovators adopt the product and turn into word of mouth carriers, the level of advertising can be gradually reduced.

Simon and Sebastian (1987) investigate the influence of advertising on the diffusion of new telephones in West Germany. They suggest and test several alternatives to integrate advertising into the Bass model. They use a cumulative measure of the total advertising efforts and find that the most valid representation of reality is a model that assumes that advertising mainly influences the demand of imitators. The lag structure of advertising response is best captured by a Nerlove-Arrow (1962) model. Furthermore, these authors found that advertising attains its maximum effect after several months.

As summarized earlier, Shankar, Carpenter, and Krishnamurthi (1998) use a generalized brand level Bass model of repeat purchases with marketing spending effects. Their analysis shows that innovative late mover brands have higher marketing spending elasticity than noninnovative late movers and the pioneer, and that their marketing spending lowers the pioneer's marketing spending elasticity.

Diffusion in the international context

The evolution of a new product in the international context has been addressed by some studies. Two key components of international market entry strategy are the international market scope (the extent of exposure to an international customer base) and the speed of rollout across countries (Fischer, Shankar, and Clement, 2005). In regard to international market scope, the brands of many large firms are typically present in multiple countries or markets with different market potentials. With respect to speed of international market rollout, brands typically follow two types of strategies: a sprinkler strategy in which a brand enters several countries around the same time (fast rollout), and a waterfall strategy in which a brand enters several markets sequentially over time (slow rollout) (Kalish, Mahajan, and Muller, 1995; Tellis Stremersch, and Yin, 2003).

Heeler and Hustad (1980) tested the forecast accuracy of the Bass model in an international setting, using time series data for 15 products in a variety of countries. Surprisingly, they find poor model fits and estimates of the estimated timing of peak sales and conclude that the model is unstable when estimated with short periods of actual sales data.

Gatignon, Eliashberg, and Robertson (1989) use data from European countries to develop a version of the Bass model for the diffusion of innovations at the individual country level. Their model allows the parameters of the process to differ systematically across industries and extends the single time-series based diffusion model to multiple time-series with simultaneous estimation of the effects of the determinants of the diffusion parameters across time periods and countries. The models use the

experience in other countries (international market scope) to forecast the penetration of an innovation in a focal country, while considering individual country
differences that systematically affect the penetration curves of similar types of innovation. In particular, the model provides estimates of the diffusion parameters even for
countries for which sales data are not available. Gatignon, Eliashberg and Robertson
(1989) find evidence of some systematic patterns of diffusion across innovations and
countries and substantive differences and similarities among international markets.

Some studies investigate the diffusion of consumer durables across multiple
countries. Takada and Jain (1991) use the Bass model for analysis of durable goods
in four major Pacific Rim countries. They find that the imitation coefficient is
positively related to time lag of product introduction between countries. Putsis
et al. (1997) simultaneously estimate a model that incorporates cross-country prior
adoption and mixing patterns for four consumer durable product categories across
ten European Community nations. Their results show that a strategy of 'seeding',
or first focusing on Germany, France, Italy, and Spain, maximizes adoption in
subsequent countries of entry. Dekimpe, Parker, and Sarvary (2000) estimate a
coupled-hazard global diffusion model for cell phones across 160 countries. They
identify two distinct stages in the diffusion process: an implementation or trial stage,
and a confirmation stage of adoption. Talukdar, Sudhir, and Ainslie (2002) propose
and estimate a model of diffusion of six product categories across 31 developed and
developing countries using the Hierarchical Bayesian estimation method. The results
show that penetration potential and time to sales peak is smaller for developing
countries as against developed countries. Country effects explain penetration level
well, whereas product effects explain variance in coefficients of innovation and
imitation. Stremersch and Tellis (2004) analyzed the same data used by Tellis,
Stremersch, and Yin (2003) and found that the growth rate of consumer durables
differs across the European countries and that country economic wealth explains
much of these differences.

Gielens and Steenkamp (2004) examine the cross-national generalizability of the
impact of key product, competitive environment, and consumer factors on the
patterns of first-year purchases of 16 000 consumers of 301 new products across
the United Kingdom, France, Germany, and Spain. They find that new products
at either the high or low extremes of novelty did better than new products in the
intermediate range. In addition, intensive marketing support, introduction under a
strong brand name, and previous introduction in another country helped the new
product succeed, and success varied with consumer characteristics.

Fischer, Shankar, and Clement (2005) develop a conceptual framework capturing
the moderating effects of international market scope and speed of rollout of late
mover brands on their market shares relative to the pioneer in the focal countries.
They develop and estimate a rigorous econometric model of relative market share
that accounts for the endogeneity of international entry strategy, order of entry,
resources, quality, and other decision variables, as well as for unobserved effects,
using pharmaceutical data on 73 brands from two product categories in eight
European markets during 1987–1996. Their results show that broader international
market scope is associated with lower late entry penalty and greater marketing
spending efficacy for late mover brands. Speed of rollout, however, is unrelated

to late entry penalty, but a waterfall rollout strategy is associated with a greater marketing spending efficacy. Thus, late mover brands that sequentially enter many large international markets can challenge the market pioneer in a country more effectively than other late mover brands. The results are consistent with Tellis, Stermersch, and Yin (2003) who also found that a waterfall strategy is advantageous.

Methodological issues in new product diffusion

The Bass (1969) model uses the ordinary least squares (OLS) method. This method does not allow the computation of standard errors for the original parameters (innovation, imitation, and market potential) of the Bass model. There have been several modifications or extensions of the estimation approaches to the Bass model. Schmittlein and Mahajan (1982) propose a maximum likelihood approach to estimate the parameters of the Bass diffusion model. Their method enables computation of approximate standard errors and determination of the required sample size for forecasting the adoption level to any desired degree of accuracy. Furthermore, they argue that the maximum likelihood estimates outperform the OLS estimates from the standpoints of goodness of fit and one-step ahead forecasts.

Srinivasan and Mason (1986) propose a nonlinear least squares (NLLS) estimation method for the Bass model. The NLLS estimation provides standard errors of the Bass model and the estimates outperform the OLS estimates. Venkatesan, Krishnan, and Kumar (2004) offer a genetic algorithm (GA) based estimation of new product diffusion model. They conclude that the estimates from the GA model provide better managerial diagnostics than the OLS estimates of the Bass model.

Other methods to forecast sales of new products

Models of new product diffusion, market growth, and product life cycle have been used to forecast the sales of new products. However, other methodologies have also been used to forecast new product sales. In a qualitative approach, Twiss (1984) explains how to develop and use a technology forecast in long-range planning. By examining past technological innovations from a market forecasting perspective and using a case study approach, the author suggests that accurate forecasting is not possible and that great precision is not needed for most long-term planning purposes. Any innovation so marginal that small errors in forecasting will swing it from profit to loss should not be considered anyway. For major innovations, one should be trying first and foremost to identify the big winners and reject the big losers. He also offers a very qualitative forecasting process that decision makers should follow to make a decision.

Teotia and Raju (1986) review economic cost models and diffusion models to forecast market penetration and offer a forecasting approach that uses both approaches sequentially. They use data from energy efficient electric motors to test the combination model empirically. They find that the combination approach of economic cost model and diffusion model may offer superior forecasts of market penetration to any approach alone. The combination model is more effective because it combines the strengths of both the economic cost model (consideration of costs factors) and the diffusion model (determination of the portion of market captured at different points in time) and is therefore able to use both cost and time in forecasting the market penetration of a new technology.

Thomas (1987) uses a case study to describe an implementation of a multi-methods approach for combining independent forecasts of a new product's market potential to improve new product planning decisions. He proposes an approach to market potential forecasting that stems from the behavioral science tradition and has logical benefits. The proposed multi-methods approach involves three steps:

- defining a concept of market potential for the particular product/market in question;
- obtaining two to six forecasts of market potential utilizing as many different and independent methods that attempt to measure the concept of market potential in question;
- evaluating the different methods with respect to the predefined criteria and deciding whether to use one method's results, a range of results, or results from combining the methods.

Urban, Hauser, and Roberts (1990) develop and apply a new product-forecasting model and measurement system for the automobile industry. The system forecasts the life cycle of a new car before introduction and develops improved introductory strategies. The authors use a consumer flow model that monitors and projects key consumer transitions in response to marketing actions. They apply the model at the Buick Division of General Motors. The analysis includes active search by consumers, dealer visits, word of mouth communications, magazine reviews, and production constraints. A test versus control consumer clinic provides data that, together with judgment and previous experience, are used to 'calibrate' the model of the sales history of the control car.

Urban, Weinberg, and Hauser (1996) address the question of how a firm can face the challenge of forecasting consumer reactions to a really-new product. Based on the introduction of an electric vehicle by General Motors, the authors combine existing forecasting methods with the Information Acceleration (IA) method to arrive at more accurate forecasts of consumer reactions.

Albers (2004) proposes alternative methods to forecasting. Using data provided by Lilien, Rangaswamy, and Van den Bulte (2000), he suggests that instead of using innovation and imitation coefficients, p and q, from the Bass model (which cannot be combined because they depend on each other) to describe the diffusion curve, one can define the diffusion curve in terms of the time to peak sales and the ratio of peak sales to the cumulative sales up to peak sales. The parameter values for p and q and the saturation level for cumulative sales can be derived from these two measures. He recommends that new product predictions should focus on the diffusion up to the peak period because the rest is of minor interest to companies.

A summary of selected studies on new product diffusion comprising the topic/problem addressed, the key findings, the model used, and the contribution for each study is shown in Table 2.1. For an in-depth review of new product diffusion models, see Mahajan, Muller, and Bass (1990) and Parker (1994).

TABLE 2.1 Selected literature on diffusion of innovation.

Study	Topic/problem	Key findings/ conclusion	Model used	Contribution
		First Purchase Diffusion Model		
Bass (1969)	Timing of adoption or initial purchase of new products.	Implies initial exponential growth of initial purchases to a peak and then exponential decay. Validated by data. Model provides good predictions of timing and magnitude of the sales peaks.	Bass model.	Develops, presents, and tests a theory of timing of initial purchase of new consumer goods. Contributes to understanding the process of new product adoption, and hence useful for long-term, forecasting.
Dodds (1973)	Long-term forecasts of cable television adoption.	Bass model provides a good description of the adoption pattern for cable television.	Bass model.	Offers model validation for the Bass model for long-term forecasts of cable television.
Tigert and Farivar (1981)	Development of a forecasting equation to aid in production scheduling and market development of a specific industry.	Model improves the Bass model and increases generalizability, particularly across time periods.	Bass model.	Develops a forecasting model to assist production scheduling.
Mahajan, Muller, and Srivastava (1990)	Overcoming shortcomings in the Rogers model of diffusion and developing adopter categories. Comparison of the Bass model with normal distribution.	Shows that following the analytical logic of the Rogers adopter categorization scheme, adopter categories can be developed using other diffusion models such as the Bass diffusion model, which overcome several of Rogers' shortcomings.	Bass model and Rogers' normal distribution of adopter categories.	Brings together two approaches to explain the diffusion process.
Easingwood, Mahajan, and Muller (1983)	Forecasting first purchases of new products.	Model overcomes the limitations imposed by uniform influence assumption in diffusion model. Estimation using data from five consumer durables validates the model.	Nonuniform influence (NUI) innovation diffusion model – Bass Model extension.	Offers a model that overcomes three limitations of the existing single adoption diffusion models.

TABLE 2.1 *(continued)*

Study	Topic/problem	Key findings/ conclusion	Model used	Contribution
Jain, Mahajan, and Muller (1991)	Modeling growth of new products facing supply restrictions from production or distribution systems.	Supply restrictions can generate negatively skewed diffusion patterns.	Bass diffusion model extension.	Suggests a parsimonious formulation integrating both supply and demand sides of the diffusion process.
Norton and Bass (1987)	Dynamic sales behavior of successive generations of high-technology products.	A model of demand growth and decline for a series of technological innovations is presented and validated with data from the semiconductor industry.	Bass diffusion model extension.	Offers a parsimonious explanation and marries prior diffusion work with substitution work, providing a model with the ability to forecast overall industry demand and market shares of various technologies.
Kim, Chang, and Shocker (2000)	A model that allows for bilateral intercategory effects (complementarity and competition among product categories) rather than a one-way intergenerational effect only.	The market potential of one category is significantly affected by others and by the overall structure of a geographic market.	Extension of Norton and Bass (1987) model.	Proposes a diffusion model for information technology products that captures both intercategory and technology substitution effects simultaneously.
Bayus (1987)	Contingent products' sales prediction	A contingent products sales model is validated with CD market data, but more detailed validation and refinement are needed.	Similar to repeat purchase models, but allows for the interaction of contingent (hardware-software) product decisions.	Offers a method to estimate hardware and software sales at the product category level.
Gatignon and Robertson (1989)	The effects of competition on the adoption of technological innovations by organizations.	Firms most receptive to innovation are in concentrated industries with limited price intensity. Supplier incentives and vertical links to buyers are important in achieving	Binary logit adoption model and multinomial choice model.	One of the initial studies of technology diffusion among organizations.

(continued overleaf)

TABLE 2.1 *(continued)*

Study	Topic/problem	Key findings/ conclusion	Model used	Contribution
		First Purchase Diffusion Model		
		adoption. Adopters can be separated from nonadopters by their information processing characteristics.		
Sinha and Chandrashekharan (1992)	Simultaneous modeling of observed heterogeneity with respect to probability and timing of eventual adoption.	Proposed model can be calibrated utilizing actual adoption data at the micro level. To increase market penetration and share, firms should act on variables that hasten the adoption decision.	Split hazard model.	Presents a model that is able to discriminate among different aspects of innovativeness and overcomes restrictive assumptions in previous models.
Chatterjee and Eliashberg (1990)	A behavioral basis for explaining adoption at the disaggregate level and consequent pattern of diffusion at the aggregate level. Considers the dynamics of consumer perceptions and impact on expected utility, and eventually on the timing of adoption.	A segmentation schema can be formulated based on individual level characteristics, true product performance, and the price of the innovation.	Analytical model considering the determinants of adoption at the individual level that allows for heterogeneity with respect to these across the population (micro-modeling approach).	Offers a model that can predict new product diffusion based on measures of individual level variables obtained via a consumer survey prior to the actual launch.
		Repeat Purchase Models		
Lilien, Rao, and Kalish (1981)	Model and an associated estimation procedure to forecast and control rate of sales of a new product when word of mouth effect is presented.	Using the proposed model at a point of product sales when sufficient historical data are not available to make inferences, optimal marketing policies can be calculated and dynamically updated. The effects of marketing variables in the trial/repeat framework can be estimated.	Repeat purchase diffusion model.	Develops a model for repeat purchases with limited historical data.

TABLE 2.1 *(continued)*

Study	Topic/problem	Key findings/ conclusion	Model used	Contribution
Rao and Yamada (1988)	Repeat purchase diffusion model.	Lilien, Rao, and Kalish (1981) model works well. The parameters can be updated when sales data are available.	Lilien, Rao and, Kalish (1981) repeat purchase diffusion model extension.	Validates an earlier model with the ability to update parameters as and when sales data become available.
Hahn, Park, Krishna-murthi, and Zoltners (1994)	Estimation of consumers' repeat purchase behavior of new product in duopolistic markets including marketing mix effects and repeat purchase rates.	The effectiveness of the firms' marketing mix on trial is related mainly to product quality attributes and market growth whereas that of word-of-mouth is associated with product class characteristics and market competitiveness.	Repeat purchase multi-segment diffusion model.	Extends existing diffusion framework by incorporating marketing mix effects and repeat purchase rates.
Shankar, Carpenter, and Krishna-murthi (1998)	Brand level repeat purchase model with competitor diffusion effects. Pioneering and late mover effects.	Innovative late movers can outsell pioneers by growing faster than the pioneers and by affecting the diffusion and marketing spending effectiveness of pioneers.	Repeat purchase generalized diffusion model with asymmetric competitor effects.	Develops a brand-level model that studies the mechanisms through which innovative late movers outsell pioneers.

Product Life Cycle (PLC)

Study	Topic/problem	Key findings/ conclusion	Model used	Contribution
Redmond (1989)	The effects of pioneer firms' initial price strategies on the development of subsequent market concentration during the growth stage of the product life cycle.	Markets pioneered by skim pricers tended to have a lower level of concentration during the growth stage, but have penetration market level concentration by the onset of the mature stage.	Regression model.	Examines aspects of pioneer's strategy that go beyond the performance outcomes for a particular firm and that extend to the structural evolution of the market itself.
Golder and Tellis (1997)	A new product category's takeoff in sales.	Price is a key variable that determines the sales takeoff of a new product.	Proportional hazard model.	Extends existing knowledge by developing an operational measure of sales takeoff and a model that predicts sales takeoff.

(continued overleaf)

TABLE 2.1 *(continued)*

Study	Topic/problem	Key findings/ conclusion	Model used	Contribution
Product Life Cycle (PLC)				
Agarwal and Bayus (2002)	Supply and demand determinants of sales takeoff is caused by outward shifting supply and demand curves.	New firm entry dominates other factors in explaining observed sales takeoff times. Sales and number of competing firms for consumer and industrial product innovations exhibit an initial period of slow growth followed by a sharp takeoff. Time between firm and sales takeoff varies considerably across products and a firm takeoff systematically occurs before sales takeoff. Firm entry into new market dominates price reductions in explaining takeoff times.	Proportional hazard model.	Adds to existing knowledge about sales takeoff times through shifting of both demand and supply curves. The takeoff times have traditionally been explained by supply side factors.
Tellis, Stremersch, and Yin (2003)	Differences in sales takeoff across international markets.	Sales takeoff occurred at an average of six years after launch and is almost half as long in the Scandinavian countries as in the Mediterranean countries.	Parametric hazard model.	Extends existing knowledge by studying sales takeoff across countries and pointing out intercountry differences.
Lilien and Weinstein (1981)	Is there a difference in the industrial marketing budgeting behavior between Europe and the US?	Advertising expenditures should decline over the life cycle.	Regression model.	Shows stability of overall relationship between strategic variables and advertising and marketing spending across the US and Europe.
Parsons (1975)	How does advertising effort change throughout the product life cycle?	Time varying demand elasticities suggest that advertising expenditures should decline over the product life cycle.	Regression model.	Shows the pattern of evolution of advertising elasticities over the product life cycle.
Winer (1979)	Time-varying effects of advertising.	Advertising expenditures should increase over the life cycle.	Varying parameter regression model.	Shows how advertising spending varies over the product life cycle.

TABLE 2.1 *(continued)*

Study	Topic/problem	Key findings/ conclusion	Model used	Contribution
Farris and Buzzell (1979)	Why and how are differences in marketing communication intensity related to basic product, market, customer, and strategy variables?	There is no evidence for a main effect of the product life cycle on advertising expenditures.	Regression model.	Identifies factors that explain the variation in advertising and promotion to sales ratios among industrial and consumer product manufacturing businesses.
Tellis and Fornell (1988)	Is there an interaction effect of product quality and the product life cycle on advertising?	The positive effect of product quality on advertising is stronger in the later than the earlier stages of the PLC.	Econometric model.	Helps resolve the conflict in the literature about the effects of advertising by stating that consumer response to advertising and the cost of producing quality are two important underlying variables that need to be included in future studies.
Shankar (2008)	What is the role of PLC and market dominance in marketing expenditures of products?	Dominant brands shift their allocation towards sales force from the growth to the mature stages, whereas weak brands shift their allocation towards advertising from the growth to the mature stage.	Econometric model with varying parameters.	Extends existing knowledge by showing that advertising and sales force expenditures are moderated by the stage in the PLC and are different for dominant and weak brands.
Lam and Shankar (2008)	Differences between customer trust, satisfaction, and loyalty relationships between early and late adopters of technological innovations.	Brand satisfaction is a key determinant of both attitudinal and behavioral loyalty for late adopters, but not for early adopters. Whereas the effect of attitudinal loyalty on behavioral loyalty is larger for late adopters than for early adopters, the effect of customer trust on attitudinal loyalty is larger for early adopters.	Latent class mixture models.	Shows the relationships among trust, satisfaction, and loyalty for different technology generations during different stages of adoption.

(continued overleaf)

TABLE 2.1 *(continued)*

Study	Topic/problem	Key findings/ conclusion	Model used	Contribution
The Role of Marketing Variables in Diffusion				
Horsky (1990)	Why durables are purchased and how the timing of purchase is determined.	Durable purchase decision depends on household's wage rate, benefits produced by the durable, and its price. Word of mouth effects do not exist in all product classes and when they do exist, they seem to be weaker than previously believed.	An aggregate diffusion model incorporating wage rate distribution across the population, such that as long as price declines over time, the sales curve will follow product life cycle curve.	Offers a model to implement optimal pricing policies and forecast sales.
Kalish (1985)	What is an optimal pricing and advertising path for a new durable monopoly?	Under certain conditions, the optimal price and advertising are monotonically decreasing over time.	Two-stage diffusion model of awareness and adoption.	Extends existing knowledge by introducing a framework for modeling innovation diffusion that includes price and advertising.
Narasimhan (1989)	The sensitivity of the optimal price path of a new durable product to the price expectations of consumers.	Price path is cyclical – in the beginning, price is at its highest level, falls monotonically over time, reaching a low price at the end of the cycle; cycle lengths are unequal. Consumer expectations impose restrictions on the optimal price path.	Model of buyers and a monopolist that includes the impact of price expectations on optimal price path of the monopolist in the presence of diffusion dynamics.	Forecasts sales, including customer expectations in the model.
Jain and Rao (1990)	The effect of price on the adoption of durables.	Price influences consumers' decisions on whether or not to buy and the diffusion process governs the timing of purchase given the decision to buy.	Modified Bass model.	Extends the existing literature by proposing a diffusion model that incorporates price.
Horsky and Simon (1983)	The effects of advertising on the sales growth	The firm could utilize advertising to control the	Bass model extension.	Provides implications for advertising policies, especially for

TABLE 2.1 *(continued)*

Study	Topic/problem	Key findings/ conclusion	Model used	Contribution
	of new infrequently purchased goods.	distribution of sales over time. The optimal advertising policy as per the model shows that the firm should advertise heavily in the initial periods, informing innovators about the new product. The advertising levels can be reduced as these innovators turn into word of mouth carriers, causing the peak in sales to occur earlier than if no advertising were used.		products with long inter purchase times.
Simon and Sebastian (1987)	The influence of advertising on the diffusion of new telephones in West Germany.	There is a substantial delay in advertising response.	Bass model.	Integrates a new marketing variable/parameter, advertising, into an established model.
Diffusion in the International Context				
Kalish, Mahajan, and Muller (1995)	How fast should a multinational firm introduce a new product into its global markets?	Multinational firms should follow the sprinkler strategy in introducing a new product to its global markets.	Analytical model using innovation diffusion models in a monopoly and a competitive game theory framework.	Shows that global competition does not necessarily force a multinational firm to introduce a new product simultaneously in all its global markets.
Heeler and Hustad (1980)	The accuracy of forecasts using various lengths of input data and for international diffusion data.	Results of the model with international data have a poor fit with estimated timing of peak sales for certain categories. The predictive value of the Bass model is restricted in the early years of a product's life and in international markets, the early	Bass model.	Explores some limitations of the Bass model and suggests that managerial intuition may be needed to supplement raw data.

(continued overleaf)

TABLE 2.1 *(continued)*

Study	Topic/problem	Key findings/ conclusion	Model used	Contribution
Diffusion in the International Context				
		point being the time when a forecast would be of the greatest value.		
Gatignon, Eliashberg, and Robertson (1989)	Innovation diffusion at the individual country level.	Countries can be classified on the basis of cosmopolitanism, sex roles, and mobility. Cosmopolitanism is related positively to propensity to innovate. Mobility and cosmopolitanism show a mixed pattern on the propensity to imitate. Propensity to innovate and imitate decrease with increased percentage of women in the workforce.	Bass model extension. Varying parameter model.	Offers significant findings relating cosmopolitanism, mobility, and sex roles to diffusion patterns. Useful methodology with a model specification based on consumer behavior and spatial diffusion theories. The model can forecast penetration of an innovation in another country, using the experience in other countries.
Takada and Jain (1991)	The diffusion of consumer durables across multiple countries.	The imitation coefficient is positively related to time lag of product introduction between countries.	Bass model extension.	Offers a model to analyze cross-national differences in the diffusion of products in multiple countries.
Putsis, Balasubramanian, Kaplan, and Sen (1997)	How do mixing patterns across countries influence the subsequent diffusion process?	A strategy of first focusing on Germany, France, Italy, and Spain will maximize adoption in subsequent countries of entry.	General model of diffusion with mixing behavior.	Presents a model of cross-country diffusion that allows for the simultaneous estimation of mixing patterns across multiple countries.
Dekimpe, Parker, and Sarvary (2000)	Global diffusion dynamics of technological innovations. The role of network externalities and installed base of existing older generation technologies that the innovation replaces.	There are two distinct stages in the global adoption process: First, the implementation or trial stage and second, the confirmation stage of adoption.	Coupled hazard global diffusion model.	Introduces the 'coupled-hazard approach' as a new methodology to study the global diffusion of technological innovations.

TABLE 2.1 *(continued)*

Study	Topic/problem	Key findings/ conclusion	Model used	Contribution
Talukdar, Sudhir, and Ainslie (2002)	Global diffusion of innovation for both developed and developing countries.	Penetration potential and time to sales peak are smaller for developing than those for developed countries. Country effects explain penetration level well, while product effects explain variance in coefficients of innovation and imitation.	Bass model extension.	Extends existing knowledge by studying the influence of various macro environmental variables on the global diffusion process.
Stremersch and Tellis (2004)	Does the pattern of growth of new products differ across European countries?	The substantial differences in the pattern of growth across European countries are explained mostly by economic wealth and not by culture.	Parametric hazard model.	First study to report strong differences across countries in both growth rate and growth duration and relatively small differences among geographic regions – Nordic (Sweden, Denmark, Norway, and Finland), mid-European and Mediterranean.
Gielens and Steenkamp (2004)	Cross-national generalizability of the impact of key product, competitive environment, and consumer factors on the patterns of consumers' first-year purchases.	New products at either the high or low extremes of novelty did better than new products in the intermediate range and new product success varies with consumer characteristics.	Hazard model.	Provides generalizable findings on new product successes in international markets.
Fischer, Shankar, and Clement (2005)	The impact of international market scope and speed of rollout of late mover brands on their market shares relative to the pioneer in the focal countries.	Broader international market scope is associated with lower late entry penalty and greater marketing spending efficacy for late mover brands. Speed of rollout is unrelated to late	Econometric model.	Offers managerial implications for late mover brands with entries across countries.

(continued overleaf)

TABLE 2.1 *(continued)*

Study	Topic/problem	Key findings/ conclusion	Model used	Contribution
		**Diffusion in the International Context**		
		entry penalty, but a waterfall strategy is associated with a greater marketing spending efficacy.		
		Methodological Issues in New Product Diffusion Models		
Schmittlein and Mahajan (1982)	A model allowing the computation of approx. standard errors for the diffusion model parameters and determination of required sample size for forecasting the adoption level to desired degrees of accuracy.	An easy to use method that can estimate the product life cycle of a new product from survey data is developed. It can also be used to assess the efficiency of different data collection and report schemes.	Maximum likelihood estimation (MLE) variant of the Bass model.	Presents a model that overcomes some limitations of the Bass model. Deviations between fitted and actual number of adopters are closer in terms of average deviations to the actual values and the errors are less systematic than those from ordinary least squares.
Srinivasan and Mason (1986)	An alternative estimation approach to MLE.	The Nonlinear Least Squares (NLS) approach produces valid standard error estimates.	NLS estimation variant of the Bass model.	Offers an improved estimation approach for the Bass model.
Venkatesan, Krishnan, and Kumar (2004)	Alternative estimation approach to ordinary least squares (OLS), MLE, and NLS estimation of the Bass model.	Under certain conditions, the Genetic algorithm (GA) estimates provide better managerial diagnostics than the OLS estimates of the Bass model or NLS estimates.	GA-based estimation variant of the Bass model.	Provides an improved method for estimation of macro-level diffusion models.
		Other Methods to Forecast Sales of New Products		
Twiss (1984)	The usefulness of forecasts of technological developments.	Technology forecasting is valuable once it is accepted that it is essentially concerned with modeling human behavior.	No model.	Offers a perspective and factors to consider in technology forecasting.

TABLE 2.1 *(continued)*

Study	Topic/problem	Key findings/ conclusion	Model used	Contribution
Teotia and Raju (1986)	Effectiveness of economic cost and diffusion models when each is used in isolation.	Combination approach to merging the two is proposed and tested to forecast the sales of energy efficient electric motors. Approach can be used with some modifications to analyze the impact of changes in various important factors that affect market penetration of the new technology. Sensitivity analyses can be easily conducted on these approaches and market penetration forecasts quickly updated.	Economic cost and diffusion model.	Presents a methodology that merges two approaches.
Thomas (1987)	Multiple measurement approaches to forecast market potential for new products.	A multiple method approach is useful in forecasting market potential of new products.	Convergence of multiple methodo-logies.	Offers an approach to combine independent forecasts of new product market potential.
Urban, Hauser, and Roberts (1990)	Prelaunch model and measurement system to the marketing planning of a new automobile.	A detailed consumer flow model that monitors and projects key consumer transitions in response to marketing actions, provides implications for advertising, dealer training and consumer incentives and is reasonably accurate.	Consumer flow model.	Presents a model to forecast sales before launch.
Urban, Weinberg, and Hauser (1996)	Forecasting consumer reaction for really new products.	Estimation of sales for a five-year period. Determination of competitive vulnerability given	A model combining managerial judgment and state-of-art	Provides a tool for forecasting really new products.

(continued overleaf)

TABLE 2.1 *(continued)*

Study	Topic/problem	Key findings/ conclusion	Model used	Contribution
		Other Methods to Forecast Sales of New Products		
		regulations. Profitability analysis conducted on an experimental/analytical basis.	market measurement.	
Albers (2004)	Forecasting the diffusion of really new products.	The diffusion curve can be defined in terms of the time to sales peak and the ratio of peak sales to the cumulative sales up to peak sales. This model reproduces the diffusion curves of 34 products accurately.	A diffusion model defined by time to peak sales and the ratio of peak sales and the ratio of peak sales to the cumulative sales up to peak sales.	Offers an alternative method to the Bass model for forecasting really new products.
Mahajan, Muller, and Bass (1990)	Evaluation of the structural and conceptual assumptions and estimation issues underlying the diffusion models of new product acceptance.	Research agenda proposed to make diffusion models theoretically more sound and practically more effective and realistic.	Number of models examined.	Provides a review of diffusion models and highlights areas worthy of further investigation and refinement.
Parker (1994)	What are the problems and potential benefits of the existing new product diffusion models?	Theoretical origins, specifications, data requirements, estimation procedures, and pre-launch calibration possibilities of diffusion models are reviewed.	Number of models reviewed.	Provides an overview of the use of market aggregate diffusion forecasting models to forecast new product diffusion.

New Product Entry Strategy and Competitor Response

A new product's market success depends on its entry strategy as well as the response of incumbents to its entry (Gatignon and Reibstein 1997; Venkatraman, Chen, and MacMillan 1997).[5] The determinants of new product entry strategy, its interrelationship with competitor response, and the drivers of competitor response

[5]The literature on order of market entry is extensive, but because our focus in this section is not on order of entry effects, but on new product marketing strategy, we do not review that literature (for a recent review of order of entry effects in physical and electronic markets, see Varadarajan, Yadav, and Shankar, 2008).

can be analyzed through the framework that appears in Figure 2.3. This framework is adapted from Shankar (1999). According to this framework, a new product's entry strategy and competitor response are determined by entrant, incumbent, and market/industry characteristics. A new product entry strategy is reflected by decisions on marketing variables such as product line length, price, advertising, and distribution.[6]

New product introduction strategy

Eliashberg and Jeuland (1986) formulate an optimal pricing strategy of a firm that introduces a new durable first and anticipates competition in the future. Using an analytical model, they show that if the Nash equilibrium pricing strategies during the duopoly period at the beginning of that period are viewed as functions of time only, they are independent of the penetration achieved by the first entrant at the time when the monopoly period ends and the duopoly period starts. The optimal penetration target of a nonmyopic monopolist (perfectly predicts competitive entry) is less than the penetration target of a myopic monopolist (completely discounts the duopoly period). During the monopoly period, the nonmyopic monopolist prices higher than the myopic monopolist and does not decrease its price as rapidly. The price charged by the first entrant – who correctly anticipates entry – immediately at the beginning of the duopoly period is lower than that it charges at the end of the monopoly period. However, if there is no differential price effect, the first entrant's price is continuous at the time of entry. For two similar competitors, the identical Nash equilibrium pricing strategies are monotonically declining over the finite time horizon. For two competitors with identical production costs, but different customer response parameters, when price differential parameter becomes large, the equilibrium strategies are always to price at production costs. For two competitors with identical customer response parameters but different costs, the high cost manufacturer's price is higher and declines more rapidly than the low cost manufacturer's price.

Mamer and McCardle (1987) develop a game theoretic model of innovation, which incorporates uncertainty and the interplay between technical uncertainty and potential competition in innovation. They show that a firm's optimal decision strategy regarding the adoption of a technological innovation of unknown profitability in the face of potential competitive innovation is characterized by a monotonic sequence of pairs of threshold values that delineate a cone-shaped continuation region. The existence of a Nash equilibrium in cone-shaped strategies is proved in the two firm case, where competition is in either substitute or complementary technologies. The potential for competition from substitute technologies decreases the probability that the firm will adopt an innovation. Substitute competition induces the firm to use a less optimistic decision strategy.

Using a game theoretic model of competition in the personal digital assistant (PDA) industry setting, Bayus, Jain, and Rao (1997) show that when firms are

---

[6]To keep the scope of this chapter manageable, we do not consider partnering strategies adopted by new firms entering a market (see Shane, Shankar, and Aravindakshan, 2006, for a review of such partnering strategies).

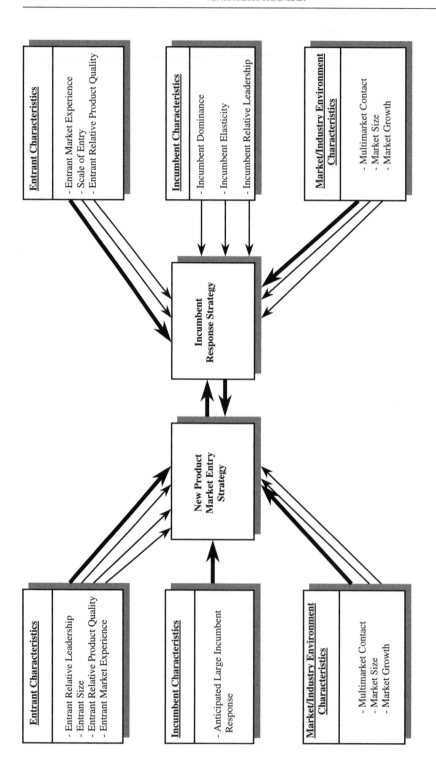

FIGURE 2.3 A framework for new product entry and competitor response strategies.

Source: Adapted from Shankar (1999).

symmetric in their estimates of market size and product development capabilities, equilibrium exists when firms enter at different times with different performance levels. In the asymmetric case, the firm with a higher estimate of market size enters first, as does the firm with a superior development process with performance levels dependent on the sensitivity of demand to performance.

Moorthy and Png (1992) use a game theoretic model to show that sequential introduction is better than simultaneous introduction when cannibalization is a problem and customers are relatively more impatient than the seller. Sequential introduction, however, is less attractive when the seller can pre-commit.

Williams (1983) focuses and extends some emerging views on technological evolution and competition. There is a generalizable pattern over the evolution of many product-market segments that includes a shift from the investment characteristics of product technology to those of process technology as the primary focus of competition. Eventually, market price falls below production costs because of shifts in demand to the innovative form of the product. The interaction of required and realized returns then provides a stopping rule for technologically-driven competition, which is different from the static case. Because technological change within a segment is noncontrollable, but predictable, the production functions and organization structures of participating firms must change in generalizable ways that can be used to predict industry structure. For the competitive organization, these changes require particular kinds of decisions that are particularly suited to the level of the organization's strategic management.

Carpenter and Nakamoto (1990) present an analytic model for new product entry strategy by a late mover in a market dominated by an incumbent brand. They offer a number of normative guidelines for price, advertising, and distribution strategies at the time of entry for different locations of the product positions contemplated by the new brand.

Gatignon, Weitz, and Bansal (1990) specify a set of hypotheses about brand introduction strategies and identify the conditions under which a given marketing mix (excluding price) can be more effective than another for continuous product innovations. Using a cross-sectional nested error component model estimated on data from pharmaceutical industry, they find that the amount of communication efforts used to introduce a brand depends on the availability of resources. Their empirical analysis supports the importance of market growth and superior quality of the new product in relation to existing products. It also shows that the competitive structure of the market is extremely important, supporting the need for competitive analysis.

By analyzing 101 new product delay announcements made by firms collected from Trade and Industry Index database and Dow Jones News Service, Hendricks and Singhal (1997) estimated the magnitude of the economic impact of being late to the market. The findings suggest that on average, delay announcements decrease the market value of a firm by 5.25 %. There are significant penalties for not introducing new products on time. Competitiveness of the industry in which the firm operates, the size of the firm, and the firm's degree of diversification are statistically significant predictors for the change in the market value of firms that announce delays in the introduction of new products.

Shankar, Carpenter, and Krishnamurthi (1999) examine the effect of the stage of the product life cycle in which a brand enters on its sales through brand growth and market response, after controlling for the order-of-entry effect and time in market. They estimate a dynamic brand sales model using 29 brands from six pharmaceutical markets and they find that the brand growth rate follows an inverted-V pattern. Growth-stage entrants grow faster than pioneers and mature-stage entrants. Competitor diffusion hurts the pioneer, has no effect on growth-stage entrants, and helps mature-stage entrants. Growth stage entrants enjoy greater response to perceived product quality than pioneers and mature-stage entrants. Pioneers enjoy higher advertising and sales force response than growth-stage entrants, which in turn, have higher response than mature-stage entrants. The research did not find a direct effect of order of entry or pioneering advantage.

Shankar (1999) develops an integrated framework for the determinants of both new product introduction and incumbent response strategies, and focuses on the interrelationship between these two aspects and on the role of multimarket contact in these strategies. He tests his model using data from the US prescription drug industry. The findings show that new product introduction strategy is influenced significantly by incumbent reaction strategy and vice versa. The relationship of a new product's marketing spending to the anticipated incumbent reaction differs across incumbents by size. For example, anticipated reactions from large incumbents lead to low spending whereas anticipated reactions from small incumbents do not pose a threat to a new brand's spending. Greater market experience helps reduce uncertainty about the effectiveness of marketing variables and contributes to increased spending. Higher spending by a new brand results in incumbent response that is significantly lower in magnitude to avoid a competitive spending war. Multimarket contact leads to both lower introduction spending and milder incumbent response.

Van Heerde, Mela, and Manchanda (2004) model the dynamic effects of product entry in markets when there is no immediate market response. Their model allows for the introduction of substantially different brands and accommodates the possibility that innovation increases uncertainty in the marketplace around the time of launch. Based on analysis of scanner data on the frozen pizza market, they find that the launch of an innovative brand

◆ makes the existing brands appear to be closer substitutes, as indicated by cross-price elasticities that increase in magnitude after launch;
◆ increases the own-brand price elasticities of existing brands over a period of time and decreases brand differentiation for the existing brands;
◆ increases the variance of the sales response equations temporarily around the time of the introduction of the innovation, which indicates increased uncertainty in sales response.

Using secondary data from the medical literature and business press, Banbury and Mitchell (1995) highlight the competitive importance of incremental product innovation in established industries. The findings suggest that effective incremental product development and rapid product introduction are critically important to business performance. Introducing incremental product innovations during its tenure as an industry incumbent strongly influences a business's market share and, indirectly, its survival in an established industry. Early adoption of innovations introduced by competitors has a smaller positive relationship with greater market share than introducing incremental product innovations. Greater market share in turn protected the firms from the impact of competitive entry and contributed to significantly lower likelihood that the business would shut down. Business survival is most influenced by its ability to support innovative products in the market, not simply by virtue of its introduction of technically innovative products.

Mahajan, Bretschneider, and Bradford (1980) present adaptive approaches to the estimation of coefficients of decision variables in the market response model. They argue that the feedback approaches to modeling structural shifts in market response are especially useful when the timing of structural changes is not known. The feedback approaches can help the analyst to assess the time effectiveness of managerial decision variables. If the effectiveness of decision variables is stable over time, these approaches would provide constant coefficients of the variables in the model, thus indicating that the popular nonadaptive approaches provide a good set of coefficients.

A new product entry into an existing market may create additional demand for the product and/or share the existing market by drawing buyers away from incumbent brands. Mahajan, Sharma, and Buzzell (1993) suggest a parsimonious modeling approach applied to data on the photo film market. They assess the impact on market size and incumbent sales of a new product entry by a new competitor into a monopoly market. A limitation of the proposed model is that it does not include the impact of pricing or advertising on the growth of individual brands.

Competitive responses to new product entry

Competitor response to new product entry plays an important role in determining the evolution of the market. Both normative and descriptive models have been developed for response to new product entry. A number of normative or game theoretic models of incumbent response have been developed. Through a seminal analytic model, Hauser and Shugan (1983) show that it is optimal for an incumbent to decrease advertising and distribution spending in a static market. In addition, if the consumers' tastes are uniformly distributed, it is optimal to decrease prices, improve product quality, and reposition the brand in the direction of the incumbent's strength. They also develop a normative model termed the 'Defender' to help the incumbent brand managers in their marketing decisions.

Kumar and Sudarshan (1988) use a decoupled response function in their model and show that the optimal defensive strategy for all incumbents is to decrease their prices, advertising, and distribution when tastes are uniformly distributed, the market is static, and advertising and distribution are decoupled. Gruca, Kumar, and Sudarshan (1992) show that the optimal response varies by the incumbent's market dominance and that a dominant incumbent (one with a market share of 50 % or more) should increase its spending, whereas a nondominant brand should reduce its spending.

Descriptive models of competitor response to new entry have used econometric analyses of data from several industries. Robinson (1988) examines the marketing reactions by incumbents to entries into oligopolistic markets. He addresses the effects of entry strategy, incumbent characteristics, and industry characteristics on incumbent reactions. Based on analysis of data from the Strategic Planning Institute on 115 new product entries, he finds that the typical incumbents do not react in the first year after entry. However, the reactions in the second year after entry are more aggressive although about half of the entrants still reported passive response.

Gatignon, Anderson, and Helsen (1989) address how established competitors in an oligopoly react to a new product entry in their market. They estimate an econometric model of demand response functions and reaction functions with data from the market for an over-the-counter gynecological product and from the airline industry. They argue that reaction time can be better understood and predicted by observing the effectiveness of a current competitor's marketing mix instruments. They find that incumbent firms react positively (retaliate) with their elastic marketing weapons and cut back (withdraw) with their inelastic marketing mix instruments.

Shankar (1997) explains the pioneer's reactions and predicts its shift in marketing mix allocation upon new entry using empirical analysis of simultaneous and sequential games. He develops equilibrium reactions under Nash and different leader–follower games and empirically illustrates the analytical results with an empirical analysis of pharmaceutical data. He finds that the type of competitive game and the anticipated impact of the late mover on the pioneer's margin and elasticities are two critical factors that significantly affect the pioneer's decisions, in addition to the pioneer's characteristics and the market conditions considered by prior research. A follower (leader) role in a marketing mix variable, a static (growing) market, a decrease (increase) in own elasticity and margin generally lead to accommodation (retaliation) in that variable. He also highlights cases in which general reactions don't hold and points out that it is necessary to look not only at one factor at a time, but also examine the combination of all the factors. The shift in pioneer's equilibrium marketing mix allocation follows changes in its relative marketing mix effectiveness. This, in turn, depends on the structure of competition, the impact of the late mover on its elasticities and margins, and the competitor's marketing mix elasticities, in addition to own elasticities.

Bowman and Gatignon (1995) develop a model of the determinants of reaction time of competitors to the introduction of a new product. They estimate their model on the PIMS data and identify significant predictors of response time, and find that response time is positively related to customers' switching costs, market share of threatening firm, and new product development time, but negatively related to market growth and the market share of reacting firm and the rate of technological change.

MacMillan, McCaffery, and Van Wijk (1985) develop a rationale for estimating the response times of competitors to easily imitated new products. Based on correlation, factor, and regression analyses of primary survey and secondary data from the banking industry, they conclude that response time is strongly associated with visibility, perceived potential, radicality, complexity, organization misfit, and strategic attack.

Using cross-sectional data, Gatignon, Robertson, and Fein (1997) estimate the effectiveness of different defense strategies when faced with a new product introduction by a competitor. The authors find that faster reactions to the new entrant have a positive impact on the perceived success of the defense strategy; the greater the breadth of reaction (number of marketing mix instruments used), however, the less successful the defense. The ability of an incumbent to maintain its market position is significantly affected by industry characteristics and the degree of competitive threat posed by the new product entry.

Kalra, Rajiv, and Srinivasan (1998) propose a conceptual framework for understanding differences in the magnitude and timing of incumbents' responses to competitive new product entries. They test the predictive power of the framework in an experimental study. The authors argue that unlike previous research, which suggests that delayed responses to competitive entry are due to either a lack of managerial competence or the managerial perception of a lack of potential threat from new product introductions, under certain conditions a delayed response may be an optimal or efficient strategy when the new product's quality is uncertain. An immediate reaction in the form of a lower price by the incumbent firm may cause consumers to believe that the new product's quality is high. Therefore, it may be better to delay the price response until consumers learn about the quality of the new product over time. Kalra, Rajiv, and Srinivasan highlight the importance of considering both the competitors and the consumers simultaneously in examining the incumbent firm's optimal reaction strategy.

Kuester, Homburg, and Robertson (1999) identify the factors that influence defense decisions to new product entries. Using a cross-sectional survey, the authors combine the analysis of the marketing instrument used to react and the speed and breadth of retaliation. Results emphasize the importance of the rival product's innovativeness in generating a reciprocal retaliation, although innovativeness slows the incumbent's reaction time. Market growth encourages rapid retaliation especially on the product mix. In concentrated markets, firms react less strongly on the product mix and exhibit slower reactions. Larger incumbents retaliate less strongly and more slowly.

In an empirical study of 509 new industrial products launched in the US, UK, and the Netherlands, Debruyne *et al.* (2002) identify the characteristics associated with competitive reactions to the launch of a new industrial product. They argue that two thirds of new product launches meet reaction by competitors after their launch, primarily in the form of price changes. Product assortment and promotional changes are less frequent and distribution policy modifications occur very rarely. The characteristics of the new product launch strategy have a significant impact on both the occurrence and nature of competitive reaction. The competitive effects of radically new products and incrementally new products differ significantly. Competitors fail to respond to radical innovations and to new products targeted at niche markets. They do react if a product can be assessed within an existing product category and thus represent an unambiguous attack. Competitors are more inclined to react to the introduction of new products that are supported by extensive communication by the innovating firm. They are also likely to react in high growth markets.

Heil and Walters (1993) develop a conceptual model to explain the strength of competitive reactions to new product introductions. They empirically test the hypothesized linkages among three market signals – hostility, consequence, and commitment – with primary data from US companies. The findings suggest that hostility and consequence signals are positively related to strength of reaction of competing firms, but commitment signals are unrelated to competing firm reactions. In general, the hostility signal has the greatest impact on reaction strength followed by the consequences signal and the commitment signal.

Robertson, Eliashberg, and Rymon (1995) address the following questions: what factors determine whether an incumbent will react to a new product announcement signal from a competitor?; what variables affect the aggressiveness of the incumbent's reaction?; and what factors influence whether the reaction will be in product or other marketing instruments? Using survey data from the US and UK, they come up with the following findings. Signal hostility is positively related to the occurrence of a reaction. An incumbent is more likely to react when it has high fixed commitments in the product category and in industries characterized by higher levels of patent protection. Aggressive reactions are more likely under conditions of high signal credibility, in industries that have high patent protection, when the signals are not hostile signals, although encouraging reactions are not likely to trigger aggressive reactions. Firms in industries in which patents are highly relevant are less likely to react in product and those with high fixed commitments in the product category show a tendency to react with alternative marketing mix instruments and hostile signals do not engender reactions in product.

Hultink and Langerak (2002) develop a framework that shows how strong and fast incumbents react to perceived market signals resulting from a new product's launch decisions (broad targeting, penetration pricing, advertising intensity, and product advantage). They explore the impacts of three perceived market signals on the strength and speed of competitive reaction. Testing the framework with cross-sectional data from 73 managers in the Netherlands, the authors find that incumbents consider high advantage new products to be hostile and consequential and consider penetration pricing and intense advertising to be hostile, especially in fast growing markets. Broad targeting is not perceived to be hostile, especially when used by entrants with an aggressive reputation. Perceived signals of hostility and commitment positively impact the strength of reaction. Perceived consequence signal positively impacts the speed of reaction.

Shankar (2006) analyzes new product introductions and deletions and proactive and reaction actions by competitor firms. He proposes a simultaneous model of product line actions and actions in price and distribution that includes both anticipation and reaction components of market leaders and followers. He estimates the model using data from the US computer printer industry. His results show that market leaders have higher product line elasticities than followers and that unlike followers, leaders have greater reaction elasticity than anticipation elasticity.

Table 2.2 provides a summary of selected studies on new product entry and competitor response. The table lists the topic/problem addressed, key findings, the model used, and contribution for each study.

IMPLICATIONS FOR MANAGEMENT OF NEW PRODUCTS

Existing research offers several implications for the development and marketing of new product innovations. We discuss these implications below.

New product diffusion models.   Managers can use appropriate diffusion models of first purchase and repeat purchase at both the category and the brand level to explain the growth of a new product and forecast its future sales. They can forecast the timing and peak level of sales, using observations from the first few periods. Managers can better assess the impact of marketing mix variables on the diffusion of new products. In particular, the impact on sales growth of a new product subject to changes in marketing variables, such as product, price, advertising, promotion, sales force, and distribution channels, can be better analyzed and simulated through models developed in the literature.

Marketing mix decisions and new product entry strategies.   As a result of the knowledge gained from research on new product entry strategies involving marketing mix variables, managers can better allocate their resources across different marketing variables such as advertising, sales promotion, sales force, and distribution. They can get a better understanding of the most effective marketing mix strategies for new products.

Managing innovations over the life cycle.   Research on product life cycle suggests that it is important to allocate resources appropriately over the life cycle of a product. In particular, firms can get a better understanding of which marketing variables to emphasize most and least in each stage of the life cycle. Some of the findings from research suggest that, in general, makers of technology-based innovations may need to market their new products differently to early and late adopters to leverage brand satisfaction and attitudinal loyalty in acquiring and retaining customers.

Managing new products in the global market.   Firms increasingly introduce new products in multiple international markets. With a better understanding of international market evolution of a new product, managers of new products can plan their introduction strategies across countries with regard to coverage of markets, timing and sequence of entry, and allocation of marketing resources.

Innovation strategy and competitor response.   Firms introducing new products can better anticipate the reactions of incumbent firms and vice versa. Knowledge of the asymmetries in elasticities among entering firms, incumbent firms, market leaders and followers, anticipation and reaction, and among marketing variables, can help managers of new products make informed decisions.

TABLE 2.2 Selected literature on new products entry strategy and competitor response.

Study	Topic/problem	Key findings/ conclusion	Model used	Contribution
New Product Introduction Strategy				
Eliashberg and Jeuland (1986)	Dynamic pricing strategies for new durable goods in a two-period context, the first period being characterized by a monopoly market structure having dynamic demand. The second period begins when a new firm enters the market and thereby changes the market structure to a duopolistic one.	The nature of pricing strategies of nonmyopic (first entrant who perfectly predicts competitive entry), myopic (totally discounts the duopolistic period), and surprised (first entrant who has a longer time horizon of the nonmyopic monopolist, but does not foresee competitive entry) monopolists are different. It is optimal for the nonmyopic firm to price its products at a higher level than the myopic monopolist. Products having higher prices (owing to cost differences) exhibit a more rapid rate of price decline.	Game theoretic model.	Presents a parsimonious model that could be the basis for researchers wishing to devise new measures for the early assessment of new product strategies.
Mamer and McCardle (1987)	A game theoretic model of innovation that incorporates uncertainty and the interplay between technical uncertainty and potential competition in innovation.	A firm's optimal decision strategy regarding the adoption of a technological innovation of unknown profitability in the face of potential competitive innovation is characterized by a monotonic sequence of pairs of threshold values, which delineate a cone-shaped continuation region. There is a Nash equilibrium in cone-shaped strategies in the two-firm case, where competition is in either substitute or complementary technologies.	Game theoretic model that extends the McCardle (1985) model of a single firm's adoption decision.	Extends knowledge base by including strategic considerations of two competitors.

TABLE 2.2 *(continued)*

Study	Topic/problem	Key findings/ conclusion	Model used	Contribution
Bayus, Jain, and Rao (1997)	When should a firm introduce a new product? What should its performance level be? How do the decisions of a competing firm affect a firm's timing and product performance decisions?	When firms are symmetric in their estimates of market size and product development capabilities, equilibrium exists when firms enter at different times with different performance levels. In the asymmetric case, the firm with a higher estimate of market size enters first, as does the firm with a superior development process with performance levels dependent on the sensitivity of demand to performance.	Game theoretic model of entry timing and product performance level decisions in a duopoly.	Provides an explanation for the inconsistent empirical findings in the literature by showing that either a market-pioneering strategy or a later-entrant strategy can be consistent with profit-maximizing behavior.
Moorthy and Png (1992)	Should a seller who faces two customer segments with differing valuations of product quality introduce two differentiated products at once or one at a time?	Sequential introduction is better than simultaneous introduction when cannibalization is a problem and customers are relatively more impatient than the seller. However, it is less attractive when the seller can pre-commit.	Game theoretic model.	Offers managerial implications for product introductions.
Carpenter and Nakamoto (1990)	Optimal positioning, advertising, and pricing strategies for late mover in a market dominated by an incumbent brand.	Preference asymmetry can contribute to the constant competitive advantage of dominant brands.	Analytical model.	Provides normative guidelines for price, advertising, and distribution strategies at the time of entry for different locations of the product positions contemplated by the new brand.
Gatignon, Weitz, and Bansal (1990)	New brand introduction strategies and impact of competitive	Importance of market share, market growth, new product quality, and competitive structure of the market	Bass model extension with the effects of variables on a firm's entry	Improves understanding of how some marketing strategic factors contribute

(continued overleaf)

TABLE 2.2 *(continued)*

Study	Topic/problem	Key findings/ conclusion	Model used	Contribution
		New Product Introduction Strategy		
	environment and firm characteristics on brand performance.	in determining new brand introduction strategies. Communication effort to introduce a brand depends only on the availability of resources and nothing else.	decision and effects of entry decision on entrant performance.	to the success of an entry strategy.
Hendricks and Singhal (1997)	The effect of not meeting promised new product introduction dates on the market value of the firm.	Delayed announcements decrease the market value of the firm by 5.25 % on average. Competitiveness of the industry in which the firm operates, size of the firm, and the firm's degree of diversification are statistically significant predictors for the change in the market value of the firms that announce delays in the introduction of new products.	Event study regression model.	Fills a gap in the literature where the empirical evidence for the economic evidence of being late to the market is limited.
Shankar, Carpenter, and Krishnamurthi (1999)	How the stage of PLC in which a brand enters affects its sales through brand growth and market response, after controlling for the order of entry effect and time in market.	Growth stage entrants reach asymptotic sales levels faster than pioneers or mature stage entrants. Growth stage entrants are also not hurt by competitor diffusion and enjoy a higher response to perceived quality than pioneers and mature stage entrants. Pioneers reach asymptotic sales levels more slowly than later entrants and pioneers sales, unlike later entrants, are hurt by competitor diffusion over time. Buyers are however more responsive to marketing spending by pioneers. Mature stage entrants are most	Dynamic sales response model with brand sales as a multiplicative function of order of entry, time in market, diffusion of competitors and marketing mix variables.	Offers implications for formulating growth strategies of pioneers, growth stage entrants, and mature stage entrants. Explores the benefits of following a growth stage entry and the advantages that can be exploited.

TABLE 2.2 *(continued)*

Study	Topic/problem	Key findings/ conclusion	Model used	Contribution
		disadvantaged, in the fact that they grow slower than growth stage entrants, have lower response to product quality than growth stage entrants, and have lowest response to market spending.		
Shankar (1999)	Determinants of both new product introduction and incumbent response strategies.	New product introduction strategy is influenced significantly by incumbent reaction strategy and vice versa. Relationship of new products marketing spending to the anticipated incumbent reaction is different for incumbents of different sizes. Higher spending by a new brand results in incumbent response that is significantly lower in magnitude. Multimarket contact leads to lower introduction spending and milder incumbent response.	Structural model involving anticipated incumbent reaction formation.	Extends prior work in the area, providing an integrated framework of new product introduction and incumbent response strategies that involves the impact of a comprehensive set of factors such as introduction strategy, response strategy, market size, entrant characteristics, incumbent characteristics, and multimarket contact. Also integrates literature on new product introduction strategy and incumbent response strategy, identifying new determinants for these strategies.
Van Heerde, Mela, and Manchanda (2004)	Market response model that copes with the challenges that dynamic environments entail: nonstationary, changes in parameters over time, missing data, and cross	Innovation makes the existing brands appear more similar, as indicated by increasing cross brand elasticities, decreases brand differentiation for the existing brands, as indicated by increase in magnitude of own brand price elasticities,	Dynamic Linear Model (DLM).	Offer a useful model for line managers concerned with the relative positioning of their brands in the marketplace. Assesses perceptions of brands in the marketplace.

(continued overleaf)

TABLE 2.2 *(continued)*

Study	Topic/problem	Key findings/ conclusion	Model used	Contribution
		New Product Introduction Strategy		
	sectional heterogeneity.	and increases the variance of the sales response equations temporarily around the time of the introduction of the innovation, indicating increased uncertainty of sales response.		
Banbury and Mitchell (1995)	How an industry incumbent's market share and business survival are affected by the firm's tendency to lead or follow its competitors when introducing important incremental product innovations.	Market share is greater the more times a firm is among the first to introduce important incremental innovations. Earlier introduction has greater impact on market share. Adopting firms have greater market share.	Regression model.	Provides an understanding of why being first to market is important in developing market share. Highlights the importance of incremental innovation.
Mahajan, Bretschneider, and Bradford (1980)	Feedback approaches to develop self-adaptive market response models based on the notion that market response varies over time.	Market response parameters can be estimated for a adaptive market response model using market feedback.	Adaptive regression model.	Demonstrates the importance of feedback approaches to modeling structural shifts in market response.
Mahajan, Sharma, and Buzzell (1993)	The impact of a new durable brand entry on market size and sales of incumbent brands.	Diffusion model on the instant photography market offers useful insights into how the market and incumbent brand sales change upon new entry.	Bass model.	Offers a practical approach to assess the impact of competitive entry, its shortcomings, and possible extensions. The model considers the impact of word of mouth communication and substitution dynamics between competing brands and multiple generations of a product.

TABLE 2.2 *(continued)*

Study	Topic/problem	Key findings/ conclusion	Model used	Contribution
		Competitive Responses to New Product Entry		
Hauser and Shugan (1983)	How should a firm adjust its marketing expenditures and its price to defend its position in an existing market from attack by a competitive new product?	It is optimal for an incumbent to decrease advertising and distribution spending in a static market. If the consumers' tastes are uniformly distributed, it is optimal to decrease prices, improve product quality, and reposition the brand in the direction of the incumbent's strength.	Analytical model.	Offers a useful model for incumbent brand managers for formulating their marketing reaction decisions.
Kumar and Sudarshan (1988)	Development of optimal defensive strategies based on an understanding of the possible reactions of the defenders.	The optimal defensive strategy for all incumbents is to decrease their prices, advertising, and distribution when tastes are uniformly distributed, market is static, and advertising and distribution are decoupled.	Decoupled response function model.	Illustrates the effect of using decoupled response function models for advertising and distribution on the derivation of optimal defense strategies.
Gruca, Kumar, and Sudarshan (1992)	What is the optimal response to competitive entry in a market characterized by a market share attraction model?	The optimal response varies by the incumbent's market dominance. A dominant incumbent should increase its spending, and a nondominant brand should reduce its spending.	Coupled response function model.	Extends knowledge base by explaining previous empirical results that could not be addressed by the decoupled models.
Robinson (1988)	Initial reactions with respect to product, distribution, marketing expenditure, and price by incumbents in oligopolistic markets.	The most common reaction pattern is either no reaction or only a single reaction. It is unusual for entrants to face reactions across the marketing mix. In high growth industries, reactions tend to be more rather than less frequent. When the market is strategically important for the	Regression model.	Offers insights into why marketing mix reactions to entry are limited.

(continued overleaf)

TABLE 2.2 *(continued)*

Study	Topic/problem	Key findings/ conclusion	Model used	Contribution
		Competitive Responses to New Product Entry		
		leading incumbent, reactions are found during first and second years following entry. Acquisition entry reduces reactions in the first year. Innovative strategies have limited positive influence on year-1 reactions.		
Gatignon, Anderson, and Helsen (1989)	How established competitors in an oligopoly react to a significant new entry in their market.	Interfirm differences in competitive reactions to entry can be predicted by observing, for each competitor, the elasticity of each marketing mix variable. Competitors will react with their effective marketing mix elements and retreat with their ineffective marketing mix instruments.	Econometric demand response and reaction models.	Suggests when a positive reaction with a marketing instrument will be observed and when a negative reaction will be observed.
Shankar (1997)	Pioneer's marketing mix reactions to new entries and shifts in their marketing mix allocation.	Pioneers who adopt a follower (leader) role with respect to a marketing mix variable in a static (growing) market and witness a decrease (an increase) in own elasticity and margin upon a new entry generally should accommodate (retaliate) in that variable. Pioneers should accommodate (retaliate) a late mover with its competitively low (high) elasticity marketing mix variable. Change in the pioneers' marketing mix allocation should follow the change in the relative marketing mix effectiveness after new entry.	Empirical industrial organization model.	Extends prior research by showing that incumbents should respond to a new entry by retaliating with their competitively strongest marketing mix variable.

TABLE 2.2 *(continued)*

Study	Topic/problem	Key findings/ conclusion	Model used	Contribution
Bowman and Gatignon (1995)	How the strategic pressures facing a firm and its organizational characteristics influence the speed of reaction to the introduction of a new product.	Market growth, market share of reacting firm, typical new product development time, the frequency of product changes in the industry, and the market share of the threatening firm appear to be significant determinants of reaction time.	Ordered logit, tobit, and regression models.	Provides an initial investigation of a generally neglected dimension and advancement toward empirical measurements and integration of key elements of a competitive defense strategy in reaction to a new product introduction.
MacMillan, McCaffery, and Van Wijk (1985)	Response times of competitors to easily imitated new products in the banking industry.	Response time is strongly related to visibility, organizational misfit, strategic attack, radicality, and complexity. Organizational inertia and strategic pressure explain significant variance in response times.	Regression model.	Offers response guidelines for firms in the banking industry.
Gatignon, Robertson, and Fein (1997)	Effectiveness of incumbent defensive strategies.	Faster reactions to the new entrant have a positive impact on perceived success of defense strategy. Greater the breadth of reaction (# of marketing mix instruments), the less successful the defense. Ability of an incumbent to maintain its market position is also significantly affected by industry characteristics and the degree of competitive threat presented by new product entry.	Regression model.	Provides characterization of the factors affecting the likelihood of competitive response to new product announcement signals.
Kalra, Rajiv, and Srinivasan (1998)	Framework to understand differences in the magnitude and timing of incumbents'	A temporal pattern of muted price reduction in the first period followed by a sharp price reduction in the second period	Game theoretic model.	Highlights the importance of considering both competitors and consumers simultaneously in

(continued overleaf)

TABLE 2.2 *(continued)*

Study	Topic/problem	Key findings/ conclusion	Model used	Contribution
		Competitive Responses to New Product Entry		
	responses to competitive entries in a model where the monopolist incumbent firm faces competitive entry.	corresponds to a delayed defensive reaction in the model. A higher than optimal competitive (duopoly) price in the first period followed by marginal reduction of price from the preentry monopolistic price represents the muted response to entry by the incumbent. Once the entrant's quality is revealed in subsequent periods through consumer usage and word of mouth, the incumbent has no incentive to maintain higher prices. The market reverts to complete information competitive prices and the incumbent lowers his prices.		examining the incumbent's optimal reaction strategy.
Kuester, Homburg, and Robertson (1999)	Defensive strategies that firms pursue when threatened by rival new products.	Importance of rival products innovativeness in generating a reciprocal retaliation, even though innovativeness slows the reaction time. Market growth encourages rapid retaliation, especially on the product mix. In concentrated markets, firms react less strongly on the product mix and exhibit slower reactions. Larger incumbents react less strongly and more slowly.	Structural equation model.	Presents models of reactions to new product entry, both from the perspectives of the incumbent and from that of the new entrant.
Debruyne *et al.* (2002)	The characteristics associated with the launch of a new industrial	Characteristics of new product launch strategy have significant impact on both occurrence	Logistic regression model.	Emphasizes the need for competitor orientation in new product launch and

TABLE 2.2 *(continued)*

Study	Topic/problem	Key findings/ conclusion	Model used	Contribution
	product that triggers competitive reaction.	and nature of competitive reactions. Competitors fail to respond to radical innovations and to new products that employ a niche strategy. They do react if a new product can be assessed within an existing product category and thus represents an unambiguous attack. Competitors are more inclined to react to the introduction of new products that are supported by extensive communication by the innovating firm. The likelihood of reaction is higher in high growth markets than low growth markets.		the antecedents of competitive reaction strategies.
Heil and Walters (1993)	Competitive reactions to new product introductions.	Market signaling variables (hostility, consequences, commitment) explain a significant portion of the variance in the perceived strength of competitive reactions to new product introductions.	Regression model.	Offers managerial implications for interpretation and utilization of new product signals. Provides empirical evidence for new product introductions carrying important competitive information not directly observable.
Robertson, Eliashberg, and Rymon (1995)	What factors determine whether an incumbent will react to a new product announcement signal from a competitor, what variables affect the aggressiveness of the	Signal hostility is positively related to the occurrence of a reaction; an incumbent is more likely to react when it has high fixed commitments in the product category and in industries characterized by higher levels of patent	Regression model.	Extends knowledge base by using survey data that complement analytical models, and secondary data sources (e.g., PIMS), which have been the dominant research paradigms in the literature on competitive reaction.

(continued overleaf)

TABLE 2.2 *(continued)*

Study	Topic/problem	Key findings/ conclusion	Model used	Contribution
		Competitive Responses to New Product Entry		
	incumbent's reaction, and what factors influence whether the reaction will be in product or other marketing instruments?	protection; firms in industries in which patents are highly relevant are less likely to react in product and those with high fixed commitments in the product category show a tendency to react with alternative marketing mix instruments and hostile signals do not engender reactions in product.		
Hultink and Langerak (2002)	How strongly and fast incumbents react to perceived market signals resulting from a new products launch decisions.	High advantage new products, penetration pricing, intense advertisement campaigns are considered hostile and consequential. Broad targeting is not considered hostile, but signals greater consequence. Perceived signals of hostility and commitment positively impact strength of reaction, but not speed of reaction. The perceived consequence signal positively impacts speed of reaction. Therefore a threatened incumbent could make a tradeoff between a strong or fast response to an entrant's new product entry. Market growth moderates the relationship between entrants' launch decisions and perceived market signals. Launch decisions that normally signal hostility,	Hierarchical moderated regression model.	Offers a managerial understanding of product launch decisions and perceptions of the resulting signals by the incumbent firm.

TABLE 2.2 *(continued)*

Study	Topic/problem	Key findings/ conclusion	Model used	Contribution
		commitment, and consequences may not be perceived as threatening by incumbents when launched by aggressive firms, because the signals are softened by the entrant's reputation for aggressiveness.		
Shankar (2006)	Analysis of new product introductions and deletions and proactive and reaction actions by competitor firms.	Market leaders have higher product line elasticities than followers and unlike followers, leaders have greater reaction elasticity than anticipation elasticity.	Structural econometric model.	Offers insights into product line decisions in a competitive environment. Model helps decompose a firm's action into anticipation and reaction and make appropriate decisions.
Williams (1983)	Competitive responses to technological evolution.	Over the evolution of many product market segments, there is a generalizable pattern, a shift from the investment characteristics of product technology to those of process technology as primary area of competition. The interaction of required and realized returns provides a stopping rule for technologically driven competition.	No model.	Provides a framework for evolving technologies.

Market/Consumer Responses

Study	Topic/problem	Key findings/ conclusion	Model used	Contribution
Moreau, Lehmann, and Markman (2001)	Psychological processes underlying the individual consumer's adoption decision.	Compared to novices, experts report higher comprehension, more net benefits, and therefore higher preferences for continuous innovations. For	Experimental study. Analysis of Variance (ANOVA).	Offers implications for segmentation, media planning, and the creation of product/brand loyalty.

(continued overleaf)

TABLE 2.2 *(continued)*

Study	Topic/problem	Key findings/ conclusion	Model used	Contribution
		Market/Consumer Responses		
		discontinuous innovations, experts entrenched knowledge is related to lower comprehension, fewer perceived net benefits, and lower preferences as compared to novices. Only when entrenched knowledge is accompanied by relevant information from supplementary knowledge base are experts able to understand and appreciate discontinuous innovations.		
Ziamou (2002)	Factors that influence consumer's judgments of uncertainty about the performance of a new interface and consumer's adoption intentions.	Consumers perceive lower uncertainty about the performance of a new interface and higher intentions to adopt a new product, when the new interface is introduced with a new functionality. When a new interface is introduced with a new functionality, imagining the product in use increases consumers' uncertainty about the performance of the new interface and decreases their intention to adopt the new product. When the interface is introduced with a pre-existing functionality, imagining the product in use decreases consumers' uncertainty about the performance of the new interface and increases their intention to adopt the new product.	Experimental study. ANOVA.	Provides guidelines for commercializing new technologies that result in new interfaces. Implications for designing communication strategies.

FUTURE RESEARCH

Existing research highlights interesting opportunities for future research. First, more research is required on repeat purchase and brand diffusion models. Should repeat purchase models be different for products with different inter-purchase times? Future research in this realm should address the following questions. Should high-technology innovations be modeled differently than low-technology innovations? Are diffusion parameters inherently different for different brands within a product category? What factors determine the differences in the diffusion parameters of brands?

Second, product life cycle curves are different for different product categories. Not all product categories exhibit smooth life cycle curves that have readily identifiable introduction, takeoff, early and late growth, maturity, and decline stages. The life cycle of fashion innovations and fad products are often short and discontinuous. Are product life cycles getting shorter? Bayus (1998) suggests that they may not, but there is a belief among managers of technology products that their product life cycles are getting compressed. We need more empirical analyses across different product categories and different time periods to explore this issue fully.

Third, not much is known about the evolution of markets for innovations that are introduced in multiple countries in different periods of time. How do new products evolve across countries, continents, and cultures both at the category level and the brand level? What new product introduction strategies are effective when an innovation is rolled out across countries? What factors determine an effective rollout strategy across countries? More research is needed on market evolution for new products and brands across countries.

Fourth, most new products introduced are line extensions, whereas some are brand extensions. How do line extensions evolve relative to the parent product and other products in the product line? What factors influence the evolution of line extensions? How is diffusion of a line extension different from that of a brand extension? What entry strategies are effective for a line extension vis-à-vis a brand extension? What competitor responses do line and brand extensions evoke? How do these responses shape the evolution of the market for line and brand extension? We need more research on market response to line and brand extension innovations.

Fifth, much research has focused on diffusion and entry strategies of goods innovations. Very little is known about diffusion and entry strategies of service innovations. Berry et al. (2005) propose a taxonomy and success drivers of different market-creating service innovations, but empirical research is needed on this issue. How are the diffusion process and entry strategy for service innovations different from those for goods innovations? Are there differences in market evolution and marketing strategies for service innovations and goods innovations?

Finally, new product entries and competitor responses have been studied primarily in terms of their impact on sales and market share. However, it is important to analyze their impact on the profits and firm values of different competitors, including the introducing firm. What entry strategies ensure both sales and profit growth and firm value? What competitor response strategies result in market growth, but improved market position and profitability for incumbents? Future research could address these important issues.

References

Agarwal, R., and Bayus, B.L. (2002). The market evolution on sales takeoff of product innovations. *Management Science*, 48(8), 1024–41.

Albers, S. (2004). Forecasting the diffusion of an innovation prior to launch. In S. Albers (ed.), *Cross-functional Innovation Management. Perspectives from Different Disciplines*, Wiesbaden: Gabler, 243–58.

Banbury, C.M., and Mitchell, W. (1995). The effect of introducing important incremental innovations on market share and business survival. *Strategic Management Journal*, 16, 161–82.

Bass, F.M. (1969). A new product growth model for consumer durables. *Management Science*, 15(5), 215–27.

Bass, F.M., Krishnan, T.V., and Jain, D.C. (1994). Why the Bass model fits without decision variables. *Marketing Science*, 13(3), 203–23.

Bayus, B.L. (1987). Forecasting sales of new contingent products: an application to the compact disc market. *Journal of Product Innovation Management*, 4(4), 243–55.

Bayus, B.L. (1998). Analysis of product lifetimes in a technologically dynamic industry. *Management Science*, 44 (June), 763–75.

Bayus, B.L., Jain, S., and Rao, A. (1997). Too little, too early: introduction timing and new product performance in the Personal Digital Assistant industry. *Journal of Marketing Research*, 34(2), 50–63.

Berry, L.L., Shankar, V., Parish, J., Cadwallader, S., and Dotzel, T. (2005). What drives the success of market-creating service innovations?, Working Paper, Texas A&M University.

Bowman, D., and Gatignon, H. (1995). Determinants of competitor response time to a new product introduction. *Journal of Marketing Research*, 32(1), 42–53.

Carpenter, G.S., and Nakamoto, K. (1990). Competitive strategies for late entry into a market with a dominant brand. *Management Science*, 36 (October), 1268–78.

Chatterjee, R., and Eliashberg, J. (1990). Innovation diffusion process in a heterogeneous population: a micromodeling approach. *Management Science*, 36 (September), 1057–79.

Davis, F.D. (1989). Perceived usefulness, perceived ease of use, and user acceptance of information technology. *MIS Quarterly*, 13(3), 319–40.

Debruyne, M., Moenaert, R., Griffin, A., Hart, S., Hultink, E.J., and Robben, H. (2002). The impact of new product launch strategies on competitive reaction in industrial markets. *The Journal of Product Innovation Management*, 19(2), 159–70.

Dekimpe, M.G., Parker, P.M., and Sarvary, M. (2000). Global diffusion of technological innovations: a coupled hazard approach. *Journal of Marketing Research*, 37 (1), 47–59.

Dodds, W. (1973). An application of the Bass model in long-term new product forecasting. *Journal of Marketing Research*, 10(3), 308–11.

Easingwood, C.J., Mahajan, V., and Muller, E. (1983). A nonuniform influence innovation diffusion model of new product acceptance. *Marketing Science*, 2(3), 273–95.

Eliashberg, J., and Jeuland, A. (1986). The impact of competitive entry in a developing market upon dynamic pricing strategies. *Marketing Science*, 5(1), 20–36.

Farris, P.W., and Buzzell, R.D. (1979). Why advertising and promotional costs vary: some cross-sectional analyses. *Journal of Marketing*, 43 (Fall), 112–22.

Fischer, M., Shankar, V., and Clement, M. (2005). Can late mover brands use international market entry strategy to challenge the pioneer? *MSI Report*, 05-004, 25–48.

Gatignon, H., Anderson, E., and Helsen, K. (1989). Competitive reactions to market entries: explaining interfirm differences. *Journal of Marketing Research*, 26(1), 44–55.

Gatignon, H., Eliashberg, J., and Robertson, T.S. (1989). Modeling multinational diffusion patterns: an efficient methodology. *Marketing Science*, 8(3), 231–47.

Gatignon, H., and Reibstein, D.J. (1997). Creative strategies for responding to competitive actions. In *Wharton on Dynamic Competitive Strategy*, G.S. Day and D.J. Reibstein (eds), New York: John Wiley & Sons, Inc., 237–55.

Gatignon, H., and Robertson, T. (1989). Technology diffusion: an empirical test of competitive effects. *Journal of Marketing*, 53(1), 35–49.

Gatignon, H., Weitz, B., and Bansal, P. (1990). Brand introduction strategies and competitive environment. *Journal of Marketing Research*, 27(4), 390–401.

Gielens, K., and Steenkamp, J-B.E.M. (2004). What drives new product success?: an investigation across products and countries. *MSI Working Paper*, 04-108.

Golder, P.N., and Tellis., G.J. (1997). Will it ever fly? Modeling the takeoff of really new consumer durables. *Marketing Science*, 16(3), 256–70.

Gruca, T., Kumar, R., and Sudarshan, K. (1992). An equilibrium analysis of defensive response to entry using a coupled response function model. *Marketing Science*, 11(4), 348–58.

Hahn, M., Park, S., Krishnamurthi, L., and Zoltners, A.A. (1994). Analysis of new product diffusion using a four-segment trial-repeat model. *Marketing Science*, 13(3), 224–47.

Hauser, J.R., and Shugan, S. (1983). Defensive marketing strategies. *Marketing Science*, 2 (Fall), 319–60.

Hauser, J.R., Tellis, G.R., and Griffin, A. (2006). Research on innovation: a review and agenda for marketing science. *Marketing Science*, 25(6), 687–717.

Heeler, R.M., and Hustad, T.P. (1980). Problems in predicting new product growth for consumer durables. *Management Science*, 26(10), 1007–20.

Heil, O.P., and Walters, R.G. (1993). Explaining competitive reactions to new products: an empirical signaling study. *The Journal of Product Innovation Management*, 10(1), 53–65.

Hendricks, K.B., and Singhal, V.R. (1997). Delays in new product introductions and the market value of the firm: the consequences of being late to the market. *Management Science*, 43(4), 422–36.

Horsky, D. (1990). A diffusion model incorporating product benefits, price, income and information. *Marketing Science*, 9(4), 342–65.

Horsky, D., and Simon, L.S. (1983). Advertising and the diffusion of new products. *Marketing Science*, 2(1), 1–18.

Hultink, E.J., and Langerak, F. (2002). Launch decisions and competitive reactions: an exploratory market signaling study. *The Journal of Product Innovation Management*, 19(3), 199–212.

Jain, D., Mahajan, V., and Muller, E. (1991). Innovation diffusion in the presence of supply restrictions. *Marketing Science*, 10(1), 83–90.

Jain, D., and Rao, R.C. (1990). Effect of price on the demand for durables: modeling, estimation, and findings. *Journal of Business & Economic Statistics*, 8(2), 163–70.

Kalish, S. (1985). A new product adoption model with price, advertising and uncertainty. *Management Science*, 31(12), 1569–85.

Kalish, S., Mahajan, V., and Muller, E. (1995). Waterfall and sprinkler new product strategies in competitive global markets. *International Journal of Research in Marketing*, 12(2), 105–19.

Kalra, A., Rajiv, S., and Srinivasan, K. (1998). Response to competitive entry: a rationale for delayed defensive reaction. *Marketing Science*, 17(4), 380–405.

Katz, M.L., and Shapiro, C. (1985). Network externalities, competition and compatibility. *The American Economic Review*, 75, 424–40.

Kim, N., Chang, D.R., and Shocker, A. (2000). Modeling intercategory and generational dynamics for a growing information technology industry, *Management Science*, 46(4), 496–512.

Kuester, S., Homburg, C., and Robertson, T.S. (1999). Retaliatory behavior to new product entry. *Journal of Marketing*, 63(4), 90–106.

Kumar, K.R., and Sudarshan, D. (1988). Defensive marketing strategies: an equilibrium analysis based on decoupled response function models. *Management Science*, 34(7), 805–15.

Lam, S.Y., and Shankar, V. (2008). Are customer trust, satisfaction, and loyalty relationships different for early and late adopters of technological innovations? Working Paper, Nanyang Technological University, Singapore.

Lambkin, M., and Day, G.S. (1989). Evolutionary processes in competitive markets: beyond the product life cycle. *Journal of Marketing*, 53(3), 4–20.

Lilien, G.L., Rao, A.G., and Kalish, S. (1981). Bayesian estimation and control of detailing effort in a repeat purchase diffusion environment. *Management Science*, 27(5), 493–506.

Lilien, G.L., Rangaswamy, A., and Van den Bulte, C. (2000). Diffusion models: managerial applications and software. In V. Mahajan, E. Muller and J. Wind (eds), *New-Product Diffusion Models*, Boston, MA: Kluwer Academic Publishers, 295–336.

Lilien, G.L., and Weinstein, D. (1981). An international comparison of the determinants of industrial marketing expenditures. *Journal of Marketing*, 48 (Winter), 46–53.

MacMillan I., McCaffery, M.L., and Van Wijk, G. (1985). Competitors' responses to easily imitated new products – exploring commercial banking product introductions. *Strategic Management Journal*, 6(1), 75–86.

Mahajan, V., Bretschneider, S.I., and Bradford, J.W. (1980). Feedback approaches to modeling structural shifts in market response. *Journal of Marketing*, 44(1), 71–80.

Mahajan, V., Muller, E., and Bass, F.M. (1990). New product diffusion models in marketing: a review and directions for future research. *Journal of Marketing*, 54(1), 1–26.

Mahajan, V., Muller, E., and Srivastava, R.K. (1990). Determination of adopter categories by using innovation diffusion models. *Journal of Marketing Research*, 27(1), 37–50.

Mahajan, V., Sharma, S., and Buzzell, R.D. (1993). Assessing the impact of competitive entry on market expansion and incumbent sales. *Journal of Marketing*, 57(3), 39–52.

Mamer, J.W., and McCardle, K.F. (1987). Uncertainty, competition, and the adoption of new technology. *Management Science*, 33(2), 161–77.

McCardle, K.F. (1985). Information acquisition and the adoption of new technology. *Management Science*, 31(11), 1372–90.

Moorthy, S., and Png, I. (1992). Market segmentation, cannibalization and the timing of product introductions. *Management Science*, 38(3), 345–59.

Moreau, P.C., Lehmann, D.R., and Markman, A.B. (2001). Entrenched knowledge structures and consumer response to new products. *Journal of Marketing Research*, 38(1), 14–29.

Narasimhan, C. (1989). Incorporating consumer price expectations in diffusion models. *Marketing Science*, 8(4), 343–57.

Nerlove, M., and Arrow, K.J. (1962). Optimal advertising policy under dynamic conditions. *Economica*, 29 (May), 129–42.

Norton J.A., and Bass, F.B. (1987). A diffusion theory model of adoption and substitution for successive generations of high-technology products. *Management Science*, 33(9), 1069–86.

Parker, P.M. (1994). Aggregate diffusion forecasting models in marketing: a critical review. *International Journal of Forecasting*, 10, 353–80.

Parker, P.M., and Gatignon, H. (1994). Specifying competitive effects in diffusion models: an empirical analysis. *International Journal of Research in Marketing*, 11(1), 17–39.

Parker, P.M., and Gatignon, H.(1996). Order-of-entry, trial diffusion, and elasticity dynamics: an empirical case. *Marketing Letters*, 7 (January), 95–109.

Parsons, L.J. (1975). The product life cycle and time varying advertising elasticities. *Journal of Marketing Research*, 12(4), 476–80.

Putsis, W.P. Jr., Balasubramanian, S., Kaplan, E.H., and Sen, S.K. (1997). Mixing behavior in cross-country diffusion. *Marketing Science*, 16(4), 354–69.

Rao, A.G., and Yamada, M. (1988). Forecasting with a repeat purchase diffusion model. *Management Science*, 34(6), 734–52.

Redmond, W.H. (1989). Effects of new product pricing on the evolution of market structure. *The Journal of Product Innovation Management*, 6(2), 99–108.

Robertson, T., Eliashberg, J., and Rymon, T. (1995). New product announcement signals and incumbent reactions. *Journal of Marketing*, 59(3), 1–15.

Robinson, W. (1988). Marketing mix reactions to entry. *Marketing Science*, 7(4), 368–85.

Rogers, E.M. (2003). *Diffusion of innovations*, Fifth edition. New York: The Free Press.

Schmittlein, D.C., and Mahajan, V. (1982). Maximum likelihood estimation for an innovation diffusion model of new product acceptance. *Marketing Science*, 1(1), 57–78.

Shane, S. (2001). Technology regimes and new firm formation. *Management Science*, 47(9), 1173–190.

Shane, S., Shankar, V., and Aravindakshan, A. (2006). The effect of partnering strategies on franchise system size. *Management Science*, 52(5), 773–87.

Shankar, V. (1997). Pioneers' marketing mix reaction to entry in different competitive game structures: theoretical analysis and empirical illustration. *Marketing Science*, 16(3), 271–93.

Shankar, V. (1999). New product introduction and incumbent response strategies: their inter-relationship and the role of multimarket contact. *Journal of Marketing Research*, 36(3), 327–44.

Shankar, V. (2006). Proactive and reactive product line strategies: asymmetries between market leaders and followers. *Management Science*, 52(2), 276–92.

Shankar, V. (2008). The role of product life cycle and market dominance in marketing expenditures of products, Working Paper, Texas A&M University.

Shankar, V., and Bayus, B.L. (2003). Network effects and competition: an empirical analysis of the videogame industry. *Strategic Management Journal*, 24(4), 375–94.

Shankar, V., Carpenter, G.S., and Krishnamurthi, L. (1998). Late mover advantage: how innovative late entrants outsell pioneers. *Journal of Marketing Research*, 35(1), 54–70.

Shankar, V., Carpenter, G.S., and Krishnamurthi, L. (1999). The advantages of entering in the growth stage of the product life cycle: an empirical analysis. *Journal of Marketing Research*, 36(2), 269–76.

Simon, H., and Sebastian, K-H. (1987). Diffusion and advertising: the German telephone campaign. *Management Science*, 33(4), 451–66.

Sinha, R.K., and Chandrasekharan, M. (1992). A split hazard model for analyzing the diffusion of innovations. *Journal of Marketing Research*, 29(1), 116–27.

Sorescu, A.B., Chandy, R.K., and Prabhu, J.C. (2003). Sources and financial consequences of radical innovation: insights from pharmaceuticals. *Journal of Marketing*, 67(4), 82–102.

Srinivasan, V., and Mason, C. (1986). Nonlinear least squares estimation of new product diffusion models. *Marketing Science*, 5(2), 169–78.

Stremersch, S., and Tellis, G.J. (2004). Understanding and managing growth of international new products. *International Journal of Research in Marketing*, 21(4), 421–38.

Takada, H., and Jain, D.C. (1991). Cross-national analysis of diffusion of consumer durables in pacific rim countries. *Journal of Marketing*, 55(2), 48–54.

Talukdar, D., Sudhir, K., and Ainslie, A. (2002). Investigating new product diffusion across products and countries. *Marketing Science*, 21(1), 97–114.

Tellis, G.J., and Fornell, C. (1988). The relationship between advertising and product quality over the product life cycle: a contingency theory. *Journal of Marketing Research*, 25(1), 64–71.

Tellis, G.J., Stremersch, S., and Yin, E. (2003). The international takeoff of new products: the role of economics, culture, and country innovativeness. *Marketing Science*, 22(2), 188–208.

Teotia, A.P.S., and Raju, P.S. (1986). Forecasting the market penetration of new technologies using a combination of economic cost and diffusion models. *Journal of Product Innovation Management*, 3(4), 225–37.

Thomas, R.J. (1987). Forecasting new product market potential: combining multiple methods. *Journal of Product Innovation Management*, 4(2), 109–19.

Tigert, D. and Farivar, B. (1981). The Bass new product growth model: a sensitivity analysis for a high technology product. *Journal of Marketing*, 45(4), 81–90.

Twiss, B.C. (1984). Forecasting market size and market growth rates for new products. *Journal of Product Innovation Management*, 1(1), 19–29.

Urban, G.L., Hauser, J.R., and Roberts, J.H. (1990). Prelaunch forecasting of new automobiles. *Management Science*, 36(4), 401–21.

Urban, G.L., Weinberg, B., and Hauser, J.R. (1996). Premarket forecasting of really-new products. *Journal of Marketing*, 60(1), 47–60.

Van Heerde, H.J., Mela, C.F., and Manchanda, P. (2004). The dynamic effect of innovation on market structure. *Journal of Marketing Research*, 41(2), 166–83.

Varadarajan, R.P., Yadav, M., and Shankar, V. (2008). First-mover advantage in the internet-enabled environment: a conceptual framework and propositions. *Journal of Academy of Marketing Science*, forthcoming.

Venkataraman, S., Chen, M.J., and McMillan, I.C. (1997). Anticipating reactions: factors that shape competitor responses. In G.S. Day and D.J. Reibstein (eds), *Wharton on Dynamic Competitive Strategy*, New York: John Wiley & Sons, Inc., 198–219.

Venkatesan, R., Krishnan, T.V., and Kumar, V. (2004). Evolutionary estimation of macro-level diffusion models using genetic algorithms. *Marketing Science*, 23(3), 451–64.

Williams, J.R. (1983). Technological evolution and competitive response. *Strategic Management Journal*, 4(1), 55–65.

Winer, R.S. (1979). An analysis of the time-varying effects of advertising: the case of Lydia Pynkam. *Journal of Business*, 52 (October), 563–76.

Ziamou, P. (2002). Commercializing new technologies: consumers' response to a new interface. *The Journal of Product Innovation Management*, 19(5), 365–74.

Part II

THE DEVELOPMENT AND INTRODUCTION OF NEW PRODUCTS

3

Understanding Customer Needs

Barry L. Bayus

The comments of the following people on an earlier draft are greatly appreciated: Sridhar Balasubramanian, Dick Blackburn, Paul Bloom, Ed Cornet, Ely Dahan, Abbie Griffin, Steve Hoeffler, Erin MacDonald, Jackki Mohr, Bill Moore, Vithala Rao, Allan Shocker, and Gal Zauberman.

INTRODUCTION

Touted as the 'most significant category innovation since toilet paper first appeared in roll form in 1890' (Kimberly Clark, 2001), dispersible (flushable) moist toilet tissue on a roll was introduced in the United States by Kimberly Clark in 2001. According to a corporate press release, Cottonelle Fresh Rollwipes was a breakthrough product that 'delivers the cleaning and freshening of pre-moistened wipes with the convenience and disposability of toilet paper' (Kimberly Clark, 2001). Internal market research seemed to indicate that there was a clear customer need for a new product to supplement dry toilet paper. Surveys and focus groups revealed that over 60 % of adult consumers had experimented with a moist cleaning method (e.g., using baby wipes, wetting a washcloth, sprinkling water on dry toilet paper) and one out of four used a moist cleaning method daily. Kimberly Clark made the obvious connection that a majority of US consumers found dry toilet paper to be limited for their real needs. Convinced that there was a huge market opportunity for a more convenient product that addressed this consumer need for a cleaner and more refreshing bathroom tissue, Kimberly Clark obtained more than 30 patents on a new product and dispenser and invested over $100 million in R&D and manufacturing to bring their Cottonelle Fresh Rollwipes to market. Backed by over $40 million in marketing programs, sales were expected to reach $150 million in the first year and $500 million after six years. Perhaps more important, a significant increase in the $4.8 billion US toilet paper market was anticipated because this innovation was a supplement, not a substitute, for existing products. Procter & Gamble also believed that there was a market opportunity for moist bathroom wipes; they quickly followed by introducing a similar product, Charmin Fresh Mates, later that year.

But, consumers were unimpressed with these new products. Sales were well below forecasts: Procter & Gamble abandoned its product after only two years and Kimberly Clark's product is confined to a regional market where executives say that sales are so small that they are financially insignificant. Despite their market research, did Kimberley Clark (and Procter & Gamble) really understand their customers' needs in this situation? The Fresh Rollwipes product was designed to be conveniently dispensed via a refillable plastic container that clipped to the standard toilet paper holder. Careful attention was paid to developing a dispenser that blended in with the consumer's bathroom. Both companies, however, underestimated the role of consumer embarrassment associated with toileting (e.g., Associated Press, 2003). Although many consumers already used some sort of makeshift wet cleaning method in the bathroom, they didn't like others knowing about it. The extra dispenser attached to the holder was right out in the open, possibly causing guests to wonder if something was wrong with household members because they were using these 'alternative' wipes. Although numerous mistakes were made in this case (e.g., Nelson, 2002), it seems clear that Kimberly Clark and Procter & Gamble did not completely understand their customers' needs.

Unfortunately, this example is not unique. New product failure rates of up to 90 % are commonly cited in the popular and academic press, and these suggest that successful innovation is the exception rather than the rule (e.g., Power, 1992; 1993; Stevens and Burley, 1997; Brand Strategy, 2003). The road to riches is littered with many stories of new product failure (e.g., Schnaars, 1989; Gershman, 1990; Kirchner, 1995; McMath and Forbes, 1998; Franklin, 2003). Not surprisingly, many pundits take these failures to mean that it is impossible to truly understand customer needs. Headlines such as 'Ignore Your Customer' (Martin, 1995), 'Shoot First, Do Market Research Later' (Elliot, 1998), and statements like 'The public does not know what is possible, we do' (Morita, 1986) fuel this viewpoint. At the same time, however, a consistent finding from benchmarking studies on the factors related to successful innovation is that understanding customer needs is a fundamental, although challenging, activity (e.g., Montoya-Weiss and Calantone, 1994; Cooper, 1999; Henard and Szymanski, 2001). There are just as many, if not more, examples in which firms used various traditional (e.g., customer surveys, focus groups) and nontraditional (e.g., ethnography, contextual inquiry, empathic design) research approaches to gain insight into their customers' needs, and to develop highly successful new products (e.g., Urban and Hauser, 1993; Leonard-Barton, 1995; Burchill and Shen, 1995; Otto and Wood, 2001; Shillito, 2001; Sanders, 2002; Squires and Byrne, 2002; Crawford and Di Benedetto, 2003; Ulrich and Eppinger, 2004). Thus, there is persuasive evidence that it is indeed possible to understand customer needs and that this insight can be used in the innovation process. Rather than ignoring customers, it is more prudent only to ignore customers' specific ideas on how to fulfill their needs – it is the company's job to develop new products!

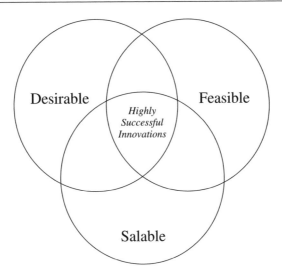

FIGURE 3.1 The innovation space.

Conceptually, understanding customer needs leads to products that are *desirable, feasible,* and *salable* (to the mass market). Note that 'product categories' are often defined by firms and not by customers (e.g., the SLR camera category, the digital camera category, the disposable camera category); thus product categories typically relate to feasible combinations of attributes that are salable (and hopefully desirable). As suggested by Figure 3.1, ideas, concepts, and new products can be classified based on their location in the desirable-feasible-salable space. Thus, highly successful innovations are desirable, feasible, *and* salable. Casual observations indicate that many existing products fall primarily in the feasible and salable region (e.g., Fresh Rollwipes), and that fresh looks at already established categories can lead to more desirable new products (e.g., consider the efforts of Oxo in the kitchen tools market and its greatly acclaimed Good Grips peeler, salad spinner, and angled measuring cup). Gizmos and gadgets such as the Segway Human Transporter are mainly in the feasible and desirable overlap (e.g., Waters and Field, 2003), but are not really salable to the mass market. Many innovations that are mainly technology-driven reside only in the feasible region for a number of years, for example directional sound systems for use in automobiles, advertising, and special office-based applications (Schwartz, 2004), brain-computer interfaces that allow the direct bi-directional interfaces between the brain, nervous system and computer (Cyberkinetics, 2004), and Michelin's Tweel, a single piece airless tire with 'spokes' that never go flat (Mayersohn, 2005). Astute business analysts note that most firms are still product-driven rather than customer-driven (i.e., firms first determine what is feasible for them to develop; they then fashion marketing strategies to sell the products and services that can deliver; only later finding out that their offerings may not really be desirable).

The primary purpose of this chapter is to review the theory and practice related to understanding customer needs. By necessity, this review will be relatively brief as this topic covers a wide spectrum of literature across the marketing, design, and engineering disciplines. This chapter provides insights into the challenges associated with identifying and interpreting customer needs, which leads to a discussion of promising directions for future research.

THE LANGUAGES OF CUSTOMER NEEDS

With respect to innovation and new product development, the language associated with 'customer needs' differs across the marketing, engineering, and industrial design literatures. Different terminology is often used interchangeably: needs, wants, attributes, features, requirements, specs, etc. For example, in their review of the product development literature, Krishnan and Ulrich (2001) indicate that a useful representation of a product is a vector of attributes, which they consider also to include customer needs, customer requirements, product specifications, engineering characteristics, and technical performance metrics. Even customers themselves often use these terms interchangeably (e.g., Captain, 2004). Customer needs are also context dependent (e.g., Green et al., 2006), particularly with respect to usage (where and how the product is used), consumer (who will use the product), and market (what competing products are available).

Any discussion of 'needs' should probably start with Maslow's (1954) widely known hierarchy of needs theory[1]. According to Maslow, there are five levels of needs ranging from basic needs that are present at birth to more complex psychological needs, which only become important once the lower level needs have been satisfied[2]. At the lowest, basic level are biological and physiological needs (e.g., air, food, drink, shelter, sleep, sex, etc.). The next level includes safety needs (e.g., security, order, law, etc.); this is followed by belongingness and love needs (e.g., family, relationships, work group, to be accepted, etc.), followed by esteem needs (e.g., achievement, independence, recognition, prestige, etc.), and self-actualization needs (e.g., self-fulfillment, realizing one's potential, personal growth, etc.).

An important insight from Maslow's theory is that there are different levels of needs and needs form a hierarchy (that may allow for lexicographic decision processes; e.g., see Olshavsky and Spreng, 1996). For example, customers expect products to be safe and useful. Products and services may be bought to perform certain tasks, as well as to be accepted and recognized by others. Products may also satisfy aesthetic, as well as self-actualization, needs. However, as noted by Sanders (1992) customers are not usually very good at expressing their needs, especially higher level needs.

---

[1]Another interesting technology 'hierarchy' proposed by Farrell (1993) consists of shelter, health, communication, tools, packaging, raw materials, and transport.

[2]Other researchers have modified Maslow's original theory to include cognitive needs (e.g., knowing, understanding, etc.), aesthetic needs (e.g., beauty, symmetry, etc.), and transcendence needs (e.g., helping others to achieve self-actualization).

Customer needs are a description of the benefits desired by 'customers'[3] (e.g., Urban and Hauser, 1993; Griffin and Hauser, 1993)[4]. Needs are essentially what the customer wants; needs are long-term in nature and cannot always be recognized or verbally described by a customer (Burchill and Brodie, 1997; Burchill *et al.*, 1997; Shillito, 2001; Mello, 2003). Importantly, needs include utilitarian as well as hedonic benefits. For example, customer needs associated with a digital camera might include 'reliving fond memories, feeling confident in taking pictures, taking great pictures'. *Wants*, on the other hand, are things that a customer believes will fulfill a known need, are short-term and temporary in nature, and can be easily influenced by psychosocial cues such as advertising, personal recommendations, and norms (e.g., Hauser, 1984; Shillito, 2001). For example, consumers may say they want an easy-to-use digital camera with at least 5.0 mega pixels, 32M internal memory, and video capability. (*Problems* are simply wants or needs expressed in negative terms; Shillito, 2001.)

Needs are concerned with 'what' is desired by customers, whereas attributes, features, requirements, and specifications deal with 'how' a need is satisfied by a specific product or service. In the economics literature, product *characteristics* are defined to be the properties of a product that are relevant to consumer choice; characteristics are quantitative in nature, can be measured objectively, and are universal (e.g., Lancaster, 1971; Rosen, 1974; Ratchford, 1975; Geistfeld *et al.*, 1977). Product *attributes* are more abstract and generally fewer in number than product characteristics, and are based on the perceptual dimensions that consumers use to make purchase decisions (e.g., Kaul and Rao, 1995)[5]. From the engineering and design literatures, *requirements* are the engineering and technical solutions to meet a customer need and *specifications* (specs) are the specific metrics associated with requirements (e.g., Shillito, 2001; Otto and Wood, 2001; Ulrich and Eppinger, 2004)[6]. As implied by this discussion, product characteristics, attributes, requirements, and specs are closely related and overlapping terms. For example, product characteristics for a digital camera might include the number of mega pixels, the available megabits of image storage, battery life, and the number of automatic modes; product attributes could include the ease of use, image quality,

---

[3]'Customer' is a general label that refers to the entire set of important stakeholders including the buyer, user, seller, and any others that are influenced by the innovation (e.g., Hauser, 1993; Gershenson and Stauffer, 1999; Karkkainen *et al.*, 2003; Molotch, 2003). In other words, needs for the complete 'customer chain' should be considered. For example, although buyers generally hate the 'impervious' blister plastic wrap for small consumer electronic products, this clamshell packaging was actually designed to satisfy retailers' need for theft reduction (Saranow, 2004).

[4]Some consultants and strategy researchers prefer to think of needs as being the 'jobs' customers are trying to get done when using a product or service (e.g., Christensen and Raynor, 2003; Ulwick, 2005). This is related to Griffin's (1996) statement that needs are the problems that a product or service solves.

[5] Shocker and Srinivasan (1974) call product attributes that are meaningful to consumers and actionable by firms 'actionable attributes'. Product *features* are generally concerned with specific attribute levels (Green 1974) or characteristics that can be specified in physical, chemical, or financial terms (Johnson and Fornell 1987).

[6] Ulrich and Ellison (1999) further propose that requirements vary in the degree to which they are 'holistic' (i.e., more holistic requirements are increasing in component complexity and the fraction of components on which performance depends). In related work, Martin (1999) develops a Generational Variety Index (a measure for the amount of redesign effort required for future product designs) and a Coupling Index (a measure of coupling among product components).

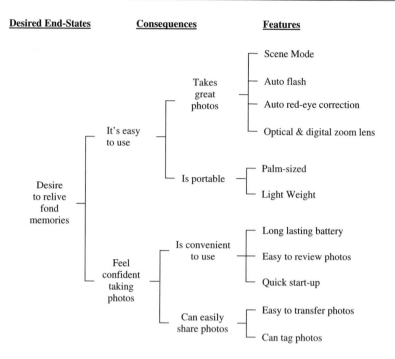

FIGURE 3.2 An example of customer needs for a digital camera.

well-known brand, and battery life; customer requirements may include usability, reliability, image quality, and battery life; and product specs can include a 4× optical zoom lens with 0.2× digital zoom, Li-Ion rechargeable battery, 5.0 mega pixels, 12 scene modes, etc.

To better grasp the challenges involved in understanding customer needs, consider the example in Figure 3.2 (see also Woodruff and Gardial, 1996; Ratneshwar *et al.*, 1999). As discussed in Shillito (2001), there are at least three levels of customer needs that are increasingly more abstract in scope: features, consequences, and desired end-states. Features are often the words a consumer uses to describe a product or service (e.g., a digital camera has an optical and digital zoom lens, auto flash and scene modes, a long lasting battery, an easy interface to share photos, etc.). Features are concrete, short-term in nature, and easy to influence. Incremental changes only result from focusing on new products with improved features.

Consequences come from possession and/or use of the product or service. For example, 'a digital camera is simple and easy to use, gives me confidence, I feel like an expert'. These expressions typically describe what the customer wants to have happen and are frequently more emotional in nature. Designing new products to satisfy consequences often leads to more creative and novel changes in existing products.

Desired end-states are the customer's underlying purposes and goals (e.g., Pieters *et al.*, 1995; Austin and Vancouver, 1996; Huffman *et al.*, 2000). As such, they are long-term and more abstract in nature (e.g., 'a digital camera allows me to relive

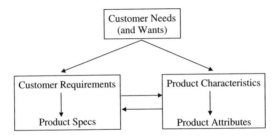

FIGURE 3.3 The languages of new product development.

fond memories'). Developing innovations with these end-states in mind can result in creative and radical changes because customer-oriented product-market structures may be very different from traditional industry defined competitive boundaries (e.g., Day *et al.*, 1979; Ratneshwar and Shocker, 1991; Shocker *et al.*, 2004).

As implied by Figure 3.2, customers typically map many discrete and continuous features onto fewer higher-level benefits (consequences and desired end-states) through a process of cognitive abstraction (e.g., Johnson and Fornell, 1987; Reynolds and Gutman, 1988).

Figure 3.3 summarizes the discussion so far. The digital camera example illustrates some of the ambiguity inherent in the language of new product development. In some cases, needs, wants, attributes, features, requirements, and specs refer to the same thing. In other instances, these terms capture very different information about what the customer really desires. Highly successful innovations come from a deep understanding of the utilitarian and hedonic benefits that customers desire, i.e., what is widely referred to as *customer needs*. Importantly, customers cannot always recognize or describe their needs in terms of consequences or end-states. Remember that customer needs are *not* a particular 'solution' (product or service), or a specific set of attributes, specs, etc. As a result, a customer needs hierarchy almost always has to be *interpreted* from the 'raw' data of a customer research study. Several general approaches for identifying customer needs will be discussed later in this chapter.

CUSTOMER NEEDS IN THE INNOVATION PROCESS

Figure 3.4 outlines the major steps involved in the 'fuzzy front-end' of the innovation process (e.g., Otto and Wood, 2001; Ulrich and Eppinger, 2004). Understanding customer needs is a key input into what has become known as the *voice of the customer* (VOC). Originating in the total quality management movement, the VOC and quality function deployment (QFD) enable marketing, design, engineering, R&D, and manufacturing to communicate effectively across functional boundaries (e.g., Hauser and Clausing, 1988; Griffin and Hauser, 1992; 1993; Shillito, 2001; Dahan and Hauser, 2002a; Akao and Mazur, 2003). This cross-functional communication is crucial to ensure that development efforts focus on innovations that are feasible, salable, and desirable (see Figure 3.1).

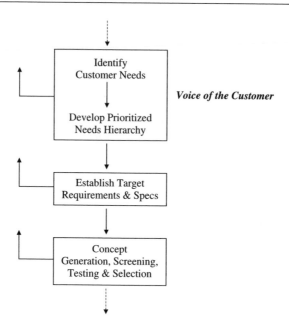

FIGURE 3.4 The fuzzy front-end of new product development.

The VOC includes identifying a set of detailed customer needs, as well as summarizing these needs into a hierarchy where each need is prioritized[7] with respect to its customer importance (e.g., Griffin and Hauser, 1993; Iansiti and Stein, 1995). Prioritizing customer needs is important because it allows the cross-functional development team to make necessary tradeoff decisions when balancing the costs of meeting a customer need with the desirability of that need relative to the entire set of customer needs. The VOC is then translated into requirements and product specs, which in turn are translated into specific product attributes that can be bundled into concepts and prototypes for further testing with customers (e.g., Dahan and Hauser, 2002a; Pullman *et al.*, 2002; Ulrich and Eppinger, 2004). Design researchers identify three research platforms (Squires, 2002):

♦ discovery research (an open-ended exploratory effort to learn about customer culture so as to develop the foundation for 'really' new products and services);
♦ definition research (which assumes there is already a product concept, and thus defines the products by identifying the customer implications associated with specific designs, products, and marketing strategies);
♦ evaluation research (which assumes there is already a working prototype, and thus helps refine and validate prototypes, design usability, market segments, and consumer preferences).

[7]There are several methods available for determining priorities, including subjective scoring by the development team as well as customer rating approaches and conjoint analysis (e.g., see Pullman *et al.*, 2002).

Practicing designers, as well as the sociology and anthropology literatures, tend to emphasize methods for understanding the complete range of customer needs. For example, many articles discuss ways to uncover embedded customer needs, including empathic design methods (e.g., Leonard-Barton, 1995; Leonard and Rayport, 1997), user-centered design (e.g., Norman and Draper, 1986; Norman, 1988; Abras *et al.*, 2004), and contextual inquiry (e.g., Holtzblat and Beyer, 1993) as well as ethnography and nontraditional market research approaches (e.g., Beebe, 1995; Patnaik and Becker, 1999; Wasson, 2000; Kelley, 2001; Squires and Byrne, 2002; Kumar and Whitney, 2003; Masten and Plowman, 2003). Used to develop the highly successful Mazda Miata Roadster[8], Kansei engineering has also been proposed as a way to expand customer needs information to include customer feelings and other hedonic benefits (e.g., Nagamachi, 1995; 2002). In addition, researchers have suggested ways to incorporate aesthetics, emotions, and experiential aspects into the identification of customer needs (e.g., Patton, 1999; Schmitt, 1999; Desmet *et al.*, 2001; Desmet, 2003). Some research also addresses the topic of determining priorities, including the use of direct rating scales (Wilkie and Pessemier, 1973; Griffin and Hauser, 1993), the analytic hierarchy process (Saaty, 1988), conjoint analysis (e.g., Green and Srinivasan, 1990; Green *et al.*, 2001), Borda counts (Dym *et al.*, 2002), and fuzzy/entropy methods (Chan *et al.*, 1999).

The engineering, quality, and operations literatures consider a new product to be a complex assembly of interacting components for which various parametric models are built to optimize performance objectives (e.g., Otto and Wood, 1998; McAdams *et al.*, 1999; Krishnan and Ulrich, 2001; Aungst *et al.*, 2003). According to Michalek *et al.* (2005, p. 43), 'engineers generally use intuition when dealing with customer needs, emphasizing the creativeness and functionality of the product concept and working toward technical objectives such are reliability, durability, environmental impact, energy use, heat generation, manufacturability, and cost reduction, among others.' Given a set of customer requirements and product specs, as well as related information on priorities, optimal values for key design variables can be determined using various standard techniques (Papalambros and Wilde, 2000). Michalek *et al.* (2005) describe how the analytical target cascading method can be used to resolve technical tradeoffs by explicitly recognizing designs that are costly and/or impossible to achieve.

By and large, the marketing literature does not directly deal with understanding customer needs (e.g., Tauber, 1974; Sanders, 1992; Eliashberg *et al.*, 1995); instead, it implicitly or explicitly focuses on the concept generation and testing stage in the innovation process (see Figure 3.4). To facilitate communication between marketing and engineering, the marketing literature generally considers a new product or service to be a bundle of 'actionable' attributes and characteristics (e.g., see the reviews in Kaul and Rao, 1995; Krishnan and Ulrich, 2001). However, as noted

[8]In the early 1990s, Mazda wanted to develop a brand new sports car for the young adult market. As part of the Kansei process of videotaping and photographing young drivers maneuvering, steering, and controlling cars, the project team concluded that 'unification of driver-machine' was the key desired end-state. As part of the design specifications, a particular sound of engine thrust was highly desired by the target customers. After extensive simulations and study of low frequency sounds with odd cycle combustion noise, a special exhaust pipe was developed that closely matched the desired sound; see Nagamachi (2002) and QFD Institute (2004).

by Shocker and Srinivasan (1974; 1979) this approach is only 'useful for locating "new" product opportunities which may not be substantially different from current alternatives' (Shocker and Srinivasan, 1979, p. 164). Most of the extensive marketing research dealing with product positioning and conjoint analysis assumes that determinant attributes have already been identified (e.g., see the reviews in Green, 1975; Shocker and Srinivasan, 1979; Green and Srinivasan, 1990; Urban and Hauser, 1993; Kaul and Rao, 1995; Srinivasan *et al.*, 2001; Green *et al.*, 2001), although novel applications are still possible (e.g., see the work of Moskowitz-Jacobs (http://www.mji-designlab.com/) in developing new foods and beverages). Moreover, marketing generally does not completely appreciate the complex interactions and constraints among product specs in developing a fully working product, and also usually underestimates the fact that some designs are totally infeasible (e.g., Aungst *et al.*, 2003; Michalek *et al.*, 2005).

The discussion to this point highlights that different research streams separately emphasize each of the critical steps in the innovation process in Figure 3.4. Moreover, the engineering and marketing (and related economics) literatures typically deal with product characteristics and attributes rather than a broader set of customer needs as defined in this chapter (see Exhibits 3.2 and 3.3). Since it is very challenging to develop systematically new products that are feasible, salable, *and* desirable without completely understanding customer needs, the relatively large number of failures reported in the press should not be that surprising (see Figure 3.1).

IDENTIFYING CUSTOMER NEEDS

One widely cited approach for determining the types of customer needs is the Kano Model of Customer Satisfaction (Kano *et al.*, 1984)[9]. Kano developed his model by adapting the ideas of Fredrick Herzberg on the asymmetry of the factors related to job satisfaction and dissatisfaction (i.e., job satisfaction is related to 'motivators' such as achievement, recognition, work itself, and responsibility, whereas job dissatisfaction is related to 'hygiene' factors such as company policy, relationship with supervisor, work conditions, and salary; Herzberg *et al.*, 1959; Herzberg, 1968). In the 1970s, Kano was working with the Konica camera company to develop some highly differentiated new products (e.g., Scholtes, 1997). Konica's sales and research groups found that customers asked only for minor improvements to the existing camera models. Kano, however, believed that really new innovations did not come from simply listening to what customers were verbally saying, but that the

---

[9]Other categories of needs have also been proposed. For example, Sanders (1992) identifies 'observable needs' (that are displayed in action and can be determined through observation by experts), 'explicit needs' (that can be expressed in words by customers), 'tacit needs' (conscious needs that customers are unable to express in words), and 'latent needs' (subconscious, possibly dormant, needs that customers are unable to express in words). Otto and Wood (2001) define 'constant needs' (needs that are intrinsic to the task of the product; e.g., the number of exposures for a camera, whether implemented on film, or the number of digital images that can be recorded), 'variable needs' (needs that might disappear; e.g., digital photography eliminates the need for long film storage life), 'general needs' (needs that apply to every customer in the population; e.g., the need for a camera to have a portable power source), and 'niche needs' (needs that only apply to a relatively small segment of the population; e.g., underwater photography).

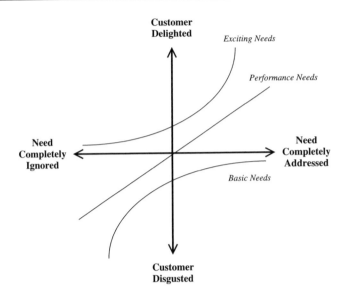

FIGURE 3.5 The Kano model of customer satisfaction.

development team had to develop a deep understanding of customers' real (latent) needs. Consequently, Konica staffers went to commercial photo processing labs to investigate the actual prints taken by customers. They found many mistakes and failures: blurry images, under and over exposure, blank film rolls. Addressing these latent needs led to features such as auto focus, built-in-flash, and automatic film rewinding that are widely available in cameras today.

The key concepts in Kano's model are summarized in Figure 3.5. The horizontal axis in this diagram indicates the degree to which a particular customer need is addressed in a (new, existing) product or service, ranging from completely absent to completely addressed. The vertical axis in this diagram indicates how satisfied the customer is for a specific implementation of a customer need, ranging from delighted to disgusted. Within this two-dimensional space, three different types of customer needs can be defined[10].

The bottom curve, labeled *basic needs*, represents needs that are taken for granted and typically assumed by the customer to be met (i.e., these are needs that 'must be' satisfied). 'The camera works out of the box', 'the camera is safe', and 'the battery can be recharged by plugging into any outlet' are examples of basic needs for a digital camera. These needs are the 'order qualifiers' and thus must be of high quality; these needs are required simply to be in the game. Completely meeting basic needs cannot greatly increase customer satisfaction, but if they are absent or below par customers will not react favorably.

[10]Other types of needs can also be defined based on the reverse of the curves in Figure 3.5, as well as needs for which the customer is indifferent (along the horizontal axis). See Center for Quality of Management (1993) and Matzler and Hintehuber (1998) for detailed discussions of methods to collect customer information that can be used to classify needs into these types.

The middle curve, labeled *performance needs*, represents needs for which customer satisfaction is roughly proportional to the performance exhibited by the product or service (i.e., these needs are 'linear' in that 'more is better'). For example, longer battery life in a digital camera and more internal memory for image storage are preferred. These needs are frequently requested by customers during the course of traditional market research studies, and are typically associated with predictable product improvements (i.e., the 'features' in Figure 3.2).

The upper curve, labeled *exciting needs*, represents needs that the customer does not expect to be satisfied. Thus, if this need is completely addressed the customer is delighted but if not, the customer does not really care. These needs are the 'order winners' for customers. For example, side airbags, global positioning systems, air-less tires that never get flat for automobiles might be exciting needs today (e.g., Mayersohn, 2005).

The underlying message of the Kano model is simple, yet powerful. Customer needs are dynamic in that an exciting need today will eventually migrate to being a performance need and will become a basic need tomorrow (e.g., automobile air conditioning was a delighter in the 1950s but is a basic need today; more recently anti-lock braking systems and cup holders that were once exciting needs have become standard equipment in most automobiles). Thus, customer expectations increase over time and, consequently, firms must continually strive to better understand evolving customer needs in order to stay competitive.

Figure 3.6 summarizes the current theory and practice for understanding customer needs. *Interpreted needs* (i.e., the voice of the customer must be 'translated' into a needs hierarchy) consist of articulated and unarticulated needs. *Articulated needs* are those needs that a customer can readily verbalize, if asked appropriately. *Unarticulated* needs are those that customers cannot easily verbalize. It is

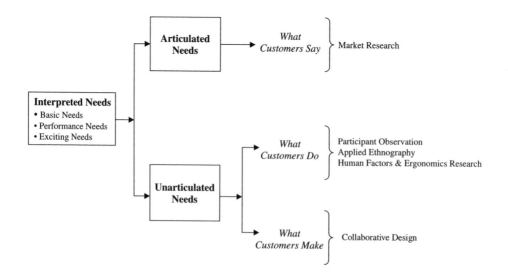

FIGURE 3.6 Approaches for understanding customer needs.

important to keep in mind that there are many reasons why customers say some things (e.g., they believe it is what the researchers want to hear; see Tourangeau *et al.*, 2000) and many reasons why they do not say other things (including that they didn't remember, didn't want to tell, didn't know how to tell, etc.).

Articulated needs generally involve information dealing with 'what customers say'. Traditional market research methods such as focus groups, personal depth interviews, surveys, email questionnaires, and product clinics can be used to collect data on articulated needs (e.g., Urban and Hauser, 1993; McDonagh-Philp and Bruseberg, 2000). Well-known market research methods include conjoint analysis, perceptual mapping, segmentation, preference modeling, and simulated test markets (e.g., see the reviews in Urban *et al.*, 1983; Green and Krieger, 1989; Urban and Hauser, 1993; Kaul and Rao, 1995; Urban, 1996; Urban *et al.*, 1997; Green *et al.*, 2001). Information on articulated needs can be obtained using category problem analysis (e.g., Tauber, 1975; Swaddling and Zobel, 1996); see Figure 3.7 for an example. Other techniques include repertory grids (Kelly, 1955), Echo procedures (Barthol, 1976), verbal protocols (Ericsson and Simon, 1984), and laddering and means-ends analysis (Reynolds and Gutman, 1988), as well as projective techniques such as product personality profiling, having customers draw their ideal product, hypnosis, and architype analysis (e.g., Shalit, 1999).

Unarticulated needs generally involve information dealing with 'what customers do' and 'what customers make' (Sanders, 1992). As suggested by Sanders and Dandavate (1999), in order to obtain a deep understanding of customer needs we need to learn about their memories as well as their current and ideal experiences. To accomplish this, we can listen to what customers say, we can interpret what customers express and make inferences about what they think, we can watch what customers do, we can observe what customers use, we can uncover what customers know, we can reach toward understanding what customers feel, and we can appreciate what customers dream. Participant observation, applied (rapid) ethnography, and contextual inquiry are the primary methods to find out what customers do. Common characteristics of these methods are that they take place in the customer's natural surroundings and that they are open-ended in nature. For example, 'listening' to what customers say can be accomplished by taking notes of conversations and audiotaping interviews; 'observing' what customers do is done by watching behaviors, making notes and mapping patterns of behavior, sketching relationships between stakeholders, photographing or videotaping the general customer environment, and using web cameras to watch activities; 'observing' what customers use can be performed by watching for unobtrusive behavior traces (e.g., wear and tear on artifacts and objects), watching, photographing, or videotaping products and services being used, and using web cameras (Sanders, 2000). For an example of observing what customers do and use, see the series of photos in Figure 3.8. These photos depict customers using barbeques at tailgating events before the big game. Key unarticulated needs discovered by the development team included a need for the capacity of a full-size grill, portability, comfort while cooking, safety, as well as quick cool down and clean up. This ethnographic fieldwork, along with other market research, led to the introduction of Char-Broil's highly successful Grill2Go portable propane grill (see Grill2Go, 2004).

**What are the relevant met and unmet needs
and problem areas for the customer?**

- *What is the essence of the consumer need?*
- *Why does the need exist?*
- *Which benefits and attributes are mandatory?*
- *Which benefits are consumers willing to "trade-off?"*
- *What benefits are available to the consumer?*
- *What benefits does the consumer most desire?*
- *What factors might drive purchase decisions in the category?*

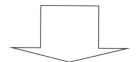

Consumer Attitudes and Behaviors

 *How often do you need to wrap food such as sandwiches? What kind of food do you need to
wrap? How long does it usually take? How do you currently wrap food? How do you know
when the food is wrapped? How do you feel when you need to wrap sandwiches? What
frustrates you when you wrap food?*

Benefits Sought

 *What are the things (tangible and intangible) you want in sandwich wrap? How
important are these benefits to you?*

Problems Consumers Encounter

 *What types of food are most difficult to wrap? What things do you dislike the most with
your current way of wrapping food? What would you change with your current
"product?"*

Solutions and Methods Used

 *How do you handle the problems you mentioned? What products do you believe are the
"gold standard" for wrapping food? What do these products do that the others do not?
Why don't you use these products?*

Aspects of Ideal Solution

 What would you like an "ideal" solution to do for you?

FIGURE 3.7 Example of category problem analysis for sandwich bags.

In addition to traditional ethnographic methods, it is possible to have customers engage in self-reporting (e.g., studies involving diaries, beepers, daily logs, disposable cameras, self-videotaping, web cameras; see Sanders, 2002), have the development team 'be the customer' (e.g., collect currently available advertising and point-of-purchase displays, analyze service and pricing options, visit retailers, talk to a salesperson, visit company web sites, call customer support, etc.; see Griffin, 1996; Otto and Wood, 2001), and/or conduct an artifact analysis of existing products and services. Human factors and ergonomics research are other approaches to better understand what customers do (e.g., Salvendy, 1997).

"I like my pig well done!" (Customers use full-sized grills, transporting them to and from the game.)

Portable grilling can be very uncomfortable!

Current grilling methods can be unsafe (people drinking before the game, vehicles, fire hazard).

"I gotta get to the game! I hope nobody steals my grill."

FIGURE 3.8 Example of ethnographic fieldwork at tailgating events.
(*Source:* Char-Broil)

Participatory and collaborative design between the development team and customer is the primary method for discovering what customers know, feel, and dream through what they make. Techniques include lead user analysis (e.g., von Hippel, 1986; von Hippel *et al.*, 1999), the use of customer toolkits (e.g., Thomke, 2003; von Hippel, 2001; Franke and Piller, 2004; Urban and Hauser, 2004), metaphor elicitation (Zaltman, 1997; Christensen and Olson, 2002), 'serious play' using LEGOs (Roos *et al.*, 2004), as well as making collages, cognitive image mapping, and Velcro modeling (Sanders, 2000; SonicRim, 2004).

The discussion in this section indicates that a variety of traditional and non-traditional market research approaches can be used to gain a rich understanding of customer needs. Indeed, as recommended by Sanders (1992) multiple methods should be used to have a complete coverage of the underlying needs. The information that can be captured from these approaches differs quite a bit. In particular, the degree to which customer needs must be *interpreted* from the original 'raw' data increases as interest moves from learning what customers say, to what customers do, to what customers make. However, in all cases the customer 'voice' must be *translated* into a hierarchy of needs. A detailed discussion of techniques for translating data from these approaches into interpreted needs is beyond the scope of this chapter. For excellent coverage of the approaches that have been successful in practice, including the use of the KJ analysis and affinity diagrams to sort the huge amount of data generally collected into a needs hierarchy, see Burchill *et al.* (1997), Burchill and Brodie (1997), Scupin (1997), Otto and Wood (2001), Shillito (2001), Mello (2003), and Ulrich and Eppinger (2004), among others.

Future Research Directions

It is clear that innovation and new product development are challenging activities. Innovations, especially those involving new technologies, are increasingly more complex with many hundreds (if not thousands) of parts, involving dispersed development teams of hundreds of people, and costing several million dollars in development before market launch (e.g., Ulrich and Eppinger, 2004). In addition, firms are under increasing pressure to shorten their development times (e.g., Bayus,

1. **Extreme User Interviews**
   Identify individuals who are extremely familiar or completely unfamiliar with the product and ask them to evaluate their experience using it.

2. **Rapid Ethnography**
   Spend as much time as you can with people relevant to the design topic. Establish their trust in order to visit and/or participate in their natural habitat and witness specific activities.

3. **Behavioral Archaeology**
   Look for the evidence of people's activities inherent in the placement, wear patterns, and organization of places and things.

4. **Social Network Mapping**
   Notice different kinds of social relationships within a user group and map the network of their interactions.

5. **Error Analysis**
   List all the things that can go wrong when using a product and determine the various possible causes.

6. **Predict Next Year's Headlines**
   Invite clients to project their company into the future, identifying how they want to develop and sustain customer relationships.

7. **Camera Journal**
   Ask potential users to keep a written and visual diary of their impressions, circumstances, and activities related to the product.

8. **Cognitive Maps**
   Ask participants to map an existing or virtual space and show how they navigate it.

9. **Empathy Tools**
   Use tools like clouded glasses and weighted gloves to experience processes as though you yourself have the abilities of different users.

10. **Activity Analysis**
    List or represent in detail all tasks, actions, objects, performers, and interactions involved in a process.

11. **Cognitive Task Analysis**
    List and summarize all of a user's sensory inputs, decision points, and actions.

12. **Unfocus Group**
    Assemble a diverse group of individuals in a workshop to use a stimulating range of materials and create things that are relevant to your project.

13. **Draw the Experience**
Ask participants to visualize an experience through drawings and diagrams.

14. **A Day in the Life**
Catalog the activities and contexts that users experience throughout an entire day.

15. **Cultural Probes**
Assemble a camera journal kit (camera, film, notebook, instructions) and distribute it to participants within one or across many cultures.

16. **Scenarios**
Illustrate a character-rich story line describing the context of use for a product or service.

17. **Experience Prototype**
Quickly prototype a concept using available materials and use it in order to learn from a simulation of the experience using the product.

18. **Bodystorming**
Set up a scenario and act out roles, with or without props, focusing on the intuitive responses prompted by the physical enactment.

19. **Try it yourself**
Use the product or prototype you are designing.

20. **Behavioral Mapping**
Track the positions and movements of people within a space over time.

21. **Role-Playing**
Identify the stakeholders involved in the design problem and assign those roles to members of the team.

22. **Behavior Sampling**
Give people a pager or phone and ask them to record and evaluate the situation they are in when it rings.

23. **Card Sort**
On separate cards, name possible features, functions, or design attributes. Ask people to organize the cards spatially, in ways that make sense to them.

24. **Shadowing**
Tag along with people to observe and understand their day-to-day routines, interactions, and contexts.

25. **Historical Analysis**
Compare features of an industry, organization, group, market segment, or practice through various stages of development.

26. **Still-Photo Survey**
Follow a planned shooting script and capture pictures of specific objects, activities, etc.

27. **Narration**
As they perform a process or execute a specific task, ask participants to describe aloud what they are thinking.

28. **Personal Inventory**
Document the things that people identify as important to them as a way of cataloging evidence of their lifestyles

29. **Character Profiles**
Based on observations of real people, develop character profiles to represent archetypes and the details of their behavior or lifestyles.

30. **Be Your Customer**
Ask the client to describe, outline, or enact their typical customer's experience.

FIGURE 3.9 Selected Method Cards from IDEO

1997; Bayus *et al.*, 1997; Reinertsen, 1997; Smith and Reinertsen, 1998), and, the costs of studies to understand customer needs are high.[11]

Under these conditions, it is not surprising that a lot of effort has been, and should continue to be, spent on developing new methods for understanding customer needs. Naturally, practicing design firms will continue to develop novel methods for understanding customer needs (e.g., see Figure 3.9 for a selected summary of IDEO's Method Cards). Academic research is also engaged in this activity. For example, Urban and Hauser (2004) describe a relatively cost effective method for 'listening in' as customers search the Internet for information and advice about automobile purchases. Using a custom designed web-based (virtual) advisor, customers can generate a large number of preferred combinations of features, and, importantly, they can also reveal their needs for 'new' combinations not currently available. Dahan and Hauser (2002b) report several other 'virtual customer' methods: interactive web-based conjoint analysis; concept testing of virtual prototypes; fast polyhedral adaptive conjoint estimation, in which large numbers of product features can be quickly screened and importance weights estimated; interactive web-based environments where customers can design their ideal virtual prototypes; the 'information pump' that allows customers to interact in a web-based game with incentives for customers to think hard and to verbalize the product features that are important to them; and stock-market-like securities trading where customers interact to identify novel and winning concepts. Finch (1999) discusses how information from customer product and service postings to Internet newsgroups gleaned from Usenet can be used to understand customer needs. Fuller *et al.* (2004) describe a method to harness the innovative ideas within online communities, along with a virtual product development lab, to generate information on customer needs. Finally, Nambisan (2002) proposes a framework of how virtual customer communities can facilitate new product development.

Information on needs must ultimately be obtained from customers, and so an important direction for future research is to incorporate findings from the consumer decision-making literature dealing with 'constructed preferences'. As reviewed by Bettman *et al.* (1998), a large body of research dealing with consumer decision making argues the following:

- ◆ preferences among options critically depends on the customer's goals;
- ◆ preferences depend on the complexity of the decision task;
- ◆ preferences are highly context dependent;
- ◆ preferences depend on what is specifically asked of customers;
- ◆ preferences depend on how the choice set is framed (e.g., losses loom larger than gains; see Kahneman and Tversky, 1979; Laibson and Zeckhauser, 1998).

---

[11] Urban and Hauser (2004) report the typical costs associated with different customer needs studies in the automobile industry. For example, qualitative/ethnographic interviews (5–10 groups of 5–10 customers each) covering 50–100 features or needs cost $40–50 000; tailored interviews for segmentation studies (800 personal interviews) including 73 scales cost $80 000; activities, interests, and opinions studies (100 000 mailed questionnaires) covering 114 features or needs cost $500 000; conjoint analyses (300 online or in-person interviews) covering 10–20 features or needs cost $50–100 000; product clinics (300 central-facility personal interviews) covering 40–50 features or needs cost $500 000.

The idea that preferences are often constructed 'on the fly' implies that the information available from customers is highly sensitive to how the concept is communicated as well as context – customers find it difficult to develop well-defined preferences and often bring multiple goals to any decision problem (Bettman *et al.*, 1998). This line of research provides a possible explanation for the inadequacy of traditional market research methods in uncovering customer needs, as well as the success attributed to empathic, ethnographic, and context specific approaches advocated by designers, sociologists, and anthropologists. Other relevant research includes work on choice bracketing (Read *et al.*, 1999), construal processes (Fischoff *et al.*, 1999), choice deferral (Dhar, 1997), contingent valuation (e.g., Kahneman *et al.*, 1999), economic modeling and rationality (McFadden, 1999), and measurement methods (Payne *et al.*, 1999). Relating work on the difficulty that customers have in making tradeoffs seems particularly promising to enhance understanding of customer needs. For example, research finds that consumers are resistant to trading off some quality to get a better price and prefer paying a higher price to get higher quality (e.g., Dhar and Simonson, 1999; Nowlis and Simonson, 1997; Luce *et al.*, 1999). Other researchers argue that some product attributes are more difficult to tradeoff than others (e.g., Tetlock, 1992, calls these 'sacred' values; Baron and Spranca, 1997, discuss 'protected' attributes). As also suggested by Bettman *et al.* (1998), continued research on the properties of customer needs (attributes) and the effects of these properties on tradeoffs is in order.

Finally, an especially interesting direction for future research is to develop a comprehensive theory around what I call *customer roadmapping*. As discussed by Sandia National Laboratories (2004), *technology* roadmapping is 'a needs-driven technology planning process to help identify, select, and develop technology alternatives to satisfy a set of product needs'. Similarly, customer roadmapping is a customer planning process to help identify and select key customer needs to be used as input into the innovation and product development process. An important component of customer roadmapping is a theory of 'universal' customer needs dimensions that can be used as a reference point for methods that collect needs information, as well as a starting point for the construction of a hierarchy of specific needs for a particular context and segment of customers. A set of universal needs dimensions would be an important input for planning purposes because it would allow comparisons and benchmarking over time and across products, categories, and markets. If systematic patterns of evolution within these universal needs dimensions can be established, customer roadmapping can be a useful forecasting tool[12]. As an example, consider the following four 'universal' customer needs dimensions that might be associated with a product or service:

- *functionality* (e.g., performance, reliability, compatibility, flexibility);
- *form* (e.g., aesthetics, durability, portability, maintainability, uniqueness);
- *usability* (e.g., ease of use, complexity);
- *cost* (e.g., acquisition, use, disposal).

---

[12]For example, consider the work of Christensen (1997) and Christensen and Raynor (2003) on 'disruptive innovations'. Although it does not seem to be based on rigorous research, they suggest a buying hierarchy in which customers want (in order): functionality, reliability, convenience, cost.

Future research might establish the validity of these four dimensions, and then develop a set of customer needs for the next level down. For example, detailed 'maps' of product functionality (McAdams *et al.*, 1999) and usability (Jordan, 1998; Han *et al.*, 2001; Babbar *et al.*, 2002) have been proposed, as have universal 'utility levers' for services (Kim and Mauborgne, 2000) and scales for uniqueness (Tian *et al.*, 2001). Reverse engineering of products can also be used to construct the evolutionary path of product attributes (Otto and Wood, 1998; McAdams *et al.*, 1999).

CONCLUSION

Understanding customer needs is a crucial input into the innovation and new product development process, and at the same time, a very challenging endeavor. This chapter has attempted to review the literature relating to customer needs that spans several disciplines. As the discussion in this chapter implies, much of the published research related to customer needs has been concerned with the cross-fertilization of ideas and concepts across disciplines (see Figure 3.10). Consequently, progress in fully integrating a deep understanding of customer needs into the innovation process has been slow. But, this review also indicates that the boundaries between the various functions are coming down. There will always be a tradeoff between the expediency and cost efficiency of practical methods for understanding customer needs versus

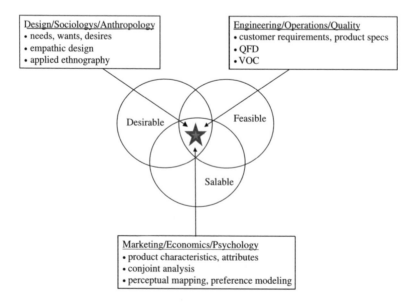

FIGURE 3.10 The cross-fertilization of research on customer needs.

methods of obtaining a deeper understanding of needs that involve more effort and resources. There also seems to be several directions that academic research can explore in the future. In all cases though, the challenge will be to integrate across multiple disciplines. But, this is what makes the topic interesting!

REFERENCES

Abras, C., Maloney-Krichmar, D., and Preece, J. (2004). User-centered design. In W. Bainbridge (ed.), *Berkshire Encyclopedia of Human-Computer Interaction*, Great Barrington, MA: Berkshire Publishing Group.

Akao, Y., and Mazur, G. (2003). The leading edge in QFD: past, present and future. *International Journal of Quality & Reliability Management*, 20(1), 20–35.

Associated Press (2003). Plans for moist toilet-paper rolls unravel. *Miami Herald*, September 2, www.miami.com/mld/miamiherald/business/6671201?1c.htm.

Aungst, S., Barton, R., and Wilson, D. (2003). The virtual integrated design method. *Quality Engineering*, 15(4), 565–79.

Austin, J., and Vancouver, J. (1996). Goal constructs in psychology: structure, process, and content. *Psychological Bulletin*, 120(3), 338–75.

Babbar, S., Behara, R., and White, E. (2002). Mapping product usability. *International Journal of Operations & Production Management*, 22(9/10), 1071–89.

Baron, J., and Spranca, M. (1997). Protected values. *Organizational Behavior and Human Decision Processes*, 70(April), 1–16.

Barthol, R. (1976). ECHO: estimating values in familiar and unfamiliar cultures. In H. Sinaiko and L. Broedling (eds), *Perspectives on Attitude Assessment: Surveys and Their Alternatives*, Champaign, IL: Pendelton Press.

Bayus, B. (1997). Speed-to-market and new product performance tradeoffs. *Journal of Product Innovation Management*, 14 (November), 485–97.

Bayus, B., Jain, S., and Rao, A. (1997). Too little and too early: introduction timing and new product performance in the Personal Digital Assistant industry. *Journal of Marketing Research*, 34 (February), 50–63.

Beebe, J. (1995). Basic concepts and techniques of rapid assessment. *Human Organization*, 54(1), 42–51.

Bettman, J., Luce, M., and Payne, J. (1998). Constructive consumer choice processes. *Journal of Consumer Research*, 25(3), 187–217.

Brand Strategy (2003). Innovation: where have all the ideas gone? *Brand Strategy*, (November), 20.

Burchill, G., and Brodie, C. (1997). *Voices into choices: acting on the voice of the customer*. Madison, WI: Joiner/Oriel Inc.

Burchill, G., and Shen, D. (1995). *Concept Engineering*. Center for Quality of Management, Cambridge, MA, Document No. ML0080.

Captain, S. (2004). Making sense of specs. *New York Times*, Dec. 23, www.nytimes.com/2004/12/23/technology/circuits/23spec.html?ex=1104642000&en=0631f3a84f5874fe&ei=5070&th.

Center for Quality of Management (1993). Special issue: Kano's method for understanding customer-defined quality. *Center for Quality of Management Journal*, 2(4), 3–36.

Chan, L., Kao, H., Ng, A., and Wu, M. (1999). Rating the importance of customer needs in quality function deployment by fuzzy and entropy methods. *International Journal of Production Research*, 37(11), 2499–2518.

Christensen, C. (1997). *The innovator's dilemma.* Boston, MA: Harvard Business School Press.

Christensen, C., and Raynor, M. (2003). *The innovator's solution.* Boston, MA: Harvard Business School Press.

Christensen, G., and Olson, J. (2002). Mapping consumers' mental models with ZMET. *Psychology & Marketing,* 19(6), 477–502.

Cooper, R. (1999). From experience: the invisible success factors in product innovation. *Journal of Product Innovation Management,* 16 (April), 115–33.

Crawford, M., and Di Benedetto, A. (2003). *New products management.* New York: McGraw-Hill/Irwin.

Cyberkinetics, Inc. (2004), www.cyberkinetics.com.

Dahan, E., and Hauser, J. (2002a). Product development: managing a dispersed process. In B. Weitz and R. Wensley (eds), *Handbook of Marketing,* Thousand Oaks, CA: Sage Publications, 179–222.

Dahan, E., and Hauser, J. (2002b). The virtual customer. *Journal of Product Innovation Management,* 19, 332–53.

Day, G., Shocker, A., and Srivastava, R. (1979). Customer-oriented approaches to identifying product-markets. *Journal of Marketing,* 43 (Fall), 8–19.

Desmet, P. (2003). A multilayered model of product emotions. *The Design Journal,* 6(2), 4–13.

Desmet, P., Overbeeke, C., and Tax, S. (2001). Designing products with added emotional value: development and application of an approach for research through design. *The Design Journal,* 4(1), 32–47.

Dhar, R. (1997). Context and task effects on choice deferral. *Marketing Letters,* 8(1), 119–30.

Dhar, R., and Simonson, I. (1999). Making complementary choices in consumption episodes: highlighting versus balancing. *Journal of Marketing Research,* 36 (February), 49–54.

Dym, C., Wood, W., and Scott, M. (2002). Rank ordering engineering designs: pairwise comparison charts and Borda counts. *Research in Engineering Design,* 13, 236–42.

Eliashberg, J., Lilien, G., and Rao, V. (1995). Minimizing technological oversights: a marketing research perspective. In R. Garud, P. Nayyar and Z. Shapira (eds), *Technological Innovation: Oversights and Foresights,* New York: Cambridge University Press, 214–32.

Elliot, H. (1998). Shoot first, do market research later. *Electronic Business,* (January), 49–50, 82.

Ericsson, K., and Simon, H. (1984). *Protocol analysis: verbal reports as data.* Cambridge, MA: MIT Press.

Farrell, C. (1993). A theory of technological progress. *Technological Forecasting and Social Change,* 44, 161–78.

Finch, B. (1999). Internet discussions as a source for consumer product customer involvement and quality information: an exploratory study. *Journal of Operations Management,* 17, 535–56.

Fischoff, B., Welsh, N., and Frederick, S. (1999). Construal processes in preference assessment. *Journal of Risk and Uncertainty,* 19(1–3), 139–64.

Franke, N., and Piller, F. (2004). Value creation by toolkits for user innovation and design: the case of the watch market. *Journal of Product Innovation Management,* 21(6), 401–15.

Franklin, C. (2003). *Why innovation fails.* Rollinsford, NH: Spiro Press.

Fuller, J., Bartl, M., Ernst, H., and Muhlbacher, H. (2004). Community based innovation: a method to utilize the innovative potential of online communities. *Proceedings of the 37th Hawaii International Conference on System Sciences,* (January), 1–10.

Geistfeld, L., Sproles, G., and Badenhop, S. (1977). The concept and measurement of a hierarchy of product characteristics. In W. Perreault (ed.), *Advances in Consumer Research,* 4, Atlanta: Association for Consumer Research, 302–07.

Gershenson, J., and Stauffer, L. (1999). A taxonomy for design requirements from corporate customers. *Research in Engineering Design,* 11, 103–15.

Gershman, M. (1990). *Getting it right the second time.* New York: Addison-Wesley.

Green, M., Linsey, J., Seepersad, C., Wood, K., and Jensen, D. (2006). Frontier design: a product usage context method. *Proceedings of DETC/CIE*, Philadelphia, PA.

Green, P. (1974). A multidimensional model of product-features association. *Journal of Business Research*, 2(2), 107–18.

Green, P. (1975). Marketing applications of MDS: assessment and outlook. *Journal of Marketing*, 39 (January), 24–31.

Green, P., and Krieger, A. (1989). Recent contributions to optimal product positioning and buyer segmentation. *European Journal of Operational Research*, 41(2), 127–41.

Green, P., Krieger, A., and Wind, Y. (2001). Thirty years of conjoint analysis: reflections and prospects. *Interfaces*, 31(3), S56–S73.

Green, P., and Srinivasan, V. (1990). Conjoint analysis in marketing: new developments with implications for research and practice. *Journal of Marketing*, 54 (October), 3–19.

Griffin, A. (1996). Obtaining customer needs for product development. In M. Rosenau, *et al.* (eds), *The PDMA Handbook of New Product Development*, New York: John Wiley & Sons, Inc., 153–66.

Griffin, A. and Hauser, J. (1992). Patterns of communication between marketing, engineering, and manufacturing – a comparison between two new product teams. *Management Science*, 38(3), 360–73.

Griffin, A., and Hauser, J. (1993). The voice of the customer. *Marketing Science*, 12(1), 1–27.

Grill2Go (2004). www.grill2go.com.

Han, S., Yun, M., Kwahk, J., and Hong, S. (2001). Usability of consumer electronic products. *International Journal of Industrial Ergonomics*, 28, 143–51.

Hauser, J. (1984). Customer research to focus R&D projects. *Journal of Product Innovation Management*, 2, 70–84.

Hauser, J. (1993). How Puritan-Bennett used the House of Quality. *Sloan Management Review*, 34(Spring), 61–70.

Hauser, J., and Clausing, D. (1988). The House of Quality. *Harvard Business Review*, 66 (May–June), 63–73.

Henard, D., and Szymanski, D. (2001). Why some new products are more successful than others. *Journal of Marketing Research*, 38(3), 362–75.

Herzberg, F. (1968). One more time: how do you motivate employees? *Harvard Business Review*, 46(1), 53–62.

Herzberg, F., Mausner, B., and Snyderman, B. (1959). *The motivation to work*. New York: John Wiley & Sons, Inc.

Holtzblat, K., and Beyer, H. (1993). Making customer-centered design work for teams. *Communications of the ACM*, (Oct.), 93–103.

Huffman, C., Ratneshwar, S., and Mick, D. (2000). An integrative framework of consumer goals. In S. Ratneshwar *et al.* (eds), *The Why of Consumption*, London: Routledge.

Iansiti, M., and Stein, E. (1995). Understanding user needs. Harvard Business School Note 9-695-051.

Johnson, M., and Fornell, C. (1987). The nature and methodological implications of the cognitive representations of products. *Journal of Consumer Research*, 14, 214–28.

Jordan, P. (1998). *An introduction to usability*. Bristol, PA: Taylor & Francis.

Kahneman, D, Ritov, I., and Schkade, D. (1999). Economic preferences or attitude expressions? An analysis of dollar responses to public issues. *Journal of Risk and Uncertainty*, 19(1–3), 203–35.

Kahneman, D., and Tversky, A. (1979). Prospect theory: an analysis of decision making under risk. *Econometrica*, 47 (March) 18–36.

Kano, N., Tsuji, S., Seraku, N., and Takahashi, F. (1984). Attractive quality and must-be quality. *Hinshitsu: The Journal of Japanese Society for Quality Control*, 14(2), 39–48.

Karkkainen, H., Elfvengren, K., and Tuominen, M. (2003). A tool for systematic assessment of customer needs in industrial markets. *International Journal of Technology Management*, 25(6/7), 588–604.

Kaul, A., and Rao, V. (1995). Research for product positioning and design decisions: an integrative review. *International Journal of Research in Marketing*, 12, 293–320.

Kelley, T. (2001). *The art of innovation.* New York: Currency Books.

Kelly, G. (1955). *The psychology of personal constructs.* New York: W.W. Norton.

Kim, W., and Mauborgne, R. (2000). Knowing a winning business idea when you see one. *Harvard Business Review*, 77 (Sept.–Oct.), 129–38.

Kimberly Clark (2001). Company press release, 18th January 2001: http://www.emailwire.com/release/First-Major-Toilet-Paper-Innovation-in-Over-100-Years.html.

Kirchner, P. (1995). *Forgotten fads and fabulous flops.* Los Angeles: General Publishing Group.

Krishnan, V., and Ulrich, K. (2001). Product development decisions: a review of the literature. *Management Science*, 47(1), 1–21.

Kumar, V., and Whitney, P. (2003). Faster, cheaper, deeper user research. *Design Management Journal*, 14(2), 50–7.

Laibson, D., and Zeckhauser, R. (1998). Amos Tversky and the ascent of behavioral economics. *Journal of Risk and Uncertainty*, 16, 7–47.

Lancaster, K. (1971). *Consumer demand: a new approach.* New York: Columbia University Press.

Leonard-Barton, D. (1995). *Wellsprings of knowledge.* Boston: Harvard Business School Press.

Leonard, D., and Rayport, J. (1997). Spark innovation through empathic design. *Harvard Business Review*, (Nov.–Dec.), 102–113.

Luce, M., Payne, J., and Bettman, J. (1999). Emotional trade-off difficulty and choice. *Journal of Marketing Research*, 36 (May), 43–159.

Martin, J. (1995). Ignore your customer. *Fortune*, 131(8), 121–24.

Martin, M. (1999). *Design for variety: a methodology for developing product platform architectures.* Ph.D. dissertation in Mechanical Engineering, Stanford University, mml.stanford.edu/Research/Papers/1999/1999.DFV.DFM.martin/1999.DFV.DFM.martin.pdf.

Maslow, A. (1954). *Motivation and personality.* New York: Harper and Row.

Masten, D., and Plowman, T. (2003). Digital ethnography: the next wave in understanding the consumer experience. *Design Management Journal*, 14(2), 75–83.

Matzler, K., and Hintehuber, H. (1998). How to make product development projects more Successful by integrating Kano's model of customer satisfaction into quality function deployment. *Technovation*, 18(1), 25–37.

Mayersohn, N. (2005). Reinventing the wheel (and the tire, too). *New York Times*, Jan. 3, www.nytimes.com/2005/01/03/automobiles/03cars.html.

McAdams, D., Stone, R., and Wood, K. (1999). Functional interdependence and product similarity based on customer needs. *Research in Engineering Design*, 11, 1–19.

McDonagh-Philp, D., and Bruseberg, A. (2000). Using focus groups to support new product development. *Engineering Designer*, 26(5), 4–9.

McFadden, D. (1999). Rationality for economists? *Journal of Risk and Uncertainty.* 19(1–3), 73–105.

McMath, R., and Forbes, T. (1998). *What were they thinking?* New York: Times Books.

Mello, S. (2003). *Customer-centric product definition.* Boston, MA: PDC Professional Pub.

Michalek, J., Feinberg, F., and Papalambros, P. (2005). Linking marketing and engineering product design decisions via analytical target cascading. *Journal of Product Innovation Management*, 22(1), 42–62.

Molotch, H. (2003). *Where stuff comes from.* New York: Taylor & Francis Books.

Montoya-Weiss, M., and Calantone, R. (1994). Determinants of new product performance: a review and meta-analysis. *Journal of Product Innovation Management*, 11(5), 397–417.

Morita, A. (1986). *Made in Japan.* New York: Penguin Books.

Nagamachi, M. (1995). Kansei engineering: a new ergonomic consumer-oriented technology for product development. *International Journal of Industrial Ergonomics*, 15, 3–11.

Nagamachi, M. (2002). Kansei engineering as a powerful consumer-oriented technology for product development. *Applied Ergonomics*, 33, 289–294.

Nambisan, S. (2002). Designing virtual customer environments for new product development: toward a theory. *Academy of Management Review*, 27(3), 392–413.

Nelson, E. (2002). The tissue that tanked. *Wall Street Journal Classroom Edition*, September, www.wsjclassroomedition.com/archive/02sep/MKTG.htm.

Norman, D. (1988). *The psychology of everyday things*. New York: Doubleday.

Norman, D., and Draper, S. (eds) (1986). *User-centered system design: new perspectives on human-computer interaction*. Hillsdale, NJ: Lawrence Earlbaum Associates.

Nowlis, S., and Simonson, I. (1997). Attribute-task compatibility as a determinant of consumer preference reversals. *Journal of Marketing Research*, 34 (May), 205–18.

Olshavsky, R., and Spreng, R. (1996). An exploratory study of the innovation evaluation process. *Journal of Product Innovation Management*, 13, 512–29.

Otto, K., and Wood, S. (1998). Product evolution: a reverse engineering and redesign methodology. *Research in Engineering Design*, 10, 226–43.

Otto, K., and Wood, S. (2001). *Product design*. Upper Saddle River, NJ: Prentice Hall.

Papalambros, P., and Wilde, D. (2000). *Principles of optimal design: modeling and computation*. New York: Cambridge University Press.

Patnaik, D., and Becker, R. (1999). Needfinding: the why and how of uncovering people's needs. *Design Management Journal*, 10(2), 37–43.

Patton, A. (1999). Deconstructing design for marketing: tools for accessing the design process. *Journal of Market Focused Management*, 4, 309–19.

Payne, J., Bettman, J. and Schkade, D. (1999). Measuring constructed preferences: towards a building code. *Journal of Risk and Uncertainty*, 19(1–3), 243–70.

Pieters, R., Baumgartner, H., and Allen, D. (1995). A means-end chain approach to consumer-goal structures. *International Journal of Research in Marketing*, 12, 227–44.

Power, C. (1992). Will it sell in Podunk? Hard to Say. *Business Week*, Aug. 10, 46–7.

Power, C. (1993). Flops: too many products fail. Here's why – and how to do better. *Business Week*, Aug. 16, 76–81.

Pullman, M., Moore, W., and Wardell, D. (2002). A comparison of quality function deployment and conjoint analysis in new product design. *Journal of Product Innovation Management*, 19, 354–64.

QFD Institute (2004). Kansei Engineering Project: Mazda Miata. www.qfdi.org/kansei_miata.htm.

Ratchford, B. (1975). The new economic theory of consumer behavior: an interpretive essay. *Journal of Consumer Research*, 2(2), 65–75.

Ratneshwar, R., and Shocker, A. (1991). Substitution in use and the role of usage context in product category structures. *Journal of Marketing Research*, 28, 281–95.

Ratneshwar, S., Shocker, A., Cotte, J., and Srinivastava, R. (1999). Product, person, and purpose: putting the consumer back into theories of dynamic market behavior. *Journal of Strategic Marketing*, 7, 191–208.

Read, D., Loewenstein, G., and Rabin, M. (1999). Choice bracketing. *Journal of Risk and Uncertainty*, 19(1–3), 171–97.

Reinertsen, D. (1997). *Managing the design factory*. New York: The Free Press.

Reynolds, T., and Gutman, J. (1988). Laddering theory, method, analysis, and interpretation. *Journal of Advertising Research*, 28, 11–31.

Roos, J., Victor, B., and Statler, M. (2004). Playing seriously with strategy. *Long Range Planning*, 37(6), 549–68.

Rosen, S. (1974). Hedonic prices and implicit markets: product differentiation in pure competition. *Journal of Political Economy*, 82 (Jan./Feb.), 34–55.

Saaty, T. (1988). *The analytic hierarchy process: planning, priority setting, resource allocation.* Pittsburgh: RWS Publications.

Salvendy, G. (1997). *Handbook of human factors and ergonomics.* New York: Wiley-Interscience.

Sanders, E. (1992). Converging perspectives: product development research for the 1990s. *Design Management Journal*, 3(4), 49–54.

Sanders, E. (2000). Generative tools for codesigning. In S. Scrivener, L. Ball and A. Woodcock (eds), *Collaborative Design*, London: Springer-Verlag, 3–12.

Sanders, E. (2002). Ethnography in NPD research: how 'applied ethnography' can improve your NPD research process. *Visions*, (April), www.pdma.org/visions/apr02/applied.html.

Sanders, E., and Dandavate, U. (1999). Design for experiencing: new tools. In C. Overbeeke and P. Hekkert (eds), *Proceedings of the First International Conference on Design and Emotion*, Delft.

Sandia National Laboratories (2004). Fundamentals of technology roadmapping. www.sandia. gov/ Roadmap/home.htm.

Saranow, J. (2004). The puncture wound I got for Christmas. *Wall Street Journal*, Dec. 30, D1, D3.

Schmitt, B. (1999). *Experiential marketing.* New York: The Free Press.

Schnaars, S. (1989). *Megamistakes: forecasting and the myth of rapid technological change.* New York: The Free Press.

Scholtes, P. (1997). *The leader's handbook.* New York: McGraw-Hill.

Schwartz, E. (2004). The sound war. *Technology Review*, (May), 50–4.

Scupin, R. (1997). The KJ method: a technique for analyzing data derived from Japanese ethnology. *Human Organization*, 56(2), 233–37.

Shalit, R. (1999). The return of the hidden persuaders. *Salon Media*, www.salon.com/ media/col/shal/1999/09/27/persuaders.

Shillito, M.L. (2001). *Acquiring, processing, and deploying voice of the customer.* New York: St. Lucie Press.

Shocker, A., Bayus, B., and Kim, N. (2004). Product complements and substitutes in the real world: the relevance of 'other' products. *Journal of Marketing*, 68 (Jan.), 28–40.

Shocker, A., and Srinivasan, S. (1974). A consumer based methodology for the introduction of new product ideas. *Management Science*, 20(6), 921–37.

Shocker, A., and Srinivasan, S. (1979). Multiattribute approaches for product concept evaluation and generation: a critical review. *Journal of Marketing Research*, 16 (May), 159–80.

Smith, P., and Reinertsen, D. (1998). *Developing products in half the time.* New York: John Wiley & Sons, Inc.

SonicRim (2004). www.sonicrim.com.

Squires, S. (2002). Doing the work: customer research in the product development and design industry. In S. Squires, and B. Byrne (eds), *Creating Breakthrough Ideas: The Collaboration of Anthropologists and Designers in the Product Development Industry*, Westport, CT: Bergin and Garvey, 103–24.

Squires, S., and Byrne, B. (eds) (2002). *Creating breakthrough ideas: the collaboration of anthropologists and designers in the product development industry.* Westport, CT: Bergin and Garvey.

Srinivasan, V., Lovejoy, W., and Beach, D. (2001). Integrated product design for marketability and manufacturing. *Journal of Marketing Research*, 34 (Feb.) 154–63.

Stevens, G., and Burley, J. (1997). 3,000 raw ideas = 1 commercial success! *Research-Technology Management*, (May–June), 16–27.

Swaddling, J., and Zobel, M. (1996). Beating the odds. *Marketing Management*, 4(4), 20–33.

Tauber, E. (1974). How market research discourages major innovation. *Business Horizons*, 17 (June), 25.

Tauber, E. (1975). Discovering new product opportunities with problem inventory analysis. *Journal of Marketing*, 39 (Jan.), 67–70.

Tetlock, P. (1992). The impact of accountability on judgement and choice: towards a social contingency model. In M. Zanna (ed.), *Advances in Experimental Social Psychology*, volume 25, San Diego: Academic Press, 331–76.

Thomke, S. (2003). *Experimentation matters: unlocking the potential of new technologies for innovation*. Boston: Harvard University Press.

Tian, K., Bearden, W., and Hunter, G. (2001). Consumers' need for uniqueness: scale development and validation. *Journal of Consumer Research*, 28 (June), 50–66.

Tourangeau, R., Rips, L., and Rasinski, K. (2000). *The psychology of survey response*. New York: Cambridge University Press.

Ulrich, K., and Ellison, D. (1999). Holistic customer requirements and the design-select decision. *Management Science*, 45(5), 641–58.

Ulrich, K., and Eppinger, S. (2004). *Product design and development*. New York: McGraw-Hill/Irwin.

Ulwick, A. (2005). *What customers want*. New York: McGraw Hill.

Urban, G., Katz, G., Hatch, T., and Silk, A (1983). The ASSESSOR pre-test market evaluation system. *Interfaces*, 13(6), 38–59.

Urban, G. (1996). New product modeling: a 30 year retrospective and future challenges. MIT Sloan Working Paper 3908-96, hdl.handle.net/1721.1/2625.

Urban, G., and Hauser, J. (1993). *Design and marketing of new products*. Englewood Cliffs, NJ: Prentice Hall.

Urban, G. and Hauser, J. (2004). Listening in to find and explore new combinations of customer needs. *Journal of Marketing*, 68 (April), 72–87.

Urban, G., Hauser, J., Qualls, W., Weinberg, B., Bohlmann, J., and Chicos, R. (1997). Information acceleration: validation and lessons from the field. *Journal of Marketing Research*, 61(1), 143–53.

von Hippel, E. (1986). Lead users: a source of novel product concepts. *Management Science*, 32(7), 791–805.

von Hippel, E. (2001). Perspective: user toolkits for innovation. *Journal of Product Innovation Management*, 18(4), 247–57.

von Hippel, E., Thomke, S., and Sonnack, M. (1999). Creating breakthroughs at 3M. *Harvard Business Review*, (Sept.–Oct.), 47–57.

Wasson, C. (2000). Ethnography in the field of design. *Human Organization*, 59(4), 377–388.

Waters, S., and Field, D. (2003). The Segway Human Transporter: developed with passion and principle. *Design Management Journal*, 14(2), 25–8.

Wilkie, W., and Pessemier, E. (1973). Issues in marketing's use of multi-attribute attitude models. *Journal of Marketing Research*, 10 (November), 428–41.

Woodruff, R., and Gardial, S. (1996). *Know your customer: new approaches to understanding customer value and satisfaction*. Cambridge, MA: Blackwell Publishers.

Zaltman, G. (1997). Rethinking market research: putting people back in. *Journal of Marketing Research*, 23 (November), 424–37.

4

Product Development as a Problem-solving Process

CHRISTIAN TERWIESCH

The author is grateful to Christoph Loch, William Lovejoy, and Karl Ulrich
for helpful comments on an earlier draft of this chapter.

Over the years, scholars of innovation have taken two different perspectives when conducting research: the macro level and the micro level. The macro-level perspective to innovation, represented in this handbook by Chapters 1, 9, and 12, searches for patterns of innovation at the industry level. This allows the researcher to study questions related to the evolution of particular technologies, the formation of standards, and the competitive behavior of firms within the industry.

However, innovations do not just happen. A researcher who analyzes innovations at the micro-level will find sophisticated new product development processes employed by organizations, project teams, and individual researchers. Since innovations typically represent solutions to existing problems and product development projects typically attempt to improve upon the problems of existing products, these processes can be thought of as problem-solving processes.

The objective of this chapter is to establish a problem-solving framework that can be used as a guide through the academic literature on product development. The problem-solving perspective has at least two advantages. First, it is sufficiently general that it allows us to abstain from favoring any one of the many existing academic disciplines associated with product development, such as marketing, operations management, organizational theory, engineering, and design. Second, the problem-solving view will reveal many similarities between the existing literature streams, illustrate how these streams have cross-fertilized each other, and point to fruitful areas of future research.

This chapter is organized as follows. Following a review of the very early work on design theory, we introduce our problem-solving framework by defining the concepts of problem representation, problem structure, reproducibility, and problem-solving

Handbook of Technology and Innovation Management. Edited by Scott Shane
© 2008 John Wiley & Sons, Ltd

processes. We then discuss how problem solving is done in organizational contexts. This includes the organizational processes related to product development as well as the associated organizational structures. We conclude by observing some similarities across the multiple lines of academic research on product development and conjecture about possible venues for future research.

PRODUCT DEVELOPMENT RESEARCH: INTELLECTUAL HERITAGE

Product design/development is frequently perceived as a young academic discipline. This is probably true if one compares it with physics or even engineering. Yet, although the management literature on this topic emerged only in the 1970s (the oldest paper referenced in the excellent literature review of Brown and Eisenhardt, 1995, was published in 1969), researchers have aspired to create a science of design for almost a century. In this section, we explore the (frequently forgotten) intellectual ancestors of product development research. Some of the early references remain highly relevant readings today and also show interesting similarities with more recent research.

Human beings have created artifacts in the form of tools, weapons, houses, and other things for thousands of years. Alexander (1964) refers to these early design efforts as unselfconscious designs. In this situation, a product is the outcome of a complex two-way interaction between the product and its environment (Figure 4.1). Alexander provides the example of the Mousgoum hut, a building form that in many ways provides a perfect design in its usage environment of Camerun, including isolation and weather protection. However, we would not say that the Mousgoums designed their houses. Rather, they kept on refining their houses in response to problems and failures in a process that was carried out over many centuries. Thus, the resulting design was as much an outcome of human involvement as it was shaped by its usage environment.

The first attempts to 'scientize' design can probably be traced back to the 1920s and the Dutch De Stijl movement (Cross, 2001). At that time, Theo van Doesburg postulated: 'Our epoch is hostile to every subjective speculation in art, science, technology, etc ... In order to construct a new object we need a *method*, that is to say an *objective system*' (van Doesburg, referenced by Cross, 2001, emphasis added by author). This objective view of design, which already was visible in the architectural

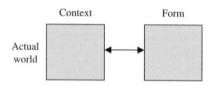

FIGURE 4.1 Form evolving as a two-way interaction with its context.
(*Source:* Alexander (1964), p. 76)

works of Frank Lloyd Wright and Charles Le Corbusier, emphasized functionalism as the basic doctrine of design.[1]

Functionalism was further refined and formalized by the German Bauhaus movement, a group of architects, engineers, and artists, including Wassily Kandinsky and Paul Klee, under the leadership of Walter Gropius. The group postulated the 'form-follows-function' principle: any product should be designed to fulfill its functional purpose, instead of being designed to look nice (unless aesthetics is an explicit function of this product) or to reflect the design tradition of a particular region, crafts guild, or designer. Products created under this paradigm can easily be recognized by their rectilinear forms and their materials (most notably glass and steel) and include Gropius' PanAm building in New York and Mies van der Rohe's various chair designs.

One implication of the form-follows-function principle is that it transformed the previously ill-structured, two-way interaction between form and context, which had been typical for the unselfconscious design, into a relatively well-defined problem. The Bauhaus emphasized the need for rational, objective analysis in the design process. As was observed by Gropius: 'First of all, we have to analyze carefully the essence of an object. Then the object has to fit perfectly with its purpose, in other words, fulfill its practical function, be easy to handle, economic and beautiful' (Gropius, referenced in Brown, 2004). Thus, design was elevated to a true profession based on scientific principles.

Alexander refers to this new approach to design as self-conscious. The approach is summarized in Figure 4.2. The process of design starts with a problem in the real (actual) world (lower left of Figure 4.2.). The role of the designer is to create a mental picture of the product's context, also referred to as the product's functions (upper left). These functions are then translated into diagrams and drawings

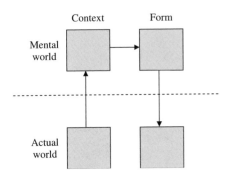

FIGURE 4.2 Form as the outcome of an analysis of its functional purpose (adapted from Alexander, 1964).

[1] The objective to create a science of design, albeit with a much narrower emphasis on building design, goes back much further. For example, 16th century architect Palladio created a scientific approach to the design of palaces and mansions, summarized in his Quattro Libri (1570). Palladio's work included formulas for room sizes and emphasized what we today would call functionalism and rational design.

(mental representations of the product's form, upper right), which a machine shop would ultimately translate into physical form (lower right). Although it seems fair to assume that the Mousgoums engaged in some informal mental representation of the problem, the self-conscious approach to design is based on an explicit abstraction of the problem from the actual world into the mental world (this typically includes some form of a symbolic representation of the problem; the concept of representation will be discussed in detail in the section 'Selection and the benefits of mental representations' on page 152).

In 1932, the Nazis shut down the Bauhaus and many of its designers emigrated to the US where they took influential academic positions in architecture and design. After leaving Germany, Walter Gropius taught at MIT and Harvard, where several years later Christopher Alexander prepared his doctoral dissertation. Alexander was inspired by the Bauhaus concepts. In his book *The synthesis of form* he describes the concept of an ensemble, consisting of form and context. He defined the objective of the designer as the creation of fit in the ensemble, a frictionless coexistence between the context and the form (Alexander, 1964, p. 27).

Mies van der Rohe moved to the Illinois Institute of Technology where he later met Herbert Simon. In his classic *The sciences of the artificial,* Simon outlined the essential ingredients for a science of design (Simon, 1969). Specifically, he suggested that utility theory be a central topic in the science of design. Simon viewed design as a search problem in which the designer had to find a set of product characteristics (design parameters) that maximize user utility.

To illustrate Simon's view of design as a search for a set of utility maximizing product characteristics, consider the example presented in Figure 4.3. The figure shows the causal network that influences user utility for the design of a laptop

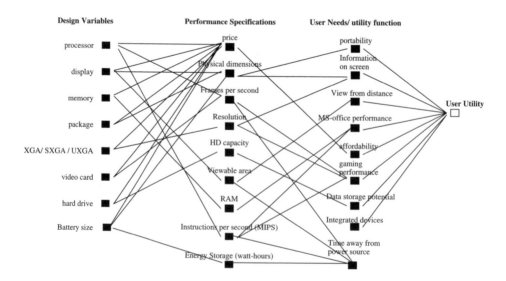

FIGURE 4.3 Design problem in the case of a laptop computer (adapted from Randall *et al.*, 2007).

computer. The utility function of the product is determined by a set of performance specifications of the product, which in turn are driven by the design parameters of the product.

In other words, a product user obtains utility to the extent that the product's functional performance fits with his or her user needs. This view of product design is an explicit quantification of the form-follows-function principle and has remained the dominant paradigm for product development up to this day (e.g., Su, 1990; Ulrich and Eppinger, 2004).

Going beyond the Bauhaus tradition, Simon and Alexander both favored formal analysis, using methods of engineering and economics, as the dominant methodology of product development. This increasing level of formalism was in line with computational and scientific advances of the time, most notably the rise of Operations Research and the continuing development of computing devices (including CAD models). The ideas led to a flourishing academic movement known as scientific design methods, also referred to as first generation design methods. This research continues in various academic disciplines today and has informed many aspects of the subsequent organizational product development literature, as we will discuss below.

The excitement about the first generation design methods, however, did not last long. Already in the early 1970s, a backlash against the formal design methods emerged and many professionals rejected their underlying values (Cross, 2001). Many designers questioned to what extent it would ever be possible to plan and manage design processes. Interestingly, even Alexander later distanced himself from his earlier theories of design.

Large parts of the design community were inspired by the work by Horst Rittel, who viewed design (and, more generally, planning) as a much more iterative and organic process (Rittel and Webber, 1973). Rittel arrived at his vision of a problem-solving process for professional disciplines by following the arguments of Karl Popper and his evolutionary theory of knowledge as outlined in *The Logic of Scientific Discovery* (Popper, 1977). This philosophical perspective made Rittel very critical of various professional planners, including designers, and Rittel accused them of taking a 'Newtonian mechanistic physics' approach to problems. Problems that were imbedded in social contexts, such as political decisions, urban planning, and product design, were to Rittel not amenable to the linear, noniterative problem-solving process favored by the Operations Research community. This view of problem solving rules out the existence of an optimal solution. Every solution should be seen as a hypothesis and is subject to continuing scientific progress.

In addition to these more philosophical observations, the growing frustration with the first generation design methods also reflected an increasing gap between the normative methods and empirical practice. Soon, a new stream of research in design emerged that was grounded on the empirically observed behavior of designers (Allen, 1966). Allen's observations of how designers actually do work, taken together with later ethnographic studies of design (see e.g., Bucciarelli, 1996), found designers to be constantly engaged in experimentation, starting with the formulations of hypotheses, followed by the creation of physical and mental models to test and refine these hypotheses.

Both of these academic views – the empirically grounded studies of Allen, as well as the philosophical reflections of Rittel – challenged the linear ('mechanistic') view of product development underlying the first generation design methods. Although coming from different perspectives, both views were also pushing the academic field of product development in the same direction: the problem-solving approach to product development.

Product Development as a Problem-Solving Process

Research on evolution, problem solving, and creativity (Campbell, 1960; Alcock, 1989) has identified three important elements of a problem-solving process:

- a mechanism that creates variation;
- a mechanism that selects one or several solutions from among this variation;
- a mechanism that inherits some or all of the characteristics from the selected variation to some future variation.

Concerning the creation of variation we have to distinguish between variations that are the outcome of pure randomness and variations that are purposefully created by a designer. Consider a product development example: the design of a safer vehicle. In this example, the problem corresponds to people dying in automotive accidents and every automotive design can be seen as a hypothesis (tentative solution) of what constitutes the safest car. One might be able to find a safe vehicle by simply trying out random variations of the vehicle geometry and its materials. However, a more effective problem solver would not just vary the vehicle geometry randomly. Instead, she would look at vehicles involved in accidents that led to traffic fatalities (problems) and consider targeted reinforcements of certain parts of the vehicle (e.g., a thicker steel for the door). The section 'Creation of variation' on page 149 discusses different forms of variations as well as the processes that lead to new variations in the product development context.

The second element of a problem-solving process is a selection mechanism. The selection mechanism separates variations that provide good solutions and those that fail to solve the problem. If the designer is able to create a mental representation of the problem, this selection can occur before we have confronted our tentative solution with the real problem (e.g., virtual crash tests). Campbell (1960) refers to this as mental selection. The section entitled 'Selection and benefits of mental representations' (page 152) elaborates on the role of problem representations in product development and the availability of mental selection models.

Third, we need a mechanism that inherits the characteristics of the selected variation to the next generation. The section 'Reproducibility of learnt actions' (page 153) introduces the concept of wicked problems, which we will define as those problems that are not even amenable to trial-and-error learning because the underlying state space is changing while we attempt to learn more about adequate solutions.

The three elements of evolutionary problem solving, creation of variation, selection, and inheritance are summarized in Figure 4.4.

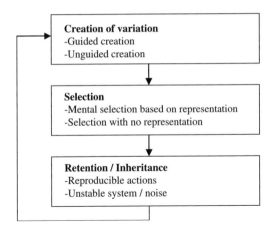

FIGURE 4.4 Elements of evolutionary problem solving.

The extent to which the creation of variation, the selection from among the variation, and the inheritance are simple or difficult in a product development setting, heavily depends on the structure of the underlying problem:

◆ If a car's safety is to be determined by the size of the bumper alone, it would be easy to create higher safety variations by simply increasing bumper size. *Thus, structured problems enable guided variation.*

◆ Complex problems in which many variables interact in potentially nonlinear ways require more knowledge to be accurately represented. Reliable, virtual crash tests have only emerged in the late 1980s, as the computations required to predict the interactions of the thousands of variables are rather complex. *Thus, mental selection is easier to the extent that the problem is structured.*

◆ If the problem is structured, we can inherit elements of one design to another design, knowing that these elements function the same way as in the previous variation.

The section 'Problem structure: Hierarchical problems and complexity' (page 154) discusses various problem structures in product development and how the problem structure influences variation, selection, and retention.

Creation of variation

Many innovations have been documented as the result of coincidences and pure luck (e.g., see Nayak and Ketteringham, 1993, for a description of the process leading to the 3M Post-Its™; another classic example is Plunkett's discovery of Teflon in the DuPont labs). But a designer searching for a solution to a problem can often do better than blind trial-and-error learning. If variation is created following a specific direction (the direction of a substantial improvement in the objectives), it is guided variation.

The easiest way of creating variation is given by parametric search, which simply takes points from the (typically multi-dimensional) solution space and evaluates the performance of the solution. In the context of Figure 4.3, the solution space is the set of eight-dimensional vectors created by the eight design variables. As we will see in 'Problem structure: Hierarchical problems and complexity' (page 154), the problem structure determines to what extent parametric search is a guided creation of variation or a pure random walk in the solution space.

The idea of creating new variations via parametric search implies that we can think of a problem solution as a combination (vector) of parameters taken from a given parameter space. Often, however, design problems exhibit nonparametric solution spaces. Consider, for example, the design of a residential home. Although variables such as square footage, the number of windows, ceiling heights, etc., might be amenable to a parametric search, many other aspects of solution spaces are not: geometric forms, the usage of spaces, and aesthetics are all very difficult to fit into the mathematical framework of design underlying Figure 4.3.

When parametric search (search 'inside the box') does not work, the creation of variation requires 'out-of-the-box' thinking. A commonly used metaphor is the puzzle in which one has to connect all nine points in Figure 4.5, using four straight lines and without taking the pencil off the paper. A problem solver who attempts to use parametric search (e.g., a back-tracking algorithm starting from one point and moving to other points) will not be able to solve the problem. It takes a new way of looking at the solution space. The lines that solve the puzzle go out of the box created by the nine dots.

Similarly, an architect working on a floor plan for a new living room might not want to limit herself to (a parametric search over) rectangular shapes. Instead, many other geometries might be considered. An active field of design and architectural research relates to the concept of 'shape grammars', a computational (rule-based) approach to geometric design problems (e.g., Stiny, 1975) that guides the designer by suggesting new shape variations.

We can abstract the problem even further. Instead of thinking of a design for a living room as geometric drawings, we can look at the purpose of the living room,

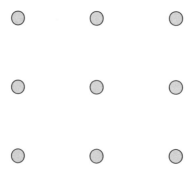

FIGURE 4.5 A problem-solving puzzle: connect all nine points using four straight lines without taking the pencil off the paper.

or the living room's functions (e.g., reading, discussions among family members). A good architect might suggest not having a living room altogether and instead combining the functions with the family room. Similarly, Ulrich and Eppinger (2004) illustrate how a clever functional representation of a power nailer leads to very creative new product concepts. Abstracting a product to its key functions also allows designers to better use their own prior experience, to look for standard solutions in existing products or knowledge reservoirs (e.g., patents, catalogs), or to search for analogies, all of which can be the source of new solution concepts. Thus, a new product concept might look to the layperson like a somewhat random thought of a genius designer, despite having been the outcome of a very structured thought process, i.e., of a guided variation.

A large body of literature exists on creativity in the field of psychology (Campbell, 1960). Most of this research is, despite its different academic discipline, very similar to the problem-solving framework outlined in this chapter. In the management literature, there also exists a body of research on creativity and brainstorming techniques. For the product development context most relevantly, Hargadon and Sutton (1996) discuss how IDEO, a leading design firm, goes about creating new solution concepts for their clients. In their ethnographic study the authors observed that IDEO's designers were permanently engaged in creating sketches of new product concepts, and many of these concepts were crafted to physical prototypes using an onsite tool shop. The authors argue that visualizing the ideas is often a great starting point to guide the creation of further variations.

In this spirit, consider the example of highway design. Assume the usage requirements dictated by an urban planner are to find a road layout for a given traffic flow: cars come from four different directions and leave in any one of the four directions. We could easily describe this design problem in various ways, including a four-by-four matrix, flow charts, graphs, or other forms. However, consider Figure 4.6, which illustrates the salient properties of the problem; namely, its connectivity and associated flows. By drawing the number of vehicles flowing in each direction via arrows with widths reflecting traffic flows, the diagram directly reveals what form the new intersection should take (Alexander, 1964). Visualization techniques hence can dramatically improve creativity and effectively guide the creation of new variation (Tufte, 2001).

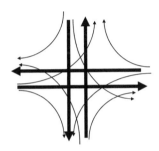

FIGURE 4.6 Traffic flow data represented in a way so that it reveals a solution.

Selection and benefits of mental representations

At the creative stage of a product development process, a team typically works according to the paradigm 'the more ideas the better'. At some point in the project, however, a team will have to select from among these variations. The use of problem representations in product development is an attempt to select between competing variations without committing the resources required for testing the product in the real market.

The word 'problem representation' is used differently across various academic disciplines. Our view of representation is inspired by research in Artificial Intelligence, which views (knowledge) representation as '... a surrogate, a substitute for the thing itself, used to enable an entity to determine consequences by *thinking rather than acting*, i.e., *by reasoning about the world rather than taking action in it*' (Davis, Shrobe, and Szolovits, 1993, emphasis added by author). This is similar to Pisano (1996), who distinguishes between learning-by-doing and learning-before-doing.

In the language of problem solving, problem representations are the foundation for mental selection (Campbell, 1960), i.e., for choosing a potential problem solution without implementing it. In a product development context, the use of mental representations corresponds to a product development team's attempt to use realistic tests of the product internally (i.e., before actually launching the product, see Sommer and Loch, 2004, for the concept of realistic tests). Such *ex ante* evaluation is typically achieved via prototypes.

Prototypes are approximations of the real product along one or multiple dimensions of interest to the designer (Ulrich and Eppinger, 2004). Prototypes enable the designer to partly develop a design with relatively little resource consumption and then to anticipate the overall quality of the design. Prototypes can take the form of drawings, physical models, computer simulations, or mathematical representations. Using prototypes in the development process allows firms to search the space of possible designs at much lower costs and at higher speed (Thomke, 1998). For example, Thomke (2003) shows how the emergence of digital crash tests has allowed automotive designers to evaluate the consequences of a crash without the costs and delays associated with physical representations of the crash problem. A virtual crash test can be seen as a symbolic representation of the car safety problem, which is more amenable to a broad search.

As another example of how a change in problem representation can improve the efficiency of the problem-solving process, consider market research tools, especially conjoint analysis. Based on the causal network in Figure 4.3 (page 146), we can represent a product development formally as the search for design parameters (DP) that influence various product attributes (functional requirements, FR) that in turn create user utility (U, the result of a multi-dimensional utility function). Hence, we can formally represent the product development problem as:

$$\underset{DP_1...DP_n}{Max} \{U(FR_1(DP_1 \ldots DP_n) \ldots .FR_1(DP_1 \ldots DP_n))\} \tag{1}$$

Conjoint analysis provides a market research tool that helps designers to predict the utility that consumers will obtain for a given set of design parameters. This is achieved by presenting consumers with a choice between several prototypes (typically in the form of verbal descriptions), and then using statistical methods to impute the underlying utility functions (e.g., Green and Srinivasan, 1990). Similar to prototyping, this approach enables the designer to quickly weed out variations that will not provide good solutions in the real world.

In addition to improving the efficiency of the problem-solving process, problem representations can also improve the effectiveness of the process. Holding overall resources constant, the improved search efficiency gained from problem representation also leads to a better solution. An automotive project that can spend $10 million on crash testing will design a safer vehicle if it performs many thousand virtual crash tests compared to crashing a handful of vehicles physically in the lab.

Despite their potential to improve effectiveness and efficiency of problem solving, changes in problem representation are also associated with a significant potential downside. Unlike mathematics, where basically all problems are solved through changes in representation, and alternative representations typically do not lose information compared to the initial problem, most representations of product development problems only provide approximations of the initial problem. The degree to which a prototype provides an accurate representation of the underlying real problem is referred to as the prototype's fidelity (e.g., Bohn, 1987; Thomke and Bell, 2001) or its comprehensiveness (Ulrich and Eppinger, 2004). Perfect fidelity is typically not achievable in any mental representation and higher fidelity is typically associated with higher costs. Hence, development teams need to make careful tradeoffs between the downside of imperfect representation and the potential benefits discussed above.

Reproducibility of learnt actions

Our model of creating variations and selecting from them has so far assumed that the designer can always go back to a previously generated solution if she so chooses. In other words, she can try out alternative solutions, and if they do not work out, she can abandon them (in search theory, this is called 'search with recall'). However, not all designers have the luxury of recall.

Rittel and Webber (1973) distinguish between tame problems and wicked problems. Wicked problems are those that exhibit the following properties, all of which make recall difficult if not impossible:

- the problem misses a definitive problem formulation (i.e., you don't understand the problem before you have solved it);
- the effectiveness of problem solutions cannot be objectively evaluated;
- there is no rule indicating if a solution is sufficiently good so that the problem-solving process can be terminated;
- the potential solution space cannot be exhaustively described;
- there is no opportunity to learn by trial-and error.

Arguably, many design problems display at least some of these properties.

Simon (1969) already recognized to a certain extent the concept of wicked problems:

> In oil painting every new spot of pigment laid on the canvas creates some kind of pattern that provides a continuing source of new ideas to the painter. The painting process is a process of cyclical interaction between painter and canvas in which current goals lead to new applications of paint, while the gradually changing pattern suggests new goals. (Simon, 1969, p. 187)

Just as in oil painting (there is no 'Undo' button on the canvas!), for wicked problems it is impossible to test a solution without changing the underlying problem. Consequently, problem definition and problem solution have to coevolve. This situation forces the designer back into the unselfconscious approach to design we introduced in Figure 4.1: there is simply no mental world (as in Figure 4.2) that allows the designer to find a good solution without changing the underlying problem.

Even late in the problem-solving process, a need exists to reconsider one's objectives and sense new opportunities for problem formulation and problem solution. This view of design is difficult to combine with the first generation design methods and favors a much more organic problem-solving approach that we will introduce below.

From an evolutionary perspective, the difficulty associated with wicked problems is that they preclude inheritance. Consider again the example of virtual prototyping. After comparing the outcomes of many different potential solutions, the designer can pick the best and inherit the desirable properties of the tested solutions to the final design. In fact, to the extent that the designer is able to guide the creation of variation, she can even inherit properties from one test to another. The problem is clearly not wicked. Now, compare this with the design of a nuclear weapon system: just alone engaging in the design, not to mention conducting nuclear tests, changes the problem. In such situations, new knowledge carries little meaning as the underlying problem has changed in the mean time.

Another enemy of inheriting knowledge from one variation to another is noise during the evaluation of a specific variation. If the designer only observes the outcomes of simulated or real crashes, but is not able to reproduce them, no real learning has occurred and the problem-solving cycle was wasted. In test settings, such situations frequently arise if tests are carried out in environments that are either highly uncertain (test outcomes are noisy, signal-to-noise ratio; Bohn, 1987) or change over time.

Problem structure: hierarchical problems and complexity

Not all problems are equally difficult to solve. Some problems have an underlying structure that makes them amenable to the idea of 'divide and conquer', i.e., dividing (also known as decomposing) the problem into subproblems and then solving (conquering) these subproblems independently. Other problems, in contrast, cannot easily be decomposed.

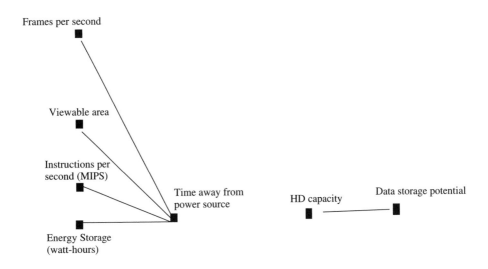

FIGURE 4.7 Illustration of an integrated system (left) and a modular system (right) (only the subsets of Figure 4.3 that are relevant to the two attributes are shown).

In product development, the problem type is largely determined by the architecture of the product. The most concise way of defining a product's architecture is based on the underlying causal structure similar to the one shown in Figure 4.3: the architecture of a product determines how the product's functions are allocated to its physical components. A product is modular if a one-to-one mapping exists between the product's functions and its physical components (e.g., Ulrich, 1995). In contrast, product attributes that are determined by multiple design parameters are labeled holistic (Ulrich and Ellison, 1999).

Figure 4.7 shows parts of our earlier example of laptop design (Figure 4.3). We observe that the user attribute 'Time away from power source' is holistic, because it is determined by several performance specifications (which in turn are driven by many design parameters). In contrast, the storage capacity of the laptop is solely determined by the size of the disk drive. If all product attributes would take this simple pattern, the product would be perfectly modular.

As discussed previously, problem structure impacts all aspects of problem solving, including the generation of variation, the possibility of using representations of the problem for selection, and inheriting elements of a solution to future variations. We will discuss each of these three aspects in turn.

First, the most important implication of problem structure on problem solving relates to the problem solver's ability to relate cause and effect and thereby her ability to created guided creation of variation. Suppose the task is to open a safe whose lock has 10 dials, each with 100 possible settings, numbered from 0 to 99 (Simon, 1969). How long will it take to open the safe by using a trial-and-error search? Since there are 10010 possible settings, the average number of trials needed to find the combination is 50 billion. Suppose, however, that the safe were defective, so that a click can be heard when any one dial is turned to the correct setting. Now, each dial can be adjusted independently and the expected number of trials is reduced to 500. Thus, the decomposability of a product has substantial implications on how fast a product development team learns and improves the product (Loch *et al.*, 2001). Once we can relate an observed effect to a cause, we are able to guide new variations in a desirable direction. Otherwise, all creation of variation takes the form of blind trial-and-error.

Second, depending on the degree of interaction between modules, it might be more or less difficult to create high-fidelity mental problem representations. High-fidelity representations require that the underlying causal structure of the problem is understood. The more interactions that exist between the subsystems of a product, the harder it is to understand fully the resulting causal structures. We label problems that are characterized by the interaction of many variables and subsystems as complex (Simon, 1969). Complex systems have a very difficult and nonlinear relationship between the variables under the control of the designer (design parameters, see Figure 4.3) and the objective function (utility). The resulting shape of the objective function is frequently referred to as a rugged solution landscape (Kauffman and Levin, 1987; Weinberger, 1990; Levinthal, 1997). In a rugged landscape, it is also very difficult to predict the performance impact of even small changes to a design. The very nature of a rugged landscape requires much more information to be accurately described. Hence, it will be much more difficult to develop high-fidelity mental representations of the problem. At the same time, attempting to optimize over an approximated solution landscape can be misleading, as it may miss out local performance peaks that are common for complex problems (Rivkin and Siggelkow, 2003).

Third, modular product architectures allow the designer to re-use prior knowledge or, put differently, to inherit knowledge to future solutions. With respect to a new product, such knowledge can take the form of standardized components, which are associated with higher scale economies and potentially higher performance (Ulrich, 1995). With respect to the development process for a new product, such knowledge might take the form of organizational routines that have been proven successful in the past. Developing new products then becomes a process of reconfiguring existing components and routines, which has many advantages in environments of uncertainty and change (Baldwin and Clark, 2000).

In addition to these three benefits, the problem structure is also likely to have a strong influence on the problem-solving process. In the case of a decomposable problem, the problem solver can attack multiple subproblems in parallel, leading to a faster completion of the overall project (e.g., think of 10 robbers opening either of the two safes defined above simultaneously). Moreover, as has been shown by Sosa *et al.* (2004), modular product architectures reduce the need for information flows across organizational subunits.

As one would expect, perfect modularity is rarely found in practice. For this reason, product development research has created several methods to describe the structures of new product development problems, specifically the interdependencies of the associated subproblems and possible ways of organizing the associated development process (see, for example, the work on the design structure matrix by Steward, 1981, and Smith and Eppinger, 1997).

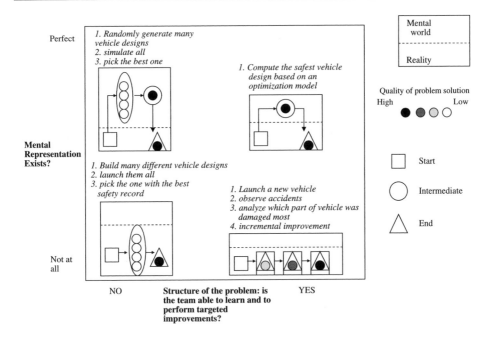

FIGURE 4.8 Different problem-solving processes in the example of automotive crash safety.

THE PROBLEM-SOLVING PROCESS

The problem-solving process is influenced by the structure of the problem and how the problem is represented. If a mental representation of the problem exists, we can use mental selection instead of incurring costly failures in the real world. Depending on the structure of the problem, we may or may not be able to learn from the past and subsequently guide new variations towards a better performance. This leads to a 2×2 logic, which is summarized by Figure 4.8.

Generic problem-solving processes

Consider the lower part of Figure 4.8 first, i.e., assume that we do not have a mental representation of the problem. To the extent that we are able to establish some structure in the problem, we will be able to improve our problem solution incrementally (lower right). In the example of creating a safe vehicle, this would correspond to first building and launching a vehicle and then using damage to the vehicle and its passengers (e.g., were passengers injured because of a deformation of the door or the steering column?) as created by real accidents to incrementally improve the safety of the vehicle. This leads to a new (safer) vehicle and the process begins all over. Iterations are performed, one-by-one, in the real world, each of them increasing the expected quality of the problem solution (darker shades in Figure 4.8). This is how the Mousgoums built (and improved) their huts.

The approach at the lower right of Figure 4.8 assumes that the problem structure is such that we can relate parts of the problem to specific parts of the solution, which in turn allows us to better target our improvements. This is exactly the benefit of feedback between cause and effect in hierarchical problem structures and modular architectures. For example, if crash safety would not be a holistic attribute, we would only have to increase the size of the bumper to find a safer car. If, however, the problem structure is such that we cannot establish such a relationship and thus are not able to intelligently guide the creation of variation, we have to rely on a more Darwinian process.

In this case, we can create random variation in vehicles, launch them all (safe and unsafe), and then empirically observe their safety based on accident statistics. Unlike in the previous case of incremental learning and improvement, learning in the Darwinian process purely happens at the population level: we do not analyze details of accident statistics (e.g., where the damage occurred on the vehicles leading to passenger fatalities), but simply look at the aggregate safety performance (e.g., number of fatalities per 100 000 miles driven for a given design) and then pick the best variant. Consequently, even after the problem has been solved (i.e., we have picked the safest vehicle), we still do not have a causal model of what creates safety.

If it is possible to create a mental representation of the problem, we again have to distinguish between two cases. Consider first the case for which the problem is structured, i.e., the product has a modular architecture and the associated complexity is low (upper right). In this case, the idea of scientific design methods (Bauhaus) applies and we can solve the problem with few iterations. In the extreme case, if we were equipped with a closed form mathematical representation of the crash safety problem, we could mathematically solve for the optimal solution (i.e., the geometry and materials of the safest possible vehicle). No iteration would be necessary at all.

If the problem is not structured we will need many trials to find a good solution (upper left). Despite computational advances (finite element analysis), from the perspective of current automotive development practice, the vehicle safety problem is still highly unstructured because of numerous interacting variables. Given the resulting rugged solution landscape, the search for a safe vehicle design is likely to include the generation of thousands of random variations of vehicle geometries. Similar to the Darwinian selection approach (lower left), we create many variants and pick the best performing one. The difference is that now the selection is carried out mentally (e.g., in a computer or a lab), which is advantageous for the project's budget and the safety of the driver populations.

Problem-solving processes in product development: a taxonomy

Obviously, the four scenarios illustrated in Figure 4.8 are extreme cases. Frequently, a problem representation may exist, but only with limited fidelity. Alternatively, it might be necessary first to build and validate a problem representation. Both cases will require additional iteration between the mental world and reality, and thus the resulting problem-solving process will combine aspects of all four patterns.

Although not necessarily in their pure form, the four different problem-solving processes outlined in Figure 4.8 exist in product development practice and have been studied in the academic literature of product development. We will label them the stage-gate process, the incremental improvement process, parallel prototyping, and Darwinian selection. There also exist two hybrid approaches that deserve discussion: the iterative (evolutionary) process and a process based on external (beta) tests. We will now discuss each of these six product development processes.

The linear (stage-gate) process. In the product development community, NASA introduced the first generation design methods and the linear (in the sense of noniterative) process in the 1960s, under the label 'Phased Project Planning.' Early publications advocating this approach included the work by Baker and Sweeney (1978), and soon led to the term 'stage-gate' process. In its initial form, the stage-gate process can be thought of as a decision tree (the nodes of the decision tree corresponding to the stage gates) in which management reviews the project and has the option to terminate the project in the case of negative information (e.g., technical infeasibility). Since its initial usage, the concept of stage-gate processes has mutated towards a very structured process with detailed targets and objectives to be met by the development team. Thus, a process that initially was responsive to new information (even if only in the form of project termination) is now commonly (and rightfully) associated with rigidity and inflexibility.

In the field of software development, phased project planning is known as the waterfall method (Boehm, 1981). The idea of the waterfall approach to managing a development project is that the project can be divided up into a set of well-defined phases, starting with requirements planning, and then going from specifications on coding and testing to systems integration. The waterfall method emphasizes a linear flow; iterations (also known as rework) should be avoided and constitute failures from the project management perspective.

In the absence of iteration, it is absolutely essential that the initial problem formulation is done correctly, which is why pre-planning has been shown as an important element of successful development for these types of projects (Eisenhardt and Tabrizi, 1995). Teams can attempt to compress the project schedule by allowing for a partial overlap between development phases. As long as the project is well planned and there exists limited uncertainty, such a concurrent approach has been shown to lead to shorter development times (Clark and Fujimoto, 1989; Krishnan *et al.*, 1997; Loch and Terwiesch, 1998; Terwiesch and Loch, 1999).

The iterative process: internal (evolutionary) and external (beta) testing. Rittel's questioning of the mechanistic worldview associated with the stage-gate process soon made its way into the software engineering literature and practice. Although it would take managerial scholars of product development until the 1990s to discover the power of this approach (and, in contrast to the design theory literature, Rittel and Webber were never credited for their achievements in the management literature), Rittel's questioning of the mechanistic worldview associated with the stage-gate process quickly made its way into the software engineering literature and practice. Boehm

(1981) refers to this approach as evolutionary prototyping, a very appropriate name given its intellectual predecessors reviewed above.

Evolutionary prototyping emphasizes frequent iterations. Depending on the quality of the mental representation of the underlying problem, such iterations can be done internally (tests, internal prototypes) or externally (see MacCormack, 2001). External prototypes, in software development known as beta-releases, correspond to iterations between the real world and the mental world. The iterations might also be necessary because of changing or incomplete problem definitions (especially in wicked problems).

In software engineering, evolutionary prototyping has long been recommended for complex projects with unclear functional requirements (Boehm, 1981). The earliest managerial work on this topic goes back to Cusumano and Selby's description of the Microsoft product development process (Cusumano and Selby, 1995). In product development, this evolutionary process is also referred to as the flexible product development process (Bhattarchya *et al.*, 1998).

Parallel prototyping. A key challenge in product development as in problem solving is to learn from observed outcomes and to use the observation to guide subsequent iterations (see references in Sommer and Loch, 2004). Unlike in the cases of the stage-gate model and the flexible development process, product development in the cases of parallel prototyping and Darwinian selection proceeds in a largely unguided manner. In the absence of a mechanism to guide the creation of new species, the two approaches rely on creating a broad range of alternative solution concepts and then picking the most promising one. The two approaches differ with respect to the timing when this selection is done.

The distinguishing element of the parallel prototyping approach is that it uses its mental representation of the problem to select a solution before its implementation. The most illustrative example of this approach is the method of high-throughput screening used in pharmaceutical development: thousands of compounds are tested for their potency in helping to cure various diseases. Based on the test outcomes, solutions are either rejected outright or advanced to further development. In a similar manner, many automotive companies explore multiple product concepts of subsystems in parallel, only to be able to pick the best performing after the test results have been observed (Ward *et al.*, 1995). By creating multiple alternative solutions in parallel, the development team hedges against a broad range of uncertain outcomes (Krishnan and Bhattarchya, 2002; Loch and Terwiesch, 2005).

When managing a product development process that relies on parallel proto-typing, a project needs to decide how many prototypes to build at any stage in the process (Dahan and Mendelson, 2001; Thomke and Bell, 2001). Moreover, the team needs to balance the cost of building multiple solutions in parallel, thereby foregoing any opportunities to learn from one implementation to the other in favor of the time benefits of a parallel approach (Loch *et al.*, 2001).

Darwinian selection. A similar tradeoff in the search strategy also needs to be made for the Darwinian selection approach. However, with this process, solutions are picked based on their performance in the real world, as opposed to the mental world. Although large costs are associated with a broad search in the real world, its main advantage is that this approach functions well for problem domains for which there does not (yet) exist a mental representation. Such problem domains tend to be new product categories with high uncertainty in technology or market requirements (Tushman and O'Reilly, 1997; McGath, 2001).

For example, Beinhocker (1999) describes how Capital One 'develops many new ideas, tries them out in the marketplace, sees what works and what doesn't, backs the winners, and unsentimentally kills the losers.' Leonard-Barton (1995) who first used the term Darwinian selection in this context describes how Sharp offered multiple PDAs in 1993, based on multiple operating systems, while others placed all their resources on one operating system. Sommer and Loch (2004) discuss how MTV experiments with shows 'on the air' and then quickly picks the most successful formats.

Incremental improvements. Last, consider the incremental improvement strategy at the lower right of Figure 4.8. This strategy favors frequent product updates with incremental enhancements of previously launched products. This practice is in line with the development strategy of Japanese automotive companies in the 1980s and 1990s. As observed by Clark and Fujimoto (1991), Japanese car makers favored model release cycles of 2–3 years, which allowed them to obtain a much fresher product line and rapid, incremental improvements compared to the European car makers that were pursuing release cycles of 6–7 years.

THE ORGANIZATIONAL CONTEXT OF PRODUCT DEVELOPMENT PROBLEM SOLVING

Product development is not carried out in a vacuum but is embedded in complex organizational systems. We view the organizational context of problem solving as a set of constraints that is imposed on the 'pure' problem-solving processes described above. Creating a safer vehicle is one problem, but doing so in the context of a large automotive company with thousands of engineers, rigid management control systems, and an ongoing battle between various internal organizations, is an entirely different challenge. We thus have to distinguish between designing an artifact and designing within the context of the organization that designs the artifact[2]

Although a headache for the professional designer, the organizational context with its insufficiencies and problems is a blessing for the organizational scholar. As we argue further below, it is our belief that after a century of design research, most of the design problems in their pure form are reasonably well understood. It is their interaction with organizations that continues to pose countless open questions. Based on the research carried out so far in this domain, we discuss research related to defining appropriate product development processes, coordinating various tasks and organizational sub-systems, and leading project organizations. This is by no means a complete list of topics that have been researched but covers the most important dimensions (see e.g., Brown and Eisenhardt, 1995; Krishnan and Ulrich, 2001).

---

[2]One might argue that both are design problems and hence should be amenable to the same methods. However, since these problems have been addressed by separate academic communities, we discuss the problem of organizational design in a separate section. The structural similarity between designing a product and designing and organization is discussed by Lovejoy (1994).

Defining product development processes: the need to match problem and process

Just as the product development community – from Simon (1969) to the present – had observed a tension between structured and more flexible processes, so did the field of organizational theory. The organizational theory literature distinguishes between situations that are certain, predictable, or routine and situations that are uncertain, unpredictable, and novel (e.g., Woodward, 1965; Galbraith, 1973). Routine situations are best approached by planning and creating bureaucratic organizational entities. In contrast, novel situations require flexibility, adaptive planning, and even improvised action (Burns and Stalker, 1961; Lawrence and Lorsch 1967; Scott, 1987).

Despite this congruency between the design literature and the organizational theory literature, these lines of thought coexisted independently for a surprisingly long time. The 1980s witnessed an increased interest of organizational scholars in the design and development of new products. This line of research quickly gained momentum and identified a number of best practices including an extensive involvement of suppliers and customers, parallel execution of development, and the use of cross-functional teams. This stream of research has led to (at least) two important findings. First, this line of research has convincingly argued that there does not exist one best product development process. A development process has to be chosen for a particular product development problem at hand, taking into account aspects of the market environment as well as the technological characteristics of the product. This finding was in sharp contrast to several articles published in the more popular business press that were postulating that certain practices such as concurrent engineering or 'the rugby team approach' to product development were superior processes *per se* (e.g., Imai *et al.*, 1985). Second, this research has identified several process configurations, consisting of project leadership and organization, project schedules, and coordination requirements, which would be mutually supportive (see Fujimoto, 1999, for the concept of configurations).

The very influential work by Eisenhardt and Tabrizi (1995) described two such configurations. The authors argue that an experiential process, which is characterized by frequent iterations and extensive internal and external testing (see above discussion of Figure 4.8), is most appropriate for environments of fast change and high uncertainty. They contrast this with the more planning-oriented product development process that emphasizes disciplined execution of a pre-defined set of tasks (see Table 4.1). Based on a data set from the global electronics industry, Eisenhardt and Tabrizi were able to show that variables of their experiential approach significantly explained higher performance in fast-changing industries (e.g., PC), while variables of the planning-oriented approach significantly explained higher performance in slowly changing industries (e.g., mainframe).

Interestingly, the tension between these two approaches and the failure of the planning-oriented approach in fast changing environments shows various similarities with our previous discussion of the Newtonian physics approach to planning and its criticism by Rittel. Developing a product for an uncertain market simply corresponds to a wicked problem. As discussed by Rittel and Webber (1973), a common problem

TABLE 4.1 Eisenhardt and Tabrizi's (1995) model of product development: comparison of compression and experiential models.

Characteristic	Compression	Experiential
Uncertainty assumption	Certainty	Uncertainty
Product innovation	Predictable series of well-defined steps	Uncertain path through foggy and shifting markets and technologies
Strategy for speed	Rationalize and then squeeze the process	Quickly build understanding and options while maintaining focus and motivation
Processes for speed	Planning	Multiple iterations
	Supplier involvement	Extensive testing
	Cut step time through CAD	Frequent milestones
	Overlap with multifunctional teams	Powerful leader
	Reward for meeting schedule	

of planners is to over-tame a wicked problem, i.e., by making decisions that ignore the need for iteration. In the product development context, for example, teams frequently over-tame the definition of the concept. A team that faces a highly unstructured problem for which it does not yet have an appropriate mental representation, yet still decides to use the stage-gate approach, will inevitably fail.

Bhattacharya *et al.* (1998) model the decision of a product development team that needs to decide at what time it should freeze its product concept. If the concept is frozen too early, it is less likely to match with the changing (and hence at the outset uncertain) market needs. If, however, the team waits too long with a concept freeze, overall costs are likely to go up. Similarly, Terwiesch and Loch (1999) find in their empirical study of various electronics industries that product development teams that face a significant amount of residual uncertainty are most effective if they are willing to engage in intensive testing and frequent iterations. In contrast, the authors find that a more schedule-oriented approach, including the common practice of overlapping subsequent development phases, is effective if most of the development uncertainty has already been resolved.

Given the need to match the type of the problem with the product development process, we extend our earlier Figure 4.8 to Figure 4.9. As before, the vertical axis corresponds to the team's ability to create an appropriate mental representation of the product. The horizontal axis corresponds to the amount of structure in the underlying product development problem. In general, the absence of such structure might be driven by the product's architecture, the resulting complexity, or other forms of unexpected interactions between variables of the problem.

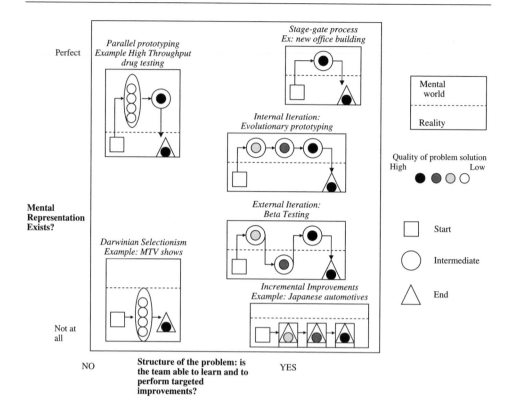

FIGURE 4.9 Different problem-solving processes and their role in product development.

Project leadership and organizational structures

In addition to defining the appropriate organizational *processes*, an important decision in the context of product development is also to define the appropriate organizational *structures*. As with other inherently cross-functional processes, organizational design in product development largely hinges on how to allocate decision authority (reporting lines) between the business functions (e.g., marketing, engineering, manufacturing) and the product development projects (see e.g., Allen, 1977; Dougherty, 1989). The resulting matrix organization can be classified into four types (Wheelwright and Clark, 1992):

- largely functional organization;
- lightweight project managers who reside outside of the functions and have a small number of liaisons in the functions to coordinate work – the majority of the people involved in the project report through their functions;
- heavyweight project manager who resides outside of the functions and has reporting authority over the majority of people on the project – the project manager also has the decision authority to define the market and shape the product concept;

◆ autonomous teams in which the entire project is set up as a separate organizational entity.

Although most R&D organizations historically had been set up with a more functional focus, the 1980s and early 1990s witnessed an increasing popularity of more project-driven organizations. This trend was strongly fueled by Clark and Fujimoto's (1989) landmark study in the automotive industry that revealed that Japanese organizations, which relied more on heavyweight project managers, were faster in creating new products than their European and US counterparts, which relied more on functional organizations. Empowering the project organizations was also identified as leading to a higher product integrity (especially important if the product has an integral product architecture, see also Clark and Fujimoto, 1991) because project organizations simplify coordination *within* a project.

The initial excitement concerning the heavyweight project management organization has since declined somewhat and research is now favoring a 'balanced matrix' (e.g., Larson and Gobeli, 1988). Subsequent research found that heavyweight project management organizations would frequently ignore the externalities that their projects might have or might not have on the rest of the organization. From a pure micro-economic perspective not surprising, this effect included the inability of projects to learn from other projects (and create knowledge that would be useful for future projects) (Nobeoka, 1995; Nobeoka and Cusumano, 1997) and to create components or subsystems that could be shared across products (Fisher *et al.*, 1999).

In several industries, including the automotive and electronic industries, organizations started to favor the development of platforms (modular architectures), which could be configured into distinctive products (from the perspective of the end user) at relatively low costs and in little time. However, such platform projects required a substantial amount of coordination across projects, which made functional organizations more attractive again (Meyer and Lehnerd, 1997).

Need for coordination (knowledge is dispersed reflecting specialization)

Product development organizations are more complex than what can be captured by simple reporting lines. In addition to defining formal organizations, product development managers need to pay special attention to the informal networks of information flows that reflect the day-to-day interactions among the many organizational units involved in the process.

An important stream of product development literature has identified various barriers to an efficient and effective information flow. This research stream has been strongly influenced by the pioneering work of Allen (1966, 1977) who was the first to develop an empirically grounded theory of information exchange in development teams. Allen's focus has been on the communication of team members among themselves as well as on the communication of team members with the outside, which is why this line of research is also referred to as the 'communication web' (Brown and Eisenhardt, 1995). It is noteworthy, however, that the importance of coordination and cross-functional communication was already an integral part of the Bauhaus movement, which had advocated the use of open floor spaces and cross functional collaboration in the 1930s.

Allen started this line of research by requesting that R&D professionals keep track of the interactions they had with other team members or with anyone outside the R&D setting. This allowed him to analyze the underlying social network, identifying two main results. First, Allen found that the physical proximity between two team members was an important variable in predicting their frequency of communication. Second, he found that successful teams included members who had information access to important stakeholders outside the project (e.g., senior management, a specific functional expertise). Allen referred to these team members as gatekeepers.

These two findings – communication intensity and the structure of the communication network – were also the themes further explored by subsequent research on this topic. For example, work by Katz and Tushman (1981), Katz (1982), Keller (1986), Zirger and Maidique (1990), Ancona and Caldwell (1992), and Moenart and Souder (1996) collectively emphasized the importance of supporting open information flows and intense cross-functional communication. Most of this research is based on the theory of organizational design (Thompson, 1967) and information processing (Galbraith, 1973). Despite its importance and success, this stream of research has matured and arguably lost some of its momentum because its basic contribution that 'communication is important and management needs to encourage open, cross-functional communication' has been made and confirmed repeatedly.

Current research on communication in product development focuses much more on the structure of the communication network (e.g., Ancona and Caldwell, 1992). Allen's gatekeeper concept has been refined in several ways with a special emphasis on the social ties to customers and senior management. This stream has reached a remarkable sophistication in network theory and has successfully applied some of the most advanced sociological methodologies to the R&D context (e.g., van den Bulte and Moenart, 1998; Sosa et al., 2004).

An additional emphasis of more recent research has been the changing dynamics of information exchange over the course of a project. Unlike in the early work by Galbraith (1973), information exchange in projects happens in the presence of an uncertainty in markets and technology that decreases over time. This has led to a set of dynamic models of information exchange (Adler, 1995; Moenart et al., 1995; Terwiesch et al., 2002).

CONCLUDING REMARKS: PAST RESEARCH AND FUTURE DIRECTIONS

We started this chapter by introducing the problem-solving framework and its usefulness in tying together the various academic disciplines that have contributed to an improved understanding of product development. The academic discipline of product development has experienced a period of dramatic growth and scholarly activity bringing together work in Marketing, Organizational Theory, Engineering, and Operations Management. The review by Krishnan and Ulrich (2001) lists more than 200 references, almost all of them published in top academic journals. If one includes the numerous articles published in other journals and adds the literature from journals such as *R&D Management, Journal of Engineering and Technology Management, Journal of Product Innovation Management,* and *IEEE Transactions on Engineering Management,* all of which are high-quality journals almost entirely dedicated to the advancement of knowledge in product development, we are likely to have a stock of articles well in excess of 1000.

This dramatic growth of the product development literature has substantially changed the nature of research published today. Consider, as a case in point, the literature on overlapping development activities in the attempt to compress the overall schedule (parallel task execution) and to improve the information flows among various parties involved in the project. The first discussion of this concept appeared in Imai *et al.* (1985), which identified overlapping development activities as a best practice that was successfully employed by Japanese development organizations. In Clark and Fujimoto (1989) the development lead-time reducing effect of overlap was first confirmed statistically. Cordero (1991) was subsequently the first to question to what extent overlap was a best practice *per se* or to what extent it would only be effective under certain project conditions. With the work of Ha and Porteus (1995), Krishnan *et al.* (1997), as well as Loch and Terwiesch (1998), the first mathematical optimization models around activity overlap appeared in *Management Science* and illustrated that activity overlap should be used only under certain conditions. At the same time, the work by Eisenhardt and Tabrizi (1995) and Terwiesch and Loch (1999) showed empirically that overlap indeed was not a panacea but would reduce development time only under specific conditions. Thus, in the timeframe of 14 years, an important research topic in product development moved from a qualitative description of the phenomena to detailed contingency models and mathematical decision support systems.

What has happened to this specific area of research in product development has happened to many others as well. Managing product development, a topic that provided virgin territory just 20 years ago, has now been settled by over 1000 articles. Not surprisingly, this has forced more recent research to be, on average, more incremental. Radically innovative ideas, so typical for the early years, have been largely replaced by a desire to achieve methodological excellence. The field has moved from qualitative descriptions to advanced econometrics and sophisticated optimization. A rather unfortunate byproduct of this trend has been an increasing fragmentation of the literature and a decline in the interdisciplinary work that was so typical for product development just two decades ago.

We end this chapter by looking back to the intellectual heritage of the product development literature. We hope that our problem-solving framework and its related review of some of the classic readings, such as the work by Simon (1969) and Alexander (1964) on design methods and the more general research on problem solving and creativity (e.g., Campbell, 1960; Rittel and Webber, 1973), have illustrated the fundamental problems of product development. In writing this chapter, we found that re-reading these classics is still exciting today and identifies numerous research opportunities that have gone unnoticed in the rapid settling of the product development landscape. For example, it appears that important aspects of the problem-solving cycle, especially the creation of variation, have received substantially less attention than other aspects (e.g., project management related topics). A similar observation can be made with respect to the interaction of creativity and organizational structures and processes.

Finally, we sincerely hope that our problem-solving framework and the literature upon which it is based can help to integrate the fragmented bodies of literature and the diverging streams of research reflective of different academic disciplines. Future research, we hope, can use the problem-solving framework as a starting point toward an integrated body of knowledge in the exciting field of product development.

REFERENCES

Adler, P.S. (1995). Interdepartmental interdependence and coordination: the case of the design/manufacturing interface. *Organization Science*, 6(2), 147–67.

Alcock, J. (1989). *Animal behavior: an evolutionary approach*, 4th edition. Sinauer.

Alexander, C. (1964). *Notes on the synthesis of form*. Harvard University Press.

Allen, T.J. (1966). Studies of the problem-solving process in engineering design. *IEEE Transactions on Engineering Management*, EM-13(2), 72–83.

Allen, T.J. (1977). *Managing the flow of technology*. MIT Press.

Ancona, D.G., and Caldwell, D.F. (1992). Bridging the boundary: external process and performance in organizational teams. *Administrative Science Quarterly*, 37, 634–65.

Baker, N.R., and Sweeney, D.J. (1978). Toward a conceptual framework of the process of organized innovation within the firm. *Research Policy*, 7, 150–74.

Baldwin, C.Y., and Clark, K. (2000). *Design rules: the power of modularity*. MIT Press.

Beinhocker, E.D. (1999). Robust adaptive strategies. *Sloan Management Review*, 95–106.

Bhattarchya, S., Krishnan, V., and Mahajan, V. (1998). Managing new product definition in highly dynamic environments. *Management Science*, 44(11), 550–64.

Boehm, B. (1981). *Software engineering economics*, Prentice Hall.

Bohn, R. (1987). Learning by experimentation in manufacturing. Working Paper No. 88-001. Harvard Business School Press.

Brown, A. (2004). The modern movement. Working paper, Wessex Design Center.

Brown, S.L., and Eisenhardt, K.M. (1995). Product development: past research, present findings, and future directions. *Academy of Management Review*, 20, 343–78.

Bucciarelli, L.L. (1996). *Designing engineers*. MIT Press.

Burns, T., and Stalker, G.M. (1961). *The management of innovation*. Tavistock.

Campbell, D.T. (1960). Blind varieties and selective retention in creative thought and other processes. *Psychological Review*, 67, 380–400.

Clark, K.B., and Fujimoto, T. (1989). Lead time in automobile development: explaining the Japanese advantage. *Journal of Technology and Engineering Management*, 6, 25–58.

Clark, K.B., and Fujimoto, T. (1991), *Product development performance: strategy, organization, and management in the world auto industry*. Harvard Business School Press.

Cordero, R. (1991). Managing for speed to avoid product obsolescence. *Journal of Product Innovation Management*, 8, 283–94.

Cross, N. (2001). Design, science, research: developing a discipline. 5th Asian Design Conference, Seoul, Korea.

Cusumano, M., and Selby, R. (1995). *Microsoft secrets*. The Free Press.

Dahan, E., and Mendelson, H. (2001). An extreme value model of concept testing, *Management Science*, 47(1), 102–16.

Davis, R., Shrobe, H., and Szolovits, P. (1993). What is a knowledge representation? *AI Magazine*, Spring, 17–33.

Dougherty, D., (1989). Interpretive barriers to successful product innovations in large firms. *Organization Science*, 3, 179–201.

Eisenhardt, K.M., and Tabrizi, B.N. (1995). Accelerating adaptive processes: product innovation in the global computer industry. *Administrative Science Quarterly*, 40, 84–110.

Fisher, M.L., Ramdas, K., and Ulrich, K.T. (1999). Component sharing in the management of product variety. *Management Science*, 45, 297–315.

Fujimoto, T. (1999). *The evolution of the Toyota Production System*. Oxford University Press.

Galbraith, J.R. (1973). *Designing Complex Organizations*. Addison Wesley.

Green, P.E., and Srinivasan, V. (1990). Conjoint analysis in marketing: new developments with implications for research and practice. *Journal of Marketing*, 54(4), 3–19.

Ha, A.Y., and Porteus, E.L. (1995). Optimal timing of reviews in concurrent design for manufacturability. *Management Science*, 41(9), 1431–40.

Hargadon, A., and Sutton, R.I. (1996). Brainstorming groups in context: effectiveness in a product design firm. *Administrative Science Quarterly*, 41(4), 685–718.

Imai, K., Ikujiro, N., and Takeuchi, H. (1985). Managing the new product development process: how Japanese firms learn and unlearn. In K.B. Clark, R.H. Hayes and C. Lorenz, *The Uneasy Alliance*, 337–75. Harvard Business School Press.

Katz, R. (1982). The effects of group longevity on project communication and performance. *Administrative Science Quarterly*, 27, 81–104.

Katz, R., and Tushman, M.L. (1981). An investigation into the managerial roles and career paths of gatekeepers and project supervisors in a major R&D facility. *R&D Management*, 11, 103–10.

Kauffman, S., and Levin, S. (1987). Towards a general theory of adaptive walks on rugged landscapes. *Journal of Theoretical Biology*, 128, 11–45.

Keller, R.R. (1986). Predictors of the performance of project groups in R&D organizations. *Academy of Management Journal*, 29, 715–26.

Krishnan, V., and Bhattacharya, S. (2002). Technology selection and commitment in new product development. *Management Science*, 48(3), 313–27.

Krishnan, V., Eppinger, S.D., and Whitney, D.E. (1997). A model based framework to overlap product development activities. *Management Science*, 43(4), 437–51.

Krishnan, V., and Ulrich, K.T. (2001). Product development decisions: a review of the literature. *Management Science*, 47(1), 1–21.

Larson, E.W., and Gobeli, D.H. (1988). Organizing for product development projects. *Journal of Product Innovation Management*, 5, 180–90.

Lawrence, P.R., and Lorsch, J.W. (1967). *Organization and environment*. Harvard University.

Leonard-Barton, D. (1995). *Wellsprings of knowledge*. Harvard Business School Press.

Levinthal, D. (1997). Adaptation on rugged landscapes. *Management Science*, 43(7), 934–50.

Loch, C.H., and Terwiesch, C. (1998). Communication and uncertainty in concurrent engineering. *Management Science*, 44(8), 1032–48.

Loch, C.H., and Terwiesch, C. (2005). Decisions under preliminary information: rush and be wrong or wait and be late? *Production and Operations Management*, 14(3), 331–43.

Loch, C.H., Terwiesch, C., and Thomke, S. (2001). Parallel and sequential testing of design alternatives. *Management Science*, 47(5), 663–78.

Lovejoy, W. (1994). Rationalizing the design process. In S. Dasu and C. Eastman (eds), *Management of design*. Kluwer.

MacCormack, A., Verganti, R., and Iansiti, M. (2001). Developing products on Internet time: the anatomy of a flexible development process. *Management Science*, 47(1), 133–50.

McGath, R.G. (2001). Exploratory learning, innovative capacity, and managerial oversight. *Academy of Management Journal*, 44(1), 118–31.

Meyer, M.H., and Lehnerd, A.P. (1997). *The power of product platforms*. The Free Press.

Moenaert, R.K., De Meyer, A., and Souder, W.E. (1995). R&D marketing communication during the fuzzy front-end. *IEEE Transactions on Engineering Management*, 42(3), 243–58.

Moenaert, R.K., and Souder, W.E. (1996). Information utility at the R&D marketing interface. *Management Science*, 42(11), 1592–1610.

Nayak, R.P., and Ketteringham, J.M. (1993). 3M's little yellow notepads: never mind, I'll do it myself. In *Breakthroughs!*, 2nd edition, Pfeiffer & Co.

Nobeoka, K. (1995). Inter-project learning in new product development. *Academy of Management Journal* (Best paper proceedings), 432–36.

Nobeoka, K., and Cusumano, M.A. (1997). Multi-project strategy and sales growth: the benefits of rapid design transfer in new product development. *Strategic Management Journal*, 18, 169–86.

Pisano.G. (1996). Learning before doing in the development of new process technology. *Research Policy*, 25(7), 1097–119.

Popper, K. (1977). *The logic of scientific discovery*. Hutchinson. First published as *Logik Der Forschung*, Springer, 1934.

Randall, T., Terwiesch, C., and Ulrich, K.T. (2007) User design of customized products, *Marketing Science*, 26(2), 268–80.

Rittel, H.W., and Webber, M.M. (1973). Dilemmas in a general theory of planning. *Policy Sciences*, 4, 155–69.

Rivkin, J.W., and Siggelkow, N. (2003). Balancing search and stability: interdependencies among elements of organizational design. *Management Science*, 49(3), 290–311.

Scott, W.R. (1987). *Organizations: rational, natural, and open systems*. Prentice-Hall.

Simon, H.A. (1969). *The sciences of the artificial*. MIT Press.

Smith, R.P., and Eppinger, S.D. (1997). A predictive model of sequential iteration in engineering design. *Management Science*, 43, 1104–20.

Sommer, S.C., and Loch, C.H. (2004). Selectionism and learning in projects with complexity and unforseeable uncertainty. *Management Science*, 50(10), 1334–47.

Sosa, M., Eppinger, S., and Rowles, C. (2004). The misalignment of product architecture and organizational structure in complex product development. *Management Science*, 50(12), 1674–89.

Steward, D.V. (1981). *Systems analysis and management: structure, strategy, and design*. Petrocelli Books.

Stiny, G. (1975). *Pictorial and formal aspects of shape and shape grammars*. Birkhäuser.

Su, N.P. (1990). *The principles of design*. Oxford University Press.

Terwiesch, C., De Meyer, A., and Loch, C.H. (2002). Exchanging preliminary information in concurrent engineering: alternative coordination strategies. *Organization Science*, 13(4), 402–19.

Terwiesch, C., and Loch, C.H. (1999). Measuring the effectiveness of overlapping development activities. *Management Science*, 45(4), 455–65.

Thomke, S. (1998). Managing experimentation in the design of new products. *Management Science*, 44, 743–62.

Thomke, S. (2003). *Experimentation matters: unlocking the potential of new technologies for innovation*. Harvard Business School Press.

Thomke, S., and Bell, D.E. (2001) Sequential testing in product development. *Management Science*, 47(2), 308–23.

Thompson, J.D. (1967). *Organizations in action*. McGraw-Hill.

Tufte, E.R. (2001). *The visual display of quantitative information*, 2nd edition. Graphics Press.

Tushman, M.L., and O'Reilly, C.A. (1997). *Winning through innovation*. Harvard Business School Press.

Ulrich, K. (1995). The role of product architecture in the manufacturing firm. *Research Policy*, 24, 419–40.

Ulrich, K.T., and Ellison, D.J. (1999). Holistic customer requirements and the design select decision. *Management Science*, 45(5), 641–58.

Ulrich, K.T., and Eppinger, S. (2004). *Product Design and Development*. Irwin McGraw Hill.

Van den Bulte, C., and Moenart, R.K. (1998). The effects of R&D team co-location on communication patterns among R&D. *Marketing, and Manufacturing, Management Science*, 44(11), 1–18.

Ward, A., Liker, J., Cristiano, J., and Sobek, D. (1995). The second Toyota Paradox: how delaying decisions can make better cars faster. *Sloan Management Review*, Spring, 43–61.

Weinberger, E. (1990). Correlated and uncorrelated fitness landscapes and how to tell the difference. *Biol. Cybernetics*, 63, 325–36.

Wheelwright, S., and Clark, K.B. (1992). *Revolutionizing product development*. The Free Press.

Woodward, J. (1965). *Industrial organization: theory and practice*. Oxford University Press.

Zirger, B.J., and Maidique, M. (1990). A model of new product development: an empirical test. *Management Science*, 36, 867–83.

5

Managing the 'Unmanageables' of Sustained Product Innovation

Deborah Dougherty

Over the past 30 years, scholars and managers alike have created, developed, and validated numerous techniques, processes, and procedures for sustained product innovation in complex organizations (Nord and Tucker, 1987; Jelinek and Schoonhoven, 1990; Bobrow, 1997; Brown and Eisenhardt, 1997). Despite the widespread availability of these best practices, many mature organizations still cannot generate multiple new products over time effectively (Benner and Tushman, 2003; Adams, 2004). There are many reasons why not, including poor strategies and leadership, the transformation of technologies and markets, and competitive forces that leave the present organization out of position. In this chapter, I argue that a mistaken view of organizational structure is one major reason for the lack of innovativeness in large, mature organizations. This mistaken view of organizational structure creates three 'unmanageables' that prevent sustained product innovation: segmentalism, rigidity, and coercive control. Organizations become segmented (Kanter, 1983), which inhibits the product and strategic integrity that innovation requires (Clark and Fujimoto, 1991); their core competencies become core rigidities, which inhibits emergence (Leonard, 1998); and coercive control robs employees of the power needed to move innovations through the organization (Dougherty and Hardy, 1996). These 'unmanageables' persist because they are assumed to be inevitable by-products of organizational age and size. In contrast, I suggest that managers create the unmanagables by how they structure their organizations. Managers can root out unmanageables by replacing them with alternative structures that enable sustained innovation.

The mistaken view of structure is to assume, however implicitly, that 'structure' and 'bureaucracy' are synonymous, so that bureaucratic structures are the only way to structure organizations. According to this view, a 'formal structure' breaks work down by functional specialty, defines jobs precisely to assure accountability, and controls everything via clear standards and hierarchy (Perrow, 1986). This view of

Handbook of Technology and Innovation Management. Edited by Scott Shane
© 2008 John Wiley & Sons, Ltd

structure focuses attention on the up and down flow of commands, controls, and communication rather than on the activities that are being commanded, controlled, and communicated. Textbooks for management, organization behavior, and strategy typically highlight the bureaucratic structure and its variations. So, even though organization theory has moved beyond this simplistic view of structure (Baum, 2002; Aldrich and Ruef, 2006), the management field continues to foster it. Economic views of organization also assume that a bureaucratic hierarchy is all that can exist (Barney and Hesterly, 2006). When managers assume that bureaucracy is the only way to structure their work settings, they create these unmanageables. Segmentalism, rigidity, and coercion do not arise from invisible forces or human cognitive limits, but instead are created by well-meaning managers, who are supported by scholars who do not examine their presumptions.

This mistaken view of structure is reinforced by three sources of confusion: that no bureaucratic structure means no structure at all; that structure *per se* is bad for innovation; and that structure is the end rather than a means. First, if one accepts the mistaken view that all formal structures are bureaucratic, eliminating the bureaucracy eliminates structure. This confusing view is reinforced by the notion that Burns and Stalker's (1961) 'organic' organizing form, which enables innovation, represents the lack of structure. Jelinek and Schoonhoven (1990) and Brown and Eisenhardt (1997) are among scholars who make this argument. Many textbooks present the 'organic' form as a 'free flowing' system that lacks formalization and standardization (e.g., Schilling, 2008; many textbooks have similar descriptions). In fact, Burns and Stalker (1961, p. 122) articulate 11 distinct approaches for structuring work that distinguish the organic from the mechanistic form. These organic dimensions lack bureaucratic formalization and standardization, but clearly are based on standards – i.e., principles – that can be readily formalized. There are many kinds of organizational structures that do not draw on the principles and logic of bureaucratic structuring (see summaries and ideas in Boland and Collopy, 2004; Zammuto *et al.*, 2007). Many managers and scholars know that alternatives to the bureaucracy exist, but many still slip easily into the fallacy of bureaucratic thinking.

A second source of confusion arises from the first: if the organic form is necessary for innovation but has no structure, then structure is bad for innovation. Popular models and myths for innovation highlight the creative individual who works around or through any structures. However, formal organizational structure is good for complex activities such as sustained product innovation, because innovation is a 'team sport' that cannot be carried out by creative loners, no matter how intrepid they might be (Tushman and O'Reilly, 1997). Formal structure, simply put, is a network of roles and relationships, and includes rules, authority relations, industry structure, the division of labor, institutional forces, and cultural norms and values. People always need to know what their jobs are, to whom they report, with whom they work, how they can go about getting resources, and what kinds of actions are not acceptable (Jelinek and Schoonhoven, 1990). And since resources are always constrained, somebody needs to decide the priority among projects, what products and businesses will get additional resources over time, and how shocks and emergencies will be dealt with. In other words, a system of authority and decision making is necessary to make these required choices and decisions.

Good structures are good for innovation. Managers must use structure to break organization-wide activities up into do-able parts, stabilize the organization, and motivate employees. Noninnovative organizations need to transform how they deal with these necessary structuring activities in order to become innovative. People working on innovation project teams can take charge of their work only if they have boundaries that help them understand their objectives, get resources, and link their performance to the enterprise (Hirschhorn, 1990; Dougherty and Takacs, 2004). R&D scientists need formal objectives to be creative (Pelz and Andrews, 1966 – creative tensions); specialized functions are vital (Damanpour, 1991); authority over innovation needs to be decentralized (Damanpour, 1991) but authority over strategy needs to be centralized (Nord and Tucker, 1987); technology mapping and platform planning delineate development paths and options that are constrained to align with capabilities (Meyer and Detore, 2001); and defining accountability and priorities enhances innovation projects by channeling resources and decision making (Brown and Eisenhardt, 1997).

Bad structures, however, are bad for innovation, because the everyday social actions necessary for innovation can be systematically inhibited with bad structures (Dougherty and Heller, 1994; Dougherty and Hardy, 1996). For example, the tendency for departmental thought worlds to comprehend user needs and technological issues in a qualitatively different and partial ways is exacerbated when managers fail to create collaborative routines and fixate on short-term closure (Dougherty 1992). The result is that inter-functional communication is short-circuited, options are not explored, and teamwork falls apart. These bad organizational structures are chosen by managers, not imposed by unnamed 'forces'.

A third source of confusion concerns the functions of organization structures. Perrow (1986) suggests that structures exist to support senior managers' dominion over the organization's resources, and indeed such dominion exists and can be exploited readily – flagrant examples include Enron and the recent fiascos in mortgages. But structures are also a tool for good management, which is the focus of this chapter. As a tool, the intent of these structures is to frame possible actions and meanings (Weick, 1993) but not to dictate specific actions. Structures are means, not ends, and the function of structures for innovation is to enable the social action of innovation: people must collectively figure out surprises on their own, improvise around problems, and come up with ways to coordinate as the work itself unfolds, because innovation by definition is new. People can make shared sense of a surprising situation, and coordinate even without a shared understanding of their joint task, provided their ideas have consistent behavioral implications (Donnellon et al., 1986). People can draw on the situation to cue knowledge, and to learn and know by doing (Tyre and von Hippel, 1997). In fact, people *will* enact the formal structures in surprising ways as they go about their everyday work (e.g., Roethlisberger and Dickson, 1939, showed that workers enacted a piece rate constraint very differently than management intended). The function of structures for innovation is simply to make these activities sensible and do-able. The question for managers and researchers is how to define the roles and relationships among the employees so that they can carry out the activities of innovation effectively, readily, and sensibly.

TABLE 5.1 Structuring for sustained product innovation.

Necessary activities of innovation	Market-technology linking in product design, business management, technology strategy	Creative problem solving continually to deal with constant surprises	Powering the process of innovation to energize and motivate such complex work
Core principle of activities	Integrity	Emergence	Empowerment
Structural imperative	Breaking innovation work up into do-able, seeable, sensible parts	Stabilizing innovation work to assure reputation, image, and work coherence	Controlling innovation work to direct attention, prioritize, and keep in sync
Unmanageables	Segmentalism	Rigidity	Coercive control
Alternate approaches for structuring innovation	Break up work into four sets of innovation problem setting and solving: horizontal flows of practice	Stabilize by redefining work as reflective practice; workers as reflective practitioners	Control by resourcing work: access to others' time, attention; own contribution; alternative solutions

Table 5.1 outlines the flow of discussion in this chapter. The columns synthesize three sets of innovative activities that must be structured so that they are enabled, shaped, and directed: continually linking markets and technologies at all levels of organizing; enabling the creative solving of surprising problems that emerge unexpectedly; and motivating employees to carry out all this difficult work. The rows reflect the structuring challenges. The first row summarizes each of the sets of innovation activities into a simple principle: integrity, emergence, and empowerment. The second row indicates a key imperative of structuring that fits with the innovation principle in a counter-intuitive way: breaking up complex work, stabilizing action, and controlling the flow of activities. The third row highlights the unmanageable, or the mistaken structural option that carries out the structural imperative in a way that prevents the innovation principle. The fourth row reframes the structural challenge to achieve the imperative in a new way, and summarizes the proposed alternative structures that can enable innovation.

STRUCTURING THE ACTIVITIES OF INNOVATION

The term 'innovation' as used in this chapter refers to sustained product innovation in complex organizations, not to R&D management *per se*, technological evolution, start-ups, IT, or networks of alliances, except as these may be directly tied to product innovation. 'Product innovation' concerns bringing new products and services into customers' use, and encompasses the whole process of conceptualizing, developing, designing, manufacturing, marketing, and distributing new products. Research demonstrates that successful product innovation requires collaboration from people with diverse functional expertise who are skilled at appreciating and anticipating issues and constraints in other functions (Souder, 1987; Clark and Fujimoto, 1991). New product teams are more successful when they have a clear product concept, strong managerial support, resources, priorities, and autonomy of action within strategic guidelines (Adams, 2004). New products themselves are more successful if they meet customers' core needs (Cooper, 1998). 'Sustained' product innovation refers to continually generating streams of new products for a variety of markets with varying degrees of innovativeness over time, so that the firm can continually adapt to shifting customer needs or competitive encroachments, take advantage of new technologies, and create new opportunities (Tushman and O'Reilly, 1997). Sustained product innovation therefore is a 'scale up' of single projects into a complex, interdependent system. Sustained innovation depends on deep marketing, technological, and manufacturing capabilities that can support a wide diversity of products and businesses (Day, 1990; Dougherty, 2001).

As noted, there are so many best practices and textbooks on managing technology, innovation, and change that it would be difficult to even summarize this vast literature. Instead, I briefly outline three key sets of activities that are necessary for sustained product innovation and a principle that captures the essence of each: market-technology linking and integrity; creative problem solving and emergence; and powering the processes of innovation and empowerment. The innovative organization needs to be structured explicitly and deliberately to enable these activities.

Integrity versus segmentalism: rethinking organizational partitions

Market-technology linking and the need for integrity. A new product is a package of features and benefits, each of which must be articulated, designed, and integrated in a way that addresses core customer needs and also that fits with what the organization can generate (Clark and Fujimoto, 1991). The principle of integrity reflects the market-technology linking at all organizational levels. Developing new products integrates functions because all functions have unique insights for a given product design (Dougherty, 1992), but each product must also mesh with the integrity of the functional capabilities in technology, manufacturing, marketing, sales, IT, etc., as these develop over time. The integrity of product families and platforms must be balanced with other firm-wide resources such as a brand that presents a common face to 'the marketplace'. Integrity extends beyond the boundaries of the organization as well, because internal functions and businesses are linked outside in a variety of alliances, partnerships, and associations (R&D, distribution, supply chain). In most industries value is created and delivered by a network of players who provide complementary assets, components, basic R&D, and so on (Chesbrough, 2003;

Floricel and Miller, 2003). Management techniques such as technology platforms, strategic portfolios, product families, networks, and alliances facilitate this complex system of integrity across these various dimensions.

The structural imperative for breaking up work.   Although it may seem counter-intuitive, the principle of integrity in innovation work matches up with the structural imperative for breaking things up. Once any organization grows beyond a small face-to-face group or a single product, the first structural imperative is to break work up in sensible ways, for two reasons. First, the specialization of labor is the hallmark of capitalism, according to Adam Smith. Separating different areas of expertise allows people in each one to concentrate deeply on their particular task, and to develop greater and greater expertise. Scientific management extends this idea to enable each step to be performed as efficiently as possible, thus reducing costs and speeding up work cycles. The second reason for breaking up work is the need to reduce complexity, by breaking work down into sensible, do-able parts. With a good definition of work units and of differentiation, people can go right to work on their tasks with others who are also working on that task or related ones. If the work of a large organization is not broken up sensibly, employees would be like day laborers, showing up every morning and waiting to be assigned tasks – not only inefficient but impossible with thousands of employees.

Moreover, the first or primary way to break work up focuses everyone's attention on the collective strategy, because the first 'cut' or boundary groups together activities that the firm's strategy says most need internal coherence (Galbraith, 1995). Good primary or first boundaries allow people to work in a self-designing manner. Everyone within the boundary naturally works with everyone else, communicating and problem solving as they go about their tasks. Boundaries are first drawn around these most essential sets of activities, so these activities become relatively self-designing, in the sense that people within the bounds communicate, interact, and engage in social actions naturally. Self-designing is good, since it reduces the need for managers to constantly tell people how to organize and coordinate. The basic question, then, is what to break up in what manner in order to enable the integrity around multiple levels of market-technology linking?

The unmanageable of segmentalism.   Unfortunately, many large, mature organizations break up their work in a way that invokes the unmanageable of segmentalism. According to Kanter (1983), segmentalism is concerned with compartmentalizing actions, events, and problems, and with keeping each piece isolated from the others: 'Segmentalist approaches see problems as narrowly as possible, independently of their context, independently of their connections to any other problems' Kanter (1983, p. 28). She says that companies with segmentalist structures have a large number of compartments that are walled off from each other: 'departments from departments, level above from level below, field office from headquarters, labor from management, or men from women' Kanter (1983). Segmentalist structures reinforce a tendency to be locally focused. The 'not invented here (NIH)' syndrome arises in teams that have been together too long because they no longer communicate much with people outside the team (Katz and Allen, 1985). People may search among familiar practices for solutions to problems, since applying 'tried and true' approaches seem less risky or more expedient (March, 1991). And people in different units have different thought worlds, where they know different things and know things differently (Dougherty, 1992), and attribute different causes to a common situation (Dearborn and Simon, 1958).

Unthinking application of the bureaucratic structure produces segmentalism, because the bureaucratic model assumes that the most important groupings of activity are by function and by level, which focuses on functional excellence apart from any collective activity and on strategic managers who can operate as they see fit. Functions are organized to work apart from each other, and levels are separated from each other, so senior managers impose the strategic objectives on lower levels (Westley, 1990). Bureaucratic structuring thus breaks big problems down into small pieces, which are separated further into product lines units, and tasks that are managed separately and often autonomously by different people. However, breaking up by functions leads to a 'silo' mentality, in which members of each function demand that problems are handed over to them to be worked on internally, without interference, and that work to be done is translated into the needs of the function, rather than the other way around. The integrity exists only within the function. Textbook alternatives such as breaking up by business unit, product category, or country of operation also do not enable innovation, because strong boundaries are drawn around work groups that have to interact, or at least draw on shared resources (Bartlett and Ghoshal, 1989). As Chandler's (1970) history suggests, more complicated cross-functional and cross-business unit structures were added as integration became more important, but these cross structures are very costly when added to a structure that is based mostly on vertical relationships (Thompson, 1967).

Segmentalism is reinforced by some innovation management literature. Historically, theorists have argued that innovation does not fit with, and may even conflict with, 'normal' or efficient work. Therefore, innovation must be managed separately, which prevents the necessary integrity of work right away – innovative activities cannot draw on or enrich the firm's resources. Early theorists proposed a variety of first cuts for segmenting work. Some said that stages of innovation needed to be managed differently (Zaltman et al., 1973; Duncan, 1976), because early stages required creativity whereas later ones required mechanistic thinking. Other first cuts include technology versus administration (dual cores – Daft, 1978; Damanpour and Evans, 1984); or parallel structures that separate innovation from mechanistic organizing (Kanter, 1983). More recently, Tushman and O'Reilly (1997) argue that large corporations need ambidextrous businesses, because the whole business units evolved different organizational architectures that have an inherent congruity. Christensen's (1997) related argument is based on resource dependence theory (Pfeffer and Salancik, 1978). Business units can become stuck on current customers; one unit can come to dominate because it controls vital resources such as customers or technology. The unit's dominance can persist even if the particular resources are no longer central, because people build up familiarity with particular customers. All this work tells managers to separate innovation from regular work, as if innovation is not regular work.

Overcoming segmentalism by horizontal organizing around innovation problems. An alternative primary cut for breaking work up is by different kinds of problems in innovation management, which embodies integrity by problem area. Innovation processes are interactive flows of problem setting and problem solving (building on Schon, 1983; see Clark and Fujimoto, 1991, and Dougherty and Heller, 1994, for discussions of innovation work as problem solving). Schon (1983) defines 'problem setting' as the artful competence of defining the decisions to be made, the ends to be achieved, and the means that may be chosen. Innovation itself is understood to be on ongoing flows of action, such as technology emergence (Leonard, 1998) or product family sequencing (Helfat and Raubitschek, 2000). Leonard (1998), for example, argues that innovation projects can drive daily business as teams dissolve and regroup according to the dictates of the business needs. Provided that just a few specific boundaries and constraints such as managing transitions from team to team, clear priorities, and clear reporting relationships are present, people can readily carry out specific innovation work and integrate their work over time (Jelinek and Schoonhoven, 1990; Brown and Eisenhardt, 1997).

There are four basic problems in innovation that need to be continually set and solved:

- ◆ corporate innovation strategy making that sets the direction(s) and determines the kinds of investments in capabilities;
- ◆ managing businesses for profit by continually bundling firm resources into new products and opportunities;
- ◆ developing technological and other specialty capabilities for the long term to support innovation;
- ◆ managing the myriad new product development teams.

Each problem is a horizontal slice of ongoing action (Barley, 1996) that integrates technologies and markets, and designing and using, but each can go on separately, provided that the other slices are constrained toward common innovation goals. Once this first cut is made, familiar structures that delineate communication flows, authority over choices and decisions, priorities, and roles and relationships can be added to channel attention in ways that meet the specific needs of the firm and its businesses. Jelinek and Schoonhoven (1990) argue that formal structures are both clear (everybody knows who his or her boss is, who is responsible for what decisions, and who relevant peers are), and fluid, in that they are changed regularly to meet shifting challenges. The structure is a tool, not a delineation of turf.

Some examples help to illustrate these differentiated flows of innovation problem setting and solving. A packaging engineer at a food company who was part of a new product team told me that because the group was organized as a team, he could work alone – which was a surprise! He explained that because the team spent several weeks together forming the product concept and strategy, he could now work alone because he understood the constraints in manufacturing. Before the project team organization, he would work in the abstract with spec sheets, but no deep appreciation. Innovation inevitably raises numerous problems for which he needed input from manufacturing. But when he called manufacturing for clarification or input, he said people would just pass him along: 'Oh, you need to talk to so-and-so, but he is on vacation for two weeks.' Although functional expertise is vital, the *primary* partition around which boundaries form is the entire activity of new product development for the particular project.

More generally, Dougherty (2001) finds that in innovative organizations, a subset of people that includes design and process engineers, sales people, financial analysts, and market researchers understand themselves to be part of the new product development community. They understand that their jobs are to apply their expertise to specific projects, working in multi-functional teams (Clark and Fujimoto, 1991; Leonard, 1998). Because project members together form the product concept (as the packaging engineer explained), they have a shared sense of the 'big picture' to which they contribute. This sense of the whole enables them to comprehend unexpected events, share ideas quickly, and continually adjust their own actions to the actions of others in a heedful manner (Weick and Roberts, 1993).

Another kind of problem to be set and solved is managing R&D, manufacturing, IT, and marketing systems to support all the projects over time, including anticipating new functionalities and opportunities. The need to bound functional capabilities from project management became clear to me from a conversation with an engineer in the early 1990s. At that time, his construction equipment firm developed new technologies in specific product development projects, which added years to their cycle times. He said it took them seven years to get a new tractor built because so much had to be reinvented, but their Japanese competitor took only three years, because they had technologies 'on the shelf'. The Japanese firm developed technologies (e.g., new transmissions, new hydraulics) apart from specific pieces of equipment, ready to be applied to specific projects as needed. The company also managed projects in product families. A chief engineer at an office equipment manufacturer brought alive the idea of managing technology separately from projects. He said he needed R&D to figure out the basic physics of their core component ahead of time, so when he brought his product team together they could concentrate on the mechanical engineering necessary to build the product so it could be manufactured and repaired quickly. In fact, developing technology and developing products are two separate problems, and as long as these processes are managed with similar strategies it is more effective to separate them.

Setting and solving project and capability problems does not necessarily involve making money. The third problem in innovation management is generating profits by bundling firm resources to fit with market, technology, and competitive trends over time. The need to separate the business management problem from others became clear when I realized that many of the very large, long established firms I studied in chemicals, office equipment, tires, textiles, or telephones industries were organized as huge bureaucracies, and so-called 'business units' were nothing more than marketing people charged with revenue goals. The more innovative of these firms had broken themselves apart into distinct but whole business units, which separated activities around distinct marketplaces. A manager explained that this 'industry focus' gave everyone in the business unit a common understanding of the whole market place and how their own work and products fit in. However, rather than manage businesses for the short term, innovation requires that businesses be managed to adjust and adapt to new opportunities, which makes product innovation a core part of the business model. Business managers oversee product portfolios and platforms to maintain the right mix; track dimensions of value for the particular business such as ease of use, quality, or delivery time; and oversee the ongoing assignment and movement among personnel.

The fourth problem is to assure that all these separate problems are being set and solved in a way that allows diverse businesses to leverage common resources. This is the strategic problem in innovation management, to set a common direction for all the businesses, functions, and projects, look for new business opportunities, and make the necessary investments in capabilities. The failure to address this corporate-wide strategic problem seems to be the primary reason for the failure to be effectively innovative (Tushman and O'Reilly, 1997). Senior managers in innovative firms do not run the businesses or choose projects, rather they manage the context within which all these flow and interact. They move charters from business to business to keep resources employed and to seize new opportunities (Galtunic and Eisenhardt, 1996), they facilitate product cannibalization, they oversee technology platforms shared by a variety of business units, they choose the emerging technologies to invest in, and they hold regular strategic meetings where businesses share new opportunities and problems.

An example of managing this strategic problem came from an innovative textile firm. A manager explained that every six months, all 50 business managers stood up in front of the board of directors and explained where they were taking their business over the next three years. They did not spend time at this forum apologizing for failing to meet last year's projections. Rather they articulated emerging opportunities. The strategic managers had the inputs to formulate their investment strategies and to make the necessary choices among opportunities. In addition, every quarter all 700 global managers were brought together to discuss new directions, problems, and technologies.

This innovative approach to breaking up the work of innovation fulfills the structural imperative for emphasizing expertise and simplifying complexity. Different sets of activities are separated to simplify and focus the work within those bounds. But the bounds are organized around emerging processes rather than around static chunks of work. Each separate flow of work embodies a complete, realistic whole that comprises a common ground. Each person can take the whole into consideration, because that whole is bounded and sensible.

Creative problem solving and emergence: rethinking the definition of everyday work

The need for emergence.   Another critical principle for organizing sustained product innovation is emergence. Product teams inevitably encounter unanticipated problems as they design and develop a new product, which means that they often must rethink the very problem they are solving – what will the product do for whom and how – as they proceed. So, although innovation team members proceed in parallel to achieve the necessary integrity, they also must shift their attention quickly to problems that affect all functions (e.g., a part cannot be made reliably after all, which affects the price, or the launch time, or the target market – Yang and

Dougherty, 1993). This emergence ripples through the whole organization, occurring within and across capabilities and businesses, as well as the innovation project domain. Clark (1985) explains how technologies can 'ripple up' the design hierarchy, because people rethink prior choices among alternative technology paths if new technologies now make previously rejected options feasible, or changes in customer needs now highlight different kinds of performance. Leonard (1998) describes large cycle changes in which whole systems such as manufacturing adapt to a new strategy, for example, which involves a simultaneous adaptation of the organization. These large cycle changes involve revisiting prior decision points, reopening issues that had been resolved, and unfreezing organizational routines. Galtunic and Eisenhardt (1996) and Helfat and Eisenhardt (2004) describe the continual strategic transformation that occurs as managers move charters for businesses or products among business units over time, to take advantage of free resources and other businesses' ebb and flow.

The structural imperative for stabilizing work. Although this may also seem counterintuitive, the principle for emergence matches up with the structural imperative for stability. Stability is necessary because organizations need to maintain consistently good reputations and brand images, which provides legitimacy over time. In addition, employees need some sense of coherence and order, and are unlikely to accept constant churning and shifting. The structuring question becomes stabilize what, in what way?

The unmanageable of rigidity. Unfortunately, many large mature organizations stabilize routines and their bureaucratic structures, which leads directly to organizational rigidity. Many forces for rigidity can arise with age, as older firms get better at replicating structures and routines that legitimate them to external parties (Hannan and Freeman, 1984), and for whom change becomes very difficult and costly (Amburgey, Kelly, and Barnett, 1993). Also, firms are subject to the 'tyranny of success', which fixates them on current businesses (Tushman and O'Reilly, 1997), and tend to prefer exploitation over exploration (March, 1991). But the fact that some large organizations do not become rigid (e.g., 3M, GE, Toyota) indicates that rigidity does not arise from 'disembodied forces afoot in the land', as Gouldner (1954) referred to institutional theory. Rigidity is created by managers' choices for stabilizing work, in particular by an unthinking reliance on bureaucratic approaches.

Unfortunately, scholars may seem to make excuses for these managerial choices. Baum and Amburgey (2002) argue: 'under conditions of uncertainty and ambiguity, however, there are severe constraints on the ability of boundedly rational individuals to consistently conceive and implement changes that improve organizational success and survival chances in the face of competition' (Baum and Amburgey, 2002, p. 305). Thus, theory says that individual organizations cannot change much and in effect do not need to worry about that. Change occurs mostly through variation and selection among organizations at the population level. Pressures for rigidity inside arise automatically and perhaps even inevitably as well. Leonard (1998) argues that core capabilities become institutionalized internally as part of the organization's taken-for-granted reality. They thus become core rigidities over time because they do not adapt readily. For example, in a high technology firm a nondominant discipline such as marketing has little power and is not developed. If the competitive situation changes and more marketing capabilities are required, the firm's technology stance becomes rigid. The organization may undervalue certain skills such as project management, and so the best people do not develop these skills.

Scholars also look at different levels of analysis and define change very differently, which further obscures what causes what. Some define change as a total transformation of form, which is rare. However, some firms do survive technological transformations if they have complementary assets and common customers (Tripsas, 1997). Long-term studies demonstrate that large organizations do change over time (Cantwell, 1989), outlasting the ongoing 'creative destruction' of market and products by developing and evolving technology capabilities. Indeed, many 'sudden' changes take years to emerge, giving firms the time to adapt. Others think of change as ongoing adjustments, so with this definition the only constant is change (Brown and Eisenhardt, 1997; Weick, 1995). Moorman and Miner (1998) point out that the presence of stable competencies is not inconsistent with improvising because routines can be the basis for adaptation.

Overcoming rigidity by redefining work as reflective practice.   An approach to enabling emergence while also providing stability is to redefine the work employees do as reflective practice, and rethink workers as professional practitioners. A major source of rigidity is the bureaucratic notions of jobs, as precisely defined lists of tasks for which the worker is held accountable. Rethinking how work is understood and carried out can produce stability without rigidity. One of Burns and Stalker's (1961) 11 properties of the mechanistic organization is 'the abstract nature of each individual task, which is pursued with techniques and purposes more or less distinct from those of the concerns as a whole; i.e., functionaries tend to pursue the technical improvement of means, rather than the accomplishment of the ends of the concern' (Burns and Stalker, 1961, p. 120). The corollary in the organic organization is 'the "realistic" nature of the individual task, which is seen as set by the total situation of the concern' (Burns and Stalker, 1961, p. 121). Dougherty's (1995) finding are consistent with Burns and Stalker's: rigidity arises not from any inevitable forces of institutionalization, but from the detachment of work from the actual realities of practice. This study suggests that core competencies become rigid because they are detached from the realities of everyday practice, not because of institutional forces. Because people focus on their own little piece of work that has been abstracted from the whole they have no common ground. Detachment leads to rigidity – people always need to make sense, but if the only source of sense is abstracted structures and roles, the sense that people make will be stilted and limited. However, effectively innovative teams in these same organizations draw on the practice of designing the product for actual use by actual customers.

To enable emergence with stability, work itself can be reconceived as, and managed as, 'reflective practice' rather than as predefined, functionary jobs. The practices of 'scholar', 'accountant', or 'architect' are structured by rules and expectations, but within those frames practitioners can enact their work in a fluid, situated manner. Rethinking work as professional practice fits innovation, because scholars have always emphasized extensive, hands-on involvement of managers at all levels in the actual practice of innovating. Maidique and Hayes (1984) argue that involvement in innovation provides senior managers with an in-depth appreciation of how the technology works and how their organization works, so they can better understand strategic possibilities. Studies emphasize the need for scientists, engineers, market researchers, and shop floor workers to learn by doing and to be actively engaged in the practice of innovation work (Pelz and Andrews, 1966; Brown and Duguid, 2000; Tsoukas and Vladimirou, 2001). If people understand themselves to be responsible for the whole practice and for contributing their expertise to it, they can understand their work in terms of its contribution to the larger whole.

'Reflective practice' highlights the spontaneous, inventive, and improvisational ways through which people get things done, such as forming relationships with customers to elicit insights that might not otherwise be revealed, interacting with colleagues over the situation, and improvising to surface problems (Schon, 1983). Being actively engaged in the details of the innovation and its emergence is important because these are complex, often tacit issues that must be 'visceralized' to be understood, to use a phrase developed by Schon (1985). The skills of practice include applying principles of the profession to unique situations and 'making do' with resources available (Lave and Wenger, 1991; Orlikowski, 2002). Reflection in action is defined as having a conversation with the situation: surfacing premises and intuitive understandings, doing frame experiments by stepping into the problem and imposing a frame on the situation, and reflecting on surprising consequences of efforts to shape the situation.

Additional structures can map out the flows of innovation activities so that people can combine designing and using in their everyday work. Many of the best practices, tools, and techniques for managing innovation map out possible pathways and frame shorter-term activities. For example, aggregate product plans combine product concepts with technology and manufacturing strategies. Ongoing operational reviews measure cycle times, yield rates, percentage of experts that are oversubscribed, capacity utilization, product quality, customer satisfaction, delivery times, market share, or profit margins – all to help keep the projects and strategies in sync (Jelinek and Schoonhoven, 1990; Leonard, 1998). These processes focus on surfacing problems so they can be addressed, rather than on eliminating variance or punishing miscreants. Fostering ongoing sensemaking keeps practices out in the open, to be evaluated and reconceived as necessary.

Powering processes of innovation and empowerment: replacing coercive control with resourcing

The need for empowerment.   A third set of activities necessary for sustained innovation concerns how to continually motivate people to do all this hard work. The critical organizing principle here is empowerment. Effective innovation work at all levels requires *very* sophisticated skills that can be enacted only if others also enact them, which means that developing these skills is not simply a matter of hiring the right people! Engineers, scientists, marketers, manufacturing people, and other special-ists all need the skills to reach beyond their specialties and absorb others' insights, while also making their own specialized insights sensible to others. They must anticipate problems in other functions and appreciate others' constraints (Clark and Fujimoto, 1991). They need 'T'-shaped skills – both a deep understanding of a specialty and an intimate understanding of the potential systemic impacts of their specialty (Iansiti, 1993). People must also shape their specialized knowledge to fit the problem at hand rather than insist that the problem appear in a certain way (Leonard, 1998). In addition, people need the skill of situated judgement (Dougherty, 1996). 'Judgement' refers to the capability to use insights and heuristics developed from experience, and to 'appreciation', which Vickers (1965) uses to refer to sizing up unstructured situations and judging the significance of various facts.

The structural imperative for controlling work.   Although also counter-intuitive, the principle of empowered workers matches up with the structural imperative for control. An organization-wide system of control can enable innovation by allowing diverse projects to share organizational resources, assuring that the needed resources are available and being used effectively, giving projects the right amount of control over specific decisions, and giving individuals access to necessary support. Proper controls can channel attention, align resources, and enable people to create synergies, and so control is good. Cardinal (2001) finds that input controls that assure diversity of perspectives, behavioral controls that govern problem solving, information flows, decision making, and output controls that avoid short-term perspectives all enhance radical innovation. Dougherty and Hardy (1996) find that successful innovators have control over the meaning of their projects, while (Damanpour, 1991) confirms the need to decentralize innovation. Innovation does indeed require direction, somebody does have to resolve the conflicts and make necessary choices, and co-workers cannot always be counted on to do the right things. Individuals, projects, and the organizational setting overall need to be controlled to support innovation.

The unmanageable of coercive control.   However, unthinking application of bureaucratic structuring can lead to coercive control, which emphasizes only one aspect of the overall system of control: that by senior managers over everything else. Coercive control produces a spiral of unmanageable effects. First, a negative kind of 'power and politics' privileges certain functions and senior managers over others (Kanter, 1983; Perrow, 1986), which demoralizes and disengages everyone else. Perrow (1986) says that a structure of domination always arises in a work organization since the possibilities for power are enormous. He argues that this structure of domination is always based on 'command and control', while Adler and Borys (1996) among others find that systems that enable work are possible as well. However, Westley (1990) shows how a top-down structure of domination can easily arise in a large, mature organization, with the result that middle managers become disempowered and de-energized when they cannot participate in strategic conversations. If managers find that people are de-energized and disengaged, rather than investigating their structure of domination, they may assume that people are lazy and opportunistic, and will satisfy their own needs at the expense of the organization's. This 'theory X' mentality says that managers must control these workers by monitoring their actions directly, and by applying clear, extrinsic (monetary), and instrumental rewards that explicitly invoke the required behavior. Purely extrinsic rewards further dampen creativity (Amabile and Conti, 1999), but managers who are intent on 'incentivizing' employees without thinking through their presumptions may continue with ineffective reward systems that reinforce coercive control. Project teams operating in the bowels of the organization without support from managers or access to resources are unlikely to innovate effectively, even if they get a bonus. Coercive control will shut down innovation.

Some innovation research reinforces unbalanced power and control systems. Ideas that highlight individual creativity or intellectual capital overlook the work context itself, and reinforce the notion that some magical individual reward system or effective recruitment is all that is needed to foster innovation. Other innovation researchers accept coercive control and develop means for individuals to push against it. Schon (1963) developed the idea of a 'product champion' as someone to force an innovation through the 'dynamically conservative' (e.g., returns to form) organization. Clark and Fujimoto (1991) find that 'heavy weight' project managers who have enough clout to push new products through the system are necessary, without questioning how adding 800 pound gorillas to a poorly structured work system would be a good management ploy. Ironically, the emphasis on forcing things through a system without thinking about why such a system exists in the first place coexists with research demonstrating that people can be truly interested in doing their jobs well (Westley, 1990; Barley, 1996). Managers do not have to force people to work effectively and to innovate, because many people do so even against great odds, in coercively controlled settings. Effective reward systems are clearly necessary, but they are certainly not sufficient.

Overcoming lack of power by redefining organizational resources. A different view of 'resources' combines managerial authority with employee empowerment. Building on structuration theory, Feldman (2004) suggests that resources are what enable people at work to do what they think they are supposed to do. These everyday resources include the authority to act, information, relationships, trust, and the organizational structure itself, since people can draw on each of these to accomplish their work. For innovation, Dougherty, Barnard, and Dunne (2005) find that people have direct access to three kinds of resources that enable them to set and solve the problems of innovation: access to other people's time and attention, control over how one's own work will contribute to the entire task (e.g., participatory control over the product concept or technology direction), and access to options available to solve situated problems. They argue that when people who work on innovation control these three everyday resources, innovation is literally energized. Senior managers in innovative organizations do not dominate specific alternatives that innovators might choose, people's time and attention, or what people know and how they know it, which means that they do not directly control what people do. Instead, managers control processes and procedures that enable these resources. They control the work overall, not the workers, which gives them much more power. They dominate the direction of activities by investing in knowledge systems and overseeing thrusts of the various businesses.

First, direct access to others' time and attention is a vital resource for innovation, because it enables teamwork, collaboration, and iterative development of problems and solutions. Direct access means that people do not have to go up and down hierarchies over multiple days just to get some input or assistance. Rather, they can go directly to the people who can provide that help. The idea comes in part from work as practice, which invokes a sense of being responsible for the whole project or business. Since everyone understands him- or herself to be responsible for the whole project, everyone can work with the expectation that they will do their part for the project. It is not only appropriate but expected that one can ask others to help, and that they will help if they have the time. Not all activities can be staffed, and so constraints exist. Senior managers need to control the amount of work and the number of projects, which means they must make the strategic decisions that define priorities among product lines and allocate time and attention to various classes of projects (e.g., radical versus derivative). Managers also decide on the amount of people resources to invest in, which presumes a well-grounded understanding of what it takes to develop and launch each of the product types (see Jelinek and Schoonhoven, 1990; Brown and Eisenhardt, 1997, on priorities and strategies).

Second, control over how one's expertise is applied to the project (be it a product, technology, or business activity) also powers everyday innovation. This resource also builds from the idea of work as reflective practice, and from the idea of breaking work up into horizontal communities of practice around different problems of innovation. Each person is an expert who is expected to contribute his or her part effectively to the project – the contributions are not second-guessed, monitored, and approved by levels of disassociated people. In addition, the contributions are based on the person having an understanding of the whole project and its role in the business or corporate strategy, because people participate in defining the product concept, technology strategy, or business strategy. That is, people have the power to help define the problems to be solved – they control what they do and why they do it. Control over one's own contribution also provides people with access to a wide variety of knowledge from other team members, since everyone is expected to make their expertise accessible to others.

Managers bound and frame the expertise. Functional or capabilities managers are responsible for developing new capabilities, and for overseeing how well their people contribute to the new product teams and how carefully the teams take functional constraints into account (e.g., limited plant capacity). Rather than dictating what each person is to do and how, the managers build the wherewithal to do innovation in particular ways – they shape the available expertise and its ongoing development. Also, capabilities managers work with business managers to identify the technological, operational, and marketing knowledge bases necessary for long-term value creation. They also are charged with keeping their capabilities connected with the businesses and product efforts, disseminating knowledge of new capabilities, and encouraging creativity and ongoing development of skills.

The third resource that powers innovation is control over the specific options that are chosen to fix problems in innovation, within strategic guidelines. Giving people on the teams this control is vital because people can learn more rapidly when they investigate several design options in parallel (Iansiti, 1993). As they learn more about the systemic effects of various alternatives, they can drop some and postpone others for future generations. The choice of particular design options or particular customer priorities is fluid, and only gradually firms up as problems are discovered, set, and solved. This resource is empty, of course, if there are not enough options available to choose from. Managers therefore must foster the development of varieties of alternatives and options, and make knowledge of these available to innovators. They do so by encouraging networking, formally sanctioning task forces to develop and disseminate ideas, and assigning the various experts with the responsibility to disseminate certain new techniques or ideas (Cusumano and Nobeoka, 1998). Managers must also develop procedures that are designed to help surface problems in the processes (not to blame individuals!), and to help resolve those problems. Although elaborate programs such as Six Sigma do this, everyday processes of ongoing operations reviews that monitor how well things are going also serve (Jelinek and Schoonhoven, 1990).

This control system affords senior managers more control over innovation in total, but spreads out resources needed to energize the everyday work of innovation. Control processes that focus on objectives to be achieved can now be included, provided they emphasize how those objectives come to be, how they emerge continually over time, and how they are interpreted. Championing and 'heavy weight' project leadership are manifestations of, and enablers for, this more basic structure of control. When people have these basic resources, the outcome is entrepreneurial, attentive, energized people. No magic reward systems or culture are needed, because these arise from the structuring of everyday work.

DISCUSSION

I have articulated three structuring options that managers can use to overcome the unmanageables of innovation and enable the integral, emergent, and empowered activities that are necessary for sustained product innovation. My basic argument is that these unmanageables are not inherent or inevitable, but rather are produced by the inappropriate structuring of everyday work. If everyday social action in the work organization is focused on separate parts, on processes that have been abstracted from the whole and thus have little intrinsic meaning, and are motivated by coercive authority, then segmentation, rigidity, and lack of power arise straightforwardly. These unmanageables are the rational outcomes of such a social system. But if structures frame core processes of innovation work in the three complementary ways outlined here, then integrated, emergent, and energized social action arises straightforwardly. These structures are:

- ◆ defining the nature of the work people do and with whom, based on four distinct kinds of innovation problems to be set and solved;
- ◆ structuring how that work is to be carried out based on work as reflective practice, where everyone takes responsibility for the whole project and actively integrates designing with using;

♦ controlling work by giving people direct access to three everyday resources: time and attention, control over the application of their own expertise, and control over specific choices made to solve problems.

The three structures are proposed as the primary or first cut at structuring work. Once these basic structures are built and reinforced as the core, the more familiar lines and boxes can be drawn to further focus people's attention and energy. This alternative view of structure in organizations highlights the socially constructed frames for everyday collective action that must be managed deliberately with that action in mind. The everyday collective action is the behavioral context (Ghoshal and Bartlett, 1996) within which individuals work and which enables them to socially enact complex, interdependent, yet situated work; namely, sustained product innovation. Innovation researchers have elaborated extensively on the kinds of social action necessary for innovation, and we know a great deal about what, exactly, we want everyone to do. Simply hiring individuals with the requisite intellectual capital, although necessary, is not sufficient, because the context truly matters (Bailyn, 1985; Amabile and Conti, 1999). Highly skilled people will leave or 'turn off' if the right kind of social action is not deliberately enabled. Banging away at intellectual capital, social capital, culture, or networks without taking the behavioral context into account makes little sense. Focusing on what people need to be able to do *together* directly is much more to the point for innovation management, rather than focusing on what they should think or believe, or on 'plumbing and wiring'-like networks that are devoid of content or context.

In conclusion, the work of innovation in large, mature organizations has to be structured, just like any complex work. Three reasonably simple yet very un-bureaucratic approaches for structuring the activities of innovation have been proposed that draw on the vast literature for organizing for innovation. These alternative structures focus managerial and scholarly attention on the everyday collective work of innovation, so that innovation can be continuously accomplished. The centrality, usefulness, and applicability of these alternatives to various competitive and industrial contexts can be explored further, and tested against the other structures.

References

Adams, M. (2004). Comparative performance assessment study findings. Presentation at the Comparative Performance Assessment Conference, PDMA Foundation, March 2004.

Adler, P., and Borys, B. (1996). Two types of bureaucracy: enabling and coercive. *Administrative Science Quarterly*, 41, 61–89.

Aldrich, H., and Ruef, M. (2006). *Organizations evolving*, 2nd edition. London: Sage

Amabile, T., and Conti, R. (1999). Changes in the work environment for creativity during downsizing. *Academy of Management Journal*, 42(6), 616–29.

Amburgey, T., Kelly, D., and Barnett, W. (1993). Resetting the clock: the dynamics of organizational change and failure. *Administrative Science Quarterly*, 38. 51–73.

Bailyn, L. (1985). Autonomy in the industrial R&D lab. *Human Resource Management*, 24, 129–46.

Barley, S. (1996). Technicians in the workplace: ethnographic evidence for bringing work into organization studies. *Administrative Science Quarterly*, 41, 404–41.

Barney, J., and Hesterly, W. (2006). Organizational economics: understanding the relationship between organizational and economic analysis. In S. Clegg, C. Hardy, T. Lawrence, and W. Nord (eds), *The Sage Handbook of Organization Studies*, London: Sage, 111–48.

Bartlett, C., and Ghoshal, S. (1989). *Managing Across Borders: The Transnational Solution*. Boston, MA: Harvard Business School Press.

Baum, J. (ed.) (2002). *The Blackwell Companion to Organizations*. Oxford, UK: Blackwell Publishers.

Baum, J., and Amburgey, T. (2002). Organizational ecology. In J. Baum (ed.), *The Blackwell Companion to Organizations*, Oxford, UK: Blackwell Publishers, 304–27.

Benner, M., and Tushman, M. (2003). Exploitation, exploration, and process management: the productivity dilemma revisited. *Academy of Management Review*, 28(2), 238–56.

Bobrow, E. (1997). *The complete idiot's guide to new product development*. New York: Alpha Books.

Boland, R., and Collopy, F. (eds) (2004). *Managing as designing*. Stanford: Stanford University Press.

Brown, J.S., and Duguid, P. (2000). Balancing act: how to capture knowledge without killing it. *Harvard Business Review*, May–June, 73–80.

Brown, S., and Eisenhardt, K. (1997). The art of continuous change: linking complexity theory and time-paced evolution in relentlessly shifting organizations. *Administrative Science Quarterly*, 42, 1–35.

Burns, T., and Stalker, G.M. (1994: originally 1961). *The management of innovation*. Oxford, UK: Oxford University Press.

Cantwell, J. (1989). *Technological innovation and multinational corporations*. Oxford, UK: Basil Blackwell.

Cardinal, L. (2001). Technological innovation in the pharmaceutical industry: the use of organizational control in managing research and development. *Organization Science*, 12(1), 19–36.

Chandler, A. (1970). *The Visible Hand*. Cambridge, MA: Harvard University Press.

Chesbrough, H. (2003). Open research. *Sloan Management Review*, Spring. 35–41.

Christensen, C. (1997). *The innovator's dilemma*. Boston, MA: Harvard Business School Press.

Clark, K. (1985). The interaction of design hierarchies and market concepts in technological evolution. *Research Policy*, 14, 235–51.

Clark, K., and Fujimoto, T. (1991). *Product development performance*. Boston, MA: Harvard Business School Press.

Cooper, R. (1998). *Product leadership: creating and launching superior new products*. Reading MA: Perseus Books

Cusumano, M., and Nobeoka, K. (1998). *Thinking beyond lean*. New York: The Free Press.

Daft, R. (1978). A dual-core model of organizational innovation. *Academy of Management Journal*, 21, 193–210.

Damanpour, F. (1991). Organizational innovation: a meta-analysis of effects of determinants and moderators. *Academy of Management Journal*, 34, 555–90.

Damanpour, F., and Evans, W. (1984). Organizational innovation and performance: the problem of organizational lag. *Administrative Science Quarterly*, 29, 392–409.

Day, G. (1990). *Market driven strategy*. New York: Free Press.

Dearborn, D., and Simon, H. (1958). Selective perception: a note on the departmental identification of executives. *Sociometry*, 140–4.

Donnellon, A., Gray, B., and Bougon, M. (1986). Communication, meaning, and organized action. *Administrative Science Quarterly*, 31, 43–55.

Dougherty, D. (1992). Interpretive barriers to successful product innovation in large firms. *Organization Science*, 3, 179–203.

Dougherty, D. (1995). Managing your core incompetencies for innovation. *Entrepreneurship Theory and Practice*, 19, 113–35.

Dougherty, D. (1996). Organizing for innovation. In S. Clegg, C. Hardy, and W. Nord (eds), *Handbook of Organization Studies*, London: Sage, 424–39.

Dougherty, D. (2001). Re-imagining the differentiation and integration of work for sustained product innovation. *Organization Science*, 12(5), 612–31.

Dougherty, D., Barnard, H., and Dunne, D. (2005). The rules and resources that generate the dynamic capability for sustained product innovation. In *Qualitative Organizational Research*, K. Elsbach (ed.), Greenwich, CN: Information Age Publishing.

Dougherty, D., and Hardy, C. (1996). Sustained product innovation in large, mature organizations: overcoming innovation-to-organization problems. *Academy of Management Journal*, 39(5), 1120–53.

Dougherty, D., and Heller, T. (1994). The illegitimacy of successful new products in large firms. *Organization Science*, 5(2), 200–18.

Dougherty, D., and Takacs, C.H. (2004). H. Takacs 2004 Heedful interrelating in innovative organizations: team play as the boundary for work and strategy. *Long Range Planning*, 37, 569–90.

Duncan, R. (1976). The ambidextrous organization: designing dual structures for innovation. In *The Management of Organizational Design*, R. Kilman and L. Pondy (eds), New York: North Holland.

Feldman, M. (2004). Resources in emerging structures and processes of change. *Organization Science*, 15, 295–309.

Floricel, S., and Miller, R. (2003). An exploratory comparison of the management of innovation in the new and old economies, *R&D Management*, 35(5), 501–25.

Galbraith, J. (1995). *Designing Organizations*. San Francisco, CA: Jossey-Bass.

Galtunic, C., and Eisenhardt, K. (1996). The evolution of intracorporate domains: divisional charter losses in high-technology, multi-divisional corporations. *Organization Science*, 7(3), 255–82.

Ghoshal, S., and Bartlett, C. (1996). Rebuilding behavioral context: a blueprint for corporate renewal. *Sloan Management Review*, 37(2), 23–36.

Gouldner, A. (1954). *Patterns of industrial bureaucracy*. New York: Free Press.

Hannan, M., and Freeman, J. (1984). Structural inertia and organizational change. *American Sociological Review*, 49, 149–64.

Helfat, C., and Eisenhardt, K. (2004). Inter-temporal economies of scope, organizational modularity, and the dynamics of diversification. *Strategic Management Journal*, 25(13), 1217–32.

Helfat, C., and Raubitschek, R. (2000). Product sequencing: co-evolution of knowledge, capabilities, and products. *Strategic Management Journal*, 21, 961–80.

Hirschhorn, L. (1990). *Managing in the new team environment*. Reading, MA: Addison Wesley.

Iansiti, M. (1993). Real world R&D: jumping the product generation gap, *Harvard Business Review*, May–June, 138–47.

Jelinek, M., and Schoonhoven, C. (1990). *The innovation marathon: lessons from high technology firms*. Oxford, UK: Basil Blackwell.

Kanter, R. (1983). *The change masters*. Boston, MA: Simon and Schuster.

Katz, R., and Allen, T. (1985). Project performance and the locus of influence in the R&D matrix. *Academy of Management Journal*, 28(1), 67–87.

Lave, J. and Wenger, S. (1991). *Situated learning*. Cambridge, UK: Cambridge University Press.

Leonard, D. (1998). *Well-springs of knowledge: building and sustaining the sources of innovation*, 2nd edition. Boston, MA: Harvard Business School Press.

Maidique, M., and Hayes, R. (1984). The art of high technology management. *Sloan Management Review*, 24, 18–31.

March, J. (1991). Exploration and exploitation in organizational learning. *Organization Science*, 2(1), 71–87.

Meyer, M., and Detore, A. (2001). Creating a platform-based approach for developing new services. *Journal of Product Innovation Management*, 18(3), 188–204.

Moorman, C., and Miner, A. (1998). Organizational improvisation and organizational memory. *The Academy of Management Review*, 23(4), 698–723.

Nord, W., and Tucker, S. (1987). *Implementing routine and radical innovations*. Lexington, MA: Lexington Books.

Orlikowski, W. (2002). Knowing in practice: enacting a collective capability in distributed organizing. *Organization Science*, 13(3), 249–73.

Pelz, D. and Andrews, F. (1966). *Scientists in organizations*. New York: John Wiley & Sons, Inc.

Perrow, C. (1986). *Complex organizations: a critical essay*, 3rd edition. New York: Random House.

Pfeffer, J., and Salancik, G. (1978). *The external control of organizations: a resource dependence perspective*. New York: Harper and Row.

Roethlisberger, F., and Dickson, W. (1939). *Management and the worker*. Cambridge, MA: Harvard University Press.

Schilling, M. (2008). *Strategic management of technological innovation*, 2nd edition. New York: McGraw-Hill Irwin.

Schon, D. (1963). Champions for radical new inventions. *Harvard Business Review*, 41(2), 77–86.

Schon, D. (1983). *The reflective practitioner: how professionals think in action*. New York: Basic Books.

Schon D. (1985). *Keynote address: Marrying science, artistry, the humanities, and professional practice*, Cornell University.

Souder, W. (1987). *Managing new product innovations*. Lexington, MA: Lexington Books.

Thompson, J. (1967). *Organizations in action*. New York: McGraw Hill.

Tripsas, M. (1997). Unraveling the process of creative destruction: complementary assets and incumbent survival in the typesetter industry. *Strategic Management Journal*, 18, 119–42.

Tsoukas, H., and Vladimirou, E. (2001). What is organizational knowledge? *Journal of Management Studies*, 38(7), 973–93.

Tushman, M., and O'Reilly, C. (1997). *Winning through innovation*. Boston, MA: Harvard Business School Press.

Tyre, M., and von Hippel, E. (1997). The situated nature of adaptive learning in organizations. *Organization Science*, 8, 71–84.

Vickers, G. (1965). *The art of judgment*. New York: Basic Books.

Weick, K. (1993). The collapse of sensemaking in organizations: the Mann Gulch disaster. *Administrative Science Quarterly*, 38, 628–52.

Weick, K. (1995). *Sensemaking in organizations*. Thousand Oaks, CA: Sage.

Weick, K., and Roberts, K. (1993). Collective mind in organizations: heedful interrelating on flight decks. *Administrative Science Quarterly*, 38(3), 357–31.

Westley, F. (1990). Middle managers and strategy: micro-dynamics of inclusion, *Strategic Management Journal*, 11, 337–351.

Yang, E., and Dougherty, D. (1993). Product innovation management: more than just making a new product. *Creativity and Innovation Management*, 2, 137–55.

Zaltman, G., Duncan, R., and Holbek, J. (1973). *Innovations and Organizations*. New York: John Wiley & Sons, Inc.

Zammuto, R., Griffith, T., Majchrzak, A., Dougherty, D., and Faraj, S. (2007). Information technology and the changing fabric of organization. *Organization Science*, 18(5), 749–62.

Part III

THE MANAGEMENT AND ORGANIZATION OF INNOVATION

6

Rival Interpretations of Balancing Exploration and Exploitation: Simultaneous or Sequential?

ERIC L. CHEN AND RIITTA KATILA

This research was supported by the National Science Foundation (Grant #0423646), Alfred P. Sloan Foundation Industry Studies Fellowship, and by Stanford Technology Ventures Program.

A long tradition of organizational literature has separated a firm's activities into two distinct realms of exploration and exploitation (March and Simon, 1958; Lawrence and Lorsch, 1967; Duncan, 1976; Mintzberg and McHugh, 1985). On the one hand, exploration encompasses behavior that increases the variance of organizational activity. As a result, its returns are often uncertain and distant in time. Exploration is 'the pursuit of knowledge, of things that might come to be known' (Levinthal and March, 1993, p. 105). On the other hand, exploitation encompasses behavior that increases the mean of organizational activity. As a result, its returns are more predictable and proximate in time (March, 1991). Exploitation is 'the use and development of things already known' (Levinthal and March, 1993, p. 105).[1]

Exploration and exploitation are particularly apt for describing different types of innovation activities, and their appropriate integration presents a consistent dilemma for innovating organizations (O'Reilly and Tushman, 2004). For instance, a typical product development strategy is likely to include exploratory projects that explore entirely new product categories as well as exploitative projects that target

---

[1] Consistent with the theoretical literature, the terms exploration and exploitation are used in this chapter to delineate specific types of *activities*. In empirical studies, exploration and exploitation are often described using outcome measures such as new product introductions or patents granted. In contrast, we focus on activities, in order to avoid tautological arguments and to enable *a priori* identification. For instance, exploitation versus exploration activities can be characterized as local versus nonlocal technology search behavior, and are not determined by the particular outcomes of search.

---

incremental improvements (Katila and Chen, 2006, 2008). Given the significance of these decisions for the entire organization and their long-term implications, an increasing stream of studies in the innovation literature has started to examine how to manage these two strategies effectively.

Several studies on technology and innovation have shown that innovative firms often use some combination of exploration and exploitation. Consequently, *balance of the two approaches* has emerged as one of the key concepts of organizational success (Tushman and O'Reilly, 1996; Katila and Ahuja, 2002; He and Wong, 2004; Laursen and Salter, 2006). Much research has argued that some degree of balance is necessary for firm survival and success: for example, scholars from a wide variety of theoretical perspectives including evolutionary (Katila and Ahuja, 2002; Laursen and Salter, 2006), organizational learning (Vermeulen and Barkema, 2001; He and Wong, 2004), organizational theory and structure (Tushman and O'Reilly, 1996), and resource-based views (Rao and Drazin, 2002); those studying product innovation, strategy, structural and human resource problems; and those using a varying set of labels such as old and new (Katila and Ahuja, 2002), stability and change (Baden-Fuller and Volberda, 1997), efficiency and flexibility (Adler, Goldoftas, and Levine, 1999), depth and breadth (Katila and Ahuja, 2002; Laursen and Salter, 2006), evolutionary and revolutionary (Tushman and O'Reilly, 1996), and exploitation and exploration (He and Wong, 2004).

Despite the significant insights regarding the importance of balancing exploration and exploitation, several rival interpretations exist on how to implement it. Our purpose in this chapter is to review these rival interpretations and synthesize previous empirical work from each approach. We also introduce an integrative framework that brings together the separate streams. By moving the discussion beyond just the elusive search for balance, the proposed framework also offers greater clarity on the strategic options that exist for firms. More specifically, it proposes that the appropriate innovation strategy for any particular firm depends on the characteristics of its environment. Firms competing in more stable environments benefit from sequentially switching between periods of exploration and exploitation while firms competing in more dynamic environments are required to explore and exploit simultaneously.

RIVAL INTERPRETATIONS OF BALANCE

Background

The scientific root of balancing exploration and exploitation lies in evolutionary biology, and is for example documented in Holland's (1975) work on complex adaptive systems. Models of adaptive systems reveal that they suffer from engaging in too much of one activity to the exclusion of the other. Exploration without exploitation results in experimentation costs without the benefits. Exploitation without exploration results in suboptimal stable equilibria. Viewing organizations as complex adaptive systems, March (1991) imports these concepts into the organizations field and argues that organizations have a similar detrimental tendency to lean towards either extreme. The subsequent proliferation of studies that have drawn upon these themes continues to support their relevance, while stressing the importance of balance, in particular for innovation (e.g., Katila and Ahuja, 2002; He and Wong, 2004; Laursen and Salter, 2006).

However, finding the appropriate balance is often difficult for firms to achieve, let alone maintain. Studies have shown that firms more often tend to lean toward too much exploitation (Benner and Tushman, 2003; Rosenkopf and Almeida, 2003), and more infrequently toward too much exploration (Miller and Friesen, 1980; Nohria and Gulati, 1996). (See also incumbent technology firms such as Dell and IBM as examples of over-exploiters, and Amazon and Apple as examples of over-explorers, frequenting the business press.) Longitudinal studies from semiconductors and chemicals similarly showcase these extreme tendencies. Sorensen and Stuart (2000, p. 106) demonstrated that older semiconductor firms in particular are likely to over-exploit, and subsequently 'produce innovations that have a lesser impact on their technological communities than do those of young firms'. In contrast, and perhaps somewhat more rarely, Ahuja and Katila (2004) documented the dangers of over-exploration in chemicals firms' scientific research: 'At high levels, exploration tends to drive out exploitation altogether. An organization that excessively exposes potential innovators to science risks their losing sight of the ultimate goal of creating useful artifacts' (p. 891).

Over time, a natural organizational tendency exists towards exploitation, making the balance point unstable. There are several reasons for this tendency. Evolutionary theory posits that organizations often become grounded in a series of common routines that favor local search behavior (Stinchcombe, 1965; Helfat, 1994; Stuart and Podolny, 1996). In addition, the rise of process management practices over the past several decades, such as programs aimed at improving quality and efficiency metrics, have often come at the cost of exploratory practices (Benner and Tushman, 2003). Similarly, the common emphasis on short-term financial performance, in particular in public firms, commonly leads to over-exploitation (Davis and Stout, 1992; Leonard-Barton, 1992; Christensen, 1997). For all these reasons, students of organizations and strategy have continued efforts to increase understanding of the dynamics of exploration and exploitation with the hope that they will lead to improved strategies for balancing the two strategies.

A review of the empirical literature that follows reveals two distinctly different conceptual approaches to balance. One approach is based on the notion that exploration and exploitation occur simultaneously within organizations. This stream stands aligned with the idea that successful complex adaptive systems must be able to balance both activities at once. A second approach argues that simultaneous balance is difficult, unnatural, and inefficient. Instead, this stream offers a sequential interpretation and posits that the tradeoff between exploration and exploitation is best overcome by periodically switching attention between them. The theoretical foundations of this approach can be traced back to studies on paradigm shifts (Kuhn, 1970; Dosi, 1982) and to the punctuated equilibrium model (Tushman and Romanelli, 1985), as well as to evolutionary processes of variation, selection, and retention (Campbell, 1969). The two approaches will be discussed next, followed by their integration.

The sequential approach

Exploration and exploitation are fundamentally conflicting activities. In fact, several researchers have questioned whether it is possible for one organization to pursue both activities simultaneously (Abernathy, 1978; Porter, 1985; Ghemawat and Costa, 1993). For example, exploration is an inefficient process – the expectation is that increased variance will not necessarily lead to any positive returns. In contrast, exploitation is fundamentally efficient. Given these incompatibilities, it is easily conceivable that an organization that tries to do both at once will succeed in neither. In response to this conflict, a set of scholars proposes that organizations should engage in the two activities *sequentially* rather than simultaneously in order to maintain a level of internal consistency. That is, the organization's innovation strategy at any point in time should focus either on increasing variety or increasing efficiency, but not on both. This interpretation of balance is temporal: periods of exploration should be moderated with periods of exploitation, and vice versa.

Early studies on the sequential approach to innovation can be traced back to the evolution of scientific paradigms (Kuhn, 1970) and technological trajectories (Dosi, 1982; Utterback, 1994). Subsequent evidence of technology S-curves (Foster, 1986; Christensen, 1992) can also be conceptualized as sequential periods of exploration and exploitation. At the beginning of the curve, significant effort and investment is required to establish a new technology or dominant design (exploration period). After this period, a dramatic increase in production and efficiency results as the innovation diffuses (exploitation period). A second inflection point in the S-curve marks the beginning of the end for that particular paradigm, at which point a new S-curve often arises, initiating a new period of exploration (Tushman and O'Reilly, 1997).

Ideas on technological paradigm shifts can also be translated into an evolutionary framework that supports the prudence of a sequential approach. In particular, Tushman and Anderson's (1986) examination of technological discontinuities offers descriptive reasons for why it may not be necessary or wise for firms to engage continuously in both exploration and exploitation. By examining patterns of technological change in multiple industries, the authors demonstrate that industries evolve through 'periods of incremental change punctuated by technological breakthroughs' (Tushman and Anderson, 1986, p. 439). In other words, industries go through periods dominated by exploitation that are interrupted by shorter periods of exploration. Similarly, Tyre and Orlikowski (1993) showed that technology evolution is characterized by natural windows of opportunity for significant change that are separated by periods of minor adjustments, and that the most innovative firms are those that take advantage of both phases: they explore significantly during windows of opportunity and exploit unceasingly during subsequent periods of minor adjustment.

Sequential models are also closely related to the processes of variation, selection, and retention (Campbell, 1969; Nelson and Winter, 1982). Indeed, the variation-selection-retention cycle mirrors that of exploration-exploitation. Exploration serves the functions of increasing variation and probing the environment to select a dominant design. Once selected, the design is retained, as well as disseminated and improved, through exploitation.

Several empirical studies also confirm the sequential interpretation of balance. For instance, Winter and Szulanski (2001) examined sequential balance in their study of business model innovation and its replication, i.e., the business process exemplified by McDonalds in which a large number of similar outlets are created for delivering a product or service. Although replication itself is a process of exploitation, Winter and Szulanski showed that an exploratory process precedes replication. This exploration phase involves experimentation leading to the discovery of a successful business model as well as an understanding of which components of the model are necessary to replicate. The success of replication strategies is evidenced by the profits achieved by the number of large corporations that employ them. Another successful example of a sequential approach is a two-stage product development model of Pixar Animation Studios. Pixar typically first explores the new technical features of a movie separately (e.g., through short films, such as *Geri's Game*) and then proceeds to exploit the successful ideas from the experiments in full feature-length films (e.g., *A Bug's Life*).

Although the exploration-to-exploitation periods and transitions are carefully crafted in the examples described above, there are also situations in which the same process occurs less as a result of strategic agency and more as a result of institutional factors. For instance, in a longitudinal study of Hollywood studio heads, Miller and Shamsie (2001) examined the relationships between exploration, exploitation, and executive tenure, and deconstructed the CEO life cycle into three distinct periods. The earliest period of the life cycle, the learning stage, is marked by a high level of product line experimentation and relatively modest financial performance. The second period, the harvest stage, is characterized by decreased experimentation and high financial performance. The final period, the decline stage, reveals even lower experimentation and a decline in financial performance. In terms of organizational learning, these CEOs begin their tenures by exploring different genres, talent, and procedures followed by exploiting the methods that are successful to the point where they become stale and outdated. Once they are replaced, the life cycle repeats itself, and over time a sequential pattern develops.

Another example that illustrates the sequential model in the context of organic growth is the Intel Corporation. The rise of Intel to its status as the world's dominant semiconductor manufacturer corresponded with the tenure of Andy Grove and his singular focus that led to coevolutionary lock-in with the personal computer market segment (Burgelman, 2002). Burgelman conceptualized this focus as strategic exploitation that originated at the top of the organizational hierarchy. The mantra 'copy exactly' coupled with countless incremental improvements to develop more efficient production were key characteristics of this strategy. However, as the growth of the PC market slowed and the development of the Internet expanded, Intel found itself in need of a transition to more exploration – one of the reasons it selected Craig Barrett as the next CEO. Grove had successfully led the firm through a period of exploitation, and Barrett was expected to transition the company into a new period of exploration. This temporal pattern is characteristic of the sequential interpretation of balance.

Empirical studies on inter-organizational resource acquisition such as acquisitions and alliances also provide support for the sequential model. Vermeulen and

TABLE 6.1 Selected papers on technology and innovation: sequential approach to balance.

Study	Sample	Exploration terms	Exploitation terms	Key findings and implications for exploration and exploitation
Organic resource development				
Tushman and Anderson (1986)	US cement, airline, and minicomputer firms, from inception to 1980	Competence-destroying	Competence-enhancing	Technological change within a product class is characterized by long periods of incremental change punctuated by discontinuities. Competence-destroying discontinuities are introduced by new firms, and competence-enhancing discontinuities by incumbents.
Winter and Szulanski (2001)	Banc One, 1970–1995	Experimentation, discovery	Replication	Firms must first engage in exploration to find a successful business model and then exploit it through replication of the model.
Burgelman (2002)	Intel Corporation, 1987–1998	Autonomous strategy (bottom-up)	Induced strategy (top-down)	Intel's success in semiconductors was a result of Grove's induced strategy towards incremental improvement. The necessity to explore more led to management turnover and a more autonomous strategy.

Inter-organizational resource acquisition

Vermeulen and Barkema (2001)	25 largest nonfinancial companies on the Amsterdam Stock Exchange, 1993; and a computer simulation	Acquisition	Greenfield (newly formed subsidiary of a firm)	Firms strike a temporal balance between the use of greenfields and acquisitions that is clearly patterned – the more a firm expands through acquisitions, the more likely it is to use greenfields, and vice versa.
Rothaermel and Deeds (2004)	325 global biotech firms in 2565 alliances, 1973–1997	Exploration alliances (upstream activities)	Exploitation alliances (downstream activities)	Biotechnology ventures that use a sequential alliance strategy (first upstream then downstream alliances) introduce more products in development and on the market.
Puranam, Singh, and Zollo (2006)	207 acquisitions of small US technology firms by large established firms, 1988–1998	Autonomy	Coordination	Successful post-acquisition integration that improves innovation performance is characterized by a sequential approach to balance. Autonomy (exploration) is more important than coordination (exploitation) immediately following the acquisition, and vice versa later.

Barkema (2001) contrasted greenfields, i.e., newly formed affiliates of a firm, with acquisitions. The authors argued that when firms create greenfields they are inclined to impose existing organizational routines and habits on the new subsidiary (that is, they engage in exploitation). In contrast, the integration of an acquired firm can lead to organizational conflict that may break the buyer out of its inertial state (that is, enable exploration). Both simulation and archival analysis revealed that once a firm has used acquisitions as a dominant method of expansion for some time, it becomes increasingly likely to use greenfields for its next expansion. Once the switch to greenfield expansions has been made, the firm will continue to utilize them for a period until it switches back to acquisitions. Over time, a clear pattern forms that follows the sequential approach. Similarly, Puranam *et al.* (2006) showed how successful buyers used a sequential model that clearly separated periods of exploration from periods of exploitation when they integrated acquisitions.

Empirical studies on alliances also confirm the sequential pattern. In a longitudinal study of strategic alliances in biotechnology, Rothaermel and Deeds (2004) modeled a product development path that proceeds from exploration to exploitation. They found that research alliances dominate early parts of the product life cycle (exploration phase) whereas commercialization alliances are more common later in the life cycle (exploitation phase). A key finding was that new ventures that followed a sequential exploration-exploitation alliance strategy introduced more products than those following other types of strategies.

Taken together, several empirical studies that have focused on a wide range of organic and inter-firm resource development activities support a sequential balance of exploration and exploitation. Early development of a new technology, business, or product is often characterized by a phase of significant exploration, followed by a focused period of exploitation. In addition, multiple mechanisms influence the transition between the two phases. Executive tenure and control can lead the firm through distinct phases, for example. In addition to these descriptive findings, normative findings demonstrate that some firms are successful precisely because they sequentially switch attention between exploration and exploitation. Table 6.1 summarizes several recent studies that have documented a sequential pattern.

The simultaneous approach

Despite the significant advances in understanding the sequential approach, another stream of literature provides equally strong support for a *simultaneous* model of balancing exploration and exploitation. In line with adaptive systems research, this stream of studies has approached exploration and exploitation as activities that reinforce each other and so must occur simultaneously. The concept of mutual learning, in which both the individual beliefs and the organizational code converge over time, is one of the fundamental features of the March (1991) model. March finds that achieving optimal organizational learning requires an appropriate balance of mutual learning rates.

Several studies on product innovation have similarly provided support for the simultaneous balance between exploration and exploitation (e.g., Katila and Ahuja, 2002; Laursen and Salter, 2006). For instance, in a longitudinal study of new product development in 124 robotics firms, Katila and Ahuja (2002) found a significant interaction effect between deep exploitation and wide exploration of technologies, indicating that at least some firms were able to engage in both approaches at the same time. Their results also provided evidence that firms that simultaneously pursue both approaches, rather than those that engage in either approach alone, are more innovative. That is, robotics firms that introduce the most new products do so by leveraging a combination of new and existing technology resources, rather than relying on new resources alone. Similarly, a recent study of corporate venture units showed that those following a simultaneous approach, which gave dual importance to both using existing capabilities and to building new capabilities, innovated more (Hill and Birkinshaw, 2006).

Danneels (2002) also looked at the dynamics of product innovation to better understand the roles of exploration and exploitation. This study defined the development of new products that draw on existing competencies as exploitation and those that require competencies that the firm does not yet have as exploration. Using field study results, he developed a 2 × 2 typology that further delineated exploration and exploitation by examining competencies both in terms of technology and customers. Pure exploration takes place when both technological and customer competencies are new to the firm, pure exploitation when both already exist in the firm. Case studies of high-tech B2B firms revealed that much new product development takes place in the remaining two quadrants outside of either pure form. In each of these quadrants, either technological or customer competence for the new product already exists in the firm but the other does not. These cases result in the firm leveraging the existing competence and combining it with the new competence. More simply stated, the firm is simultaneously exploiting its existing technologies (or customers) to explore a new customer market (or technology). This process closely resembles the recombinatory process that takes place in 'technology brokering', in which old knowledge is applied to new uses to create superior designs (Hargadon and Sutton, 1997).

The above papers on simultaneous balance all emphasize organic development of resources. Other work has also demonstrated the significance of the model in the context of inter-organizational resource acquisition. Research on acquisitions, for example, has been particularly influential. Karim and Mitchell (2000) focused on acquisitions in the medical sector as a vehicle to extend existing resources and to obtain new ones. They suggested two contrasting roles for acquisitions: acquisitions can deepen existing resource bases (path-dependent change, i.e., exploitation) and they can move the firm to new areas that require substantially different resources (path-breaking change, i.e., exploration). Their data support both types of change: acquiring firms deepen existing resources by retaining target firm product lines that are similar to their own, while, at the same time, extend into new areas by retaining target firm medical categories that are distinct from their own. Ahuja and Katila (2001) similarly showed that successful buyers in the chemicals industry balance exploration and exploitation by acquiring target firms that are somewhat related but not too similar. Finally, in line with March's (1991) model, Karim and Mitchell (2000) suggested that in successful acquisitions both the buyer and the target learn from each other, thus supporting the simultaneous interpretation of balance.

TABLE 6.2 Selected papers on technology and innovation: simultaneous approach to balance.

Study	Sample	Exploration terms	Exploitation terms	Key findings and implications for exploration and exploitation
Organic resource development				
Tushman and O'Reilly (1996, 1997)	Multiple case studies of mainly US-based firms	Revolutionary change	Evolutionary change	Successful technology firms manage dual strategies where they support exploitation in mature divisions and exploration in divisions that need to be revitalized.
Katila and Ahuja (2002)	124 robotics companies in Europe, Japan, and North America, 1985–1996	Search scope	Search depth	Firms that balance their efforts on two fronts by simultaneously both reusing their existing knowledge (search depth) and exploring new knowledge (search scope) introduce new products more frequently.
He and Wong (2004)	206 manufacturing firms in Singapore and Malaysia, 1999–2000	Exploratory innovation strategy	Exploitative innovation strategy	Firms that explore and exploit simultaneously, and invest in both strategies at equal levels, grow faster (but do not have significantly higher product innovation).
Katila and Chen (2006)	71 industrial automation companies in Japan, Europe, and the US, 1984–1998	Early-mover	Late-mover	Firms create the most innovative product portfolios when they move early in some technology areas while simultaneously moving late in others.

Inter-organizational resource acquisition

		Exploration (turnover)	Exploitation (socialization)	
March (1991)	Simulation model of impact of employee socialization and turnover rates on organizational knowledge			Organizations with hiring strategies that balance short-term exploitation (old, mean-seeking activity) with long-term exploration (new, variance-seeking activity) live longer and perform better.
Rao and Drazin (2002)	Recruitment of portfolio managers in 588 US mutual funds, 1986–1994	Novices	Veterans	Firms that introduce new products more frequently, balance exploration and exploitation in recruiting. New firms recruit industry veterans to gain industry experience and old firms recruit novices to gain new ideas.
Karim and Mitchell (2004)	Johnson & Johnson; 88 medical sector business units (incl. 54 acquired), 1975–1997	Boundary-redefinition	Routines	Innovation stems from maintaining a deep understanding of organizationally-embedded routines (exploitation) while undertaking redefinition of unit and firm boundaries (exploration).

Taken together, several empirical studies reviewed above, both from organic and inter-organizational perspectives, provide significant support for a simultaneous model of balance. The authors show that a simultaneous balance of exploration and exploitation may be difficult to implement, but often produces beneficial results. For example, the findings showed that some firms are able to explore and exploit simultaneously, and those that did so introduced new products more frequently, adapted to rapidly changing environments more swiftly, and created more value through acquisitions. The main insight of this set of studies is that exploration and exploitation need not always be competing activities, but can and should be complementary. Table 6.2 summarizes recent studies that document a simultaneous pattern.

TOWARD AN INTEGRATIVE FRAMEWORK

Balancing the dual processes of exploration and exploitation is a constant struggle for firms and their managers. As a result, innovation researchers across a wide variety of theoretical disciplines and empirical focuses have offered insights on the subject. The above review of the current literature shows that these interpretations can be categorized into two approaches: simultaneous and sequential. Given these rival interpretations, several new questions arise. One is how to reconcile the two approaches, which are based on fundamentally different theoretical perspectives on balance. Another question is how to resolve empirical findings that offer support for both interpretations and show that both approaches can support and stimulate innovation. Third, it is unclear which types of challenges underlie the successful implementation of each approach. Simultaneous and sequential approaches demonstrate different prescriptions for stimulating innovation, and are likely to present distinct managerial challenges as well. In this section, we propose a framework that begins to integrate the two approaches.

Integrated model of balance

One approach to resolving an apparent contradiction between simultaneous and sequential approaches is to take into account that organizations face a spectrum of different competitive environments. Since early contingency theory, scholars have pointed out that successful organizations create a fit with their environmental conditions (Lawrence and Lorsch, 1967; Thompson, 1967). For example, the strategies needed to succeed in 'high-velocity' markets (Brown and Eisenhardt, 1998) differ from those required in more stable environments. Although several environmental characteristics are likely to be significant for balance, in this chapter we differentiate between two types of environments, stable and dynamic, because of their significance for innovation activities. More stable environments have lengthy production cycles and follow clear technological trends whereas demands for successful innovation are likely to change rapidly and in more unpredictable ways in dynamic environments.

First, several arguments support the idea that the simultaneous approach is more appropriate in dynamic environments. In landscapes where conditions are constantly changing, it is vital that firms simultaneously explore and exploit. One major implication of managing under these conditions is that careful, long-term strategic planning is less effective. Instead, firms must continually explore for new opportunities, and be prepared to exploit them as they arise. Firms competing in more dynamic markets do not have time to switch from exploration to exploitation mode because the window of opportunity is often very short. Thus, the best strategy for firms facing highly dynamic environments is to engage in simultaneous exploration and exploitation.

Comparatively, in more stable, established environments, firms are afforded the luxury of sequential switching. Industries such as cement and airlines analyzed by Tushman and Anderson (1986) are characterized by significant periods of stability before being punctuated by major change. Given these features, firms are able to predict more accurately environmental conditions and their evolution, and can concentrate on either exploration or exploitation depending on the environmental state.

Our analysis of empirical studies described above and summarized in Tables 6.1 and 6.2 provide support for this integrative model. Studies that emphasized the simultaneous approach typically include firms in more dynamic, technology-based industries. Firms analyzed by Brown and Eisenhardt (1997), Katila and Ahuja (2002), and Danneels (2002) competed in information technology, robotics, and B2B products, respectively. Similarly, Karim and Mitchell (2000) focused on medical sector product lines in which new, competing devices were steadily being generated by a wide array of firms. In contrast, studies that provided support for a more sequential approach focused on more stable industries such as cement, airlines, and minicomputers (Tushman and Anderson, 1986). Each of these industries is characterized by long and predictable product technology life cycles, and by conditions that are relatively stable with the rare exception of disruption events. Other industries that offer support for a sequential approach range from semiconductors (Burgelman, 2002) to feature films (Miller and Shamsie, 2001). In each case, firms engage in lengthy periods of exploitation equated with high performance, and only shift to an exploration phase when the industry is in search of a new dominant design. For example, Intel made famous the predictable speed of technological advance in semiconductors (Moore's Law).

Although the studies reviewed above show clear support for the environmental contingency model, several recent studies have also proposed an alternative approach to integrate the simultaneous and sequential approaches. Rather than posit the two approaches as competing alternatives, these studies argue for an 'open source' model where firms do not need to make a choice between exploration and exploitation, but can pursue both simultaneously, mainly by 'outsourcing' exploration (e.g., Laursen and Salter, 2006). For example Katila (2002) demonstrated how new product innovators explore externally created knowledge while simultaneously exploiting their internal knowledge. In this view, firms can explore and exploit sequentially, as long as the organization is able to effectively use others' 'simultaneous' exploration. Other authors have proposed similar solutions where exploration and exploitation occur simultaneously but are structurally (rather than temporally) separated or where the organizational context is simultaneously supportive for both exploration and exploitation (Gibson and Birkinshaw, 2004). These integrative models provide intriguing avenues for future work, and further emphasize the importance of integrating the two approaches.

Implementation challenges

In addition to new solutions to resolving the tension between exploration and exploitation, several open questions also remain about implementation. The sequential approach has emphasized the processes of variation, selection, and retention that enable organizations to evolve into an efficient form. Furthering the biological analogy, those firms that are unable to evolve or adapt are naturally-selected out. However, the same adaptive mechanisms that increase environmental fit put high performing incumbents at risk when faced with sudden changes in the landscape (Christensen, 1997). In related terms, adaptive processes refine exploitation faster than exploration (March, 1991). This imbalance is further magnified in more stable environments where firms face greater inertial pressures that result from the establishment of organizational routines (Stinchcombe, 1965) and institutionalization (Meyer and Rowan, 1977). Thus, due to this skew towards exploitation, the fundamental source of imbalance in the sequential approach is maladaptation. As a result, most innovation studies have focused on examining how to increase exploratory activity and improve its outcomes (e.g., Leonard-Barton, 1992; Ahuja and Lampert, 2001; Rosenkopf and Nerkar, 2001).

In contrast, the simultaneous approach to balance is subject to being at a dissipative equilibrium (Brown and Eisenhardt, 1998). Therefore, the fundamental source of imbalance for firms is a tendency to slip either into too much exploration or too much exploitation. But with some exceptions (Gersick, 1991; Brown and Eisenhardt, 1998; Ahuja and Katila, 2004), few empirical studies have discussed the case of over-exploration. Instead, the majority of proposed solutions are part of the same research stream that treats too much exploitation as the main problem and increased exploration as the lofty goal.

To summarize, the sequential approach tends to adapt towards too much exploitation while the simultaneous approach is subject to dissipative equilibrium that can easily destabilize in either direction. However, the majority of the innovation studies have focused on only one side of the solution – namely, improving mechanisms for exploration – even though under-exploitation may provide equally important challenges.

DISCUSSION

Early work on organizations established the fundamental organizational tendencies towards path-dependent behavior. Our subsequent understanding of the tradeoffs between exploration and exploitation highlighted the dangers of such path-dependent tendencies and the desirability of balancing the two activities, especially in the context of innovation. This chapter reviewed the current innovation literature on exploration–exploitation balance. Although both concepts are heavily cited in the literature, the meaning of their balance is often ambiguous and multifaceted. In trying to uncover the concept, we reviewed in detail the modes of activity being considered, the types of knowledge that are created and utilized, and the methods of managerial behavior employed. Our review revealed rival interpretations of balance and called for an integrative framework that is more specific about the terms and activities being discussed.

Our review illustrated empirical studies supporting both a simultaneous and a sequential approach to balancing exploration and exploitation. The simultaneous approach, following a complexity theory foundation, advocates organizations engaging in both activities at the same time. Although subject to unstable equilibrium, a balance that enables complementarities between exploration and exploitation has proven beneficial. The sequential approach, following an evolutionary theory foundation, advocates organizations alternating between each activity in turn. In this approach the challenge is to avoid the pitfall of a stable but unbalanced equilibrium towards too much exploitation. Based on features of environmental turbulence, a framework was proposed to reconcile these two interpretations in which the simultaneous approach performs better in dynamic environments and the sequential approach in stable environments.

Our review of the balance literature also reveals two main avenues for future research. First, studies of innovation have almost uniformly made the assumption that more exploration is better. Few empirical investigations have been directed at the problem of over-exploration, and, even fewer, to better understanding effective exploitation. However, our discussion on the dissipative equilibrium that characterizes simultaneous balance indicates that firms are just as likely to err in one direction as in the other. More empirical studies of entrepreneurial firms in emerging industries and more studies on effective exploitation by incumbent firms are fruitful directions for future work.

Second, we need to better understand the relationship between the simultaneous and sequential approaches. The first integrative framework proposed in this paper couples each approach with a particular type of environment. However, there is an opportunity to conceptualize environments in a more realistic manner, as continuous rather than as binary states, and to determine the point at which one approach outperforms the other. In addition, our framework mirrors current organization theory in that it assumes for the most part that environments are exogenous and unchanging. In reality, organizations do not compete under constant conditions, and do impact their environments. In fact, they are likely to consciously attempt to change the competitive landscape in their favor, and to interact across increasingly permeable organizational boundaries (e.g., Katila and Chen, 2006, 2008; Laursen and Salter, 2006). One hypothesis is that leading firms in emergent industries attempt to manage the uncertainty by making the environment more stable as it matures (Thompson, 1967). As a result, they are also able to move from a simultaneous approach to a sequential one that may be easier to manage because it demands focus on only one activity at a time and avoidance of maladaptation in only one direction. A related issue that could be examined in more detail in future work is the effects of different types of environments, such as how environmental complexity and munificence affect the choice of innovation strategies (e.g., Katila and Shane, 2005).

REFERENCES

Abernathy, W.J. (1978). *The productivity dilemma: roadblock to innovation in the automobile industry.* Baltimore, MA: Johns Hopkins University Press.

Adler, P.S., Goldoftas, B., and Levine, D.I. (1999). Flexibility versus efficiency? A case study of model changeovers in the Toyota Production System. *Organization Science*, 10(1), 43–68.

Ahuja, G., and Katila, R. (2001). Technological acquisitions and the innovation performance of acquiring firms: a longitudinal study. *Strategic Management Journal*, 22, 197–220.

Ahuja, G., and Katila, R. (2004). Where do resources come from? The role of idiosyncratic situations. *Strategic Management Journal*, 25(8/9), 887–907.

Ahuja, G., and Lampert, C.M. (2001). Entrepreneurship in the large corporation: A longitudinal study of how established firms create breakthrough inventions. *Strategic Management Journal*, 22, 521–43.

Baden-Fuller, C., and Volberda, H.W. (1997). Strategic renewal. *International Studies of Management and Organization*, 27(2), 95–120.

Benner, M., and Tushman, M.L. (2003). Exploitation, exploration, and process management: the productivity dilemma revisited. *Academy of Management Review*, 28(2), 238–56.

Brown, S.L., and Eisenhardt, K.M. (1997). The art of continuous change: linking complexity theory and time-paced evolution in relentlessly shifting organizations. *Administrative Science Quarterly*, 42, 1–34.

Brown, S.L., and Eisenhardt, K. (1998). *Competing on the edge – strategy as structured chaos.* Boston, MA: Harvard Business School Press.

Burgelman, R.A. (2002). Strategy as vector and the inertia of co-evolutionary lock-in. *Administrative Science Quarterly*, 47, 325–57.

Campbell, D.T. (1969). Variation and selective retention in socio-cultural environments. *General Systems*, 14, 69–85.

Christensen, C.M. (1992). The limits of the technology S-curve. Parts I and II. *Production and Operations Management*, 1, 334–66.

Christensen, C.M. (1997). *The innovator's dilemma: when new technologies cause great firms to fail.* Boston, MA: Harvard Business School Press.

Danneels, E. (2002). The dynamics of product innovation and firm competencies. *Strategic Management Journal*, 23(12), 1095.

Davis, G.F., and Stout, S.K. (1992). Organization theory and the market for corporate control: a dynamic analysis of the characteristics of large takeover targets, 1980–1990. *Administrative Science Quarterly*, 37(4), 605–33.

Dosi, G. (1982). Technological paradigms and technological trajectories. *Research Policy*, 11, 147–62.

Duncan, R.B. (1976). The ambidextrous organization: designing dual structures for innovation. In R.H. Kilmann, L.R. Pondy, and D. Slevin (eds), *The Management of Organization*, New York: North-Holland, vol. 1, 167–88.

Foster, R. (1986). The S-curve: a new forecasting tool. *Innovation. The attacker's advantage.* New York: Summit Books, Simon and Schuster.

Gersick, C. (1991). Revolutionary change theories: a multi-level exploration of the punctuated equilibrium paradigm. *Academy of Management Review*, 16, 10–36.

Ghemawat, P., and Costa, J. (1993). The organizational tension between static and dynamic efficiency. *Strategic Management Journal*, 14(8), 59–73.

Gibson, C.B., and Birkinshaw, J. (2004). The antecedents, consequences, and mediating role of organizational ambidexterity. *Academy of Management Journal*, 47(2), 209–26.

Hargadon, A., and Sutton, R.I. (1997). Technology brokering and innovation in a product development firm. *Administrative Science Quarterly*, 42, 716–49.

He, Z.-L., and Wong, P.-K. (2004). Exploration vs. exploitation: an empirical test of the ambidexterity hypothesis. *Organization Science*, 15(4), 481–94.

Helfat, C.E. (1994). Evolutionary trajectories in petroleum firm R&D. *Management Science*, 40, 1720–47.

Hill, S., and Birkinshaw, J. (2006). Ambidexterity in corporate venturing: simultaneously using existing and building new capabilities. *Academy of Management Proceedings*, C1–C6.

Holland, J.H. (1975). *Adaptation in natural and artificial systems: an introductory analysis with applications to biology, control and artificial intelligence*. Ann Arbor, MA: University of Michigan Press.

Karim, S., and Mitchell, W. (2000). Path-dependent and path-breaking change: reconfiguring business resources following acquisitions in the U.S. medical sector, 1978–1995. *Strategic Management Journal*, 21(11), 1061–81.

Karim, S., and Mitchell, W. (2004). Innovating through acquisition and internal development. *Long Range Planning*, 37(6), 525–47.

Katila, R. (2002). New product search over time: past ideas in their prime? *Academy of Management Journal*, 5, 995–1010.

Katila, R., and Ahuja, G. (2002). Something old, something new: a longitudinal study of search behavior and new product introduction. *Academy of Management Journal*, 45(6), 1183–94.

Katila, R., and Chen, E. (2006). Never too early, never too late: effects of search timing on product innovation. *Academy of Management Best Paper Proceedings*, Atlanta: Academy of Management: OMT: O1–O6.

Katila, R., and Chen, E. (2008). Effects of search timing on product innovation: the value of not being in sync. *Administrative Science Quarterly*, in press.

Katila, R., and Shane, S. (2005). When does lack of resources make new firms innovative? *Academy of Management Journal*, 48(5), 814–29.

Kuhn, T. (1970). *The structure of scientific revolutions*. Chicago, IL: University of Chicago Press.

Laursen, K., and Salter, A. (2006). Open for innovation: the role of openness in explaining innovation performance among U.K. manufacturing firms. *Strategic Management Journal*, 27(2), 131–50.

Lawrence, P.R., and Lorsch, J.W. (1967). *Organization and environment: managing differentiation and integration*. Boston, MA: Harvard University Press.

Leonard-Barton, D. (1992). Core capabilities and core rigidities: a paradox in managing new product development. *Strategic Management Journal*, 13, 111–25.

Levinthal, D.A., and March, J.G. (1993). The myopia of learning. *Strategic Management Journal*, 14, 95–112.

March, J.G. (1991). Exploration and exploitation in organizational learning. *Organization Science*, 2(1), 71–87.

March, J., and Simon, H. (1958). *Organizations*. New York: John Wiley & Sons, Inc.

Meyer, J.W., and Rowan, B. (1977). Institutionalized organizations: formal structure as myth and ceremony. *American Journal of Sociology*, 83, 340–63.

Miller, D., and Friesen, P.H. (1980). Momentum and revolution in organizational adaptation. *Academy of Management Journal*, 23(4), 591–614.

Miller, D., and Shamsie, J. (2001). Learning across the life cycle: experimentation and performance among the Hollywood studio heads. *Strategic Management Journal*, 22, 725–45.

Mintzberg, H., and McHugh, A. (1985). Strategy formation in an adhocracy. *Administrative Science Quarterly*, 30, 160–97.

Nelson, R.R., and Winter, S.G. (1982). *An evolutionary theory of economic change*. Cambridge, MA: Belknap – Harvard University Press.

Nohria, N., and Gulati, R. (1996). Is slack good or bad for innovation? *Academy of Management Journal*, 39(5), 1245–64.

O'Reilly, C.A., III, and Tushman, M.L. (2004). The ambidextrous organization. *Harvard Business Review*, 82(4), 74–81.

Porter, M.E. (1985). *Competitive advantage*. Boston, MA: Free Press.

Puranam, P., Singh, H., and Zollo, M. (2006). Organizing for innovation: managing the coordination-autonomy dilemma in technology acquisitions. *Academy of Management Journal*, 49(2), 263–80.

Rao, H., and Drazin, R. (2002). Overcoming resource constraints on product innovation by recruiting talent from rivals: a study of the mutual fund industry, 1986–94. *Academy of Management Journal*, 45(3), 491–507.

Rosenkopf, L., and Almeida, P. (2003). Overcoming local search through alliances and mobility. *Management Science*, 49(6), 751–66.

Rosenkopf, L., and Nerkar, A. (2001). Beyond local search: boundary-spanning, exploration and impact in the optical disc industry. *Strategic Management Journal*, 22, 287–306.

Rothaermel, F.T., and Deeds, D.L. (2004). Exploration and exploitation alliances in biotechnology: a system of new product development. *Strategic Management Journal*, 25, 287–306.

Sorensen, J.B., and Stuart, T.E. (2000). Aging, obsolescence and organizational innovation. *Administrative Science Quarterly*, 45(1), 81–112.

Stinchcombe, A.L. (1965). Social structure and organizations. In J.G. March (ed.), *Handbook of Organizations*, 142–93. Chicago, IL: Rand McNally and Company.

Stuart, T., and Podolny, J. (1996). Local search and evolution of technological capabilities. *Strategic Management Journal*, 17, 21–38.

Thompson, J.D. (1967). *Organizations in action*. New York: McGraw-Hill.

Tushman, M.L., and Anderson, P. (1986). Technological discontinuities and organizational environments. *Administrative Science Quarterly*, 31, 439–65.

Tushman, M.L., and O'Reilly, C.A., III. (1996). Ambidextrous organizations: managing evolutionary and revolutionary change. *California Management Review*, 38(4), 8–30.

Tushman, M.L., and O'Reilly, C.A., III. (1997). *Winning through innovation: a practical guide to leading organizational change and renewal*. Boston, MA: Harvard Business School Press.

Tushman, M., and Romanelli, E. (1985). Organizational evolution: a metamorphosis model of convergence and reorientation. In L.L. Cummings, and B.M. Staw (eds), *Research in Organizational Behavior*, Vol. 7, 171–222. Greenwich, CT: JAI Press.

Tyre, M., and Orlikowski, W. (1993). Exploiting opportunities for technological improvement. *Sloan Management Review*, 35(1), 13–26.

Utterback, J. (1994). *Mastering the dynamics of innovation*. Boston, MA: Harvard Business School Press.

Vermeulen, F., and Barkema, H.G. (2001). Learning through acquisitions. *Academy of Management Journal*, 44(3), 457–76.

Winter, S., and Szulanski, G. (2001). Replication as strategy. *Organization Science*, 12(6), 730–43.

7

R&D Project Selection and Portfolio Management: A Review of the Past, a Description of the Present, and a Sketch of the Future

D. Brunner, L. Fleming[1], A. MacCormack, and D. Zinner

Introduction

The selection of R&D projects has been recognized as an important problem since the 1950s and 1960s, and its importance has grown with intensifying global competition and accelerating technological change. Academics and practitioners have proposed hundreds of techniques to help managers decide which projects to fund. Yet despite the volume of proposed solutions, project selection has turned out to be an extremely difficult problem. A few selection techniques have become popular in industry, but none has proved wholly satisfactory.

Given this context of an unsolved managerial and academic problem, we develop a review of existing literature, a description of current managerial challenges, and a sketch of future research. The literature review begins by describing the major families of project selection techniques. We have included the techniques that attract significant attention in the academic literature, as well as those techniques that are common in practice. Each section comprises a brief explanation of the technique; a discussion of its strengths, weaknesses, and use in industry; and pointers to seminal papers, surveys, case studies, or other informative articles. The project selection problem can also be decomposed into two parts, which we examine separately: how to determine the value of individual projects, and how to choose a portfolio of projects that are optimal given the firm's objectives (Baker and Freeland, 1975; Winkofsky *et al.*, 1980). These two components are closely related, but a clear distinction can be drawn between project evaluation models that focus

[1]Corresponding author at lfleming@hbs.edu.

Handbook of Technology and Innovation Management.   Edited by Scott Shane
© 2008 John Wiley & Sons, Ltd

on the former and portfolio selection models that attempt to address the latter.[2] Following the literature review, we describe two current managerial challenges that cannot be solved with current tools. For example, managers within industries with highly skewed returns such as pharmaceuticals and movies must plan a portfolio where the modal project loses money, the average outcome is negative, and the occasional blockbuster reaps most of the returns. Many industries are also moving to distributed models of research and development. Where firms used to develop all of their projects internally, they must now manage a distributed network of opportunities and outcomes. We conclude by outlining what we see as the most salient issues for research, based on our review and description of current challenges.

For those seeking more information on the field in general, there is no shortage of survey papers and books. Reviews of the early literature may be found in Baker and Pound (1964), Cetron *et al.* (1967), and Dean (1968). The survey by Steele (1988) is particularly insightful, if somewhat dated. Helpful recent works include practitioner-oriented handbooks by Martino (1995) and Cooper *et al.* (1998). Martino includes an annotated bibliography comprising over 50 articles. Two studies of actual management practices illuminate the nature of the theory-practice gap: Liberatore and Titus (1983) and Cooper *et al.* (2001).

Project Evaluation Models

Project evaluation models seek to determine the absolute or relative value of individual projects. Outputs from these models can be used to make go/no go decisions about particular projects or to rank projects against each other (Cooper *et al.*, 2001). However, these models are of limited value in selecting project portfolios. Indeed, a portfolio constructed by selecting those projects valued most highly by a project evaluation model is almost certain to be suboptimal, because these models do not effectively account for interactions between projects. Nor do project evaluation models offer any insight into how resources should be allocated among the most attractive projects. Portfolio selection models, discussed in the subsequent section, seek to address these issues.

We divide project evaluation models into economic value models and scoring models. *Economic value models* estimate financial returns based on revenue and cost forecasts. They incorporate only factors with direct and quantifiable impact on financial outcomes. *Relative value models* evaluate projects by comparing them against fixed scales or other projects. In contrast to economic value models, relative value models can – and often do – include nonfinancial criteria. In the following sections, we describe both approaches in more detail.

Economic value models

Economic value models are probably the most popular R&D project selection methodology. According to a recent study, they are used by 77 % of firms (Cooper

---

[2]Note that these terms are by no means standard in the field; taxonomies of project selection techniques have appeared in literature surveys since the 1960s, but none seems to have become dominant. The taxonomy used here is our own, although it borrows heavily from others, especially those of Baker and Freeland (1975) and Hall and Nauda (1990).

et al., 2001). The wide use of economic value models reflects many important strengths, some of which are quite obvious. To begin with, economic value models seek to evaluate projects based on profitability, which is generally the single most important criterion for project selection in industrial R&D. The outputs of economic value models are convenient, absolute measures of project value in forms familiar to financially-oriented managers (Steele, 1988).

In addition to generating useful outputs, the process of using economic value models can be valuable in itself. Using economic value models can help clarify and quantify assumptions, aid understanding of project dynamics, facilitate cross-functional communication and process planning, and add analytical rigor to the evaluation process. The benefits of using a standard, quantitative evaluation methodology can reach back to the project generation stage. In an article describing the adoption of a net present value-based economic value model at General Motors, Bordley writes, 'We quickly discovered that the main benefits of the project-selection system were not in discovering the best projects to fund but in stimulating researchers to develop better projects' (Bordley, 1998).

Despite their popularity, economic value models suffer from significant limitations. Perhaps most fundamentally, their outputs are not accurate. The models omit many criteria that are difficult to quantify but have significant influence on project profitability, such as timing of major activities and cash flows, project interdependencies, human resources, strategic fit, brand impact, and capability-building. Consequently, the set of projects with the highest value is unlikely to represent a truly optimal portfolio. Furthermore, economic value models rely on estimates of future sales and costs likely to be highly inaccurate (Roussel *et al.*, 1991; Cooper *et al.*, 1998). The problem is compounded by the analytical structure and quantitative output of economic value models, which suggest levels of rigor and certainty that are both unjustified and potentially deceptive (Roussel *et al.* 1991).

Several categories of economic value models can be distinguished based on the way they handle risk. Basic cost-benefit models generally account for risk by adding a risk premium to the rate used to discount future cash flows or by multiplying cash flows by one or more probabilities of success. More sophisticated models seek to make explicit the level and nature of risk inherent in different projects. These models include decision tree models, Monte Carlo simulations, and real options models. We describe each family of models in more detail below.

Basic cost-benefit models. These models include well-known measures of financial returns such as net present value (NPV), internal rate of return (IRR), and payback period. Other measures can be used to quantify different aspects of financial return. For example, Cooper *et al.* (1998) describe a simple 'productivity index' used by some firms to quantify return per unit of R&D expenditure.

Basic cost-benefit models are the simplest and most convenient variety of economic value model, but they also have the least satisfactory treatment of uncertainty. By incorporating only the revenues and costs expected to be incurred if a project succeeds, they effectively assume that each project involves a single go/no go decision. This tends to undervalue long-term, high-risk projects, because firms can usually cut their losses by terminating projects with deteriorating prospects early (Cooper *et al.*, 1998). Thus the actual risk is lower than it would be if the firm had to commit the full cost of the project upfront. As we describe below, project risks can be modeled more realistically using decision trees and real options.

Another problem results from the use of discounted cash flow analysis, the cornerstone of most cost-benefit models. The risk premium for each project should be set based on the premium observed for comparably risky assets – an extremely difficult task for unique research and development projects, especially since the level of risk (and, therefore, the appropriate discount rate) often varies over the life of the project. In practice, firms often use a standard discount rate, which is unlikely to be an accurate reflection of the project's riskiness. Excessively high discount rates can bias project valuations in favor of short-term, low-risk projects (Hodder and Riggs, 1985; Doctor *et al.*, 2001).

Decision tree models.   These models use a technique from decision analysis for quantifying the value of a choice based on the value and likelihood of possible outcomes and subsequent decisions. The expected value of a choice is calculated by summing the value of each possible outcome weighted by the probability of its occurrence. Although not as widely used as basic cost-benefit models, decision trees are commonly used in industry (Liberatore and Titus, 1983; Doctor *et al.*, 2001).

Decision tree models offer several benefits over basic cost-benefit models, especially for long-term projects involving a number of well-defined risks. To begin with, they account for the fact that management can decrease project risk by making funding decisions in multiple stages. Decision tree models also facilitate a more rigorous approach to dealing with the probability of success. Rather than relying on a holistic estimate, they enable the probability of success to be estimated based on the probabilities of certain influential events, represented by branches of the tree. From a process perspective, decision tree models aid understanding of project flow and facilitate the specification of stage gates by explicitly identifying key decisions and milestones. The major weakness of decision tree models is that the values of the branches are generally calculated using discounted cash flow techniques, the shortcomings of which were discussed above (Doctor *et al.*, 2001).

Monte Carlo simulations.   These models are a technique for transforming the output of a given economic value model into a probability distribution of a project's financial outcomes. Rather than assigning a single value to each of the model's input parameters and computing a single output value, a probability distribution is assigned to each input parameter. Then, computer software is used to conduct an 'experiment' in which the value of each input parameter is chosen randomly based on that parameter's probability distribution and the output value of the model is computed. The 'experiment' is repeated hundreds or thousands of times, yielding a distribution showing the range and likelihood of possible project outcomes. Although Monte Carlo simulations are far less common than basic cost-benefit models and decision tree models, they are used by a significant minority of firms – over 10 %, according to one study (Liberatore and Titus, 1983).

Monte Carlo simulations can be used to better understand the range of likely project outcomes and its sensitivity to uncertain input parameters (Doctor *et al.* 2001). However, as Monte Carlo simulations simply compute the results of another economic value model for a large number of input values, they share the shortcomings of the underlying model. Moreover, since the distribution of input parameters are rarely known with any precision, the primary value of Monte Carlo simulations may be underscoring the uncertainty of project outcomes by substituting ranges for deceptive point estimates.

Real options.   These models are so named because they signify the tangible investment parallel of a financial call option (Dixit and Pindyck, 1994; Amram and Kulatilaka, 1999). In an R&D context, the price of the option represents the small, but immediate costs of exploratory R&D projects or pilot programs. The knowledge created through these efforts may be appropriated through patents or other intellectual property. Thus, the firm has the choice to further develop, license, sell, or ignore the project altogether. Managers can value the R&D project based on the theory of financial contracts, which is dependent on the exercise price of the option (the larger cost to fully develop the product), expected payoffs (the projected market revenues), the uncertainty of those payoffs, and the length of time to make that decision (Black and Scholes, 1973).

Perhaps, the greatest contribution of real options models is the change in the conceptual approach they bring in valuating R&D projects, or what authors have called 'strategic options perspective' or 'real option reasoning' (Bowman and Hurry, 1993; Sanchez, 1993; McGrath and Nerkar, 2004). Real option valuation calls for active management of R&D investments. Compared to popular ROI or NPV analyses that assume the trajectory of the project will passively follow the pre-ordained path generated by the analysis, real options assume that decisions will be re-evaluated as the time horizon shortens and uncertainties are reduced. Because the methodology recognizes the value of flexibility and volatility, real option valuations often lead managers to invest in small or even negative NPV projects (Bowman and Moscowitz 2001). Unlike the economic value models, real options demonstrate the value in investing in growing, uncertain markets, precisely the domain of most R&D projects (Mitchell and Hamilton, 1988).

One of the advantages of real options models is that they clearly separate two types of uncertainty: technical risk and market risk (Boer 2000). Technical risk represents the probability of successfully developing the project and bringing it to market. Understandably, an increase in the difficulty and risk of completing a project uniformly lowers its real-option value. Market risk represents the volatility in demand once the product is on the market. An elevation in market risk increases the probability that the project will sell very high or very low quantities. But because the firm has the right to simply abandon the option if it is 'out of the money', the downside losses are constrained. Thus, an increase in market risk increases real-option valuations.

Although the theory of real options is a growing field in academia, the methodology has not caught on in practice. A 2001 survey of 451 executives across 30 industries by Bain & Company estimated that only 9% used them, and almost a third had tried and abandoned the use of real options (Teach, 2003).

Critics offer several of reasons why implementing real options is so difficult. First, real investment decisions are more complex than financial options. Not only is the sophisticated mathematics hard to communicate to corporate executives, transforming these scenarios into the five or six variables of the Black-Scholes-Merton model may oversimplify the decision. R&D decisions are often 'compound options'; a venture in one phase helps resolve uncertainties, but then offers the option for investment in future phases. Without fixed expiration dates, managing these options is often difficult and failing to exercise the option optimally can lead to significantly reduced valuations (Copeland and Tufano, 2004).

Similarly, data on the volatility of the market risk of a product are not readily available. Although investors can research the historic price fluctuations of a specific stock, how does one estimate the range of potential box office receipts of a movie sequel or the drug sales of an untested pharmaceutical? Without informed proxies, estimating the option value of an R&D project can be as misinformed as other methodologies.

Even though the advantage of the real option framework is that it assumes active management of ongoing projects, many firms find it difficult to change policies mid-course. Firms find they cannot easily abandon options that are 'out of the money'. Eliminating or re-allocating research personnel and equipment is difficult to accomplish politically, and in reality, a decision to invest in a preliminary research program often creates a path-dependence that obligates future funding (Teach, 2003).

Useful articles. With the notable exception of real options, most economic value models are relatively old technologies that attract relatively little academic attention – at least in the context of R&D project evaluation – and few early articles stand out as seminal. Consequently, the most useful articles may be case studies and articles from the managerial literature. One such article, written from the perspective of a practitioner, is Bordley's (1998) insightful description of how implementing a basic cost-benefit model contributed to improving R&D management at GM. Another is a case study by Doctor *et al.* (2001), which provides an instructive discussion on the use of decision trees, real options, and Monte Carlo simulations at a diversified multinational firm. From the managerial literature, Hodder and Riggs's (1985) article on the misuse of discount cash flow techniques is helpful for anyone seeking to avoid common pitfalls that often bias economic value model outputs against long-term, high-risk projects. Monte Carlo simulations trace their origins to Hertz's (1964) influential article on evaluating the riskiness of capital investments. An overview of real options can be found in two seminal books by Dixit and Pindyck (1994) and Amram and Kulatilaka (1999).

Relative value models

Relative value models are used to make subjective estimates of project value in terms of some conception of project quality. The meaning of 'project quality' varies by model, but it generally functions as a proxy for criteria that are difficult to measure directly, such as profitability (Cooper, 1981). Yet, although the outputs of relative value models may be correlated with profitability, the relationship is extremely imprecise, and in practice relative value models provide no appreciable insight into expected financial returns.

Relative value models can be divided into two categories based on how they measure value. *Comparative models* measure the value of projects relative to each other, whereas *scoring models* measure projects against one or more fixed scales. Both categories are described in more detail below.

Comparative models.   There are many types of comparative models with varying degrees of sophistication. As its name suggests, *pairwise comparison* methods rank projects from best to worst based on the results of comparisons between pairs of projects. Comparisons may be performed once on the basis of a vague, subjective criterion such as 'attractiveness', or they may be repeated using distinct criteria. Two simple pairwise comparison methods are described in Martino (1995). Another method for ranking projects is *Q-sort*, in which projects are sorted into groups based on a subjective evaluation of their strength with regard to a given criterion. Extensions to the Q-sort method have been proposed that use repeated applications of the Q-sort method interspersed with discussions to help groups reach a consensus on project rankings (Souder, 1978).

A more sophisticated comparative model is the *analytic hierarchy process* (AHP) developed by Saaty (1980). Since its introduction, several authors have described how the general AHP technique can be adapted for evaluating R&D project (see, for example, Liberatore, 1987; Brenner, 1994; Hsu *et al.*, 2003). The first step in applying AHP is to create a hierarchy of evaluation criteria. For example, project attractiveness might have strategic fit, market attractiveness, and technical feasibility as subcriteria, and in turn market attractiveness might have several subcriteria such as market size and intensity of competition. At each point where the hierarchy branches, pairwise comparisons and matrix operations are used to assign weights to each of the subcriteria indicating their importance relative to the parent criterion. Then, the same process of pairwise comparisons and matrix operations are used to calculate weights for the available R&D projects with respect to each of the lowest-level criteria in the hierarchy. Finally, matrix operations are used to collapse the weights up the hierarchy and determine a single vector of weights for the project set. A concise explanation of AHP for practitioners is available in Martino (1995).

Comparative models have two serious limitations. First, they do not provide any information on the actual quality of a given project, which managers are likely to find unsatisfactory. Second, when large numbers of projects need to be considered, methods that rely on pairwise comparisons of every project against every other become tedious and time-consuming. Probably as a result of these shortcomings, comparative models are not widely used. (Liberatore and Titus, 1983; Fahrni and Spatig, 1990; Cooper *et al.*, 1998; Cooper *et al.*, 2001). Cooper *et al.* (1998) suggest that comparative approaches may be useful at the 'idea stage', 'when almost no information is available'. Comparative models may also be useful in selecting and weighting the criteria incorporated in other project evaluation models (Souder, 1978).

Scoring models.   These models use algebraic expressions to calculate holistic project scores from project subscores on a set of evaluation criteria. Many variants are possible: criteria may be few or many, subjective or objective, quantitative or qualitative; the algebraic expression used to combine the subscores may be additive, multiplicative, or hybrid; criteria may or may not be weighted equally. Typical criteria include cost, profitability, probability of technical success, market attractiveness, development time, and strategic fit, among others (Steele, 1988). The simplest form of scoring model is the *checklist*, in which projects are given binary subscores against a list of criteria. In such simple models, it may be helpful to simply display the subscores as a graphical 'profile' rather than aggregating them into a holistic score (Martino, 1995).

Scoring models began to appear in the operations research literature during the late 1950s and early 1960s. One of the first scoring models, proposed by Mottley and Newton (1959), computed a score by multiplying subscores on five, equally weighted criteria: promise of success, time to completion, cost of project, strategic need, and market gain. Subscores were one, two, or three, signifying a low, medium, or high value for the criterion. Another representative example is the model described by Dean and Nishry (1965), which used a weighted sum of 36 subscores, 16 based on technical criteria and 20 on market criteria.

Clearly, the effectiveness of a scoring model is largely determined by the choice of criteria and weights. Some researchers have proposed criteria and weights derived from statistical analysis of actual data on project performance or decision-maker behavior (Schwartz and Vertinsky, 1977; Cooper, 1981; Stahl and Harrell, 1983). Others have recommended techniques to help management determine appropriate criteria and weights. There does not seem to be any consensus on optimal scoring model structure.

Although not as popular as economic value models, scoring models are common in industry (Liberatore and Titus, 1983; Steele, 1988; Cooper *et al.*, 2001). Cooper *et al.* (2001) found that 38 % of firms use scoring models and 20 % use checklists. However, scoring models and checklists were the dominant project selection method at only 5 % and 3 % of firms, respectively, indicating that these models usually play a supporting role in the selection process (Cooper *et al.*, 2001). Scoring models are regarded by managers as particularly well-suited to early stages of development, when making financial predictions is difficult or impossible (Cooper *et al.*, 1998). At stage gates, checklists can be used to kill projects that do not meet certain basic requirements (Cooper *et al.*, 1998).

Scoring models have many strengths: for example, in contrast to economic value models, scoring models can incorporate nonfinancial criteria that may have important – but unquantifiable – impact on total project profitability. Scoring models are also relatively convenient: they are easy to understand, have manageable data requirements, and output a single score reflecting project attractiveness (Cooper *et al.*, 1998; Steele, 1988). Unlike comparative approaches, scoring model outputs have some meaning for single projects: a score toward the high end of the scale indicates that the project was evaluated favorably against most heavily weighted criteria, whereas a low score indicates weakness along some or all dimensions. Additional insight may be gained by examining a project's subscores and determining where its strengths and weaknesses lie.

Scoring models are also helpful from a process perspective. Cooper *et al.* (1998) observe that applying a scoring model forces management to think carefully about project attributes, facilitates discussion, and ensures that key criteria are not over-looked. Since scoring models are relatively straightforward, firms can create their own proprietary models. Steele (1988) points out that the process of creating a scoring model gives managers an opportunity to think about and agree upon evaluation criteria.

Of course, scoring models are not without limitations. The results, although more meaningful than the rankings produced by comparative models, do not provide an absolute measure of value. Furthermore, scoring model results can be misleading: as with economic value models, the quantitative outputs of scoring models suggest far more precision than can be justified given the subjectivity of the subscores and criteria weights (Cooper *et al.*, 1998). Finally, as with all project evaluation models, scoring models evaluate projects in isolation, so the set of highest ranked projects is almost certain to represent an unbalanced and suboptimal portfolio. For example, even if strategic fit is included among the model criteria, the highest scoring projects could all be minor improvements, when the firm may need to invest in platform projects. In fact, the shortcomings of scoring models may be deeper than neglecting balance: a scoring model that favors projects aligned with current corporate strategy 'may optimize for the current strategy at the expense of the company's future choices' (Raynor and Leroux, 2004). Informative discussions of scoring models include a practical tutorial in Martino (1995) and reviews of several industry examples in Cooper *et al.* (1998).

PORTFOLIO SELECTION

The preceding section described models for evaluating projects in isolation. However, the problem faced by most companies is selecting a portfolio of projects. *Portfolio selection models* have been developed to address this problem. They fall into four major categories:

- *Mathematic programming models* use quantitative optimization techniques to identify optimal portfolios.
- *Portfolio diagrams* facilitate portfolio selection decisions by displaying the distribution of available projects with respect to a set of criteria.
- *Strategic frameworks* impose a high-level structure to guide resource allocation decisions.
- *Procedural approaches* use a variety of approaches, but stress the value of interaction over the content of the approach.

Mathematical programming models

Mathematical programming models structure the portfolio selection problem as an objective function to be maximized subject to a set of constraints. For their inputs, these models generally rely on measures of project value generated by economic value models or scoring models. For example, a very basic model might define the objective function as the sum of the economic values of the selected projects and use R&D budget as a constraint. Hundreds of variants, some quite sophisti-cated, have been proposed to deal with the complexities of the portfolio selection problem (Schmidt and Freeland, 1992). Families of approaches that appear fre-quently in the literature include linear programming, nonlinear programming, zero-one programming, goal programming, and dynamic programming, among others.

Mathematical programming models are rigorous, quantitative, and fairly adapt-able (Steele, 1988). They received considerable attention from management sci-entists, especially during the 1960s. However, it has been recognized since the early 1970s that mathematical programming models are *almost never used in indus-try* (Souder, 1973; Baker, 1974; Liberatore and Titus, 1983; Souder and Mandakovic, 1986; Steele, 1988; Schmidt and Freeland, 1992; Chien, 2002). This disuse can be attributed to a number of major shortcomings. Mathematical models have difficulty dealing with uncertainty, project interdependencies, and interrelated or hetero-geneous evaluation criteria (Jackson, 1983; Chien, 2002). The more sophisticated models have highly impractical data requirements and employ abstruse mathemati-cal formulae (Jackson, 1983; Souder and Mandakovic, 1986; Steele, 1988). Indeed, given the extreme uncertainty of the underlying inputs, complex quantitative mod-els appear to be 'methodological overkill' (Steele, 1988). Furthermore, even given accurate inputs and a well-designed objective function, portfolios chosen by the models are unlikely to be optimal since the models do not incorporate high-level strategic needs.[3]

Why, then, has so much effort been expended on mathematical programming models? One possible explanation looks to the role of government agencies, which have been an important driving force behind the development of these mod-els (Steele, 1988). Government agencies must evaluate large numbers of projects and demonstrate methodological rigor, but they have little visibility into contextual factors important in corporate settings. 'Devoting effort to improved, more rigorous and quantified selection techniques,' Steele states, 'is at least one way of demon-strating awareness and concern over the need to spend money wisely' (Steele, 1988). Whatever the reason, work in the field continues and new mathematical programming models still appear in the literature.

The literature on mathematical programming models comprises hundred of papers. Some papers are cited more frequently than others, but none seem influen-tial enough to be considered seminal. For those seeking to get a general sense of the field, the survey by Gear *et al.* (1971) provides succinct descriptions of nine represen-tative models (1971). Souder's (1973) comparison of nonlinear, linear, zero-one, and profitability index programming models is also instructive. The chapter on mathematical programming in Martino (1995) includes a straightforward tutorial as well as references to several more recent articles. Additional references may be found in the general survey articles cited in the introductory section of this chapter.

---

[3]Although these shortcomings probably provide ample reason for the unpopularity of mathematical programming models, other explanations are possible. In their case study of the (incomplete) adoption of mathematical programming models for R&D project selection at BMW, Loch *et al.* (2001) call attention to the difficulties of transferring technology from academic institutions into business practice.

Portfolio diagrams

Portfolio diagrams provide visual summaries of selected characteristics for the set of available projects. They often take the form of bubble charts, in which each project is represented by a bubble whose size and location indicate its performance along three dimensions. Common dimensions of portfolio diagrams include NPV estimates generated by economic value models and estimates of riskiness or market attractiveness (Cooper et al., 1998). In essence, these frameworks can give management insight into the mix of project characteristics that project evaluation models collapse into single numbers. Well-designed diagrams may also highlight portfolio imbalances, although they do not indicate whether or not such imbalances are desirable (Cooper et al., 1998). Portfolio diagrams, unlike mathematical programming models, do not provide any answers.

In stark contrast to mathematical programming models, portfolio diagrams are virtually ignored in the academic literature, but quite common in practice. A recent survey found bubble charts in use at over 40 % of firms, and at 13 % of firms they were the dominant project selection method (Cooper et al., 2001). Descriptions of portfolio diagrams used by firms including 3M and Procter & Gamble can be found in Cooper et al. (1998).

Strategic frameworks

All the approaches discussed thus far, both for project evaluation and portfolio selection, are bottom-up techniques. They take one or more R&D projects and evaluate them, individually or in groups, seeking to identify the best projects or portfolios. High-level corporate priorities play a supporting role; at most, they may be factored into the choice of evaluation criteria. Strategic frameworks take the opposite approach: they begin by using strategic objectives to draw the broad contours of the R&D portfolio, and then proceed to evaluate and select individual projects within the context of this high-level blueprint. Cooper et al. (1998) call this the 'strategic buckets' approach, because a strategic framework specifies the R&D areas or 'buckets' of strategic importance to the firm. By first establishing the firm's high level areas of focus, strategic frameworks seek to ensure that the mix of R&D projects meet the strategic needs of the company.

Several strategic frameworks appear in the literature. Aggregate project planning, proposed by Wheelwright and Clark (1992), recommends defining strategic buckets by the degree of change along relevant competitive dimensions, such as product or process change. Typical categories resulting from this exercise include incremental or derivative projects; platform projects (those that involve a change to the 'system-level' solution); breakthrough projects (those that develop new product categories); and advanced development projects (those that are geared to investigating technologies that may be applied to future products). Wheelwright and Clark's (1992) framework takes the resources committed to R&D (a strategic variable) and allocates them between different project types according to a 'mix' governed by a firm's strategy and its competitive environment. Project evaluation occurs only between 'like' projects. In comparison, Raynor and Leroux (2004) advocate a scenario-based approach for distinguishing between 'core' projects that will be needed in all scenarios, 'contingent' projects needed only in particular scenarios, and superfluous projects that can be eliminated. This approach also provides some guidance for resource allocation, recommending that core projects be fully funded and contingent projects funded at a level sufficient to keep them viable in case they become needed.

Much like portfolio diagrams, strategic frameworks are common in industry, but have been largely neglected by the academic literature in terms of how to build an 'optimal' portfolio. We found only one academic journal article proposing a strategic framework, and that was written by researchers at a consulting firm (Raynor and Leroux, 2004). Indeed, it seems that strategic frameworks trace their origins to practitioners, consultancies, and the managerial literature rather than to academic theory. Cooper *et al.* (2001) found that 65 % of businesses use strategic frameworks to allocate resources to 'different buckets or envelopes', making strategic frameworks the second most popular project selection methodology after economic value models. Many firms use hybrid approaches, in which economic value models, scoring models, or portfolio diagrams are used to select projects within these buckets (Cooper *et al.*, 2001).

This popularity has good reason, because strategic frameworks offer many benefits. In contrast to bottom-up models that focus on examining characteristics of particular project and portfolio options, strategic frameworks give priority to the firm's high level strategic needs. They provide a methodology for management to formulate an explicit technology strategy and assemble an R&D project portfolio compatible with that strategy. Strategic frameworks also help management detect and address portfolio deficiencies. For example, a top-down process allows managers to assess whether the portfolio of potential projects that emerge from a bottom-up approach is skewed towards certain project types. Work by Wheelwright and Clark (1992) suggests that without this guidance, firms typically find that they allocate too many resources to derivative or incremental projects, at the expense of riskier projects involving a greater degree of novelty. The great limitation of strategic frameworks, however, is that they are nothing more than frameworks to support decision-making: by themselves, strategic frameworks produce no answers. There are no hard and fast rules for determining the appropriate set of strategic buckets, or for allocating resources between or within these buckets.

Procedural approaches

Observing the gap between academic research and managerial practice, and noting that much of the value from project selection models seems to derive from the process of using them rather than from their outputs, some authors have suggested other directions (Souder 1978; Souder and Mandakovic, 1986; Hall and Nauda, 1990). For the most part, these proposals focus on the procedural dimensions of the project selection problem, which are generally ignored by the models discussed above.

Procedural approaches often seek to leverage existing project selection models as decision aids by integrating them into interactive processes. For instance, Souder (1978) recommends a 'nominal-interacting' process in which traditional models are incorporated into cycles of structured discussions that facilitate information-sharing and consensus-building. Hall and Nauda (1990) describe a selection process employing priority-setting, solicitation of project proposals, scoring, and portfolio diagrams. Recent examples include the decision support systems proposed by Stummer and Heidenberger (2003) and Ghasemzadeh and Archer (2000). Some authors have also suggested using artificial intelligence technologies, such as expert systems, to support human decision makers (Liberatore and Stylianou, 1995; Rao et al., 1999)

Another approach is to focus on the flow of projects through the development pipeline. For example, Gino and Pisano (2004) use a pipeline model to explore the linkage between project selection policies, risk aversion, and outcome volatility. Compared to the volume of work on project selection models, however, procedural approaches have attracted relatively little interest, and they do not appear to be used in practice (Liberatore and Titus, 1983; Cooper et al. 2001)

LESSONS FROM THE FIELD

The preceding discussion has critiqued the various models and methods proposed in the literature for project and portfolio selection at a high level. However, a deeper exposure to the problems raised by particular managerial contexts and the practices that have evolved as a result of these contexts can provide useful insights into the challenges facing future researchers in this arena. In this respect, we identify two specific contextual cases that raise challenges to existing theory, and use qualitative data from industry interviews to highlight firms' approaches to dealing with these challenges.

Environments with high uncertainty over project outcomes

In industries characterized by high uncertainty over the outcome of individual projects, the application of existing project evaluation and portfolio management techniques proves problematic. This problem is particularly striking in industries where there is no clear understanding of the causal model linking a product's design to its performance in the marketplace. For example, both the movie industry and the video game industry exhibit such characteristics. In these industries, the distribution of returns is highly skewed; the result is that a few successes (or 'hits') have to pay for a large number of failures (see De Vany, 2004; MacCormack et al., 2004). Furthermore, there are few proven 'ingredients' to increase the chances that a project will succeed. For example, although a 'star' director or actor may increase a film's revenue expectations, no effect on the distribution of *profits* has yet been found empirically (De Vany, 2004).

In such environments, each individual project can have a very large distribution of potential financial outcomes (much of it negative). Furthermore, in most cases these distributions are nonlinear (for example, in the drug industry, there is a high chance of project failure plus the distribution of returns for drugs that do make it to the market is highly skewed). A further complication is that there are likely to be several different 'types' of projects, each of which has a different payoff profile. In such scenarios, it is likely that the optimal portfolio would consist of a *mix* of different project types, with some 'safe' bets and some 'speculative' bets providing options for growth.

It is useful to focus on a single industry to illustrate the challenge of project and portfolio management when facing extreme (and potentially differing) levels of uncertainty over project outcomes. In this respect, we highlight the dynamics in the $10 billion video game industry, an industry in which over 1000 new games are launched each year, only 10 % of games make a profit, and the top 5 % generate more than half of industry sales (see MacCormack *et al.*, 2004). Within this context, the success of new game concepts is extremely unpredictable (e.g., *Grand Theft Auto*, a game about theft and violent crime, is one of the best selling games of all time). So how do video game publishers such as Electronic Arts and Activision handle this uncertainty?

The first observation that can be made is that not all game development projects face similar levels of uncertainty. In any given year, many of the top selling games are actually sequels of previously successful games. Sequels are more predictable in terms of revenues hence their development can be managed accordingly. In many ways, the challenge in this industry is to develop new 'breakthrough' game concepts, which eventually turn into a stream of highly profitable sequels. Although projects to develop such breakthrough concepts are extremely uncertain, there are ways to mitigate some of the risks. One way is to develop games that exploit existing brands or franchises, for example, through the use of professional sports sponsorships, such as football or basketball. Another is to partner with outside developers of intellectual property (IP) (e.g., a movie studio) to develop games that are marketed alongside a complementary product (e.g., a major film release). In these cases, the brand, franchise, or IP owners typically seek compensation for the rights to their use via an auction among competing game publishers. The challenge for a publisher is to evaluate whether the benefits of these IP rights (in terms of increased profit expectations and decreased uncertainty over project outcomes) are sufficient to justify the price of the IP.

In essence, the challenge of portfolio management in the video game industry is one of selecting an optimal portfolio of different project types, each of which provides an 'option' on a future product market position with a different payoff profile. Although the most profitable and predictable types of projects are sequels, it is clear that a portfolio consisting only of sequels would have few prospects for growth; hence the need to explore other types of projects with greater risk, but potentially greater rewards. Resolving this problem requires combining existing theories that evaluate projects in terms of option values with portfolio models and strategic frameworks that help firms identify the optimal allocation of resources across different project types. To date, these models and frameworks have viewed projects only as having deterministic or binary outcomes (i.e., they tend to assume that a project will result in a successful product).

Recent field work suggests that managers in the video game industry deal with high levels of uncertainty by using heuristics that seek to construct an optimal portfolio by starting from the revenue and profit objectives of the firm, and then working backwards to identify a set of projects that would meet these targets. A quote from one industry executive illustrates such a heuristic:

> I start with our revenue targets for three to four years down the road. I plug in the sequels I know we will do – annual updates of our most popular games or games for movie sequels. I then try to anticipate which of the licensing deals we are negotiating with proven 'properties' will pan out. When I add these up, I see the potential gaps in our portfolio. So I look to fill these with other licensed deals or original game concepts. For the latter, we try to actively manage the high risk of failure. For example, we might seed an internal development team to exploit a new market niche that we think is unfilled – for example, a game that mixes two types of genre. Or we might contract with an external 'studio' that has already built a strong reputation for a certain game-type or has a particular technical skill we want to exploit.[4]

The latter strategy – contracting with outside resources to fill portfolio gaps – indicates another way that firms deal with high levels of uncertainty over the outcomes of individual projects. In the video game industry, thousands of small (i.e., 5–30 people) development 'studios' provide a constant source of new game concepts that they attempt to sell to publishers. At any one time, publishers maintain a portfolio of contracts with outside studios, many of which are geared to developing original game concepts. Although many of these projects fail, such a relationship has two advantages: first, if a game should prove successful, the publisher can acquire the studio, securing the development team for future sequels; and second, if a game should fail, the publisher has developed knowledge of the skills and capabilities of the studio that may prove valuable in addressing future opportunities as they arise in the industry.

Environments where firms fund projects using external R&D resources

The mutually beneficial relationship between publishers and external studios noted above highlights another contextual challenge facing models of project and portfolio selection. Recent work on the management of innovation highlights that firms increasingly look outside their organizational boundaries in an attempt to maximize the value generated from the use of their internal R&D capabilities (Chesbrough, 2003; Iansiti and Levien, 2004). For example, Chesbrough (2003) notes that Procter & Gamble plan to source a significant number of innovations from outside the firm, using their product development and marketing expertise to generate a larger return from these innovations than might otherwise be the case. Merck's 2000 annual report asserts the need to 'reach out to universities, research institutions, and companies worldwide to bring the best technology...into Merck'. Iansiti and Levien (2004) argue that without a detailed understanding of the external 'ecosystem' upon which a firm depends, its approach to managing innovation is likely to be suboptimal, and in some cases might be catastrophic.

Several dynamics have driven firms to be more aware of the need to actively manage *external* resources in their innovation efforts. The first is the increasing

---

[4]Interview with Video Game Industry executive, 25th August, 2004.

amount of aggregate R&D accounted for by small firms and start-ups – by 1999, this had risen fourfold to 22.5 % as compared to the figure in 1981 (Chesbrough, 2003). The second is the increasing distribution of talent around the globe, and the potential differences in the cost and ability of these resources, as compared to a firm's own employees. The third is the trend towards open architectures and standards in many industries that can bring a reduction in levels of vertical integration and an increase in the need for coordination across component providers (e.g., see Baldwin and Clark, 2000). Finally, there is evidence that the traditional model for long-term R&D – a wholly-owned central research facility – is viewed as outdated by firms (Tennenhouse, 2004) and is not always associated with better outcomes (Lim, 2004).

Given these trends in the broader environment, the management of projects and capabilities *external* to a firm is likely to be of increasing importance in many industries, and indeed, may provide a valuable source of competitive advantage. There is therefore a need to examine the unique challenges that are generated by the requirement to manage external resources, as well as a need for frameworks to help managers decide when to source projects using internal resources, when to rely on outside capabilities, and how to optimize a portfolio that uses both.

In this respect, we find it informative to focus on one particular context to understand how firms approach these problems, and from these observations, speculate as to the conceptual underpinnings for the models we see used in practice. For this purpose, we draw upon evidence of how Intel has structured its exploratory research activities in the computer industry to leverage outside capabilities and resources (for a detailed description, see Tennenhouse, 2004; MacCormack and Herman, 2004).

In 1999, Intel set up an organization known as Intel Research, with the aim of funding 'disruptive' research projects that fell outside of its silicon 'roadmap', the plan that provides guidance for the majority of Intel's R&D efforts, ensuring Moore's Law continues to hold into the future. Intel Research's agenda was to identify emerging new technologies that might threaten Intel's existing businesses and models, or might lead to significant new ones. The effort was therefore intended to act as an early warning system for technology-based opportunities and threats.

David Tennenhouse was recruited from the Defense Advanced Research Projects Agency (DARPA) to lead Intel Research's efforts. But rather than establish an in-house facility to conduct research on newly emerging technologies – one established approach to performing exploratory research – Tennenhouse developed a different approach, based upon 'sensing' the environment to identify promising new research areas, and then building a portfolio of projects around these areas. Critical to this approach was the coordinated use of university research grant funding, small 'lablets' that were run jointly with academia, corporate venture funding, and projects run in Intel's existing R&D facilities.

The main sensing mechanism by which Intel identified potentially new emerging technologies was its university grant funding program, which sponsored over 300 research projects across a variety of academic disciplines and locations. Once a promising research thread was detected, this was designated a 'sector', and a coordinated portfolio of projects created to further advance the technology.

This portfolio included additional university grants, internal research efforts called 'Strategic Research Projects' (which used existing R&D resources, but were paid for by Intel Research), and complementary investments made by Intel's corporate venture capital arm, Intel Capital.

In support of these exploratory research efforts, Intel opened four 'lablets', research facilities run jointly with a sponsoring university but funded by Intel. Each facility was co-directed by one Intel manager and one academic on a 2-year leave of absence from the university. The projects undertaken in each lablet were selected by the academic director, but were staffed with both university students and Intel employees. Each lablet typically had three to four major projects running concurrently.

Intel's unique approach to exploratory research creates a number of challenges for its managers with regard to project evaluation and portfolio selection. Specifically, Intel Research has no staff of its own, but uses its budget to fund research activities within a variety of organizations, some of which are inside Intel, some of which are outside the firm, and some of which are 'hybrid' organizations that mix internal and external resources. Furthermore, the objectives for these investments vary according to whether they are primarily 'sensing' efforts, or represent part of a coordinated strategy for developing a specific 'sector'. So how should Intel Research allocate resources between sensing activities and sector development? And how should it think about the optimal allocation of resources among the different organizational modes that it has available (e.g., should it fund 50 additional research grants or open an additional lablet)?

One way of thinking about this problem conceptually is to view Intel's project investments as representing the 'nodes' in a network of sensors, each of which generates valuable information (and ultimately, useful assets) related to the environment in which it is situated. The value of each project can therefore be thought of in terms of the option value associated with the information that is likely to come from that part of the environment *in future*. With this view, the design of a project portfolio becomes a problem in network design. The optimal structure will depend, among other things, on the likelihood of important technologies emerging in each part of the external environment, the levels of uncertainty surrounding these technologies, the size of their potential impact on Intel's business, and the costs and benefits of examining these technologies under different organizational modes. Critically, this view suggests there is likely to be greater value in a portfolio that adopts multiple methods for sensing and responding to emerging new technologies (and hence taps more parts of the external environment) in contrast to one that focuses on only a single approach. In particular, the ability to triangulate information from diverse sources is likely to prove valuable, given the inherent ambiguity in the types of opportunities that the firm is looking to identify.

FUTURE DIRECTIONS

We conclude by highlighting four opportunities for future research: the continuing lack of practical application and adoption of most research, and more substantive questions such as managing a portfolio of projects with extremely skewed potential outcomes, understanding the interdependence between portfolio projects, and managing external options, particularly across a complex and interdependent network. The first area has been previously and repeatedly identified. Indeed, the field of R&D project selection has always been characterized by a conspicuous and persistent gap between theory and practice. As academics have developed ever more sophisticated quantitative models, practitioners have preferred simpler economic analyses, qualitative scoring techniques, and strategic approaches. Academia and industry do interact to some degree: there are examples of quantitative models being applied in practice, and practical scoring techniques do appear in the academic literature. Nevertheless, the gap has remained surprisingly broad. It appears as a recurring theme in literature surveys spanning several decades (Baker and Pound, 1964; Souder, 1972; Steele, 1988).

This lack of progress is surprising because the strategic role of R&D project selection is widely recognized. Almost every paper on the subject begins by describing the critical importance of wise R&D investments to the long-term prospects of the firm. Yet academic models almost invariably treat project selection as a technical problem much akin to supply chain management or production scheduling. When the resulting models have not been adopted, academics have tried to make the models more user-friendly, interactive, and powerful, rather than re-examining the underlying approach.

Since many well-trained and talented academics have made substantial contributions in this area, it is not a question of a lack of effort. Much of the disconnect results from analytical modeling that remains divorced from the realities that face practitioners. This presents an opportunity to ground all work, whether analytical, empirical, or normative, in a better understanding of the challenge. Although this approach will probably make closed form solutions more difficult (for example, an assumption of independence between projects), we believe simulation methods offer promise in this task. Analytical researchers can also take cues from the work of the Carnegie School (March and Simon, 1958) and recent work in behavioral economics (Bromiley and Fleming, 2004; Gino and Pisano, 2004). Resulting work would require inherent consideration of fundamental biases and provide more accurate – and useable – research.

If researchers accept the goal of practical relevance and impact, they must devote some attention to the details of technology transfer. Rather than building a better theoretical mousetrap with consideration of use only after the thought, researchers would do well to begin with a better understanding of the context of use. Researchers need not take an active role in the diffusion of their technology into practice (although given the increasing protection for academic intellectual property and the need for such solutions, there should certainly exist pecuniary incentives to do so), but models would diffuse faster if researchers considered how they might be used. Although practitioners bear some responsibility for their continued reliance on blunt and inaccurate tools, we suspect that if researchers discovered a clear advantage, the adoption of the improved mousetraps would quickly follow. Finally, the authors would welcome more realistic modeling, in the hopes that it might liven an otherwise dry literature.

We make more substantive arguments in the three remaining areas of research opportunity. The first is motivated by our description of the video gaming industry, but it has wide applicability in any context of skewed returns, for example, the pharmaceutical industry and other industries that rely upon occasional blockbusters to fund the vast majority of (usually) failed projects. One obvious agenda would be to deepen the current managerial response of separating projects by type and risk. There exists little systematic research about how projects within a highly skewed context should be categorized and how the risk profiles for each project type should be selected. Furthermore, what capital and organizational structure should support these arrangements? Should the risk always be shifted to small and creative populations of experimenters, as is the case in the video gaming industry and in some respects, the biotechnology industry? Clearly, many opportunities lie in both description and normative modeling.

Such work would also greatly benefit from a better understanding of the underlying dynamics of interdependent and chaotic systems. Highly skewed distributions have already been widely studied (Zipf, 1949; Ijiri and Simon, 1977; De Vany 2004). This literature might inform the descriptive work, yet it will probably have little to add to the normative modeling. Despite identification of such distributions across an impressive range of phenomena, including firm sizes (Ijiri and Simon, 1977), earthquakes and financial panics (Bak and Chen, 1991), and patent distributions (Harhoff *et al.*, 1999), we are unaware of any widely accepted predictive models. It remains to be seen if managerial prescriptions for industries with highly skewed outcomes can be developed without an understanding of the underlying dynamics in such contexts.

The notion of interdependence also forms the basis of our third and fourth research opportunities. Specifically, almost all research to date on project and portfolio selection has ignored the interdependence that usually exists between projects. The basis for such interdependence can be simple, for example, the limited number of qualified personnel that can be assigned to projects, or the potential cannibalization of sales of related products. More often, however, it is exceedingly complex: for example, in predicting how the learning that occurs within each project will impact a firm's overall research and commercialization capability. Project selection is often the basis for changing the competitive basis of a firm (Wheelwright and Clark, 1992), and yet it is extremely difficult to understand the interactions between current projects and future learning and capability development. Furthermore, although a manager can make a broad prescription (for example, we need to move into nano-technology) it remains extremely difficult to predict what *combination* of specific competencies will be most important, even just a few years ahead (for example, what combinations of biological and mechanical nano-tech will constitute the next breakthrough). Progress has been slow on these issues because complex interdependencies are so difficult for the human mind to comprehend and manage. They also are multivariate in nature, which makes analytical solutions even more difficult to find. Even a breakthrough such as options pricing in the field of finance theory is likely to illuminate only one facet of the problem.

Although interdependence makes our fourth recommendation even more challenging, we believe that there remains much opportunity in learning how to manage projects and portfolios that bridge organizational boundaries. Most project selection models assume a set of potential projects generated by a firm's existing R&D base. The majority assume a fixed pool of available projects, from which projects are selected. This approach is a holdover from a time when there was little technological crossover and the future of the firm could be found in its research labs. Now, future products and processes must leverage technological inputs from a wide variety of fields, many of which lie outside their traditional areas of expertise. The phenomenon has been identified and described (Chesbrough, 2003), but there remains much opportunity, both qualitative and normative.

To begin with, the literature needs a basic typology of the external opportunities or options that are available to a firm's managers. What should a firm's sensors observe and look for, and how should they accomplish that goal? For example, how does a firm monitor its competitors versus university research (keeping in mind that universities may now also compete)? What types of absorptive capacity (Cohen and Levinthal, 1990) must be developed to understand the opportunities across various contexts? Strategies must also be formulated and validated; for example, when does a firm buy another firm, license the technology, or begin an in-house development project, in response to an identified threat? How do IP and scientific commons issues influence these choices? Only after these phenomena have been described, can the analytical modeling and empirical validation work proceed.

In many ways this prescription resembles recent high-profile efforts to provide firms with the tools to manage inter-organizational networks. The opportunity and challenge, however, remains daunting, mainly due to the interdependencies that exist across external project selection and portfolio options. It is difficult enough to manage the simple hub and spoke network described at Intel, but even more challenging would be to provide guidance on how to manage the interdependencies between these outside options. For example, given potentially cross-fertilized projects in widely disparate technologies managed by different technical staff, how does one identify, value, and execute the brokerage opportunity? And how does one incorporate this into financial and optimization models? Networks may well be the metaphor for future management, but with the exception of simple case studies, they may remain poorly exploited unless the academy can provide further guidance on their design and detailed operation.

CONCLUSION

This chapter covered a variety of topics, both old and new, on project and portfolio management. We first described the literature on project selection methods, followed by portfolio methods. Most of this voluminous (and still growing) literature remains unapplied in practice. We then described two current practitioner contexts, including management in an industry with excessively skewed returns and management in an industry where much research and development takes place outside of the firm.

Based on the current state of the literature and our descriptions of current practice, we prescribe four areas for future research. First, we suggest that academics build models more thoroughly grounded in managerial and behavioral reality, even though this will increase their analytical difficulty. Second, we outline an academic research agenda that would help managers in industries with highly skewed returns, though we note that breakthroughs might need to wait until we have a better understanding of the causal mechanisms of chaotic and interdependent systems. Building on the interdependence theme, we suggest that all project and portfolio research would benefit from a more thorough consideration of tightly coupled projects. Finally, we suggest that future research explore the opportunities of managing networked portfolios across firm boundaries; understanding the interdependence between projects remains an attractive though difficult goal. Hopefully the next literature review in this field will report that the first problem has been solved, because academics have made progress on the other three.

References

Amram, M., and Kulatilaka, N. (1999). *Real options: managing strategic investment in an uncertain world*. Boston, MA: Harvard Business School Press.

Bak, P., and Chen, K. (1991). Self-organized criticality. *Scientific American*, 264, 46–53.

Baker, N.R. (1974). R&D project selection models: an assessment. *IEEE Transactions on Engineering Management*, 21(4), 165–71.

Baker, N., and Freeland, J. (1975). Recent advances in R&D benefit measurement and project selection methods. *Management Science*, 21(10), 1164–75.

Baker, N., and Pound, W.H. (1964). R&D project selection: where we stand. *IEEE Transactions on Engineering Management*, 11(4), 124–34.

Baldwin, C., and Clark, K. (2000). *Design rules*. Cambridge, MA: MIT Press.

Black, F., and Scholes, M. (1973). The pricing of options and corporate liabilities. *Journal of Political Economy*, 81, 631–54.

Boer, F.P. (2000). Valuation of technology using 'real options'. *Research-Technology Management*, 43, 26–30.

Bordley, R.F. (1998). R&D project selection versus R&D project generation. *IEEE Transactions on Engineering Management*, 45(4), 407–13.

Bowman, E.H., and Hurry, D. (1993). Strategy through the option lens: an integrated view of resource investments and the incremental-choice process. *Academy of Management Review*, 18, 760–82.

Bowman, E.H., and Moscowitz, G.T. (2001). Real options analysis and strategic decision making. *Organization Science*, 12(6), 772–7.

Brenner, M.S. (1994). Practical R&D project prioritization. *Research Technology Management*, 37(5), 38–42.

Bromiley, P., and Fleming, L. (2004). A behavioral model of R&D allocation. Working Paper, Harvard Business School.

Cetron, M.J., Martino, J., and Roepcke, L. (1967). The selection of R&D program content – survey of quantitative methods. *IEEE Transactions on Engineering Management*, 14(1), 4–13.

Chesbrough, H. (2003). *Open innovation: the new imperative for creating and profiting from new technology*, Boston, MA: Harvard Business School Press.

Chien, C-F. (2002). A portfolio-evaluation framework for selecting R&D projects. *R&D Management*, 32(4), 359–68.

Cohen, W.M., and Levinthal, D.A. (1990). Absorptive capacity: a new perspective on learning and innovation. *Administrative Science Quarterly*, 35, 128–52.

Cooper, R.G. (1981). An empirically derived new product project selection model. *IEEE Transactions on Engineering Management*, 28(3), 54–61.

Cooper, R.G., Edgett, S.J., and Kleinschmidt, E.J. (1998). *Portfolio management for new products*. Reading, MA: Addison-Wesley.

Cooper, R., Edgett, S., and Kleinschmidt, E. (2001). Portfolio management for new product development: results of an industry practices study. *R&D Management*, 31(4), 361–80.

Copeland T., and Tufano, P. (2004). A real-world way to manage real options, *Harvard Business Review*, 82(3), 90–9.

De Vany, A. (2004). *Hollywood economics: how extreme uncertainty shapes the film industry*. New York: Routledge Taylor & Francis Group.

Dean, B.V. (1968). *Evaluating, selecting, and controlling R&D projects*. New York: American Management Association.

Dean, B.V., and Nishry, M.J. (1965). Scoring and profitability models for evaluating and selecting engineering projects. *Operations Research*, 13(4), 550–69.

Dixit, A.K., and Pindyck, R.S. (1994). *Investment under uncertainty*. Princeton, NJ: Princeton University Press.

Doctor, R.N., Newton, D.P., and Pearson, A. (2001). Managing uncertainty in research and development. *Technovation*, 21, 79–90.

Fahrni, P., and Spatig, M. (1990). An application-oriented guide to R&D project selection and evaluation models. *R&D Management*, 20(2), 155–71.

Gear, A.E., Lockett, A.G., and Pearson, A.W. (1971). Analysis of some portfolio selection models for R&D. *IEEE Transactions on Engineering Management*, 18(2), 66–76.

Ghasemzadeh, F., and Archer, N.P. (2000). Project portfolio selection through decision support. *Decision Support Systems*, 29: 73–88.

Gino, F., and Pisano, G. (2004). R&D performance volatility: a behavioral model. Working Paper, Harvard Business School.

Hall, D.L., and Nauda, A. (1990). An interactive approach for selecting IR&D projects. *IEEE Transactions on Engineering Management*, 37(2), 126–33.

Harhoff, D., Narin, F., Scherer, F.M., and Vopel, K. (1999). Citation frequency and value of patented innovation. *Review of Economics and Statistics*, 81(3), 511–15.

Hertz, D.B. (1964). Risk analysis in capital investment. *Harvard Business Review*, 42(1), 95–106.

Hodder, J.E., and Riggs, H.E. (1985). Pitfalls in evaluating risky projects. *Harvard Business Review*, 63(1), 128–35.

Hsu, Y-G., Tzeng, G-H., and Shyu, J.Z. (2003). Fuzzy multiple criteria selection of government-sponsored frontier technology R&D projects. *R&D Management*, 33(5), 539–51.

Iansiti, M., and Levien, R. (2004). *The keystone advantage*. Boston, MA: Harvard Business School Press.

Ijiri, Y., and Simon, H.A. (1977). *Skew distributions and the sizes of business firms*. Amsterdam: North-Holland.

Jackson, B. (1983). Decision methods for selecting a portfolio of R&D projects. *Research Management*, 16(5), 21–6.

Liberatore, M.J. (1987). An extension of the analytic hierarchy process for industrial R&D project selection and resource allocation. *IEEE Transactions on Engineering Management*, 34(1), 12–8.

Liberatore, M.J., and Stylianou, A.C. (1995). Expert support systems for new project development decision making: a model framework and applications. *Management Science*, 41(8), 1296–316.

Liberatore, M.J., and Titus, G.J. (1983). The practice of management science in R&D project management. *Management Science*, 29(8), 962–74.

Lim, K. (2004). The relationship between research and innovation in the semiconductor and pharmaceutical industries (1981–1997). *Research Policy*, 33(2), 287–321.

Loch, C.H., Pich, M.T., Terwiesch, C., and Urbschat, M. (2001). Selecting R&D projects at BMW: a case study of adopting mathematical programming models. *IEEE Transactions on Engineering Management*, 48(1), 70–80.

MacCormack, A., and Herman, K. (2004). Intel outside: building a research SensorNet., *Harvard Business School Case* No. 605-051.

MacCormack, A., Herman, K., and D'Angelo, E. (2004). Activision: the Kelly Slater's Pro Surfer Project. *Harvard Business School Case* No. 604-075.

March, J., and Simon, H. (1958). *Organization*. Cambridge, MA: Blackwell Publishing.

Martino, J.P. (1995). *Research and development project selection*. New York: John Wiley & Sons, Inc.

McGrath R.G., and Nerkar, A. (2004). Real options reasoning and a new look at the R&D investment strategies of pharmaceutical firms. *Strategic Management Journal*, 25, 1–21.

Mitchell G.R., and Hamilton, W.F. (1988). Managing R&D as a strategic option. *Research-Technology Management*, 27, 15–22.

Mottley, C.M., and Newton, R.D. (1959). The selection of projects for industrial research. *Operations Research*, 7(6), 740–51.

Rao, S.S., Nahm, A., Shi, Z., Deng, X., and Syamil, A. (1999). Artificial intelligence and expert systems applications in new product development – a survey. *Journal of Intelligent Manufacturing*, 10, 231–44.

Raynor, M.E., and Leroux, X. (2004). Strategic flexibility in R&D. *Research Technology Management*, 47(3), 27–32.

Roussel, P.A., Saad, K.N., and Erickson, T.J. (1991). *Third generation R&D: managing the link to corporate strategy*. Boston, MA: Harvard Business School Press.

Saaty, T.L. (1980). *The analytic hierarchy process*. New York: McGraw-Hill.

Sanchez R. (1993). Strategic flexibility, firm organization, and managerial work in dynamic markets: a strategic options perspective. In *Advances in Strategic Management*, P., Shrivastrava, A. Huff, and J. Dutton (eds), Greenwich, CT: JAI Press, 251–91.

Schmidt, R.L., and Freeland, J.R. (1992). Recent progress in modeling R&D project-selection processes. *IEEE Transactions on Engineering Management*, 39(2), 189–200.

Schwartz, S.L., and Vertinsky, I. (1977). Multi-attribute investment decisions: a study of R&D project selection. *Management Science*, 24(3), 285–301.

Souder, W.E. (1972). A scoring methodology for assessing the suitability of management science models. *Management Science*, 18(10), B–526–B–543.

Souder, W.E. (1973). Analytical effectiveness of mathematical models for R&D project selection. *Management Science*, 19(8), 907–23.

Souder, W.E. (1978). A system for using R&D project evaluation methods. *Research Management*, 21(5), 29–37.

Souder, W.E., and Mandakovic, T. (1986). R&D project selection models. *Research Management*, 29(4), 36–42.

Stahl, M.J., and Harrell, A.M. (1983). Identifying operative goals by modeling project selection decisions in research and development. *IEEE Transactions on Engineering Management*, 30(4), 223–28.

Steele, L.W. (1988). Selecting R&D programs: what we've learned. *Research Technology Management*, 31(2), 17–36.

Stummer, C., and Heidenberger, K. (2003). Interactive R&D portfolio analysis with project interdependencies and time profiles of multiple objectives. *IEEE Transactions on Engineering Management*, 50(2), 175–83.

Teach, E. (2003). Will real options take root? *CFO Magazine*, July, 73–6.

Tennenhouse, D. (2004). Intel's open collaborative model of industry-university research. *Research Technology Management*, 49(4), 19–26.

Wheelwright, S.C., and Clark, K.B. (1992). *Revolutionizing product development*. New York: The Free Press.

Winkofsky, E.P., Mason, R.M., and Souder, W.E. (1980). R&D budgeting and project selection: a review of practices and models. In *Management of Research and Innovation*, B.V. Dean and J.L. Goldhar (eds), Amsterdam: North-Holland, 183–97.

Zipf, G.K. (1949). *Human behaviour and the principle of least-effort*. Cambridge MA: Addison-Wesley.

8

Managing the Innovative Performance of Technical Professionals

RALPH KATZ

In 1987, a distinguished task force was sponsored by the US National Research Council to study and report on how US companies could regain their international competitiveness through the ways in which they organized, managed, and coordinated their business strategies and technological efforts (NRC, 1987). Given the record trade deficits, the poor productivity growth, and the alarming loss of technical leadership in an increasing number of high technology industries – trends that were all occurring at that time – the task force was asked to uncover those key problem areas in the management of technology that could be improved to help mitigate, and it was hoped, turn around this growing decline in global leadership. Seven major technology-related needs or issues facing US industries were identified by the task force as becoming increasingly important to the future competitiveness of American businesses. Improvements in the following areas were targeted:

- How to integrate technology into the firm's overall strategic objectives, including the allocation of resources and the planning for technical developments and acquisitions.
- How to get into and out of technologies faster and more efficiently, including the selection, prioritization, timing, and assessment of alternative technological investments.
- How to assess and evaluate technology more effectively, especially with respect to financial concerns and the company's ability to compete in future markets.
- How best to accomplish technology transfer, including the transfer and dissemination of internal R&D results as well as the assimilation of external technical developments.
- How to reduce new product development time, including the links among design, engineering, and manufacturing as well as the lag between idea and/or product conception and market delivery.

Handbook of Technology and Innovation Management.   Edited by Scott Shane
© 2008 John Wiley & Sons, Ltd

- How to manage large, complex, and interdisciplinary projects as large coordinated systems of interrelationships and cross-functional integrations to meet budget, schedule, and performance goal pressures.
- How to manage the organization's internal use of technology, including the smooth introduction and use of operational support technologies such as information systems, robotics, automation, and financial tools and models.

Although one can readily understand why these seven strategic areas would be crucial for any company's long-term success, the task force report also emphasized an eighth overarching requirement: the need to leverage more effectively the motivations and contributions of the organization's technical professionals. There is an enormous literature and a wealth of research and information written in the area of management, but most of it has little to do with the management and leadership of technical professionals and technical project teams ensconced in the process of developing new product and/or service-related innovations. In R&D, many of the tasks and projects that are worked on are fundamentally different from the tasks and projects performed by individuals who are running and supporting the operating part of the organization (Von Glinow and Mohrman, 1990; Von Glinow, 1988; Katz and Allen, 2004a). In their work on managing professional intellect, Quinn, Anderson, and Finkelstein (1996) clearly acknowledge the distinction between professional intellect based on the cognitive knowledge and self-motivation that comes up with creative breakthroughs and technical advances versus the organization's need to have most of their professional employees focus their activities on well-defined processes that yield highly reliable, measurable results. Organizations and their customers primarily want professional know-how delivered predictably but with the most relevant advanced capability. People rarely need or even want surgeons, accountants, pilots, or nuclear maintenance personnel to behave creatively (for example, especially during the surgery). Instead, professionals are typically required to repeat the use of their skills and talents on relatively similar, though complex problems. Clearly, they must be prepared for those emergencies or unexpected circumstances that require creative responses, but the bulk of their efforts and attention are primarily concentrated on delivering consistent, high-quality accomplishments.

There are lots of dimensions underlying the ways in which repetitive, operational tasks differ from those activities that are nonrepetitive, i.e., to do something new that no one else in the organization or the world has yet done. Meyer (1998) and others have nicely articulated a number of these dimensions as contrasted in Table 8.1.

The implications of these differences are significant. If you try, for example, to manage and deal with the uncertainty that is inherent in innovation with the same techniques and thinking designed for the relative certainty of operations, you'll probably run into trouble. In innovative settings, you expect things not to work and are delighted when they do in fact work; whereas in operations, you expect things to always work and are upset when they do not. Kirton's Adaption-Innovation theory (KAI) is founded on a similar set of assumptions (Kirton, 2003). Although all people solve problems and are creative, the theory sharply distinguishes between individuals' levels and styles of problem solving, creativity, and decision making, ranging along a continuum from high adaptation to high innovation. The key distinction is that

TABLE 8.1 Comparison of repetitive and nonrepetitive operational tasks.

Repetitive, operational and supportive tasks	Nonrepetitive, innovative and creative tasks
Uncertainty is low and incremental	Uncertainty is high and discontinuous
Steps are pre-defined and sequential	Steps are undefined, nonlinear, and iterative
Variability and rework costs money	Variability and rework are necessary for learning
Facts and information are clear	Facts and information are fuzzy
Easy to measure inputs and outputs	Hard to measure inputs and outputs
Clear, straightforward goals and objectives	Unclear, ambiguous, and even conflicting requirements
Feedback is objective and short term	Feedback is subjective and long term
Performance is measurable and controllable	Performance is creative and motivational
Underlying knowledge is known and explicit	Underlying knowledge is developing and tacit
Decisions are logical and programmable	Decisions are intuitive and nonprogrammable

the more adaptive professionals prefer their problems to be associated with more structure and consensual agreement, whereas the more innovative are comfortable solving problems with less structure and less consensual agreement. In short, an organization setting that is managed, structured, and designed to do the same thing well repetitively is not going to be good for doing something once; similarly, an organization that is managed, structured, and designed for doing something once is not going to be good for doing something repetitively – innovation and operations are essentially opposing logics. Before it was acquired by IBM, for example, Lotus Computer discovered that the creative people hired by the company to come up with its originally innovative and market dominant products (such as the Lotus 1-2-3 spreadsheet) no longer felt comfortable with or valued the organizational and management cultures that had emerged to run the businesses of the company that now had over 1000 employees (Sutton, 2002).

INTERNAL MOTIVATION FOR ENHANCING INNOVATIVE, CREATIVE PERFORMANCE

In performing these nonrepetitive kinds of tasks and projects, there are three basic ways in which professionals can focus their efforts and direct their time. They can be productive, nonproductive, or creative in the way they carry out their day-to-day assignments and activities. Although managers can be trained and given techniques and tools to measure and deal with the differences in performance and quality results of tasks occurring within the first two categories, the third category of creative time is much more difficult to control or measure simply because so much of it takes place in unexpected ways and depends so much on the individual's or group's internal motivational state for working with the results. It is easy to see the outcome differences between productive and nonproductive tasks – how many lines of code were written or bugs found, or how many products were manufactured or sold. It is very hard, on the other hand, to know whether an experiment that didn't get the desired results was nonproductive or creative – did one learn or gain insights from the experiment or did one become confused or give up?

Most managers would readily agree that the benefits of having internally driven motivated professionals are clear, but it is a very difficult thing to direct, maintain, and understand. Although the presence of motivation does not guarantee high performance or success, its absence seems to result in long-term problems. Strongly motivated employees and project teams push themselves to overachieve, stretching their thinking and working arduously to accomplish considerably more than even brighter and more technically competent peers. In fact, as technical leaders gain experience, they soon realize just how important it is to have the kind of excitement that motivates people to be creative and move their innovative ideas and advances more quickly through the organization. They are much better off having technical professionals with *A-rated* motivations and *B-rated* capabilities than the other way around. Or as Thomas Edison once remarked: 'I have more respect for the person who gets there than for the brilliant person with a thousand ideas who does nothing' (Israel, 1998).

PSYCHOLOGICAL NEED-BASED MODELS OF MOTIVATION

Generalized cognitive models of the motivation process, as reviewed by Steers and Porter (1995), can be characterized by three basic common denominators. Motivation is primarily concerned with:

- what energizes particular behaviors;
- what directs or channels these behaviors;
- how these behaviors are sustained or altered.

The first component concentrates on those needs, drives, or expectations within individuals or work settings that trigger certain behaviors, whereas the second component emphasizes the goals and visions of the individuals and groups toward which the energized behaviors are directed. The last component of any motivational model has to deal with feedback, focusing on those forces within individuals or their work environments that can either reinforce and intensify the energy and direction of desired behaviors or shift them to another course of action, thereby redirecting their efforts.

Although a wide range of motivational models has been put forth, most are psychological in nature, focusing on the willingness of a professional to undertake action in order to satisfy some need. An unsatisfied need creates tension, which stimulates a drive within the individual to identify particular goals that, if attained, will satisfy the need and lead to a reduction of tension. In some sense, motivated employees are in a state of tension, and they undertake activities and behave in ways to relieve this tension: the greater the tension, the greater the drive to bring about and seek relief. Cognitive models of this type require managers to understand the psychological needs of their R&D workforce, because when technical professionals are working hard at some set of activities, they are motivated by a desire to achieve the goals they value. Consequently, if organizations want motivated engineers and scientists, they must create the kinds of job assignments, careers, and work-related conditions that allow these professionals to satisfy their individual needs.

Maslow's hierarchy of needs

Arguably one of the most venerable models of motivation, Maslow's (1954) hierarchy of needs theory claims that within every individual there exists a hierarchy of five classes of needs:

1. *Physiological:* These involve bodily needs such as hunger, shelter, and sex.
2. *Safety:* These include one's needs for security and protection from physical and and emotional harm.
3. *Social:* These include one's needs for affection and a sense of belonging and acceptance.
4. *Self-esteem:* These include one's internal needs for self-respect, autonomy, and achievement, as well as one's external needs for status and recognition.
5. *Self-actualization:* This involves the need for self-fulfillment, to grow and achieve one's full potential.

Based on the hierarchical nature of this model, as each class of needs becomes more satisfied, the next class of needs in the hierarchy becomes more dominant. Maslow separated the five classes of needs into lower (physiological and safety) and higher (social, self-esteem, and self-actualization) orders. He then suggested that lower-order needs are satisfied *externally* through wages, bonuses, job security, and the like, while higher-order needs are satisfied *internally* through the individual's own sense of personal growth and development. Since satisfied needs no longer motivate, individuals tend to move up the hierarchy as their lower-order needs are met. (One can of course move down the hierarchy as lower needs, such as job security, become threatened.) The managerial implications of this motivational model are rather straightforward. RD&E settings should be organized and led to satisfy the higher-order needs of their technical professionals. To be strongly motivated, technologists need to feel that their jobs are both important and meaningful and that their contributions are truly valued by their organizations, their professions, and even by society. Nevertheless, many organizations still have trouble providing job experiences that consistently give their professional employees the opportunities for the growth and achievement they desire.

Herzberg's two-factor theory of motivation

In the belief that an individual's attitude toward work can greatly affect success or failure in the job, Herzberg (1966) asked professional employees to write two separate paragraphs: one to describe a situation in which they felt exceptionally satisfied about their jobs and one describing a situation in which they felt especially dissatisfied. After analyzing hundreds of paired-comparisons from these critical incident descriptions, Herzberg observed that the kinds of issues professionals mentioned and described when they felt good about their jobs were distinctly different from the replies given when they felt bad. After categorizing these paired comparison responses, Herzberg concluded that certain job characteristics, labeled 'motivators', are more influential with respect to job satisfaction whereas other characteristics, labeled 'hygiene-factors', are more strongly connected with job dissatisfaction. Motivating or intrinsic-type factors included items involving achievement, recognition, responsibility, challenging work, and opportunities for growth and advancement, whereas hygiene or extrinsic-type factors associated with job dissatisfaction were connected with items such as company policies, administrators, supervisory relationships, working conditions, salary, and peer relationships.

Based on this empirical divergence, Herzberg argued that it may not be very meaningful to measure or think about satisfaction and dissatisfaction as end points along a single dimension or continuum. Instead, one should consider satisfaction and dissatisfaction as two independent factors comprised by very different items. There are intrinsic factors that lead to greater levels of job satisfaction, and consequently more motivated individuals within the workplace. And then there are separate hygiene-type factors that mostly affect one's level of job dissatisfaction. The basic notion underneath this two-factor theory is that managers who focus on improving hygiene-type factors may succeed in reducing employee dissatisfaction but such efforts will probably not increase job motivation. Most likely, such managers are placating their workers rather than motivating and engaging them. When hygiene factors are adequate, employees may not be dissatisfied but neither will they feel motivated. As in Maslow's theory, if organizations want to enhance the motivations of technical professionals, they have to emphasize the intrinsic aspects of jobs and create the organizational changes and climates that result in positive energies that foster creative and innovative performances rather than instituting policies and changes that lower dissatisfactions but can also yield complacency in place of excitement.

McClelland's theory of needs

Additional psychological models have been developed to look at motivation as a function of the *fit* between the individual and the organizational job setting. McClelland and his colleagues, for example, contend that individuals' needs and motives can be measured along three critical dimensions (Boyatzis, 1982; McClelland and Boyatzis, 1982). The *need for affiliation* describes an individual's desire for friendly and close interpersonal relationships. Employees with a high need for affiliation want to be well liked and accepted by their colleagues. They prefer job situations that are cooperative rather than competitive, environments in which relationships are built on high levels of mutual trust and understanding. A second dimension depicts an individual's *need for power*, that is, the drive to influence others and have an impact. People with a high need for power strive for control, prefer competitive situations, and seem to enjoy being in charge. The third dimension captures a person's *need for achievement,* the desire to excel or succeed at some challenging activity or project. Individuals with a high need for achievement, seek to overcome obstacles in order to do things better or more efficiently than they were done in the past. They work to accomplish difficult goals that have intermediate levels of risk, and they are willing to accept the personal responsibility for a project's success or failure rather than leaving the outcome to chance or to the actions of others.

Studies in R&D settings have consistently found that technical professionals with a high need for achievement are more motivated and successful in entrepreneurial activities (Roberts, 1991), although a high need to achieve does not necessarily lead to being a good technical manager. In fact, McClelland (1988) reported from his most recent research that the best managers have a relatively low need for affiliation but a relatively high need for power – a need for power, however, that is not unbridled but is carefully kept under restraint by the individual. Since innovation often requires entrepreneurial risk-taking behavior, R&D managers can either select professionals with high achievement needs to lead such efforts or they can establish appropriate training programs to stimulate the achievement needs of those technologists undertaking entrepreneurial-type projects and activities (Goleman, McKee, and Boyatzis, 2002).

Schein's career anchor model

As discussed by Schein (1996), an individual's career anchor is his or her self-concept, consisting of self-perceived talents and abilities; basic values; and most importantly, the individual's evolved sense of motives and needs. Career anchors develop as one gains occupational and life experiences and once they are formed, they function as a stabilizing force, making certain job and career changes either acceptable or unacceptable to the individual. The research showed that most people's self-concepts revolve around eight categories reflecting basic values, motives, and needs. And as careers and lives evolve, Schein discovered that most individuals employ one of these eight categories as their motivational and decision-making anchor, the aspect of their jobs and careers that they come to value the most and will *not* give up:

1. *The managerial anchor:* Technical professionals in this category are motivated by the complex set of activities comprising general management, seeking higher levels of responsibility and authority within the business organization rather than remaining within their technical specialty. To be successful, they must develop the analytical competence to work with conceptual problems under conditions of uncertainty and incomplete information; they must develop the interpersonal competence to lead people toward the more effective achievement of organizational and business goals; and they must develop the emotional competence to remain strong and make tough decisions in highly pressured, stressful situations without feeling debilitated or paralyzed.
2. *The technical-functional anchor:* These professionals are motivated by the technical challenges of the actual work they do. Their careers lie in

using the knowledge and skills of their technical disciplines and not the managerial process itself. They are usually most comfortable supervising professionals like themselves or who work in the same disciplinary area. In contrast to the managerial anchor professionals, it is the nature of the technical work and not the supervising that excites them and so they would prefer not to be promoted to job positions outside their technical areas.

3. *The security-stability anchor:* These professionals have an underlying need for security, seeking to stabilize their careers by linking them to particular organizations, and are more willing than other anchor types to accept the organization's definition of their careers. They rely on the organization to recognize their needs and provide them with the best possible job options and opportunities. This type of professional often experiences stress and has considerably more difficulty in times of uncertainty, particularly when the organization wants the person to become more responsible for his or her career.

4. *The entrepreneurial creativity anchor:* Some professionals have a strong desire to create something of their own, which becomes the fundamental operating need. These professionals are strongly interested in commercializing new products or services or in creating something with which he or she can be clearly identified. They often express a strong desire to be on their own and away from the constraints of established organizations. Technical entrepreneurs start their own companies not just because they want to make a great deal of money or to be autonomous but because they truly believe in what they are doing and their former organization would not let them continue to do it. They have a strong need to create or build something and can easily become restless with the demands and routines of running a business. Often, they are more concerned with the exploitation and commercialization of good ideas that have been created and worked on by others.

5. *The autonomy-independence anchor:* Some professionals strongly prefer not to be bound by the traditional norms and policies that are present in most large organizations. These creative individual contributors are primarily driven by their own sense of freedom and autonomy. They have an overriding need to do things their own way, at their own pace, and along their own standards. They find organizational life to be restrictive, irrational, and somewhat intrusive. As a result, they prefer to pursue more independent careers, often seeking work as consultants, professors, independent contractors, or R&D staff professionals for whom the technical ladder of promotion is most appropriate (Katz and Allen, 2004b).

6–8. *The lifestyle, service-dedication, and pure challenge anchors:* According to Schein (1996), there are a few professionals in each of these small anchor categories. Some professionals focus on careers that can be integrated with a total lifestyle, permitting themselves to stabilize their life patterns without significant disruptions. They do not define their careers in terms of economic or organizational security but rather in terms of a larger life system. Most are in dual career situations, seeking work settings that provide them with the flexibility they need to integrate family concerns, including working at home, flexible schedules, leaves of absence, or day-care coverage. What these professionals want from their organizations is an understanding attitude and respect for their lifestyle pressures and needs. Other individuals report that they need to do something meaningful and significant from a societal point of view. Professionals anchored in service want to work in organizations and have careers that allow them to contribute to significant societal issues. And finally, a small group of people define their careers in terms of facing tough challenges, solving difficult problems, or simply winning out over competitors.

Since the career anchors of technical professionals vary so widely, Schein (1996) argues that constructive career management is only possible when individuals know their own needs and biases, analyzing their own career anchors, gaining more self-insight, and then proactively managing their own career paths. And in order to keep their professionals highly motivated, organizations should also create more flexible career paths and incentive systems in order to meet this wide range of pluralistic needs.

All these cognitive theories of motivation imply that when technical professionals are well matched with their jobs, it is rarely necessary to force or manipulate them into working hard to perform their jobs well. When there is a good *fit* between individuals and the jobs, the individuals will usually have very high levels of internal work motivation, feeling good both about themselves and what they are accomplishing. Good performance becomes self-rewarding, which in turn, serves as an incentive for continuing to do well. In similar fashion, poor performance creates unhappy feelings, which prompts the person to try harder in the future to avoid unpleasant outcomes and regain the intrinsic rewards that good performance can bring. The result is a self-perpetuating cycle of positive work motivation powered through the intrinsically rewarding nature of the work itself. The critical issue is for organizations to structure and design requisite project activities in such a way that professionals also find the work personally rewarding and satisfying.

It is the nature of this *fit* between the individual and the job that makes internal motivation a dynamic rather than a static concept. It is constantly changing over time depending on how well the individuals' needs fit the demands of the tasks performed (Chatman and Barsade, 1995; Katz, 2004b). Typically, when an individual chooses or self-selects to work on a given project, the fit and associated motivation starts at a higher level than if the professional had to be asked or assigned to work on a given project. This is why in almost all the examples and stories of high performing project teams, the core team members were not assigned but chose or agreed through some process to work on the project (Katz, 2004b). It is also why managers and project leaders will tell you that it is far easier to motivate professionals who in a way had self-selected to work for them rather than were assigned to work for them, just as it is easier for professors to teach students in an elective course rather than one that is required – they come as active participants rather than as passive observers. It is also why the process of the ways in which technical and cross-functional personnel are allocated among the project teams in a matrix organizational structure is such an important motivation factor (Katz and Allen, 1985; Allen and Henn, 2007) and why 'heavyweight' project teams are so strongly preferred by project managers (Clark and Wheelwright, 1992). But as professionals continue to perform their jobs over time, the nature of the *fit* can change. The individual's needs and concerns can change or the dimensions of the task requirements of the job can change, or both can change. And it is how these two aspects of the work setting change, i.e., the professionals' sense of their own needs and concerns coupled with the task requirements of their jobs, which lead either to higher levels of intrinsic motivation and creative performance or result in lower levels of intrinsic motivation and more routine performance.

MOTIVATIONAL TASK DIMENSIONS

Although there are a large number of cognitive models and theories about individual needs and the drivers of individual needs, such as the ones previously described, there are few frameworks for analyzing how technical professionals perceive the various task dimensions of their jobs even though it is generally acknowledged that a professional's true calling comes from the nature of the work he or she is asked to do. Put simply, people in general, and technical professionals in particular, like to do *neat* things – 'to boldly go where no man has gone before'. If a technical revolution is taking shape, the more creative, highly motivated R&D professionals in that area just don't want to miss it! If organizational employees believe their work is challenging, innovative, significant, and exciting, then no demands are so difficult that they cannot eventually be met (Kidder, 1984). In his feature story on *techies*, for example, Alpert (1992) points out that during the interviews not a single engineer or programmer mentioned career advancement as a primary goal; instead, they talked about technical challenges, i.e., the work itself, as their chief reward.

Although extrinsic factors such as salary, benefits, security, and working conditions are also important, decades of research convincingly shows that they do not instill the kind of commitment and excitement needed in creative work environments where employees are expected to stretch their thinking, push their ideas, and persevere to find solutions to tough, unyielding problems (Badawy, 1988). Are the professionals' managers trying to motivate their staff by reducing dissatisfaction or are they creating the task demands and job environments that foster the creative tension, the positive energy that leads to excitement (Farris and Cordero, 2002). It is important to remember that 'fat rats don't run mazes' (Manners, Steger, and Zimmerer, 1998). The intrinsic motivational potential of any specific job, then, is dramatically influenced by how the professional views the job assignment on which he or she is working at a given point in time, including how tasks, information, reward, and decision-making processes are organized, structured, and managed. Even in highly pressured and stressful job situations, professionals reported that their work was still truly motivational because they felt they were also having *fun* doing it (Kidder, 1984; Katz, 2004a; Arndt, 2006; Lashinsky, 2006). In some sense, then, highly motivating work assignments should be similar to the kinds of activities individuals or professionals would choose to do for fun on their own.

A 'work-fun' analogy

To pursue this analogy, let's assume that many professionals enjoy playing golf or even like to go bowling. Let's further assume that one of the underlying reasons they like to golf or bowl is that it is a use of their own skills and abilities. They perform the activities by themselves based on their own individual styles and competencies. They can set their own target scores and strive to achieve these scores at their own pace without being dependent on someone else's progress and capabilities. The majority of their educational years of experience also asked them to take courses, prepare homework, solve problems, complete exams, and get final grades as individuals. This *individualism*, however, can be very problematic in organizations when the professional is now required to work interdependently with others who may not be as technically creative or as capable as themselves. It is one thing to work with or be on a project with someone who is at least as talented and as motivated as oneself. It is much more difficult to work with someone who is less capable or less motivated. And since the technical capabilities and priorities of individual team members are rarely uniformly distributed, professionals have to learn how to work and interact with others on either end of these distributions. If not, the R&D professional is likely to end up working apart rather than interdependently, which in turn can lead to the silos, with uneven motivations, that characterize far too many cross-functional project teams. It is in the higher performing project teams that one finds the kinds of interaction, leadership, and mutual accountability that are needed for enabling project team members to value and respect the energy, commitment, involvement, and contribution of each other (Larson and LaFasto, 1989; Hackman, 2002). Naturally, frustrations can also occur in bowling or golfing if one does not develop the patience and sensitivity for learning to have fun with others who cannot play as well or who play at a slower or more methodical pace.

Most likely, technical employees also like to bowl or play golf because they have a complete understanding of the game from beginning to end. As previously discussed, they have a more *holistic* view of their team and their goal, seeing themselves playing an active and genuine role during the game because their contributions are valued and respected (Katzenbach and Smith, 1993). As a result, they feel they are significant and somewhat equal players or colleagues within the overall team effort. Status and positional differences are minimal because all scores and contributions matter. No employee would be excited to play, for example, if one was told that one's score or contribution would never count – or that one's score was going to be canceled or shelved – or if everyone else's scores were seen as more pivotal. Over the last few years, I have come across many technical professionals, who had been highly motivated in the past in excellent organizations but who frustratingly left, primarily because their technical efforts were being shelved and not commercialized.

Even though the goals and objectives of the games are clear, bowlers and golfers are given a lot of autonomy within which to play. They are free to develop their own style and pace within the rules and constraints of the game. They also know how well they are performing while playing. Feedback is quick and unequivocal – and they know how they are doing comparatively. But again, no one would like to bowl or golf if the alleys or fairways were draped hiding the pins or greens, or if one was told to come back in six months for a performance appraisal. Nor would anyone enjoy the game if a boss stood by with constant reminders such as 'Move to your left, watch the red line, keep your grip steady, your arm straight'. And finally, who would want to play if, as soon as one achieved a terrific score, the CEO ended up congratulating the boss rather than the player? It is doubtful that anyone would truly find bowling or golfing *fun* under these kinds of conditions.

Task dimensions

If work is to be viewed in the same vein as having fun, a job's tasks should have some of the same characteristics as golfing and bowling. But what are these task characteristics that elicit such high levels of intrinsic work motivation? Referring to Hackman and Oldham's (1980) framework, Figure 8.1 shows that people are more motivated when they feel their jobs require them to use a wide *variety* of skills and abilities. All too often, professionals become disenchanted when narrowly defined tasks allow them to use only a small portion of their overall competencies and educational training, or when assignments might involve only mundane technologies rather than the newer ones that are developing within their disciplines. Previous research clearly indicates that the broader the range of skills and abilities tapped early in a person's career, the more likely it is that the person will remain to become a more effective and successful contributing member of the organization (Katz, 2004c). The key is not how many different projects individuals are asked to work on, but whether they are able to develop the cumulative knowledge, perspective, and credibility essential for continued success within the organization's particular setting and culture.

In his seminal study, for example, Pelz (1988) discovered that technical professionals were judged most effective when they had spent time in activities along

Dimensions of task characteristics	Definitions
Skill variety	The degree to which the job requires the use of different skills, abilities, and talents
Task identity	The degree to which the person feels that he or she is part of the whole job or project activity from beginning to end
Task significance	The degree to which the job is considered important by and has impact on the lives of others
Autonomy	The degree to which the job provides freedom, independence, and discretion in how the work is carried out
Feedback	The degree to which the person is provided with clear and direct information about the effectiveness of his or her performance

FIGURE 8.1 A framework for work motivation (adapted from Hackman and Oldham, 1980).

the research, development, and technical service continuum rather than concentrating in only one of these domains. Young professionals not only have to solidify their technical reputations by focusing their efforts and accomplishments in a major project and/or technical area, but they must also have enough challenge and range in their tasks and networks to take the kinds of initiatives and come up with the kinds of ideas that will help them become the organization's future high flyers and star performers (Kelley, 1998; McCall, 1998).

But getting ones technical career off to a good start is not a forgone conclusion. The research of Dalton and Thompson (1993) indicates that the establishment of a 'professional identity' is the critical first step in a successful technical career. It usually involves landing a challenging first assignment and demonstrating technical competency. It then evolves into gaining independence from direct supervision while working in an area of proficiency that allows the new professional to become one of the company's experts. At this stage aspiring professionals are sought after for their technical know-how. They've become a member of the 'technical club' with all the informal information exchanges and networking necessary for continued competence development.

Interestingly enough, it is not just the technical aspects of the work that are important. Of the many job-related experiences investigated in my own studies of technical professionals' early career years, the ones that were most predictive for achieving higher managerial promotions were the opportunities to work on jobs that helped familiarize them with the ways in which the organization dealt with business and financial information. Most likely, these fiscally related experiences provided these individuals with more chances for developing into, or of being seen, as broader contributors. They were perceived as more capable of putting together the kinds of *business* plans that make those managing existing operations and finances more comfortable – at least in terms of focus, scope, and language – rather than the more one-sided, narrow *technical* arguments that are all too often put forward by their technical colleagues (Badawy, 1982; Badawy, 1993).

It is extremely important for technical managers to learn how to frame or 'couch' their ideas into the business screens and financial terminology that are specifically used by those who run and evaluate the organization's day-to-day pressures and interests. Even General Electric's ex-CEO, Jack Welch, points out in his autobiography that as a Ph.D. chemical engineer, he was sufficiently 'green' in the intricacies of finance that he asked his staff to prepare a book translating all of GE's financial jargon into layman's terms so he could be more conversant with the businesses (Welch, 2001).

Two other analogous and important characteristics of work in Figure 8.1 are *task identity* and *task significance*. Work assignments are just much more fun and motivating when people are given a complete picture of the project and feel as if they are *real* contributing members. And it is through the kinds of communications, involvements, and reward systems that take place that employees build perceptions of these task dimensions. Consider, for example, the experience of an extremely important 25-person R&D project team working feverishly in a major well-known organization. These 25 engineers struggled together for several years to accomplish a product breakthrough development with technical superiority that added significant value to customers in the marketplace. What really mattered however to this technical team after all these years of effort was not just pay raises, promotions, or managerial praise and recognition; they truly wanted the opportunity to present their *breakthrough* as a team at their discipline's annual international conference in order to impress their colleagues and sort of 'stick it' to their competitors. Rather than rewarding this team, to enhance its motivational commitment for future accomplishments, the organization simply replied that traditional Human Resource Management (HRM) practices and procedures allowed for *only* one or two project members to present results at a conference (even though the company was planning to spend many hundreds of millions of dollars to promote and build its future business around this breakthrough). You can, of course, predict how this perfunctory response affected the future enthusiasm of this team, whose members had put their lives 'on hold' to meet incredible deadlines. Their dimensions of task identity and significance plummeted virtually overnight. Money, title, and praise may be very visible on report cards, but they are not always the most valued incentives – what really drives most technical innovators is excitement in their work, pride in their accomplishments, and the ability to receive recognition from those whose opinions they value. They want their 'names' on or even in the product!

Another task characteristic in Figure 8.1 for inducing high levels of motivation is autonomy – the degree of freedom one has in carrying out work requirements. As autonomy increases, individuals become more reliant on their own efforts, initiatives, and decisions. They feel more personal responsibility and are willing to accept more personal accountability for work outcomes. In designing motivating work environments, however, managers must distinguish between *strategic* autonomy and *operational* autonomy – between *what* has to be done in terms of goals, expectations, direction, and constraints versus *how* one chooses to meet the goals and accomplish the work (Kanter, 2000). Many managers, unfortunately, confuse or even reverse these two aspects of autonomy. Rather than clarifying expectations and establishing clear parameters that would enable people to make decisions and take initiatives within well-defined boundaries, organizations often give too much free reign with aphorisms such as 'take risk' or 'don't be afraid to fail'. Then, as they get increasingly nervous, they try to control and micromanage the work, imposing all kinds of unanticipated constraints and changes. In studies on and interviews with technical employees, for example, the research often describes how management gives initial research assignments to technical professionals with well-intentioned but rather unclear mandates such as 'go be creative', 'be more innovative', or 'go think great thoughts'. The professionals then go off on their own trying desperately to be creative and innovative. Many would eventually emerge months or even years later with wonderful new ideas and products only to discover that the organization was no longer interested in pursuing something in that particular area, something that risky, or something that required that much money or time, etc. Managers need to *empower* the other way around. They should clarify expectations and conditions as much as possible and then give people the freedom to function within those definitions (Smith and Alexander, 1988). Constraints need not be constraining – they can be empowering as long as there are some degrees of freedom for tradeoffs and not the 'better, faster, cheaper' strategy that so many managers demand.

To sustain intrinsic motivation, individuals also need to see and hear about the results of their work. Achievement provides a source of both personal and collegial recognition that drives continuous innovative behavior. This comes from setting stretch goals that encourage both curiosity and risk taking, thereby providing opportunities for overachievement and creative success. It is the feedback from those who they respect the most that motivates professionals and ties their success to the goals of their peer groups and organization. If professionals cannot determine whether they are performing well or poorly, they have no basis for trying to improve. Thus, the remaining motivating task characteristic in Figure 8.1 is *feedback* – the degree to which individuals receive clear, unambiguous information about their performance. Although professionals often feel that they are excellent judges of their own roles and performances, they still need to calibrate their activities and career progress. They especially want to know how others whom they respect and whose opinions they value judge their abilities, efforts, contributions, and success. When a technologist values the opinions of others on his or her team and wants to perform to their expectations then those other team members have 'social control' over that technical professional. In her survey of US engineers, Westney (1987) found that engineers wanted to perform well most importantly in the eyes of their peers and colleagues.

As managers gain experience, they soon learn one of the more important tenants of motivation: it is easier to destroy morale than to create excitement. Only by examining how jobs are organized and perceived along Hackman and Oldham's (1980) model of five task dimensions can managers hope to foster the settings in which professionals might find themselves having fun as they do their work. Furthermore, extant research with technical professionals seems to show that feedback is the most deficient task characteristic and the one around which technologists complain the most (Katz, 1998). There are probably at least three reasons for this. First, in innovative settings where one is trying to do something that has never been done before, it is very hard to define or measure what good work is. Trying to explain what constitutes 'good code', for example, is very difficult to do ahead of time. Only after one sees it can one really say whether the code was 'neat' or poorly done. One may also not be able to determine for quite some time whether a new idea is truly creative or dumb – brilliant or just plain foolish. Or to say it another way, the most creative idea and the stupidest idea often look the same in the early stages.

A second reason for feedback being low is simply that most technical managers and leaders are not particularly comfortable or well trained at giving constructive feedback. Third, most technical professionals are not particularly good at receiving feedback, especially feedback that may not be totally positive. It is not uncommon to discover that many creative individuals have never received feedback or been given anything but uniform praise (Humphrey, 1987). This can make the transmission of what was intended as constructive interaction into a troublesome and unpleasant exchange.

Although R&D professionals may complain about inadequate communication and feedback about job performance and career opportunities, it is not the most powerful task dimension for establishing high levels of work motivation. The most critical dimension by far for elevating motivation is task significance. Professionals become more excited and energized when they feel they are working on something important – something that clearly makes a difference within the business unit (Meyer, 1997). Interestingly enough, even though task significance is the most influential task characteristic for influencing motivation, the dimension that often surfaces from surveys is autonomy. But one should be very careful in interpreting self-report surveys. It is easy for professionals to say they want a lot of autonomy; it does not necessarily mean they will thrive under autonomy. And autonomy decoupled from a sense of significance can lead to very dissatisfying and frustrating work experiences (Katz, 2004b).

Multidimensional task dimensions

As just described, one can easily examine any job for its motivational potential by determining whether it is relatively strong or weak with respect to each of these five task characteristics. One of the problems, however, in managing and motivating R&D professionals is that there are at least two ways of looking at each of these task characteristics (Figure 8.2).

Hackman and Oldham's (1980) framework, for example, deals with skill variety. Organizations hire professional employees because they need them – they want to *use* their knowledge and technical skills. The individual's prior education, training, and work experiences are all strongly considered in decisions to hire new personnel and in the distribution of critical work assignments. On the other hand, professionals not only want to be used, they also want to grow. They want to learn – to *extend* their knowledge and capabilities. That's the professional norm! What makes a job especially exciting is the belief that the professionals will learn a heck of a lot as

Task dimensions	Organization's orientation priority	Professional's orientation priority
Skill variety	To utilize one's skills and abilities	To learn and develop new skills and abilities
Task identity	To become a contributing member of the organization	To become a contributing member of the profession
Task significance	To work on projects that are important to the organization	To work on projects that are exciting within the profession
Autonomy	Strategic clarity	Operational autonomy
Feedback	Subjective data and information processes	Objective data and information processes

FIGURE 8.2 Multidimensional framework for work motivation.

they carry out their assignments. Put simply, they not only want to utilize what they already know, they also want to keep up-to-date, incorporating relevant leading-edge thinking and advances from their discipline areas into their project's requirements. In a rapidly changing environment, keeping up with the latest knowledge is essential for sustained success and some techies are manic about keeping abreast of the latest developments.

Executives and professionals would readily agree that *both* skill utilization and skill extension are crucial elements of any job environment, but the organization must deal with the reality that there are major differences in how these two groups order their relative priorities. Such priority differences are not very problematic when there are lots of slack resources and good times. They can become very de-motivating and counterproductive, however, if priority disagreements lead to conflicts that are left unresolved especially under conditions of stress and uncertainty. Without active leadership intervention, stress will tend to exacerbate these priority differences. HRM's tuition reimbursement programs, for example, are usually one of the first things to go when the firm feels monetarily stressed. In research interviews, engineers often complained that their organizations would not fund their taking certain technical courses because the technologies were not part of the firm's product line. Yet, the engineers countered that they could not effectively adopt the technologies until they take the courses – the proverbial catch 22. In such cases, technical professionals become increasingly cynical, often deciding to leave the firm or enroll in an MBA program. Professionals working in organizations want to be viewed as an investment and not as an expense (Baldwin, Danielson, and Wiggenhorn, 1998).

In a similar vein, the organization's managers and knowledge workers often view the dimensions of task identity and task significance in very different ways. Are the technical employees primarily members of their organization or members of their profession? In essence, they have one head but two hats. Are they software or hardware engineers at IBM or are they IBM employees doing software design or hardware engineering? Most managers would contend that technologists should perceive themselves first as organizational contributors and second as members of their profession. Many professionals, however, prioritize their orientations, scientists, and Ph.D.s in particular the opposite way around (Allen and Katz, 1992). A similar pattern often occurs with respect to task significance. Is it more important to work on projects that are important to the organization or on technical issues that are exciting to the profession? Is it more important to incorporate the most sophisticated technological developments and features or to focus on technological advances and features that fit within infrastructure of use, that are manufacturable, reliable, cost effective, etc. Once again, most professionals would prefer to come up with breakthrough, elegant solutions for problems defined as important by their fields. Business managers, in contrast, would prefer they concentrate on technical advances that are 'good enough' – enabling technologies that can be quickly turned into products and services that solve customer problems and eventually make money (Steele, 1988).

Many professionals see themselves as having studied a body of knowledge and internalized a code of conduct that supersedes the companies in which they work.

They therefore want to influence (but not necessarily lead or make) decisions that determine project strategies as well as how their expertise will be used and applied. These individual contributors often have strong beliefs and personalities and are more motivated when *pulled* rather than *pushed*. They want to know *why* something is asked and they want to mull over ideas, information, assignments, and strategies and then be able to challenge any with which they are uncomfortable or disagree. These professionals respond best to leaders who have an empathetic understanding of their technical problem-solving worlds and who make their lives easier by respecting their expertise, supporting them in their technical efforts, providing them with the best available tools, equipment, and information, and protecting them from nonproductive hierarchical demands and inflexible bureaucratic constraints.

There are, as previously discussed with respect to such decision-making and leadership processes, two kinds of autonomy: *strategic* and *operational*. If organizations want to enrich jobs and motivate employees through empowerment, that is, giving them the freedom to function independently and make decisions based on their own careful professional judgments, then managers need to establish as much strategic focus and clarity as possible and then let their technical personnel function autonomously within these clearly defined goals and boundary conditions. In developing new products and services, project teams are constantly making critical decisions and tradeoffs. And the clearer the leadership is about its expectations and constraints, its proverbial *lines in the sand*, the easier it is to empower project teams effectively. Managers have to be careful not to do the reverse, confusing people with unclear directives and support while simultaneously maintaining rigid control over the means by which they asked their people to do things differently, i.e., to be creative and innovative.

And of course, there are two kinds of feedback: *subjective* and *objective*. Although both types are important and have to be integrated, when objective data conflicts with a manager's subjective gut, i.e., his or her more intuitive feeling and understanding, the subjective element is more likely to dominate. But remember, technical professionals come from perhaps the most objective environments, namely educational and university institutions. When taking courses, students are told what to read, when to read, and even how long it should take them to do the assignments. They are told which formulas to memorize and, when tested, they are given all the information needed to solve carefully-crafted technical problems. There is, moreover, a single correct solution to each problem, and answers are individually scored to give each student an objective piece of feedback, namely a grade. Finally, if one passes any prescribed sequence of courses, one will graduate in a pre-defined time frame. All this programmed structure fits nicely with the educational philosophy propagated within technical professions – cultures in which analyses and decisions that are based on logical thinking, clear discussions, and reliable, unambiguous data are highly valued.

In the world of work, however, the opposite conditions typically apply. Technologists soon discover that problems are not well-defined or self-contained but are intertwined with all sorts of history, politics, and behavioral-type issues. Nor are they given all the formulas, tools, and information needed to come up with appropriate solutions. In fact, they usually have to figure out what it is they need, where to get it, what may or may not be valid information, who they can believe, and what may or may not be acceptable. A given problem may not even be solvable. Promotions and rewards, moreover, are not guaranteed. And unlike the university, feedback is no longer based on objective test answers graded by professors who have more expertise than the students. Feedback is now based on the subjective perceptions of one's boss who may actually have much less technical knowledge and understanding about the tasks on which the individual has worked. In short, the critical skill for performing in the university is *solving* carefully structured and communicated problems. The real skill in the real world, however, is being able to *formulate* a comprehensive definition of what are often incomplete and ill-defined problems and solution approaches.

Organizations and their HRM functions need to understand that they can never permanently 'eliminate' the differences highlighted in Figure 8.2. Instead, they need to make sure that their practices, policies, and procedures are flexible enough to deal with both dimensions of the professional's job setting. Without recognizing these differences, organizational policies run the risk of destroying morale and excitement rather than helping to create them. Whereas the former is easy to do, the latter is the much more difficult. In fact, it is the latter, i.e., sustaining excitement and technical vitality, that is the real challenge. Recent research has shown just how fast *winning* firms can become *losers* if they allow themselves to become too complacent and too stress free (Tushman and O'Reilly, 1997). Differences and stress *per se* are not necessarily bad by themselves – they are often needed for generating creativity and energetic change. The critical question is whether the organization's leadership can take these differences and stressful requirements and focus them into *positive energy* or *creative tension*.

Job tenure stages

Research studies by Katz (2004b), Kozlowski and Hults (1987), and Dalton and Thompson (1993) also show that technical professionals pass through three broad stages as they perform their work over time in a relatively stable job environment: *socialization, innovation,* and *stabilization*. During the socialization period, professionals are primarily concerned with understanding and coming to terms with their new and unknown social and task environments. Newcomers must learn the customary norms of behavior within their groups, how reward systems operate, the expectations of their superiors, and a host of other considerations that are necessary for them to function meaningfully in their new settings. This 'breaking-in' period is not only true for those joining the organization but also for veteran employees assigned to new job positions or groups who must also 're-socialize' themselves, because they, too, must now deal with unfamiliar tasks and colleagues. Both newcomers and veterans have to learn not only the technical aspects of their new jobs, but also the behaviors and attitudes that are necessary and acceptable for becoming a true contributing member of their new job assignments. It is during this stage, therefore, that professionals are most responsive to the task significance and feedback dimensions of their jobs and rather unreceptive to levels of autonomy that serve to prolong their socialization or re-socialization processes.

As professionals gain familiarity with their work settings, they are freer to focus their energies and concerns less on socialization and more toward performance and achievement. In this job stage of innovation, employees become increasingly capable of acting on their own in a more exciting and undistracted manner. As they progress, they are more capable of deciphering their new job surroundings and can direct their attention from their previous concerns for 'psychological safety and acceptance' to concerns for influence and achievement. Opportunities to change the status quo and to respond to new challenging demands within their job settings become increasingly more pertinent during this stage. Essentially, they are highly motivated and become responsive to all the task dimensions of their jobs. As the length of time spent in the same job environment stretches out, however, professionals gradually enter the stabilization phase, in which there is a slow shift away from a high level of involvement and receptivity to the challenging aspects in their jobs and toward a greater degree of unresponsiveness to the task dimensions. Their motivations shift from creative performance to routine performance; from excitement to complacency. Motivation and satisfaction now comes from maintaining predictability and routine, from being left alone rather than from the creative tension of facing new problems and challenges.

In time, even the most engaging job assignments and responsibilities can appear less exciting, little more than habit, to people who have successfully mastered and become accustomed to their everyday task requirements. It makes sense then that with long-term job stability, employees' perceptions of their present tasks and possibilities for the future will become increasingly impoverished. If professionals cannot perceive, redefine, or expand their jobs for continued change and growth, their work enthusiasm will deteriorate. If cycles of new job challenges occur or if development possibilities are continued even within a given job, the stabilization period may be held off indefinitely.

Motivational dualism and the need for the ambidextrous organization

In many organizations today, HRM concentrates on the functioning aspects of the organization. It develops policies and practices that primarily support the ongoing operations, including job descriptions, performance appraisals, reward/recognition systems, and educational/training programs. Given this emphasis, the HRM function in many organizations has failed to gain strong credibility among technical professionals or within the innovating technical community *per se*. All too often, R&D mistrusts HRM, viewing it as too soft, irrelevant, naive, and unrealistic. To help overcome this barrier, HRM needs to understand the subtle but important differences that I have just been discussing between the organization's managers and its technical professionals.

It needs more than ever before to deal with these motivational challenges of *dualism* and *job tenure*. That is, HRM has to carry out its responsibilities efficiently to support the organization's existing operations while at the same time its policies and practices must be robust enough to support effectively the motivations of technical professionals necessary to sustain its future creative and innovative success. No matter how they are structured and organized, corporations must manage both sets of concerns simultaneously. As a result, HRM must help build internally those contradictory and inconsistent structures, competencies, and cultures that not only foster more efficient and reliable processes but also encourage the kinds of experiments and explorations needed to re-create the future, even though such innovative activities are all too often seen by those running the organization as a waste of resources or threat to its current priorities and prior basis of success.

But even getting an agreement on a common definition of innovation demonstrates the challenge that underlies this dilemma. Innovative activities have generally been classified as either radical or incremental, continuous or discontinuous, competence-enhancing or competence-destroying, and most recently as sustaining or disruptive (Katz, 2004d). These classifications have focused on which types of innovating activities are most important for enhancing sustained organizational success. But most astute managers understand the necessity for both, and the need to identify and somehow manage the issues associated with these apparent contradictory innovation approaches. The simple point is that organizations need to have split personalities to manage simultaneously both approaches and do it well. A singular strong cohesive organizational culture can easily undermine this need for multiplicity – the ability to create ambidextrous organizations that concurrently work to commercialize the different kinds of innovation streams (Tushman and O'Reilly, 1997).

Although it is easy to say that organizations should internalize both sets of concerns, it is a very difficult thing to do. Witness for example the experiences of Procter & Gamble (P&G) over the last 10 or so years. In the beginning, analysts claimed that P&G was doing an excellent job at managing its existing businesses but regrettably was not growing the company fast enough through the commercialization of new brands or new product categories. P&G then impressively introduced a number of very successful new products (Swiffer, Whitestrips, Thermacare, and Febreze to name a few) that were collectively bringing in considerably more than a billion dollars in added revenue per year. The analysts then switched gears acknowledging P&G's new product initiatives but criticizing them for taking their eye off its existing brands and losing important market share to very aggressive competitors. It is not particularly surprising that these same analysts now wanted P&G to de-emphasize its new venture strategies and investments in order to concentrate on protecting and strengthening its major bedrock brands. The pendulum just seemed to keep on swinging.

Product heaven

The unfortunate reality is that there is usually much disagreement within a company as to how to carry out this dualism, instead of the back and forth pendulum. Amid the demands of everyday pressures, decision makers representing different parts of the organization rarely agree on the relative merits of allocating resources and management attention among the range of competing projects and technical activities; that is, those that directly benefit the organization's more salient and immediate needs versus those that will fuel long-term future growth. Consider the reactions of individuals representing different organizational functions to a very simple question such as 'What is heaven to you from a product line point of view?'. Manufacturing managers would typically respond that in their heaven there would be only *one* product with no design changes. This would enable them to build the most reliable processes for high volume output that they hope would be defect free. Marketing managers, on the other hand, would have a diametrically opposite point of view. In their heaven, there would be *unlimited* product variation in order for them to customize and personalize their products and services as rapidly as possible to each individual customer. This would enable them to be close to their customers to gain as much market share as possible. R&D personnel would give yet a third response. From their point of view, heaven would be characterized by their ability to work on the most exciting, state-of-the-art, technical *breakthrough* products that would (they hope) deliver superior value to the marketplace. And naturally this would be more easily achieved if there were unlimited resources and no time constraints. This heavenly description would obviously scare the daylights out of the finance (e.g., the controller) function who see their heaven as one with strong monetary, budget, and schedule *controls* so they could both predict and report accurate accounting- and financial-type statements. This would minimize uncertainty and yield the strong financial controls necessary to sustain growth, profitability, and overall market value.

None of these points of view in and of themselves are wrong; in fact, they are all necessary. The organization needs manufacturing and operations to work continuously towards greater efficiencies and lower costs, especially as product lines become more mature, customers expect better values, and competition becomes much more grounded in relative costs. At the same time, the organization does not want marketing people – it needs people who know the markets. It has to know the customers and the changes that are taking place in the many markets in which the organization does business so that appropriate products can be successfully developed, distributed, and sold.

But unfortunately, not all needs are easily identifiable or articulated. Customers cannot readily visualize new products or new benefits beyond a logical extrapolation of their current experiences. Although they can tell you about their explicit uses and experiences with current products and services, they cannot easily tell you what might be technologically feasible. The R&D function, therefore, must not only work with marketing and manufacturing on improving existing product line features and services, but should also strive to develop the future products and services that meet unarticulated or tacit needs. Finance, on the other hand, needs to ensure that the organization remains fiscally responsible and sound and that the new products, services, acquisitions, strategic initiatives, etc. are not out of control. At the same time, it must work not just to control R&D, marketing, and manufacturing but also to support and work with these functions over time to determine the combined functional strategies that will enable the company to make money from new innovative initiatives.

The critical factor, for example, that allowed Xerox to become so successful in commercializing its new copying machines was not the photostatic technological breakthrough *per se*. After all, when it was first introduced, *Business Week*'s evaluation of Xerox's new product was very pessimistic. In its September 19, 1959, evaluation, *Business Week* concluded: 'Office copying is a field where Haloid (Xerox) will find plenty of competition. Most of the 30 or so copying machine manufacturers are already in it with a variety of products and services including such strong competition as 3M (thermofax) and Kodak (verifax).' What fooled the experts and permitted the ultimate success of Xerox was finance's leasing strategy that allowed customers primarily to pay only for copies made rather than having to make a huge capital outlay to purchase very expensive machines. Amazingly enough, businesses never believed they would ever need to or make a lot of copies. But once the machines were installed and available, users soon uncovered all kinds of *new* needs and uses. And as we all know today, the amount of copies being made has probably grown exponentially over time despite predictions of *paperless* offices. Many similar examples can be found in the cross- functional implementation strategies of other successful breakthrough products. The implication for the HRM function is not getting the functional areas to think alike, to be similar, or to be harmonious (at least one major company actually titled their HRM VP, the VP of Harmony). The trick is to have them benefit from these differences when they are motivated to work together to execute and steer their business strategies. Functional areas do not have to be *team players*, they should be *people playing and working together as a team*. Much too frequently this approach runs amok in the execution of HRM policies and practices, including its feedback and reward systems, where there is in fact great pressure to consolidate HRM systems to a *one size fits all* approach. All this despite the desire to create and maintain organization subcultures that support the differing motivational needs of the ambidextrous organization.

REFERENCES

Allen, T., and Henn, G.W. (2007). *The organization and architecture of innovation*. Burlington, MA: Elsevier.

Allen, T., and Katz, R. (1992). Age, education and the technical ladder. *IEEE Transactions on Engineering Management*, 39, 237–45.

Alpert M. (1992). Engineers. *Fortune Magazine*, September 21, 87–95.

Arndt, M. (2006). Creativity Overflowing. *Business Week*, May 8, 50–3.

Badawy, M.K. (1982). *Developing managerial skills in engineers and scientists*. New York: Van Nostrand Reinhold.

Badawy, M.K. (1988). What we have learned about managing human resources. *Research-Technology Management*, September–October, 19–35.

Badawy, M.K. (1993). *Management as a new technology*. New York: McGraw-Hill

Baldwin, T., Danielson, C., and Wiggenhorn, W. (1998). Evolution of learning strategies in organizations: from employee development to business. *IEEE Engineering Management Review*. 26(11), 50–7.

Boyatzis, R. (1982). *The competent manager: a model for effective performance*. New York: John Wiley & Sons, Inc.

Chatman, J., and Barsade, S. (1995). Personality, organizational culture, and cooperation. *Administrative Science Quarterly*, 40, 423–43.

Clark, K., and Wheelwright, S. (1992). Organizing and leading 'heavyweight' development teams. *California Management Review*, 34(3), 201–14.

Dalton, G., and Thompson, P. (1993). *Novations: strategies for career management*. Provo, UT: Novations Group.

Farris, G., and Cordero, R. (2002). Leading your scientists and engineers 2002. *Research-Technology Management*, November–December 13–22.

Goleman, D., McKee, A., and Boyatzis, R. (2002). *Primal leadership*. Cambridge, MA: Harvard Business School Press.

Hackman, J.R. (2002). *Leading teams: setting the stage for great performances*. Cambridge, MA: Harvard Business School Press.

Hackman, J.R., and Oldham, G.R. (1980). *Work redesign*. Reading, MA: Addison-Wesley.

Humphrey, W. (1987). *Managing for innovation: leading technical people*. Englewood Cliffs, NJ: Prentice-Hall.

Herzberg, F. (1966). *Work and the nature of man*. Cleveland, OH: World Publishing.

Israel, P. (1998). *Edison: a life of invention*. New York: John Wiley & Sons, Inc.

Kanter, R.M. (2000). When a thousand flowers bloom: structural, collective and social conditions for innovation in organizations. In *Entrepreneurship: The social science view*, R. Swedberg (ed.), New York: Oxford University Press.

Katz, R. (1998). Motivation leads To innovation. *Information Week 500*, September, 290–97.

Katz, R. (2004a). How a team at Digital Equipment designed the 'Alpha' chip. In *The human side of managing technological innovation*, 2nd edition. R. Katz (ed.), New York: Oxford University Press, 121–33

Katz, R. (2004b). Managing creative performance in R&D teams. In *The Human Side of Managing Technological Innovation*, 2nd edition. R. Katz (ed.), New York: Oxford University Press, 161–70

Katz, R. (2004c). Organizational Socialization and the Reduction of Uncertainty. In *The Human Side of Managing Technological Innovation*, 2nd edition, R. Katz (ed.), New York, NY: Oxford University Press, 34–47.

Katz, R. (2004d). Managing technological innovation in organizations. In *The human side of managing technological innovation*, 2nd edition. R. Katz (ed.), New York: Oxford University Press, 685–700

Katz, R., and Allen, T. (1985). How project performance is influenced by the locus of power in the R&D matrix. *Academy of Management Journal*, 28(1), 67–87.

Katz, R., and Allen, T. (2004a). Organizational issues in the introduction of new technologies. In *The human side of managing technological innovation*, 2nd edition. R. Katz (ed.), New York: Oxford University Press, 450–63.

Katz, R., and Allen, T. (2004b). Managing dual ladder systems in RD&E settings. In *The human side of managing technological innovation*, 2nd edition. R. Katz (ed.), New York: Oxford University Press, 545–59.

Katzenbach, J.R., and Smith, D.K. (1993). The discipline of teams. *Harvard Business Review*, 17, 111–20.

Kelley, R.E. (1998). *How to be a star performer*. New York: Random House.

Kidder, T. (1984). *The soul of a new machine*. New York: Modern Library.

Kirton, M. (2003). *Adaption-innovation: in the context of change and diversity*. London, UK: Routledge.

Kozlowski, S., and Hults, B. (1987). An exploration of climates for technical updating and performance. *Personnel Psychology*, 55, 314–30.

Larson, C.E., and LaFasto, F.M. (1989). *Teamwork*. Newbury Park, CA: Sage Publications.

Lashinsky, A. (2006). Razor's edge. *Fortune*, June 12, 124–32.

Manners, G. Steger, J., and Zimmerer, T. (1988). Motivating your R&D staff. In *Managing Professionals in Innovative Organizations*. In R. Katz (ed.), New York: Oxford University Press, 19–26.

Maslow, A. (1954). *Motivation and personality*. New York: Harper and Row.

McCall, M.W. (1998). *High flyers: developing the next generation of leaders*. Cambridge, MA: Harvard Business School Press.

McClelland, D. (1988). *Human motivation*. New York: Cambridge University Press.

McClelland, D.C., and Boyatzis, R.E. (1982). Leadership motive pattern and long-term success in management. *Journal of Applied Psychology*, 67, 737–43.

Meyer, C. (1997). Managing the volunteer workforce. *Inc. Magazine*, December, 73–81.

Meyer, C. (1998). *Relentless growth: how silicon valley innovation strategies can work in your business*. New York: The Free Press.

NRC Report. (1987). *Management of technology: the hidden competitive advantage*. National Academy Press, Report No: CETS-CROSS-6.

Pelz, D.C. (1988). Creative tensions in the research and development climate. In *Managing professionals in innovative organizations*. R. Katz (ed.), New York: Harper Business, 37–48.

Quinn, J.B., Anderson, P., and Finkelstein, S. (1996). Managing professional intellect: making the most of the best. *Harvard Business Review*, March–April, 71–9.

Roberts, E. (1991). *Entrepreneurs and high technology: lessons From MIT and beyond*. New York: Oxford University Press.

Schein, E. (1996). Career anchors revisited: implications for career development in the 21st century. *Academy of Management Executive*, 10, 80–8.

Smith, D.K., and Alexander, R.C. (1988). *Fumbling the future: how Xerox invented, then ignored, the first personal computer*. New York: William Morrow & Company.

Steele, L. (1988). Managers' misconceptions about technology. In *Managing professionals in innovative organizations*. R. Katz (ed.), New York: Harper Press, 280–87.

Steers, R.M., and Porter, L.W. (1995). *Motivation and work behavior*. New York: McGraw-Hill.

Sutton, R. (2002). *Weird ideas that work*. New York: The Free Press.

Tushman, M., and O'Reilly, C. (1997). *Winning through innovation*. Cambridge, MA: Harvard Business School Press.

Von Glinow, M.A. (1988). *The new professionals: managing today's high-tech employees*. Cambridge, MA: Ballinger Press.

Von Glinow, M.A., and Mohrman, S.A. (1990). *Managing complexity in high-tech organizations*. New York: Oxford University Press.

Welch, J. (2001). *Jack: straight from the gut*. New York: Warner Books.

Westney, E. (1987). *Imitation and innovation: the transfer of Western organizational patterns to Meiji Japan*. Cambridge, MA: Harvard University Press.

Part IV

TECHNOLOGY STRATEGY

9

The Economics and Strategy of Standards and Standardization

SHANE GREENSTEIN AND VICTOR STANGO

THE IMPORTANCE OF STANDARDS

Today's worldwide information infrastructure encompasses a broad spectrum of activities in which technological standards are important. That infrastructure involves both simple and sophisticated equipment – everything from wireless communication devices, to microprocessors, to thousands of miles of copper cables. The rapid pace of technological change has increased the importance of this infrastructure and highlights the strong links between technological standards, firm strategy, market performance, and economic welfare.

By default, decentralized market mechanisms, private firms, and standards development organizations shape the development and diffusion of standards. However, there are several open questions regarding the efficacy of this process. When is coordination on a common standard valuable? Do markets choose the 'right' standards? When and how do firms use standards as strategic (anticompetitive) weapons? Does open cooperation among firms in the form of joint ventures and alliances improve matters? When might nonmarket institutions such as standards bodies improve upon market-mediated standards outcomes? And how do property rights for standards affect the efficiency of their adoption? These questions have received considerable interest in the last two decades. We discuss this burgeoning area of interest and offer some observations on the 'state of the art' in economic thinking about standards.

We start by presenting a set of definitions of standards in economic research, before proceeding to outline the different ways in which standards are chosen by market and nonmarket processes. Then, we outline the conclusions of the current research regarding what we term the short-run issues involving standards and strategy. We then discuss long-run issues before a final concluding section. We draw on thinking from academic theory and empirical and case studies. This

Handbook of Technology and Innovation Management. Edited by Scott Shane
© 2008 John Wiley & Sons, Ltd

discussion serves as a complement and update to other surveys of standards and standard-setting.[1]

DEFINITIONS

Network effects

Standards are important in markets with *network effects*, which can be thought of as complementary relationships in value creation among market participants.[2] The most straightforward instances of markets with network effects are those where consumers and firms form literal communication networks that connect consumers and firms. Email, telephones, and fax machines, for example, are goods that involve information flows from one party to another. In these communication networks operating on a common network allows communication with more users, which is valuable. This is a *direct network effect,* in that the value of the network to any user is directly proportional to the total number of users on the network. It can become a *network externality* if users do not incorporate the effect their adoption has on the decision of others.

Another sort of network effect is an *indirect network effect.* This type of network effect arises in markets for video game consoles and games, computer hardware and software, audio/visual equipment, or any market in which buyers purchase and consume *system goods.* Buyers assemble these system goods by purchasing *components,* often from different sellers. For example, the audio/visual system consists of components (receiver, CD player, speakers, etc.) purchased separately and then assembled by the consumer. There are many such examples of system goods in 'traditional' markets – razors and razor blades, for example, are a system good. Wrenches, nuts, and bolts are also a system good.[3] System goods using electronic protocols to interoperate have become much more prevalent in high-tech markets.

In markets with indirect network effects, the value of any component does not depend directly on the number of other users of that component (hence the terminology), but rather on the availability of complementary and compatible components. For example, a PC is more valuable as the set of available software for that PC grows. In this case, adoption by other users can indirectly benefit any one user by affecting the variety of complementary components. For example, greater adoption of Playstation consoles should generate greater variety in Playstation game titles, by allowing game producers to take advantage of scale economies.

Notice that the use of 'network' here is not the conventional definition used by engineers. Economists view telecommunications networks as more than just their

---

[1] David and Greenstein (1990) is the most comprehensive and closely related; see Stango (2004) for a more narrowly focused discussion of standards wars. Our discussion here draws on both these surveys.

[2] For a comprehensive survey of the broader literature on network effects, see Farrell and Klemperer (2003).

[3] In the traditional parlance of economics, these goods simply have been considered *complements.* The central advance of the literature on system goods is that it recognizes that firms choose the set of complementary goods available to consumers through their compatibility decisions.

physical linkages and electronic signals, more than just the physical equipment extant at any given time. Although many buyers and sellers of the same information technology may not buy equipment or services from the exact same supplier, they still may be a subset of the same economic network if they use compatible equipment.

Standards

Economists take an expansive definition of the term standard. A simple definition, and one that is closer to the parlance of tech industry participants, is that *standards* are specifications that determine the *compatibility* of different components in a network industry.[4] In the simplest case, compatibility standards define the physical fit of two components. Familiar examples are modular phone jacks on telephone cords and handsets, and compatible telephone switches. More complex are the standards that determine electronic communication channels. The need for these standards is obvious, since successfully filtering, transmitting, and translating signals across telecommunication networks requires precise engineering. Similar needs arise in the design of circuitry linking computers, their operating systems, and application software programs.

Economists also use the term standard more broadly, referring to a system good or technology that may consist of a set of technical standards. For example, audio playback technology has had several standards during the last three decades: LPs, audiocassettes, eight-tracks, CDs, and more recently MP3s. These technologies are differentiated not only by their characteristics (such as sound quality and production cost), but also by the fact that music recorded on one standard cannot be played back using the equipment of another standard. This is a result of the numerous technology-specific compatibility standards associated with each system. Standards with similar features include video playback, where the Betamax and VHS standards competed in the early 1980s, and home video games, where a variety of standards have competed since the 1980s.

Although standards have recently come to the fore of strategic discussions in high-tech markets, standards act similarly in many traditional markets. Nuts on the Metric standard will only work with Metric bolts. Razors manufactured by Schick will not work with Gillette razor blades. Similarly, if a client computer using the TCP/IP and send-mail protocol transmits data to another client computer using the same protocol, we say they use the same standard, and otherwise they do not work together.

STANDARDS AND STANDARDIZATION

Economic costs and benefits of standardization

Standards are interesting from an economic and strategic standpoint because many markets face a strong trend toward *standardization* – the adoption of a common specification for a standard by consumers and/or firms. Put simply, standardization

---

[4]This usage does not refer to quality or reference standards.

can generate significant economic benefits for market participants. There are also costs associated with standardization. In this section, we discuss the variety of economic factors driving these benefits and costs. Understanding what these factors are and how they spur (or hinder) standardization is critical to understanding how market processes may or may not function efficiently in their choice of standards.

Scale economies.   Standards may reduce the economic costs of large-scale production. For example, automobile tires are standardized across similarly-sized automobiles produced by different firms. This reduces average production costs at any given firm and avoids duplicate design expenditures. There are a wide variety of standards (in markets other than automobile parts) that transparently serve this purpose. For example, this motive is a key driver of standardized IT installations by large businesses. The standardization eliminates the differences between installations in distinct locations, ultimately reducing the fixed costs of operation.

The desire to achieve scale economies does not necessarily engender a demand for standardized technologies that display network effects. In practice, however, most of the markets subject to these types of demands also display features of competition between bundles of products that embed distinct standards. Sometimes these standardized bundles of components are called 'platforms'. Accordingly, buyers often demand distinct platforms as a way to reduce the number of standards, and achieve internal costs in service, maintenance, and upgrade activities (Bresnahan and Greenstein, 1996, 1999).

It is important to emphasize the scale-based benefits of standardization because so many technology products display scale benefits over the entire range of demand. Consequently, it is possible to confuse the scale-based benefits of standardization with the network benefits. For example, has standardization on operating systems occurred because of network benefits, as is commonly assumed, or simply because OS technology is a natural monopoly? This is potentially important, because market structure and pricing may differ depending on the source of standardization.

Network effects.   Of course, regardless of scale economies it is the case that markets with strong network effects tend toward standardization. This operates in two ways depending on the type of network benefit. In markets with direct network effects there is a clear demand-side benefit to standardization on a common system, because consumer surplus at any price is unequivocally greater with full standardization. Thus, we expect that communication-network based markets should achieve standardization, through *compatibility* in the technology used for communication.

For example, email systems today display near-complete standardization; senders with different email and Internet service providers can communicate with little difficulty. The same is (almost completely) true for operating systems, file transfers, fax technology, languages, and a host of other communication networks where there are large demand-side benefits to standardization.

Indirect network effects also spur standardization, but in a slightly different way. In such markets, the benefit from common adoption of a standard most often comes from increased availability of complements to the standard (or platform). To continue the tire example from the previous section, it is not simply the case that standardization of tires stems from economies of scale. Standardization also makes after-sales and service cheaper for all tire buyers and distributors. This effect operates in a host of other markets. Audio/visual equipment displays near-complete standardization across manufacturers; CD players produced by one manufacturer are largely compatible with receivers, televisions, and other equipment produced by other manufacturers.[5] This stems from the fact that the value of any one component (e.g., a brand of CD player) depends directly on the supply of complementary components (amplifiers). Standardization generates benefits for consumers by encouraging greater product variety.

Although network effects do spur standardization, there are two important clarifying points to make regarding the nature of such standardization. First, network effects need not lead to complete standardization. In some cases, network effects may be small enough that incompatibility can persist. This was the case in the commercial era of the Internet dominated by bulletin boards (prior to 1994). Standardization came about when the Internet commercialized and firms reacted by making PCs, data-transmission networks, and all intermediaries compatible with Internet standards, i.e., TCP/IP and World Wide Web standards. The increase in network effects then led to more complete standardization.

Alternatively, although network effects may be substantial, firms may take actions that hinder standardization. For example, email communications are largely standardized, but other communication networks in a closely related market – instant messaging services – are incompatible without great effort. AOL's Instant Messenger service does not work with those of other Internet service providers except those who pay licensing fees to AOL. Similar issues arise in markets with indirect network effects. Razors and razor blades are not standardized; most Gillette razor blades will not work with Schick razors, and vice versa. Partial compatibility also can arise in markets subject to network effects. Credit cards are an example of a market in which there is partial compatibility between components (cards issued by banks and merchants who may accept cards). Nearly all merchants accept credit cards. However, there are competing credit card networks (such as VISA and Discover) that are incompatible with each other – a customer cannot use a Discover card to conduct a transaction on the VISA network of banks and merchants. Similarly, although there are strong indirect network effects between ATMs and ATM cards (cards become more valuable as more ATMs are deployed), this market does not display complete compatibility; consumers must pay fees to use other banks' ATMs.

A second point is that whereas it is sometimes assumed that standardization implies monopoly, this relationship is a function of *sponsorship*. In a sponsored process, one or more entities, suppliers, or cooperative ventures own property rights to a technology that is critical to standardization. Thus, standardization can lead to dominance by the sponsors of the standard. This is the case, for example, in operating systems, where standardization has occurred on a proprietary technology (Windows). Patents create sponsorship as well. Compact disk technology was a sponsored standard at

---

[5]Small instances of incompatibility exist, but these are generally instances of backward compatibility between new technologies and old technologies, (e.g., optical cable versus standard cable) rather than instances in which firms contemporaneously chose incompatibility.

its inception, although Philips has since licensed the technology to other industry participants. In contrast, an unsponsored process has no identified originator with a proprietary interest, yet follows well-documented specifications. For example, the standards determining compatibility between audio/visual components are unsponsored. Hence, the market can remain fragmented even while displaying nearly complete standardization. We will discuss the differences in firm strategy and market outcomes stemming from sponsorship at some length below.

Product variety. Although standardization generates benefits for consumers by allowing them to construct a wider array of composite goods, it may also reduce differentiation between individual components and the associated composite goods if the process of standardization restricts the dimensions of product differentiation. As an example, suppose that razor blade manufacturers decided to standardize the production of razors and razor blades so that all blades and razors would be fully interoperable (i.e., any company's razor blade would fit any other razor). Doing so might require eliminating product differentiation that consumers find valuable (such as the number of blades on the razor, or whether the razor is disposable). In such cases, standardization might reduce consumer welfare.

The locus of competition: systems versus components. In many markets, standardization is important because it changes the dimensions on which firms compete. For example, Macintosh and PC computers operate on different standards; one cannot use a Macintosh software program or hard drive on a PC. This creates differentiation between the two systems, which may soften price competition. For example, it allows Mac to target particular market segments (e.g., graphics-intensive applications) through its system design. In contrast, within the PC system itself there is a great deal of standardization; monitors, printers, and other components are all fully interoperable, therefore creating competition at the component level.

This distinction provides a straightforward explanation for small margins in PC hardware, because all suppliers are nearly alike in their final product – i.e., there is little basis for any player to differentiate from any other except on price. This one facet of the market explains why it is possible for a supplier, Dell Computer in this case, to have a high market share through focusing on low-cost distribution and investing in process engineering (for cost reduction). It also explains why other firms, such as IBM, Compaq, and HP could not make high margins in their respective PC division in the same time period.

The importance of this distinction is that because standardization can change the dimensions on which firms compete, firms have incentives to choose (when possible) a level of standardization that provides them with the greatest profitability. If, for example, standardization intensifies competition because components are less differentiated than entire systems, suppliers may resist standardization. In this view, standardization reduces the product to a 'commodity' and, though attractive to users, will necessarily not be chosen by firms. It is also important to consider in policy discussions of forcing standardization; standardization will not only change the set of choices available to consumers, but also may fundamentally alter the competitive environment.

The sunk costs of adoption.   Many technologies that standardize are durable goods, which provide a flow of services over time. For example, consumers typically hold audio/visual components for several years. Operating systems (which are components of computer systems) are another example of a good that is purchased infrequently.

Product durability is important in the adoption decision because it introduces sunk costs of adoption. Most components cannot be resold at their initial purchase value. Another product feature in many systems market is the 'hardware/software' aspect of components. Certain systems are assembled through the assembly of a durable component (hardware) and a more frequently purchased add-on (software). Finally, some system markets are 'subscription' markets (e.g., credit cards and ATMs).

When sunk costs of both new and existing technologies are large, new technologies may have trouble penetrating the market. For example, during the last few decades a host of new audio playback technologies have become available, beginning with 8-track and cassette tapes, moving through CDs and continuing to the all-digital formats currently available. Yet, the transitions between these technologies have not been as rapid as one might expect. Although each new technology offers substantial benefits, old technologies are less costly to continue using. Thus, large transition costs (or opportunity costs of transition) can deter rapid standardization on new technologies by discouraging adoption. These transition costs are directly related to the sunk costs of committing to new technologies.

Expectations and coordination.   Finally, because of the myriad effects of the product features above, it is often extremely difficult for adopters to forecast the process of standardization. Adopters may be uncertain about the relative merits of competing technologies, what other adopters will do, whether firms will leave them stranded if widespread adoption does not arise, or a host of other variables.

This uncertainty can hinder standardization in a number of ways. Because adopters of a new technology know that the value of the adoption often depends on what other adopters do (due to network effects, for example), *coordination* is a key element of standardization. Coordination is particularly important when adopters are diffuse (say, consumers or producers of complementary components in related unconcentrated markets).

When coordination is important, adopters' expectations about how the market will evolve play a critical role in the process of standardization. Slight differences at the outset of a market in consumer expectations can 'tip' the market dramatically. For example, suppose that two new network goods are competing. If they are otherwise identical but consumers expect that most other consumers will adopt good 'A', every consumer will perceive good 'A' if it generates strong network benefits – leading it to be adopted by 100 % of consumers. This might occur even if technology A is fundamentally inferior to its alternatives. This is a case of *coordination failure* among adopters.

Coordination failure may also stall adoption rather than lead to standardization on the wrong technology. Adopters may find it valuable to wait for uncertainty to resolve before making a commitment to adoption. In instances where components are incompatible, require significant sunk costs of adoption, and uncertainty is severe, the option value of delaying purchases may be extremely high and new technologies may stall.

Owing to these issues, it comes as no surprise that firms place tremendous strategic importance on affecting consumer expectations. Firms may do this through advertising or persuasion. More sophisticated strategies often involve commitments by firms to stay in the market, or on a particular price path. Alternatively, firms attempt to spread fear uncertainty and doubt (FUD) on rival networks. Vendors recognize the strategic importance of locking users into a standard and spend, or waste, considerable resources on manipulating its development. This represents a cost of standardization. For example, new format suppliers in such diverse market settings as DiVX (Dranove and Gandal, 2003), hand-helds (McGahan, Vadasz, and Yoffie, 1997), and early operating systems in PCs (Gandal, Greenstein and Salant, 1999), all faced problems from their inability to generate commitment by application developers.

The key questions involving standardization

The factors discussed above all influence the economic costs and benefits of standardization on common technologies. It is clear that given these factors, some markets will display strong trends toward standardization. Beyond this, however, the question then becomes whether market and nonmarket processes lead to technological evolution that is efficient. Do markets display an efficient level of standardization? If a market standardizes on a common technology, will it choose the correct standard? How severe is coordination failure? We now turn to these questions and attempt to characterize the received wisdom regarding them.

THE ECONOMICS AND STRATEGY OF STANDARDIZATION

There are two central problems that focus economists' analysis of standardization. Both arise from analyzing competitive behavior in a *standards war* between competing alternatives. The first issue concerns whether unfettered market processes choose the efficient 'winner'. Another is that markets may not migrate efficiently between standards, stalling on an inefficient technology. Both of these are related outcomes of the 'lock-in' problem. There are a host of prominent historical episodes in which these questions were important: IBM versus DEC in minicomputers, MS Word versus Word Perfect in word processing, FDDI versus ATM in network communications, and US Robotics versus Rockwell in 56K modems. The VHS/Betamax duel in the VCR markets is another well-known case.

Standards wars also commonly arise as subplots to related larger product market duels. Various banks may belong to incompatible ATM networks, and United Airlines and American Airlines sponsor competing airline reservation systems. If recent experience is any guide, this type of market structure is likely to characterize many, if not most, private economic networks in the future information infrastructure.

In what follows, we discuss the economic literature on standards largely in the context of the lock-in problem. We address the extent to which the factors above (such as direct and indirect network effects, or sunk costs) affect lock-in. Our focus in this section is on *de facto* standardization – the process by which markets choose among competing standards, or a new standard that stands to supplant an existing standard.[6] We first discuss wars between unsponsored standards, before moving on to a discussion of wars between sponsored standards. After discussing the implications of the distinction between direct and indirect network effects, we summarize the existing empirical work on standards.

Wars between unsponsored standards

A fundamental question involving unsponsored standards wars is whether they exhibit *multiple equilibria* in adoption.[7] If these equilibria differ in the economic welfare associated with them, lock-in is possible if the market settles on an inefficient equilibrium. As an example, communication networks are classic examples of markets that might exhibit multiple equilibria, because they display strong network externalities. Consider the decision faced by adopters of a new communication standard such as the fax machine. If no consumers have fax machines, no one consumer will want to adopt the first fax machine, because a fax machine has no stand-alone value if it cannot communicate with other machines. Thus, adoption by none is a plausible outcome. There may be other outcomes as well, involving adoption by many or all consumers. But the fact that the market can become locked-in at zero adoption is a potentially serious concern, because society as a whole is worse off at zero adoption than unanimous adoption.

An early paper modeling the circumstances under which the market might become locked-in is Arthur (1989).[8] Arthur outlines a model of adopter choice between two unsponsored technologies in which adopters may face what the author calls *increasing returns*. These increasing returns are network externalities: benefits to adoption that increase with the number of other consumers adopting the same technology. Arthur does not directly motivate his work as explaining economies' failure efficiently to choose or move between standards, but he notes several anecdotal examples from the case literature on standards (e.g., narrow gauge railroads).[9]

Arthur (1989) provides general conditions under which a market will become locked in to an inferior standard. His definition of lock-in is a situation in which a government subsidy could not move the market toward the more efficient standard. The manner in which lock-in occurs in Arthur's model is a function of the timing

---

[6]For the most part, in the discussion below we abstract from the compatibility choice, taking competition between standards as given. Research focusing instead on compatibility choices made by firms falls into two areas. One addresses compatibility between (horizontally) competing networks when there are network externalities (see Besen and Farrell, 1994, for a survey). The other addresses compatibility between components in system markets: Katz and Shapiro (1994) is a good survey. The latter survey also deals with issues related to standards wars; we reference their discussion below. See Gandal (2002) for a survey of some public policy issues related to compatibility and standardization. These public policy issues are related to the literature on tying, which can be viewed as a form of incompatibility. See Carlton and Waldman (2002), Choi and Stefanadis (2001), and Church and Gandal (1996, 2000) for analyses of tying in system markets.

[7]See Farrell and Klemperer (2003) for a discussion and examples.

[8]Arthur (1996) provides more detail on lock-in.

[9]Similarly, some of the work below refers generally to technology adoption with network effects rather than the adoption of standards *per se*. We use the term 'standard' throughout for consistency.

of adoption and payoffs. He posits a situation in which adopters move sequentially, and more importantly receive payoffs that are a function of the number of adopters that have previously chosen each standard. In this setting, standards adoption displays *path dependence*: later adopters' decisions depend strongly on the decisions of previous adopters. In this situation, it is possible that early adopters choose the 'inefficient' standard. An inefficient standard is one such that at some point in the adoption process, a different prior adoption path would have yielded greater total benefits to all adopters. Intuitively, such a standard would be one with high intrinsic benefits to early adopters but small network effects.[10] This standard would 'win', because its high intrinsic benefits are attractive to early adopters when the network is small. However, it becomes inefficient as later adopters come on board because it generates relatively small network benefits. A key assumption of Arthur's model is that economic agents must move sequentially in their adoption decisions. Arthur also assumes that agents must commit to a standard and cannot defer adoption. Nor does Arthur allow coordination or side-payments among the adopters.

Farrell and Saloner (1985) examine a sequential unsponsored standard adoption game with network externalities. They focus on the impact of imperfect information and note that when agents are certain about other agents' benefits from adoption, then adoption decisions are always efficient. This result holds even if agents have different preferences for the new standard.

When agents are uncertain about each others' benefits from adoption, the market can exhibit lock-in, or what Farrell and Saloner (1985) call *excess inertia*: the propensity to become trapped on an inferior standard.[11] The intuition Farrell and Saloner describe is a situation in which '[b]oth firms are fence-sitters, happy to jump on the bandwagon [of the new standard] if it gets rolling but insufficiently keen to set it rolling themselves'. Interestingly, Farrell and Saloner note that pre-play communication may exacerbate excess inertia when agents have different preferences for the new standard. This occurs because adopters misrepresent their preferences in order to influence the adoption decisions of others. This has implications for the performance of standards bodies, which foster pre-commitment communication.

Markets with unsponsored standards also may often swell and shrink for many reasons that may have only a tenuous connection to the long-term economic welfare of market participants. They become subject to 'bandwagon effects' (Rohlfs, 2001). In a characteristic bandwagoning effect, networks may be slow to start when they are small. Many potential adopters will sit on the fence, waiting to make expensive and unrecoverable investments until a large fraction of other users choose a clear technical standard. Networks may not develop at all if most participants are lukewarm about a new standard due to technical uncertainty, for example, even though all would collectively benefit from it. Alternatively, bandwagons may also gather speed remarkably quickly once a network becomes large enough to justify investments by

---

[10]Intrinsic benefits are those received by the adopter regardless of the number of other adopters.

[11]More precisely, Farrell and Shapiro (1992) define *symmetric excess inertia* as a situation in which every adopter prefers the new standard, but that adoption does not occur. They use the term *excess inertia* to refer more generally to a situation when adoption of the new standard does not occur, even though the market-wide benefits from adoption of the new standard exceed the market-wide benefits from using the old standard. In the second instance, some firms may prefer the old standard.

potential adopters who, in the early phase of development, had delayed making commitments. The lack of communication between all the potentially affected decision-makers exacerbates such bandwagons, though professional organizations can often provide communication channels to bridge some of the troubles.

The QWERTY debate.   The early literature motivates the problems examined in their theoretical analysis by reference to a few classic examples of excess inertia. The most well-known of these is the QWERTY keyboard, so named for the first five letters on the top row of a standard typewriter keyboard. An influential paper by David (1985) argues that the QWERTY keyboard design was chosen early in the market but is inefficient given the current standard. In particular, the QWERTY keyboard is designed to minimize key sticking on manual typewriters. The thrust of the argument is that this is no longer a concern. Because computer keyboards cannot stick, there is no gain to a design that minimizes key sticking. Furthermore, the argument is that superior alternatives to the QWERTY design exist in terms of learning costs and ultimate typing speed, and that the costs of switching are vastly outweighed by the benefits. This implies that the market is locked-in to an inferior standard.

This example has been hugely influential. Nearly every theoretical paper on standards wars mentions it at least in passing and QWERTY remains the most common example. This is important because the validity of the QWERTY story itself has come under question. Liebowitz and Margolis (1990) present contrary evidence suggesting that the superiority of alternative keyboards has never been firmly established. They note that classic tests of the leading alternative (the 'Dvorak') are in retrospect inconclusive and possibly tainted by the influence of Dvorak himself, who held a patent on his design.[12] In addition, the critique is not restricted to the QWERTY example. Arguments have also been made that Betamax was in fact an inferior VCR standard and that this, rather than lock-in and inertia, explains the dominance of VHS.[13]

Unfortunately, the arguments above are based on somewhat anecdotal evidence. Given the paucity of hard evidence regarding the QWERTY case, it is unlikely that the debate can ever be resolved conclusively. However, the debate raises the larger point that there exists little hard empirical evidence of lock-in. Given the strong policy prescriptions implied by the debate on excess inertia and lock-in, the scant evidence on these questions suggests that conducting empirical tests of lock-in stands as one of the most important areas for future research in standards. This is not an easy undertaking. Lock-in and inertia are extremely difficult to identify. Because standards are not priced in the traditional sense, their impact on welfare is difficult to measure. Furthermore, comparing welfare under different standards requires careful counterfactual analysis because when trends toward standardization are strong, it is most common to observe only market performance under the winning standard. Later in this survey we discuss some encouraging recent empirical work on this front.

[12]An even more compelling argument that the persistence of the QWERTY keyboard does not stem from network effects is raised by the fact that any individual user can now re-program a computer keyboard in any configuration and re-train privately. This suggests that the private costs of re-training at the individual level are greater than the private benefits.

[13]See Liebowitz and Margolis (1996) for more detail on the Beta/VHS case history.

Fuller specifications of wars between unsponsored standards. Later work refines these intuitions and highlights some new insights. Farrell and Saloner (1986) examine a setting in which an older unsponsored standard faces competition from a new, superior unsponsored standard. The novelty of their model is that the older standard has an *installed base*: a group of users that have committed to using the standard.[14] The importance of installed base in Farrell and Saloner's model is that it highlights the degree to which adopters of a new standard can strand existing users of an older standard; consequently, the model exhibits insufficient friction.

Farrell and Saloner (1986) highlight another important issue in standards wars: 'preannouncements'. In their model, the arrival of the new standard is unanticipated, so a preannouncement notifying consumers of its impending arrival can change adoption decisions. A somewhat surprising result of their analysis is that preannouncements can reduce welfare. This occurs because some consumers who would have adopted the old standard without the announcement wait for the imminent new standard, strengthening the degree to which users of the old standard are stranded.

Another promising line of recent research considers richer specifications of consumer and firm behavior than those in the early literature. Choi (1994) models the option of waiting, where adopters can defer their adoption decision until learning more about the competing standards. The network externality in his model is what might be termed generational, in that it captures the failure of current adopters to consider the effects of their actions on past or future adopters.[15] Choi does allow adopters to forecast how their and others' actions will affect future benefits to adopting one standard or another, and act accordingly. In this respect his model is richer than Arthur's (1989). Interestingly, he finds that there are excessive incentives for early adoption.

Wars between sponsored standards

Although the literature examining unsponsored standards is important because many standards lack owners, many standards are sponsored. This sponsorship can arise implicitly through proprietary information or the control of an interface, or explicitly through patenting. This introduces additional dimensions to the problems because owners of competing standards can behave strategically, through their choices of prices or other choice variables. The canonical example of a war between sponsored standards is that between Betamax and VHS. Many of the classic issues in standards wars arose here: it is commonly argued that Betamax lost despite many technical factors that were superior (though that factual assertion is also debated), in part due to the strategic decisions made by the two sponsors. This locked the market into an inefficient standard.

The genesis of the economic literature on sponsorship lies in Katz and Shapiro's (1986) work examining competition between (potentially) sponsored standards.

---

[14]The bulk of their paper is devoted to a model in which older consumers have committed irrevocably to the old standard, while new consumers can choose between the old and new standards.

[15]Current adopters generate useful information about the quality of each standard by adopting now, but do not value that information. Nor do they consider that adopting a standard different from that adopted by prior adopters 'strands' those who have already adopted.

Katz and Shapiro identify a broad set of features of equilibrium in their model, including whether the market chooses the efficient standard. They differentiate standards by assuming that their relative superiority changes over time (in a two-period model).

As a benchmark result, Katz and Shapiro first establish that price will equal marginal cost when standards are unsponsored and there is free entry. This leads to inefficient adoption of the standard because buyers do not consider the network externality they generate through their adoption; this effect may cause markets to become locked-in on the wrong standard.[16] Katz and Shapiro also consider an intermediate case, and find that a sponsored but inferior standard may 'win' and become locked-in when competing against a superior but unsponsored standard. The intuition for this is that the holder of property rights to a standard will expend monopoly rents to spur adoption by investing in an 'installed base'.

Analyzing the case of competing sponsored standards, Katz and Shapiro observe the somewhat counter-intuitive outcome that the market may exhibit *excess momentum* or *insufficient friction*.[17] These terms refer to situations in which the market is biased against an old but superior standard, and moves too swiftly to a new but inferior standard. In the Katz and Shapiro model this happens through *stranding*, in which adopters of the standard ignore the network benefits that they confer on adopters of the alternative standard.

Katz and Shapiro (1992) consider the role of installed base in a setting with sponsored standards.[18] In their model, owners of an old and new standard compete on prices; the owner of the new standard also chooses when to introduce the new standard. Consumers are nonstrategic, in that they take other consumers' adoption decisions as given.[19] In general, Katz and Shapiro show that the private incentives for new standard introduction exceed social incentives; the new standard comes to market too soon and may take over the market even when such an outcome is not socially desirable. In essence this is because the owner of the new standard can subsidize its (inefficient) adoption.

Beyond this early work, there has also been a recent wave of work focusing on sponsorship of standards. Clements (2005) examines whether sponsorship can solve excess inertia and momentum. His dynamic model considers a situation in which consumers in different 'generations' consider the contemporaneous benefits accruing to others through their adoption and coordinate accordingly. Consumers do not, however, consider benefits accruing to past or future generations. This framework is therefore similar to that in Katz and Shapiro (1986). Clements notes that when consumers are homogeneous, sponsorship guarantees efficient adoption;

---

[16]The externality may cause lock-in, but also may lead to *under-adoption* of an efficient standard. Under-adoption occurs when the standard is adopted by fewer than the socially efficient number of market participants. This can lead to inefficient *splitting*, in which the market holds more than one standard when it would be optimal for all participants to choose the same standard.

[17]This occurs as a minor case in Farrell and Saloner (1985). Katz and Shapiro (1986) use slightly different language, terming this outcome 'excessive foresight'.

[18]Katz and Shapiro also consider firms' compatibility and licensing decisions, but since these involve compatibility choice we do not discuss them here.

[19]Allowing consumers to consider the effect that their decisions have on the adoption decisions of others resolves the multiple equilibrium problem in their model.

there is no such guarantee in the unsponsored case. However, when Clements allows for consumer heterogeneity he finds that markets move too swiftly or too slowly between standards even if they are sponsored. This inefficiency persists because even a monopolist is unable to transfer surplus efficiently across different generations of consumers. Clements considers a number of extensions limiting sponsors' behavior, such as a constraint that prices must be nonnegative, or a limitation on the length of the sponsorship period after which the standard becomes open. He suggests that these extensions would bias the market toward excess inertia.

Choi and Thum (1998) examine the adoption of standards both when markets are competitive and when markets are monopolistic.[20] They extend the Katz and Shapiro (1986) model by allowing consumers to wait for the new standard rather than commit to the old standard. The insight of this extension is that there is 'insufficient waiting'; when an optimal strategy involves waiting for the superior new standard, consumers will adopt the current inferior standard because they do not consider the benefit they would generate for future adopters. This represents excess inertia of a sort, because the new standard does not achieve universal adoption when it should, and occurs when the new standard is competitively supplied. In contrast to the result in Katz and Shapiro (1986), Choi and Thum (1998) also find that a monopolistic owner of the new standard may worsen insufficient waiting; because the monopolist will set high prices for the new standard, waiting becomes less attractive to consumers.[21]

Shy (1996) presents a model that incorporates varying consumer preferences over the quality of standards and varying sizes of standards' installed bases. Shy also uses an overlapping generations framework to conduct the analysis, which is richer than the standard two- or three-period models used in much previous work. Shy's focus is on the speed of technological change rather than the existence of inertia or momentum, but his work does have promise in modeling a fuller model of consumers' and firms' intertemporal decision-making in standards wars.

The importance of direct and indirect network effects

Does the specification of network effects overstate the extent to which markets generate inefficiency?[22] The arguments about excess inertia and momentum hinge on the difference between indirect and direct network effects, and a claim that many standards are characterized by indirect network effects. This is important because in their simplest specification, indirect network effects are pecuniary or market-mediated.[23] For example, a market-mediated network effect arises when two firms operate on the same standard and consequently produce products that

[20]Competitively and monopolistically supplied standards correspond to unsponsored and sponsored standards.

[21]Because the monopolist does not offer the new standard early in the game, it is unable to transfer surplus across time by pricing low initially to spur adoption.

[22]This discussion and that below on sponsorship draw from Katz and Shapiro (1994) and Liebowitz and Margolis (1994).

[23]Below we discuss richer models in which indirect network effects are not completely market-mediated because they affect product variety.

have complementary demands. An example might be a computer operating system producer and separate company writing software for that OS.

An important dimension of this argument is market structure. For example, there will be no inefficiency if markets for the two products are perfectly competitive. Inefficiencies will arise if the products exhibit economies of scale over the range of demand, but two-part pricing or volume discounts can mitigate them (with the associated distributional consequences).[24] As a point of contrast, where the network effect is direct, inefficiencies are more likely to arise regardless of market structure or the degree of integration.

This issue has been taken up by Chou and Shy (1990) and Church, Gandal, and Krause (2003), who argue that indirect network effects may cause true externalities in hardware/software markets where consumers purchase complementary components of a system and assemble them into system goods.[25] Church, Gandal, and Krause (2003) note that the externality will operate if the following assumptions hold:

◆ software production exhibits increasing returns;
◆ there is free entry in software;
◆ consumers have a preference for variety.

This is an important point for two reasons. First, it seeks to provide a clear case in which indirect network effects might *per se* generate inefficiency. Second, establishing a rough theoretical (micro-)equivalence between direct and indirect network effects implies that many of the lessons from the early standards literature, which were cast in terms of direct network effects, can be applied to markets with indirect network effects.

The particular issue of standards adoption in markets with indirect network effects has also received attention. Church and Gandal (1993) examine a model of oligopolistic (i.e., sponsored) hardware and software competition, in which different firms produce the hardware and software. In their model, hardware firms differ in their marginal cost and in the fixed cost associated with software development on their standard. This second cost is particularly important, as the indirect network externality operates through the number of software varieties available. The number of varieties depends on the software's fixed costs, and the demand for software as determined through hardware pricing. In a line of questioning similar to that in Katz and Shapiro (1986), Church and Gandal (1993) ask whether the market will sometimes adopt an inferior standard. They find this to be the case; the market may adopt a standard with lower software fixed costs even though the other standard could yield higher social welfare if priced by a regulator.

---

[24]Chou and Shy (1990) present a model in which economies of scale lead to inefficiency in markets with indirect network effects.

[25]The terms hardware and software refer to situations in which consumers purchase one (usually) durable component – hardware – and may match it with more than one complementary component – as is the case, for example, with literal hardware and software, but which is also true about operating systems and word processing programs. Church and Gandal (1993) consider a setting in which hardware and software are provided by separate firms, while Church and Gandal (1996) consider a setting in which hardware and software are provided by integrated firms.

Church and Gandal (1996) present an alternative model that also involves sponsorship, although it differs in that single integrated firms sell both hardware and software. They consider whether an incumbent (monopoly) supplier of hardware and software can deter entry by a superior standard. The key parameter in their model is the 'monopoly premium' – the difference between the monopoly and duopoly prices. When this premium is large, the market can settle on the wrong (incumbent) standard; this is qualitatively similar to excess inertia. Interestingly, this result does draw a distinction between indirect and direct network effects – for the latter, excess inertia seems less likely from a theoretical perspective. Church and Gandal explain this distinction by noting that it is the hardware producer's ability to commit to software production that gives it an advantage, by granting it a large installed base.

Clements (2004) provides another comparison between direct and indirect network effects, for the case in which there are two competitive hardware providers and a free-entry software market characterized by economies of scale. Clements concludes that direct and indirect network effects operate differently; direct network effects are more likely to yield insufficient incentives for the market to settle on a single standard, whereas indirect effects are more likely to provide excessive incentives. The second result stands in contrast to the conclusions in Church and Gandal (1996); this exists because of differences between the models, in their specification of hardware competition and the effects of software variety on consumer welfare.[26]

Real-world studies of standardization

In search of empirical validation for the arguments discussed in the previous section, economists have turned their attention to studies of actual markets in which these issues are important. This has proven difficult. By nature standards wars involve few players. This leads to a paucity of observations, exacerbated by the fact that many standards wars are resolved quickly. In many case, therefore, there is little cross-sectional or time-series variation in market outcomes to exploit. As an example, the operating system market standardized extremely quickly. Given the variety of possible explanations for this, it is extremely difficult to estimate their importance – did Microsoft win due to network effects, product quality, or some other (e.g., anticompetitive) activity? One can only answer these questions by observing variation in these effects, the decisions made by market participants, and their impact on outcomes. But in many markets with network effects, we essentially have 'one observation'. It is even more difficult to answer questions about the efficiency of the market outcome. Should the market 'switch' to an alternative at this point? What would be the welfare implications of a switch?

As a consequence of these limitations, much early empirical work on standards is case-oriented. Work by Gabel (1987, 1991), Grindley (1995), Kahin and Abbate

[26]Church and Gandal (1996) assume that consumers benefit directly from software entry, as they purchase more than one variety of software. Clements (2004) assumes that consumers purchase one variety of software. The strategic behavior of hardware producers in Church and Gandal (1996) also affects the market outcome.

(1995), Von Burg (2001), Rohlfs (2001), and Postrel (1990) falls into this category. This work is interesting and informative, though limited in some cases by the fact that the data involved do not allow sophisticated statistical analysis.

Recently, however, data constraints have relaxed to the point where researchers have been able to apply standard econometric techniques to the analysis of standards.[27] Dranove and Gandal (2003), for example, study application entry in the DVD/DiVX war. In Dranove and Gandal's study, there were two technically different formats competing, and one of those specifications quickly failed in the marketplace. Dranove and Gandal find that the 'preannouncement' of the DiVX standard affected the adoption of DVD technology. Saloner and Shepard (1996) examine the timing of adoption of a new standard (ATM machines), although they do not discuss the efficiency of adoption. They argue that competitive incentives accelerate adoption by the providers who follow the first adopter. Gandal, Greenstein, and Salant (1999) show that the diffusion of a new standard (the DOS operating system) was affected by the availability of complementary software, but similarly do not attempt to ascertain whether the transition was efficient.

Another example of this line of research is a paper by Ohashi (2003), which estimates the importance of network effects in the VHS/Beta standards battle.[28] Ohashi estimates the strength of the relationship between each standard's installed base and consumer demand for each standard, finding economically significant indirect network effects. Ohashi is able to use these estimates to calculate the size of the benefit from standardization, and also to examine what would have happened had SONY (the owner of the Beta standard) priced its VCRs differently. An interesting result of the analysis is that although it appears that consumers valued the VHS standard early in the battle, it would have been possible for Beta to capture the market if it had used its first-mover advantage to build an installed base through low pricing.

To conclude the section, economic thinking about standardization focuses on efficiency, as typified by the likelihood of lock-in. There are three phases to a canonical model of a standards war: First, an economic opportunity arises from a technical upgrade. Second, competition develops between different implementations of that upgrade. Third, resolution of the conflict occurs when one of the implementations wins in a competitive battle. In general, this research has shown that there are clearly defined theoretical circumstances in which lock-in can occur. Less is known empirically.

This leaves a number of open questions, however. How many markets fit the assumptions of these models? Furthermore, if we accept that unfettered market mechanisms can lead to lock-in, what does that imply? Can other quasi-market mechanisms that allow cooperation solve these problems, or is there scope for government intervention? We now turn to a discussion of these issues.

---

[27]This discussion omits mention of the growing empirical literature that focuses on establishing the existence of either direct or indirect network effects, rather than on standards *per se*; See, e.g., Farrell and Klemperer (2003) for a discussion of this literature.

[28]This paper is part of a larger recent literature using structural techniques to estimate the importance of network effects. Rysman (2004) is an early paper examining network effects in the Yellow Pages market. Nair *et al.* (2004) estimate the magnitude of indirect network effects between Personal Digital Assistants (PDAs) and PDA software.

NONMARKET PROCESSES OF STANDARDIZATION

Although in many cases standardization occurs through competition (either sponsored or unsponsored), nonmarket processes may also shape the outcome. These processes take a variety of forms. Confronted with an incipient or active standards war, firms may behave cooperatively to settle things through joint ventures, consortia, or other alliances. More formal processes of standardization also exist precisely to spur coordination. Standards Development Organizations (SDOs) and Standard-Setting Organizations (SSOs) have become prominent institutional features of technology markets, serving to foster cooperative standardization. Finally, governments have become involved in standard-setting where they perceive lock-in or coordination problems to be particularly severe. In this section we discuss these alternative processes.

Consortia and alliances

As we discussed earlier, coordination is a central problem in standardization. Clearly, if firms can internalize network effects through integration they can in many cases mitigate inefficiencies in standardization and/or avoid costly standards wars. For example, banks have integrated into markets for both ATM cards and ATM machines, internalizing (at least partially) the indirect network effect between these two services. Work by Knittel and Stango (2007, 2008) estimates that the provision of ATM machines by banks has an economically significant relationship with the value that consumers attach to ATM cards.

Even when firms do not integrate, they can solve the problem of indirect network effects by forming joint ventures, consortia, or writing other contracts that align their incentives properly. Consortia usually consist of groups of like-minded participants (for technical or market reasons), who assemble for with the intent of the proposed standardization activity. The general appeal of these groups lies in the efficacy of their processes, usually outside the ambit of more established institutions with broader membership. For example, banks have formed shared ATM networks (such as Star, Plus, and Cirrus) as joint ventures to internalize the network externality associated with allowing customers access to any banks' ATM machines, and create a sponsor for the standard.[29]

Consortia generate a number of benefits. They resolve uncertainty if they agree on a common standard, accelerating the development of complementary components. Success is more likely when all the companies (who may directly compete in a particular component market) find a common interest in developing products that complement their competitive offering.

Unfortunately, consortia are not a perfect solution to coordination problems. They can easily fall prey to some of the same structural impediments that prevented network development in their absence. The experience with the development of Unix standards in the 1980s amply illustrates these weaknesses. Many firms perceived strategic alliances as tools to further their own economic interests and

[29]Knittel and Stango (2008) provide evidence on the link between consumers' use of these networks and the expansion of ATMs nationwide.

block unfavorable outcomes. As a result, two different consortia, OSF and Unix international, originally sponsored two different Unix standards. Industry participants lined up behind one or another based on economic self-interest. In the early 1990s different consortia (and firms) have sponsored slightly different forms of Unix, confusing the marketplace once again.

Another issue associated with consortia is that they often engage in ostensibly pro-competitive activities that nonetheless skirt antitrust law. There is a tension between the benefits accruing from integration and the antitrust issues involved with such cooperative behavior. The recent antitrust cases against Mastercard and VISA illustrate the importance of this issue.

Standards development organizations

In contrast to *de facto* standards, *de jure* standards are those that emerge through explicit industry consensus, usually mediated within a formalized industry process. Examples of these come from committees organized by IEEE, ANSI, and other industry associations. *De jure* standards can emerge from an industry standards body, or ratified by a standards organization such as ANSI.[30] In cases where a sponsored standard is considered for *de jure* ratification, it is often a condition of ratification that the sponsor must surrender property rights to the standard.

Standards development organizations (SDOs) play many useful roles in solving network coordination problems, especially those related to lack of communication. They can serve as a forum for affected parties to educate each other about the common perception of the problems they face. They can also serve as a legal means to discuss and plan the development of a network of compatible components, as well as document agreements about the technical specification of a standard and disseminate this information to interested parties. They can also serve as an informal forum to settle competing claims about technical efficacy of alternative approaches to similar problems.

And perhaps most importantly, their standards can serve as a focal point to designers who must choose from among many technical solutions when embedding a standard in a component design. These groups then are most likely to succeed when market participants mutually desire interoperability, need to establish a mechanism for communication, and need a mechanism to develop or choose one of many technical alternatives. For example, this was the role taken by grocers groups in the development of barcodes for retail products. It is also the role taken by the ITU in the development and up-grading of interoperability standards for fax machines.

Voluntary standards groups are no panacea for the structural impediments to network development. They will fail to produce useful standards when the self-interest of participants prevents it in any event. Designers thus must have some economic incentives for embedding a technical standard in their product, since use is optional. A dominant firm need not follow the recommendations of a voluntary

[30] The American National Standards Institute (ANSI) is a sub-group of ISO (the International Standards Organization) handling standards in the United States. ISO is an umbrella group containing a host of standards bodies.

standardization group. Moreover, it is not likely to do so if it believes that it can block entry and successfully market its products without the standard. IBM's marketing of systems using EBCDIC rather than ASCII serves as one such example (Brock, 1975).

SDOs also fall prey to many of the classic problems in public choice. User interests tend to be systematically unrepresented, because users tend to be diffuse and not technically sophisticated enough to master many issues. In addition, large firms have an advantage in volunteering resources that influence the outcome, such as volunteering trained engineers who will write standards that reflect their employers' interests. Finally, insiders have the advantage in manipulating procedural rules, shopping between relevant committees, and lobbying for their long-term interests. This can lead to extraordinary investment in the process to influence outcomes or to 'free-riding' off the activities of the organization.

Although the discussion above raises a number of issues, there has been relatively little formal treatment of them by economists. One of the few studies of nonmarket processes of standard-setting is Farrell (1996). Farrell studies the performance of standard-setting bodies, focusing on the tradeoffs between the delays inherent in achieving consensus and the benefits of avoiding a costly standards war. His key notion is of 'vested interests', which are asymmetries between the payoffs of the 'winner' and 'loser' after a standard has been adopted (the winner is that whose proposed standard is adopted). These vested interests cause delay and impede consensus. Farrell discusses how strategies to reduce vested interest can improve outcomes; he mentions a number of these, including forcing early standardization and requiring that owners license their standard as a condition of its ratification by a standards body. Farrell (1989, 1995) discusses a similar point in a less formal way, suggesting that weakening intellectual property protection can help markets settle on correct standards more quickly.[31]

Cabral and Kretschmer (2007) model policy design in standard-setting. They use the Arthur (1989) model as their baseline, with the major difference being that consumers have different preferences over the (two) competing standards. They model the policymaker as having (initially) imperfect information regarding which standard is preferred by more consumers. The policymaker gains information regarding which standard is preferred by observing consumers' sequential adoption decisions. It is therefore valuable for the policymaker to delay 'lock-in' to the standard in order to acquire better information. This incentive can in fact cause the policymaker to support the 'lagging' standard, where the lagging standard is one with fewer adopters at any point in time.

Greenstein and Rysman (2007) offer a detailed analysis of the coordination costs behind the standardization of 56K modems. They focus primarily on market events and standard-setting activities during early deployment. Because so much activity focused on the ITU's processes they argue that the canonical model for a standards war is misleading in the case of 56K. They highlight two common and sharply contrasting views about the relationship between deployment and negotiations at the ITU. One view emphasizes the way in which market events

---

[31] The primary focus of his discussion – particularly in the 1989 piece – is on compatibility and whether markets achieve efficient levels of adoption rather than markets' choice between competing standards, but the intuition applies.

strongly shape negotiations. The other view argues that decisions were based on engineering choices, not on business incentives. They eventually argue for a middle ground between these two views. Firm participation inside the SDO varied with market circumstances and intellectual property holdings. The situation compelled participation and managerial attention of all interested parties, but each came to the SDO with asymmetric negotiating positions. They argue that had the positions been different, negotiations would also have been different.

As yet, there is little work comparing markets to nonmarket processes. Funk and Methe (2001) is one exception. They explicitly compare the effects of market- and committee-based processes on adoption of new standards. Another exception is Farrell and Saloner (1988), who compare the performance of committees to that of markets, in an attempt to better understand the situations in which industry standards bodies can improve on market outcomes. The committee's purpose is to allow pre-adoption communication, while the market exhibits less communication and allows firms to commit unilaterally to a standard. The issue Farrell and Saloner (1988) examine is a bit different from that discussed here, in that both competing standards are equally attractive from society's point of view but failure to coordinate on a common standard is harmful. They find that committees delay coordination but can improve outcomes by helping to choose the better standard more often. A related line of inquiry is taken by Simcoe (2007), who examines the speed of standards adoption by an SDO. He finds that this speed is correlated with a number of factors, including the technical complexity of standards and the makeup of the standards body.

Beyond this work, there has been little other formal examination of nonmarket processes in determining standards. This seems to be a fruitful area for future research. It would be useful, for example, to see a model that captures the benefit that a standards body or public agency has on resolving potential adopters' uncertainty when they can delay committing to a standard. Anecdotally, this effect of uncertainty is viewed as a serious issue in standards wars.[32] Another area that might inform policy is an examination of the institutional structure of standards bodies.[33] Work on the 'economic theory of regulation' has deepened our understanding of how competition between interest groups affects regulatory outcomes.[34] Again, there is anecdotal evidence that standards bodies often serve as forums for this interest group competition. For example, if a standards body is not representative of all market participants affected by standard-setting, it may settle on a standard that is inefficient from society's point of view.

Mandated standards

Government bodies may also shape the development of standards or the economic networks that grow up around standards. They often do so because important public policy issues are at stake, for example when domestic and foreign firms

[32]The competition between British Satellite Broadcasting and Sky TV in satellite television is a well-known example. BSB and Sky offered incompatible formats. The fact that consumers could not forecast the winning standard was cited as a reason for the slow penetration of satellite TV in the United Kingdom.

[33]Weiss (1993) makes a similar point.

[34]The economic theory of regulation derives from work by Becker (1983), Peltzman (1976), and Stigler (1971).

use standardization as a competitive weapon. Governments are often reluctant to become involved, because external forces such as fast-paced technical change outstrip the ability of any administrative process to guide events. This makes it easier to leave decisions to market participants. When to rely on a market process instead of on government decision-making is an open and active topic of debate, one that usually hinges on tradeoffs between imperfect market processes and imperfect government intervention.

Again, this area has seen very little work. The exceptions are the rich analyses in Besen and Johnson's (1986) study of FM radio and color television, and Farrell and Shapiro's (1992) study of the US HDTV standards development process.

Long-Run Issues in Standardization

The discussion until now has treated standardization as a choice between exogenously available technologies. This abstracts from a number of long-run issues, the most important being that standards are the result of innovation. Thus, the interaction between standardization and innovation is strong.

Standardization may both encourage and discourage innovation. Because well-defined technical standards may provide component suppliers a more secure set of interfaces around which to design a product, they may encourage research and development into the design of new components for a network. Secure telecommunication transmission standards were important in hastening innovation in customer premises markets, such as facsimile machines and modems, and in other markets that interconnected with telephones, such as Internet Service Providers. Indeed, the success of third parties in US communications network comes partly from AT&T standardizing the technology of its network, as well as the Federal Communication Commission's intervention to standardize interconnection in places where AT&T could have done so, but did not.

On the other hand, an installed base of users may also create an unintended hindrance for innovation on a mature network. An existing substitute network may hinder the growth of a new network, because the technology embedded in much existing equipment may be inappropriate for a new application, raising its cost. In addition, minority interests may be burdened with higher costs on an existing network, but may not be large enough to justify setting up a new network. For example, the existing AM network hindered the post-WWII growth of the FM network.

Market structure in network markets also affects innovation. Placing a single sponsor in charge of a standard is a natural solution to coordination problems. The structure of a single firm internalizes all design decisions and upgrading and maintenance problems. Unifying control within a single firm generally eliminates competing designers, providing users with certainty about who controls the evolution of standards and their ultimate compatibility. This can speed technical change.

We cannot overemphasize this potential benefit from single-firm sponsorship, especially in markets subject to uncertain and rapid changes in technology. Many readers will recognize this as the traditional model of telephone networks under

AT&T's pre-divestiture leadership and as IBM's vision for integrating computers and telecommunications under the System Network Architecture model. Many other firms have also tried to adopt this model, though competition often forces them into standards wars.

Unfortunately, single-firm sponsorship by a single supplier also raises many issues. Generally, large firms have disproportionate influence upon market processes, which they manipulate to their advantage, potentially to the detriment of society's long-term interests. For example, this was the central issue in the US government's case against Microsoft in the browser wars. The browser introduced by Netscape had the potential to open up a new distribution channel and a new source for information. The largest incumbent in the PC market, Microsoft was initially unprepared to respond to the new entrants, who offered competitive alternatives to existing Microsoft products and by-passed other Microsoft's APIs. In such a setting, Microsoft had a strong incentive to use its coordinating abilities to slow down development of this alternative until it could technically catch up, which it did with successive releases of upgrades to Internet Explorer. These incentives translated into multiple actions, such as restrictions on assembler behavior and differential treatment of firms friendly to Netscape's commercial interests (Bresnahan, 2005).

These long-run issues affect prices as well as innovation. Events in the video game market illustrate how complex these issues can become. Microsoft entered in the late 1990s with the X-Box. This entry came at considerable cost in terms of sunk R&D expenses and variable losses over the early generations of the platform. Because the firm was a small player at first it had considerable difficulty generating cooperation from the largest developers. It had to subsidize console sales to consumers because it lacked applications. Since the royalty fees from developers hardly made up for the expense, the firm lost billions of dollars on the first generation. Yet, Microsoft has been very open that they are not benchmarking their own behavior by the break-even standard in the earliest generations. Thus, its pricing strategy is more oriented toward establishing a long-term presence. Given these factors, it is extremely difficult to make a welfare assessment in the market.

CONCLUSIONS

The emergence of standardization in markets with network effects is justifiably receiving greater attention than ever before, from academics, industry observers, and policymakers. At this point, the questions are well known: Do markets select the right standards? Do they move between standards too swiftly or too slowly? How do nonmarket mechanisms perform by comparison?

Answers are less readily forthcoming. Certainly, theoretical work in network economics has clarified our understanding of the circumstances under which the classic problems associated with lock-in can occur. But this literature has also shown that many outcomes are possible. Decentralized market mechanisms may produce desirable outcomes or distort them, depending on the market structure, chance historical events, and changes in the costs of technicalalternatives. Diffuse market structures produce coordination problems and communication difficulties, but also much innovation. More concentrated market structures will alleviate some of the communication problems, but strategic interests will distort incentives away from optimal outcomes. Administrative processes may ameliorate communication problems, but internal political battles will distort outcomes in other ways.

Unfortunately, because there has been relatively little empirical study of standards, many key questions remain unanswered. At this point, one of the largest gaps in the theoretical literature is the relative lack of work modeling the performance of standards bodies relative to markets. Because so many standards are set in practice through these bodies, the welfare effects of a better understanding of how standards bodies perform could be enormous. A similar gap exists regarding public sector standard-setting. Most existing work on standards examines the extent to which market outcomes are efficient. Little work exists clarifying the circumstances under which a policymaker might improve on the market.

Beyond the theoretical issues, it seems clear that hard empirical analysis of standards wars and the performance of standards bodies can be fruitful. Most existing work in the area has been limited to straightforward tests for the existence of network effects. As discussed above, there has been some encouraging recent empirical work; in particular, state-of-the-art empirical techniques now allow the welfare calculations that are at the heart of the debate on standards. This provides reason to be optimistic that our understanding of the economics of standardization will improve.

References

Arthur, W.B. (1989). Competing technologies, increasing returns, and lock-in by historical events. *Economic Journal*, 99, 116–31.

Arthur, W.B. (1996). *Increasing returns and path dependence in the economy*. University of Michigan Press.

Becker, G.S. (1983). A theory of competition among pressure groups for political influence. *Quarterly Journal of Economics*, 98, 371–400.

Besen, S., and Farrell, J. (1994). Choosing how to compete: strategies and tactics in standardization, *Journal of Economic Perspectives*, 8, 117–31.

Besen, S.M. and Johnson, L.L. (1986). Compatibility standards, competition, and innovation in the broadcasting industry. Rand Report R-3453-NSF, November.

Bresnahan, T. (2005). The economics of the Microsoft case. http://www.stanford.edu/~tbres/research.htm.

Bresnahan, T., and Greenstein, S. (1996). Technical progress and co-invention in computing and in the use of computers. *Brookings Papers on Economics Activity: Microeconomics*, 1–78.

Bresnahan, T., and Greenstein, S. (1999). Technological competition and the structure of the computing industry. *Journal of Industrial Economics*, 47(1), 1–40.

Brock, G., (1975). Competition, standards and self-regulation in the computer industry. In R. Caves and M. Roberts (eds), *Regulating the Product: Quality and Variety*, Ballinger Publishing.

Cabral, L.M.B., and Kretschmer, T. (2007). Standard battles and public policy. In S. Greenstein and V. Stango (eds), *Standards and Public Policy*, Cambridge, MA: Cambridge University Press, 329–44.

Carlton, D., and Waldman, M. (2002). The strategic use of tying to preserve and create market power in evolving industries. *RAND Journal of Economics*, 33, 194–220.

Choi, J.P. (1994). Irreversible choice of uncertain technologies with network externalities. *RAND Journal of Economics*, 25, 382–401.

Choi, J.P., and Stefanadis, C. (2001). Tying, investment and the dynamic leverage theory. *RAND Journal of Economics*, 32, 52–71.

Choi, J.P., and Thum, M. (1998). Market structure and the timing of technology adoption with network externalities. *European Economic Review*, 42, 225–44.

Chou, C., and Shy, O. (1990). Network effects without network externalities. *International Journal of Industrial Organization*, 8, 259–70.

Church, J., and Gandal, N. (1993). Complementary network externalities and technology adoption. *International Journal of Industrial Organization*, 11, 239–60.

Church, J., and Gandal, N. (1996). Strategic entry deterrence: complementary products as installed base, *European Journal of Political Economy*, 12, 331–54.

Church, J., and Gandal, N. (2000). System competition, vertical merger and foreclosure, *Journal of Economics and Management Strategy*, 9, 25–51.

Church, J., Gandal, N., and Krause, D. (2003). Indirect network effects and adoption externalities. CEPR Discussion Paper No. 3788. Available at SSRN: http://ssrn.com/abstract=383802.

Clements, M.T. (2004). Direct and indirect network effects: are they equivalent? *International Journal of Industrial Organization*, 22, 633–45.

Clements, M.T. (2005). Inefficient standard adoption: inertia and momentum revisited. *Economic Inquiry*, 43, 507–18.

David, P. (1985). CLIO and the economics of QWERTY. *American Economic Review*, 75, 332–7.

David, P., and Bunn, J. (1988). The economics of gateway technologies and network evolution: lessons from electrical supply history. *Information Economics and Policy*, 3, 165–202.

David, P.A., and Greenstein, S. (1990). The economics of compatibility standards: an introduction to recent research. *Economics of Innovation and New Technology*, 1, 3–41.

Dranove, D., and Gandal, N. (2003). The DVD vs. DIVX standard war: empirical evidence of preannouncement effects. *Journal of Economics and Management Strategy*, 12, 363–86.

Evans, D. (2003). The antitrust economics of two-sided markets. *Yale Journal on Regulation*, 20(2), 325–82.

Farrell, J. (1989). Standardization and intellectual property. *Jurimetrics Journal*, 30, 35–50.

Farrell, J. (1995). Arguments for weaker intellectual property protection in network industries. *StandardView*, 3, 46–9.

Farrell, J. (1996). Choosing the rules for formal standardization. mimeo, University of California Berkeley.

Farrell, J., and Klemperer, P. (2003). Coordination and lock-in: competition with switching costs and network effects. In R. Schmalensee and R. Willig (eds), *Handbook of Industrial Organization 3*. North Holland.

Farrell, J., and Saloner, G. (1985). Standardization, compatibility and innovation. *RAND Journal of Economics*, 16, 70–83.

Farrell, J., and Saloner, G. (1986). Installed base and compatibility: innovation, product preannouncements, and predation. *American Economic Review*, 76, 940–55.

Farrell, J., and Saloner, G. (1988). Coordination through committees and markets. *RAND Journal of Economics*, 19, 235–52.

Farrell, J., and Shapiro, C. (1992). Standard setting in high-definition television. *Brookings Papers on Economic Activity. MicroEconomics*, 1–77.

Funk, J.L., and Methe, D.T. (2001). Market- and committee-Based mechanisms in the creation and diffusion of global industry standards: the case of mobile communication. *Research Policy*, 30, 589–610

Gabel, H. (1991). *Competitive strategies for product standards*. McGraw-Hill.

Gabel, H.L. (1987). *Product standardization and competitive strategy. Advanced Series in Management*, vol. 11. Elsevier Science.

Gandal, N. (2002). Compatibility, standardization and network effects: some policy implications. *Oxford Review of Economic Policy*, 18(1), 80–91.

Gandal, N., Greenstein, S., and Salant, D. (1999). Adoptions and orphans in the early microcomputer market. *Journal of Industrial Economics*, XLVII, 87–105.

Greenstein, S., and Rysman, M. (2007). Coordination costs and standard setting: lessons from 56K modems. In S Greestein and V Stango (eds), *Standards and Public Policy*, Cambridge, MA: Cambridge University Press, 123–59.

Grindley, P. (1995). *Standards strategy and policy*. Oxford University Press.

Kahin, B., and Abbate. J. (1995). *Standards policy for information infrastructure*. MIT Press.

Katz, M.L., and Shapiro, C. (1986). Technology adoption in the presence of network externalities. *Journal of Political Economy*, 94, 822–41.

Katz, M.L., and Shapiro, C. (1992). Product introduction with network externalities. *Journal of Industrial Economics*, 40, 55–83.

Katz, M.L., and Shapiro, C. (1994). Systems competition and network effects. *The Journal of Economic Perspectives*, 8, 93–115.

Knittel, C., and Stango, V. (2007). How does incompatibility affect prices? Evidence from ATMs. *Journal of Industrial Economics*.

Knittel, C., and Stango, V. (2008). Incompatibility, product attributes and consumer welfare: evidence from ATMs. B.E. Press Advances in *Economic Analysis and Policy*, 8(1). Available at http://www.bepress.com/bejeap/vol8/iss1/art1/.

Liebowitz, S.J., and Margolis, S.E. (1990). The fable of the keys. *Journal of Law and Economics*, 22, 1–26.

Liebowitz, S.J., and Margolis, S.E. (1994). Network externality: an uncommon tragedy. *Journal of Economic Perspectives*, 8, 113–50.

Liebowitz, S.J., and Margolis, S.E. (1996). Should technology choice be a concern of antitrust policy? *Harvard Journal of Law and Technology*, 9, 283–318.

McGahan, A.M., Vadasz, L.L., and Yoffie, D. (1997). Creating value and setting standards. In D. Yoffie (ed.), *Competing in an Age of Convergence*, Harvard University Press, 240–54.

Nair, H., Chintagunta, P., and Dube, J-P (2004). Empirical analysis of indirect network effects in the market for Personal Digital Assistants. *Quantitative Marketing and Economics*, 2(1), 23–58.

Ohashi, H. (2003). The role of network effects in the U.S. VCR market, 1978–86. *Journal of Economics and Management Strategy*, 12(4), 447–94.

Peltzman, S. (1976). Toward a more general theory of regulation. *Journal of Law and Economics*, 19, 211–48.

Postrel, S.R. (1990). Competing networks and proprietary standards: the case of quadraphonic sound. *Journal of Industrial Economics*, 39, 169–85.

Rohlfs, J. (2001). *Bandwagon Effects in High Technology Industries*. MIT Press.

Rysman, M. (2004). Competition between networks: a study of the market for Yellow Pages. *Review of Economic Studies*, 71, 483–512.

Saloner, G., and Shepard, A. (1996). Adoption of technologies with network externalities: an empirical examination of the adoption of automated teller machines. *RAND Journal of Economics*, 26, 479–501.

Shy, O. (1996). Technology revolutions in the presence of network externalities. *International Journal of Industrial Organization*, 14, 785–800.

Simcoe, T. (2007). Delay and de jure standardization: exploring the slowdown in Internet standards development? In S. Greenstein and V. Stango (eds) *Standards and Public Policy*, Cambridge, MA: Cambridge University Press, 260–95.

Stango, V. (2004). The economics of standards wars. *Review of Network Economics*, 3(1), 1–19.

Stigler, G. (1971). The theory of economic regulation. *Bell Journal of Economics and Management Science*, 2, 3–21.

Von Burg, U. (2001). *The triumph of ethernet, technological communities and the battle for the LAN standard*, Stanford University Press.

Weiss, M.B.H. (1993). The standards development process: a view from political theory. *StandardView*, 1, 35–41.

10

Intellectual Property and Innovation

ROSEMARIE H. ZIEDONIS

Laura Berdish provided exceptional assistance with the journal searches
and ISI citation counts reported in this chapter. I also thank Giovanni Dosi,
David Hsu, Tim Simcoe, Scott Stern, Georg von Graevenitz, Minyuan Zhao,
and Arvids Ziedonis for useful suggestions and Faria Jabbar for additional
assistance.

INTRODUCTION

Scholars of innovation and firm strategy have long recognized that intellectual property shapes the creation and use of new technologies. Although better known for his writings on the personal or 'tacit' dimension of knowledge, Michael Polanyi also emphasized that legal rights to creative works and new discoveries could affect the pace and direction of innovative activity. In a 1944 article on patent reform, he voiced the following concerns:

> The law ... aims at a purpose which cannot be rationally achieved. It tries to parcel up a stream of creative thought into a series of distinct claims, each of which is to constitute the basis of a separately owned monopoly. But the growth of human knowledge cannot be divided into such sharply circumscribed phases. Ideas usually develop gradually by shades of emphasis, and even when, from time to time, sparks of discovery flare up and suddenly reveal a new understanding, it usually appears that the new idea has been at least partly foreshadowed in previous speculations. (Polanyi, 1944, pp. 70–71)

Edith Penrose, whose writings on the competitive advantage and growth of firms remain foundational in the field of strategy, shared Polanyi's interest in the relationship between proprietary rights and innovation. In a 1950 article with Fritz Machlup, for example, she reviewed attempts by 19th century scholars to wrestle, somewhat unsuccessfully, with several fundamental questions: Where should governments 'draw the line' between one innovation and another? Are there conditions under which alternative mechanisms, such as prizes or R&D subsidies, would promote

Handbook of Technology and Innovation Management. Edited by Scott Shane
© 2008 John Wiley & Sons, Ltd

scientific and technological progress more effectively? More generally, how can individuals and the organizations that employ them build upon the discoveries of others while simultaneously justifying the time and expense of their own endeavors? These questions continue to unite a large and growing body of research that spans the fields of economics, law, public policy, and business.

This chapter discusses recent advances in the literature on intellectual property and innovation, particularly as they inform research by management scholars. Throughout the chapter, the term 'intellectual property' (IP) is used to refer to various legal entitlements for new inventions and creative works. The main forms of protection include patents (for novel, useful, and nonobvious inventions of commercial relevance), trade secrets (for business-sensitive information that is safeguarded appropriately), copyrights (for creative expressions such as songs, films, books, or computer programs), and trademarks (for distinctive brands or logos). Landes and Posner (2003) describe these rights in more detail and discuss the tradeoffs among them.

From a policy perspective, the primary reason for assigning property rights to creations of the mind (or 'intellect') is to encourage innovative activity. Patents, for example, confer the right to exclude others from making, using, or selling a protected invention for a period of time that typically is limited to 20 years. As Abraham Lincoln famously stated, the period of exclusive protection is designed to add the 'fuel of interest to the fire of genius'.[1] By helping to deter imitation during the period of exclusivity, patents can increase the financial incentives for bringing improved goods and services to market. As part of this arrangement, information about the invention is made public through descriptions and drawings contained in published patent documents, thus spreading news about the discovery. Indeed, the word 'patent' is derived from *litterae patentes* in Latin, which means open letter.

From a research perspective, understanding how IP affects innovative activity naturally requires input from multiple disciplines. When designing policy levers used in IP systems, economists and legal scholars make crucial assumptions about how organizations and individuals will respond to the incentives or barriers introduced by such rights. When investigating broader forces affecting firm performance or the diffusion of technological knowledge, management scholars make assumptions (often implicitly) about the effects of legal IP protection.

Recognizing the multi-disciplinary nature of the topic, this chapter casts a relatively wide net over the literature on IP and innovation before focusing on issues more relevant for management scholars. To do so, 19 peer-reviewed journals were selected from the fields of management, law, and economics. Searches of these journals retrieved almost 600 articles published between 1986 and 2006 that include various IP-related terms in their titles, abstracts, or keywords. As discussed in the next section, the results of this exercise suggest that scholarly interest in IP has grown considerably over the past two decades. I then explore possible explanations for this heightened interest. To illuminate issues of particular salience in the field, I identify a subset of IP-related articles that are frequently cited in other academic

---

[1]The quote is attributed to Lincoln's 1859 lectures on discoveries and inventions, as cited in Fisk (1998, p. 1129).

publications.[2] I report the highly cited articles and identify prominent themes that run among them. I use these themes to organize my discussion of recent findings, methodological advances, and unanswered questions. The chapter ends with some brief conclusions.

The target audience for this chapter is scholars interested in technology and innovation management, strategy, or entrepreneurship. My objective is to illuminate linkages across disciplinary boundaries and to identify a few promising avenues for future research. The chapter is written to complement more extensive reviews of the recent literature on IP and innovation that have been targeted primarily towards economics and public policy audiences. For example, Jaffe (2000), Gallini (2002), FTC (2003), and von Graevenitz *et al.* (2007) discuss in greater depth the large and growing literature on the economics of patents (and on the strategic value and use of such rights).[3] Gallini and Scotchmer (2002) and Landes and Posner (2003) review the economic rationale for IP systems more thoroughly and discuss the effectiveness of alternative instruments such as prizes and R&D subsidies used to entice innovative activity. Similarly, although managerial insights often emerge from studies discussed in this chapter, the primary focus is on advances that inform research in the field. More practitioner-oriented issues regarding the effective management of IP assets – such as the specific terms of license agreements, whether to file for international protection, or how to seek remedies in the event of unauthorized use or imitation – although important, are beyond the scope of this chapter. Such issues are often context-specific and require input from legal counsel.

TRENDS IN THE PUBLICATION OF IP-RELATED ARTICLES, 1986–2006

Table 10.1 reports the journals from which the research-oriented articles related to IP and innovation were identified. Although far from comprehensive, the list includes prominent peer-reviewed outlets in management (e.g., the *Strategic Management Journal* and *Management Science*), economics (e.g., the *American Economic Review* and *Quarterly Journal of Economics*), law and economics (e.g., the *Journal of Law, Economics, and Organization* and the *Journal of Law and Economics*), and finance (e.g., the *Journal of Financial Economics* and the *Journal of Finance*). Owing to their significance as outlets for research on innovation, specialized journals such as *Research Policy*, *Economics of Innovation and New Technologies* (*EINT*), and *Industrial*

---

[2]A similar approach has been used to identify influential articles and topics in the broader fields of management (Judge *et al.*, 2007) and economics (Kim *et al.*, 2006).

[3]Jaffe (2000) and Gallini (2002) focus on a series of legislative and judicial actions since the late 1970s that strengthened and expanded the protection afforded by patents in the United States. von Graevenitz *et al.* (2007) identify working papers and articles that have emerged since these earlier reviews, including studies that investigate the effects of controversial legal rulings in the 1990s that affected the patentability of computer software and business methods. Readers interested in an international perspective will also find the von Graevenitz *et al.* (2007) article useful, because the authors discuss patent-related initiatives in Europe and Japan and describe procedures for filing and enforcing patents in those jurisdictions. Finally, the FTC (2003) report, which is based on a series of hearings held in 2002 and 2003, is a wonderful resource for those interested in learning more about the patent experiences of 'real managers'. Testimonies made by executives from a wide mix of companies and industrial sectors are posted on the FTC web site at: http://www.ftc.gov/opp/intellect/ (last viewed June 2007).

TABLE 10.1 List of selected journals.

Journal name	Abbreviation
Academy of Management Journal	AMJ
Administrative Science Quarterly	ASQ
American Economic Review	AER
Economics of Innovation and New Technology	EINT
Industrial and Corporate Change	ICC
International Journal of Industrial Organization	IJIO
Journal of Finance	JOF
Journal of Financial Economics	JFE
Journal of Industrial Economics	JIE
Journal of Law and Economics	JLE
Journal of Law, Economics, and Organization	JLEO
Journal of Legal Studies	JLS
Management Science	MS
Organization Science	OS
Quarterly Journal of Economics	QJE
Rand Journal of Economics	RJE
Research Policy	RP
Review of Economics and Statistics	RESTAT
Strategic Management Journal	SMJ

and Corporate Change (*ICC*) also are included. Each journal was searched for articles published between 1986 and 2006 that contain one or more of the following terms in their titles, abstracts, or keywords: intellectual property, intangible asset, intellectual capital, patent, trademark, copyright, or secret (secrecy). Book reviews, research notes, and articles in conference proceedings are excluded.

Although providing a useful snapshot of recent studies, this approach is not without important limitations. First, although the list of journals is wide-ranging, the search terms are defined quite narrowly – in part to keep the exercise manageable in scope. An unfortunate drawback is that relevant articles are omitted due to failure to match the specific search terms. Consider, for example, Cohen and Levinthal's (1990) influential article on 'absorptive capacity'. The article does not match the IP search terms listed above in its title, abstract, or keywords and is not retrieved in this search. Nonetheless, as Cohen *et al.* (2000) note elsewhere, IP rights play a fundamental role in shaping the incentives of firms to absorb and make use of external technologies, whether by facilitating inter-organizational contracting or by deterring internalization efforts due to risks of possible infringement.[4] Expanding the search to include terms such as 'innovation', 'technology', 'knowledge', or

[4]Similarly, as discussed in the later section 'Additional insights from highly-cited articles', a growing strand of research in strategy emphasizes the importance of difficult-to-imitate resources and capabilities as a source of competitive advantage. Although IP rights relate to core principles in both the 'resource'- and 'knowledge'-based view of the firm, many articles on these topics do not include IP-specific search terms in their titles, keywords, or abstracts and therefore are not retrieved by the search.

'research and development' would retrieve a much larger body of work but also would increase the number of articles that speak more tangentially to IP-related issues. Influential works also may have been excluded due to publication as books or in journals not included on the list. Legal scholars, for example, tend to publish in law reviews that are not subjected to the peer-review process. Thus, writings by prominent IP legal scholars, such as Rebecca Eisenberg, Mark Lemley, or Robert Merges, are under-represented in the sample.[5] Similarly, among the influential writings by Suzanne Scotchmer and colleagues on the economics of patents and cumulative innovation, the most highly cited is Scotchmer's 1991 synthesis in the *Journal of Economic Perspectives* (*JEP*), a journal not included in the search.[6]

Despite these limitations, a large set of articles – 592 in total – was retrieved using the search terms and journals reported above. Figure 10.1 plots the annual number of 'IP-related' articles identified by publication year. Between 1986 and the mid-1990s, the number of IP articles published in these journals remained quite stable, at roughly 20 publications per year. During the past decade, however, the annual number of IP publications has climbed sharply, with over 80 IP articles identified in 2006 alone.

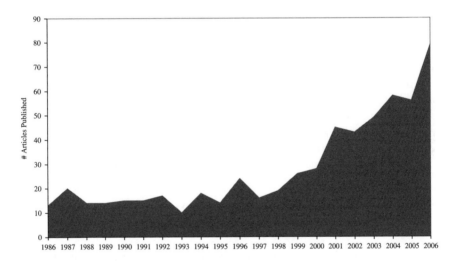

FIGURE 10.1 Annual number of IP-related articles published in selected journals (by publication year, 1986–2006).

[5]As illustrated by a large body of work by Mark Lemley and colleagues, legal scholars are increasingly engaged in research that bridges into issues regarding the strategic use and management of IP (e.g., Allison *et al.*, 2004; Lemley and Shapiro, 2005). Ronald Mann's article on the role of patents in the venture financing of software startups nicely illustrates this type of work (Mann, 2005); his paper is filled with insightful quotes based on interviews with entrepreneurs, venture capitalists, and investment bankers. I encourage readers to search law journals (or working papers by legal scholars posted, for example, on the Social Science Research Network at ssrn.com) for articles that provide insight into the phenomenon or institutional context of focal interest in their studies.

[6]*JEP* solicits articles directly from authors, and so it is not among the peer-reviewed journals in Table 10.1.

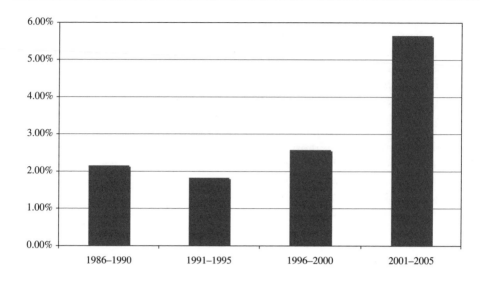

FIGURE 10.2 IP-related articles as a share of total articles published in selected journals (by 5-year intervals, 1986–2005).

This expansion in the literature could, of course, simply reflect an overall increase over time in the annual number of articles published by these journals. Figure 10.2 suggests that something more substantive is going on. Of the total number of articles published in these journals, the estimated share related to IP grew from 2 % in the 1980s to almost 6 % in the most recent five-year interval.[7] Given the general-interest nature of many of the journals, the low overall percentage is not surprising. For example, the search retrieved only ten IP-related articles in the finance journals (*JOF* and *JFE*), eight of which were published between 2002 and 2006.

WHY IS INTEREST IN IP GROWING WITHIN THE ACADEMIC COMMUNITY?

The proliferation of IP-related articles could be driven by many factors. Prominent among these is the more widespread availability and use of patent-based statistics. When Schmookler (1966) conducted his pioneering work using patent data to trace the sources of technological change, he spent a year in the basement at the US Patent and Trademark Office (PTO) and manually categorized the information contained in original patent documents.[8] Although far less heroic, some of us may recall trips to regional patent depositories to retrieve data, floppy disks in hand.

[7]The start year of each journal was used to determine this percentage. The total number of research articles published annually by each journal was then estimated by multiplying the number of full-length articles appearing in the September (or Fall) issue by the number of issues a journal published that year.

[8]As reported in Griliches and Hurwicz (1972, p. 88). I thank Mike Scherer, author of other landmark studies in the 1960s using patent statistics (Scherer 1965a, 1965b), for pointing me toward this reference. In personal correspondence, Scherer also recalled how the formation of the PTO's Office of Technology

Today, electronic databases with information on millions of US patents are available for free from the NBER web site[9] or can be purchased from private vendors, such as Micropatent or Delphion. Meanwhile, advances in computing power and statistical software packages have facilitated the use of these data.

Within the community of management scholars, anecdotal evidence from the Academy of Management (AOM) meetings suggests that interest in patents as a data source has grown considerably in recent years. When inaugural versions of professional development workshops on the uses (and abuses) of patent data were organized in the late 1990s, the workshops were held in small rooms and attracted 30 or so participants. By 2007, the 'patent data' workshops had become institutionalized as an annual event involving hundreds of participants from across the entrepreneurship, technology and innovation management, and business policy and strategy divisions of the Academy.[10]

Patent data are being used to investigate a wide range of issues relevant to the study of technology and innovation management. Sorenson and Stuart (2000), for example, investigate the effects of organizational aging on the innovation process in biotechnology and semiconductors. By tracing changes in the 'vintage' of technologies referenced in a firm's portfolio of patents, the authors show that firms tend to 'turn inward' and forego use of state-of-the-art discoveries as they grow older, a result that is suggestive of strong inertial forces. In a similar spirit, Benner and Tushman (2002) use patent data to distinguish between 'exploitative' and 'exploratory' innovations.[11] Integrating information on the quality management initiatives of paint and photography companies, the authors find that managerial processes aimed at creating more reliable (lower-variance) outcomes paradoxically can undermine an organization's ability to produce path-breaking discoveries. These studies illustrate how information reported in patent documents can be used to trace changes in the internal innovative activities of firms. As discussed in the next section, numerous studies also use patent data, and the citations they contain, to investigate how firms identify and recombine technological knowledge from *external* sources.

Although it is now quite common to use patent data to trace various dimensions of innovative activity, authors making use of such data frequently remain silent on how the exclusionary rights conferred by patents alter the dynamics of focal interest in the study (e.g., by influencing the pace or direction of a firm's innovative activities). It is possible, therefore, that the proliferation of IP-related studies reflects greater use of patents as a data source without necessarily indicating growing scholarly interest in how IP rights *per se* affect firm behavior or performance.

Assessment and Forecast in the 1970s facilitated his own research by making patent statistics available in electronic databases.

[9]The NBER patent database is available for download at: http://www.nber.org/patents/. Hall *et al.* (2001) discuss the database and define key variables and their construction. See also the National University of Singapore patent database, which is available at: http://patents.nus.edu/.

[10]Additional information about these professional development workshops is available on the AOM web site: http://www.aomonline.org/. A reading list prepared for the 2005 workshop, organized by Kwanghui Lim then of the National University of Singapore, is available at: http://kwanghui.com/aom2005/(last visited June 23, 2007).

[11]As Jaffe and Trajtenberg (2002) discuss, earlier work uses patent data to construct similar proxies for the 'originality' or 'basicness' of technologies embedded in patented inventions.

Over the past two decades, however, IP also assumed a more central role in economic activity, thus providing scholars with more substantive reasons for understanding the relationship between IP (as property rights) and the introduction, exchange, or adoption of technological discoveries. The trend towards a 'knowledge' or 'information'-based economy is widely documented. In a Brookings Institute study, for example, Blair and Kochan (2000) report that the proportion of shareholder value attributed to intangible assets rose from 17 % in 1978 to almost 70 % by 1998 for corporations traded on US stock exchanges. Hall (2001) reports similar trends and documents further that growth and productivity gains in the US economy are increasingly fueled by the ownership and utilization of nonphysical assets. As the quest for profitability and growth increasingly rests on assets that are intangible in nature, the mechanisms firms use to build and protect those assets arguably increase in importance as phenomena of study.

A second (albeit more subtle) shift has occurred in the organization of innovative activity. In their recent book, *The Financing of Innovation,* Lamoreux and Sokoloff (2007) show that multiple organizations were involved in the development and launch of influential inventions such as electricity and aircraft, whether in the creation and refinement of initial discoveries (the 'entrepreneurs'), the supply of funds used to support such activities (the 'financiers'), or the provision of complementary distribution or marketing services required to bring new products to market (the 'complementary asset owners,' using terminology popularized by Teece, 1986). Several scholars show that these boundary-spanning commercialization activities have grown widespread over the past few decades (Arora *et al.* 2001; Chesbrough, 2003). Gompers and Lerner (2001) report, for example, that the amount of venture capital provided to entrepreneurial firms in the US grew from negligible sums in the 1970s to more than $17 billion in investments in 1998 alone. Kortum and Lerner (2000) show further that funds invested in these innovation-intensive startups produced larger numbers of patentable inventions than equivalent R&D investments made by established corporations. In combination, these studies underscore the increased vibrancy of startups as sources of new technologies and products.[12] Meanwhile, significant cutbacks have occurred at prominent corporate R&D labs such as the Bell Labs System of AT&T or the PARC facility at Xerox (Chesbrough, 2003). In addition, statistics from the National Science Foundation suggest that the supply base of innovation has grown more fragmented over the past two decades. According to the NSF (2007), the share of US industrial R&D spending comprised by firms with fewer than 1000 employees increased from 4.4 % in 1980 to more than 25.3 % by 2003.

As discussed in Chapter 15 on the financing of innovation, the organizational separation of research, financing, and commercialization activities creates a context rife with expropriation hazards (Arrow, 1962) and potential problems of adverse selection (Akerlof, 1970). A number of questions naturally follow. To what extent, if

---

[12]As discussed in Chapter 13 on technology entrepreneurship, the innovative activities of small firms have also been propelled by changes in policies affecting the commercialization of technologies from public research institutions and universities. For additional discussion, see Jaffe and Lerner (2001) and Mowery *et al.* (2004).

at all, do ownership rights to new discoveries (and their acquisition or enforcement) facilitate these inter-organizational collaborations? Are there conditions under which an aggressive use of IP rights or their accumulation could *undermine* the ability of firms to tap into external sources of innovation? Do proprietary, enforceable rights to innovative output sustain a higher degree of organizational separation than would otherwise be expected? Finally, how do the ownership and control rights to new technologies affect the formation of new firms, including the incentives of a firm's employees to join or form rival companies? These questions, which lie at the intersection of firm strategy, innovation management, and entrepreneurship, motivate a small but growing stream of research that is discussed in the next section.

A final explanation for heightened interest in IP within the academic community relates to shifts in the institutional environment. The past few decades have witnessed major reforms in the laws and policies governing IP protection, both in the US and in most industrialized countries. In the US, for example, copyright protection has been lengthened in term and extended to content secured by encryption devices (Littman, 2001), stiffer penalties have been imposed for theft of trade secrets and infringement of patents (Landes and Posner, 2003), and the subject matter eligible for patent protection has been expanded to include genetically altered organisms, computer software, and methods of doing business (von Graevenitz *et al.*, 2007).

The US patent system nonetheless remains in a state of flux, with some even claiming that the system is 'broken' (Jaffe and Lerner, 2004). The US Patent and Trademark Office has granted record numbers of patents in areas ranging from semiconductors and computer software to business methods and human gene sequences, raising concerns about the costs and feasibility of navigating through mazes of overlapping rights in these areas (Heller and Eisenberg, 1998; Shapiro, 2001). Lerner (1995) estimates, for example, that US firms spent over $1 billion defending or enforcing patents in courts in 1991 while investing only $3.7 billion in basic R&D that year. More recent studies suggest that legal disputes over IP in the US have become both more frequent and more costly (Landes and Posner, 2003; Bessen and Meurer, 2006). Perhaps in response to such concerns, the US Supreme Court agreed to hear more IP-related cases in 2006 than it had accepted since 1965 (Lemley and Sampat, 2007). Meanwhile, bills to reform certain aspects of the US patent system remain pending before Congress.

Outside the US, governmental bodies and institutions continue to wrestle with how to strike an appropriate balance between proprietary rights and the ability of others to consume, build upon, or use IP-protected assets, often reaching divergent solutions. The patent protection afforded to computer software algorithms remains considerably stronger in the US than it is in Europe (von Graevenitz *et al.*, 2007). Meanwhile, database compilations qualify for special forms of protection in Europe that are not available in the US (Bitton, 2006). The 1994 Trade-Related Aspects of Intellectual Property (TRIPs) agreement created minimum standards for IP protection in signatory nations, but implementation of the agreement remains slow and controversial.[13]

---

[13]See von Graevenitz *et al.* (2007) for more detailed discussion of this landmark agreement.

These shifts and heterogeneity in the institutional environment provide valuable opportunities for research aimed at disentangling the effects of IP rights on innovation. In turn, as legislatures, courts, and institutional bodies face difficult decisions on how best to define the length, duration, and standards for protection, authors of studies that shed light on the effects of IP policies on individual- and organization-level behavior have opportunities to weigh in on such debate.

The sheer volume of proprietary rights being awarded in key industrial sectors (and the inherent 'fuzziness' of their boundaries) simultaneously magnifies concerns about rent *expropriation* and hold-up by outside patent owners (Shapiro, 2001; FTC, 2003). The basic concern is that outside patent owners have incentives to delay assertion of their legal rights to exclusivity until after firms have invested considerable sums into the development, manufacture, and sale of related products. Not only can patent owners threaten an injunction at that point (thus enhancing their bargaining position in license negotiations), but also firms can find it difficult to invent around patented inventions that have been integrated within manufacturing processes or product designs. Firms bringing technologically complex products to market therefore may be vulnerable *ex post* to rent-seeking lawsuits brought by external patent owners. The recent conflict between Research-in-Motion (RIM), the maker of Blackberry hand-held devices, and NTP Inc., a patent holding company, illustrates the potential stakes involved. After four years of legal wrangling and faced with a possible halt in sales on the US market, RIM paid NTP more than $600 million to settle its claims of patent infringement.[14]

Concerns about patent 'hold-up' are amplified in standards-setting contexts (Shapiro, 2001). The costs of switching to an alternative standard mean that the bargaining power of entities owning essential patents increases dramatically once a common platform has been established. A nascent strand of research investigates the options available to firms, standards organizations, and anti-trust authorities in response to these high-stakes dilemmas. See, for example, recent work by Lemley (2002), Lerner and Tirole (2006), and Rysman and Simcoe (2007).

In summary, evidence from the 19 peer-reviewed journals suggests that the literature on IP and innovation has grown considerably over the past two decades. This heightened interest in IP within the academic community is likely to reflect a combination of factors. First, patent data have become more widely accessible and easier to use, thus opening doors for research on a wide range of innovation-related topics. Second, corporate wealth has become increasingly tied to assets that are intangible rather than physical in nature, thus calling attention to the mechanisms firms use to safeguard and leverage those important assets. Third, markets to commercialize new technologies and ideas have become more fragmented, which raises questions about the role of IP in boundary-spanning activities. Finally, shifts in IP policies and institutions have generated unique opportunities and demand for empirical research. These factors should not be viewed as mutually exclusive. Shifts in legal IP regimes, for example, could affect the private value of IP protection while simultaneously altering the organization of innovative activity.

[14]von Graevenitz *et al.* (2007) discuss other examples of patent 'hold-up' and discuss linkages with anti-trust and competition policies.

ADDITIONAL INSIGHTS FROM HIGHLY-CITED ARTICLES

This section takes a closer look at recent IP-related articles that are particularly influential, as evidenced by the number of citations they have received in other academic studies. As Kim *et al.* (2006) and Judge *et al.* (2007) discuss, citations to academic articles can reflect numerous factors, including the significance of an article's contributions, the provocative nature of the study or its findings, and the author's reputation as a leading scholar on the subject. In other instances, citations can reflect 'herding' tendencies where articles are frequently cited even if they are infrequently read. Although prone to many interpretations, citation counts nonetheless remain the most common metric used to estimate the 'impact' or 'influence' of academic publications.

Citation counts were compiled for each IP-related article identified from the searches reported earlier. Following standard practice, the Social Science Citations Index on ISI's Web of Knowledge was used to identify citations. When working papers listed in ISI by the same author(s) shared the same title as a published article on the list, citations to the earlier working paper were included. The information was downloaded from ISI citations in June 2007. As a result, the true impact of recent articles (with fewer years 'at risk' of being cited) will be biased downward relative to that reported for older articles in the group.

The results of this exercise are quite interesting. Of the 592 IP-related articles identified, only 28 had received 100 or more ISI citations by June 2007. This relatively small number could reflect the fact that many of the articles identified are quite new, as suggested by the trends reported earlier in Figure 10.1.

Table 10.2 lists the highly-cited articles, rank-ordered by the number of citations they received. David Teece's 1986 article 'Profiting from technological innovation' tops the list, with 866 citations. Of the five remaining articles with more than 300 citations, three are by Adam Jaffe – as solo-authored work or in collaboration with Manuel Trajtenberg and Rebecca Henderson. These articles are discussed in more detail below.

Overall, the articles listed in Table 10.2 nicely illustrate the fact that scholarship related to IP spans multiple disciplines. As shown in the second column, the authors represent a mix of institutional affiliations from business schools, economics departments, and schools of law.[15] Similarly, no single journal dominates the field as an outlet for research. Six of the 28 highly cited articles are published in the *Rand Journal of Economics*, five appear in *Research Policy*, and four are in the *Strategic Management Journal*. The remaining articles are distributed widely among the journals.

As a group, the highly-cited articles offer several vantage points on IP and innovation. Echoing points made earlier, one set of articles focuses on the use of patent data as an input into empirical research on innovation. Among these articles, some introduce new methods for utilizing such data in large-sample studies (e.g., Jaffe, 1986; Trajtenberg, 1990; Jaffe *et al.*, 1993), some validate the interpretation of such data (e.g., Narin *et al.*, 1987), while others use the data to probe more deeply into

---

[15] The authors of two articles (Narin *et al.*, 1987, 1997) are from consulting firms that specialize in the generation and use of patent-based statistics.

TABLE 10.2 Articles receiving more than 1000 cites by June 2007.[a]

Rank	Author (Department affiliation)[b]	Article title	Journal[c]	Year	# Cites[d]
1	Teece, David J. (business)	Profiting from Technological Innovation: Implications for Integration, Collaboration, Licensing and Public Policy	RP	1986	866
2	Jaffe, Adam B. (economics); Trajtenberg Manuel (economics); Henderson, Rebecca (business)	Geographic Localization of Knowledge Spillovers as Evidence by Patent Citations	QJE	1993	606
3	Jaffe, Adam B. (economics)	Technological Opportunity and Spillovers of R&D: Evidence from Firms' Patents, Profits, and Market Values.	AER	1986	381
4	Landes, William M. (law); Posner, Richard A. (law)	An Economic Analysis of Copyright Law	JLS	1989	341
5	Jaffe, Adam B. (economics)	Real Effects of Academic Research	AER	1989	305
6	Anderson, Philip (business); Tushman, Michael L. (business)	Technological Discontinuities and Dominant Designs: A Cyclical Model of Technological Change	ASQ	1990	289
7	D'Aspremont, Claude (economics); Jacquemin, Alexis (economics)	Cooperative and Noncooperative R&D in Duopoly with Spillovers	AER	1988	251
8	Mowery, David C. (business); Oxley, Joanne E. (business); Silverman, Brian S. (business)	Strategic Alliances and Interfirm Knowledge Transfer	SMJ	1996	220
9	Katz, Michael L. (economics)	An Analysis of Cooperative Research and Development.	RJE	1986	184

TABLE 10.2 *(continued)*

Rank	Author (Department affiliation)[b]	Article title	Journal[c]	Year	# Cites[d]
10	Mansfield, Edwin (business)	Patents and Innovation: an Empirical Study	MS	1986	177
11	Hall, Richard (business)	The Strategic Analysis of Intangible Resources	SMJ	1992	169
12	Landes, William M. (law); Posner, Richard A. (law)	Trademark Law: an Economic Perspective	JLE	1987	161
13	Narin, Francis; Hamilton, Kimberly S.; Olivastro, Dominic (consulting)	The Increasing Linkage between US Technology and Public Science	RP	1997	149
14	Trajtenberg, Manuel (economics)	A Penny for Your Quotes: Patent Citations and the Value of Innovations	RJE	1990	145
15	Henderson, Rebecca (business); Cockburn, Iain (business)	Scale, Scope, and Spillovers: The Determinants of Research Productivity in Drug Discovery	RJE	1996	137
16	Oldham, Greg (business); Cummings, Anne (business)	Employee Creativity: Personal and Contextual Factors at Work	AMJ	1996	129
17	Ahuja, G. (business)	Collaborative Networks, Structural Holes, and Innovation: A Longitudinal Study	ASQ	2000	123
18	Almeida, Paul (business); Kogut, Bruce (business)	Localization of Knowledge and the Mobility of Engineers in Regional Networks.	MS	1999	120
19	Hall, Richard (business)	A Framework Linking Intangible Resources and Capabilities to Sustainable Competitive Advantage	SMJ	1993	119
20	Hall, Bronwyn H. (economics); Ziedonis, Rosemarie H. (business)	The Patent Paradox Revisited: An Empirical Study of Patenting in the US Semiconductor Industry, 1979–1995	RJE	2001	116

(continued overleaf)

TABLE 10.2 *(continued)*

Rank	Author (Department affiliation)[b]	Article title	Journal[c]	Year	# Cites[d]
21	Chatterjee, Savan (business); Wernerfelt, Birger (business)	The Link Between Resources and Type of Diversification: Theory and Evidence	*SMJ*	1991	115
22	Narin, Francis; Noma, Elliot; Perry, Ross (consulting)	Patents as Indicators of Corporate Technological Strength	*RP*	1987	112
23	Acs, Zoltan J. (economics & finance); Audretsch, David B. (economics)	Innovation, Market Structure, and Firm Size	*RESTAT*	1987	110
24	Gilbert, Richard (economics); Shapiro, Carl (economics)	Optimal Patent Length and Breadth	*RJE*	1990	107
25	Kortum, Samuel (economics); Lerner, Josh (business)	What is Behind the Recent Surge in Patenting	*RP*	1999	104
26	Mowery, David C. (business); Nelson, Richard R. (policy); Sampat, Bhaven N. (economics); Ziedonis, Arvids A. (business)	The Growth of Patenting and Licensing by US Universities: An Assessment of the Effects of the Bayh–Dole Act of 1980	*RP*	2001	101
27	Klemperer, Paul (economics)	How Broad Should the Scope of Patent Protection Be?	*RJE*	1990	100
28	Conner, Kathleen R. (business); Rumelt, Richard P. (business)	Software Piracy: An Analysis of Production Strategies	*MS*	1991	100

Notes:
[a]Based on searches of journals listed in Table 10.1 between 1986 and 2006. Search terms are reported in the text.
[b]Author affiliations in the publication year were identified from information reported on the article or, if missing, from the author's c.v.
[c]Journal abbreviations are reported in Table 10.1.
[d]Total # ISI Citations received by June 2007; citations to working papers reported in ISI (same title, same authors) are included.

the determinants of innovative performance (e.g., Henderson and Cockburn, 1996; Mowery *et al.*, 1996; Almeida and Kogut, 1999; Ahuja, 2000).

A second set of studies, published primarily in strategy journals, casts IP as part of a larger bundle of resources that can confer advantages to firms against rivals (e.g., Chatterjee and Wernerfelt, 1991; Hall, 1992, 1993). In other instances, however, strategy scholars explicitly assume that IP rights are either absent (Anderson and Tushman, 1990) or weak (Teece, 1986), thus allowing the authors to shift theoretical attention to broader forces influencing technological change and firm performance.

A final set of studies shifts analytical attention to the relationship between legal IP regimes and innovation, offering both normative (design of 'optimal' IP systems) and positive (observed effects of IP on behavior) perspectives. Not surprisingly, influential articles on the design of optimal IP systems are by legal scholars (Landes and Posner, 1987, 1989) and economic theorists (Gilbert and Shapiro, 1990; Klemperer, 1990).[16] Articles on how IP laws and policies shape innovative activity 'in the real world' are written by a more diverse group of scholars from across the fields of business, public policy, and economics (Kortum and Lerner, 1999; Hall and Ziedonis, 2001; Mowery *et al.*, 2001).

Collectively, therefore, the highly cited articles reveal three prominent themes in the recent literature:

- the use of patent data as a 'paper trail' with which to trace innovative activity;
- the value of IP as a strategic asset (thus shifting attention to its accumulation and use);
- the role of IP as a policy lever (motivating research on how IP policies and laws affect behavior).

These themes map broadly onto the factors discussed earlier, which are likely to underpin the growing interest in IP within the academic community. In the remainder of this section, I highlight selected articles from Table 10.2 that relate to these topics and highlight emerging issues and potential avenues for continued research.

Use of patent data as a 'paper trail' of innovative activity

The articles in Table 10.2 illustrate two common uses of patent data in studies of innovation and technological change.[17] First, patents generated from an organization's R&D activities can be used to construct an indicator of innovative productivity.

---

[16]Table 10.2 also includes formal economic models by D'Aspremont and Jacquemin (1988) and Katz (1986). In these models, IP enters indirectly by affecting the spillovers associated with R&D investments. When IP protection is strong, firms are assumed to be better positioned to recoup profits from their R&D investments.

[17]These articles are part of a much larger body of work using patents as proxies for innovative activity. Building on his earlier studies, Scherer (1982) uses patents to trace patterns of technology flows across industries. In related work, Soete (1981, 1987) and Dosi *et al.* (1990) use patent data to investigate the relationship between technical change and technology flows across countries. Griliches (1990) and Jaffe and Trajtenberg (2002) provide more comprehensive reviews of empirical studies using patent-based statistics.

Second, the citations reported in patent documents can also be used to trace the linkages between generations of patented discoveries, thus providing indirect evidence of knowledge flows. In both instances, patent data provide a visible 'paper trail' of innovative activity that otherwise would be difficult for scholars to observe. Despite significant methodological advances over the past two decades, the appropriate use and interpretation of patent-based statistics remains a matter of considerable debate within the field, as discussed below.

Patent-based indicators of innovative performance. Much of the literature using patent data to capture the 'innovativeness' of firms builds on methods introduced by Hausman *et al.* (1984) for estimating 'knowledge production functions'. The authors used annual R&D spending to estimate inputs used in the production of technological knowledge and annual patent filings to capture the output from such activity. These methods provide a useful vehicle to economists and management scholars seeking to track changes in firm-level R&D productivity or innovative 'performance'.

Two articles in Table 10.2 illustrate the diverse ways in which such methods can be applied. Cockburn and Henderson (1998) use the approach to demonstrate scale and scope economies in the performance of R&D, an issue of central interest in both economics and strategy. Anchored in the sociology literature on inter-organizational networks, Ahuja (2000) uses a similar 'knowledge-production-function' methodology to estimate how direct and indirect ties with alliance partners affect the innovativeness of firms in the chemical industry. Similar methods have been used to investigate the innovative impact of other corporate development activities, such as technology-driven acquisitions (e.g., Ahuja and Katila, 2001; Puranam and Srikanth, 2007), collaborations with university scientists (e.g., Cockburn and Henderson, 1998), and minority equity investments in startups (e.g., Dushnitsky and Lenox, 2005; Wadhwa and Kotha, 2006).

Despite such widespread use, it is well documented that patents can paint a distorted picture of innovative activity. As noted by Griliches (1990), technological discoveries may remain unpatented either because they do not qualify for such protection or because innovators elect to safeguard the discovery through trade secrets instead. Additionally, the propensity for filing patents can differ substantially across industrial sectors (Cohen *et al.*, 2000; Hall and Ziedonis, 2001), the quality of the examination process that 'screens out' low-quality inventions varies across countries (von Graevenitz *et al.*, 2007), and budgetary constraints of patent agencies affect the rate at which applications are reviewed and granted (Griliches, 1990). Finally, the private value of patented inventions is notoriously skewed: a few are extremely valuable while most are not.[18]

A variety of approaches have been adopted in response to these limitations of using patent data. Recognizing that the motives for patenting (and the propensity to keep discoveries secret) can differ dramatically across sectors, some restrict

---

[18]As discussed below, Trajtenberg's influential 1990 study in Table 10.2 underscores this point in the context of medical devices (Trajtenberg, 1990). Similar evidence is reported from patent renewal data in pharmaceuticals (Grabowski and Vernon, 1992) and a cross-industry survey of German patent holders (Harhoff *et al.*, 1999).

attention to a single industry setting (e.g., Cockburn and Henderson, 1996; Ahuja, 2000). Alternatively, if multiple sectors are included for purposes of generalizability or comparison, regressions using patent-based output measures as the dependent variable can be run separately for each industrial sector (e.g., Sorenson and Stuart, 2000; Benner and Tushman, 2002).

Even within a sector, however, some caution may be needed when using patents to infer time-varying changes in innovative productivity. In semiconductors, for example, Hall and Ziedonis (2001) find that reforms in US patent policies in the mid-1980s triggered an upsurge in patenting behavior driven largely by concerns about litigation risks and hold-up posed by outside patent owners. More recently, Hall (2005) shows that the 1980s reforms stimulated an unexpected jump in patenting within the information technology (IT) sector more generally, suggesting that the effects were not confined to the semiconductor segment. Cohen *et al.* (2000) provide additional evidence from a 1994 survey of R&D lab managers that the primary motive for patenting in IT and other 'complex products' industries is defensive in nature. If these strategic motives for filing patents vary across sectors or grow more pronounced within a sector over time, false inferences could be reached about the 'true' levels of innovative productivity from using simple knowledge-production-function estimates.

To clarify the latter point, consider the drawbacks of naïvely applying such methods to estimate the innovative performance of software firms. In the early development of the software industry, firms primarily relied on copyrights, not patents, to protect software algorithms. A series of court rulings in the 1990s, however, altered the IP landscape and led to more prolific patenting of software and Internet-related inventions (Graham and Mowery, 2003; Bessen and Hunt, 2004). Patent-based indicators therefore would understate (perhaps severely) the true production of innovative software technologies in the early period relative to years following the court rulings. This example illustrates the benefits to scholars of investigating the legal and policy landscape germane to the empirical context of focal interest in their research; doing so can reveal alternative explanations or possible sources of measurement error that would be difficult to discern from simply downloading patent data and plugging them into econometric regressions.

In response to criticisms of the distortions created by patent data, some scholars have turned fruitfully to alternative sources of information about new discoveries and technological advances. Among the articles in Table 10.2, for example, Narin *et al.* (1987) supplement patent filings with peer ratings of the quality of a company's research, reporting a high degree of correlation between the measures. In a study on employee creativity, Oldham and Cummings (1996) use both patent-based indicators (of invention disclosures) and nonpatent measures (of supervisor ratings) to measure the creativity of employees within a firm.

Although time-intensive, information drawn from news articles and trade journals can also be used to construct indicators of new and improved products brought to market or to identify significant technological enhancements. The Acs and Audretsch (1987) study in Table 10.2 nicely illustrates this approach. Instead of patents, the authors use announcements of innovations reported in trade journals to investigate the relationship between innovative productivity and firm size.[19] More recently, Lerner (2006) integrates evidence from *Wall Street Journal* articles and patent documents in a study on the sources of innovation in financial services. Armed with both sets of data, Lerner shows that smaller (and less profitable) firms produce a higher share of innovations in financial services than they patent. These results corroborate evidence reported in earlier studies (e.g., Lerner, 1995; Cohen *et al.*, 2000) that resource-constrained organizations may generate a higher share of innovations than they choose to patent when compared with organizations with deeper pockets. Scholars relying on patent-based statistics alone to assess the innovativeness of organizations with divergent resource endowments should be aware of these findings.

The literature has moved beyond the use of simple patent counts as proxies for the 'innovativeness' of firms or other organizations. Trajtenberg (1990), listed in Table 10.2, is a pioneering study on this topic. In the paper, Trajtenberg introduces and validates a method for employing the number of times a patent is cited, or referenced, in subsequent patents as a means for sorting influential from more trivial inventions. The basic logic is explained as follows:

> During the examination process, the examiner searches the pertinent portion of the 'classified' patent file. His purpose is to identify any prior disclosures of technology... which might anticipate the claimed invention and preclude the issuance of a patent; which might be similar to the claimed invention and limit the scope of patent protection...; or which, generally, reveal the state of the technology to which the invention is directed... If such documents are found, they are made known to the inventor and are 'cited' in any patent which matures from the application... Thus, the number of times a patent document is cited may be a measure of its technological significance. (Trajtenberg, 1990, 173–174)[20]

As Jaffe and Trajtenberg (2002) discuss, this method for using citation-weighted patent counts to estimate innovative productivity has been widely adopted and refined in subsequent studies. Hall, Jaffe, and Trajtenberg (2005), for example, show that citation-weighted patents are strongly related to the market value of public US manufacturing firms. They also find, however, that the effect is nonlinear – highly cited patents are worth far more than those with less than average counts of citations – and that simple patent counts yield little information in estimates of market value beyond that conveyed by R&D spending. These findings are relevant for management scholars interested in using patent-based performance indicators (whether as simple counts or with citation-weighted adjustments) in the context of their studies.

[19]Cohen (1995) provides an extensive review of the large literature on this topic.

[20]Harhoff *et al.* (1999) and Hall *et al.* (2005) provide additional evidence linking patent citations to economic value, while Lanjouw and Schankerman (2004) compare the statistical power of citation-weighted patents relative to alternative indicators of value. Sampat (2005) further suggests that the share of citations added by examiners on a patent application provides an *ex ante* measure of value. Sampat's argument is that firms will devote more attention and resources toward prior art searches before submitting a patent application when the anticipated private value of a patent is high. Consistent with this argument, he finds a statistically significant (and negative) correlation between the share of examiner-added cites and counts of forward citations.

The use of patent citations to trace knowledge flows. The linkages revealed in patent citations are also popular means for tracing flows of technological knowledge, thanks in part to methods introduced in the study of Jaffe, Trajtenberg, and Henderson (hereafter, JTH) (1993), listed in Table 10.2. By using the 'paper trail' provided by patent citations, JTH contributed the first systematic evidence that knowledge of technological advances originating from university-based research flows first to local areas before diffusing to other geographic locations – that is, it is geographically localized. To identify such effects, the authors estimate the proportion of university patents that are cited by inventors in the same state and in the same metropolitan area relative to the share of local cites to 'control patents' matched by vintage and 3-digit patent class. The control patents serve an important purpose; they enable the authors to disentangle citations due to spillover-localization from those that otherwise would be anticipated due to pre-existing patterns of technological or industrial activity within a region.

The methodology introduced by JTH paved the way for a large body of subsequent research using patent citations to trace knowledge flows across geographic, technological, and organizational boundaries. Recent examples include Rosenkopf and Nerkar (2001), Almeida *et al.* (2003), Alcacer and Chung (2007), and Hoetker and Agarwal (2007). Among the articles in Table 10.2, Almeida and Kogut (1999) use a JTH-type methodology to trace the dissemination of important semiconductor inventions across firm boundaries. The authors further document that firms facilitate the inward transfer of technological knowledge by hiring inventively productive employees from rivals. These findings resonate with the view that the process of technological discovery has an important 'tacit' dimension (Polanyi, 1966). In a similar vein, the Mowery, Oxley, and Silverman (hereafter, MOS) (1996) study listed in Table 10.2 shows (again, using evidence from patent citations) that alliances facilitate the transfer of technological knowledge between firms, particularly when supported by equity investments. Instead of employing case-control groups such as the JTH and Almeida and Kogut (1999) studies, MOS use a 'before' versus 'after' set-up that tests for shifts in the technological capabilities of firms prior to and following the formation of an alliance.

The patent-based evidence reported in the Almeida and Kogut (1999) and MOS (1996) studies enables the authors to devise novel tests drawn from the 'resource-based view,' which has emerged as an influential theoretical framework within strategy. Building on earlier work by Penrose (1959), the resource-based view highlights the importance of 'sticky' and difficult-to-imitate resources as a source of firm profit and growth (Wernerfelt, 1984; Barney, 1991; Peteraf, 1993). A related strand of research on the 'knowledge-based view' elevates in strategic importance the role of knowledge embedded in individuals within organizations. In the latter view, developed in articles by Kogut and Zander (1992) and Grant (1996a, 1996b), the capacity of firms to integrate and utilize knowledge that is tacit (and thereby less prone to inadvertent leakage or imitation) is cast as a potentially powerful source of sustainable advantage. Positioned within these strands of thought, Almeida and Kogut (1999) and MOS (1996) highlight two mechanisms that firms can use to facilitate the inward transfer of such knowledge: the mobility of employees and R&D collaborations. The effectiveness of these and other mechanisms used to facilitate the inward transfer of technological knowledge across organizational boundaries is the subject of a large number of more recent studies (e.g., Rosenkopf and Almeida, 2001; Song *et al.*, 2003; Gomes-Casseres *et al.*, 2006).

Since few alternative sources for tracing knowledge flows exist, it is not surprising that scholars have turned eagerly to the use of evidence drawn from patent citations.[21] Nonetheless, the appropriate use and interpretation of such data remains the subject of continued debate within the field.

One concern regarding the use of patent citations as evidence of knowledge flows hinges on a fact previewed earlier in the excerpt from Trajtenberg's 1990 study – the citations are often added by examiners in the process of reviewing the application rather than the inventor or organization that submits the application. This fact has long been noted in the literature, with examiner-added citations being treated as 'noise' in citations-based estimates of knowledge flows and spillovers (Jaffe, Fogarty, and Banks, 1998). Starting in 2001, the PTO added an asterisk on published patent documents to indicate the subset of citations added by patent examiners. A series of recent papers have used this newly available information to investigate more explicitly the biases introduced by examiner-added cites. The findings of these studies are quite provocative. Thompson (2006) and Alcacer and Gittelman (2006) report that examiners are disproportionately more likely to insert citations to more recent inventions, suggesting that examiners pay particular attention to state-of-the-art technologies when evaluating an application's eligibility for patent protection. More surprising is that examiner-added citations represent a large share of total citations included on patent documents. Although the authors use a different sample of patents, the estimates reported in both the Thomspon (2006) and Alcacer and Gittelman (2006) studies suggest that examiners add roughly 40 % of all citations listed in US patents. In a related study, Sampat (2005) shows further that the share of examiner-added citations varies significantly across industrial sectors, with higher shares reported in IT-related sectors relative to life science and chemical sectors.

Does the prevalence of examiner-added citations necessarily undermine the use of patent citations in the investigation of knowledge flows? Not necessarily. In some cases, authors are interested in using the data to 'position' firms along technological dimensions or to test for technological linkages between inventions. In these instances, measurement could be *improved* by the addition of references by examiners, particularly for state-of-the-art inventions. In other instances, however, citations are used to infer that the inventor and/or organization submitting the application 'learned of' (and explicitly built upon) the technological discoveries embedded in inventions listed as prior art on a patent. Here, the results of these recent studies warrant more careful consideration. At a minimum, authors should be aware of the biases reported in these studies and discuss how such biases affect inferences being made in the study. The Sampat (2005) findings suggest that using the patent citations to discern differential rates of learning across industrial sectors is especially problematic. If citations made since 2001 are available, the robustness

[21]References contained in the scientific literature provide an alternative data source. See, for example, Fleming and Sorenson (2004), Azoulay, Ding, and Stuart (2006), and Murray and Stern (2006).

of results could also be tested with a restricted sample that omits examiner-added citations. (See Alcacer and Gittelman, 2006, for additional discussion on this point.) Finally, additional insights could be gleaned from supplemental surveys and interviews. Examples of studies using this last approach include the survey of NASA inventors conducted by Jaffe *et al.* (1998) and recent work by Fleming *et al.* (2007), where field interviews were used to establish that collaborations reported in patent citations captured (in a meaningful but imperfect manner) actual interpersonal relationships among inventors.

More generally, little is known about the strategic factors that weigh in on the decision to include citations in patent applications or to forego an intensive prior art search before submitting a patent application. Anecdotal evidence reported in Rivette and Klein (2000) and Ziedonis (2004) suggests, for example, that the 'paper trail' left by patent citations can be used to identify potential targets for royalty-seeking licenses. In this event, including references to prior art may amplify rather than reduce litigation risks.[22] Similarly, Sampat (2005) notes that firms in some sectors may be reluctant to conduct extensive prior art searches due to concerns of willful infringement. A recent paper by Lampe (2007) provides evidence supportive of this latter view using patent citation data from the US semiconductor industry. More specifically, he finds that applicants are significantly more likely to cite patents that are technologically 'close', a result that is attributed to concerns of the enhanced damages that must be paid if an inventor's patent is subsequently shown to be infringing. These issues clearly invite further study[23] and highlight the theoretical importance of understanding how these uncertainties and 'fuzzy boundaries' affect IP acquisition, exchange, and value.

In addition to the recent debate over examiner-added cites, a recent article by Thompson and Fox-Kean (2005) has attracted considerable attention by challenging the validity of the matching criteria used in Jaffe *et al.*'s influential 1993 article. More specifically, the authors suggest that the method JTH use to select control groups of patents (in particular, their use of patent classes measured at

---

[22]The term 'litigation risk' is sometimes used loosely in the strategy and innovation literatures. Note that there are two conceptually distinctive issues linking litigation risks with prior art citations. The first pertains to the risk that the patentee's *own* rights will be invalidated if subsequently challenged: if others find prior art that establishes obviousness or lack of novelty, the rights run the risk of being rendered invalid. The second issue pertains to the risk that *others* will sue the patentee for infringement. Here, the role of prior art citations is more ambiguous. On one hand, prior art citations may represent an attempt to 'invent around' an earlier patent to avoid infringement (thus arguably reducing litigation risk). As legal scholars note, however, 'determining when a patented device has been "designed around" enough to avoid infringement is a difficult determination to make. One cannot know for certain that changes are sufficient to avoid infringement until a judge or a jury has made that determination' (Moore *et al.*, 1999, p. 564). Moreover, if citations are used to identify potential targets for litigation or licensing and their existence fuels concerns of enhanced damages in event of subsequent dispute (by providing evidence that the citing party knew about the patented invention but proceeded without a license in light of that awareness), patentees have incentives to *refrain* from including certain citations. Empirical research on how firms manage these tradeoffs is lacking. The recent working paper by Lampe (2007) represents a laudable step toward filling this gap in the literature.

[23]Looking forward, there may be opportunities for additional research on this topic by exploiting differences in citations contained within patent 'pairs', where the same invention is awarded a patent in multiple national jurisdictions. As Harhoff and Reitzig (2004) discuss, citations added by examiners at the European Patent Office are 'objective' in the sense that all citations are added by examiners. I thank Georg von Graevenitz for pointing out this fact.

the 3-digit level) can induce spurious evidence of localization. Thompson and Fox-Kean's basic concern is that 3-digit classes are overly broad for the purpose of identifying control groups of patents given the high degree of technological heterogeneity within classes. In turn, the authors recommend that control samples of patents be matched based on 6-digit patent classes instead.

In response to this critique, Henderson *et al.* (2005) caution against use of the more restrictive matching criteria. More specifically, they note that 'it is exceedingly difficult to establish the extent to which subclasses correspond to anything akin to well-circumscribed technologies' (2005, p. 462). The authors also point out that use of ever-stricter matching criteria can expand the time horizon required to identify 'similar' patents, thus introducing other distortions.

Debate over the appropriate methods for using patent citations to trace knowledge flows continues. Using a more flexible choice-based sampling framework, a recent study by Singh (2005) validates the general findings from the 1993 JTH study: knowledge flows are significantly stronger than would otherwise be expected within regions (and firms) than across regional and firm boundaries.[24] More recently, Thompson (2006) proposes an alternative identification strategy that exploits differences in citations made by examiners and patent applicants. Unfortunately, however, distinguishing examiner-added citations from others listed in the patent document is difficult prior to 2001 when such data were first published on the PTO web site.

In summary, major strides have been made over the past two decades in the use of patent-based statistics. In addition to the two main uses discussed above (compilation of performance indicators and evidence of knowledge flows), scholars have used the 'paper trails' provided by patents in numerous other ways. For example, Jaffe (1986) gauges the technological proximity of firms and other patenting organizations by comparing distributions of patent portfolios across technology classes. In a similar spirit, Silverman (1999) uses the data to construct better measures of a firm's technological resources, which he uses to predict subsequent paths of diversification. As suggested earlier, patent data have also been used to estimate the extent to which firms draw on frontier (versus older-generation) technologies (Sorenson and Stuart, 2000) or perform research that is 'exploratory' in nature (Benner and Tushman, 2002). More recently, Ziedonis (2004) uses prior art citations to estimate the dispersion of ownership rights in markets for technology.[25] In other recent studies, Fleming *et al.* (2006) use citations to estimate the 'complexity' of knowledge inputs, while Zhao (2006) uses patent data to examine the internal organization of inventive teams by multinational corporations. Despite such widespread use of patent-based statistics, valuable insights into the generation or diffusion of technological innovations are often gained from alternative sources such as news articles, industry data, and field interviews. Hopefully the discussion above will motivate continued research in that direction.

[24]Singh (2005) further shows that being in the same region or firm has little additional effect on the probability of knowledge flows among inventors with pre-existing ties with one another, thus highlighting the importance of interpersonal networks on observed patterns of knowledge diffusion.

[25]The resulting index of ownership 'fragmentation' provides a means of identifying systematic sources of heterogeneity among firms in their abilities to rely on *ex ante* contracting solutions to mitigate patent hold-up problems featured in the theoretical literature (Heller and Eisenberg, 1998; Shapiro, 2001).

IP as a strategic asset

A second prominent theme in the literature pertains to the value (and limitations) of IP as a strategic asset.[26] This theme is central to David Teece's (1986) influential article on 'Profiting from technological innovation' listed in Table 10.2. Drawing on survey evidence by Mansfield (1986) among others (discussed more fully below), Teece emphasizes that patents provide a relatively *ineffectual* means for safeguarding against imitation in all but a handful of sectors such as the life sciences and chemicals. In turn, he argues that the owners of the specialized 'complementary assets' required to manufacture, service, and distribute innovative new goods and services stand to capture the lion's share of profits (Teece, 1986). As discussed in a recent special issue of *Research Policy* in honor of this paper (Chesbrough *et al.*, 2006), Teece's article has motivated a large body of subsequent research in strategy and technology management, which tests and refines predictions on how the profits from innovation will be divided.

Other articles in Table 10.2 further investigate the links between intangible resources (including employee know-how and proprietary rights such as IP) and the profitability, growth, and market value of firms – relationships of longstanding interest within strategy and economics (e.g., see Scherer, 1965a; Scherer and Ross, 1990). Based on a survey of 95 chief executives from British companies, for example, Hall (1992) finds that corporate reputations and employee know-how are perceived to be the most important determinants of firm success, whereas legal forms of protection such as patents and copyrights fall much lower in the queue. In Hall (1993), the author categorizes different types of intangible assets and synthesizes their relationship with one another in creating what he refers to as 'capability differentials'. In a more formal model, Conner and Rumelt (1991) investigate the relationship between the assertion of IP rights and the profits earned by software firms, revealing conditions under which firms reap greater profits by *refraining* from the deployment of legal IP assets in response to acts of piracy and imitation.

Echoing arguments made earlier by Teece (1986), these studies collectively underscore an important point: the strategic value of IP is not only driven by the legal environment but also hinges on how well firms are positioned to appropriate the gains from innovation without such protection (e.g., due to control of unique distribution channels, superior manufacturing capabilities, or reputations for superior service). Teece (1986) and Hall (1992, 1993) highlight the importance of corporate reputations in regards to reliability and superior service. Conner and Rumelt (1991) emphasize the added benefits that can arise from the early adoption of technologies in industries characterized by positive network externalities. This latter insight from the Conner and Rumelt (1991) study – that firms do not necessarily maximize profits by restricting access to proprietary technologies – resonates closely with arguments developed in recent work by Chesbrough (2003), Anand and Galetovic (2004) and von Hippel (2005). Our understanding of where firms draw the line between 'opening up' (e.g., via widespread licensing) and 'walling off' innovative discoveries, and

---

[26]The literature on this topic is vast and is reviewed more extensively by von Graevenitz *et al.* (2007). For sake of brevity, my discussion in this section focuses on issues and research opportunities that relate most closely to articles featured in Table 10.2.

the performance implications of those decisions, nonetheless remains quite limited. Additional research on this important topic is needed.

A nascent strand of research is extending this literature on IP as a strategic lever in other promising directions. As previewed earlier, the organizational separation of research, financing, and commercialization activities raises a number of questions about the role of IP rights in such boundary-spanning activities. These questions have attracted considerable theoretical attention in the recent literature, as illustrated in formal models by Aghion and Tirole (1994), Arora (1996), Anton and Yao (1994, 1995), Gans and Stern (2000), and Hellman (2007).

Empirical evidence on how IP rights influence the commercialization activities of firms has also started to surface, although establishing the counterfactual (e.g., of the propensity or mode of inter-organizational activity that would have taken place had the property regime been different) remains exceedingly difficult. As one response to this identification problem, Oxley (1999) exploits cross-national differences to test the effects of IP effectiveness on the governance of inter-firm partnerships. Her evidence suggests that when IP rights are more effective, firms tend to rely on less hierarchical modes of contracting. This result is consistent with the view that the availability of effective IP protection facilitates inter-organizational transactions.

Gans *et al.* (2002) provide corroborating evidence based on a survey of the commercialization strategies of 118 technology startups, showing that startups with greater control over IP are significantly more likely to cooperate with established firms when bringing new products to market. In a more recent study, Gans *et al.* (2008) exploit lags in the timing of patent grants and provide additional evidence that formal patent rights facilitate technology transfer activities. Finally, using cross-sectional data from the 1994 Carnegie Mellon survey of US R&D lab managers, Arora and Ceccagnoli (2006) find that the availability of more effective patent protection stimulates licensing activity. Collectively, these studies suggest that IP rights can facilitate innovation-related collaborations, as suggested in formal models by Aghion and Tirole (1994), Arora (1996), and Gans and Stern (2000). Nonetheless, empirical evidence remains limited to a handful of settings.

A related line of research investigates the effects of IP on patterns of entry and new firm formation. The general argument is that, by creating a property right to intangible assets, the patent system encourages activities that otherwise would have been internalized by firms to be performed by third parties, in line with transactions cost arguments made in the Oxley (1999) study mentioned earlier. In turn, entrepreneurial opportunities are created for firms that specialize in the out-sourced activities.

Again, however, empirical research on this topic confronts a vexing methodological problem: pinpointing the effect of IP protection from other factors affecting entry is difficult. Hall and Ziedonis (2001), for example, present qualitative and quantitative evidence that a 'pro-patent' shift in US policies facilitated entry by specialized firms in the semiconductor industry; identifying the marginal effect of patent reforms on entry was complicated, however, by the fact that technological factors (unrelated to the shift in patent policies) simultaneously pulled the industry toward greater vertical specialization. In a study of the chemical industry, Arora *et al.* (2001) provide corroborating evidence that the availability of strong patent rights facilitated the formation of specialized firms providing engineering services.

As discussed in Chapter 15, patents may also provide a mechanism that helps entrepreneurs overcome their reluctance to disclose embryonic ideas to suppliers of capital, thus facilitating markets for venture financing. Evidence reported by Shane (2001a, 2001b), based on cross-sectional data on patents assigned to the Massachusetts Institute of Technology, is consistent with the view that patents facilitate the formation of new firms: he finds that the more effective patent protection is in a given sector, the greater the likelihood that entrepreneurial ventures will be formed to commercialize early-stage technologies.

More direct evidence on the hypothesis that patent protection facilitates the financing of early-stage technologies remains limited. As mentioned earlier, Kortum and Lerner (2000) find that venture-backed startups produce more patents per dollar invested relative to established firms. It is unclear from the evidence reported in the study, however, whether these startups are simply more innovatively productive relative to established firms (which is the authors' interpretation) or whether they have a higher propensity to patent because doing so facilitates their ability to secure the outside resources required to grow the company. Mann (2005) and Mann and Sager (2007) provide mixed support for the 'patents facilitate financing' hypothesis in the context of venture-backed software startups, whereas Hall and Ziedonis (2001) provide indirect evidence supportive of this view in the semiconductor industry. To investigate these issues more fully, future studies ideally would include startups that sought but did not receive venture financing in the sample.

A recent formal model by Hellmann (2007) also raises the intriguing possibility that policies affecting the ownership and control rights to technological discoveries alter patterns of spin-off activity. Similar in spirit to earlier work by Aghion and Tirole (1994), the allocation of property rights to innovative output is cast as a central choice variable for firms. Hellmann (2007) derives conditions under which the allocation of such rights to employees enables firms to profit from entrepreneurial exits through the generation of spin-offs while simultaneously shifting the internal production of innovations. The model therefore brings insights from the property rights literature into the literature on organizational spawning and spin-offs (e.g., Agarwal *et al.*, 2004; Klepper and Sleeper, 2005; Gompers *et al.*, 2005).

To test hypotheses emerging from this work, scholars would need to find instances where firms 'switched policies' from centralized to more delegated IP ownership policies or varied in the policies they employed in different product groups or subsidiaries. Even then, interpretation could be difficult because the adoption of such policies is nonrandom. On a more practical matter, most US corporations require individuals to assign over IP ownership rights to discoveries they produce as part of their employment contract (Merges, 1999). As a result, it is unclear whether scholars would observe heterogeneity in practices among modern for-profit organizations. Scholars therefore may need to look for variation within alliance-related activities (as per Lerner and Merges, 1998) or to nonprofit or university settings where policies governing the allocation of IP rights vary more widely. Alternatively, Fisk (1998) and Lamoreaux and Sokoloff (1999) provide intriguing accounts of firms in the early 20th century moving from a 'shop rights' regime (where patent ownership rights were allocated to employees but licensed back to their employers) to one in which courts looked more favorably upon corporations owning rights to patents invented by their employees. To my knowledge, little is known about how this shift in internal policies altered the entrepreneurial activities of employees or the types of inventions they created.

IP as a policy lever

The third main theme represented by the studies in Table 10.2 relates to questions posed in the introduction: How should governments 'draw the line' of exclusionary protection between one innovation and another? Is the system of IP rights promoting the progress of science and technology as originally intended? If not, how should the various aspects of the system be adjusted? More generally, how have firms and other organizations responded to shifts in the legal IP environment over the past few decades? Here, attention shifts to the role of IP as a policy lever for governments.

As suggested earlier, one set of studies on this topic is normative in spirit and investigates how IP rights should be designed. From Table 10.2, Landes and Posner (1987, 1989) for example examine the economic rationale for trademarks and copyrights. In the context of patents, Gilbert and Shapiro (1990) and Klemperer (1990) model changes in various dimensions of protection (including the scope, or 'breadth', of coverage and the duration, or 'length', of protection) and their effects on R&D investments. Consistent with the earlier findings of Nordhaus (1969), the Gilbert–Shapiro and Klemperer models generally show that increases in the longevity and breadth of patents strengthen incentives to innovate.[27] As von Graevenitz et al. (2007) discuss, formal models in this tradition typically assume that a single patent confers significant market power to protected processes or products and that patent rights are well-defined and valid (thus assuming away transactions costs and uncertainties underpinning their exchange). These models also typically assume that absent of patents, perfect competition would prevail. Alternative mechanisms for appropriating gains from innovation are therefore cast as ineffectual.[28]

A separate set of studies in Table 10.2 investigates how IP rights work in the 'real world', thus helping to identify conditions under which key assumptions in formal models are likely to hold true or to be violated. There are two main approaches to conducting empirical research on this topic. One approach, like that used in the Hall (1992, 1993) studies mentioned above, is to solicit input directly from managers. An alternative approach, used by Kortum and Lerner (1999), Hall and Ziedonis (2001), and Mowery et al. (2001), is to exploit changes in IP laws and policies. The first approach provides insights that are difficult to discern through examination of more aggregated data. Unless the surveys are repeated to the same respondents at different points in time, scholars can nonetheless find it

---

[27]Scotchmer (1991) and Gallini (2002) show that increases in the lifetime of patents may reduce levels of innovation if profits anticipated by future innovators are reduced.

[28]Gallini and Scotchmer (2002) and von Graevenitz et al. (2007) review more recent models in economics that relax these assumptions. Merges and Nelson (1990) and Mazzoleni and Nelson (1998) offer earlier, thoughtful critiques of the IP design literature in economics.

difficult to establish causality due to the cross-sectional nature of the data.[29] The latter approach can provide a useful 'before' versus 'after' set-up that allows more flexibility for hypothesis testing. Even then, causality can be difficult to establish. The true counterfactual – innovative activity that would have taken place had regime shifts not occurred – is rarely observable.

Mansfield's 1986 article in Table 10.2 illustrates the survey-based method. Randomly selecting a sample of 100 US firms across 12 industries, Mansfield asked R&D executives what proportion of their inventions would not have been developed had patent protection been unavailable. Only in two industries, pharmaceuticals and chemicals, was patent protection judged to be essential.[30] Larger-scale surveys of R&D lab managers conducted in the US (Levin *et al.*, 1987; Cohen *et al.*, 2000), Japan (Cohen *et al.*, 2002), and Europe (e.g., Arundel and Kabla, 1998; Arundel, 2001) generally corroborate Mansfield's findings. Although in some industries, such as pharmaceuticals, patents are seen as critical for appropriating the gains from innovation, firms in most industries predominantly rely on other mechanisms, including secrecy, lead time, and the exploitation of superior manufacturing or design capabilities. Collectively, this body of empirical evidence suggests that one of the assumptions typically invoked in formal models (that innovation rents would be dissipated by perfect competition if patents did not exist) fails to characterize the competitive dynamics in many industrial sectors.

Three of the remaining studies in Table 10.2 (Kortum and Lerner, 1999; Mowery *et al.*, 1996; and Hall and Ziedonis, 2001) use panel data to examine shifts in IP regimes. Mowery *et al.* (1996) investigate the effects of a specific US policy initiative, the Bayh-Dole Act of 1980, on university patenting and licensing activities. As Rothaermel *et al.* (2007) discuss in a recent review of the literature on the commercialization of university-based research, the Bayh-Dole Act and its effects have attracted worldwide attention within the academic and policy communities. By providing blanket permission for universities performing federally funded research to apply for patents based on the results of such research and to license those inventions to other parties, including to startups, the Act has been credited with stimulating entrepreneurial activity and economic growth in regions surrounding major universities.

Even though the patenting and licensing activities at US universities increased in years following the Act, Mowery *et al.* (1996) find little evidence that the Act itself *caused* the growth in these activities. Instead, the authors attribute the growth to other factors, including increases in federal funding for basic biomedical research at universities in the late 1960s and the related rise of research in biotechnology that began in the early 1970s, which set the stage for rapid growth. The authors also point out that a simultaneous shift in policies governing the patentability of 'engineered molecules' played an important contributing role, thus making it even more difficult

---

[29]Recent studies by Arora and Ceccagnoli (2006) and Cassiman and Veugelers (2006) discuss the limitations of survey data in greater detail and illustrate clever attempts to overcome such limitations.

[30]More specifically, executives from pharmaceuticals reported, on average, that 65 % of their products would not have been developed absent patent protection. The average percentage in chemicals was 30 %. In all other sectors, the percentages fell below 20 %, suggesting that the lion's share of innovative activity would have been performed even if patent protection were unavailable.

to attribute the growth in university patenting and licensing to the Bayh-Dole Act. From a methodological perspective, the study illustrates the importance of thinking carefully about the counterfactual (of patterns expected had a given policy shift not occurred) even when clear shifts in behavior are observed predating and following IP reforms.

The Kortum and Lerner (1999) and Hall and Ziedonis (2001) studies investigate a broader 'pro-patent' shift in US policies that is widely attributed to the 1982 creation of a centralized patent appellate court. Kortum and Lerner (1999) first document a striking empirical trend: the past few decades have witnessed dramatic growth in patenting activity within the US. Based on time trends in aggregate R&D spending and rates of patenting, however, they are unable to establish a causal link between the upsurge in patenting and reforms in US patent policy. Instead, they attribute the trend to gradual improvements in the internal management of R&D, which could produce higher rates of patenting per R&D dollar. By using firm-level data to estimate 'patent yields' from R&D spending, Hall and Ziedonis (2001) show that the rate at which US firms were receiving patents had in fact remained quite stable from the late 1970s through the mid-1990s and even declined in pharmaceuticals. In sharp contrast, the patenting rates of firms in semiconductors (and computers, to a lesser extent) jumped upward soon following the reforms. The escalation in patenting in semiconductors was particularly puzzling since R&D lab managers from electronics-related sectors consistently rank patents among the *least* effective mechanisms for appropriating the returns to R&D investments in surveys mentioned above (e.g., Levin *et al.*, 1987; Cohen *et al.*, 2000).

To investigate this paradoxical behavior, Hall and Ziedonis (2001) conducted interviews with industry representatives and analyzed the patenting behavior of US semiconductor firms during 1979–1995, a period that pre-dates and follows the 1980s reforms. In doing so, they identified two divergent effects of the 'pro-patent' shift. On the one hand, the strengthening of patent rights seemed to facilitate entry by specialized design firms in the industry. In interviews, stronger patents were viewed to be especially critical to these firms in attracting venture capital funds and establishing a proprietary stake in niche product markets.[31] The interviews also suggested, however, that managers in firms with complex manufacturing facilities had grown increasingly concerned about being 'held-up' by outside patent owners and had responded strategically to the reforms by amassing larger portfolios of patents, as discussed in an earlier section. Consistent with this insight, the quantitative evidence showed that the upsurge in patenting following the reforms was driven disproportionately by capital-intensive firms.

The Mowery *et al.* (1996), Kortum and Lerner (1999), and Hall and Ziedonis (2001) studies illustrate that, even though shifts and heterogeneity in IP regimes provide opportunities for research, such settings still require that scholars think carefully about identification. In addition to looking closely at patterns of behavior that predate and follow IP reforms, interviews with managers involved in making

---

[31] As discussed earlier, it is exceedingly difficult to estimate the extent to which specialized firms would have entered the industry without the reforms in US patent policy. The interviews were useful in discerning a causal mechanism by which the strengthening of patent rights would, on the margin, facilitate the entry by such firms.

decisions of focal interest in the study (whether in allocating resources toward patenting activities or the patenting and licensing of university technologies) can yield insights that would otherwise be difficult to gain from data alone. Sakakibara and Bransetter (2001) further illustrate the potential complementarities between qualitative and quantitative methods; to investigate the effects of a policy shift that broadened the scope of patent protection in Japan on R&D investments, the authors conducted both econometric regressions and interviews with business practitioners.

As discussed earlier, the past two decades have witnessed significant reforms to IP regimes both in the US and internationally. Even so, the strength and availability of IP protection continues to vary considerably across countries, particularly in areas such as pharmaceuticals and software. Although posing methodological challenges to authors, these shifts and heterogeneity in IP regimes invite continued research along several important dimensions.

As suggested earlier, the strengthening of IP rights in the US is widely believed to have elevated patent 'hold-up' problems for firms producing technologically complex products (FTC, 2003). In 2006, the Supreme Court made a series of rulings that stand to alter the bargaining power between patent owners and defendants in legal disputes over IP (Lemley and Sampat, 2007). The effects of these rulings on IP litigation risk and incentives to innovation will be important to investigate looking forward. Similarly, standards boards continue to experiment with how best to entice the submission of high quality technologies while safeguarding against patent 'hold-up' problems once standards have been adopted (Lemley, 2002; Rysman and Simcoe, 2007). Although Lerner and Tirole (2006) model 'forum shopping' among standards-setting organizations, it is unclear how IP ownership and licensing policies influence the decisions of firms to participate in standards-setting organizations or the types of technologies they choose to disclose.

Numerous opportunities exist for continued research in the international arena, particularly in the wake of the TRIPS agreement and its gradual implementation among signatory nations of the World Trade Organizations. Recent studies have contributed new insights to the larger body of work on international IP reforms.[32] Branstetter et al. (2006), for example, examine a series of reforms in the 1980s and 1990s that strengthened the effectiveness of IP protection in 16 countries. Their evidence suggests that US multinationals responded to the strengthened protection by transferring more technologies to affiliates located in reforming countries. In another recent study, Qian (2007) presents new evidence in the context of reforms targeted toward pharmaceutical patents. Using matched samples of countries and tests for 'within country' changes following the establishment of stronger patent regimes in pharmaceuticals between 1978 and 2002, Qian (2007) shows that the effects of the reforms vary significantly among countries at different stages of development. More specifically, she finds that the adoption of stronger patent laws in pharmaceuticals stimulates domestic innovation in the sector only in countries with relatively high levels of economic development, educational attainment, and economic freedom: in other countries in the sample, patent reforms *failed* to stimulate shifts in domestic patenting, R&D expenditures, or pharmaceutical-related exports. In earlier work, Scherer and Weisburst (1995) report similar evidence that the

---

[32]von Graevenitz et al. (2007) review the literature on this topic.

legitimization of drug product patents in Italy in the early 1980s failed to trigger significant changes in the R&D and patenting activities of Italian pharmaceutical companies.

IP reforms continue to unfold that invite future examination. A prominent example is India's 2005 enactment of stronger patent laws in pharmaceuticals. Given the large size of the Indian market for pharmaceutical products and the vibrancy of its supply base of generic manufacturers, the effects of the 2005 Patent Act in India on pharmaceutical innovations, drug pricing, and patterns of international technology transfer are important to investigate in the future.

Finally, although patent reforms have drawn the lion's share of attention among scholars of IP and innovation, far less is known about the effects of significant shifts in the legal treatment of other forms of IP both within the United States and internationally. For example, the 1998 Digital Millennium Copyright Act made it a criminal offense to break through encryption devices that protect copyrighted content. Although legal scholars argue that this Act has affected the reverse engineering activities of firms (e.g., Littman 2001; Lunney 2001), the evidence remains largely anecdotal. Given the importance of reverse engineering as a vehicle for learning about (and improving upon) innovations made by rivals, this topic seems naturally well-suited for scholars interested in technology management and innovation. As mentioned earlier, major industrialized countries continue to vary in the legal protection they afford to software algorithms, business methods, and compilations of data. Although these divergent policies have existed for quite some time, surprisingly little is known about their effects on firm strategy and innovative activity. Similarly, it is widely recognized that trade secrets and distinctive brands (i.e., trademarks) are valuable assets for innovation-intensive companies (Cohen *et al.*, 2000; Landes and Posner, 2003). Nonetheless, empirical research on the strategic management of trade secret and trade market protection, and possible sources of complementarities among these and other forms of IP protection, remains limited – certainly in comparison to patent-related studies.[33]

CONCLUSION

> Intellectual property is the foundation of the modern information economy. It fuels the software, life sciences, and computer industries, and pervades most of the products we consume. Gallini and Scotchmer (2002, p. 51)

Based on the evidence from 19 peer-reviewed journals, interest in IP within the academic community has grown considerably over the past two decades. The proliferation of IP-related studies partly reflects the more widespread use of patent data, and the citations they contain, in studies of innovation. It is now quite common to use patent data to compile various indicators of innovative performance and to

---

[33]A nascent stream of research is moving in this direction. Hannah (2005) provides a fascinating account of organizational factors that affect the extent to which trade secret policies affect employee-level behavior. Recent working papers by Graham and Somaya (2006) and von Graevenitz (2007) provide new insights by investigating factors that affect the strategic management (and value) of copyright and trademark-related assets.

trace patterns of knowledge flows. Even so, patents can provide distorted views of innovative activity and can be altered by shifts in the legal environment. As illustrated by the studies discussed above, additional insights can be gleaned from use of complementary data sources or from interviews with business practitioners.

Scholars of innovation and the determinants of firm performance also have more substantive reasons to pay greater attention to the accumulation, use, and exchange of IP-related assets. The basis of competitive advantage in advanced economies rests critically on the management of intangible assets, thus elevating the strategic value of ownership and control rights to know-how, creative works, and technological or scientific discoveries. Due to the proliferation of IP rights over the past few decades, firms are also likely to face continued challenges in safeguarding against rent expropriation by outside property owners. Given the high stakes involved, the interplay between legal rights, innovation, and firm performance is likely to remain a salient topic for continued research. Finally, as discussed above, governments continue to experiment widely with how best to define the 'rules of the game' that affect the availability, strength, and enforceability of patents as well as other forms of IP protection. Although posing methodological challenges to authors, these shifts and variation in IP regimes naturally set the stage for continued research.

Exclusionary rights to technological discoveries and ideas shape the overall process of innovation. It is important to understand the broader, strategic value of patents as intangible assets and their intended and unintended effects on the creation and use of new technologies. I hope that this chapter helps stimulate additional research on these complex yet important topics of longstanding interest to scholars of strategy and technology management.

REFERENCES

Acs, Z.J., and Audretsch, D.B. (1987). Innovation, market structure, and firm size. *The Review of Economics and Statistics*, LXIX (4), 567–74.

Agarwal, R., Echambadi, R., Franco, A.M., and Sarkar, M.B. (2004). Knowledge transfer through inheritance: spin-out generation, growth, and survival. *Academy of Management Journal*, 47(4), 501–22.

Aghion, P., and Tirole, J. (1994). The management of innovation. *Quarterly Journal of Economics*, CIX, 1183–1209.

Ahuja, G. (2000). Collaborative networks, structural holes, and innovation: a longitudinal study. *Administrative Science Quarterly*, 45, 425–55.

Ahuja, G., and Katila, R. (2001). Technology acquisitions and the innovative performance of acquiring firms: a longitudinal study. *Strategic Management Journal*, 22(3), 197–220.

Akerlof, G.A. (1970). The market for lemons: quality, uncertainty, and the market mechanism. *Quarterly Journal of Economics*, 84, 488–500.

Alcacer, J., and Chung, W. (2007). Location strategies and knowledge spillovers. *Management Science*, 53(5), 760–76.

Alcacer, J., and Gittelman, M. (2006). How do I know what you know? Patent examiners and the generation of patent citations. *Review of Economics and Statistics*, 88(4), 774–79.

Allison, J.R., Lemley, M.A., Moore, K.A., and Trunkey, R.D. (2004). Valuable patents. *Georgetown Law Journal*, 92(3), 435–79.

Almeida, P., and Kogut, B. (1999). Localization of knowledge and the mobility of engineers in regional networks. *Management Science*, 45(7), 905–17.

Almeida, P., Dokko, G., and Rosenkopf, L. (2003). Startup size and the mechanisms of external learning: increasing opportunity and decreasing ability? *Research Policy*, 32, 301–15.

Anand, B., and Galetovic, A. (2004). Strategies that work when property rights don't. In G. Libecap (ed.), *Advances in the Study of Entrepreneurship, Innovation, and Economic Growth*, 15, 261–304.

Anderson, P., and Tushman, M.L. (1990). Technological discontinuities and dominant designs: a cyclical model of technological change. *Administrative Science Quarterly*, 35, 604–33.

Anton, J., and Yao, D. (1994). Expropriations and inventions: appropriable rents in the absence of property rights. *The American Economic Review*, 84, 190–209.

Anton, J., and Yao, D. (1995). Start-ups, spin-offs, and internal projects. *Journal of Law, Economics & Organization*, 11(2), 362–78.

Arora, A. (1996). Contracting for tacit knowledge: the provision of technical services in technology contracts. *Journal of Development Economics*, 50, 223–56.

Arora, A., and Ceccagnoli, M. (2006). Patent protection, complementary assets, and firms incentives for technology licensing. *Management Science*, 52(2), 293–308.

Arora, A., Fosfuri, A., and Gambardella, A. (2001). *Markets for technology: the economics of innovation and corporate strategy*. MIT Press.

Arrow, K.J. (1962). Economic welfare and the allocation of resources for inventions. In R. Nelson (ed.), *The Rate and Direction of Inventive Activity: Economic and Social Factors*. Princeton University Press.

Arundel, A. (2001). The relative efficacy of patents and secrecy for appropriation. *Research Policy*, 30, 611–24.

Arundel, A., and Kabla, I. (1998). What percentage of innovations are patented? Empirical estimates for European firms. *Research Policy*, 27, 127–41.

Azoulay, P., Ding, W., and Stuart, T. (2006). The impact of academic patenting on the rate, quality, and direction of (public) research output. NBER Working Paper No. 11917.

Barney, J. (1991). Firm resources and sustained competitive advantage. *Journal of Management*, 17, 99–120.

Benner, M.J., and Tushman, M. (2002). Process management and technological innovation: a longitudinal study of the photography and paint industries. *Administrative Science Quarterly*, 47(4), 676–706.

Bessen, J., and Hunt, R.M. (2004). An empirical look at software patents. Federal Reserve Bank of Philadelphia, working paper 03–17.

Bessen, J., and Meurer, M.J. (2006). The patent litigation explosion, working paper, Boston University School of Law.

Bitton, M. (2006). A new outlook on the economic dimension of the database protection debate. *IDEAS – The Intellectual Property Law Review*, 47, 93–169.

Blair, M.M., and Kochan, T.A. (eds) (2000). *The new relationship: human capital in the American corporation*. The Brookings Institution.

Branstetter, L.G., Fisman, R., and Foley, C.F. (2006). Do stronger intellectual property rights increase international technology transfer? Empirical evidence from U.S. firm-level panel data. *Quarterly Journal of Economics*, 121(1), 321–49.

Cassiman, B., and Veugelers, R. (2006). In search of complementarity in innovation strategy: internal R&D and external knowledge acquisition. *Management Science*, 52(1), 68–82.

Chatterjiee, S., and Wernerfelt, B. (1991). The link between resources and type of diversification: theory and evidence. *Strategic Management Journal*, 12(1), 33–48.

Chesbrough, H. (2003). *Open innovation: the new imperative for creating and profiting from technology.* HBS Press.

Chesbrough, H., Birkinshaw, J., and Teubal, M. (2006). Introduction to the research policy 20th anniversary special issue of Profiting from Innovation by David J. Teece. *Research Policy*, 35, 1091–9.

Cockburn, I.M., and Henderson, R. (1998). Absorptive capacity, coauthoring behavior, and the organization of research in drug discovery. *The Journal of Industrial Economics*, XLVI(2), 157–82.

Cohen, W.M. (1995). Empirical studies of innovative activity. In P. Stoneman (ed.), *Handbook of the Economics of Innovation and Technical Change*. Basil Blackwell.

Cohen, W.M., Goto, A., Nagata, A., Nelson, R.R., and Walsh, J.P. (2002). R&D Spillovers, patents and the incentives to innovate in Japan and the United States. *Research Policy*, 31, 1349–67.

Cohen, W.M., and Levinthal, D.A. (1990). Absorptive capacity: a new perspective on learning and innovation. *Administrative Science Quarterly*, 35, 569–96.

Cohen, W.M., Nelson, R.R., and Walsh, J. (2000). Protecting their intellectual assets: appropriability conditions and why U.S. manufacturing firms patent (or not). NBER Working Paper 7552 (Feb).

Conner, K.R., and Rumelt, R.P. (1991). Software piracy: an analysis of protection strategies. *Management Science*, 37(2), 125–39.

D'Aspremont, C., and Jacquemin, A. (1988). Cooperative and noncooperative R&D in duopoly with spillovers. *American Economic Review*, 75(5), 1133–7.

Dosi, G., Pavitt, K., and Soete, L. (1990). *The economics of technical change and international trade.* New York University Press.

Dushnitsky, G., and Lenox, M.J. (2005). When do incumbents learn from entrepreneurial ventures? Corporate venture capital and investing firm innovation rates. *Research Policy*, 34(5) 615–39.

Federal Trade Commission (FTC) (2003). *To promote innovation – the proper balance of competition and patent law and policy.* Available at: http://www.ftc.gov/opp/intellect/ (last visited June 2007).

Fisk, C.L. (1998). Removing the fuel of interest from the fire of genius: law and the employee-inventor, 1830–1930. *The University of Chicago Law Review* 65, 1127–98.

Fleming, L., King, C., and Juda, A. (2007). Small worlds and regional innovative advantage. *Organization Science*, 19(6), 938–54.

Fleming, L., and O. Sorenson (2004). Science as a map in technological search. *Strategic Management Journal*, 25, 909–28.

Fleming, L., Sorenson, O., and Rivkin, J. (2006). Complexity, networks and knowledge flow. *Research policy*, 35(7), 994–1017.

Gallini, N. (2002). The economics of patents: lessons from recent U.S. patent reform. *Journal of Economic Perspectives*, 16(2), 131–54.

Gallini, N., and Scotchmer, S. (2002). Intellectual property: when is it the best incentive mechanism? In A. Jaffe, J. Lerner and S. Stern (eds), *Innovation Policy and the Economy*, volume 2, 51–77.

Gans, J.S., Hsu, D.H., and Stern, S. (2002). When does start-up innovation spur the gale of creative destruction? *RAND Journal of Economics* 33, 571–86.

Gans, J.S., Hsu, D.H., and Stern, S. (2008). The impact of uncertain intellectual property rights on the market for ideas: evidence from patent grant delays. *Management Science*, 54, 982–97.

Gans, J.S., and Stern, S. (2000). Incumbency and R&D incentives: licensing the gale of creative destruction. *Journal of Economics and Management Strategy*, 9(4), 485–511.

Gilbert, R., and Shapiro, C. (1990). Optimal patent length and breadth. *Rand Journal of Economics*, 21(1), 106–12.

Gomes-Casseres, B., Hagedoorn, J., and Jaffe, A.B. (2006). Do alliances promote knowledge flows? *Journal of Financial Economics*, 80(1), 5–33.

Gompers, P., and Lerner, J. (2001). The venture capital revolution. *Journal of Economic Perspectives*, 15, 145–68.

Gompers, P., Lerner, J., and Scharfstein, D. (2005). Entrepreneurial spawning: public corporations and the genesis of new ventures: 1986–1999. *Journal of Finance*, 60(2), 577–614.

Grabowski, H.G., and Vernon, J.M. (1992). Brand loyalty, entry, and price competition in pharmaceuticals after the 1984 drug act. *Journal of Law and Economics*, 35(2), 331–50.

Graham, S., and Mowery, D. (2003). Intellectual property protection in the software industry. In *Patents in the Knowledge-Based Economy*, W. Cohen and S. Merrill (eds), National Academy Press.

Graham, S., and Somaya, D. (2006). Vermeers and Rembrandts in the same attic: complementarity between copyright and trademark leveraging strategies in software. Working paper, Georgia Institute of Technology.

Grant, R.M. (1996a). Prospering in dynamically-competitive environments: organizational capability as knowledge integration. *Organization Science*, 7, 375–87.

Grant, R.M. (1996b). Toward a knowledge-based theory of the firm. *Strategic Management Journal*, 17, 109–22.

Griliches, Z. (1990). Patent statistics as economic indicators: a survey. *Journal of Economic Literature*, 27, 1661–707.

Griliches, Z., and Hurwicz, L. (eds) (1972). *Jacob Schmookler: patents, invention, and economic change*. Harvard University Press.

Hall, B.H. (2005). Exploring the patent explosion. *Journal of Technology Transfer*, 30, 35–48.

Hall, B.H., Jaffe, A.B., and Trajtenberg, M. (2001). The NBER patent citation data file: lessons, insights and methodological tools. NBER Working Paper 8498.

Hall, B.H., Jaffe, A.B., and Trajtenberg, M. (2005). Market value and patent citations. *RAND Journal of Economics*, 36(1), 16–38.

Hall, B.H., and Ziedonis, R.H. (2001). The patent paradox revisited: an empirical study of patenting in the US semiconductor industry, 1979–95. *RAND Journal of Economics*, 32(1), 101–28.

Hall, R. (1992). The strategic analysis of intangible assets. *Strategic Management Journal*, 13, 135–44.

Hall, R. (1993). A framework for linking intangible resources and capabilities to sustainable competitive advantage. *Strategic Management Journal*, 14, 607–18.

Hall, R.E. (2001). The stock market and capital accumulation. *American Economic Review*, 91(5), 1185–202.

Hannah, D. (2005). Should I keep a secret? The effects of trade secret procedures on employees' obligations to protect trade secrets. *Organization Science*, 16(1), 71–84.

Harhoff, D., Narin, F., Scherer, F.M., and Vopel, K. (1999). Citation frequency and the value of patented inventions. *Review of Economics and Statistics*, 81, 511–15.

Harhoff, D., and Reitzig, M. (2004). Determinants of opposition against EPO patent grants – the case of biotechnology and pharmaceuticals. *International Journal of Industrial Organization*, 22, 443–80.

Hausman, J.A., Hall, B.H., and Griliches, Z. (1984). Econometric models for count data with an application to the patents-R&D relationship. *Econometrica*, 52, 909–38.

Heller, M.A., and Eisenberg, R.S. (1998). Can patents deter innovation? The anticommons in biomedical research. *Science*, 280, 698–701.

Hellmann, T. (2007). When do employees become entrepreneurs? *Management Science*, 53(6), 919–33.

Henderson, R., and Cockburn, I. (1996). Scale, scope, and spillovers: the determinants of research productivity in drug discovery. *RAND Journal of Economics*, 27(1), 32–59.

Henderson, R., Jaffe, A., and Trajtenberg, M. (2005). Patent citations and the geography of knowledge spillovers: a reassessment: comment. *American Economic Review*, 95(1), 461–4.

Hoetker, G., and Agarwal, R. (2007). Death hurts, but it isn't fatal: the postexit diffusion of knowledge created by innovative companies. *Academy of Management Journal*, 50(2), 446–67.

Jaffe, A. (1986). Technological opportunity and spillovers of R&D: evidence from firms patents, profits, and market value. *American Economic Review*, 76(5), 984–1001.

Jaffe, A. (1989). Real effects of academic research. *American Economic Review*, 79(5), 957–70.

Jaffe, A. (2000). The U.S. patent system in transition. *Research Policy*, 29, 531–57

Jaffe, A.B., Fogarty, M.S., and Banks, B.A. (1998). Evidence from patents and patent citations on the impact of NASA and other federal labs on commercial innovation. *Journal of Industrial Economics*, XLVI(2), 183–205.

Jaffe, A., and Lerner, J. (2001). Reinventing public R&D: patent policy and the commercialization of national laboratory technologies. *RAND Journal of Economics*, 32, 167–98.

Jaffe, A., and Lerner, J. (2004). *Innovation and its discontents: how our broken patent system is endangering innovation and progress, and what to do about it.* Princeton University Press.

Jaffe, A.B., and Trajtenberg, M. (2002). *Patents, citations and innovation: a window on the knowledge economy.* MIT Press.

Jaffe, A.B., Trajtenberg, M., and Henderson, R. (1993). Geographic localization of knowledge spillovers as evidenced by patent citations. *Quarterly Journal of Economics*, 108, 577–98.

Judge, T.A., Cable, D.M., Colbert, A.E., and Rynes, S.L. (2007). What causes a management article to be cited – article, author, or journal? *Academy of Management Journal*, 50(3), 491–506.

Katz, M.L. (1986). An analysis of cooperative research and development. *Rand Journal of Economics*, 17(4), 527–543.

Kim, E.H., Morse, A., and Zingales, L. (2006). What has mattered to economics since 1970. *Journal of Economic Perspectives*, 20(4), 189–202.

Klemperer, P. (1990). How broad should the scope of patent protection be? *Rand Journal of Economics*, 21(1), 113–30.

Klepper, S., and Sleeper, S. (2005). Entry by spin-offs. *Management Science*, 51(8), 1291–306.

Kogut, B., and Zander, U. (1992). Knowledge of the firm, combinative capabilities and the replication of technology. *Organization Science*, 3(3), 283–301.

Kortum, S., and Lerner, J. (1999). What is behind the surge in patenting? *Research Policy*, 28, 1–22.

Kortum, S., and Lerner, J. (2000). Assessing the contribution of venture capital to innovation. *RAND Journal of Economics*, 31, 674–92.

Lampe, R. (2007). Strategic citation. Stanford University Economics Department, SSRN working paper # 984123.

Lamoreaux, N.R., and Sokoloff, K.L. (1999). Inventors, firms, and the market for technology in the late nineteenth and early twentieth centuries. In N.R. Lamoreaux, D.M.G. Raff and P. Temin, (eds), *Learning by Doing in Firms, Markets, and Countries*, University of Chicago Press.

Lamoreaux, N.R., and Sokoloff, K.L. (eds) (2007). *The financing of innovation in the United States 1870 to present.* MIT Press.

Landes, W.M., and Posner, R.A. (1987). Trademark law: an economic perspective. *Journal of Law and Economics*, 30(2), 265–309.

Landes, W.M., and Posner, R.A. (1989). An economic analysis of copyright law. *Journal of Legal Studies*, 18(2), 325–63.

Landes, W.M., and Posner, R.A. (2003). *The economic structure of intellectual property law*. Belknap Press of Harvard University Press.

Lanjouw, J.O., and Schankerman, M. (2004). Patent quality and research productivity: measuring innovation with multiple indicators. *The Economic Journal*, 114, 441–65.

Lemley, M.A. (2002). Intellectual property rights and standards setting organizations. *California Law Review*, 75(3), 424–40.

Lemley, M.A., and Sampat, B.N. (2007). Is the patent office a rubber stamp? SSRN working paper Stanford Public Law Working Paper No. 999098, available at http://www.ssrn.com/.

Lemley, M.A., and Shapiro, C. (2005). Probabilistic patents, 19. *Journal Of Economic Perspectives*, 19(2), 75–98.

Lerner, J. (1995). Patenting in the shadow of competitors. *Journal of Law and Economics*, 38, 563–95.

Lerner, J. (2006). The new new financial thing: the origins of financial innovations. *Journal of Financial Economics*, 79, 223–55.

Lerner, J., and Merges, R.P. (1998). The control of technology alliances: an empirical analysis of the biotechnology industry. *Journal of Industrial Economics*, 46(2), 125–56.

Lerner, J., and Tirole, J. (2006). A model of forum shopping. *American Economic Review*, 96, 1091–113.

Levin, R.C., Klevorick, A.K., Nelson, R.R., and Winter, S.G. (1987). Appropriating the returns from industrial research and development. *Brookings Papers on Economic Activity*, (3), 783–820.

Littman, J. (2001). *Digital Copyright*. Prometheus Books.

Lunney, G.S. (2001). The death of copyright: digital technology, private copying, and the digital millennium copyright act. *Virginia Law Review*, 87, 813.

Machlup, F., and Penrose, E. (1950). The patent controversy in the nineteenth century. *The Journal of Economic History*, 10(1), 1–29.

Mann, R.J. (2005). Do patents facilitate financing in the software industry? *Texas Law Review*, 83, 961–1030.

Mann, R.J., and Sager, T.W. (2007). Patents, venture capital, and software start-ups. *Research Policy*, 36, 193–208.

Mansfield, E. (1986). Patents and innovation: an empirical study. *Management Science*, 32(2), 173–181.

Mazzoleni, R., and Nelson, R.R. (1998). Economic theories about the benefits and costs of patents. *Journal of Economic Issues*, 32(4), 1031–52.

Merges, R.P. (1999). The law and economics of employee inventions. *Harvard Journal of Law and Technology*, 13(1), 1–53.

Merges, R.P., and Nelson, R.R. (1990). On the complex economics of patent scope. *Columbia Law Review*, 90(4), 839–916.

Moore, K.P., Michel, P.R., and Lupo, R.V. (1999). *Patent Litigation and Strategy*. West Group.

Mowery, D.C., Nelson, R.R., Sampat, B.N., and Ziedonis, A.A. (2001). The growth of patenting and licensing by U.S. universities: an assessment of the effects of the Bayh-Dole Act of 1980. *Research Policy*, 30(1), 99–119.

Mowery, D.C., Nelson, R.R., Sampat, B.N., and Ziedonis, A.A. (2004). *Ivory tower and industrial innovation: university-industry technology transfer before and after the Bayh-Dole Act*. Stanford University Press.

Mowery, D.C., Oxley, J.E., and Silverman, B.S. (1996). Strategic alliances and interfirm knowledge transfer. *Strategic Management Journal*, 17: 77–91.

Murray, F., and Stern, S. (2006). Do formal intellectual property rights hinder the free flow of scientific knowledge? An empirical test of the anti-commons hypothesis. *Journal of Economic Behavior and Organization*, 63, 648–87.

National Science Foundation (NSF) (2007). Research and development in industry: 2003. NSF-07-314, available at: http://www.nsf.gov/statistics/nsf07314/.

Narin, F., Hamilton, K., and Olivastro, D. (1997). The increasing linkage between U.S. technology and public science. *Research Policy*, 26, 317–30.

Narin, F., Noma, E., and Perry, R. (1987). Patents as indicators of corporate technological strength. *Research Policy*, 16, 143–55.

Nordhaus, W. (1969). *Invention, Growth, and Welfare: A Theoretical Treatment of Technological Change*. (Cambridge, Mass: MIT Press).

Oldham, G., and Cummings, A. (1996). Employee creativity: personal and contextual factors at work. *Academy of Management Journal*, 39(3), 607–34.

Oxley, J.E. (1999). Institutional environment and the mechanism of governance: the impact of intellectual property protection on the structure of inter-firm alliances. *Journal of Economic Behavior and Organization*, 38, 283–309.

Peteraf, M. (1993). The cornerstones of competitive advantage: a resource-based view. *Strategic Management Journal*, 14, 179–91.

Penrose, E.T. (1959). *The theory of the growth of the firm*. John Wiley & Sons, Inc.

Podolny, J.M., and Stuart, T.E. (1995). A role-based ecology of technological change. *American Journal of Sociology*, 100, 1224–60.

Polanyi, M. (1944). Patent reform. *Review of Economic Studies*, XI.

Polany, M. (1966). *The tacit dimension*. Anchor Day.

Puranam, P., and Srikanth, K. (2007). What they know vs. what they do: how acquirers leverage technology acquisitions. *Strategic Management Journal*, 28, 805–25.

Qian, Y. (2007). Do additional national patent laws stimulate domestic innovation in a global patenting environment? A cross-country analysis of pharmaceutical patent protection, 1978–2002. *Review of Economics and Statistics*, 89(3), 436–53.

Rivette, K.G., and Kline, D. (2000). *Rembrandts in the attic: unlocking the hidden value of patents*. Harvard University Press.

Rosenkopf, L., and Almeida, P. (2001). Overcoming local search through alliances and mobility. *Management Science*, 49(6), 751–66.

Rosenkopf, L., and Nerkar, A. (2001). Beyond local search: boundary-spanning, exploration, and impact in the optical disc industry. *Strategic Management Journal*, 22, 287–306.

Rothaermel, F.T., Agung, S.D., and Jiang, L. (2007). University entrepreneurship: a taxonomy of the literature. *Industrial and Corporate Change*, 16(4), 691–791.

Rysman, M., and Simcoe, T. (2007). Patents and the performance of voluntary standard setting organizations, working paper. University of Toronto Rotman School of Management.

Sakakibara, M., and Branstetter, L. (2001). Do stronger patents induce more innovation? Evidence from the 1988 Japanese patent law reforms. *RAND Journal of Economics*, 32, 77–100.

Sampat, B.N. (2005). The determinants of patent quality: an empirical analysis. Columbia University working paper.

Scherer, F.M. (1965a). Corporate inventive output, profits, and growth. *Journal of Political Economy*, 73, 290–97.

Scherer, F.M. (1965b). Firm size, market structure, opportunity, and the output of patented innovations. *American Economic Review*, 55, 1097–123.

Scherer, F.M. (1982). Industrial technology flows in the United States. *Research Policy*, 227–45.

Scherer, F.M., and Harhoff, D. (2000). Policy implications for a world with skew-distributed returns to innovation. *Research Policy*, 29, 559–66.

Scherer, F.M., and Ross, R. (1990). *Industrial market structure and economic performance*, 3rd edition. Houghton Mifflin Company.

Scherer, F.M., and Weisburst, S. (1995). Economic effects of strengthening pharmaceutical patent protection in Italy. *Industrial and Corporate Change*, 1009–24.

Schmookler, J. (1966). *Invention and economic growth*. Harvard University Press.

Scotchmer, S. (1991). Standing on the shoulders of giants: cumulative research and the patent law. *Journal of Economic Perspectives*, 5(1), 29–41.

Scotchmer, S. (2004). *Innovation and incentives*. MIT Press.

Shane, S. (2001a). Technology regimes and new firm formation. *Management Science*, 47, 1173–90.

Shane, S. (2001b). Technology opportunities and new firm creation. *Management Science*, 47, 205–20.

Shapiro, C. (2001). Navigating the patent thicket: cross licenses, patent pools, and standard-setting. In A. Jaffe, J. Lerner and S. Stern (eds), *Innovation Policy and the Economy*, 1, 119–50.

Silverman, B. (1999). Technological resources and the direction of corporate diversification: toward an integration of the resource-based view and transaction cost economics. *Management Science*, 45(8), 1109–24.

Singh, J. (2005). Collaborative networks as determinants of knowledge diffusion patterns. *Management Science*, 51(5), 756–70.

Soete, L. (1981). A general test of the technology gap trade theory. *Review of World Economics*, 117(4), 638–60.

Soete, L. (1987). The impact of technological innovation on international trade patterns: the evidence reconsidered. *Research Policy*, 16, 101–30.

Song, J., Almeida, P., and Wu, G. (2003). Learning-by-hiring: when is mobility more likely to facilitate interfirm knowledge transfer? *Management Science*, 49(4), 351–65.

Sorensen, J., and Stuart, T. (2000). Aging, obsolescence and organizational innovation. *Administrative Science Quarterly*, 45, 81–112.

Stuart, T., and O. Sorenson (2003). Liquidity events and the geographic distribution of entrepreneurial activity, *Administrative Science Quarterly* 48, 175–201.

Teece, D.J. (1986). Profiting from technological innovation: implications for integration, collaboration, licensing, and public policy. *Research Policy*, 15, 285–305.

Thompson, P. (2006). Patent citations and the geography of knowledge spillovers: evidence from inventor- and examiner-added citations. *Review of Economics and Statistics*, 88(2), 383–8.

Thompson, P., and Fox Kean, M. (2005). Patent citations and the geography of knowledge spillovers: a reassessment. *American Economic Review*, 95(1), 450–60.

Trajtenberg, M. (1990). A penny for your quotes: patent citations and the value of innovations. *Rand Journal of Economics*, 21, 172–87.

von Graevenitz, G. (2007). Which reputation does a brand owner need? Evidence from trademark opposition. GESY Discussion Paper #215, University of Munich.

von Graevenitz, G., Wagner, S., Harhoff, D., Hall, B.H., and Hoisl, K. (2007). The strategic use of patents and its implications for enterprise and competition policy. Report ENTR/05/82, European Commission.

Von Hippel, E. (2005). *Democratized Innovation*. (Cambridge, Mass: MIT Press).

Wadhwa, A., and Kotha, S. (2006). Knowledge creation through external venturing: evidence from the telecommunications equipment manufacturing industry. *Academy of Management Journal*, 49(4), 1–17.

Wernerfelt, B. (1984). A resource-based view of the firm. *Strategic Management Journal*, 5(2), 171–80.

Zhao, M. (2006). Conducting R&D in countries with weak intellectual property rights protection. *Management Science*, 52(8), 1185–99.

Ziedonis, R.H. (2004). Don't fence me In: fragmented markets for technology and the patent acquisition strategies of firms. *Management Science*, 50(4), 804–20.

11

Orchestrating Appropriability: Towards an Endogenous View of Capturing Value from Innovation Investments

Henry Chesbrough

Introduction

In this chapter, we revisit the motivating question of Teece's seminal (1986) paper: why do some firms profit from their innovation investments, whereas others do not? Teece's answer, as we will review below, blended elements of technological characteristics (particularly the character of knowledge), the degree of appropriability conveyed through intellectual property (IP), and the nature of the complementary assets required to commercialize the innovation.

In Teece's account, firms operating in 'tight appropriability regimes' would be able to capture value from their innovation investments, whereas firms operating in 'weak' regimes would be at risk of failing to do so. He took the degree of appropriability to be exogenously determined, as have scholars conducting empirical research on perceived appropriability within industries (Levin, *et al.*, 1987).

Yet Teece's own insight into complementary assets suggests that a firm's own actions can ameliorate the appropriability problem. If the firm owns or can access the requisite complementary assets, the firm may profit from innovation activities even in weak appropriability regimes. This motivates the present chapter, in that it points the way toward firm actions that can alter the degree of appropriability in their industry. To put it differently, it suggests that appropriability may be endogenously determined – at least to some degree.

This is a potentially important contribution to the strategic management literature, which has largely followed Teece, Levin *et al.*, and others, in treating appropriability as exogenous. It may also explain potential anomalies in the exogenous view of appropriability, such as the apparent ability of some firms in an industry to protect their ideas, processes, and technologies, whereas other firms in the same industry appear to be unable to do so.

Handbook of Technology and Innovation Management. Edited by Scott Shane
© 2008 John Wiley & Sons, Ltd

The next section of the paper will review the role of appropriability in the strategic management literature. Then, we explore some specific mechanisms that are largely or entirely under the control of the firm's managers, which directly affect the degree of appropriability of a firm's innovation investments. The fourth section considers the potential costs of these endogenous mechanisms, with particular attention paid to complementary assets. The final section brings the various mechanisms together, to explore possible orchestration strategies that collectively enhance the appropriability of a firm's innovation investments.

APPROPRIABILITY AND FIRM STRATEGY

So, why do some firms profit from their innovation investments, whereas others do not? As Teece (1986) noted, the aim of his article was 'to explain why a fast second or even a slow third might outperform the innovator' (p. 285). Teece's answer to the question blended elements of technological characteristics (particularly the character of knowledge), the degree of appropriability conveyed through IP, and the nature of the complementary assets required to commercialize the innovation. Firm strategy, in turn, needed to take all these core parameters into account.

The story of EMI in medical CT scanners was the archetypal example in Teece (1986). Its initial successful entry into this new category demonstrated the utility of its innovation. Yet its subsequent failure revealed the company's inability to access the requisite complementary assets, and – importantly for our purposes – its failure effectively to leverage IP to stay ahead of the followers. The followers were able to move in, and take over the industry. 'By 1978, EMI has lost market leadership to Technicare which in turn was quickly overtaken by GE.... Though royalties continued to flow to EMI, the company had failed to capture the lion's share of the profits generated by the innovation it had pioneered and successfully commercialized.' (Teece, 1986, pp. 298–9). EMI and Technicare were replaced by GE, owing to the latter's superior marketing and sales channels, as well as GE's superior manufacturing capability. Teece termed these 'complementary assets' (Teece, 1986).

Complementary assets can be generic, specialized, or co-specialized (Teece, 1986). Generic assets are easy to replicate, and hence are not a source of competitive advantage. Specialized and co-specialized assets are difficult to replicate, and are a type of specific asset in Williamson's (1985) conception. These are the assets of potential strategic importance. The value of this complementary asset is the sum of its specific use, plus its residual value in its next best alternative use, as well as any generic use. This is shown in Figure 11.1.

As shown in the figure, the key value in a complementary asset derives from its quasi-rent, the amount of value gained by deploying the asset in its specialized use, as opposed to the value gained in the next-best use.

In this chapter, we pay particular attention to intermediate markets, whereby an upstream technology supplier licenses its know-how and IP to downstream developers and producers.[1] In these markets, the question of appropriability is

---

[1] See Teece (2000) and Arora, Fosfuri, and Gambardella (2001).

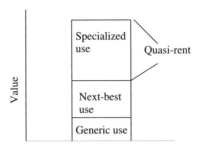

FIGURE 11.1 Partitioning the value of a specialized complementary asset.

more nuanced and intriguing than in the EMI scanner story above, in large part because the ownership of the requisite knowledge assets, complementary assets, and IP assets may all lie in different hands. As intermediate markets grow in importance in industries ranging from software, semiconductors, and telecommunications, to petroleum engineering, an increasing number of situations have emerged wherein the owner of the technology, the owner of the complementary assets, and the owner of the requisite IP all differ. These different owners with their respectively different assets influence these markets for technology, and in turn, affect the appropriability of innovation investments.

Before teasing apart these different assets, it will be useful to review some prior empirical literature that examined the role of complementary assets in firm strategy. No attempt has been made to compile exhaustively every study in this vein. Instead, illustrative studies have been chosen that provide a rich internal view of complementary assets. Each study supports the importance of complementary assets but also illustrates an endogenous component to those complementary assets.

Selected prior empirical studies of complementary assets

Mitchell (1989) examined the effect of innovation upon firms in the medical diagnostic equipment industry. He probed the emergence of new subfields within medical equipment, which were enabled by technical advances in imaging and related technologies. The causal mechanism driving his analysis was based upon economic incentives. The firm's incentive to enter was contingent on the costs of delay (firms rationally want to wait and see what the risks and benefits of entry might be, particularly if the new subfield might substitute for sales of their current products), versus the risks of being pre-empted by the entry of rival firms, who might become entrenched before the firm could establish itself in the new field (if the firm waited too long). Here the appropriability of investments was determined by the interplay of the costs of delay versus the costs of pre-emption.

In one carefully constructed analysis (Mitchell, 1989),[2] he found evidence that incumbents that perceive a threat to their core products are more likely to enter. He

---

[2]One example of Mitchell's more thorough analysis is his explicit treatment of the issues of right-censorship, i.e., the condition where a firm is in the sample but has not (yet) entered a new subfield.

also reported findings that incumbents that possess relevant complementary assets are more likely than other rivals to enter into a new subfield. Mitchell (1992) later extended this research by explicitly comparing and contrasting the role of market-related supporting assets (such as a direct sales force) to the role of technically related assets, such as prior experience in similar technological areas, in the behavior of medical equipment firms. He found evidence indicating that market-related assets were associated with greater incumbent survival, and with higher market shares, whereas incumbents with prior technical experience encounter a more mixed set of outcomes. Prior technical experience exhibited a slightly negative effect upon incumbent survival and short-term share. The 1992 study found that prior technical experience may impair incumbents' initial adaptation to innovation, resulting in a 'trap' (p. 342) within an inferior technical trajectory, and 'mistakes' (p. 343). This hints at one of the potential downsides for developing and maintaining complementary assets (here, prior technical experience): they may impose costs of their own that constrain later adaptation.

A research program by Tripsas (1997) examined the impact of technological change in the typesetter industry. Tracking the events of a century in that industry, she identified three separate waves of technical change that hit the firms in the industry. Interestingly, although these changes were quite extensive, not all the leaders in the industry were displaced. Many firms indeed were driven out, but a few persisted.

This persistence prompted her to examine the mechanisms that appeared to promote this longevity, despite the turbulent technical environment. She found that the presence or absence of key complementary assets (Teece, 1986) such as manufacturing, sales networks, and font libraries, enhanced the ability of incumbent firms to survive the technological shift (Tripsas, 1997). She also found that firms with 'external integrative capability' were better able to respond to nonincremental innovation shocks. This integrative capability included internal investments in research and development that improved the firm's absorptive capacity to access knowledge from the external environment. It also included investments in transferring knowledge throughout the firm, particularly investments that promoted the sharing of knowledge across functional groups such as R&D, manufacturing, and sales.

A final mechanism Tripsas found of enhanced longevity was the existence of dispersed research sites in different locations. These different sites appeared to stimulate rivalry between the sites on the one hand, and promoted greater variation in technological approaches that a firm pursued on the other hand. Thus, although technological changes rendered the technology of one research site obsolete, the different technical path of another site sometimes enabled the incumbent firm to shift to that technology platform at the other site, instead of fighting a losing battle to sustain the now-obsolete technology base. It is perhaps obvious, but nonetheless worth noting, that the knowledge transfer mechanisms and the maintenance of multiple R&D sites are again entirely determined by actions of a given firm, not by some exogenous factor.

In work with Joseph Bower (Christensen and Bower, 1996), Christensen linked the disruption of the *external* value network to the inertia created by the *internal* resource allocation process inside incumbent hard disk drive firms (see also Christensen, 1997). They showed that established disk drive firms listened carefully to their established customers, and their internal resource allocation procedures channeled funds among competing projects towards those projects that served these established customers. When architectural changes such as new form factors emerged that served their established customers, they found that US incumbent hard disk drive firms had little difficulty adjusting to the new technology. This type of technology they termed 'sustaining'. When new form factors emerged that served different customers in remote markets that did not interest current customers, though, these same incumbents were late to enter the new form factors, and were generally ineffective when they did enter. This type of technology was termed 'disruptive'. Christensen essentially argued that firms could readily appropriate the value of sustaining investments, although they were unlikely to do so with disruptive investments. Here, appropriability was not dependent upon exogenous factors, but instead upon the internal tensions in allocating resources within the firm.

Sull (1997; Sull *et al.*, 1997) has published results from a detailed study of incumbent behavior in the US tire industry. There are at least two characteristics of this research program that are relevant to the question of appropriability. One is that the technology transition from bias ply to radial ply tires that Sull studied was an obvious transition to incumbent tire manufacturers. Because it was signaled well in advance of the event, and because it was not a particularly complex technological change, the usual cognitively limited causal explanations for incumbent difficulties with technology transition (e.g., Henderson and Clark, 1990) ought not to apply. Incumbents ought to have known what was coming, and ought to have known what to do to respond to it, well in advance of having to do it.

The other salient characteristic of this research program is that Sull had unusually deep access to internal records of the incumbent tire firms, and so was able to reconstruct detailed records of investment at the individual tire plant level for each of the US incumbent firms. This unusually detailed evidence indicated that, despite the obvious character of the technical shift, US incumbent tire firms nonetheless stumbled badly in responding to the radial technological transition. The causal explanation he offered for this finding derived from the commitments that management at each incumbent firm had to stakeholders of each firm, including customers, employees, and the surrounding community. In other contexts, analysts often praise firms for 'high commitment workforce policies', and for 'staying close to the customer' (Peters and Waterman, 1982). Presumably these commitments were also appropriate for the US tire industry at an earlier point in time. By the time of the advent of radial tires, though, these commitments prevented incumbent firms from taking actions such as tire plant closures or conversions that would have preserved many hundreds of millions of dollars in shareholder value. Note that these commitments were internally constructed by the actions of the US tire firms, and were not imposed by some exogenous circumstance.

Stepping back from these individual empirical studies, it is clear that the appropriability mechanisms that each identified emanated more from internal actions of focal firms, than they did from overall industry-level characteristics. In Mitchell's and especially in Sull's work, it is also clear that the actions that firms took to enhance the appropriability of their innovation investments at one point in time, later became a source of strategic inertia for the firm.

ENDOGENOUS APPROPRIABILITY MECHANISMS: IMPLICATIONS FOR STRATEGY

Strategy has been argued by many to be the search for rents (Williams, 1994). The work of Michael Porter (1980; 1985) established a source of rents from entry barriers into an industry, along with switching costs faced by consumers. Porter's analysis, in turn, was informed by a longstanding literature in industrial organization, spearheaded by the work of Bain (Caves and Porter, 1977; Gilbert, 1989).

An even older stream of economic analysis by David Ricardo identified the role of scarcity in creating rents. This venerable insight has been rediscovered by the resource-based view (RBV) of the firm (Wernerfelt, 1984; Barney, 1989; Mahoney and Pandian, 1992). Building on the observation by Rumelt (1982) that profitability varied within an industry as much or more as it did between industries, this approach seeks to understand the sources of variation in rents between firms in the same industry. In the RBV construction, strategic rents come from assets that are inimitable, or difficult to imitate. This is simply scarcity by another name, albeit now in an advanced industrial economic context. Assets that are easily imitated or readily exchanged cannot be a source of sustainable advantage. The RBV analysis identified the source of Ricardian rents to come from within the firm, rather than from the Porterian rents arising from the external entry barriers to an industry.

The Teece (1986) analysis and the subsequent development of dynamic capabilities (Teece, Pisano, and Shuen, 1997) identify a third source of strategic rents for the firm. These are Schumpeterian rents, the rents that arise from innovation. These do not arise from incremental innovation; rather, they derive from the Schumpeterian innovation that 'strikes at the very lives' of established firms. These rents are rooted in fundamentally improved products and processes. Like the Ricardian rents of the RBV approach, these rents also emanate from within the firm. Unlike the Ricardian rents, though, these rents are likely to be transient, as the waves of innovative activity overtake and make obsolete previous improvements in products and processes. In contrast to the static conceptions of 'industry' that underlie Porterian strategy, the Schumpeterian innovation process is dynamic, showing scant regard for current industry boundaries, and eroding previously high industry barriers in its wake (while possibly throwing up new barriers).

Although we follow this last line of analysis in identifying the sources of rents, the analysis does not go far enough into the actions of firms that can influence those rents. Therefore, the next section considers the potential separation of complementary assets from the IP that undergirds those assets.

The Potential Costs of Complementary Assets When IP is Separately Owned

In 1995, the US Department of Justice (DOJ) issued its guidelines licensing IP.[3] These guidelines drew a distinction between the market for goods, the market for technology, and the market for innovation. The market for goods relates to product market offerings. The market for technology involves the trading of IP, while the market for innovation involves the conduct of research that may lead to future development of products and services. Here we will focus on the second category, the market for technology, or the market for knowledge assets in our terminology. As discussed in Teece (1982; 1998), Gans, Hsu, and Stern (2002), and Arora, Fosfuri, and Gambardella (2001), this can be conceived to be a market lying upstream from producers of goods and services in the product market, and the presence of this upstream market may have powerful effects on innovation within the industry of the upstream and downstream firms.

Implicit in the dynamic capabilities analysis is the assumption that the IP that supports Schumpeterian innovation is fully controlled by the innovating firm, as in Teece (1986). This does not consider situations such as those contemplated in the DOJ guidelines above, where IP ownership may differ from the ownership of the requisite knowledge assets and complementary assets, and where this separation may create blocking situations that impede the innovating firm. Yet Teece himself made the conceptual distinction in one of his early articles (Teece, 1982). More recently, he has begun to tease apart the innovation of a given firm from the intellectual capital that underlies this innovation.[4]

This distinction leads to additional insights in the challenge of profiting from innovation. Under certain conditions, it also leads to insights that qualify the findings of the Teece (1986) article. We argue below that the dimension of IP affects the apportionment of Schumpeterian rents from innovation.

Teece's 1986 paper implicitly assumed that the owner of the knowledge assets and the complementary assets also controlled the relevant IP that pertained to those assets. In GE's case, this was probably the case, as it had a strong internal R&D program, supported by a large patent portfolio in medical equipment technology, manufacturing processes, trademarks for its brands, and so on. However, the emergence of intermediate markets creates conditions where that ownership of the knowledge assets, the IP assets, and complementary assets need not coincide.

Consider the case of Qualcomm in cellular telephony, or of Rambus in high transfer speed DRAM devices. In each instance, the technology supplier (Qualcomm or Rambus) has developed a new and valuable technology. This led to substantial know-how, as well as IP assets (primarily patents). Each company licenses these assets to manufacturers of cell phones or DRAMs, respectively. The licensee must still develop the final product, manufacture the product, and market and sell the product. So the licensee must own or have access to the usual complementary assets

---

[3]US Department of Justice, Antitrust Guidelines for the Licensing of Intellectual Property, Washington, DC, Department of Justice: Federal Trade Commission, April 6, 1995.

[4]See Teece's 1998 article 'Capturing value from knowledge assets', which won the Accenture award, and his 2000 book *Managing intellectual capital.*

in Teece's sense of the term, and yet the licensee must further access knowledge assets and IP assets from a technology supplier.

In addition to intermediate markets, there are a number of other circumstances that can cause a firm practicing a technology (and therefore has the requisite know-how to utilize an innovation) not to have the necessary IP rights to protect its ability to continue to operate. One instance is due to the ambiguity of patent claims granted by the patent authorities, which takes time and money to resolve.[5] This ambiguity can be exploited to block, or impair, a competitor. It can also arise where a firm has misappropriated a technology (wittingly through unauthorized copying,[6] or unwittingly through parallel discovery and deployment). It can even arise when a company pursues an innovation opportunity, but neglects to file for relevant legal protection of the IP undergirding its pursuit.

When one considers that the owners of the know-how, the complementary assets, and the IP may all be different, the gains from innovation are also affected. A fourth possible role (which will be discussed later) is that of the orchestrator of these different assets. The gains from innovation are likely to be allocated among the four asset owners. Here is a brief description of each:

◆ *Knowledge Assets* – this is the product and process knowledge needed to effect the innovation. These can be embodied in physical artifacts and processes as well, but they often have a significant tacit component, and are hard to transfer.

◆ *Complementary Assets* – these are the assets needed to commercialize the innovation, to bring it to market effectively. These may be generic in character, specific, or co-specialized (Teece, 1986). Examples of such assets include manufacturing and distribution assets, as well as a brand.

◆ *Intellectual Property* – this refers to the patents, trade secrets, and copyrights that are relevant to the ability to practice the innovation. In the case of patents, if it includes a blocking patent, then such IP conveys the ability to exclude the owners of the other assets from making, using, or selling the infringing items.[7]

◆ *Orchestration Capabilities* – these are the abilities to orchestrate the above assets in a coherent way, such that the innovation can be commercialized effectively, and will not be blocked. Done well, the orchestrator can assure itself of the gains from innovation, and even discern future paths for profitable innovation. Without proficiency here, the innovating firm may lose, even if it is well positioned with regard to complementary assets and know-how.

---

[5]As Lanjouw and Lerner (2001) discuss, the high costs of patent litigation can 'tilt the table' for less financially endowed competitors. Plaintiffs, for example, often file for preliminary injunctive relief, which seeks to force a defendant to cease production of the offending item, pending the outcome of litigation. This can cause significant damage, even if the eventual outcome is favorable to the defendant.

[6]Of course, misappropriation is only effective if you're not caught. Two years ago, an arbitrator ruled that Caterpillar Inc. had willfully misappropriated the intellectual property from a research joint venture with Clean Fuels Technology Inc. (CFTI) and then transferred that IP to another joint venture with Lubrizol Corp. without the knowledge of CFTI. Unfortunately, CFTI was able to discover the misappropriation, and successfully pursued a remedy. See 'Caterpillar is Found to Have Defrauded Ex-Partner Over Clean Fuels Technology', *Wall Street Journal*, January 19, 2000.

[7]Not all the focal innovation may be covered by IP, and what portion is covered may or may not block others. Frequently, it is possible to invent around or design around the claims covered by the IP. This is an essential element of appropriability in Teece (1986).

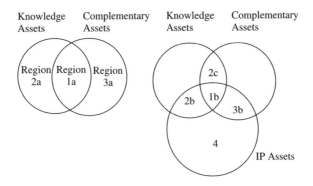

FIGURE 11.2 Underlying assets supporting innovation.

The first three of these elements are combined visually on the left side of Figure 11.2, which separates the elements so that they intersect, but do not overlap entirely with each other.

A firm's knowledge assets are shown in the circle on the left, while the complementary assets needed to commercialize the technology effectively are shown on the right. At least three conditions are possible:

- In Region 1a, the firm's knowledge assets coincide with the firm's complementary assets, and it is here where the firm can successfully profit from its innovation.
- In Region 2a, the firm has the knowledge assets, but lacks the complementary assets necessary to commercialize the technology. It is here where many firms fail to profit from their innovation activities.
- In Region 3a, the firm lacks the knowledge assets, but possesses the complementary assets. This firm has the opportunity to be a successful follower, because of these latter assets. Alternatively, the firm could contract with a firm in Region 2a, and extract a healthy portion of the rents from the innovation.

In a related analysis, Chesbrough and Teece (1996) argued that when firms possessed relevant complementary assets, 'virtual' outsourcing of particular technologies may be 'virtuous', because the firm would not have to negotiate for access to the requisite complementary assets to commercialize an externally accessed innovation. This stood in contrast to Region 2a, where outsourcing the innovation was argued to be hazardous.

Subsequent empirical work by other scholars has extended upon these insights. Tripsas (1997) showed how complementary assets assisted firms in navigating the complex technology transitions that arose in the typesetting industry over a period of a hundred years. Silverman (1999) provided a rigorous empirical methodology that predicted diversification moves by corporations into new businesses, based on the presence of complementarities between the old and new business. This empirical work, though, follows Teece (1986) in paying little attention to the potential separation of IP ownership from knowledge or complementary assets.

The right side of Figure 11.2 shows that conceptually, the technology or innovation is separable from the underlying IP that is relevant to practicing the technology. Regions 1b, 2b, 2c, and 3b are areas where untangling these concepts extend the earlier insights in profiting from innovation. As we will discuss, under certain conditions *a firm's complementary assets can become a hostage that confers additional leverage upon the IP holder.*

- ◆ In Region 1b, all three concepts are aligned within the firm. The firm possesses the technology, the associated IP, and the requisite complementary assets. This represents an effective orchestration of the requisite elements. Here, the prediction of the Teece (1986) article is again borne out: the firm can expect to profit from its innovation investments in this region.[8]
- ◆ In Region 3b, the firm lacks the technology, but owns the relevant IP and requisite complementary assets. Here, the firm is in a strong position to access the missing technology from outside the firm, and then take it to market. As noted in Chesbrough and Teece (1996), here, virtual is indeed virtuous. The firm need not invent the technology, or even possess the knowledge assets to drive the technology's development, in order to profit from it.
- ◆ In Region 2b, the firm has the knowledge and the IP, but lacks the complementary assets. As above for region 2a, the firm must negotiate access to the requisite complementary assets. Failure to gain such access on reasonable terms could again thwart the firm's ability to commercialize its innovation.
- ◆ In Region 2c, by contrast, the firm has the knowledge and the complementary assets, but lacks the IP associated with the innovation. Here, contrary to Teece (1986), *the firm is actually at risk of holdup or expropriation from the IP owner, even though it controls the requisite complementary assets.* If the IP owner is in region 4, lacking the technology and the complementary assets, it may nonetheless be positioned to use the IP to extract rents from the innovator. Indeed, the presence of complementary assets held by the innovator in region 2c *adds to the leverage of the IP holder* over the innovating firm.

This last conclusion requires some analysis. Assume that firm C has the technology and complementary assets necessary to commercialize the investment. However, firm D owns the legal rights to the IP that are embodied in the technology. Firm D can not only extract the rents from the technology itself, but also extract an additional amount from Firm C amounting to the specialized portion of the latter firm's complementary assets. This specialized portion, shown in Figure 11.1 as the quasi-rent, is at risk, if another firm can assert its IP rights over innovations that the complementary asset supports. The remaining value of the complementary asset is not at risk, because the asset could be placed in its next best use by firm C and continue to earn that level of value.

---

[8]In Teece (1986), the firm would utilize its own technology and supply it in the product market. Left unexamined is the additional possibility of whether the firm might also profit from licensing its technology to other firms who also possess relevant complementary assets. Arora *et al.* (2001) examine this possibility, and find that the firm must balance the *revenue effect* from additional receipts for its technology against *the rent dissipation effect* from increased product market competition downstream. A related treatment of these issues can be found in Chesbrough (2006), chapters 3 and 4.

In Williamson's (1985) terms, the quasi-specific value of the complementary asset serves as a hostage, which could be forfeit if the innovator was blocked by the IP owner's claim. The more firm C has invested in the specialized portion of its complementary assets, the greater the quasi-rent from deploying that asset to best advantage, and hence the greater the leverage firm D has over it in a negotiation about appropriating the rents from innovation.

If it has not obtained access to the technology in advance, Firm C is at substantial risk of losing the investments it has made in pursuit of innovation to the owners of the IP (here, firm D) whose claims 'read on' the innovation. The amount at risk could be quite substantial, as much as the total expected profits from the innovation, plus the quasi-rents from any specific investments B has already made to support that stream of profits.[9] To the extent that there are alternative technology suppliers, the presence of these feasible alternatives constrains the ability of D to hold up firm C. Even here, though, the switching costs for C also confers some market power on D. To the extent that endogenous investments in complementary assets increase quasi-rents and switching costs for C, they actually impair C's ability to profit from its investments.

Although this analysis has considered the context of intermediate technology markets as an instance where such hazards could arise, there are other contexts in which these considerations occur as well. One example is the 'submarine patents' held by IP owners such as Jerome Lemelson. Here, there may be little or no real contribution to know-how to practice the technology, but through strategic maneuvering the IP owner nonetheless has obtained a valid claim. If the claim is found to be valid, the division of rents from an innovation would have to include compensation for use of those assets.

Orchestrating Appropriability

The foregoing analysis suggests the emergent need for a new role that was previously latent in appropriating the gains from innovation: the orchestration role. As defined above, this role brings together the requisite know-how, IP, and complementary asset classes, so that the innovation investments made lead to an acceptable return. This role includes a capability for systems integration, in understanding the possible ways that the technical components of a technology might be put together, both from current and possible alternative suppliers.

At a mundane level, orchestration might simply be viewed as checking to be sure that one owns or has effective access to the requisite know-how, IP, and

[9]In 1990 Eastman Kodak paid $909 million in damages (including interest) to Polaroid for its 1986 conviction for infringement of several of Polaroid's instant camera patents. This included treble damages for 'willful' infringement. Kodak's loss to Polaroid stands as the largest single judgment awarded to an IP holder in US court. Polaroid's patents were blocking patents in the instant camera market, but this was not clear (to Kodak, at least) at the outset – an example of the *ex ante* ambiguity of patent claims. But Kodak's total loss exceeded even this amount, because Kodak was forced to repurchase all of its channel inventory, and rebate the purchase price of its cameras to consumers who bought the infringing camera. Kodak's distribution capability (a complementary asset) ended up increasing the total cost to Kodak of infringing Polaroid's patents, by increasing the number of units of channel inventory that had to be repurchased.

complementary assets. If one or more of these assets is not readily at hand, however, the orchestration role becomes more strategic. In essence, the orchestration role must seek to offset or neutralize ones' own complementary assets as a hostage, in the bargaining over the gains from Schumpeterian innovation. Without such a role, the Teecian prescription of advising innovators to focus on accessing complementary assets may be overturned.

Although orchestration strategies could apply equally to all three classes of assets discussed, we focus here on how an alert orchestrator could seek to offset or neutralize advantages held by independent owners of IP. Below we sketch five orchestration strategies, which are not intended to be exhaustive, but do illustrate the wide range of options available to the innovating firm:

- countersuit;
- cross-licensing;
- voluntary divestiture of downstream operations;
- providing safe harbor;
- pre-emptive publishing.

Countersuit.   In the example above, Firm C may consider the possibility of counter-suit against firm D, owing to the ambiguity of protection over the IP at issue. It may well be that Firm C can mount a plausible action against Firm D, because the scope of D's patent claims is not entirely clear, and/or Firm D's operations (in this or another business) may be alleged to infringe on some other IP held by firm C. And if Firm D also possesses complementary assets to support its own product market activities, those latter complementary assets may then serve as a hostage against Firm D's interests, offsetting firm C's complementary assets at risk from the initial suit.

Cross-licensing.   Cross-licensing is a well-known strategy for realizing design freedom (e.g., Grindley and Teece, 1997; Shapiro, 2000; Hall and Ziedonis, 2001). In many complex technologies, though, the costs of design are dwarfed by the costs of the requisite complementary assets to commercialize the design – a fact not yet recognized by strategy scholars.[10] In such instances, firms' cross-licensing may have less to do with seeking design freedom for its developers, and more to do with realizing the ability to utilize their own specific complementary assets to their best use in future. Their ability to continue to use their specialized complementary assets could be at risk if others can exert IP claims against the firm. This is an additional reason why competing firms (each with significant complementary assets) often seek out cross-licensing arrangements, a reason not previously noted in the literature. Cross-licensing confers the freedom to employ one's own complementary assets to their best advantage, reducing the chance that they can be used by an IP owner against the firm.

The cross-licensing analysis is more intriguing if there is an asymmetry in the complementary asset positions of the two competing firms. If firm C possesses significant complementary assets, while firm D does not, firm C faces the asymmetric

---

[10]For example, a new microprocessor design may require a few hundred human years of time, for a cost of a couple of hundred million dollars. However, the fabrication facility to make the design might cost ten times that amount.

threat of losing the quasi-specific value of its complementary assets, while firm D simply calculates its probability of winning or losing a litigation action against firm C. In this instance, *D's weakness* (its lack of the requisite complementary assets to profit from innovation) *turns into strength*, because it improves firm D's bargaining position over firm C. Firm C's strength, its ownership of key complementary assets, similarly becomes a liability, because firm D gains leverage in a negotiation with firm C due to the specialized character of C's complementary assets.[11]

Voluntary divestiture. This suggests a novel third orchestration strategy of voluntary divestiture of downstream operations. In the example above, Firm C might choose to spin off or discontinue downstream operations that employed its complementary assets, and become a competing technology supplier to firm D. A specialized 'technology supplier' firm that owns valuable IP, but lacks any operations or complementary assets, might actually be a superior organizational mode for pursuing a rent extraction strategy against innovating firms in a weak appropriability regime.[12] Such a specialized supplier voluntarily would eschew these downstream activities, in order to avoid having them be targeted by the party they wish to sue in a countersuit.

Consider the case of Qualcomm in the wireless telephony marketplace. Qualcomm used to be a manufacturer of telephone handsets and equipment as well as semiconductor chips used in phones. Its differentiation in the market was based on its CDMA technology, and Qualcomm became a licensor of the technology, to try to make it a *de facto* standard. In the past three years, Qualcomm has shifted its strategy to focus exclusively upon its CDMA technology, and leverage it to become the key standard in next generation wireless communications. The company intends to make money from licensing its IP for its CDMA and related technologies. In the process, the company has chosen to divest itself of all its product operations in handsets. When Qualcomm announced these moves, analysts attributed this withdrawal to Qualcomm's inability to fund its technology development as well as its products.

Be that as it may, our analysis suggests an additional motivation for why Qualcomm voluntarily withdrew from the product market: to maximize its bargaining position in the upstream IP market. Qualcomm's products competed in an environment of complex or cumulative technologies (Nelson and Winter, 1982; Pavitt, 1999), where one technology builds upon other, closely related technologies. In order to participate in selling handsets and chips, Qualcomm had to make significant investments in a number of technology and complementary assets. It is difficult in this industry to have 100 % ownership of all the IP involved in the products one builds. Qualcomm could not be sure that its downstream products would not infringe to at least some degree upon other companies' IP, particularly the IP of other companies in the telecommunications market.

---

[11] There are a number of testable propositions emerging from this section. We predict that, in a weak appropriability regime, greater levels of complementary assets held by both parties would lead to a greater likelihood of cross-licensing. We also predict that, again in a weak appropriability regime, if significant asymmetries in complementary assets exist, revenues in any cross-licensing for a given amount of IP (or holding IP constant) would flow towards the party with the lesser amount of such assets.

[12] Here we depart from Gans, Hsu, and Stern (2002), who find that the 'cooperative strategy' of licensing to a downstream business is more likely when appropriability is strong, and less likely when weak. We argue that the firm has a third option in a weak appropriability regime, the option of divesting itself of its own operating assets to enhance its bargaining power.

The ambiguity of IP claims, the complex nature of the underlying technologies, and the significant investments in technology and complementary assets, all impaired Qualcomm's ability to maximize its profits from its IP. If Qualcomm wished to maximize the revenues it could earn from licensing its CDMA technology, it would gain more leverage in its negotiations with other handset manufacturers if it deprived them of a chance to countersue for infringement of their own IP in the handset market. Qualcomm's withdrawal from making handsets allowed it to remove potential hostages from negotiations over its CDMA technology, thereby strengthening its negotiating position in the upstream market.

A second example of this orchestration strategy comes from Rambus, an innovative designer of dynamic random access memories (DRAMs) in the semiconductor industry. The semiconductor industry is one studied by many scholars, and one where cross-licensing and defensive patenting has been extensively reported (e.g., Cohen, Nelson, and Walsh, 2000; Hall and Ziedonis, 2001). Rambus has designed – and carefully built a wall of patents around – a chip-to-chip interface that speeds the flow of data into and out of the DRAMs, alleviating the bottleneck of DRAMs in personal computer system performance. The company's business model is *not* to enter into manufacturing of devices using the Rambus design; instead, the goal is to license its technology to other companies.

Rambus' organizational mode cleverly places it in a position to avoid having to water down the strength of its IP claims by trading those for access to other IP it would need to compete as a manufacturer of DRAM devices. It also avoids having to raise the capital to finance or access complementary assets in manufacturing Rambus-enabled DRAMs, assets that ironically could compromise its negotiating leverage in the IP market. Its strategy is likely to lead to far greater revenues from its IP than it would have obtained, had it chosen to enter into the downstream product market as well.

Safe harbor. A fourth orchestration strategy is to use one's complementary assets and IP to provide a safe harbor to innovation partners, in order to protect the latter's innovation against countersuits by other parties. Tensilica is a new entrant in the microprocessor market (Chesborough, 2003, chapter 8). It has an innovative technology to permit low power operation, and field programmability of its device. But the company lacks much of the surrounding IP needed to manufacture microprocessors. Intel, by contrast, has a much stronger IP portfolio, and has demonstrated its willingness to litigate aggressively with its portfolio to deter entry into its microprocessor markets (Jackson, 1997). When a startup company such as Tensilica wants to compete with a powerhouse like Intel in the low-power microprocessor market, it has to worry a great deal about Intel's ability to impair its business through the threat of patent infringement litigation. Given the complexity of microprocessors, and the complexity of their manufacture, it is difficult at best to assure a young startup's investors, as well as its intended customers, that the startup's activities will not infringe another company's IP rights. How can Tensilica resolve this uncertainty, and convince its investors and customers to support its innovative efforts?

They resolved this problem by finding a safe harbor through working with IBM, a partner with an even better semiconductor IP portfolio than that of Intel. IBM agreed to serve as Tensilica's foundry, to make its devices. IBM has a wonderful portfolio of semiconductor patents, earned over many years of R&D in the industry. IBM has leveraged this portfolio to enter into cross-licensing agreements with virtually all the major industry players (including Intel), often receiving payments, in addition to access to other companies' IP in return for access to its own. This network of agreements and strong internal IP makes IBM a safe foundry for younger companies seeking to enter into the industry. IBM is likely to earn a healthy margin acting as Tensilica's manufacturer. And that margin consists not only of a return to IBM for its manufacturing expenses in the capital-intensive production of semiconductors, but also of a margin in return for providing Tensilica an IP insurance policy.

Pre-emptive publishing.   A final and very different orchestration strategy for complementary asset holders would be to pre-empt IP holders by proactively publishing one's knowledge, in order to create an intellectual commons. Creating such a commons would forfeit the chance to capture value from one's own IP, but it similarly could prevent another firm from extracting IP rents from one's own operations and complementary assets. If one has sufficiently strong complementary assets and technology, one may be able to win in the market without owning the IP, so long as no one else can stake that claim, and block the firm from leveraging its assets in pursuing future innovations.

The Intel Corporation actively sponsors university research in a number of areas of technological interest to the firm.[13] It also spends many billions of dollars each year in R&D, to create critical complementary assets such as the latest generation semiconductor fabrication facilities, sales and marketing, and advertising. At the time of writing, Intel owns and operates more semiconductor fabrications facilities (known as 'fabs') than any other company in the world. Intel goes to great lengths to ensure that its fabs can keep operating.

This philosophy animates Intel's approach to funding university research. Intel does not prevent its funding recipients in universities from publishing; indeed, it encourages publishing, because the published results cannot then be patented by other firms, and used to exclude Intel in its operations.[14] Intel also maintains the *Intel Technical Journal,* which it publishes precisely to establish particular discoveries in the public domain, where they cannot be used against Intel's large and growing complementary asset base.

Intel's approach to allowing its funding recipients to publish their knowledge, and its sponsorship of its own journal to publish some of Intel's own knowledge, deprives Intel of the ability to extract rents from the use of that knowledge. However, Intel

---

[13]Intel's university research funding program is analyzed in chapter 6 of Chesbrough (2003).

[14]Under the Bayh-Dole Act of 1980, universities can patent research discoveries funded by public monies as well. In the case where Intel has funded at least a portion of the work being patented, negotiates in advance with the university to assure Intel royalty-free access to the patent, if one is subsequently received.

may be willing to forfeit these opportunities in the upstream technology market, if by publishing this knowledge it increases the chance that its extensive complementary assets may continue to be employed to commercialize new semiconductor products. If Intel can 'win' in the product market by virtue of its complementary assets, it can afford to play for a 'tie' in the upstream IP that utilizes those assets.

CONCLUSION

We began by re-examining the question that prompted David Teece in his exploration of complementary assets: why do some firms profit from their innovation investments, and others not? The emergence of intermediate markets for technology gives a new importance to this question, both for antitrust policy, and for firm strategy. Particularly for the latter concern, the rise of intermediate markets creates situations where the ownership of the IP that undergirds a technology may *not* align with the ownership of the requisite complementary assets needed to practice the technology.

Such situations render the appropriability of innovation investments potentially problematic, even when the innovator owns or has access to the requisite complementary assets. For now the innovator must also own or gain access to the requisite IP assets as well, in order to profit from its innovation investments. There are strategic dimensions involved in gaining this access, and alert innovators must take steps to neutralize the threat that an alert IP owner may pose. One result of these strategic issues is that the ownership of complementary assets may confer leverage of the IP owner, unless steps are taken to neutralize that leverage. A variety of orchestration tactics are sketched, to illustrate the range of potential problems that this alignment of IP may entail, as well as the steps companies are taking to address them.

Once we begun to ponder these orchestration moves, we come to understand that the appropriability of innovation investments is at least partially endogenous in its character. Although industry characteristics or other exogenous factors may influence the appropriability of an innovator's investments, there are also factors under the innovator's control that must be brought to bear as well. We should expect to see significant variation in appropriability within industries, in addition to variation between industries. And we should not be surprised if innovators with complementary assets sometimes fail to profit from their innovation investments, when competing in industries with active intermediate markets.

REFERENCES

Arora, A., Fosfuri, A., and Gambardella, A. (2001). *Markets for Technology*. MIT Press.
Barney, J. (1989). Firm resources and sustained competitive advantage. *Journal of Management*, 17(1), 99–120.
Caves, R., and Porter, M. (1977). From entry barriers to mobility barriers. *Quarterly Journal of Economics*, 91, 241–61.
Chesbrough, H.W. (1999a). The differing organizational impact of technological change: a comparative theory of national institutional factors. *Industrial and Corporate Change*, 8, 3.

Chesbrough, H.W. (1999b). Arrested development: the experience of European hard disk drive firms in comparison with US and Japanese firms. *Journal of Evolutionary Economics*, 9(3), 287–330.

Chesbrough, H.W. (2003). *Open innovation: the new imperative for creating and profiting from technology.* Harvard Business School Press.

Chesbrough, H.W. (2006). *Open business models: how to thrive in the new innovation landscape.* Harvard Business School Press.

Chesbrough, H., and Teece, D. (1996). When is virtual virtuous: organizing for innovation. *Harvard Business Review*, Jan/Feb., 65–74.

Christensen, C. (1997). *The innovator's dilemma.* Harvard Business School Press.

Christensen, C., and Bower, J. (1996). Customer power, strategic investment, and the failure of leading firms. *Strategic Management Journal*, 17, 197–218.

Cohen, W., Nelson, R., and Walsh, J. (2000). Protecting their intellectual assets: appropriability conditions and why US manufacturing firms patent (or not). NBER working paper #7552, National Bureau of Economic Research.

Gans, J.S., Hsu, D.H., and Stern, S. (2002). When does start-up innovation spur the gale of creative destruction? *RAND Journal of Economics*, 33(4), 571–86.

Gilbert, R. (1989). Mobility barriers and the value of incumbency. In R. Schmalensee and R. Willig (eds), *Handbook of Industrial Organization*, volume 1, North-Holland, 476–535.

Grindley, P., and Teece, D. (1997). Managing intellectual capital: licensing and cross-licensing in semiconductors and electronics. *California Management Review*, 39(2), 8–41.

Hall, B., and Ziedonis, R. 2001. The patent paradox revisited: an empirical analysis of patenting in the US semiconductor industry from 1979–1995. *Rand Journal of Economics*, 32(1), 101–28.

Henderson, R., and Clark, K. (1990). Architectural innovation: the reconfiguration of existing product technologies and the failure of established firms. *Administrative Science Quarterly*, 35, 9–30.

Jackson, T. (1997) *Inside Intel: Andy Grove and the rise of the world's most powerful chip company.* Dutton.

Lanjouw, J., and Lerner, J. (2001). Tilting the table? The use of preliminary injunctions. *Journal of Law and Economics*, 44 (October), 573–96.

Levin, R.C., Levorick, A.K., Nelson, R.R., and Winter, S.G. (1987). Appropriating the returns from industrial research and development. *Brookings Papers on Economic Activity*, 3, 783–820.

Mahoney, J., and Pandian, R. (1992). The resource based view within the conversation of strategic management. *Strategic Management Journal*, 13, 363–80.

Mitchell, W. (1989). Whether and when: probability and timing of incumbents' entry into new subfields. *Administrative Science Quarterly*, 34, 208–30.

Mitchell, W. (1992). Dual clocks: entry order influences on incumbent and newcomer market share and survival when specialized assets retain their value. *Strategic Management Journal*, 12, 85–100.

Nelson, R.R., and Winter, S.G. (1982). *An evolutionary theory of economic change.* Belknap Press.

Pavitt, K. (1999). *The nature and economic importance of national innovation systems.* Edward Elgar.

Peters, T., and Waterman, R. (1982). *In search of excellence.* Harper and Row.

Porter, M. (1980). *Competitive strategy.* Free Press.

Porter, M. (1985). *Competitive advantage.* Free Press.

Rumelt, R. (1982). Diversification strategy and profitability. *Strategic Management Journal*, 3, 359–69.

Shapiro, C. (2000). *Navigating the patent thicket: cross licensing, patent pools, and standard setting*, National Bureau of Economic Research.

Silverman, B. (1999). Technological resources and the direction of corporate diversification: toward an integration of the resource-based view and transaction cost economics. *Management Science*, 45(8), 1109–24.

Sull, D. (1997). No exit: overcapacity and plant closure in a declining industry. London Business School working paper.

Sull, D.N., Tedlow, R.S., and Rosenbloom, R.S. (1997). Managerial commitments and technological change in the US tire industry. *Industrial and Corporate Change*, 6, 2.

Teece, D.J. (1982). Towards an economic theory of the multiproduct firm. *Journal of Economic Behavior and Organization*, 3, 39–63.

Teece, D.J. (1986). Profiting from technological innovation: implications for integration, collaboration, licensing, and public policy. *Research Policy*, 15, 285–305.

Teece, D.J. (1998). Capturing value from knowledge assets. *California Management Review*, 40(3), 55–79.

Teece, D.J. (2000). *Managing intellectual capital*. Oxford University Press, 2000.

Teece, D.J., Pisano, G., and Shuen, A. (1997). Dynamic capabilities. *Strategic Management Journal*, 18(7), 509–33.

Tripsas, M. (1997). Unraveling the process of creative destruction: complementary assets and incumbent survival in the typesetter industry. *Strategic Management Journal*, 18, 119–42.

US Department of Justice (1995). *Antitrust guidelines for the licensing of intellectual property*. Department of Justice, Federal Trade Commission.

Wernerfelt, B. (1984). A resource based view of the firm. *Strategic Management Journal*, 5, 171–80.

Williams, J. (1994). Strategy and the search for rents. In R. Rumelt, D. Schendel, and D. Teece (eds), *Fundamental Issues in Strategy*, Harvard Business School Press.

Williamson, O.E. (1985). *The economic institutions of capitalism*. Free Press.

12

Individual Collaborations, Strategic Alliances and Innovation: Insights from the Biotechnology Industry

PAUL ALMEIDA, JAN HOHBERGER, AND PEDRO PARADA

INTRODUCTION

The knowledge intensive areas of our economy are characterized by rapid innovation fueled by technological and scientific advances. For firms competing in knowledge-based industries, continuous access to new information, know-how, and ideas is essential to success (Bierly and Chakrabarti, 1996). Firms create new knowledge through investments in R&D but, given the rapid pace of knowledge development around the world and the numerous scientific and technological frontiers along which innovation takes place, no firm can internally develop all the knowledge needed for success. Firms must, therefore, continuously access knowledge from other organizations including domestic and international firms, government laboratories, and universities (Arora and Gambardella, 1990; Powell *et al.*, 1996).

One of the approaches taken by firms to monitor external knowledge development, and to absorb this knowledge when useful, is to engage in strategic alliances. Strategic alliances are used in numerous industries to gain access to ideas, know-how, and expertise from other organizations (Inkpen, 1998). Empirical research has confirmed that alliances are an important source of scientific and technological knowledge (Mowery *et al.*, 1996; Powell *et al.*, 1996; Ahuja, 2000) and contribute to firm success (Stuart, 2000).

However, organizational collaborations in the form of strategic alliances are not the only source of external knowledge. Recent research, both conceptual and empirical, suggests that individual knowledge flows are an important form of learning. For instance, research on localized knowledge spillovers (Saxenian, 1994; Porter, 2000) explains that firms learn from each other through mechanisms other than formal alliances and that often individual employees play an important role in the sharing of ideas and information between firms. The role of the individual in creating knowledge bridges across organizations was highlighted in the early work of Diana

Handbook of Technology and Innovation Management. Edited by Scott Shane
© 2008 John Wiley & Sons, Ltd

Crane (1972) where she described the role of the 'invisible college of scientists' that helped diffuse knowledge within scientific communities. Research by Rappa and Debackere (1992) suggests similar activities between experts in technological communities, which also results in inter-firm knowledge diffusion. More recently, ethnographic research on web-based communities (Madanmohan and Navelkar, 2004) describes how the Internet facilitates the exchange of knowledge between individuals in distant locations and in a wide spectrum of technologies.

This individual-level exchange of knowledge can be expected to be particularly important in knowledge intensive industries. For example, Olk (1998) explores how individual-level relationships affect the formation process and structure of R&D consortia. The focus on the individual as a conduit for inter-firm knowledge flows is also evident from the work on mobile engineers and innovation in semiconductors (Almeida and Kogut, 1999). In biotechnology, research has highlighted the role played by collaborations between university star scientists and firms (Zucker et al., 2002) and the importance of communities of practice in sharing non-local knowledge (Gittelman, 2007). The preponderance of prior research suggests that individuals play an important role in facilitating and harnessing inter-organizational knowledge flows.

Though we have reason to believe that individuals collaborate (often informally) across firms, and access knowledge from external sources (Liebeskind et al., 1996; Gittelman and Kogut, 2003), several questions remain on the table. Do firms benefit from these individual-level collaborative activities? Do these activities enhance the innovativeness of the firms that employ these collaborating scientists? And, what is the relationship between strategic alliances and individual collaborations as regards firm innovation? We elaborate on the role of individual and organizational collaborations and its impact on innovation. Our main purpose it to establish basic propositions to guide future research on individual-level collaborations, its relationship to strategic alliances, and its impact on innovation. We build on some examples from the biotechnology industry as an example of a knowledge intensive industry. Next we explore the link between strategic alliances and innovation, individual collaborations and innovation, and the overall relation of strategic alliances, individual collaborations, and innovation. We build propositions for each relationship. Finally we present our conclusions and propositions for future research.

THE BIOTECHNOLOGY INDUSTRY: PREVIOUS RESEARCH FINDINGS

A knowledge intensive industry, such as biotechnology, is characterized by continuous scientific and technological change. Compared to traditional pharmaceutical firms that have developed their competitive advantage through capabilities linked to medicinal chemistry, biotechnology firms usually have expertise in the rapidly evolving field of molecular biology. Molecular biology has opened an array of new frontiers for research (including genomics, proteomics, genetic engineering, and gene therapy) and has also spawned hundreds of technologies (related to target identification, clinical trials, screening, bioinformatics) that can be applied to research processes (Pisano, 2002).

Thus there are an ever increasing number of 'locks and keys' particularly for pharmaceutical research and drug development and no firm can develop mastery on more than a few. In this rapidly changing industry, the sources of new scientific and technological knowledge come from an array of fields and a number of specialized firms, academic laboratories, and government institutions from around the globe (Arora and Gambardella, 1990; Powell *et al.*, 1996). Success in this industry can be related to expertise in basic science and also to associated technologies to test, develop, and commercialize scientific ideas (Bartholomew, 1997). In order to succeed in this industry, every firm must reach across their organizational boundaries to the sources of new knowledge capabilities on both the scientific and technological fronts (Liebeskind *et al.*, 1996.). Olk *et al.* (2005) look at the impact of personal and organizational ties on strategic alliance characteristics and performance in an international setting. Rothaermel and Hess (2007) show that individual level, firm level, and network level factors are not only important in their own right but also interact with each other with regard to innovative output. We focus next in exploring the individual level collaboration and the firm level collaboration in the form of strategic alliances.

Strategic alliances and innovation

The idea that alliances can lead to inter-firm learning is well documented in the strategic management literature. Hamel *et al.* (1989) explained that alliances can be used as part of a learning strategy. Subsequently, empirical and conceptual studies have supported this idea (Lyles and Salk, 1996; Dussauge *et al.*, 2000; Inkpen, 2000). For example, Rosenkopf and Almeida (2003) and Mowery *et al.* (1996) both use patent data to show that alliances facilitate inter-firm knowledge flows. Grant and Baden-Fuller (2004) suggest that strategic alliances may be useful not just for acquiring knowledge from partners but also for exploiting complementarities or 'accessing' partners' advantages. Thus, alliances may not only serve as a source of knowledge but also enhance the efficiency with which knowledge is applied in the firm.

In biotechnology, it can be argued that strategic alliances are extremely important to innovation. Given the technological and scientific changes taking place in the industry, and given the resource limitations of most stand-alone biotechnology firms, these organizations may need to follow a broad-based alliance strategy to avoid mediocrity. The literature suggests that biotechnology firms appear to follow strategies that use external alliances for knowledge acquisition to keep up with rapid changes in technology on a number of fronts as well as to access partners' capabilities (Powell *et al.*, 1996). Rothaermel and Deeds (2004) suggest that in biotechnology alliances can play the role of enhancing exploration and exploitation (the emphasis changes to the latter with increases in firm size). Baum *et al.* (2000) look at strategic alliances formed by biotechnology start-ups in Canada and find that alliances provide early access to information and enhance innovative performance. Looking at biotechnology firms in the Boston, MA, area, Owen-Smith and Powell (2004) show that geographic location and organizational form affect the inter-firm flow of knowledge across firms. Thus, although few studies explicitly measure inter-firm knowledge flows associated with alliances, the weight of conceptual and empirical literature suggests that strategic alliances can enhance innovation.

Individual collaborations and innovation

Though strategic alliances have many potential benefits to both accessing and exploiting knowledge, they are difficult to manage and costly to maintain (Gulati and Singh, 1998). This is especially true for small biotechnology firms that are often constrained in terms of their managerial and financial resources. Furthermore, the potential sources of useful information and knowledge are numerous and scattered and it may not be possible for even large firms to form alliances to access every possible source of relevant knowledge (Pisano, 2002). Most firms form only a limited number of strategic alliances in targeted areas. Over a 25-year period, on average each biotechnology firm formed an average of eight alliances (Rothaermel and Deeds, 2004).

Research suggests that an alternative mechanism of knowledge acquisition in biotechnology may be through the communities of practice to which the scientists belong (Liebeskind *et al.*, 1996). Scientists in biotechnology firms often have strong links to scientists in other firms, universities, and research institutions. Biotechnology firms usually grant their scientists a degree of autonomy to engage with members of the scientific community (Powell *et al.*, 1996). These communities extend beyond geographic and firm boundaries and can be useful sources for knowledge and information. They have a strong social dimension (common language and norms) that governs the flow of knowledge between researchers (Knorr-Cetina, 1999). Scientists simultaneously belong to organizational and scientific communities (Brown and Duguid, 2001) and often facilitate the flow of knowledge between these communities.

In biotechnology, these communities often give rise to research collaborations of scientists across firm boundaries that in turn strengthen the ties between scientists. Cockburn and Henderson (1998) suggest that collaboration enhances the productivity of a scientist's research. The product of these collaborations is often the publication of scientific papers. Why do scientists publish their research arising from individual or collaborative activities? Stephan (1996) points to the importance of 'priority' in scientific discovery and published papers establish the link between the individual and the discovery. Although organizations may or may not always supply incentives for their scientists to collaborate across firm boundaries, these collaborations provide organizations with an additional source of knowledge and expertise, and allow insights and access to the knowledge from a wider spectrum (geographically, organizationally, and scientifically) than formal alliances may permit. Cockburn and Henderson (1998) find that in the pharmaceutical industry, 'connectedness' between for-profit firms and publicly-funded research increases their performance in drug discovery.

Firms whose employees have engaged in a larger number of collaborations can be seen to have greater access to a common stock of community knowledge that sets the foundation for further knowledge development. These individual collaborations can be expected to enhance in-house innovative capabilities along developing technological or scientific trajectories, help monitor collaborative R&D processes elsewhere, and point the firm in the direction of future scientific research.

Individual collaborations, strategic alliances, and innovation

We proposed that strategic alliances and individual collaborations individually enhance innovation. This leads to questions regarding the relative roles that these two knowledge-acquiring mechanisms play with respect to firm innovativeness. One line of argument could be that the two types of collaborations act as complements. The informal collaboration of scientists across organizations could serve to enhance the formation and exploitation of formal strategic alliances or vice versa. Stuart *et al.* (2007) find that for biotechnology firms, the external networks of scientists of a firm facilitate the organizations' ability to identify and absorb university research. Scientists' connections within the research community permit them to evaluate the quality and potential fit of research conducted in other organizations and hence allow them to play a key role in evaluating biotechnology firms as potential alliance partners (Liebeskind *et al.*, 1996). The trust and understanding (Zaheer *et al.*, 1998; Brass *et al.*, 2004) built through informal collaborations could also enhance the management of these alliances, making them more useful as knowledge sharing mechanisms. Furthermore, individual collaborations could help a firm's scientists scan and search the market of ideas and technologies beyond the firm's reach and this knowledge combined with the knowledge sourced through strategic alliances could enhance the innovativeness of the firm. Rosenkopf and Almeida (2003) show that firms use informal means such as hiring of experts to fill gaps in their knowledge base. Perhaps informal collaborations could be used to complement the knowledge base acquired by more formal means.

An opposing view is that firms may not be able to employ two very different mechanisms for external sourcing, because they are dependent on fundamentally distinct organizational capabilities and routines. Various organizational attributes (structure, systems, processes, culture, and leadership) may align the organization more towards formal (strategic alliances) or informal (individual collaborations) forms of learning. After all, individual collaborations rise out of scientific communities that are characterized by unique norms and rules that are very different from those that lead to the formation of strategic alliances between firms (Merton, 1973; Dasgupta and David, 1994). By concentrating on one learning mechanism, firms build competences in one area and lose the ability to benefit from alternative forms of learning (Levitt and March, 1988). Previous research supports the idea that firms create and specialize in using different learning mechanisms, e.g. recruiting and retaining star scientists creates internal R&D capabilities, developing alliance capabilities, or superior acquisition and integration capabilities (Rothaermel and Hess, 2007). Proficiency in one innovation mechanism could impede them from developing expertise in alternative ones and therefore create competency traps (Levinthal and March, 1993). These arguments suggest that strategic alliances and individual collaborations may have a negative impact on each other and may not play complementary roles as regards firm innovativeness. Given the above arguments, the relationship between the two types of collaboration and their effect on firm innovativeness deserves careful examination.

The Biotechnology Industry: The View from Within the Industry

To better understand the role of individual collaborations in innovation, we conducted semi-structured interviews with ten scientists (senior scientific officers) from two European firms and eight US firms. Every interviewee had a Ph.D. and three previously held leading positions in university laboratories.

Our interviews suggest that individual collaborations are indeed an important part of the research process of biotechnology firms. When researchers need additional insights or knowledge inputs in areas they are investigating, they identify potential collaborators based on their personal and professional networks or simply based on an Internet search. As one researcher put it, they 'go down the list' until a suitable collaborator is found. The researchers in biotechnology firms and their academic partners have different motivations for collaboration. For researchers within firms, these collaborations are usually targeted to fill a particular knowledge gap that emerges during the research process. Although the immediate motivation for collaboration may be to successfully conduct research that leads to patentable inventions, this activity often leads to co-authored publications as well. This may explain why such a large percentage of publications in scientific journals have co-authors from different organizations. Small firms particularly use publications to gain legitimacy in the scientific and investment community. For university researchers, individual collaborations with firms are a source of funding, tools, and knowledge.

Our interviewees suggest that firms, in addition to individual collaborations, need strategic alliances to enhance their knowledge. They also highlight differences between the two. Individual collaborations are strongly rooted in the scientific community whereas strategic alliances are often driven by non-scientific managers. The researchers acknowledge that individual collaborations, usually with academic researchers, are much more informal in nature and are usually initiated and managed by the individuals themselves. Individual collaborations are based on personal relationships between researchers, whereas strategic alliances are more formal in nature and are planned and executed within the organizational bureaucracy. Individual collaborations are formed and managed based on the characteristics and knowledge of the individual researchers, whereas strategic alliances are based on broader organizational characteristics and capabilities. From the point of view of a scientist, the time and cost in building and maintaining strategic alliances often makes them unattractive. Scientists perceive individual collaboration to be faster and more flexible.

Our interviewees confirm that firms need to patent and publish scientific articles to protect their intellectual property and gain legitimacy. Particularly for small biotech companies that often have no products and markets, patents are a good indicator of innovative output, and are often used by potential investors to gage the success of firms. The publication of scientific articles is encouraged directly

TABLE 12.1 Main differences of individual collaborations and strategic alliances.

	Individual collaborations	*Strategic alliances*
Motivation for collaboration	Fill a particular knowledge gap	Formal agreement or contract
Collaborator identification	Personal and professional networks	Hierarchy driven
Type of knowledge	Basic and applied	Usually applied
Link to	University or research labs	Firm-to-firm
Outcome	Patents or publications	Usually patents
Role of patent or publication	Legitimacy	Protection of intellectual property
	Protection of intellectual property Source of funding	Current or future revenue stream

Source: authors, based on field research

and indirectly by the firm. The researchers, all of whom have both co-authored publication and patents, also agreed that co-authored publications are a good measure of the extent of individual collaborations and suggest that there is a direct link between the success of individual collaborations and subsequent patents.

An interesting question is to what extent both relationships provide access to different types of knowledge. Conventional wisdom suggests that universities are the source of knowledge related to basic research, whereas firms are the source of more applied knowledge. Our interviews suggest a muddier picture. Although it is true that most basic advances in the field are derived from university research, they are also a source of applied knowledge. A large number of interviewees suggest that firms gain substantial applied knowledge oriented towards the development of products through collaboration with universities. Table 12.1 summarizes the different roles played by Individual Collaborations and Strategic Alliances.

DISCUSSION

Our main proposition is that individual collaborations across organizations have a positive effect on innovation. Though prior research has suggested that actions of individual scientists and engineers play a role in the circulation of knowledge (Crane, 1972; Zucker *et al.*, 2002), the phenomenon of individual level collaboration and its effect on innovation has rarely been evaluated in empirical research. The actions of individuals are often less observable than firm-level actions and therefore hard to track. Fortunately, collaborations by biotechnology (and other) scientists do leave a paper trail. This trail seems appropriate to evaluate and illustrate the extent of these collaborations and their impact on innovation.

We believe that firms use two independent sources of knowledge for innovation. The two sources span levels of analysis (individual and organizational). By looking at the influence of strategic alliances, we build on a well-established stream of research that considers the effect of collaboration at the organizational level. We move beyond the emphasis on strategic alliances as collaborative mechanisms by highlighting the importance of individual collaborations on firm level innovation, thus highlighting the role of the underlying sociology of individuals in influencing observable organizational outcomes. In this way we add to the growing body of research that focuses on the implications of phenomena such as mobility of engineers (Song *et al.*, 2003) or hiring of star scientists. Our research agenda makes the point that it is necessary to move beyond the study of strategic alliances if we are to understand fully the impact of the range of collaborative arrangements on firm innovation.

Although strategic alliances positively impact organizational innovativeness, research points out that these alliances are difficult to form and manage, and small firms may be limited in their ability to learn in this way. Managers often see formal alliances as strategic learning tools and yet have difficulty fully exploiting them for success (Gulati and Singh, 1998; Kale *et al.*, 2002). We suggest that an alternative form of collaborations, those conducted at the individual-level, can significantly enhance a firm's knowledge base. The value of individual collaborations may not be fully recognized by researchers or understood by managers. The choice of learning mechanisms between strategic alliances and individual collaborations may have a strategic angle as well. If both mechanisms are useful for learning, the use of individual collaborations may have an advantage. They are less easily observable and therefore, due to the causal ambiguity associated with this mechanism of learning, are less likely to be imitable, suggesting implications for the sustainability of advantages obtained by employing this mechanism.

An issue worth investigating is the relative roles that strategic alliances and individual collaborations play in the innovative process. It seems that these two collaborative mechanisms provide access to distinct knowledge pools. Strategic alliances are generally firm-to-firm linkages whereas individual collaborations are more oriented towards firm-to-university (or research laboratory) linkages. This would suggest that these knowledge sources could play complementary roles. Field research indicates that firms would like to tap into both sources of knowledge but they may need different capabilities and routines to harness each mechanism effectively. For example, strategic alliances are often supported by formal organizational processes and structures (Dyer and Singh, 1998), whereas our interviews indicate that individual collaborations are much more informal in nature and enhanced by organizational flexibility. It may be difficult for organizations to combine the organic approach to manage individual collaborations with a more structured approach for organizational alliances.

FUTURE RESEARCH

Despite its importance for firms, research on individual collaborations is still scarce and therefore provides researchers an interesting avenue for future inquiry. For example, recent theoretical contributions (Dansereau *et al.*, 1999; Felin and Foss, 2005; Felin and Hesterly, 2007) have criticized the assumptions of single-level research as being limited because firm outcomes are often based on multi-level determinants that interact. Empirical research has begun to address this issue more specifically. For example, Rothaermel and Hess (2007) show that individual level, firm level, and network level factors are not only important in their own right but also interact with each other with regard to innovative output. We extended this line of multilevel research by proposing that firms' innovative output is influenced by organizational level collaboration *and* individual level collaborations, as well as the interaction effects between these levels. However, less is known about the process of how different levels affect each other. In-depth case study research might be needed to provide necessary data richness to extend our understanding of these micro processes.

Similarly, although a strong body of literature supports the view that single strategic alliances create value for firms, research focuses more and more on the perspective of a firm's alliance portfolio. A number of studies showed that the alliance portfolio is an interesting unit of analysis that raises a number of important theoretical and empirical issues that merit further scholarly research (Parise and Casher, 2003; Lavie, 2007). However, most existing studies have theoretically and empirically neglected interdependencies, such as synergies and conflicts that can occur between individual alliances in a firm's alliance portfolio. The study of individual collaborations not only presents a second form of an alliance portfolio but also raises the question of how two different alliance portfolios interact with each other.

Finally, during our interviews with senior managers we observed the importance of this topic for biotech firms. However, we also perceived the ambiguity of managers about how to deal with individual collaborations. Several managers asked directly for advice or at least descriptive findings to compare their behavior with other firms. Currently, procedures to manage individual collaborations are mainly based on personal experience of the senior staff or the founder. Therefore, biotech firms can benefit directly from research that reduces this ambiguity and provides orientation regarding managing individual collaborations to firms.

CONCLUSION

We highlight the important role that individual collaborations play in the innovative processes. We emphasize that researchers and managers alike must move beyond considerations of strategic alliances when exploring collaborative avenues for knowledge acquisition. Individual collaborations provide a different access to external knowledge, which needs distinct organizational capabilities. In the future, firms may learn how to develop capabilities linked with both types of collaborative activities simultaneously, to help them be more successful. Researchers need to investigate how organizations can meet this challenge.

REFERENCES

Ahuja, G. (2000). Collaboration networks, structural holes, and innovation: a longitudinal study. *Administrative Science Quarterly*, 45(3), 425.

Almeida, P., and Kogut, B. (1999). Localization of knowledge and the mobility of engineers in regional networks. *Management Science*, 45(7), 905–18.

Arora, A., and Gambardella, A. (1990). Complementarity and external linkages: the strategies of the large firms in biotechnology. *Journal of Industrial Economics*, 38(4), 361.

Bartholomew, S. (1997). National systems of biotechnology innovation: complex interdependence in the global system. *Journal of International Business Studies*, 28(2), 241.

Baum, J.A.C., Calabrese, T. and Silverman, B.S. (2000). Don't go it alone: alliance network composition and startups' performance in Canadian biotechnology. *Strategic Management Journal*, 21(3), 267–94.

Bierly, P., and Chakrabarti, A. (1996). Generic knowledge strategies in the U.S. pharmaceutical industry. *Strategic Management Journal*, 17(Winter Special Issue), 123–35.

Brass, D.J., Galaskiewicz, J., and Greve, H.R. (2004). Taking stock of networks and organizations: a multilevel perspective. *Academy of Management Journal*, 47, 795–817.

Brown, J.S., and Duguid, P. (2001). Knowledge and organization: a social-practice perspective. *Organization Science*, 12(2), 198–212.

Cockburn, I.M., and Henderson, R.M. (1998). Absorptive capacity, coauthoring behavior, and the organization of research in drug discovery. *Journal of Industrial Economics*, 46(2), 157–82

Crane, D. (1972). *Invisible colleges. Diffusion of knowledge in scientific communities*. University of Chicago Press.

Dansereau, F., Yammarino, F.J., and Kohles, J.C. (1999). Multiple levels of analysis from a longitudinal perspective: Some implications for theory building. *Academy of Management Review*, 24(2), 346.

Dasgupta, P., and David, P. (1994). Towards a new economics of science. *Research Policy*, 23, 487–521.

Dussauge, P., Garrette, B., and Mitchell, W. (2000). Learning from competing partners: outcomes and durations of scale and link alliances in Europe, North America and Asia. *Strategic Management Journal*, 21(7), 99–126.

Dyer, J., and Singh, H. (1998). The relational view: cooperative strategy and sources of interorganizational competitive advantage. *Academy of Management Review*, 23(4), 660–79.

Felin, T., and Foss, N. (2005). Strategic organization: a field in search of micro-foundations. *Strategic Organization*, 3(4), 441–55.

Felin, T., and Hesterly, W.S. (2007). The knowledge-based view, nested heterogeneity, and new value creation: philosophical considerations on the locus of knowledge. *Academy of Management Review*, 32(1), 195–218.

Gittelman, M. (2007). Does geography matter for science-based firms? Epistemic communities and the geography of research and patenting in biotechnology. *Organization Science*, 18, 724–741.

Gittelman, M., and Kogut, B. (2003). Does good science lead to valuable knowledge? Biotechnology firms and the evolutionary logic of citation patterns. *Management Science*, 49(4), 366.

Grant, R.M., and Baden-Fuller, C. (2004). A knowledge assessing theory of strategic alliances. *Journal of Management Studies*, 41(1), 61–81.

Gulati, R., and Singh, H. (1998). The architecture of cooperation: managing coordination costs and appropriation concerns in strategic alliances. *Administrative Science Quarterly*, 43(4), 781.

Hamel, G., Doz, Y., and C.K. Prahalad, C.K. (1989). Collaborate with your competitors and win. *Harvard Business Review*, 67(1), 133–40.

Inkpen, A.C. (1998). Learning, knowledge acquisition, and strategic alliances. *European Management Journal*, 16(2), 223–30.

Inkpen, A.C. (2000). Learning through joint ventures: a framework of knowledge acquisitions. *Journal of Management Studies*, 37(7), 1019–34.

Kale, P., Dyer, J.H., and Singh, H. (2002). Alliance capability, stock market response, and long-term alliance success: the role of the alliance function. *Strategic Management Journal*, 23(8), 747–67.

Knorr-Cetina, K. (1999). *Epistemic culture*. Harvard University Press.

Lavie, D. (2007). Alliance portfolios and firm performance. A study of value creation and appropriation in the US software industry. *Strategic Management Journal*, (28)12, 1187–1212.

Levinthal, D.A., and March, J.G. (1993). The myopia of learning. *Strategic Management Journal*, 14, 95–112.

Levitt, B., and March, J.G. (1988). Organizational Learning. *Annual Review of Sociology*. 14, 319–40.

Liebeskind, J.P., Oliver, A.L., Zucker, L., and Brewer. M. (1996). Social networks, learning and flexibility: sourcing scientific knowledge in new biotechnology firms. *Organization Science*, 7(4), 428–43.

Lyles, M.A., and Salk, J.E. (1996). Knowledge acquisition from foreign parents in international joint ventures: an empirical examination in the Hungarian context. *Journal of International Business Studies*, 27(5), 877–903.

Madanmohan, T.R., and Navelkar, S. (2004). Roles and knowledge management in online technology communities: an ethnography study. *International Journal of Web Based Communities*. 1(1), 71–89.

Merton, R.K. (1973). *The sociology of science. Theoretical and empirical investigations*. University of Chicago Press.

Mowery, D., Oxly, J., and Silverman, B. (1996). Strategic alliances and interfirm knowledge transfer. *Strategic Management Journal*, 17(2), 77–91.

Olk, P. (1998). A knowledge-based perspective on the transformation of individual-level relationships into interorganizational structures: the case of R&D consortia. *European Management Journal*, 16(1), 36–49.

Olk, P., Gabbay, S., and Chung, T. (2005). The impact of personal and organizational ties on strategic alliance characteristics and performance: a study of alliances in the USA, Israel, and Taiwan. In A. Arino, P. Ghemawat, and J.E. Ricart (eds), *Creating Value Through International Strategy*. Palgrave Publishing, 201–213.

Owen-Smith, J., and Powell, W.W. (2004). Knowledge networks as channels and conduits: the effects of spillovers in the Boston biotechnology community. *Organization Science*, 15(1), 5–21.

Parise, S., and Casher, A. (2003). Alliance portfolios: designing and managing your network of business-partner relationships. *Academy of Management Executive*, 17(4), 25–39.

Pisano, G. (2002). Pharmaceutical biotechnology. In R.R. Nelson, D.G. Victor, and B. Steil (eds), *Technological Innovation and Economic Performance*. Princeton University Press.

Porter, M.E. (2000.) Location, competition, and economic development: local clusters in a global economy. *Economic Development Quarterly*, 4(1), 15–34.

Powell, W., Koput, K.W., and Smith-Doerr, L. (1996). Interorganizational collaboration and the locus of innovation: network learning in biotechnology. *Administrative Science Quarterly*, 41(1), 116–45.

Rappa, M.A., and Debackere, K. (1992). Technology communities and the diffusion of knowledge. *R&D Management*, 22(3), 209–20.

Rosenkopf, L., and Almeida, P. (2003). Overcoming local search through alliances and mobility. *Management Science*, 49(6), 751–66.

Rothaermel, F.T., and Deeds, D.L. (2004). Exploration and exploitation alliances in biotechnology: a system of product development. *Strategic Management Journal*, 25(3), 202–21.

Rothaermel, F.T., and Hess, A.M. (2007). Building dynamic capabilities: innovation driven by individual, firm and network level effects. *Organization Science*, 18(3), 358–73.

Saxenian, A. (1994). Lessons from silicon valley. *Technology Review*, 97(5), 42.

Song, J., Almeida, P., and Wu, G. (2003). Learning-by-hiring: when is mobility more likely to facilitate interfirm knowledge transfer? *Management Science*, 49(4), 351–65.

Stephan, P.E. (1996). The economics of science. *Journal of Economic Literature*, XXXIV (September), 1199–235.

Stuart, T.E. (2000). Interorganizational alliances and the performance of firms: a study of growth and innovation rates in a high-technology industry. *Strategic Management Journal*, 21(8), 791–811.

Stuart, T.E., Ozdemir, S.Z., and Ding, W.W. (2007). Vertical alliance networks: the case of university-biotechnology-pharmaceutical alliance chains. *Research Policy*, 36(4), 477–98.

Zaheer, A., McEvily, B., and Perrone, V. (1998). Does trust matter? Exploring the effects of interorganizational and interpersonal trust on performance. *Organization Science*, 9, 141–59.

Zucker, L.G., Darby, M.R., and Armstrong, J.S. (2002). Commercializing knowledge: university science, knowledge capture, and firm performance in biotechnology. *Management Science*, 48(2), 149–70.

Part V

WHO INNOVATES?

13

Technology-Based Entrepreneurship

David H. Hsu

This chapter addresses the field of technology-based entrepreneurship (TBE). My goal is to provoke discussion and hopefully spur research in a few directions rather than attempt an exhaustive treatment of the subject. Technology entrepreneurship is a field that draws from two research areas: the study of technical innovation on the one hand, and the study of entrepreneurship on the other. Like these research areas, rather than being oriented around any particular academic discipline, the field tends to be organized around a phenomenon. In my discussion throughout this chapter, I will therefore be drawing on multiple academic disciplines that contribute to our understanding of TBE, though my bias is on management issues associated with the phenomenon.[1] In addition, although I use a framing of new ventures developed to commercialize innovation, most of the discussion will also be of relevance to entrepreneurial efforts within the setting of established firms.

The study of TBE appears to have emerged in the early 1960s (Roberts, 2004), perhaps with the rise of research-based new ventures emerging from Silicon Valley and the Boston area companies. Although academic interest in TBE appears to have grown alongside the economic importance of the phenomenon, scholars at least since Joseph Schumpeter have understood entrepreneurs as efficiency-inducing change agents in the economy. One might argue that efficiency in the capitalist system is importantly driven by entrepreneurial actors who seize on previously unexploited economic opportunities. From a societal standpoint, it might be necessary to have a lot of experimentation in business ventures to discover the 'right' ones, and although there might be organizational failure in such a system, overall social efficiency may be enhanced by entrepreneurial experimentation. For the entrepreneurs of new firms that survive and flourish,

---

[1] There is also obvious overlap with some of the other chapters contained in this volume. When this is likely to be the case, I will concentrate my discussion on a few points and refer the interested reader to more in-depth discussion in the other chapters.

Handbook of Technology and Innovation Management. Edited by Scott Shane
© 2008 John Wiley & Sons, Ltd

there may be tremendous associated wealth creation – and it is these rewards that can help induce entrepreneurial entry. TBE is distinguished from other forms of entrepreneurial entry by being innovation-based, which may be construed as a barrier to entry. The job creation and potential economic development effects have led some national governments, such as Singapore, to promote TBE as an industrial policy (known as 'technopreneurship' in Singapore).

Although such macroeconomic effects may be quite important, I will concentrate my remarks and discussions to studies of individual- or firm-level behavior. Also, though there are many public policy implications for some of the topics that are discussed, the main purpose of this chapter is to explore business policy. As such, the decision maker will most often be an entrepreneur or potential entrepreneur, and research questions are framed from this perspective.

This chapter is organized to dovetail a stylized process of new venture development: new venture origins, human and financial resource assembly, strategizing, and growth and harvesting. Each of these areas is broad, and so my approach is to identify certain aspects and key questions that technology-based entrepreneurs face at each of these phases of venture development. I then discuss the approaches used in the literature to tackle these questions, and end each section with some thoughts on potential directions for future research in each domain.

New Venture Origins

The recent literature has underscored the proposition that entrepreneurial opportunities are ephemeral and transitory (e.g., Shane and Venkataraman, 2000), and so such windows of opportunity can open and shut over time. This structure, coupled with the high rate of entrant failures (e.g., Dunne, Roberts, and Samuelson, 1988), has led some researchers to ask whether entrepreneurial entry is economically rational, or in the alternative, entrepreneurs exhibit over-optimism and/or misperceived risk (e.g., Camerer and Lovallo, 1999; Moskowitz and Vissing-Jorgenson, 2002). In an early study, Cooper et al. (1988) found that 68 % of their surveyed entrepreneurs thought that the odds of their business succeeding was better than other businesses similar to theirs (only 5 % thought their odds were worse). Camerer and Lovallo (1999) find that their experimental subjects accurately forecast negative industry profits and enter anyway, and Moskowitz and Vissing-Jorgenson (2002) find that private equity returns do not seem to offer a premium to public equity. Although these three studies offer evidence from three methods (survey-based, experimental, and empirical) that appear consistent with the proposition that overconfidence is at the root of entrepreneurial entry, it may still be worthwhile to rule out explicitly more rational economic explanations. Two such explanations come to mind: first, entrepreneurs might be aware of the positively-skewed distribution of risk and reward associated with striking out on their own, but prefer buying a 'lottery ticket' in the off-chance that they end up in the right tail of the distribution. Second, individuals may have sufficiently high utility for nonpecuniary benefits associated with entrepreneurial activities that some expected monetary effects are overwhelmed.[2]

[2]It would be interesting to study if and how individual overconfidence interacts with technology quality.

After the entry decision is made, at least two types of knowledge are important as inputs into the entrepreneurial process for technology-based ventures: commercial and technical knowledge. It might be argued that the relative importance of technical as compared to commercial knowledge diminishes with stage of new venture development (and vice versa). For the moment, let us hold technical knowledge constant and discuss the role of commercial knowledge in the new venture formation process (in the next section, I discuss the effects of variation in technical knowledge).

Commercial knowledge

An important recent theme in the literature is that there may be substantial differences among entrants, particularly in the 'pre-history' of new venture development. These studies collectively consider the characteristics of the parent organization from which entrepreneurs were 'spawned', as well as the prior experience of the entrepreneurial individual or team. Although some studies emphasize one dimension or the other, I discuss them together because they shed insight into reasons for observed entrant heterogeneity.

In addressing the area of entrepreneurial origins of high-technology firms, it is hard to ignore the importance of new ventures that spin-off from more established firms. Bhide (1994, p. 151), in a survey of the Inc. '500' fastest growing private companies, for example, found that 71 % had 'replicated or modified an idea encountered through previous employment'. Examples from the electronics industries (e.g., semiconductors, lasers, and hard disk drives) come readily to mind. Spin-offs of Fairchild Semiconductor (e.g., Intel, Advanced Micro Devices, and National Semiconductor) and Xerox Corporation (e.g., 3Com and Adobe) are often cited as examples of this phenomenon.[3] One set of studies has examined the characteristics of the spawning parent, asking the question: What types of parent organizations are more likely to spin-off progeny? In a cross-industry study of spawned venture capital-backed firms, Gompers, Lerner, and Scharfstein (2005) contrast two alternate views of the spawning process. In the first, would-be entrepreneurs prepare themselves (including through a process of social contagion), and become entrepreneurs by being exposed to the entrepreneurial process and developing network links with suppliers and customers while working at an established organization. A second view of the spin-off process is that bureaucratic organizations are reluctant to commercialize innovations, and so frustrated individuals leave the parent firm to strike out on their own. Although both accounts are likely to be true to a certain extent, Gompers, Lerner, and Scharfstein (2005) find more support for the employee learning rather than the organizational failure view in explaining venture capital-backed spin-offs. A second study, Agarwal et al. (2004), examined spin-offs in the hard disk drive industry and found that incumbents with both strong market pioneering and technical knowledge generated fewer spin-offs

---

[3]Anton and Yao (1994) found that there are conditions under which inventor-employees will start their own spin-off even though joint profits would have been larger had the parent organization exploited the invention (due to incentive conflicts arising from inventions that require little start-up capital and have weak or no property rights).

than did firms with competence in only one of these areas. These results seem consistent with the view that individuals compare their opportunity costs of staying with an incumbent organization with their beliefs about the potential size of an entrepreneurial opportunity when considering a spin-off venture.

A related domain of research has tried to better understand what exactly is transferred from the parent to the spin-off organization. The studies in this arena have found that the parent organization's capabilities at the time of spin-off are significantly related to the progeny's subsequent performance. Agarwal *et al.* (2004) found this result in the hard drive industry using probability of spin-off survival as the performance metric. This effect may not be confined to technology-intensive industries. Phillips (2002) found that spin-offs of Silicon Valley law firms received resources and routines from the parent organization, which increased survival likelihoods of the spin-off while decreasing them for the parent. As in the legal market, commercializing technical products requires specialized human capital, so there are some linkages between the two settings. Burton, Sorensen, and Beckman (2002) suggest that status effects are transferred from the parent organization to the offspring. In their study of Silicon Valley high-tech firms, they find that the status of the entrepreneurs' previous employers is positively related to the likelihood that the start-up secures financing at the founding of the new venture. The status effect is consistent with the view that resource providers regard the reputation of entrepreneurial affiliates as a signal of entrepreneurs' underlying quality.

Another set of studies in the spin-off literature has tried to understand the effects of experience associated with prior employment. The emergence and early history of the automobile industry has been the subject of a few studies in this regard. Klepper (2002) found that 'while diversifying firms on average outperformed *de novo* entrants, *de novo* entrants founded by individuals that worked for the leading automobile firms outperformed all firms and dominated the industry' (p. 645). Similarly, Carroll *et al.* (1996) found that entrants with pre-production experience and prototypes in the auto industry had lower mortality rates relative to those without such experience. Both studies suggest important heterogeneity among new entrants in this industry, and the results are consistent with the hypothesis that knowledge of quality production processes and/or business relationships with key actors such as suppliers or customers are associated with organizations' ability to innovate and effectively commercialize innovations, which may ultimately correlate with firm performance. Consistent with these auto studies, research in other industries also suggests that experienced entrants, especially those that have a background in a related industry, are advantaged relative to *de novo* entrants when new industries are born. Klepper and Simons (2000) find, for example, that 'no non-radio producer ever captured a significant share of the television market' (p. 998).

Finally, in a study that is not situated in the spin-off literature, Shane (2000) studies the effects of prior experience on how individuals recognize and interpret an entrepreneurial opportunity. For a given technology developed at MIT (three-dimensional printing), which was available for licensing, different individuals perceived different commercial opportunities depending on their prior knowledge and experience. This study nicely illustrates a fundamental point about the nature of entrepreneurial opportunities: the information set about potential ways to exploit a given entrepreneurial opportunity is not uniform across individuals – but rather is heterogeneous across the population of potential entrepreneurs. Furthermore, individuals are likely to differ in their opportunity costs to engaging in entrepreneurship, as well as in their beliefs about the likely size of a given entrepreneurial opportunity.

It appears that recognition of technology-based entrepreneurial opportunities is a complex function of active search, problem solving ability, prior knowledge, and serendipity. If the four elements identified here are indeed elements of the entrepreneurial production function, new venture creation would appear to involve opportunity recognition and entrepreneurial opportunity creation based on entrepreneurial conjectures (Shane and Venkataraman, 2000). Moreover, several of the inputs depend on individual investments rather than stable individual or personality differences.

Overall, the research discussed in this section has highlighted two important issues: first, there are significant differences among entrepreneurial founding teams (especially in their pre-venture history), and second, that some organizational 'genetic' material is passed on from incumbent to spin-off organization. Looking to the future, it would be interesting to further investigate three issues. First, a deeper understanding of what exactly is typically 'inherited' from incumbent organizations (and why?) would be worthwhile. Second, although the within-industry studies in this literature that track the origins of the entrants from the beginning of the industry allow detailed analyses that shed a great deal of insight on entry in emergent industries, it would be interesting from a prescriptive standpoint to better understand what might be important in more generic situations. Restated, because most individuals can treat innovations that become the basis of new industries as exogenous events for which timing is highly uncertain, what general entrepreneurial skills and experience importantly separate would-be entrepreneurs in non-new industry settings?[4]

Finally, the results of these studies also suggest that potential selection effects in the entry process are important (and should be considered when doing studies of this kind). Klepper and Simons (2000) find that more experienced radio firms were more likely to enter television manufacturing (and succeed when they did so). In a broader assessment of this literature, Helfat and Lieberman (2002) conclude that there seems to be growing evidence that entry is more likely to succeed if founders feel that their resources and capabilities are well suited to entry, again suggesting an important potential selection effect leading to observed entrants.

Technical knowledge

So far the technical component of technology-based venture origins has been left untouched. In this section, therefore, I discuss three dimensions of technical knowledge as it relates to entrepreneurial origins: local technological search, knowledge spillovers, and intellectual property.

---

[4]Not only can entrants differ with respect to prior industry work experience (in a related or unrelated industry), but they may also differ in their founding experience. Such 'serial entrepreneurs' might be advantaged in the timing and valuation of received external financial resources (Hsu, 2007), as well as in resource attainment more generally.

Individuals are likely to vary in their degree of technical knowledge that may be germane to new venture formation. In this section, it will be useful to consider a setting in which commercial knowledge is fixed, and examine the effects of changes in technical knowledge. Individuals or teams of individuals have different stocks of technical knowledge and training, and so may have differential abilities to recognize and understand the commercial consequences of technical knowledge. Although founders can assemble entrepreneurial team members with diverse knowledge sets (Eisenhardt and Schoonhoven, 1990) with varied implication organizational behavior (Beckman, 2006), the corresponding authority transfer given to additional founding team members can have business policy and 'imprinting' effects on the venture's subsequent development (more on this below).

With a given collection of founders, the technological search process of the new venture is often characterized as locally circumscribed. The underpinnings for this behavior have been explored at multiple levels of analysis, ranging from individual-level explanations of bounded rationality (March and Simon, 1958) to firm-level capabilities, routines, and learning myopia (Nelson and Winter, 1982). New venture 'imprinting' by their founders (Stinchcombe, 1965) and firms' initial conditions (Cockburn, Henderson, and Stern, 2000) also suggest alternative mechanisms by which firms' search behavior is perpetuated. To the extent that the founders' entrepreneurial conjectures are correct, and entry is profitable, local search processes may not be as problematic, though the transitory nature of entrepreneurial opportunities might make such entry timing difficult.

In environments in which innovation is important as the basis for competition, firms and their managers may be particularly concerned about the long-term competitive effects of local search (March, 1991). Not surprisingly, then, there has been considerable interest in mechanisms associated with overcoming local search, particularly in the context of firms in research and development-based industries. For example, Mowery, Oxley, and Silverman (1996) examine strategic alliances as a mechanism for overcoming local search. Engineers are mobile, and their movement is another means by which firms can overcome local search (Rosenkopf and Almeida, 2003). Even with a given technological starting point, entrepreneurs will draw on knowledge from other technological domains in varying intensities, representing another possible means to overcome local search behavior (Hsu and Lim, 2007). This study also finds that firms' degree of technological search is responsive to changes in the business and commercialization environment, a finding consistent with Cockburn, Henderson, and Stern (2000), who find that initial founding effects are indeed important, but are not all-encompassing in determining organizational practices on innovation.

A second area of research related to technical knowledge observes that because appropriability of technical knowledge is imperfect (authors of such knowledge are rarely able to capture the full financial return associated with their invention), agents in the economy have the possibility of capturing knowledge spillovers. The ability to recognize and integrate extramural knowledge – an actor's absorptive capacity (Cohen and Levinthal, 1990) – represents an alternative path (outside of own knowledge generation) to exploiting technical knowledge. The circumstances surrounding the commercialization of biotechnology illustrate the phenomenon of new organizations choosing geographic locations to attempt specialized scientific knowledge capture. At the beginning of commercial applications of biotechnology (recombinant DNA technology), the relevant technical knowledge was highly specialized and primarily resident in institutions of higher education (Kenney, 1986). Commercial operations disproportionately located their operations near such knowledge centers (and their associated 'star' scientists) in hopes of being able to capture potential knowledge spillovers (Zucker, Darby, and Brewer, 1998). More generally, the locality of knowledge flows as evidenced through patent citations (Jaffe, Trajtenberg, and Henderson, 1993) suggests that knowledge exchange tends to be local, perhaps as a result of knowledge tacitness that can become 'unstuck' (Von Hippel, 1994) through social interactions. Recent evidence suggests, however, that the Jaffe, Trajtenberg, and Henderson (1993) results may need revisiting, as a different method of constructing control patents attenuates the locality of patent citations effect (Thompson and Fox-Kean, 2005).

Geographic location may also be important to new venture creation for a reason other than knowledge spillovers. Certain geographic areas may be associated with different cultures of risk taking and career norms, which may differ even within technology intensive regions (e.g., Silicon Valley versus Boston's Route 128 area (Saxenian, 1994)). In regions in which entrepreneurial failure is stigmatized, individuals tend to be more hesitant to experiment with new ventures, which can lead to higher costs of start-up capital (Landier, 2006).

A final area of technical knowledge is intellectual property existence and strength as applied to knowledge transfer relevant to venture creation. Intellectual property licensing in this regard has recently received attention because of the potential for value enhancement both to the technology owner (e.g., corporations and universities (Arora, Fosfuri, and Gambardella, 2001; Gans, Hsu, and Stern, 2002)) as well as to start-up licensees of intellectual property (e.g., Shane, 2001a; 2001b). University technology licensing is a fortuitous setting to study technology transfer as the basis for ventures both because of data availability (through, for example, the Association of University Technology Managers, AUTM) and because the possibility of strategic effects of potential self-commercialization is remote (these conditions may not be true in the corporate setting). The empirical context of university technology licensing is an interesting setting in its own right as a source of technological input to new ventures. 214 US academic institutions accounted for a total of 450 new startups through technology licensing in the fiscal year 2002, and since 1980, 4320 new companies have formed based on university technology licenses, with 2741 still operating as of fiscal year 2002 (http://www.autm.net/about/dsp.licensing_surveys.cfm). Using data from technology licensed from MIT, Shane (2001a; 2001b) found support for enhanced likelihoods of new venture formation as a function of patent radicalness, importance, scope, and effectiveness. Again in the MIT context, Agrawal and Henderson (2002) found that knowledge diffusion via patenting among electrical engineering and computer science faculty represented only a minority of overall knowledge flows (scientific paper publishing and graduate student training were perhaps more important). In situations in which relevant knowledge is complex, tacit, and/or embryonic, which is typically true in university technologies, there may be few substitutes for inventor involvement and/or scientific exchange to aid commercial development of the invention, though inventors may have to be given appropriate incentives to do so (Jensen and Thursby, 2001).

In summary, recent contributions have added to our understanding of the technical knowledge inputs to the origins of technology-based ventures. I conclude this section by mentioning one potential research area spurred by this discussion: What explains organization-level heterogeneity in the ability to absorb extramural knowledge in settings in which the sources of relevant technical knowledge are more diffuse and/or uncertain? This is a difficult problem to address, and may require a different initial research strategy than constructing a large dataset, because the mechanism of capturing knowledge spillovers may be better understood in ways that may be difficult to address immediately if a larger dataset comes at the likely expense of more granular detail. Although much of the research in technology-based entrepreneurship (and innovation) has made progress by studying the medical science areas (where we know a great deal about the institutional features of the phenomenon, and for which we now have readily-available data sources), much interesting economic activity takes place in other institutional settings – and the field would benefit from studies drawn from a broader domain of industrial fields.

RESOURCE ASSEMBLY

After developing and evaluating the venture idea, the next step in the process of venture development is to secure human and financial resources. Although this conceptualization of linear development is very much stylized (i.e., in the process of trying to obtain resources, the venture idea and business model may be amended), I use this scheme for expositional ease. The main challenges that technical entrepreneurs face during the resource assembly stage are recruiting talented technical workers and managers and convincing financial resource holders to fund the new venture. These challenges are exacerbated for early stage ventures with mostly intangible, intellectual-based assets. I concentrate on relatively early stage ventures in this discussion because ventures that receive early buy-in from resource holders are likely to be the ones that benefit from a virtuous upward cycle of business development, and so entrepreneurial challenges may be most demanding in the early stages of development. I discuss the literature addressing human resource and then financial resource assembly, and conclude by posing some possible future directions in this literature.

A preliminary observation is worth noting before jumping into the discussion: it is important to establish some baseline expectations of why entrepreneurs differ in resource assembly. It would seem that the market for resources is relatively efficient in the sense that ventures of a given quality are matched with resources of commensurate quality. Quality in this setting might include at least the following dimensions:

- *ex ante* levels of human and social capital; and
- *ex ante* technological quality.

It might be useful to conceptualize these quality dimensions as 'controls' in an analysis, because these dimensions are well-established in the literature.

In this discussion of recruiting human resources, I first briefly consider recruiting managers and executives in start-ups. I then devote more attention to examining the technical labor market in the context of new ventures. Personnel at start-ups are typically compensated in a scheme that has a fixed component (wage) and a variable one (equity). Although the fixed component is likely to be smaller than for employment at more established firms, the entrepreneurial contract is meant to allow employee sharing of potential upside gains. Liquidity on the variable component of compensation is usually deferred (sometimes forever!), possibly making recruitment challenging as potential employees examine their opportunity costs. Although my focus here is not on optimal compensation schemes, it may be useful to consider the relative weighting of rewarded dimensions of merit in allocating equity to personnel. Because compensation schemes are meant to induce managerial and employee behavior, a clearer understanding of *what behavior* should be rewarded in the context of high-technology ventures is in order. Some candidate dimensions of personnel merit include: venture idea origination and evaluation, business plan preparation, commitment to the venture, skills and relevant business experience, and level of responsibility, and so on. Relevant compensation policy decisions, for example, might include the relative equity weighting assigned to historical contributions (e.g., venture idea origination) versus forward-looking contributions (e.g., effort toward shipping a product).

Most of my discussion in this section, however, is on other dimensions of human resource assembly. Stern (2004) finds that in the Ph.D. biologist labor market (which spans academia and private industry), scientists are willing to tradeoff monetary returns for utility-generating job dimensions (such as the ability to pursue, at least in part, their own scientific agenda). Henderson and Cockburn (1994) find that in the setting of pharmaceutical drug discovery efforts, human resource policies that promote scientists based on public science norms (publishing in top peer-reviewed academic journals) are associated with drug discovery productivity. This finding is consistent with the proposition that scientists working in pharmaceutical drug discovery value avoiding private industry-specific career investments (retaining the option of potentially crossing boundaries between academia and industry), and so higher ability scientists may be attracted to business environments featuring 'open science' policies.

Evidence on human resource practices and recruiting from a broader set of high-tech industries featuring entrepreneurial companies comes from the Stanford Project on Emerging Companies (SPEC). Baron, Burton, and Hannan (1996) describe this longitudinal dataset of Silicon Valley firms spanning technology-intensive industrial segments, and categorize firms into one of five archetypes according to the founders' organization of human resource practices (there is variation of human resource models within industries in their sample). These archetypes take into account employee attachment, coordination and control, and new venture selection of employees. Hannan, Burton, and Baron (1996) find that some human resource archetypes are less stable than others from the viewpoint of transition rates to nonfounder CEOs, but are also the same employment models that experienced higher rates of initial public offerings.

Both the Henderson and Cockburn (1994) and the SPEC studies link business policies to organizational performance outcomes. Armed with these results, it would seem that founders and managers of technology-oriented entrepreneurial ventures would rapidly converge on the performance-enhancing practices identified by these studies. As Henderson (1994) reports, a simple change in promotion policy without accompanying changes to accommodate the exchange of knowledge across external and internal boundaries of the firm should not be considered an organizational competence. To the extent that adoption of an optimal human resource archetype is contingent on post-founding factors, we may believe that changing human resource policies might be worthwhile. Baron, Hannan, and Burton (2001), however, find that such organizational changes can be disruptive, leading to higher employee turnover rates. In any case, a deeper understanding of what accounts for the slow diffusion of organizational practices that have been associated with firm performance (or the persistent *non*-diffusion of such practices) would seem worthwhile.

I also discuss two additional areas for possible future research in the area of human resource assembly for entrepreneurial ventures. First, much of what we know about corporate open science policies comes from the health science industries (and primarily from drug discovery efforts in pharmaceutical or biotechnology firms). It would be interesting to investigate the policy's generality and boundary conditions (under what circumstances do costs of such policies exceed benefits?). Lewis and Yao (2003) have made some progress in this area by modeling how such open R&D policies can vary as a function of the business environment (including labor market, product development, and intellectual property conditions).

Since human resource assets are typically disproportionately important to the long run competitiveness of innovation-intensive firms, losing valuable scientists or engineers with specialized knowledge stocks could devastate firms. A second potential area of research would therefore examine productivity consequences of knowledge worker turnover, both for the knowledge worker, as well as for the firms involved. Groysberg, Nanda, and Nohria (2004) suggest that mobility of star investment bank professionals is associated with productivity losses both individually and for the firm the knowledge worker joins. Do the same results hold for scientists and engineers?

A second major input to new venture development is financial resources. Evans and Leighton (1989) find that men with greater assets are more likely to switch into self-employment, inferring that entrepreneurs face liquidity constraints. A focal point in this literature has been on venture capital (VC), which is not surprising given the fact that this institutional form has taken steps to design specialized mechanisms to permit funding new ventures (e.g., Gompers and Lerner, 1999; Hsu and Kenney, 2005).[5] Because the financing of innovation is covered elsewhere in this volume, my discussion here is brief, and I do not propose specific research directions in this area.

[5]For early stage firms, more informal means of financing (through 'angel' investors and friends and family) are also likely to be important. Systematic studies of angel investors have been elusive, however, due to the typically informal and private nature of this market. Corporate venture capital (CVC) represents another source of entrepreneurial funding. Dushnitsky (2004) studies the conditions under which an entrepreneur chooses to approach a CVC versus an independent venture capitalist.

The recent empirical literature on VC has highlighted not only the financial intermediation role of VCs, but also their extra-financial role in start-up business development. This literature has highlighted the role of VCs in business development, including start-up product development, human resource management professionalization, and strategic alliance formation (Hellmann and Puri, 2000, 2002; Hsu, 2006).

Two main mechanisms have been proposed to enable entrepreneurial funding. The first is a contractual approach in which financial resource holders offer funding under rather stringent conditions, which serves the function of screening entrepreneurial type (e.g., Kaplan and Strömberg, 2003). A second research stream has suggested that when the quality of a start-up cannot be directly observed, external actors rely on the quality of the start-up's affiliates as a signal of the start-up's own quality. (e.g., Megginson and Weiss, 1991, and Stuart, Hoang, and Hybels, 1999). This certification-based approach may help legitimate startups and entrepreneurs without a prior track record.

The first research stream emphasizes the VC's problem (designing the appropriate mechanisms) and the second highlights the entrepreneur's potential actions more directly (whether to affiliate with highly reputable partners, and at what cost?). Notice that these streams are most relevant in settings in which little or no external information is available about the qualities of the entrepreneurs (i.e., career experience is missing or not relevant to the entrepreneurial undertaking). Although several studies have documented performance benefits associated with 'leasing' a reputation via certification, my own research in this domain suggests that start-ups wishing to affiliate with a high reputation VC pay a monetary price (Hsu, 2004). The finding is consistent with the view that entrepreneurs who are tied into more connected networks at reputable VC firms expect to come across more opportunities for start-up growth, but must pay a premium for such access.

STRATEGIZING

One of the main issues confronting start-ups is the question of how to earn returns from their innovative efforts when industry incumbents typically have much greater resources and could ostensibly compete successfully against entering start-ups. In this section, I review four prescriptive themes in the literature that might guide start-up entry strategy:

- entering into a niche;
- exploiting relative organizational flexibility;
- differentiating product or service offerings;
- cooperating with industry incumbents.

The first start-up strategy is the conventional wisdom to enter in a discreet market niche, making sure to stay below the radar screen of industry incumbents (e.g., Yoffie and Kwak, 2001). The idea is that inconspicuous entry allows entrants to improve their offerings without established incumbents perceiving an immediate threat to their business, allowing entrants to improve their capabilities and learn over time while avoiding direct head-to-head competition in the near term. This phenomenon is consistent with Romanelli's (1989) finding in the minicomputer industry that a 'specialist', or niche-targeted strategy, is associated with new venture survival. Consider the experience of Southwest Airlines: founded in 1972, the airline got its start serving cities in Texas on short-haul flights, which were meant to compete against other modes of transportation (not necessarily other airlines). In the 1980s, the airline expanded to California and certain cities in the US Midwest, and by the 1990s, Southwest moved into the highly competitive US eastern seaboard, as well as into the American southeast and northwest. The question, of course, is whether a controlled growth strategy is available in contexts in which technical change, rather than operational efficiency (for example), tends to drive competitive outcomes. Incumbents, particularly multi-divisional ones, have the potential of realizing economies of scale and/or scope in their operations (see Henderson and Cockburn, 1996, for evidence in pharmaceutical drug discovery). Early stage entrants rarely can achieve these economies, especially if they follow a niche entry and controlled growth strategy. Therefore, for technology intensive new ventures, the scale of entry decision is probably a more complex decision that will weigh marginal technological and feature improvements as compared to extant offerings (taking into account cost considerations), intellectual property characteristics, potential network effects, as well as the usual firm-level strategic considerations such as industry structure.

A second possible entry strategy is to exploit the start-up's organizational flexibility relative to industry incumbents. For example, when Dell entered the personal computer market in 1984, Compaq used an extensive network of distributors and resellers to sell its computers. Compaq's sales model meant forecasting demand, and given the rate of price depreciation on computers and inventory expenses, inaccurate forecasts were costly. Dell's direct distribution model economized on inventory because products were not assembled until after they were sold. Compaq's strategy of emulating the direct sales model while retaining its prior distribution channels was largely unsuccessful, as governance costs for the dual sales channels were high. This anecdote illustrates the conventional wisdom that entrants, by starting from a clean slate, are necessarily more flexible. Although new ventures at their inception are probably less constrained relative to ongoing operations with respect to organizational design decisions, business environment shifts, as are common in technologically dynamic settings, would suggest that organizational flexibility *after* founding is also quite important. Several studies, however, suggest important 'imprinting' effects and other constraints imposed from founding conditions. Starting with Stinchcombe's (1965) proposition that founding conditions have long-lived effects, researchers have found support for the proposition in the context of corporate strategy (Boeker, 1989; Romanelli, 1989), top management teams (Eisenhardt and Schoonhoven, 1990), human resource management (Hannan, Burton, and Baron, 1996), and interfirm network structures (Marquis, 2003).[6] It would be

---

[6]Levinthal (1997), through simulation studies, finds that imprinting effects do not depend on lack of organizational change; rather, the combination of firms' local search in a rugged fitness landscape (in which the value of a particular organizational feature depends on a variety of other organizational features) results in founding organizational form persistence.

interesting in future research to delve more into the origins and evolution of organizational flexibility and explicitly address the causal mechanisms of organizational response, which is particularly important in technology-intensive settings. Why might such responses differ by organizational size or age, for example?[7]

A third start-up entry strategy is to differentiate the new product or service offering, preferably reinforced with intellectual property protection. Differentiation can result from technical innovation, and theoretical evidence (Reinganum, 1983) suggests that when innovations are sufficiently radical and the inventive process is stochastic, incumbent firms have weaker incentives to invest in research and development relative to entrants. Using direct measures of innovation, Acs and Audretsch (1988) find that although innovation size is not statistically different between small and large firms, industries composed of large firms tend to have more innovations, but higher innovative activity in such industries is associated with smaller rather than larger firms.[8] These findings are consistent with the proposition that entrants try to differentiate their offerings through innovation. Another means by which new ventures can differentiate themselves is to adopt a novel business and revenue model, which can have performance consequences for entrepreneurial firms (Zott and Amit, 2007). Research in this domain is emergent, and it would be interesting to address the appropriability of business and revenue model innovations in future research. In fast-paced business environments, competitive leads (regardless of source) are likely to be temporary, even if appropriability conditions are perfect, and so development strategy would ideally extend beyond initial entry strategy.

A different strategy from those noted above involves entrepreneurial start-ups deciding to develop products or services jointly with industry incumbents to diffuse potential competition and/or to tap into complementary assets that might be expensive or difficult for the start-up innovators to acquire. Various forms of cooperative product development between innovators and established firms, ranging from technology licensing to strategic alliances and even to outright acquisition, have increasingly been subjects of study (e.g., Gulati, 1998; Gans, Hsu, and Stern, 2002; Mathews, 2006). This academic interest in cooperative behavior appears to mirror the tremendous growth in actual inter-organizational cooperative behavior in the real world.

A better understanding of the determinants of when start-up innovators decide to develop their products jointly with established firms (such as frequently observed in the biotechnology industry (e.g., Lerner and Merges, 1998)) as opposed to competing with them (such as is often true in the hard disk drive industry (e.g., Christensen, 1997)), impacts both the nature of competition in high-tech industries and potentially social efficiency as well. In particular, social gains might result from dividing innovative labor according to comparative advantage (start-ups innovate while

---

[7]Henderson and Clark (1990) provide a framework for understanding the disruptive impact of architectural knowledge on established firms' competitiveness and illustrate the phenomenon in the semiconductor photolithographic alignment industry. Future research efforts might investigate whether the disruptive impact of architectural innovation is an inevitable outcome of organizational bureaucratization and growth.

[8]In a broader review of empirical studies of innovation and market structure, however, Cohen and Levin (1989) state: 'The most notable feature of this considerable body of empirical research on the relationship between firm size and innovation is its inconclusiveness.' (p. 1069).

established firms commercialize) and avoiding duplication of development efforts (leaving aside the possible effect of duplicative R&D effort spurring technical progress). Gans, Hsu, and Stern (2002) examine three effects that may determine start-up commercialization strategy:

- the role of formal intellectual property (patents) in negotiating with established firms;
- the role of venture capitalists as information brokers, lowering transaction costs of cooperation;
- the relative costs of entry and associated complementary assets necessary for entry (Teece, 1986; Tripsas, 1997).

Gans, Hsu, and Stern (2002) develop a novel dataset to test these factors, and find that each of the three factors has a quantitatively significant effect on the probability of start-up cooperation. For example, firms with patents associated with their projects are 23 % more likely to pursue a cooperative strategy than firms without patents associated with their projects. The results are consistent with the notion that patents allow start-up innovators to enter negotiations in the first place with prospective collaboration partners. The results also suggest that although patents affect the absolute return to innovation (regardless of start-up commercialization strategy), they also enhance start-up bargaining power due to the ability for start-ups to credibly threaten product market entry in the absence of a cooperative agreement (which increases the relative return to a cooperative strategy).

A follow-on paper, Gans, Hsu, and Stern (2008), provides evidence for the causal role of formal patent rights in enabling technology transfer. Although efficiency might favor cooperation as soon as the inventor is able to transfer the key knowledge to the licensee, uncertainty about the scope of patent protection might delay the achievement of such an agreement. The authors contend that the timing of cooperation is thus a key strategic choice. The hypothesis is that patent allowances (the administrative notification prior to formal patent grant) mitigate intellectual property scope uncertainty, and will therefore boost the hazard rate of engaging in the ideas market, though the effect of such allowances depends on the commercialization environment in which the new venture operates.

To test these ideas, Gans, Hsu, and Stern (2008) assembled a dataset that combines information on the timing of patent allowances with data on the timing of cooperative licensing by start-up entrepreneurs, exploiting the significant empirical variation in the timing of patent allowance to identify the role of patent grants on the timing of technology licenses.[9] Empirical findings suggest that the hazard rate for achieving a cooperative licensing agreement increases 70 % with the allowance of formal intellectual property rights, and the boost is most pronounced in the time period immediately following patent allowance. In addition, the overall rate of licensing and the importance of patent allowance on the licensing hazard rate depend on the strategic and institutional environment in which firms operate. Patent allowance plays a particularly important role for technologies with longer

---

[9]Much of the prior literature explicitly or implicitly assumes that patent rights are conferred coincidentally with invention, and the literature is increasingly recognizing the importance of treating patent rights as probabilistic rather than determined across various stages of the patenting cycle.

technology life cycles or that lack alternative mechanisms for appropriation such as copyright or reputation. The authors conclude that delays in the patent grant system impacts the market for ideas transfer (Gans, Hsu, and Stern, 2008).

GROWTH AND LIQUIDITY

Growth of the new enterprise is typically not linear, because there are likely to be continuous challenges for the entrepreneurial team. It is almost a truism to characterize the process of new venture business development in the following ways: 'The only certainty is uncertainty' and 'double the expected time and effort put into the venture, and cut the business plan projections in half, and you will have reality'. From a research standpoint, the gray boundaries of the growth stage of venture development compound the research difficulties. In particular, it is not clear when a fledgling start-up graduates from early stage status and into the growth phase. Should the decision rule be based on employee size, age, or product development, for example? And can we use the selected criteria to meaningfully compare firms across industries? Also, several of the issues associated with maturing firms are covered by other literatures. For example, growth issues start to converge with the strategy literature and some harvesting issues converge with the finance literature.

It is worthwhile to list some of the major entrepreneurial management challenges during the growth phase before discussing some of the associated research issues:

- meeting projections and milestones;
- raising additional financing to fund further development (perhaps preparing for a liquidity event);
- motivating, retaining, and further recruiting managers and scientific employees;
- refining business and revenue models;
- positioning or repositioning product portfolios, including strategic entry or exit of product or service lines;
- managing product development including expansion and possible entry into new products and/or markets; managing multiple lines of business;
- sustaining innovation and keeping ahead of actual or potential competitors;
- professionalizing organizational practices (including corporate governance);
- developing the formal and informal sides of the organization, including scaling a corporate culture alongside the necessary level of organizational bureaucratization;
- managing the scope of the firm (including integration or outsourcing decisions for downstream commercialization assets such as manufacturing or distribution channels);
- preparing for a liquidity event (e.g., an initial public offering, a merger/ acquisition, or a management buyout).

Unlike in the other sections, I do not have a strong view on the few key research questions that face ventures in the growth phase of development. The challenges during this phase are sufficiently diffuse that a deeper understanding of many of the foregoing issues would be interesting. In addition, as ventures develop, their needs and challenges of growth are more diffuse relative to earlier stages of new venture development. For this reason, perhaps, there is no natural focal point in these studies. My strategy here is to discuss a few topics that may have applicability across areas.

One important theme is the development of corporate leadership and governance among technology-based entrepreneurial firms. Since venture capitalists tend to fund such enterprises, and because VCs typically acquire equity stakes in exchange for their cash infusions (which may have corporate control implications), several studies in this area have not surprisingly examined their role in start-ups' corporate governance. Baker and Gompers (2003) find that VC-backed firms are more likely to build 'professional' boards of directors in the sense of having more independent directors, which is linked to corporate value, at least at larger firms (Gompers, Ishii, and Metrick, 2003).

An intriguing question is why (and under what circumstances would) founder-entrepreneurs voluntarily give up control rights (such as the right to be replaced as CEO) to venture capitalists? The results of Hellmann's (1998) model suggest that such rights are necessary to give VCs the incentive to find professional managers to increase the value of the venture. This finding is consistent with the view that VCs act as more than traditional financial intermediaries (simply taking capital from savers and channeling financial resources to users). Further evidence in this regard comes from Lerner (1995) who found enhanced VC representation on biotechnology firm's boards of directors around the time of CEO turnover (there was no such increase among other directors).

The rate of founder-CEO turnover among technology-based start-ups appears substantial. Hannan, Burton, and Baron (1996) find that in the SPEC study of Silicon Valley area start-ups, the likelihood that a nonfounder is appointed CEO reaches about 40 % 40 months after the venture is founded, and 80 % after 80 months (departures for voluntary and involuntary reasons are not distinguished in their data). More recently, Boeker and Karichalil (2002) found empirical evidence that the likelihood of founder departure increases with firm size, decreases with founder ownership, and has a U-shape relationship with firm growth. Wasserman (2003) reports two events that are related to founder-CEO departure: VC funding rounds and product development completion. Looking to the future in this literature, it would be interesting to construct a baseline for the rate of founder-CEO departures to be expected (after all, different management challenges are likely to be associated with various stages of venture development, and market efficiency requires replacing ineffective top managers) and then compare actual rates of departure to that benchmark. More fundamentally, it would be interesting to examine potential differences in business policy decision making between founder-CEOs and outside CEOs in the setting of entrepreneurial firms. Are there biases by founder-CEOs? If so, what accounts for the biases?

Despite the importance of entrepreneurial harvesting events – exit timing and mode issues are important to growth-oriented start-ups because of their effects on entrepreneurs' incentives to engage in new venture activity in the first place – there has been limited work done by management scholars on the liquidity phase of venture development. In an interesting study, Sorenson and Stuart (2003) examine the regional consequences (new venture founding rates) of prior biotechnology IPOs and acquisitions. They find that liquidity events accelerate founding rates in the same and adjacent regions, though the results are moderated by state-level heterogeneity in enforceability of post-employment 'non-compete' covenants. Graebner and Eisenhardt (2004) examine entrepreneurial motivations for merging their venture. Further research on the causes and consequences of liquidity (or the absence of liquidity) events would be welcome.

Below I highlight a few other potential research questions in the domain of venture growth that might be interesting to investigate in future research:

- Black and Gilson (1998) argue that stock market-centered capital markets foster venture capital markets (affecting the supply of entrepreneurial ventures) more so than bank-centered ones, because legal environments affecting entrepreneurial exit affect the entrepreneurs' incentives to enter in the first place. It would be interesting to better understand what accounts for differential rates of VC and entrepreneurial activity *within* stock market- or bank-centered capital markets.
- How much conflict (and exercise of control rights) is there between entrepreneurs and VCs in timing and mode of exit?
- How much *entrepreneurial* skill dispersion is there in the timing of exits? (Lerner, 1994, finds that seasoned VCs appear to be able to take biotechnology firms public near market peaks.)
- Do entrepreneurs prepare their ventures for certain exit events? How? When? How would we know?
- What factors are involved in entrepreneurs' decision to abandon a venture?

CONCLUDING THOUGHTS

In this chapter, I have discussed a wide range of management issues related to technology-based entrepreneurial business development. The discussion was organized around research issues faced at different stages of venture development: venture origins, resource assembly, strategizing, and growth and harvesting issues. I will not attempt to summarize the discussion or the areas I have highlighted for potential future research here. Instead, I conclude with a few methodological points that apply to future empirical research in the field. Data are hard to come by to study emerging ventures. Researchers will have to employ creative and entrepreneurial means to obtain interesting data for future research. In addition, multiple or even non-standard methods may have to be employed to make progress. Finally, I would encourage researchers to consider ambitious data collection efforts, preferably longitudinal, to address research questions in this field.[10] There appears to be increasing interest in technology-based entrepreneurship among management researchers. My hope is that this chapter has usefully discussed some of the recent research in the field and that future research will be stimulated by some of the discussion contained here.

[10]Some recent examples include the panel data assembled by the Stanford Project on Emerging Companies by Baron, Burton, and Hannan and the MIT licensing data by Shane.

References

Acs, Z., and Audretsch, D. (1988). Innovation in small and large firms: an empirical analysis. *American Economic Review*, 78, 678–90.

Agarwal, R., Echambadi, R., Franco, A.M., and Sarkar, M.B. (2004). Knowledge transfer through inheritance: spin-out generation, development, and survival. *Academy of Management Journal*, 47, 501–22.

Agrawal, A., and Henderson, R. (2002). Putting patents in context: exploring knowledge transfer from MIT. *Management Science*, 48, 44–60.

Anton, J.J., and Yao, D. (1994). Expropriation and inventions: appropriable rents in the absence of property rights. *American Economic Review*, 84, 190–209.

Arora, A., Fosfuri, A., and Gambardella, A. (2001). *Markets for technology: economics of innovation and corporate strategy*. MIT Press.

Association of University Technology Managers (AUTM). http://www.autm.net/about/dsp.licensing_surveys.cfm.

Baker, M., and Gompers, P. (2003). The determinants of board structure at the initial public offering. *Journal of Law and Economics*, 46, 569–98.

Baron, J.N., Burton, M.D., and Hannan, M.T. (1996). The road taken: origins and evolution of employment systems in emerging companies. *Industrial and Corporate Change*, 5, 239–75.

Baron, J.N., Hannan, M.T., and Burton, M.D. (2001). Labor pains: change in organizational models and employee turnover in young, high-tech firms. *American Journal of Sociology*, 106, 960–1012.

Beckman, C.M. (2006). The influence of founding team company affiliations on firm behavior. *Academy of Management Journal*, 49, 741–58.

Bhide, A. (1994). How entrepreneurs craft strategies that work. *Harvard Business Review*, 72, 150–61.

Black, B.S., and Gilson, R.J. (1998). Venture capital and the structure of capital markets: banks vs. stock markets. *Journal of Financial Economics*, 47, 243–77.

Boeker, W. (1989). Strategic change: the effects of founding and history. *Academy Management Journal*, 32, 489–515.

Boeker, W., and Karichalil, R. (2002). Entrepreneurial succession: factors influencing the departure of founding managers. *Academy of Management Journal*, 45, 818–26.

Burton, M.D., Sorensen, J., and Beckman, C. (2002). Coming from good stock: career histories and new venture formation. *Research in the Sociology of Organizations*, 19, 229–62.

Camerer, C., and Lovallo, D. (1999). Overconfidence and excess entry: an experimental approach. *American Economic Review*, 89, 306–18.

Carroll, G.R., Bigelow, L.S., Seidel, M.L., and Tsai, L.B. (1996). The fates of *de novo* and *de alio* producers in the American automobile industry 1885–1981. *Strategic Management Journal*, 17, 117–37.

Christensen, C.M. (1997). *The innovator's dilemma: when new technologies cause great firms to fail*. Harvard Business School Press.

Cockburn, I., Henderson, R., and Stern, S. (2000). Untangling the origins of competitive advantage. *Strategic Management Journal*, 21, 1123–45.

Cohen, W., and Levin, R. (1989). Empirical studies of innovation and market structure. In R. Schmalensee and R. Willig (eds), *Handbook of Industrial Organization*, Vol. 2, North Holland, 1059–107.

Cohen, W.C., and Levinthal, D.A. (1990). Absorptive capacity: a new perspective on learning and innovation. *Administrative Science Quarterly*, 35, 128–52.

Cooper, A.C., Woo, C.Y., and Dunkelberg, W.C. (1988). Entrepreneurs' perceived chances for success. *Journal of Business Venturing*, 3, 97–108.

Dunne, T., Roberts, M.J., and Samuelson, L. (1988). Patterns of firm entry and exit in U.S. manufacturing industries. *RAND Journal of Economics*, 19, 495–515.

Dushnitsky, G. (2004). Limitations to inter-organizational knowledge acquisition: the paradox of corporate venture capital. Best Paper Proceedings of the 2004 Academy of Management Conference.

Eisenhardt K., and Schoonhoven, K. (1990). Organizational growth: linking founding team, strategy, environment, and growth among U.S. semiconductor ventures, 1978–1988. *Administrative Science Quarterly*, 40, 84–110.

Evans, D.S., and Leighton, L.S. (1989). Some empirical aspects of entrepreneurship. *American Economics Review*, 79, 519–35.

Gans, J.S., Hsu, D.H., and Stern, S. (2002). When does start-up innovation spur the gale of creative destruction? *RAND Journal of Economics*, 33, 571–86.

Gans, J.S., Hsu, D.H., and Stern, S. (2008). The impact of uncertain intellectual property rights on the market for ideas: evidence from patent grant delays. *Management Science*, 54, 982–97.

Gompers, P.A., Ishii, J.L., and Metrick, A. (2003). Corporate governance and equity prices. *Quarterly Journal of Economics*, 118, 107–55.

Gompers, P., and Lerner, J., (1999). *The venture capital cycle*. MIT Press.

Gompers, P., Lerner, J., and Scharfstein, D. (2005). Entrepreneurial spawning: public corporations and the formation of new ventures, 1986–1999. *Journal of Finance*, 60, 577–614.

Graebner, M.E., and Eisenhardt, K.M. (2004). The seller's side of the story: acquisition as courtship and governance as syndicate in entrepreneurial firms. *Administrative Science Quarterly*, 49, 366–403.

Groysberg, B., Nanda, A., and Nohria, N. (2004). The risky business of hiring stars. *Harvard Business Review*, 82, 92–100.

Gulati, R. (1998). Alliances and networks. *Strategic Management Journal*, 19, 293–317.

Hannan, M.T., Burton, M.D., and Baron, J.N. (1996). Inertia and change in the early years: employment relations in young, high technology firms. *Industrial and Corporate Change*, 5, 503–36.

Helfat, C., and Lieberman, M. (2002). The birth of capabilities: market entry and the importance of pre-history. *Industrial and Corporate Change*, 11, 725–60.

Hellmann, T. (1998). The allocation of control rights in venture capital contracts. *RAND Journal of Economics*. 29, 57–76.

Hellmann, T., and Puri, M. (2000). The interaction between product market and financing strategy: the role of venture capital. *Review of Financial Studies*, 13, 959–84.

Hellmann, T., and Puri, M. (2002). Venture capital and the professionalization of start-up firms: empirical evidence. *Journal of Finance*, 62, 169–97.

Henderson, R. (1994). The evolution of integrative capability: innovation in cardiovascular drug discovery. *Industrial and Corporate Change*, 3, 607–30.

Henderson, R., and Clark, K. (1990). Architectural innovation: the reconfiguration of existing product technologies and the failure of established firms. *Administrative Science Quarterly*, 35, 9–30.

Henderson, R., and Cockburn, I. (1994). Measuring competence? Exploring firm effects in pharmaceutical research. *Strategic Management Journal*, 15, 63–84.

Henderson, R., and Cockburn, I. (1996). Scale, scope, and spillovers: the determinants of research productivity in drug discovery. *RAND Journal of Economics*, 27, 32–59.

Hsu, D.H. (2004). What do entrepreneurs pay for venture capital affiliation? *Journal of Finance*, 59, 1805–44.

Hsu, D.H. (2006). Venture capitalists and cooperative start-up commercialization strategy. *Management Science*, 52, 204–19.

Hsu, D.H. (2007). Experienced entrepreneurial founders, organizational capital, and venture capital funding. *Research Policy*, 36, 722–41.

Hsu, D.H., and Kenney, M. (2005). Organizing venture capital: the rise and demise of American research and capital corporation, 1946–1973. *Industrial and Corporate Change*, 14, 579–616.

Hsu, D.H., and Lim, K. (2007). The antecedents and innovation consequences of organizational knowledge brokering capability. mimeo. Wharton School, University of Pennsylvania.

Jaffe, A., Trajtenberg, M., and Henderson, R. (1993). Geographic localization of knowledge spillovers as evidenced by patent citations. *Quarterly Journal of Economics*, 103, 577–98.

Jensen, R., and Thursby, M. (2001). Proofs and prototypes for sale: the licensing of university inventions. *American Economic Review*, 91, 240–59.

Kaplan, S., and Strömberg, P. (2003). Financial contracting theory meets the real world: an empirical analysis of venture capital contracts, *Review of Economic Studies* 70, 281–315.

Kenney, M. (1986). *Biotechnology: the university-industrial complex*. Yale University Press.

Klepper, S. (2002). The capabilities of new firms and the evolution of the US automobile industry. *Industrial and Corporate Change*, 11, 645–66.

Klepper, S., and Simons, K.L. (2000). Dominance by birthright: entry of prior radio producers and competitive ramifications in the U.S. television receiver industry. *Strategic Management Journal*, 21, 997–1016.

Landier, A. (2006). Entrepreneurship and the stigma of failure. mimeo. New York University.

Lerner, J. (1994). Venture capitalists and the decision to go public. *Journal of Financial Economics*, 35, 293–316.

Lerner, J. (1995). Venture capitalists and the oversight of private firms. *Journal of Finance*, 50, 301–18.

Lerner, J., and Merges, R. (1998). The control of strategic alliances: an empirical analysis of the biotechnology industry. *Journal of Industrial Economics*, 46, 125–56.

Levinthal, D. (1997). Adaptation on rugged landscapes. *Management Science*, 43, 934–50.

Lewis, T.R., and Yao, D.A. (2003). Innovation, knowledge flow, and worker mobility. mimeo. Duke University.

March, J.G. (1991). Exploration and exploitation in organizational learning. *Organization Science*, 2, 71–87.

March, J.G., and Simon, H.A. (1958). *Organizations*. John Wiley & Sons, Inc.

Marquis, C. (2003). The pressure of the past: network imprinting in intercorporate communities. *Administrative Science Quarterly*, 48, 655–89.

Mathews, R.D. (2006). Strategic alliances, equity stakes, and entry deterrence. *Journal of Financial Economics*, 80, 35–79.

Megginson, W., and Weiss, K. (1991). Venture capital certification in initial public offerings. *Journal of Finance*, 46, 879–903.

Moskowitz, T.J., and Vissing-Jorgenson, A. (2002). The returns to entrepreneurial investment: a private equity premium puzzle? *American Economic Review*, 92, 745–78.

Mowery, D.C., Oxley, J.E., and Silverman, B.S. (1996). Strategic alliances and interfirm knowledge transfer. *Strategic Management Journal*, 17 (Winter special issue), 77–91.

Nelson, R.R., and Winter, S.G. (1982). *An evolutionary theory of economic growth*. Harvard University Press.

Phillips, D.J. (2002). A genealogical approach to organizational life chances: the parent-progeny transfer among Silicon Valley law firms, 1946–1996. *Administrative Science Quarterly*, 47: 474–506.

Reinganum, J.F. (1983). Uncertain innovation and the persistence of monopoly. *American Economic Review*, 73, 741–48.

Roberts, E. (2004). A perspective on 50 years of the engineering management field. *IEEE Transactions on Engineering Management*, 51, 398–403.

Romanelli, E. (1989). Environments and strategies of organization start-up: effects on early survival. *Administrative Science Quarterly*, 34, 369–87.

Rosenkopf, L., and Almeida, P. (2003). Overcoming local search through alliances and mobility. *Management Science*, 49, 751–66.

Saxenian, A. (1994). *Regional advantage: culture and competition in Silicon Valley and Route 128*. Harvard University Press.

Shane, S. (2000). Prior knowledge and the discovery of entrepreneurial opportunities. *Organization Science*, 11, 448–69.

Shane, S. (2001a). Technological opportunities and new firm creation. *Management Science*, 47, 205–20.

Shane, S. (2001b). Technology regimes and new firm formation. *Management Science*, 47, 1173–190.

Shane S., and Venkataraman, S. (2000). The promise of entrepreneurship as a field of research. *Academy of Management Review*, 25, 217–26.

Sorenson, O., and Stuart, T.E. (2003). Liquidity events and the geographic distribution of entrepreneurial activity. *Administrative Science Quarterly*, 48, 175–201.

Stern, S. (2004). Do scientists pay to be scientists? *Management Science*, 50, 835–53.

Stinchcombe, A.L. (1965). Social structure and organizations. In J. March (ed.), *Handbook of Organizations*. Rand-McNally, 142–93.

Stuart, T.E., Hoang, H., and Hybels, R. (1999). Interorganizational endorsements and the performance of entrepreneurial ventures. *Administrative Science Quarterly*, 44, 315–49.

Teece, D. (1986). Profiting from technological innovation: implications for integration, collaboration, licensing and public policy. *Research Policy*, 15, 285–305.

Thompson, P., and Fox-Kean, M. (2005). Patent citations and the geography of knowledge spillovers: evidence from inventor- and examiner-added citations. *American Economics Review*, 95, 450–60.

Tripsas, M. (1997). Unraveling the process of creative destruction: complementary assets and incumbent survival in the typesetter industry. *Strategic Management Journal*, 18, 119–42.

Von Hippel, E. (1994). 'Sticky information' and the locus of problem solving: implications for innovation. *Management Science*, 40: 429–39.

Wasserman, N. (2003). Founder-CEO succession and the paradox of entrepreneurial success. *Organization Science*, 14, 149–72.

Yoffie, D., and Kwak, M. (2001). *Judo strategy*. Harvard Business School Press.

Zott, C. and Amit, R. (2007). Business model design and the performance of entrepreneurial firms. *Organization Science*, 18, 181–99.

Zucker, L., Darby, M., and Brewer, M. (1998). Intellectual human capital, and the birth of U.S. biotechnology enterprises. *American Economic Review*, 88, 290–306.

14

Knowledge Spillover Entrepreneurship and Innovation in Large and Small Firms

David B. Audretsch

Introduction

Where do new opportunities come from and what is the response of decision makers when confronted by such new opportunities? The disparate approaches pursued to answer these questions distinguish the literature on entrepreneurship from that on firm innovation. The model of the knowledge production function of the firm has assumed the firm to be exogenous, while opportunities are endogenously created through purposeful investments in the creation of new knowledge, such as expenditures on research and development and augmentation of human capital.

By contrast, in the entrepreneurship literature the opportunities are generally viewed as exogenous, but the startup of the new firm is endogenous to characteristics specific to the individual. The focus of the entrepreneurship literature in general, and entrepreneurship theory in particular, has been on the cognitive process by which individuals recognize entrepreneurial opportunities and then decide to attempt to actualize them through the process of starting a new business or organization. This approach has typically taken the opportunities as given and focused instead on differences across individual-specific characteristics, traits, and conditions to explain variations in entrepreneurial behavior.

The purpose of this chapter is to reconcile these two disparate literatures on entrepreneurship and firm strategy. We do this by considering entrepreneurship to be endogenous – not just to differences in individual characteristics but also to differences in the context in which a given individual, with an endowment of personal characteristics, propensities, and capabilities, finds herself.

We do not contest the validity of the pervasive entrepreneurship literature identifying individual specific characteristics as shaping the decision to become an entrepreneurial. What we do propose, however, is that such differences in

Handbook of Technology and Innovation Management.   Edited by Scott Shane
© 2008 John Wiley & Sons, Ltd

the contexts in which any given individual finds herself, might also influence the entrepreneurial decision.

Rather than taking entrepreneurial opportunity as exogenous, this chapter places it in the main center of attention by making it endogenous. Entrepreneurial opportunity is posited to be greater in contexts that are rich in knowledge but limited in those contexts with impoverished knowledge. According to the *Endogenous Entrepreneurship Hypothesis*, entrepreneurship is an endogenous response to investments in knowledge made by firms and nonprivate organizations that do not fully commercialize those new ideas, thus generating opportunities for entrepreneurs. Thus, although most of the literature typically takes entrepreneurial opportunities to be exogenous, this chapter suggests that they are, in fact, endogenous, and systematically created by investments in knowledge.

A summary and conclusions are provided in the last section. In contrast to the prevalent approach in entrepreneurship theory, this chapter concludes that entrepreneurial opportunities are not exogenous but rather systematically generated by investments in ideas and knowledge that cannot be fully appropriated and commercialized by those incumbent firms and organizations creating the new knowledge.

WHERE DOES OPPORTUNITY COME FROM?

The entrepreneurial firm

Why do (some) people start firms? This question has been at the heart of considerable research, not just in economics but also throughout the social sciences. Herbert and Link (1989) have identified three distinct intellectual traditions in the development of the entrepreneurship literature. These three traditions can be characterized as the German Tradition, based on von Thuenen and Schumpeter, the Chicago Tradition, based on Knight and Schultz, and the Austrian Tradition, based on von Mises, Kirzner, and Shackle.

Stevenson and Jarillo (1990) assume that entrepreneurship is an orientation towards opportunity recognition. Central to this research agenda are the questions 'How do entrepreneurs perceive opportunities and how do these opportunities manifest themselves as being credible versus being an illusion?'. Krueger (2003) examines the nature of entrepreneurial thinking and the cognitive process associated with opportunity identification and the decision to undertake entrepreneurial action. The focal point of this research is on the cognitive process identifying the entrepreneurial opportunity along with the decision to start a new firm. Thus, a perceived opportunity and intent to pursue that opportunity are the necessary and sufficient conditions for entrepreneurial activity to take place. The perception of an opportunity is shaped by a sense of the anticipated rewards accruing from and costs of becoming an entrepreneur. Some of the research focuses on the role of personal attitudes and characteristics, such as self-efficacy (the individual's sense of competence), collective efficacy, and social norms. Shane (2000) has identified how prior experience and the ability to apply specific skills influence the perception of future opportunities. Shane and Eckhardt (2003) and Shane and Venkataraman

(2001) introduce the concept of the entrepreneurial decision resulting from the cognitive processes of opportunity recognition and ensuing action. They suggest that an equilibrium view of entrepreneurship stems from the assumption of perfect information. By contrast, imperfect information generates divergences in perceived opportunities across different people. The sources of heterogeneity across individuals include different access to information, as well cognitive abilities, psychological differences, and access to financial and social capital.

It is a virtual consensus that entrepreneurship revolves around the recognition of opportunities and the pursuit of those opportunities (Venkataraman, 1997). Much of the more contemporary thinking about entrepreneurship has focused on the cognitive process by which individuals reach the decision to start a new firm. According to Sarasvathy *et al.* (2003, p. 142): 'An entrepreurial opportunity consists of a set of ideas, beliefs and actions that enable the creation of future goods and services in the absence of current markets for them'. The authors provide a typology of entrepreneurial opportunities as consisting of opportunity recognition, opportunity discovery, and opportunity creation.

In asking the question of why some start firms, while others don't, scholars have focused on differences across individuals (Stevenson and Jarillo, 1990). As Krueger (2003, p. 105) observes, 'The heart of entrepreneurship is an orientation toward seeing opportunities', which frames the research questions, 'What is the nature of entrepreneurial thinking and What cognitive phenomena are associated with seeing and acting on opportunities?'. The traditional approach to entrepreneurship essentially holds the context constant and then asks how the cognitive process inherent in the entrepreneurial decision varies across different individual characteristics and attributes (McClelland, 1961; Shaver, 2003). As Shane and Eckhardt (2003, p 187) summarize this literature in introducing the individual-opportunity nexus: 'We discussed the process of opportunity discovery and explained why some actors are more likely to discover a given opportunity than others.' Some of these differences involve the willingness to incur risk, while others involve the preference for autonomy and self-direction, and still others involve differential access to scarce and expensive resources, such as financial capital, human capital, social capital, and experiential capital. This approach focusing on individual cognition in the entrepreneurial process has generated a number of important and valuable insights, such as the contribution made by social networks, education and training, and familial influence. The literature certainly leaves the impression that entrepreneurship is a personal matter largely determined by DNA, familial status, and access to crucial resources.

The incumbent large firm

In contrast to the prevalent thinking concerning entrepreneurial startups, the most predominant theory of firm innovation does not assume that opportunities are exogenous to the firm. Rather, innovative opportunities are the result of systematic effort by firms and the result of purposeful efforts to create knowledge and new ideas, and subsequently to appropriate the returns of those investments through commercialization of such investments. Thus, while the entrepreneurship literature has taken entrepreneurial opportunities to be exogenous, the literature on firm innovation and technological change has taken the creation of such innovative opportunities to be endogenous.

The traditional starting point in the literature on innovation and technological change for most theories of innovation has been the firm (Griliches 1979; Chandler, 1990; Cohen and Levin 1989). In such theories firms are exogenous and their performance in generating technological change is endogenous (Cohen and Klepper, 1991; 1992).

The most prevalent model of technological change is the model of the knowledge production function, formalized by Zvi Griliches in 1979. According to the model of the knowledge production function, incumbent firms engage in the pursuit of new economic knowledge as an input into the process of generating the output of innovative activity. The most important input in this model is new economic knowledge. As Cohen and Klepper (1991; 1992) point out, the greatest source generating new economic knowledge is generally considered to be R&D. Other inputs in the knowledge production function have included measures of human capital, skilled labor, and educational levels. Thus, the model of the knowledge production function from the literature on innovation and technological change can be represented as

$$I_i = \alpha R D_i^\beta H K_i^\gamma \varepsilon_i \qquad (1)$$

where I stands for the degree of innovative activity, RD represents R&D inputs, and HK represents human capital inputs. The unit of observation for estimating the model of the knowledge production function, reflected by the subscript i, has been at the level of countries, industries, and enterprises.

Thus, in this view of firm innovation, the firm exists exogenously. It undertakes purposeful investments to create knowledge endogenously, which results in the output of innovative activity. Opportunities are not exogenous, but rather the result of purposeful and dedicated investments and efforts by firms to create new (knowledge) opportunities and then to appropriate them through commercializing their innovations.

THE INNOVATION PARADOX

When it came to empirical validation of the model of the knowledge production function, it became clear that measurement issues played a major role. The state of knowledge regarding innovation and technological change has generally been shaped by the nature of the data that were available to scholars for analyses. Such data have always been incomplete and, at best, represented only a proxy measure reflecting some aspect of the process of technological change. Simon Kuznets (1962) observed that the greatest obstacle to understanding the economic role of technological change was a clear inability of scholars to measure it. More recently, Cohen and Levin (1989, p. 146) warned

> A fundamental problem in the study of innovation and technical change in industry is the absence of satisfactory measures of new knowledge and its contribution to technological

progress. There exists no measure of innovation that permits readily interpretable cross-industry comparisons.

Measures of technological change have typically involved one of the three major aspects of the innovative process:

- a measure of the inputs into the innovative process, such as R&D expenditures, or else the share of the labor force accounted for by employees involved in R&D activities;
- an intermediate output, such as the number of inventions that have been patented;
- a direct measure of innovative output.

These three levels of measuring technological change have not been developed and analyzed simultaneously, but have evolved over time, roughly in the order of their presentation. That is, the first attempts to quantify technological change at all generally involved measuring some aspects of inputs into the innovative process (Scherer, 1965; 1967; Mueller, 1967; Grabowski, 1968; Mansfield, 1968). Measures of R&D inputs – first in terms of employment and later in terms of expenditures – were only introduced on a meaningful basis to enable inter-industry and inter-firm comparisons in the late 1950s and early 1960s.

A clear limitation in using R&D activity as a proxy measure for technological change is that R&D reflects only the resources devoted to producing innovative output, but not the amount of innovative activity actually realized. That is, R&D is an input and not an output in the innovation process. In addition, Kleinknecht (1987a and b), Kleinknecht and Verspagen (1987), and Kleinknecht and Reijnen (1991) have systematically shown that R&D measures incorporate only efforts made to generate innovative activity that are undertaken within formal R&D budgets and within formal R&D laboratories. They find that the extent of informal R&D is considerable, particularly in smaller enterprises. And, as Mansfield (1984) points out, not all efforts within a formal R&D laboratory are directed towards generating innovative output in any case. Rather, other types of output, such as imitation and technology transfer, are also common goals in R&D laboratories.

When systematic data measuring the number of inventions patented were made publicly available in the mid-1960s, many scholars interpreted this new measure not only as being superior to R&D but also as reflecting innovative output. In fact, the use of patented inventions is not a measure of innovative output, but rather a type of intermediate output measure. A patent reflects new technical knowledge, but it does not indicate whether this knowledge has a positive economic value. Only those inventions that have been successfully introduced in the market can claim that they are innovations as well.

Empirical estimation of the model of the knowledge production function, represented by Equation 1, was found to be stronger at broader levels of aggregation such as countries or industries. For example, at the unit of observation of countries, the empirical evidence (Griliches, 1984) clearly supported the existence of the knowledge production function. This is intuitively understandable, because the most innovative countries are those with the greatest investments to R&D. Less innovative output is associated with developing countries, which are characterized by a paucity of new economic knowledge.

Similarly, the model of the knowledge production function was found to be empirically corroborated at the level of the industry (Scherer, 1982; Griliches, 1984). Again, this seems obvious because the most innovative industries also tend to be characterized by considerable investments in R&D and new economic knowledge Industries such as computers, pharmaceuticals, and instruments are not only high in R&D inputs that generate new economic knowledge, but also in terms of innovative outputs (Scherer, 1983; Acs and Audretsch, 1990). By contrast, industries with little R&D, such as wood products, textiles, and paper, also tend to produce only a negligible amount of innovative output.

Where the relationship became less robust was at the disaggregated microeconomic level of the enterprise, establishment, or even line of business: there is no direct deterministic relationship between knowledge inputs and innovative output. Although innovations and inventions are related, they are not identical. The distinction is that an innovation is a new product, process, service, or organizational form that is introduced into the market, whereas an invention may or may not be introduced into the market.

Besides the fact that many, if not most, patented inventions do not result in an innovation, a second important limitation of patent measures as an indicator of innovative activity is that they do not capture all the innovations actually made. In fact, many inventions that result in innovations are not patented. The tendency of patented inventions to result in innovations, and of innovations to be the result of inventions that were patented, combine into what Scherer (1983) has termed 'the propensity to patent'. It is the uncertainty about the stability of the propensity to patent across enterprises and across industries that casts doubt upon the reliability of patent measures According to Scherer (1983, pp. 107–108):

> The quantity and quality of industry patenting may depend upon chance, how readily a technology lends itself to patent protection, and business decision-makers' varying perceptions of how much advantage they will derive from patent rights. Not much of a systematic nature is known about these phenomena, which can be characterized as differences in the propensity to patent.

Mansfield (1984, p. 462) has explained why the propensity to patent may vary so much across markets:

> The value and cost of individual patents vary enormously within and across industries . . . . Many inventions are not patented. And in some industries, like electronics, there is considerable speculation that the patent system is being bypassed to a greater extent than in the past. Some types of technologies are more likely to be patented than others.

The implications are that comparisons between enterprises and across industries may be misleading. According to Cohen and Levin (1989), 'There are significant problems with patent counts as a measure of innovation, some of which affect both within-industry and between-industry comparisons.'

Thus, even as superior sources of patent data were introduced, such as the new measure of patented inventions from the computerization by the US Patent Office, the reliability of these data as measures of innovative activity has been severely challenged. For example, Pakes and Griliches (1980, p. 378) warn that 'patents are a flawed measure (of innovative output); particularly since not all new innovations are patented and since patents differ greatly in their economic impact.' And in addressing the question, 'Patents as indicators of what?', Griliches (1990, p. 1669) concludes that

> Ideally, we might hope that patent statistics would provide a measure of the (innovative) output .... The reality, however, is very far from it. The dream of getting hold of an output indicator of inventive activity is one of the strong motivating forces for economic research in this area.

It was not until well into the 1970s that systematic attempts were made to provide a direct measure of the innovative output. Therefore, it should be emphasized that the conventional wisdom regarding innovation and technological change was based primarily upon the evidence derived from analyzing R&D data, which essentially measure inputs into the process of technological change, and patented inventions, which are a measure of intermediate output at best.

The most ambitious major database providing a direct measure of innovative activity is the US Small Business Administration's Innovation Data Base (SBIDB). The database consists of 8074 innovations commercially introduced in the US in 1982. Acs and Audretsch (1987; 1988; 1990) analyzed these data to examine the relationships between firm size and technological change and market structure and technological change, where a direct rather than indirect measure of innovative activity is used.

The knowledge production function has been found to hold most strongly at broader levels of aggregation. The most innovative countries are those with the greatest investments to R&D. Little innovative output is associated with less developed countries, which are characterized by a paucity of production of new economic knowledge. Similarly, the most innovative industries also tend to be characterized by considerable investments in R&D and new economic knowledge. Industries such as computers, pharmaceuticals, and instruments are not only high in R&D inputs that generate new economic knowledge, but also in terms of innovative outputs (Audretsch, 1995). By contrast, industries with little R&D, such as wood products, textiles, and paper, also tend to produce only a negligible amount of innovative output. Thus, the knowledge production model linking knowledge generating inputs to outputs certainly holds at the more aggregated levels of economic activity.

Where the relationship becomes less compelling is at the disaggregated microeconomic level of the enterprise, establishment, or even line of business. For example, although Acs and Audretsch (1990) found that the simple correlation between R&D inputs and innovative output was 0.84 for four-digit standard industrial classification (SIC) manufacturing industries in the United States, it was only about half, 0.40, among the largest US corporations.

At the heart of the conventional wisdom has been the widely accepted hypothesis that large enterprises are able to exploit at least some market power as the engine of technological change. This view dates back at least to Schumpeter, who in *Capitalism, Socialism and Democracy* (1942, p. 101) argued that, 'The monopolist firm will generate a larger supply of innovations because there are advantages which, though not strictly unattainable on the competitive level of enterprise, are as a matter of fact secured only on the monopoly level.' The Schumpeterian thesis, then, is that large enterprises are uniquely endowed to exploit innovative opportunities. That is, market dominance is a prerequisite to undertaking the risks and uncertainties associated with innovation. It is the possibility of acquiring quasi-rents that serves as the catalyst for large-firm innovation.

In one of the most important studies, Scherer (1984) used the US Federal Trade Commission's Line of Business Data to estimate the elasticity of R&D spending with respect to firm sales for 196 industries. He found evidence of increasing returns to scale (an elasticity exceeding unity) for about 20 % of the industries, constant returns to scale for a little less than three-quarters of the industries, and diminishing returns (an elasticity less than unity) in less than 10 % of the industries.

Although the Scherer (1984) and Soete (1979) studies were restricted to relatively large enterprises, Bound *et al.* (1984) included a much wider spectrum of firm sizes in their sample of 1492 firms from the 1976 COMPUSTAT data. They found that R&D increases more than proportionately along with firm size for the smaller firms, but that a fairly linear relationship exists for larger firms. Despite the somewhat more ambiguous findings in still other studies (Mansfield, 1981; 1983; Mansfield *et al.*, 1982), the empirical evidence seems generally to support the Schumpeterian hypothesis that research effort is positively associated with firm size.

The studies relating patents to firm size are considerably less ambiguous. Here the findings unequivocally suggest that 'the evidence leans weakly against the Schumpeterian conjecture that the largest sellers are especially fecund sources of patented inventions' (Scherer, 1982, p. 235). In one of the most important studies, Scherer (1965) used the Fortune annual survey of the 500 largest US industrial corporations. He related the 1955 firm sales to the number of patents in 1959 for 448 firms. Scherer found that the number of patented inventions increases less than proportionately along with firm size. Scherer's results were later confirmed by Bound *et al.* (1984). Basing their study on 2852 companies and 4553 patenting entities, they determined that the small firms (with less than $10 million in sales) accounted for 4.3 % of the sales from the entire sample, but 5.7 % of the patents.

Thus, just as there are persuasive theories defending the original Schumpeterian hypothesis that large corporations are a prerequisite for technological change, there are also substantial theories predicting that small enterprises should have the innovative advantage, at least in certain industries. As described above, the empirical evidence based on the input measure of technological change, R&D, tilts decidedly in favor of the Schumpeterian hypothesis. However, as also described above, the empirical results are somewhat more ambiguous for the measure of intermediate output – the number of patented inventions. It was not until direct measures of innovative output became available that the full picture of the process of technological change could be obtained.

Using the measure of innovative output from the US SBIDB, Acs and Audretsch (1990) showed that, in fact, the most innovative US firms were large corporations. Furthermore, the most innovative American corporations also tended to have large R&D laboratories and be R&D intensive. At first glance, these findings based on direct measures of innovative activity seem to confirm the conventional wisdom. However, in the most innovative four-digit standard industrial classification (SIC) industries, large firms, defined as enterprises with at least 500 employees, contributed more innovations in some instances, while in other industries small firms produced more innovations. For example, in computers and process control instruments small firms contributed the bulk of the innovations. By contrast in the pharmaceutical preparation and aircraft industries the large firms were much more innovative.

Probably their best measure of innovative activity is the total innovation rate, which is defined as the total number of innovations per 1000 employees in each industry. The large-firm innovation rate is defined as the number of innovations made by firms with at least 500 employees, divided by the number of employees (thousands) in large firms. The small-firm innovation rate is analogously defined as the number of innovations contributed by firms with fewer than 500 employees, divided by the number of employees (thousands) in small firms.

The innovation rates, or the number of innovations per 1000 employees, have the advantage in that they measure large- and small-firm innovative activity relative to the presence of large and small firms in any given industry. That is, in making a direct comparison between large- and small-firm innovative activity, the absolute number of innovations contributed by large firms and small enterprises is somewhat misleading, since these measures are not standardized by the relative presence of large and small firms in each industry. When a direct comparison is made between the innovative activity of large and small firms, the innovation rates are presumably a more reliable measure of innovative intensity because they are weighted by the relative presence of small and large enterprises in any given industry. Thus, although large firms in manufacturing introduced 2445 innovations in 1982, and small firms contributed slightly fewer, 1954, small-firm employment was only half as great as large-firm employment, yielding an average small-firm innovation rate in manufacturing of 0.309, compared to a large-firm innovation rate of 0.202 (Acs and Audretsch, 1988; 1990).

Thus, there is considerable evidence suggesting that, in contrast to the findings for R&D inputs and patented inventions, small enterprises apparently play an important generating innovative activity, at least in certain industries. By relating the innovative output of each firm to its size, it is also possible to shed new light on the Schumpeterian hypothesis. Acs and Audretsch (1991) find that there is no evidence that increasing returns to R&D expenditures exist in producing innovative output. In fact, with just several exceptions, diminishing returns to R&D are the rule. This study made it possible to resolve the apparent paradox in the literature that R&D inputs increase at more than a proportional rate along with firm size, while the generation of patented inventions does not. That is, although larger firms are observed to undertake a greater effort towards R&D, each additional dollar of R&D is found to yield less in terms of innovative output.

The model of the knowledge production function therefore became less compelling in view of a wave of studies that found that small enterprises were an engine of innovative activity in certain industries. The apparent contradiction between the organizational context of knowledge inputs, principally R&D, and the organizational context of small firm innovative output resulted in the emergence of what has become known as the *Innovation Paradox*: Either the model of the knowledge production did not hold, at least at the level of the enterprise (for a broad spectrum across the firm-size distribution), or else the appropriate unit of observation had to be reconsidered. In searching for a solution, scholars chose the second interpretation, leading them to look beyond the boundaries of the firm for sources of innovative inputs.

THE KNOWLEDGE SPILLOVER THEORY OF ENTREPRENEURSHIP

The endogenous entrepreneurship hypothesis

Resolution to the *Innovation Paradox* came after rethinking not the validity of the model of the knowledge production function, but rather the implicit assumptions of independence and separability underlying the decision-making analytical units of observation – the established incumbent firm and the new entrepreneurial firm. Just as the prevailing theories of entrepreneurship have generally focused on the cognitive process of individuals in making the decision to start a new firm, so that the decision-making criterion are essentially internal to the decision-making unit – in this case the individual, the model of the knowledge production function generally limited the impact of the firm's investments in creating new knowledge to that decision-making unit – in this case the firm.

That these decision-making units – the firm and the individual – might actually not be totally separable and independent, particularly with respect to assessing the outcome of knowledge investments, was first considered by Audretsch (1995), who introduced *The Knowledge Spillover Theory of Entrepreneurship*.

The reason for challenging the assumptions of independence and separability between (potential) entrepreneurs and firms emanates from a fundamental characteristic of knowledge that differentiates it from the more traditional firm resources of physical capital and (unskilled) labor. Arrow (1962) pointed out that knowledge differs from these traditional firm resources due to the greater degree of uncertainty, higher extent of asymmetries, and greater cost of transacting new ideas.

The expected value of any new idea is highly uncertain, and as Arrow pointed out, has a much greater variance than would be associated with the deployment of traditional factors of production. After all, there is relative certainty about what a standard piece of capital equipment can do, or what an unskilled worker can contribute to a mass-production assembly line. By contrast, Arrow emphasized that when it comes to innovation, there is uncertainty about whether the new product can be produced, how it can be produced, and whether sufficient demand for that visualized new product might actually materialize.

In addition, new ideas are typically associated with considerable asymmetries. In order to evaluate a proposed new idea concerning a new biotechnology product, the decision maker might not only need to have a Ph.D. in biotechnology, but also a specialization in the exact scientific area. Such divergences in education, background, and experience can result in a divergence in the expected value of a new project or the variance in outcomes anticipated from pursuing that new idea, both of which can lead to divergences in the recognition and evaluation of opportunities across economic agents and decision-making hierarchies. Such divergences in the valuation of new ideas will become greater if the new idea is not consistent with the core competence and technological trajectory of the incumbent firm.

Thus, because of the conditions inherent in knowledge – high uncertainty, asymmetries, and transactions cost – decision-making hierarchies can reach the decision not to pursue and try to commercialize new ideas that individual economic agents, or groups or teams of economic agents, think are potentially valuable and should be pursued. The basic conditions characterizing new knowledge, combined with a broad spectrum of institutions, rules, and regulations impose what could be termed as *The Knowledge Filter*. The knowledge filter is the gap between new knowledge and what Arrow (1962) referred to as economic knowledge or commercialized knowledge: the greater the knowledge filter, the more pronounced this gap between new knowledge and new economic, or commercialized, knowledge.

The knowledge filter is a consequence of the basic conditions inherent in new knowledge. Similarly, it is the knowledge filter that creates the opportunity for entrepreneurship in the knowledge spillover theory of entrepreneurship. According to this theory, opportunities for entrepreneurship are the duality of the knowledge filter. The higher is the knowledge filter, the greater are the divergences in the valuation of new ideas across economic agents and the decision-making hierarchies of incumbent firms. Entrepreneurial opportunities are generated not just by investments in new knowledge and ideas, but also in the propensity for only a distinct subset of those opportunities to be fully pursued by incumbent firms.

Thus, as Audretsch pointed out in 1995, the knowledge theory of entrepreneurship shifts the fundamental decision-making unit of observation in the model of the knowledge production function away from exogenously assumed firms to individuals, such as scientists, engineers, or other knowledge workers – agents with endowments of new economic knowledge. When the lens is shifted away from the firm to the individual as the relevant unit of observation, the appropriability issue remains, but the question becomes, 'How can economic agents with a given endowment of new knowledge best appropriate the returns from that knowledge?' If the scientist or engineer can pursue the new idea within the organizational structure of the firm developing the knowledge and appropriate roughly the expected value of that knowledge, she has no reason to leave the firm. On the other hand, if she places a greater value on her ideas than do the decision-making bureaucracy of the incumbent firm, she may choose to start a new firm to appropriate the value of her knowledge.

In the knowledge spillover theory of entrepreneurship the knowledge production function is actually reversed. The knowledge is exogenous and embodied in a worker. The firm is created endogenously in the worker's effort to appropriate the value of her knowledge through innovative activity. Typically an employee from an established large corporation, often a scientist or engineer working in a research laboratory, will have an idea for an invention and ultimately for an innovation. Accompanying this potential innovation is an expected net return from the new product. The knowledge worker would expect to be compensated for her potential innovation accordingly. If the company has a different, presumably lower, valuation of the potential innovation, it may decide either not to pursue its development, or that it merits a lower level of compensation than that expected by the employee.

In either case, the knowledge worker will weigh the alternative of starting her own firm. If the gap in the expected return accruing from the potential innovation between the inventor and the corporate decision maker is sufficiently large, and if the cost of starting a new firm is sufficiently low, the employee may decide to leave the large corporation and establish a new enterprise. Since the knowledge was generated in the established corporation, the new startup is considered to be a spin-off from the existing firm. Such startups typically do not have direct access to a large R&D laboratory. Rather, the entrepreneurial opportunity emanates from the knowledge and experience accrued in the R&D laboratories with their previous employers. Thus the knowledge spillover view of entrepreneurship is actually a theory of endogenous entrepreneurship, where entrepreneurship is an endogenous response to opportunities created by investments in new knowledge in a given context that are not commercialized because of the knowledge filter.

The *Endogenous Entrepreneurship Hypothesis* posits that entrepreneurship is a response to investments in knowledge and ideas by incumbent organizations that are not fully commercialized by those organizations. Thus, those contexts that are richer in knowledge will offer more entrepreneurial opportunities and therefore should also endogenously induce more entrepreneurial activity, *ceteris paribus*. By contrast, those contexts that are impoverished in knowledge will offer only meager entrepreneurial opportunities generated by knowledge spillovers, and therefore would endogenously induce less entrepreneurial activity.

But what is the appropriate unit of observation to be used to frame the context and observe the entrepreneurial response to knowledge investments made by incumbent organizations? In his 1995 book, Audretsch proposed using the industry as the context in which knowledge is created, developed, organized, and commercialized. The context of an industry was used to resolve the paradox concerning the high innovative output of small enterprises given their low level of knowledge inputs that seemingly contradicted the Griliches model of the firm knowledge production:

> The findings in this book challenge an assumption implicit to the knowledge production function – that firms exist exogenously and then endogenously seek out and apply knowledge inputs to generate innovative output.... It is the knowledge in the possession of economic agents that is exogenous, and in an effort to appropriate the returns from that knowledge, the spillover of knowledge from its producing entity involves endogenously creating a new firm. (Audretsch, 1995, 179–180)

What is the source of this entrepreneurial knowledge that endogenously generated the startup of new firms? The answer seemed to be through the spillover of knowledge from the source leading to commercialization via the startup of a new firm:

How are these small and frequently new firms able to generate innovative output when undertaken a generally negligible amount of investment into knowledge-generating inputs, such as R&D? One answer is apparently through exploiting knowledge created by expenditures on research in universities and on R&D in large corporations. (Audretsch, 1995, p. 179)

The empirical evidence supporting the knowledge spillover theory of entrepreneurship was provided from analyzing variations in startup rates across different industries reflecting different underlying knowledge contexts (Audretsch, 1995). In particular, those industries with a greater investment in new knowledge also exhibited higher startup rates while those industries with less investment in new knowledge exhibited lower startup rates, which was interpreted as the mechanism by which knowledge spillovers are transmitted.

In subsequent research, Klepper and Sleeper (2000) showed how spin-offs in the automobile industry exhibited a superior performance when the founder came from a high-performing incumbent firm, as compared to a low-performing incumbent firm, or even from outside of the industry. Klepper and Sleeper interpreted this result as indicating that the experience and ability to absorb human capital within the context of the incumbent firm influenced the subsequent entrepreneurial performance.

Thus, compelling evidence was provided suggesting that entrepreneurship is an endogenous response to the potential for commercializing knowledge that has not been adequately commercialized by the incumbent firms. This involved an organizational dimension involving the mechanism transmitting knowledge spillovers – the startup of new firms.

The localization hypothesis

The *Endogenous Entrepreneurship Hypothesis* involves the organizational interdependency between entrepreneurial startups and incumbent organizations investing in the creation of new knowledge (Audretsch, Keilbach, and Lehmann, 2006; Audretsch, 2007). A second hypothesis emerging from the knowledge spillover theory of entrepreneurship, *The Localizational Hypothesis*, has to do with the location of the entrepreneurial activity.

An important theoretical development is that geography may provide a relevant unit of observation within which knowledge spillovers occur. The theory of localization suggests that because geographic proximity is needed to transmit knowledge and especially tacit knowledge, knowledge spillovers tend to be localized within a geographic region. A wave of recent empirical studies by Jaffe (1989), Jaffe, Trajtenberg, and Henderson (1993), Acs, Audretsch, and Feldman (1992; 1994), Audretsch and Feldman (1996), and Audretsch and Stephan (1996) has supported the importance of geographic proximity for knowledge spillovers.

As it became apparent that the firm was not completely adequate as a unit of analysis for estimating the model of the knowledge production function, scholars began to look for externalities. In refocusing the model of the knowledge production to a spatial unit of observation, scholars confronted two challenges. The first one was theoretical. What was the theoretical basis for knowledge to spill over yet, at the same time, be spatially within some geographic unit of observation? The second challenge involved measurement. How could knowledge spillovers be measured and identified? More than a few scholars heeded Krugman's warning (1991, p. 53) that empirical measurement of knowledge spillovers would prove to be impossible because 'knowledge flows are invisible, they leave no paper trail by which they may be measured and tracked.'[1]

In confronting the first challenge, which involved developing a theoretical basis for geographically bounded knowledge spillovers, scholars turned to the emerging literature of the new growth theory. In explaining the increased divergence in the distribution of economic activity between countries and regions, Krugman (1991b) and Romer (1986) relied on models based on increasing returns to scale in production. By increasing returns, however, Krugman and Romer did not necessarily mean at the level of observation most familiar in the industrial organization literature – the plant, or at least the firm – but rather at the level of a spatially distinguishable unit. In fact, it was assumed that the externalities across firms and even industries yield convexities in production. In particular, Krugman (1991b), invoking Marshall (1920), focused on convexities arising from spillovers from the following:

◆ a pooled labor market;
◆ pecuniary externalities enabling the provision of nontraded inputs to an industry in a greater variety and at lower cost;
◆ information or technological spillovers.

That knowledge spills over was barely disputed. Some 30 years earlier, Arrow (1962) identified externalities associated with knowledge due to its nonexclusive and nonrival use. However, what has been contested is the geographic range of knowledge spillovers: knowledge externalities are so important and forceful that there is no reason that knowledge should stop spilling over just because of borders, such as a city limit, state line, or national boundary. Krugman (1991b), and others, did not question the existence or importance of such knowledge spillovers. In fact, they argue that such knowledge externalities are so important and forceful that there is no reason for a political boundary to limit the spatial extent of the spillover.

In applying the model of the knowledge production function to spatial units of observation, theories of why knowledge externalities are spatially bounded were needed. Thus, it took the development of localization theories explaining not only that knowledge spills over but also why those spillovers decay as they move across geographic space.

Studies identifying the extent of knowledge spillovers are based on the model of the knowledge production function applied at spatial units of observation. In what is generally to be considered to be the first important study re-focusing the knowledge production function, Jaffe (1989) modified the traditional approach to estimate a model specified for both spatial and product dimensions. Empirical estimation of Equation (1) essentially shifted the knowledge production function from the unit

[1]Lucas (2001) and Lucas and Rossi-Hansberg (2002) impose a spatial structure on production externalities in order to model the spatial structure of cities. The logic is that spatial gradients capture some of the externalities associated with localized human capital accumulation.

of observation of a firm to that of a geographic unit. Implicitly contained within the knowledge production function model is the assumption that innovative activity should take place in those regions where the direct knowledge-generating inputs are the greatest, and where knowledge spillovers are the most prevalent. Jaffe (1989) dealt with the measurement problem raised by Krugman (1991a) by linking the patent activity within technologies located within states to knowledge inputs located within the same spatial jurisdiction.

Jaffe (1989) found empirical evidence supporting the notion that knowledge spills over for third-party use from university research laboratories as well as industry R&D laboratories. Acs, Audretsch, and Feldman (1992) confirmed that the knowledge production function represented by Equation (1) held at a spatial unit of observation using a direct measure of innovative activity: new product introductions in the market. Feldman (1994) extended the model to consider other knowledge inputs to the commercialization of new products. The results confirmed that the knowledge production function was robust at the geographic level of analysis: the output of innovation is a function of the innovative inputs in that location.

Although this literature has identified the important role that knowledge spillovers play, it provides little insight into the questions of why and how knowledge spills over. What happens within the black box of the knowledge production is vague and ambiguous at best. The exact links between knowledge sources and the resulting innovative output remain invisible and unknown. None of the above studies suggesting that knowledge spillovers are geographically bounded and localized within spatial proximity to the knowledge source actually identifies the precise mechanisms that transmit the knowledge spillover; rather, the spillovers were implicitly assumed to exist automatically, or fall like 'manna from heaven', but only within a geographically bounded spatial area.

One explanation was provided by the knowledge spillover theory of entrepreneurship, which suggests that the startup of a new firm is a response to investments in knowledge and ideas by incumbent organizations that are not fully commercialized by those organizations. Thus, those contexts that are richer in knowledge will offer more entrepreneurial opportunities and therefore should also endogenously induce more entrepreneurial activity, *ceteris paribus*. By contrast, those contexts that are impoverished in knowledge will offer only meager entrepreneurial opportunities generated by knowledge spillovers, and therefore would endogenously induce less entrepreneurial activity.

Access to knowledge spillovers requires spatial proximity. Jaffe (1989) and Audretsch and Feldman (1996) made it clear that spatial proximity is a prerequisite to accessing such knowledge spillovers, but they provided no insight about the actual mechanism transmitting such knowledge spillovers. As for the Romer (1986) and Lucas (1993) models, investment in new knowledge automatically generates knowledge spillovers. Their only additional insight involves the spatial dimension – knowledge spills over but the spillovers are spatially bounded. Since we have just identified one such mechanism by which knowledge spillovers are transmitted – the startup of a new firm – it follows that knowledge spillover entrepreneurship is also spatially bounded, in that local access is required to access the knowledge facilitating the entrepreneurial startup. Therefore, new firm startups tend to locate close to knowledge sources, such as universities, in order to access spillovers.

Systematic empirical support for both the *Localization Hypothesis* and the *Endogenous Entrepreneurship Hypothesis* is provided by Audretsch, Keilbach, and Lehmann (2005), who show that the startup of new knowledge-based and technology firms is geographically constrained within close geographic proximity to knowledge sources. Based on data from Germany in the 1990s, their evidence shows that startup activity tends to cluster geographically around sources of new knowledge, such as R&D investments by firms and research undertaken at universities. Their findings provide compelling support for the *Knowledge Spillover Theory of Entrepreneurship* in that entrepreneurial activity is systematically greater in locations with a greater investment in knowledge and new ideas.

Similarly, the research laboratories of universities provide a source of innovation-generating knowledge that is available to private enterprises for commercial exploitation. Jaffe (1989) and Acs, Audretsch, and Feldman (1992), for example, found that the knowledge created in university laboratories 'spills over' to contribute to the generation of commercial innovations by private enterprises. Acs, Audretsch, and Feldman (1994) found persuasive evidence that spillovers from university research contribute more to the innovative activity of small firms than to the innovative activity of large corporations. Similarly, Link and Rees (1990) surveyed 209 innovating firms to examine the relationship between firm size and university research. They found that, in fact, large firms are more active in university-based research. However, small- and medium-sized enterprises apparently are better able to exploit their university-based associations and generate innovations. Link and Rees (1990) conclude that, contrary to the conventional wisdom, diseconomies of scale in producing innovations exist in large firms. They attribute these diseconomies of scale to the 'inherent bureaucratization process which inhibits both innovative activity and the speed with which new inventions move through the corporate system towards the market' (Link and Rees, 1990, p. 25).

Conclusions

Something of a dichotomy has emerged between the literatures on entrepreneurial opportunities and firm innovation and technology management. On the one hand, in the entrepreneurship literature, opportunities are taken as being exogenous to the fundamental decision-making unit – the individual confronted with an entrepreneurial decision. On the other hand, in the model of the knowledge production function, opportunities are decidedly endogenous and the result of purposeful investments into the creation of new knowledge and ideas through expenditures on R&D and augmentation to human capital. This dichotomy between the literatures on firm innovation and entrepreneurship reflects implicit assumptions about the independence and separability of the two essential decision-making units – the incumbent organization and the (potential) entrepreneur.

This chapter has drawn on emerging theories of entrepreneurship that challenge the assumption that opportunities are exogenous. The *Knowledge Spillover Theory of Entrepreneurship* inverts the assumptions inherent in the model of the knowledge production function for the firm. Rather than assuming that the firm is exogenous and then endogenously creates new knowledge and innovative output through purposeful investments in R&D and human capital, this view instead starts with an individual exogenously endowed with a stock of knowledge and ideas. The new firm is then endogenously created in an effort to commercialize and appropriate the value of that knowledge.

The prevalent and traditional theories of entrepreneurship have typically held the context constant and then examined how characteristics specific to the individual impact the cognitive process inherent in the model of entrepreneurial choice. This often leads to a view that is remarkably analogous to that concerning technical change in the Solow (1956) model – given a distribution of personality characteristics, proclivities, preferences, and tastes, entrepreneurship is exogenous. One of the great conventional wisdoms in entrepreneurship is that 'Entrepreneurs are born not made': either you have it or you don't. This leaves virtually no room for policy or for altering what nature has created.

This chapter has presented an alternative view. We hold the individual attributes constant and instead focus on variations in the context. In particular, we consider how the knowledge context will impact the cognitive process underlying the entrepreneurial choice model. The result is a theory of endogenous entrepreneurship, where (knowledge) workers respond to opportunities generated by new knowledge by starting a new firm. In this view entrepreneurship is a rational choice made by economic agents to appropriate the expected value of their endowment of knowledge. Thus, the creation of a new firm is the endogenous response to investments in knowledge that have not been entirely or exhaustively appropriated by the incumbent firm.

In the endogenous theory of entrepreneurship, the spillover of knowledge and the creation of a new, knowledge-based firm are virtually synonymous. Of course, there are many other important mechanisms facilitating the spill over of knowledge that have nothing to do with entrepreneurship, such as the mobility of scientists and workers, and informal networks, linkages, and interactions. Similarly, there are certainly new firms started that have nothing to do with the spillover of knowledge. Still, the spillover theory of entrepreneurship suggests that there will be additional entrepreneurial activity as a rational and cognitive response to the creation of new knowledge. Those contexts with greater investment in knowledge should also experience a higher degree of entrepreneurship, *ceteris paribus*. Perhaps it is true that entrepreneurs are made. But more of them will discover what they are made of in a high-knowledge context than in an impoverished knowledge context. Thus, we are inclined to restate the conventional wisdom and instead propose that entrepreneurs are not necessarily made, but are rather a response – and in particular a response to high-knowledge contexts that are especially fertile in spawning entrepreneurial opportunities.

References

Acs, Z.J., and Audretsch, D.B. (1987). Innovation, market structure and firm size. *Review of Economics and Statistics*, 69(4), 567–75.

Acs, Z.J., and Audretsch, D.B. (1988). Innovation in large and small firms: an empirical analysis, *American Economic Review*, 78(4), 678–90.

Acs, Z.J., and Audretsch, D.B. (1990). *Innovation and small firms*. MIT Press.

Acs, Z.J., and Audretsch, D.B. (1991). R&D, firm size, and innovative activity. In Z.J. Acs and D.B. Audretsch (eds), *Innovation and Technological Change*, The University of Michigan Press, 39–60.

Acs, Z.J., Audretsch, D.B., Braunerhjelm, P., and Carlsson, B. (2004). *The missing link: the knowledge filter and entrepreneurship in endogenous growth*. Centre for Economic Policy Research (CEPR) discussion paper.

Acs, Z.J., Audretsch, D.B., and Feldman, M.P. (1992). Real effects of academic research. *American Economic Review*, 82(1), 363–67.

Acs, Z.J., Audretsch, D.B., and Feldman, M.P. (1994). R&D spillovers and recipient firm size. *Review of Economics and Statistics*, 100(2), 336–67.

Agarwal, R., Echambadi, R., Franco, A., and Sarker, M.B. (forthcoming). Knowledge transfer through inheritance: spin-out generation, development and performance. *Academy of Management Journal*.

Arrow, K.J. (1962). Economic welfare and the allocation of resources for invention. In R.R. Nelson (ed.), *The Rate and Direction of Inventive Activity*, Princeton University Press, 609–26.

Audretsch, D.B. (1995). *Innovation and industry evolution*. MIT Press.

Audretsch, D.B. (2007). *The entrepreneurial society*. Oxford University Press.

Audretsch, D.B., and Feldman, M.P. (1996). R&D spillovers and the geography of innovation and production. *American Economic Review*, 86(3), 630–40.

Audretsch, D.B., Keilbach, M., and Lehmann, E. (2006). *Entrepreneurship and Economic Growth*. Oxford University Press.

Audretsch, D.B., and Stephan, P.E. (1996) Company-scientist locational links: the case of biotechnology. *American Economic Review*, 86(3), June, 641–52.

Bound, J., Cummins, C., Griliches, Z., Hall, B.H., and Jaffe, A. (1984). Who does R&D and who patents? In Z. Griliches (ed.), *R&D, Patents, and Productivity*, University of Chicago Press, 21–54.

Chandler, A. (1990). *Scale and Scope: The Dynamics of Industrial Capitalism*. Harvard University Press.

Cohen, W.M., and Klepper, S. (1991). Firm size versus diversity in the achievement of technological advance. Z.J. Acs and D.B. Audretsch (eds), *Innovation and Technological Change: An International Comparison*, University of Michigan Press, 183–203.

Cohen, W.M., and Klepper, S. (1992). The tradeoff between firm size and diversity in the pursuit of technological progress. *Small Business Economics*, 4(1), 1–14.

Cohen, W.M., and Levin, R.C. (1989). Empirical studies of innovation and market structure. In R. Schmalensee and R. Willig (eds), *Handbook of Industrial Organization*, Volume II, North Holland, 1059–107.

Feldman, M.P. (1994). Knowledge complementarity and innovation. *Small Business Economics*, 6, 363–72.

Grabowski, H.G. (1968). The determinants of industrial research and development: a study of the chemical, drug, and petroleum industries. *Journal of Political Economy*, 76(4), 292–306.

Griliches, Z. (1979). Issues in assessing the contribution of R&D to productivity growth. *Bell Journal of Economics*, 10, 92–116.

Griliches, Z. (1984). *R&D, Patents and Productivity*. University of Chicago Press.

Griliches, Z. (1990). Patent statistics as economic indicators: a survey. *Journal of Economic Literature*, 28(4), 1661–707.

Henbert, R.F., and Link, A.N. (1989). In search of the meaning of entrepreneurship. *Small Business Economics*, 1(1), 39–49.

Jaffe, A.B. (1989). Real effects of academic research. *American Economic Review*, 79(5), 957–70.

Jaffe, A., Trajtenberg, M. and Henderson, R. (1993). Geographic localization of knowledge spillovers as evidenced by patent citations. *Quarterly Journal of Economics*, 63, 577–98.

Kleinknecht, A. (1987a). Measuring R&D in small firms: How much are we missing? *The Journal of Industrial Economics*, 36(2), 253–56.

Kleinknecht, A. (1987b). Firm size and innovation. *Small Business Economics Journal*, 1(3), 215–22.

Kleinknecht, A., and Reijnen, J.O.N. (1991). More evidence on the undercounting of small firm R&D. *Research Policy*, 20(6), 579–87.

Kleinknecht, A., and Verspagen, B. (1987). R&D and market structure: The impact of measurement and aggregation problems. *Small Business Economics Journal*, 1(4), 297–301.

Klepper, S., and Sleeper, S. (2000). Entry by spinoffs. Unpublished manuscript, Carnegie Mellon University.

Krueger, N.F. Jr. (2003). The cognitive psychology of entrepreneurship. In Z.J. Acs and D.B. Audretsch (eds), *Handbook of Entrepreneurship Research*, Springer Publishers, 105–40.

Krugman, P. (1991a). Increasing returns and economic geography. *Journal of Political Economy*, 99, 483–99.

Krugman, P. (1991b). *Geography and trade*. MIT Press.

Kuznets, S. (1962). Inventive activity: problems of definition and measurement. In R.R. Nelson (ed.), *The Rate and Direction of Inventive Activity*, National Bureau of Economic Research Conference Report, 19–43.

Link, A.N., and Rees, J. (1990). Firm size, university based research, and the returns to R&D. *Small Business Economics*, 2(1), 25–32.

Lucas, R.E. (1993). Making a miracle. *Econometrica*, 61, 251–72.

Lucas, R.E. (2001). Externalities and cities. *Review of Economic Dynamics*, 4(2), 245–74.

Lucas, R.E., and Rossi-Hansberg, E. (2002). On the internal structure of cities. *Econometrica*, 70(4), 445–76.

Mansfield, E. (1968). *Industrial research and technological change*. W.W. Norton, for the Cowles Foundation for Research Economics at Yale University, 83–108.

Mansfield, E. (1981). Composition of R&D expenditures: relationship to size of firm, concentration, and innovative output. *Review of Economics and Statistics*, 63, 610–5.

Mansfield, E. (1983). Industrial organization and technological change: recent empirical findings. In J.V. Craven (ed.), *Industrial Organization, Antitrust, and Public Policy*, Kluwer-Nijhoff, 129–43.

Mansfield, E., Romeo, A., Schwartz, M., Teece, D., Wagner, S., and Brach, P. (1982). *Technology transfer, productivity, and economic policy*, W.W. Norton.

Marshall, A. (1920). *Principles of Economics. An Introductory Volume*, 8th Edition, Macmillan.

McClelland, D. (1961). *The achieving society*. Free Press.

Mueller, D.C. (1967). The firm decision process: an econometric investigation. *Journal of Political Economy*, 81(1), 58–87.

Nelson, R.R. (1959). The simple economics of basic scientific research. *Journal of Political Economy*, 67(2), 297–306.

Pakes, A. and Griliches, Z. (1980). Patents and R&D at the firm level: A first report. *Economics Letters*, Elsevier, 5(4), 377–81

Romer, P.M. (1986). Increasing returns and long-run growth. *Journal of Political Economy*, 94(5), 1002–37.

Sarasvathy, S.D., Dew, N., Velamuri, S.R., and Venkataraman, S. (2003). Three views of entrepreneurial opportunity. In Z.J. Acs and D.B. Audretsch (eds), *Handbook of Entrepreneurship Research*, Springer Publishers, 141–60.

Scherer, F.M. (1965). Firm size, market structure, opportunity, and the output of patented inventions. *American Economic Review*, 55, 1097–125.

Scherer, F.M. (1967). Market structure and the employment of scientists and engineers. *American Economic Review*, 57, 524–30.

Scherer, F.M. (1982). Industrial technology flows in the United States. *Research Policy*, 11(4), 227–45.

Scherer, F.M. (1983). The propensity to patent. *International Journal of Industrial Organization*, 1, 107–28.

Scherer, F.M., (1984). *Innovation and growth: Schumpeterian perspectives*. MIT Press.

Schumpeter, J.A., (1942). *Capitalism, socialism and democracy*. Harper and Row.

Shane, S. (2000). Prior knowledge and the discovery of entrepreneurial opportunities. *Organization Science*, 11, 448–69.

Shane, S., and Eckhardt, J. (2003). The individual-opportunity nexus. In Z.J. Acs and D.B. Audretsch (eds), *Handbook of Entrepreneurship Research*, Springer Publishers, 161–94.

Shaver, K.G. (2003). The social psychology of entrepreneurial behavior. In Z.J. Acs and D.B. Audretsch (eds), *Handbook of Entrepreneurship Research*, Springer Publishers, 331–58.

Soete, L.L.G. (1979). Firm size and inventive activity: The evidence reconsidered. *European Economic Review*, 12(4), 319–40.

Solow, R. (1956). A contribution to the theory of economic growth. *Quarterly Journal of Economics*, 70, 65–94.

Stevenson, H.H., and Jarillo, J.C. (1990). A paradigm of entrepreneurship: Entrepreneurial management. *Strategic Management Journal*, 11, 17–27.

Venkataraman, S. (1997). The distinctive domain of entrepreneurship research: An editor's perspective. In J. Katz and R. Brockhaus (eds), *Advances in Entrepreneurship, Firm Emergence and Growth, vol. 3*, JAI Press, 119–38.

15

The Financing of Innovation

Bronwyn H. Hall

This is a revision of an article published in the *Oxford Review of Economic Policy*, January 2002. I am grateful to the editor of this handbook, Scott Shane, for comments and to the Munich School of Management, Ludwig-Maximilians University for hospitality when the revision was prepared.

INTRODUCTION

An important problem in the managing of technology is the financing of technological development and innovation. Even in large firms, technology managers often report that they have more projects that they would like to undertake than funds to spend on them.[1] There are a number of reasons for this phenomenon: low expected returns due to an inability to capture the profits from an invention, the uncertainty and risk associated with the project, and over-optimism on the part of managers. This chapter reviews these arguments in more detail and considers the evidence, both theoretical and empirical, on the extent of the problem.

Economists have long held the view that innovative activities are difficult to finance in a freely competitive market place. Support for this view in the form of economic-theoretic modeling is not difficult to find and probably begins with the classic articles of Nelson (1959) and Arrow (1962), although the idea itself was alluded to by Schumpeter (1942).[2] The argument goes as follows: the primary output of innovation investment is the knowledge of how to make new goods and services, and this knowledge is nonrival: use by one firm does not preclude its use by another. To the extent that knowledge cannot be kept secret, the returns to the investment in it cannot be appropriated by the firm undertaking the investment, and therefore such firms will be reluctant to invest, leading to the underprovision of R&D and other innovation investments in the economy.

---

[1] See, for example, Peeters and van Pottelsberghe (2003). The author has also heard this claim in conversations with R&D managers of a variety of firms.

[2] See, for example, footnote 1, Chapter VIII of *Capitalism, Socialism and Democracy*.

Handbook of Technology and Innovation Management.   Edited by Scott Shane
© 2008 John Wiley & Sons, Ltd

Since the time when this argument was fully articulated by Arrow (1962), it has of course been developed, tested, modified, and extended in many ways. For example, Levin *et al.* (1987) and Mansfield *et al.* (1981) found using survey evidence that imitating a new invention was not costless, but could cost as much as 50–75% of the cost of the original invention. This fact will mitigate but not eliminate the underinvestment problem. Empirical support for the basic point concerning the positive externalities created by research that was made by Arrow is widespread, mostly in the form of studies that document a social return to R&D that is higher than the private level (Griliches, 1992; Hall, 1996).

This line of reasoning is already widely used by policymakers to justify such interventions as the intellectual property (IP) system, government support of innovative activities, R&D tax incentives, and the encouragement of research partnerships of various kinds. In general, these incentive programs can be warranted even when the firm or individual undertaking the research is the same as the entity that finances it. However, Arrow's (1962) influential paper also contains another argument, again one which was foreshadowed by Schumpeter and which has been addressed by subsequent researchers in economics and finance: the argument that an additional gap exists between the private rate of return and the cost of capital when the innovation investor and financier are different entities.

This chapter concerns itself with this second aspect of the market failure for innovation investment: even if problems associated with incomplete appropriability of the returns to R&D are solved using IP protection, subsidies, or tax incentives, it may still be difficult or costly to finance R&D and other innovative activities using capital from sources external to the firm or entrepreneur. That is, there is often a wedge, sometimes large, between the rate of return required by an entrepreneur investing his or her own funds and that required by external investors. By this argument, unless an inventor is already wealthy, or firms already profitable, some innovations will fail to be provided purely because the cost of external capital is too high, even when they would pass the private returns hurdle if funds were available at a 'normal' interest rate.

In the following, I begin by describing some of the unique features of R&D investment. Many of these features also characterize innovative activity when it is more broadly defined to include the marketing, product development, and employee training associated with an innovation. Then I discuss the various theoretical arguments why external finance for R&D might be more expensive that internal finance, before going on to review the empirical evidence on the validity of this hypothesis and the solutions that have been developed and adopted by the market and some governments.

RESEARCH AND DEVELOPMENT AS INVESTMENT

From the perspective of investment theory, innovation investments have a number of characteristics that make them different from ordinary investment. First and most importantly, in practice 50% or more of the R&D portion of this investment is the wages and salaries of highly educated scientists and engineers. Their efforts create an intangible asset, the firm's knowledge base, from which profits in future years will be generated. To the extent that this knowledge is 'tacit' rather than codified, it is embedded in the human capital of the firm's employees, and is therefore lost if they leave or are fired.

This fact has an important implication for the conduct of R&D investment. Because part of the resource base of the firm itself disappears when such workers leave or are fired, firms tend to smooth their R&D spending over time, in order to avoid having to lay off knowledge workers. This implies that R&D spending at the firm level typically behaves as though it has high adjustment costs (Hall, Griliches, and Hausman, 1986; Lach and Schankerman, 1988), with two consequences, one substantive and one that affects empirical work in this area. First, the equilibrium required rate of return to R&D may be quite high simply to cover the adjustment costs. Second, and related to the first, is that it will be difficult for empirical studies to measure the impact of changes in the costs of capital on such investment, because such effects can be weak in the short run due to the sluggish response of R&D to any changes in its cost.

A second important feature of R&D investment is the degree of uncertainty associated with its output. This uncertainty tends to be greatest at the beginning of a research program or project, which implies that an optimal R&D strategy has an options-like character and should not really be analyzed in a static framework. R&D projects with small probabilities of great success in the future may be worth continuing even if they do not pass an expected rate of return test. The uncertainty here can be extreme and not a simple matter of a well-specified distribution with a mean and variance. There is evidence (Scherer, 1998) that the distribution of profits from innovation sometimes takes the form of a Pareto distribution where the variance does not exist. When this is the case, standard risk-adjustment methods will not work well.

An important characteristic of uncertainty for the financing of investment in innovation is the fact that as investments are made over time, new information arrives that reduces or changes the uncertainty. The consequence is that the decision to invest in any particular project is not a once and for all decision, but has to be reassessed throughout the life of the project. In addition to making such investment a real option, the sequence of decisions complicates the analysis by introducing dynamic elements into the interaction of the financier (either within or without the firm) and the innovator. I discuss the implications for the source of financing of innovation in the next section of this chapter.

The natural starting point for the analysis of any type of investment financing is the 'neo-classical' marginal profit condition, suitably modified to take the special features of R&D into account. This condition sets the marginal product of capital equal to the pre-tax rate of return on investment in that capital. Because the financial markets supply capital at an interest rate that is evaluated after corporate tax is paid, the investment decision will depend on the depreciation rate and tax treatment of the particular capital asset. The user cost formulation directs attention to the following determinants of R&D financing:

- Tax treatment such as tax credits, which are clearly amenable to intervention by policy makers.

- Economic depreciation δ, which in the case of R&D is more properly termed obsolescence. This quantity is sensitive to the realized rate of technical change in the industry, which is in turn determined by such things as market structure and the rate of imitation. Thus it is difficult to treat δ as an invariant parameter in this setting.
- The marginal costs of adjusting the level of the R&D program.
- The investor's required rate of return.

The last item has been the subject of considerable theoretical and empirical interest, on the part of both industrial organization and corporate finance economists. Two broad strands of investigation can be observed: one focuses on the role of asymmetric information and moral hazard in raising the required rate of return above that normally used for conventional investment, and the other on the requirements of different sources of financing and their differing tax treatments for the rate of return. The next section discusses these factors.

THEORETICAL BACKGROUND

This section reviews the reasons why the impact of financial considerations on the investment decision may vary with the type of investment and with the source of funds in more detail. To do this, I distinguish between those factors that arise from various kinds of market failures in this setting and the purely financial (or tax-oriented) considerations that affect the cost of different sources of funds.

One of the implications of the well-known Modigliani-Miller theorem (Modigliani and Miller, 1958; Miller and Modigliani, 1961) is that a firm choosing the optimal levels of investment should be indifferent to its capital structure, and should face the same price for all types of investment (including investments in creating new products and processes) on the margin. The last dollar spent on each type of investment should yield the same expected rate of return (after adjustment for nondiversifiable risk). A large literature, both theoretical and empirical, has questioned the bases for this theorem, but it remains a useful starting point.

There are several reasons why the theorem might fail to hold in practice:

- uncertainty coupled with incomplete markets may make a real options approach to the R&D investment decision more appropriate;
- the cost of capital may differ by source of funds for non-tax reasons;
- the cost of capital may differ by source of funds for tax reasons;
- the cost of capital may also differ across types of investments (tangible and intangible) for both tax and other reasons.

With respect to innovation investment, economic theory advances a plethora of reasons why there might be a gap between the external and internal costs capital; these can be divided into three main types:

- asymmetric information between innovator and investor;
- moral hazard on the part of the innovator or arising from the separation of ownership and management;

♦ tax considerations that drive a wedge between external finance and finance by retained earnings.

Asymmetric information problems

In the R&D setting, the asymmetric information problem refers to the fact that an inventor frequently has better information about the likelihood of success and the nature of the contemplated innovation project than potential investors. Therefore, the marketplace for financing the development of innovative ideas looks like the 'lemons' market modeled by Akerlof (1970). The lemons' premium for R&D will be higher than that for ordinary investment because investors have more difficulty distinguishing good projects from bad when the projects are long-term R&D investments than when they are more short-term or low-risk projects (Leland and Pyle, 1977). When the level of R&D expenditure is a highly observable signal, as it is under current US and UK rules, we might expect that the lemons problem is somewhat mitigated, but certainly not eliminated.[3]

In the most extreme version of the lemons model, the market for R&D projects may disappear entirely if the asymmetric information problem is too great. Informal evidence suggests that some potential innovators believe this to be the case in fact. And as will be discussed below, venture capital systems are viewed by some as a solution to this 'missing markets' problem.

Reducing information asymmetry via fuller disclosure is of limited effectiveness in this arena, due to the ease of imitation of inventive ideas. Firms are reluctant to reveal their innovative ideas to the marketplace and the fact that there could be a substantial cost to revealing information to their competitors reduces the quality of the signal they can make about a potential project (Bhattacharya and Ritter, 1985; Anton and Yao, 1998). Thus the implication of asymmetric information coupled with the costliness of mitigating the problem is that firms and inventors will face a higher cost of external than internal capital for R&D due to the lemons' premium.

Some empirical support for this proposition exists, mostly in the form of event studies that measure the market response to announcements of new debt or share issues. Both Alam and Walton (1995) and Zantout (1997) find higher abnormal returns to firm shares following new debt issues when the firm is more R&D-intensive. The argument is that the acquisition of new sources of financing is good news when the firm has an asymmetric information problem because of its R&D strategy. Similarly, Szewcxyk, Tsetsekos, and Zantout (1996) find that investment opportunities (as proxied by Tobin's q) explain R&D-associated abnormal returns, and that these returns are higher when the firm is highly leveraged, implying a higher required rate of return for debt finance in equilibrium.

---

[3]Since 1974, publicly traded firms in the US have been required to report their total R&D expenditures in their annual reports and 10-K filings with the SEC, under FASB rule No. 2, issued October 1974, if such expenditures are 'material'. In 1989, a new accounting standard, SSAP 13, obligated similar disclosures in the UK. Most continental European countries do not have such a requirement, although they may evolve in that direction due to international harmonization of accounting standards, at least for publicly traded firms.

Moral hazard problems

Moral hazard in R&D investing arises in the usual way: modern industrial firms normally have separation of ownership and management. This leads to a principal-agent problem when the goals of the two conflict, which can result in investment strategies that are not share value maximizing. Two possible scenarios may coexist: one is the usual tendency of managers to spend on activities that benefit them (growing the firm beyond efficient scale, nicer offices, etc.) and the second is a reluctance of risk-averse managers to invest in uncertain R&D projects. Agency costs of the first type may be avoided by reducing the amount of free cash flow available to the managers by leveraging the firm, but this in turn forces them to use the higher cost external funds to finance R&D (Jensen and Meckling, 1976). Empirically, there seem to be limits to the use of the leveraging strategy in R&D-intensive sectors. See Hall (1990, 1994) for evidence that the LBO/restructuring wave of the 1980s, viewed by most researchers as driven by the need to reduce free cash flow in sectors where investment opportunities were poor, was almost entirely confined to industries and firms where R&D was of no consequence.

According to the second type of principal-agent conflict, managers are more risk averse than shareholders and avoid innovation projects that will increase the riskiness of the firm. If bankruptcy is a possibility, managers whose opportunity cost is lower than their present earnings and potential bondholders may both wish to avoid variance-increasing projects that shareholders would like to undertake. The argument of the theory is that long-term investments can suffer in this case. The optimal solution to this type of agency cost would be to increase the long-term incentives faced by the manager rather than reducing free cash flow.

Evidence on the importance of agency costs as they relate to R&D takes several forms. Several researchers have studied the impact of anti-takeover amendments (which arguably increase managerial security and willingness to take on risk while reducing managerial discipline) on R&D investment and firm value. Johnson and Rao (1997) find that such amendments are not followed by cuts in R&D, while Pugh, Jahera, and Oswald (1999) find that adoption of an Employee Stock Ownership Plan (ESOP), which is a form of anti-takeover protection, is followed by R&D increases. Cho (1992) finds that R&D intensity increases with the share that managerial shareholdings represent of the manager's wealth and interprets this as incentive pay mitigating agency costs and inducing long-term investment.

Some have argued that institutional ownership of the managerial firm can reduce the agency costs due to the free-riding by owners that is a feature of the governance of firms with diffuse ownership structure, whereas others have held that such ownership pays too much attention to short term earnings and therefore discourages long-term investments. Institutions such as mutual and pension funds often control somewhat larger blocks of shares than individuals, making monitoring firm and manager behavior a more effective and more rewarding activity for these organizations.

There is some limited evidence that this may indeed be the case. Eng and Shackell (2001) find that firms adopting long-term performance plans for their managers do not increase their R&D spending but that institutional ownership is associated with higher R&D; R&D firms tend not to be held by banks and insurance companies. Majumdar and Nagarajan (1997) find that high institutional investor ownership does *not* lead to short-term behavior on the part of the firm; in particular, it does not lead to cuts in R&D spending. Francis and Smith (1995) find that diffusely held firms are less innovative, implying that monitoring alleviates agency costs and enables investment in innovation.

Although the evidence summarized above is fairly clear and indicates that long-term incentives for managers can encourage R&D and that institutional ownership does not necessarily discourage R&D investment, it is fairly silent on the magnitude of these effects, and whether these governance features truly close the agency cost-induced gap between the cost of capital and the return to R&D.

In the presence of uncertainty and the revelation of innovation success probability over time, the possibility of asymmetric information and moral hazard in the investor-innovator relationship creates further problems for achieving the optimal contract. For example, it is often observed that entrepreneurs or R&D managers wish to continue projects that investors would like to terminate (Cornelli and Yosha 2003), presumably because the possibility of an ultimate benefit to them looms large and they do not face the investment cost in the case of failure. If they are also over-confident, they will be even more biased toward continuation. Asymmetric information about the project will imply that the investor has relatively more difficulty than the innovator even in determining the probability of success. The combination of information rents and agency costs will lead to inefficient funding of projects over time as well as inefficient (too low) levels of funding.

In a recent paper, Bergemann and Hege (2005) have analyzed these tradeoffs in a multi-stage investment financing decision under changing uncertainty, with renegotiation allowed. They look at the choice between relationship financing (where the investor is able to monitor the progress of the project accurately) and arm's length financing (where the investor must rely on the innovator for information). The investor is able to speed up or slow down the rate of financing, depending on the progress of the project and his or her expectations of success. In general, Bergemann and Hege find that agency costs lead to nonoptimal stopping rules for projects, stopping them too soon on average. Surprisingly, arm's length contracts can lead to higher project values, because in these the investor can precommit to a stopping rule, which eliminates any benefit to the entrepreneur from attempts to prolong the project.

Capital structure and R&D

In the view of some observers, the leveraged buyout (LBO) wave of the 1980s in the US and the UK arose partly because high real interest rates meant that there were strong pressures to eliminate free cash flow within firms (Blair and Litan, 1990). For firms in industries where R&D is an important form of investment, such pressure should have been reduced by the need for internal funds to undertake such investment and indeed Hall (1993, 1994) and Opler and Titman (1993) find that firms with high R&D intensity were much less likely to do an LBO. Opler and Titman (1994) find that R&D firms that were leveraged suffered more than other firms when facing economic distress, presumably because leverage meant that they were unable to sustain R&D programs in the fact of reduced cash flow.

In related work using data on Israeli firms, Blass and Yosha (2003) report that R&D-intensive firms listed on the US stock exchanges use highly equity-based sources of financing, whereas those listed only in Israel rely more on bank financing and government funding. The former are more profitable and faster-growing, which suggests that the choice of where to list the shares and whether to finance with new equity is indeed sensitive to the expected rate of return to the R&D being undertaken. That is, investors supplying arms-length finance require higher returns to compensate them for the risk of a 'lemon'.

Although leverage may be a useful tool for reducing agency costs in the firm, it is of limited value for R&D-intensive firms. Because the knowledge asset created by R&D investment is intangible, partly embedded in human capital, and ordinarily very specialized to the particular firm in which it resides, the capital structure of R&D-intensive firms customarily exhibits considerably less leverage than that of other firms. Banks and other debtholders prefer to use physical assets to secure loans and are reluctant to lend when the project involves substantial R&D investment rather than investment in plant and equipment. In the words of Williamson (1988), 'redeployable' assets (that is, assets whose value in an alternative use is almost as high as in their current use) are more suited to the governance structures associated with debt. Alderson and Betker (1996) provide empirical support for this idea, finding that liquidation costs and R&D are positively related across firms. The implication is that the sunk costs associated with R&D investment are higher than that for ordinary investment.

In addition, servicing debt usually requires a stable source of cash flow, which makes it more difficult to find the funds for an R&D investment program that must be sustained at a certain level in order to be productive. For both these reasons, firms are either unable or reluctant to use debt finance for R&D investment, which may raise the cost of capital, depending on the precise tax treatment of debt versus equity.[4] Confirming empirical evidence for the idea that limiting free cash flow in R&D firms is a less desirable method of reducing agency costs is provided by Chung and Wright (1998), who find that financial slack and R&D spending are correlated with the value of growth firms positively, but not correlated with that of other firms. Czarnitzki and Kraft (2002) find that more leveraged German firms have lower innovation output (measured by patents), especially when ownership of the firm is dispersed.

Taxes and the source of funds

Tax considerations that yield variations in the cost of capital across source of finance have been well articulated by Auerbach (1984) among others. He argued that under the US tax system during most of its history the cost of financing new investment by debt has been less that of financing it by retained earnings, which is in turn less than

---

[4]There is also considerable cross-sectional evidence for the US that R&D intensity and leverage are negatively correlated across firms: see Friend and Lang (1988), Hall (1992), and Bhagat and Welch (1995).

that of issuing new shares. If dividends are taxed, financing with new shares is more expensive than financing with retained earnings because the alternative use of such earnings is paying out as taxable dividends. And except for the unlikely case where the personal income tax rate is much higher than the sum of the corporate and capital gains rates, debt financing will be the least expensive source of funds because the interest is deductible at the corporate level. Shareholders normally pay tax at a higher rate on retained earnings that are paid out than on those retained by the firm and invested.[5] It implicitly assumes that the returns from the investment made will be retained by the firm and eventually taxed at the capital gains rate rather than the rate on ordinary income.

It is also true that the tax treatment of R&D and other innovation investments in most OECD economies is very different from that of other kinds of investment: because R&D, marketing costs, training costs, etc. are expensed as they are incurred, the effective tax rate on the corresponding assets is lower than that on either plant or equipment, with or without an R&D tax credit in place. This effectively means that the economic depreciation of innovation assets is considerably less than the depreciation allowed for tax purposes – which is 100 % – so that the required rate of return for such investment would be lower. In addition some countries offer a tax credit or subsidy to R&D spending, which can reduce the after-tax cost of capital even further.[6]

The conclusion from this section of the paper is that the presence of either asymmetric information or a principal-agent conflict implies that new debt or equity finance will be relatively more expensive for R&D than for ordinary investment, and that considerations such as lack of collateral further reduce the possibility of debt finance. Together, these arguments suggest an important role for retained earnings in the R&D investment decision, independent of their value as a signal of future profitability. In fact, as has been argued by both Hall (1992) and Himmelberg and Petersen (1994), there is good reason to think that positive cash flow may be more important for R&D than for ordinary investment. The next section reports on a series of empirical tests for this proposition.

TESTING FOR FINANCIAL CONSTRAINTS

The usual way to examine the empirical relevance of the arguments that R&D investment in established firms can be disadvantaged when internal funds are not available, and recourse to external capital markets required, is to estimate R&D investment equations and test for the presence of 'liquidity' constraints, or excess sensitivity to cash flow shocks. This approach builds on the extensive literature developed for testing ordinary investment equations for liquidity constraints (Fazzari, Hubbard,

---

[5] A detailed discussion of tax regimes in different countries is beyond the scope of this survey, but it is quite common in several countries for long-term capital gains on funds that remain with a firm for more than one year to be taxed at a lower rate than ordinary income. Of course, even if the tax rates on the two kinds of income are equal, the inequalities will hold. Only in the case where dividends are not taxed at the corporate level (which was formerly the case in the UK) will the ranking given above not hold.

[6] See Hall and Van Reenen (2000) for details.

and Petersen, 1988; Arellano and Bond, 1991). It suffers from many of the same difficulties as the estimates in the investment literature, plus one additional problem that arises from the tendency of firms to smooth R&D spending over time.

The ideal experiment for identifying the effects of liquidity constraints on investment is to give firms additional cash exogenously, and observe whether they pass it on to shareholders or use it for investment and/or R&D. If they choose the first alternative, either the cost of capital to the firm has not fallen, or it has fallen but they still have no good investment opportunities. If they choose the second, the firm must have had some unexploited investment opportunities that were not profitable using more costly external finance. A finding that investment is sensitive to cash flow shocks that are *not* signals of future demand increases would reject the hypothesis that the cost of external funds is the same as the cost of internal funds. However, lack of true experiments of this kind forces researchers to use econometric techniques such as instrumental variables to attempt to control for demand shocks when estimating the investment demand equation, with varying degrees of success.

Econometric work that tests the hypothesis that financing constraints matter for R&D investment has largely been done using standard investment equation methodology. Two main approaches can be identified: one uses a neoclassical accelerator model with ad hoc dynamics to allow for the presence of adjustment costs, and the other an Euler equation derived from the forward-looking dynamic program of a profit-maximizing firm that faces adjustment costs for capital.[7]

The accelerator model begins with the marginal product equal to the cost or rate of return for capital and adds lags to the equation to reflect the fact that it takes time to adjust capital to its optimal level. Time dummies are generally included in the equation to capture the conventional cost of capital, assumed to be the same for all firms, and firm-specific costs related to financing constraints are included by adding current and lagged values of the cash flow/capital ratio to this equation.

The Euler equation approach is based on the idea that firms will shift investment between periods until the cost of capital in each period is equalized. When the firm changes its financial position (that is, the shadow value of additional funds for investment changes) between one period and the next, it will invest as though it is facing a cost of capital greater than the market interest rate (when the shadow value falls between periods) or less than the market interest rate (when the shadow value rises between periods). When estimating the model, the changes in financial position are modeled in a number of different ways:

- ◆ as a function of such things as dividend behavior, new share, or debt issues;
- ◆ as a function of the cash flow-capital ratio;
- ◆ by stratifying the firms into two groups, financially constrained and financially unconstrained.

This last was the method used by Fazzari, Hubbard, and Petersen (1988) in the paper that originated this literature.

---

[7]A detailed consideration of the econometric estimation of these models can be found in Mairesse, Hall, and Mulkay (1999). See also Hall (1991).

During the past few years, various versions of the methodologies described above have been applied to data on the R&D investment of US, UK, French, German, Irish, and Japanese firms. The firms examined are typically the largest and most important manufacturing firms in their economy. For example, Hall (1992) found a large positive elasticity between R&D and cash flow, using an accelerator-type model and a very large sample of US manufacturing firms. The estimation methodology here controlled for both firm effects and simultaneity. Similarly, and using some of the same data, Himmelberg and Petersen (1994) looked at a panel of 179 US small firms in high-tech industries and found an economically large and statistically significant relationship between R&D investment and internal finance.

Harhoff (1998) found weak but significant cash flow effects on R&D for both small and large German firms, although Euler equation estimates for R&D investment were uninformative due to the smoothness of R&D and the small sample size. Combining limited survey evidence with his regression results, he concludes that R&D investment in small German firms may be constrained by the availability of finance. Bond, Harhoff, and Van Reenen (1999) find significant differences between the cash flow impacts on R&D and investment for large manufacturing firms in the UK and Germany. German firms in their sample are insensitive to cash flow shocks, whereas the investment of non-R&D-doing UK firms does respond. Cash flow helps to predict whether a UK firm does R&D, but not the level of that R&D. The authors interpret their findings to mean that financial constraints are important for UK firms, but that those doing R&D are a self-selected group that face fewer constraints. This is consistent with the view that the desire of firms to smooth R&D over time combines with the relatively high cost of financing it to reduce R&D well below the level that would obtain in a frictionless world.

Mulkay, Hall, and Mairesse (2001) perform a similar exercise using large French and US manufacturing firms, finding that cash flow impacts are much larger in the US than in France, both for R&D and for ordinary investment. Except for the well-known fact that R&D exhibits higher serial correlation than investment (presumable because of higher adjustment costs), differences in behavior are between countries, not between investment types. This result is consistent with evidence reported in Hall *et al.* (1999) for the US, France, and Japan during an earlier time period, which basically finds that R&D and investment on the one hand, and sales and cash flow on the other, are simultaneously determined in the US (neither one 'Granger-causes' the other), whereas in the other countries, there is little feedback from sales and cash flows to the two investments. Using a nonstructural R&D investment equation together with data for the US, UK, Canada, Europe, and Japan, Bhagat and Welch (1995) found similar results for the 1985–1990 period, with stock returns predicting changes in R&D more strongly for the US and UK firms.

More recently, Bougheas, Goerg, and Strobl (2001) examined the effects of liquidity constraints on R&D investment using firm-level data for manufacturing firms in Ireland and also found evidence that R&D investment in these firms is financially constrained, in line with the previous studies of US and UK firms.

Brown (1997) argues that existing tests of the impact of capital market imperfections on innovative firms cannot distinguish between two possibilities: capital markets are perfect and different factors drive the firms' different types of expenditure; or capital markets are imperfect and different types of expenditure react differently to a common factor (shocks to the supply of internal finance). He then compares the sensitivity of investment to cash flow for innovative and noninnovative firms. The results support the hypothesis that capital markets are imperfect, finding that the investment of innovative firms is more sensitive to cash flow.

The conclusions from this body of empirical work are several: first, there is solid evidence that debt is a disfavored source of finance for R&D investment; second, the 'Anglo-Saxon' economies, with their thick and highly developed stock markets and relatively transparent ownership structures, typically exhibit more sensitivity and responsiveness of R&D to cash flow than continental economies; third, and much more speculatively, this greater responsiveness may arise because they are financially constrained, in the sense that they view external sources of finance as much more costly than internal, and therefore require a considerably higher rate of return to investments done on the margin when they are tapping these sources. However, it is perhaps equally likely that this responsiveness occurs because firms are more sensitive to demand signals in thick financial equity markets; a definitive explanation of the 'excess sensitivity' result awaits further research.[8] In addition to these results, the evidence from Germany and some other countries suggests that small firms are more likely to face this difficulty than large established firms (not surpisingly, if the source of the problem is a lemons' premium).

From a policy perspective, these results point to another reason why it may be socially beneficial to offer tax incentives to companies in order to reduce the cost of capital they face for R&D investment, especially to small and new firms. Many governments, including those in the US and the UK, currently have such programs. Such a policy approach simply observes that the cost of capital is relatively high for R&D and tries to close the gap via a tax subsidy. However, there is an alternative approach relying on the private sector that attempts to close the financing gap by reducing the degree of asymmetric information and moral hazard rather than simply subsidizing the investment. I turn to this topic in the next section.

SMALL FIRMS, STARTUP FINANCE, AND VENTURE CAPITAL

As should be apparent from much of the preceding discussion, any problems associated with financing investments in new technology will be most apparent for new entrants and startup firms. For this reason, many governments already provide some form of assistance for such firms, and in many countries, especially the US, there exists a private sector 'venture capital' industry that is focused on solving the problem of financing innovation for new and young firms. This section reviews what we know about these alternative funding mechanisms, beginning with a brief

---

[8] It is also true that much of the literature here has tended to downplay the role of measurement error in drawing conclusions from the results. Measurement error in Tobin's q, cash flow, or output is likely to be sizable and will ensure that all variables will enter any specification of the R&D investment equation significantly, regardless of whether they truly belong or not. Instrumental variables estimation is a partial solution, but only if all the errors are serially uncorrelated, which is unlikely.

look at government funding for startups and then discussing the venture capital solution.

Government funding for startup firms

Examples of such programs are the US Small Business Investment Company (SBIC) and Small Business Innovation Research (SBIR) programs. Together, these programs disbursed \$2.4 billion in 1995, more than 60 % of the amount from venture capital in that year (Lerner, 1998a). In Germany, more than 800 federal and state government financing program have been established for new firms in the recent past (OECD, 1995). In 1980, the Swedish established the first of a series of investment companies (along with instituting a series of measures such as reduced capital gains taxes to encourage private investments in startups), partly based on the US model. By 1987, the Swedish government's share of venture capital funding was 43 % (Karaomerliolu and Jacobsson, 1999). Recently, the UK has instituted a series of government programs under the Enterprise Fund umbrella, which allocate funds to small and medium-sized firms in high technology and certain regions, as well as guaranteeing some loans to small businesses (Bank of England, 2001). There are also programs at the European level.

A considerable body of evidence exists as to the effectiveness and 'additionality' of these programs. In most cases, evaluating the success of the programs is difficult due to the lack of a 'control' group of similar firms that do not receive funding.[9] Therefore most of the available studies are based on retrospective survey data provided by the recipients; few attempt to address the question of performance under the counterfactual seriously. A notable exception is the study by Lerner (1999), who looked at 1435 SBIR awardees and a matched sample of firms that did not receive awards, over a ten-year post-award period. Because most of the firms are privately held, he is unable to analyze the resulting valuation or profitability of the firms, but he does find that firms receiving SBIR grants grow significantly faster than the others after receipt of the grant. He attributes some of this effect to 'quality certification' by the government, which enables the firm to raise funds from private sources as well.[10]

A number of recent studies have looked more closely at the twin questions of whether such subsidies displace R&D investments that would have been done anyway and whether they lead to increased innovation output. David et al. (2000) surveys those studies done earlier and Hall (2005) looks at more recent analyses. Although the results are mixed, the usual finding is that firms receiving subsidies do perform more R&D, but not as much more as the size of the subsidy, and that they patent slightly more. That is, there is some replacement of the firm's own R&D, and the productivity in terms of innovation is slightly lower, as one might have expected given the multiple goals of such subsidies.

[9]See Jaffe (2002) for a review of methodologies for evaluation such government programs. For a complete review of the SBIR program, including some case studies, see the National Research Council (1998).

[10]Also see Spivack (2001) for further studies of such programs, including European studies, and David et al. (2000) and Klette et al. (2000) for surveys of the evaluation of government R&D programs in general.

Venture capital

Many observers view the rise of the venture capital (VC) industry, especially that in the United States, as a 'free market' solution to the problems of financing innovation. In fact, many of the European programs described above have as some of their goals the provision of seed capital and the encouragement of a VC industry that addresses the needs of high technology startups. Table 15.1 shows why this has been of some concern to European policymakers: the amount of VC available to firms in the US and Europe was roughly comparable in 1996, but the relative allocation to new firms (seed money and startups) in Europe was much less, below 10 % of the funds as opposed to 27 %. A correspondingly greater amount was used to finance buyouts of various kinds.

In the US, the VC industry consists of fairly specialized pools of funds (usually from private investors) that are managed and invested in companies by individuals knowledgeable about the industry in which they are investing. In principle, the idea is that the lemons' premium is reduced because the investment managers are better informed and moral hazard is minimized because a higher level of monitoring than that used in conventional arm's length investments is the norm. But the story is more complex than that: the combination of high uncertainty, asymmetric information, and the fact that R&D investment typically does not yield results instantaneously not only implies option-like behavior for the investment decision but also has implications for the form of the VC contract and the choice of decision maker. That is, there are situations in which it is optimal for the investor (VC) to have the right to shut down a project and there are other situations in which optimal performance is achieved when the innovator has control.

A number of studies have documented the characteristics and performance of the VC industry in the United States. The most detailed look at the actual operation of the industry is that by Kaplan and Stromberg (2000), who examine 200 VC contracts and compare their provisions to the predictions of the economic theory of financial contracting under uncertainty. They find that the contracts often provide for separate allocation of cash flow rights, control rights, voting rights, board positions, and liquidation rights, and that the rights are frequently contingent on performance measures. If performance is poor, the VCs often gain full control of the firm. Provisions such as delayed vesting are often included to mitigate hold-up by the entrepreneur as suggested by Anand and Galetovic (2000).

TABLE 15.1 Venture capital disbursements by stage of financing (1996).

	United States	*Europe*
Total VC disbursements (millions $)	9,420.6	8,572.0
Share seed and startups	27.1 %	6.5 %
Share for expansion	41.6 %	39.3 %
Share other (incl. buyouts)	31.3 %	54.2 %

Source: Rausch (1998) and author's calculations.

Kaplan and Stromberg conclude that these contracts are most consistent with the predictions of Aghion and Bolton (1992) and Dewatripont and Tirole (1994), all of whom study the incomplete contracts that arise when cash flows can be observed but not verified in sufficient detail to be used for contract enforcement. Put simply, the model VC contract is a complex debt-equity hybrid (and in fact, frequently contains convertible preferred securities and other such instruments) that looks more like debt when the firm does poorly (giving control to the investor) and more like equity when the firm does well (by handing control to the entrepreneur, which is incentive-compatible).

In a series of papers, Lerner (1992, 1995) studied a sample of VC-financed startups in detail, highlighting the important role that investing and monitoring experience has in this industry. He found that the amount of funds provided and the share of equity retained by the managers are sensitive to the experience and ability of the capital providers and the maturity of the firm being funded. VCs do increase the value of the firms they fund, especially when they are experienced investors. Firms backed by seasoned VC financiers are more likely to successfully time the market when they go public, and to employ the most reputable underwriters.

At a macro-economic level, VC funding tends to be pro-cyclical but it is difficult to disentangle whether the supply of funding causes growth or productivity growth encourages funding (Gompers and Lerner, 1999a,b; Kortum and Lerner, 2000; Ueda, 2001). The problem here is very similar to the identification problem for R&D investment in general: because of feedback effects, there is a chicken-egg simultaneity in the relationship. Some evidence (Majewski, 1997) exists that new and/or small biotechnology firms turn to other sources of funding in downturns, but that such placements are typically less successful (Lerner and Tsai, 2000), due to the misallocation of control rights (when the startup firm is in a weak bargaining position, control tends to be allocated to the more powerful corporate partner, but this has negative consequences for incentives).

The limited evidence from Europe on the performance of VC-funded firms tends to confirm that from the US. Engel (2001) compares a matched sample of German firms founded between 1991 and 1998 and finds that the VC-backed firms grew faster than the non-VC-backed firms. Lumme et al. (1993) compare the financing and growth of small UK and Finnish firms. This approach permits a comparison between a financial market-based and a bank-centered economy, and indeed, they find that small UK firms rely more on equity and less on loan finance and grow faster than small Finnish firms. Further evidence on small UK high technology firms is provided by Moore (1993), who looks at 300 such firms, finding that the availability and cost of finance is the most important constraint facing these firms, but that they are affected only marginally more than other types of small firms. That is, the financing 'gap' in the UK may be more related to size than to R&D intensity.

For Japan, Hamao, Packer, and Ritter (1998) find that the long run performance of VC-backed Initial Public Offerings (IPOs) is no better than that for other IPOs, unlike Lerner's evidence for the United States. However, many VCs in Japan are subsidiaries of major securities firms rather than specialists as in the US. Only these VCs have low returns, whereas those that are independent have returns more similar to the US. They attribute the low returns to conflicts of interest between the VC subsidiary and the securities firm that owns it, which affects the price at which the IPO is offered. This result highlights the importance of the institutions in which the venture capital industry is embedded for the creation of entrepreneurial incentives.

Black and Gilson (1998) and Rajan and Zingales (2001) take the institutional argument further. Both pairs of authors emphasize the contrast between arms' length market-based financial systems (e.g., the US and the UK) and bank-centered capital market systems (e.g., much of continental Europe and Japan), and view venture capital as combining the strengths of the two systems, in that it provides both the strong incentives for the manager-entrepreneur characteristic of the stock market system and the monitoring by an informed investor characteristic of the bank-centered system. They emphasize the importance of an active stock market, especially for newer and younger firms, in order to provide an exit strategy for VC investors, and to allow them to move on to financing new startups. Thus, having a VC industry that contributes to innovation and growth requires the existence of an active IPO (Initial Public Offering) market to permit successful entrepreneurs to regain control of their firms (and incidentally to provide powerful incentives for undertaking the startup in the first place) and also to ensure that the VCs themselves are able to use their expertise to help to establish new endeavors.

CONCLUSIONS

Based on the literature surveyed here, what do we know about the costs of financing innovation investments and the possibility that some kind of market failure exists in this area? Several main points emerge:

◆ There is fairly clear evidence, based on theory, surveys, and empirical estimation, that small and startup firms in R&D-intensive and high technology industries face a higher cost of capital than their larger competitors and than firms in other industries. In addition to compelling theoretical arguments and empirical evidence, the mere existence of the VC industry and the fact that it is concentrated precisely where these startups are most active suggests that this is so. In spite of considerable entry into the VC industry, returns remain high, which does suggest a high required rate of return in equilibrium.

◆ The evidence for a financing gap for large and established R&D firms is harder to establish. It is certainly the case that these firms prefer to use internally generated funds for financing investment, but less clear that there is an argument for intervention, beyond the favorable tax treatment that currently exists in many countries.[11]

[11]It is important to remind the reader of the premise of this chapter: I am focusing *only* on the financing gap arguments for favorable treatment of R&D and ignoring (for the present) the arguments based on R&D spillovers and externalities. There is good reason to believe that the latter is a much more important consideration for large established firms, especially if we wish those firms to undertake basic research that is close to industry but with unknown applications (the Bell Labs model).)

◆ The VC solution to the problem of financing innovation has its limits. First, it does tend to focus on only a few sectors at a time, and to make investment with a minimum size that is too large for startups in some fields. Second, good performance of the VC sector requires a thick market in small and new firm stocks (such as NASDAQ or EASDAQ) in order to provide an exit strategy for early stage investors.

◆ The effectiveness of government incubators, seed funding, loan guarantees, and other such policies for funding R&D deserves further study, ideally in an experimental or quasi-experimental setting. In particular, studying the cross-country variation in the performance of such programs would be desirable, because the outcomes may depend to a great extent on institutional factors that are difficult to control for using data from within a single country.

REFERENCES

Aghion, P., and Bolton, P. (1992). An incomplete contracts approach to financial contracting. *Review of Economic Studies*, 77, 338–401.

Akerlof, G.A. (1970). The market for 'lemons': quality, uncertainty, and the market mechanism. *Quarterly Journal of Economics*, 84, 488–500.

Alam, P., and Walton, K.S. (1995). Information asymmetry and valuation effects of debt financing. *Financial Review*, 30(2), 289–311.

Alderson, M.J., and Betker, B.L. (1996). Liquidation costs and accounting data., *Financial Management*, 25(2), 25–36.

Anand, B.N., and Galetovic, A. (2000). Weak property rights and holdup in R&D. *Journal of Economics and Management Strategy*, 9(4), 615–42.

Anton, J.J., and Yao, D.A. (1998). The sale of intellectual property: strategic disclosure, property rights, and incomplete contracts. The Wharton School, University of Pennsylvania: working paper.

Arellano, M., and Bond, S. (1991). Some tests of specification for panel data: Monte Carlo evidence and an application to employment equations. *Review of Economic Studies*, 58, 277–97.

Arrow, K.J. (1962). Economic welfare and the allocation of resources for invention. In R. Nelson (ed.), *The Rate and Direction of Inventive Activity*. Princeton University Press.

Auerbach, A.J. (1984). Taxes, firm financial policy, and the cost of capital: an empirical analysis. *Journal of Public Economics*, 23, 27–57.

Bank of England. (2001). *Finance for Small Firms – An Eighth Report*. London: Domestic Finance Division, Bank of England.

Bergemann, D., and Hege, U. (2005). The financing of innovation: learning and stopping. *Rand Journal of Economics*, 36(4), 719–52.

Bhagat, S., and Welch, I. (1995). Corporate research and development investments: international comparisons. *Journal of Accounting and Economics*, 19(2/3), 443–70.

Bhattacharya, S., and Ritter, J.R. (1985). Innovation and communication: signaling with partial disclosure., *Review of Economic Studies*, L, 331–46.

Black, B.S., and Gilson, R.J. (1998). Venture capital and the structure of capital markets: banks versus stock markets. *Journal of Financial Economics*, 47, 243–77.

Blair, M.M., and Litan, R.E. (1990). *Corporate leverage and leveraged buyouts in the eighties*. Brookings Institution.

Blass, A.A., and Yosha, O. (2003). Financing R&D in mature companies: an empirical analysis. *Economics of Innovation and New Technology*, 12(5), 425–48.

Bond, S., Harhoff, D., and Van Reenen, J. (1999). Investment, R&D, and financial constraints in Britain and Germany., Institute of Fiscal Studies Working Paper No. 99/5.

Bougheas, S., Georg, H., and Strobl, E. (2001). Is R&D financially constrained? Theory and evidence from Irish manufacturing. University of Nottingham.

Brown, W. (1997). R&D intensity and finance: are innovative firms financially constrained? London School of Economics Financial Market Group.

Cho, S. (1992). Agency costs, management stockholding, and research and development expenditures. *Seoul Journal of Economics*, 5(2), 127–52.

Chung, K.H., and Wright, P. (1998). Corporate policy and market value: A q theory approach. *Review of Quantitative Finance and Accounting*, 11(3), 293–310.

Cornelli, F., and Yosha, O. (2003). Stage financing and convertible debt. *Review of Economic Studies*, 70, 1–32.

Czarnitzki, D., and Kraft, K. (2002). Innovation indicators and corporate credit ratings: evidence from German firms. *Economic Letters*, 82, 377–84.

David, P.A., Hall, B.H., and Toole, A.A. (2000). Is public R&D a complement or a substitute for private R&D? A Review of the econometric evidence. *Research Policy*, 29, 497–530.

Dewatripont, M., and Tirole, J. (1994). A theory of debt and equity: diversity of securities and manager-shareholder congruence. *Quarterly Journal of Economics*, 109, 1027–54.

Eng, L., and Shackell, M. (2001). The implications of long term performance plans and institutional ownership for firms' research and development investments. *Journal of Accounting, Auditing and Finance*, 16(2), 117–39.

Engel, D. (2001). Hoeheres Beschaeftigungswachstum Durch Venture Capital? Mannheim: ZEW Discussion Paper No. 01–34.

Fazzari, S.M., Hubbard, R.G., and Petersen, B.C. (1988). Financing constraints and corporate investment. *Brookings Papers on Economic Activity*, 1988(1), 141–205.

Francis, J., and Smith, A. (1995). Agency costs and innovation: some empirical evidence. *Journal of Accounting and Economics*, 19(2/3), 383–409.

Friend, I. and Lang, H.H.P. (1988). An empirical test of the impact of management self-interest on corporate capital structure. *Journal of Finance*, 43, 271–83.

Gompers, P.A., and Lerner, J. (1999a). What drives venture capital fundraising? NBER Working Paper No. 6906.

Gompers, P.A., and Lerner, J. (1999b). *Capital formation and investment in venture markets: implications for the Advanced Technology Program*. Advanced Technology Program, NIST, U.S. Dept. of Commerce.

Griliches, Z. (1992). The search for R&D spillovers. *Scandinavian Journal of Economics*, 94, S29–S47.

Hall, B.H. (1990). The impact of corporate restructuring on industrial research and development. *Brookings Papers on Economic Activity*, 1990(1), 85–136.

Hall, B.H. (1991). Firm-level investment with liquidity constraints: what can the Euler equations tell us? University of California at Berkeley and the National Bureau of Economic Research. Photocopied.

Hall, B.H. (1992). Research and development at the firm level: does the source of financing matter? NBER Working Paper No. 4096 (June).

Hall, B.H. (1993). R&D tax policy during the eighties: success or failure? *Tax Policy and the Economy*, 7, 1–36.

Hall, B.H. (1994). Corporate capital structure and investment horizons in the United States, 1976–1987, *Business History Review*, 68, 110–43.

Hall, B.H. (1996). The private and social returns to research and development. In B.L.R. Smith and C.E. Barfield (eds), *Technology, R&D, and the Economy*, 140–83. Brookings Institution and the American Enterprise Institute.

Hall, B.H. (2005). Government policy for innovation in Latin America. Report to the World Bank, available at http://www.econ.berkeley.edu/~bhhall/bhpapers.html.

Hall, B.H., Griliches, Z., and Hausman, J.A. (1986). Patents and R&D: is there a lag? *International Economic Review*, 27, 265–83.

Hall, B.H., Mairesse, J., Branstetter, L., and Crepon, B. (1999). Does cash flow cause investment and R&D: an exploration using panel data for French, Japanese, and United States firms in the scientific sector. In D. Audretsch and A.R. Thurik (eds), *Innovation, Industry Evolution and Employment*. Cambridge University Press.

Hall, B.H., and van Reenen. J. (2000). How effective are fiscal incentives for R&D? A new review of the evidence. *Research Policy*, 29, 449–69.

Hamao, Y., Packer, F., and Ritter, J.R. (1998). Institutional affiliation and the role of venture capital: evidence from initial public offerings in Japan. FRB of New York Staff Report No. 52.

Harhoff, D. (1998). Are there financing constraints for R&D and investment in German manufacturing firms? *Annales d'Economie et de Statistique*, 49/50, 421–56.

Himmelberg, P., and Peterson, B.C. (1994). R&D and internal finance: a panel study of small firms in high-tech industries. *Review of Economics and Statistics*, 76, 38–51.

Jaffe, A. (2002). *Oxford review of economic policy*. Oxford University Press.

Jensen, M.C., and Meckling, W. (1976). Theory of the firm: managerial behavior, agency costs, and ownership structure. *Journal of Financial Economics*, 3, 305–60.

Johnson, M.S., and Rao, R.P. (1997). The impact of antitakeover amendments on corporate financial performance. *Financial Review*, 32(4), 659–89.

Kaplan, S.N., and Stromberg, P. (2000). Financial contracting theory meets the real world: an empirical analysis of venture capital contracts. NBER Working Paper No. 7660.

Karaomerliolu, D.C., and Jacobsson, S. (1999). *The Swedish venture capital industry – an infant, adolescent, or grown-up?* Chalmers Institute of Technology.

Klette, T.J., Møen, J., and Griliches, Z. (2000). Do subsidies to commercial R&D reduce market failures? Microeconometric evaluation studies. *Research Policy*, 29, 471–96.

Kortum, S., and Lerner, J. (2000). Assessing the contribution of venture capital to innovation. *Rand Journal of Economics*, 31(4), 674–92.

Lach, S., and Schankerman, M. (1988). Dynamics of R&D and investment in the scientific sector. *Journal of Political Economy*, 97(4), 880–904.

Leland, H.E., and Pyle D.H. (1977). Informational asymmetries, financial structure, and financial intermediation. *Journal of Finance*, 32, 371–87.

Lerner, J. (1992). Venture capitalists and the decision to go public. Harvard Business School Working Paper No. 93-002.

Lerner, J. (1995). Venture capitalists and the oversight of privately-held firms. *Journal of Finance*, 50, 301–18.

Lerner, J. (1998b). 'Public venture capital': rationale and evaluation. In National Research Council (ed.), *SBIR: Challenges and Opportunities*. Board on Science, Technology, and Economic Policy, NRC.

Lerner, J. (1999). The government as venture capitalist: the long-run effects of the SBIR program. *Journal of Business*, 72, 285–318.

Lerner, J., and Tsai, A. (2000). Do equity financing cycles matter? Evidence from biotechnology alliances. NBER Working Paper No. 7464 (January).

Levin, R.C., Klevorick, A.K., Nelson, R.R., and Winter, S.G. (1987). Appropriating the returns from industrial research and development. *Brookings Papers on Economic Activity*, 1987(3), 783–832.

Lumme, A. *et al.* (1993). New, technology-based companies in Cambridge in an international perspective. University of Cambridge Small Business Research Centre Working Papers 35 (September).

Mairesse, J., Hall, B.H., and Mulkay, B. (1999). Firm-level investment in France and the United States: an exploration of what we have learned in twenty years. *Annales d'Economie et de Statistique* No. 55–56, 27–69.

Majewski, S.E. (1997). Using strategic alliance formation as a financing mechanism in the biotechnology industry. UC Berkeley: photocopied.

Majumdar, S.K., and Nagarajan, A. (1997). The impact of changing stock ownership patterns in the United States: theoretical implications and some evidence. *Revue d'Economie Industrielle*, 82, 39–54.

Mansfield, E., Schwartz, M., and Wagner, S. (1981). Imitation costs and patents: an empirical study. *Economic Journal*, 91, 907–18.

Miller, M.H., and Modigliani, F. (1961). Dividend policy, growth, and the valuation of shares. *Journal of Business*, 34, 411–33.

Modigliani, F., and Miller, M.H. (1958). The cost of capital, corporation finance and the theory of investment. *American Economic Review*, 48, 261–97.

Moore, B. (1993). Financial constraints to the growth and development of small high-technology firms. University of Cambridge Small Business Research Centre Working Paper 31 (July).

Mulkay, B., Hall, B.H., and Mairesse, J. (2001). Investment and R&D in France and in the United States. In Deutsche Bundesbank (ed.), *Investing Today for the World of Tomorrow*. Springer Verlag.

National Research Council. (1998). *SBIR: Challenges and Opportunities*. Board on Science, Technology, and Economic Policy, NRC.

Nelson, R.R. (1959). The simple economics of basic scientific research. *Journal of Political Economy*, 49, 297–306.

OECD. (1995). *Venture capital in OECD countries*. Organization for Economic Cooperation and Development.

Opler, T.C., and Titman, S. (1993). The determinants of leveraged buyout activity: free cash flow vs. financial distress costs. *Journal of Finance*, 48(5), 1985–99.

Opler, T.C., and Titman, S. (1994). Financial distress and corporate performance. *Journal of Finance*, 49(3), 1015–40.

Peeters, C., and van Pottelsberghe de la Potterie, B. (2003). Measuring innovation competencies and performances: a survey of large firms in Belgium. Institute of Innovation Research, Hitotsubashi University, Japan, Working Paper #03-16.

Pugh, W.N., Jahera, J.S. Jr., and Oswald, S. (1999). ESOPs, takeover protection, and corporate decision making. *Journal of Economics and Finance*, 23(2), 170–83.

Rajan, R.G., and Zingales, L. (2001). Financial systems, industrial structure, and growth. *Oxford Review of Economic Policy*, 17, 467–82.

Rausch, L.M. (1998). Venture capital investment trends in the United States and Europe. National Science Foundation Division of Science Resource Studies Issues Brief, 99–303.

Scherer, F.M. (1998). The size distribution of profits from innovation. *Annales d'Economie et de Statistique*, 49/50, 495–516.

Schumpeter, J. (1942). *Capitalism, Socialism, and Democracy*. Harper and Row (reprinted 1960).

Spivack, R.N. (2001). *The economic evaluation of technological change*. Conference Proceedings of the Advanced Technology Program, National Institute of Standards and Technology, Washington, DC.

Szewczyk, S.H., Tsetsekos, G.P., and Zantout, Z.Z. (1996). The valuation of corporate R&D expenditures: evidence from investment opportunities and free cash flow., *Financial Management*, 25(1), 105–10.

Ueda, M. (2001). Does innovation spur venture capital? Universitat Pompeu Fabra. *Upside* magazine, December 2001 issue.

Williamson, O.E. (1988). Corporate finance and corporate governance. *Journal of Finance*, 43, 567–91.

Zantout, Z.Z. (1997). A test of the debt monitoring hypothesis: the case of corporate R&D expenditures. *Financial Review*, 32(1), 21–48.

16

The Contribution of Public Entities to Innovation and Technological Change

MARYANN P. FELDMAN AND DIETER F. KOGLER

The authors would like to thank Barry Bozeman, Elizabeth Graddy, Chandler Stolp, and David Wolfe for comments and suggestions on this chapter. We have benefited from discussion with Wendy Dobson, Al Link, Maryellen Kelley, and Don Siegel.

Innovation – the realization of economic value from new ideas – is recognized to be an activity best accomplished by the private sector. Motivated by profits, market share, and growth potential, companies develop new products, processes, and organizational forms. The market adjudicates their success, rewarding those companies that produce goods and services valued by consumers. Indeed, the idea of the invisible hand of the market driving the winds of creative destruction, which then result in innovation, technological change, and economic growth, is a most romantic and intoxicating image.

Yet, in many ways, the efforts of the private sector are only the visible tip of the iceberg that defines innovation and technological change in the economy. Under the surface, typically unobserved and underappreciated are public entities – governments, universities, nonprofit foundations, voluntary membership organizations, and other institutions that are instrumental in providing resources, offering incentives, and defining opportunities for the private sector. It has not been popular to talk about the role of government, or to acknowledge the role of nonmarket forces in innovation and technological change perhaps since Ronald Reagan and Margaret Thatcher defined an agenda that viewed government as bureaucratic and inefficient. Indeed, this vision is so pervasive that William Baumol's recent book (2002), *The Free-Market Innovation Machine: Analyzing the Growth Miracle of Capitalism*, gives scarce mention to public organizations and does not even have an index entry for government. Nevertheless, communities of scholars have examined the contribution of public entities from a variety of perspectives that will be reviewed here.

The Internet offers an example of the instrumental role of public entities in innovation and technological change (Mowery and Simcoe, 2002; Rogers and Kingsley, 2004; Greenstein, 2007). The origins of the Internet, or more generally computer networking, date back to the early 1960s, when the US Department of Defense (DoD) prioritized funding for the development of decentralized communication and transportation redundancies in the event of nuclear attack. Defense applications were the primary concern and this intersected with the opportunity provided by scientific advances in mathematics and computer science. Based on the assumption that a strong national computer industry would be necessary for competitiveness, the DoD favored a broad research agenda that included funding granted to federal labs and grants to academia and industry (Langlois and Mowery, 1996). A loose governance structure favored experimentation with few restrictions, open sharing rather than proprietary technologies, and collaboration. By the mid-1980s infrastructure investments were needed. The National Science Foundation (NSF) not only provided substantial funding, but also more importantly, 'encouraged and expanded the involvement of many other groups in providing network services as well as using them' (Kahn 1994, p. 17). A variety of private firms, both large, established entities and new startups, entered the industry.

One of the most significant developments was the NSF's decision to mandate the adoption of the TCP/IP (Transmission Control Protocol/Internet Protocol) standard to universities that it funded. Since virtually every American research university received NSF funding this mandate enforced a standard that accelerated the diffusion of the Internet and also exposed a generation of students to the technology (Goldfarb, 2006).

By the early 1990s, with the technological backbone in place, the commercial potential of the Internet was becoming apparent. There was significant and contentious debate about the most appropriate governance mechanisms to support the continued development of infrastructure. The US government withdrew its oversight and turned over responsibilities to the Internet Society (ISOC), a public membership consortium that brings together a variety of stakeholders: corporations, nonprofit, trade, and professional organizations, foundations, educational institutions, government agencies, other international organizations, and individual members (Mowery and Simcoe, 2002). Despite their different agendas, all members in the ISOC share the common goal of advancing the Internet, such as discussing infrastructure standards. At this point government public entities remain crucial actors in the advancement of this technology.[1]

Certainly the availability of personal computers and the invention of the WWW spurred the development of commercial content and applications; however, three significant US government policies influenced the progress of the Internet (Mowery and Simcoe, 2002). First, regulatory policies assured low rates for telecommunications that increased access. Second, antitrust policies promoted competitive markets

[1]The Internet Society's web site, http://www.isoc.org/index.shtml, provides a concise guide to the major Internet bodies and members of the organization.

and encouraged entrepreneurship. Third, intellectual property policies placed key elements of the Internet in the public domain and lowered entry barriers for new firms mainly by promoting open standards rather than proprietary technology. In addition, changes in federal policies allowed pension plans and other public entities to invest in venture capital, which financed many new firms in related sectors. The net result has been the creation of a general purpose technology associated with innovation and economic growth in the 1990s (Lipsey, Bekar, and Carlaw, 1998).

The remainder of this chapter considers the literature on the role of public entities. Recent work has established the importance of government investment in infrastructure to economic growth and competitiveness (Klein and Luu, 2003; La Porta *et al.*, 1999). We begin by considering why a coherent system of institutions, as suggested by the systems of innovation literature, is instrumental for innovation and technological change. The following section will discuss the role that government, in particular the local levels of government, plays in this context. Next, the subsequent sections address the contributions made by the nonprofit sector, universities, and government laboratories to the process of innovation and technological change. Given that we have made a case for the importance of public entities, we outline some of the fundamental difficulties in the evaluation of nonmarket transactions. The chapter draws to a close with reflective conclusions and the realization that public entities typically carry out tasks in the economy that are essential to the process of innovation and technological change. Efforts to privatize all aspects of innovation and technological change or to impose private sector metrics on public sector science and technology investments may ultimately have the perverse effect of diminishing economic growth.

Coherent Systems of Institutions

Understanding differences in economic performance and growth has been a motivating question, starting with the publication of Adam Smith's *Wealth of Nations* in 1776. As a result, a large body of literature explores differences in the performance of national economies – why is it that some nations thrive while others languish or decline (Mankiw, Phelps, and Romer, 1995; Temple, 1999). At the time when firms were small and underdeveloped, national economies were seen as the fundamental unit of analysis.

Well in advance of Adam Smith's publication, public entities were actively trying to influence innovation and economic growth. Notably, Jean-Baptiste Colbert, the French minister of finance for King Louis XIV (1665–1683), actively worked to improve French manufacturing by hiring skilled labor from Italy and England, constructing infrastructure beneficial to industry, and instituting what we would now describe as a friendly business climate (Sargent, 1899). Colbert is notable for his quotations: 'The art of taxation consists in so plucking the goose as to obtain the largest possible amount of feathers with the smallest possible amount of hissing' (Sargent, 1899). He summed up his motivation for industrial policy as, 'It is simply, and solely, the abundance of money within a state [which] makes the difference in its grandeur and power' (Sargent, 1899). Unfortunately, the King was harder for Colbert to control than the economy and these gains were not long lasting.

One of the important dimensions of innovation is its pronounced tendency to cluster both temporally and spatially. Over the course of history we have witnessed that innovation and progress have flourished in certain societies, such as Florence under the Medicis, Hollywood in the 1920s, and perhaps currently Silicon Valley. We characterize these instances as a golden-age realized through the unique confluence of events, opportunity, the actions of individuals and collectives, and the support of public institutions. The public sector, either monarchy or any form of elected or appointed government, defines a system of institutions that regulate the functioning of markets, provides infrastructure and opportunity, protects property rights, and generally mitigates risk. Most importantly, taken together, these institutions define a system of innovation, together with a set of interlocked institutions that provide incentives for the creation of new ideas and reward the inherent risk of engaging in innovation and the commercializing of new activities. Historical context and path dependence certainly play a role. Although there are no guarantees of an ensuing golden-age it is surely more likely that innovation and technological progress, followed by economic growth, are likely to take place when the system is coherent and the various institutional pieces fit together. Of course, system coherence provides the threshold upon which private sector activity may flourish.

The Industrial Revolution is the typical starting point for thinking about systems of innovation and technological change. Rosenberg and Birdzell (1986) answer the question of *How the West Grew Rich* by considering how institutional reforms and social changes, which started in 15th century Europe, laid the foundation for the Industrial Revolution, and the subsequent economic success of the West. Building upon the scientific advances of the Renaissance, monarchies, as the principal form of public governance, put in place a set of institutions advantageous for commerce and trade. In addition, the fragmentation of European geopolitical jurisdictions created experimentation in institutional forms and functions that were subsequently adapted and improved upon. Diverse factors such as religious beliefs congruent with commerce, new forms of economic organization favoring meritocracy over kinship, predictable accounting and business standards, and the establishment of a legal structure for property rights and dispute resolution, facilitated economic development, innovation, and technological progress. Although taxation is never viewed favorably it is certainly preferable to government seizure of assets. Seemingly trivial innovations, for example double entry bookkeeping, allowed for the evaluation of the profitability of an enterprise and its various activities for the first time. This practice diffused quickly through guilds and trade associations, and as a result, commercial activity and trade flourished. A variety of activities that appear to be private owe their existence to public entities and institutions, which created the incentives and background conditions that allowed private enterprise to thrive.

Contemporary scholars (see, for example, Scotchmer, 2004) accord great importance to the establishment of intellectual property rights, and though property rights are certainly important, these appear to be only one of the structural elements that encouraged economic growth. Governing bodies and public entities were instrumental in the introduction and formation of these institutional changes, and although the 'inventions of technology spring more readily to mind than the inventions of institutions ... the contribution of new institutions to Western economic growth was unmistakable, and in some cases essential' (Rosenberg and Birdzell, 1986, p. 139). These factors are still relevant, as highlighted by De Soto's (2000) examination of economic growth in South America and other developing countries.

Economists traditionally do not put much emphasis on institutions, but when they mention them they are typically portrayed as constraints on the free market, creating inefficient rigidity rather than providing incentives. For example:

> institutions consist of a set of *constraints* on behavior in the form of rules and regulations; a set of procedures to detect deviations from the rules and regulations; and, finally, a set of moral, ethical, behavioral norms which define the contours that constrain the way in which the rules and regulations are specified and enforcement is carried out. (North 1984, p. 8)

Certainly, institutions define the opportunity set. If we want to move away from this view of the institution to something that is more positive and enabling, we need to employ a different rhetoric, namely, seeing institutions as human constructs designed to achieve civic objectives that advance the welfare of a community. For example, traffic rules guarantee that individuals drive in certain, predictable ways, thereby creating conditions that allow more efficient transportation. For another often-cited example, individuals can engage in innovation more aggressively because of intellectual property rights, which remove the fear that other agents will appropriate ideas and usurp the gains that should accrue to the inventor. In addition, predictable implementation and enforcement of laws and regulations promote competition and innovation by penalizing opportunistic actions. This suggests that institutions facilitate the efficient performance of human activity, creativity, and inquiry, all of which are broader constructs than the task of focusing on market transactions and immediately measurable outcomes. North (2005) argues that economic growth depends on society's ability to create institutions that are productive, stable, and fare. Moreover, institutions are not static; they adapt to changing political and economic situations. For example, recent increased concerns about globalization and competitiveness have increased focus on science and innovation.

Innovation is now widely understood to be nonlinear, iterative, and interactive; a social process that often involves continuous improvement to existing products and processes (c.f., Bozeman and Rogers, 2002). Innovation, is thus, shaped in a path-dependent fashion by past insights, decisions, responses to events, and technological choices. In the 1980s, a series of influential books in the systems of innovation literature described differences between countries, and broke new ground by considering how institutions work together to create conditions that enable innovation and economic growth (Freeman, 1987; Lundvall, 1992; Nelson, 1993; Edquist and Johnson, 1997). The innovation systems approach underlines the idea that innovation processes are grounded in a complex web of institutional practices and organizational relationships that condition and shape the path along which innovation develops. Certainly, Michael Porter's (1990) *The Competitive Advantage of Nations*, which describes national forces that define a firm's capabilities, is part of this intellectual trajectory. Interestingly, in Porter's conceptualization, government is delineated as a background factor with the implication that the legal and regulatory conditions are essential and understanding them is a prerequisite to firm performance.

A common thread in these literatures is the idea that technological capabilities, as embodied in a country's firms, are a key source of competitive advantage, which leads to the conclusion that these capabilities can be built or constructed by national action. The literature is largely silent on exactly how this might be done, although there is growing emphasis on socio-cultural factors that define public attitudes about market relationships and collective action. A related literature on *Varieties of Capitalism* (Albert, 1993; Hall and Soskice, 2001) defines an emerging sub-discipline of comparative political economy, and also examines the institutional foundations of national comparative advantage. This literature argues that firm behavior is defined by a highly contextual interpretation of market relationships that are dependent on culture and social norms of behavior. This literature contrasts the viewpoint that firms are footloose, and that choice of location does not matter.

Different institutional systems produce companies with different strengths and capabilities. In *How We Compete*, Suzanne Berger (2005) examines how national systems interact with company characteristics to determine firm strategy and competitive success in the face of globalization and the modular disintegration of the value chain.

Of course, institutions and incentives are calibrated to specific industrial sectors and epistemic communities, and based on the general approach, new concepts such as *technological systems* (Carlsson and Jacobsson, 1997), *sectoral systems of innovation* (Breschi and Malerba, 1997), and *social systems of innovation* (Amable, Barré, and Boyer 1997) constitute a further critique and refinement of the original systems of innovation theory. The Triple Helix model, which focuses on the interplay among universities, business, and government, may be interpreted as yet another variant of the national systems of innovation literature that focuses on the new emerging mission for research universities (Etzkowitz and Leydesdorff, 2000; Etzkowitz, 2003). In sum, the system of innovation literature is informative but largely descriptive, perhaps due to the complexity of the topic.

The idea that innovation is geographically mediated implies that innovation systems may be conceptualized at the sub-national level and led to the systematic study of regional systems of innovation (Scott, 1988; Porter, 1990; Feldman, 1994; Cooke and Morgan, 1998). The literature starts from the premise, as reviewed in Chapter 12 in this volume, that innovation benefits from a series of factors that are geographically defined, suggesting that location may provide an advantage to innovative activity. Interest in the regional scale was also based on the realization that the local advantages that Alfred Marshall (1920) described were active in Italian industrial districts that provided flexible, localized production systems based on small firms (Pyke, Beccattini, and Sengenberger, 1990). Interest in this type of regional innovation system is predicated on the economic success of Silicon Valley as a paradigm of innovation, technological change, and wealth creation. Saxenian (1994) provided a comparison of the competitive advantage between Silicon Valley and Boston, which emphasized socio-cultural factors that influence cooperation, the sharing of ideas, and attitudes towards risk and failure that affected innovation and ultimately influenced the competitive success of firms.

Local entrepreneurial spirit or business climate is, of course, notoriously difficult to measure, although that does not deter researchers from trying. There are a variety of scorecards and beauty contests that rank places (World Economic Forum, 2005; Forbes, 2006). These efforts provide benchmarks and aggregate useful data, but may be forcing conformity to perform on a specifically chosen metric. Research at the local geographic level of inquiry now considers how variation in institutions such as 'noncompete' agreements (Gilson, 1999; Stuart and Sorensen, 2003), availability of venture capital (Sorenson and Stuart, 2001), and local industrial organization (Rosenthal and Strange, 2003; Aharonson, Baum, and Feldman, 2007) influence a firm's capabilities and success.

Integral to these literatures is the idea that firms' core competencies and competitiveness are shaped by the locations in which they originate and operate. In contrast to the view that firms are footloose and able to scan the landscape for the location that best suits their needs, there is an increased recognition of the interdependencies between firms and the places in which they operate. This idea is part of the stream of evolutionary economics, which begins with the work of Nelson and Winter's (1982) *An Evolutionary Theory of Economic Change* and has inspired a variety of scholars to theorize on the interdependence of institutions and firms, the role of human agency in defining systems of innovation, and the importance of collective action. There is evidence that local environments are further shaped by the actions of entrepreneurs (Feldman, 2001a).

The New Growth theory builds on these insights. It stands in contrast to neo-classical growth theory, which recognizes technical knowledge but considers it to be a product of nonmarket forces, and thus fails to explain what causes technology to improve over time (Solow, 1957). The New Growth theory emphasizes the endogenous character of knowledge and technical progress, which results in increasing returns mainly due to the nonrival, and not excludable, qualities of these inputs (Romer, 1990; Grossman and Helpman, 1992). This strand of literature is a further development of exogenous models of growth, which is, to a certain extent, a direct result of the shift from an economy that is driven by the exchange of ordinary goods and services that are subject to diminishing returns, to a market that is dominated by knowledge inputs and innovation that are subject to increasing returns and thus difficult for markets to allocate. In sum, this theory caused lasting changes in the perception surrounding the significance of historic events in shaping development trajectories, the relevance of the regulatory framework in influencing economic growth, and the importance of place in providing a particular advantage (Romer, 1996). The New Growth theory also considers technological progress as an endogenous product of economic activity rather than an exogenous determined factor (Jones, 2002). Endogeneity implies that causality is difficult to assign and that the precise impact of any one factor such as a specific government program is difficult to evaluate.

Most importantly, the literature indicates that the innovation system at whatever level considered, should form a coherent logic. This suggests that emulation of any one part of a system or any specific policy may not produce the desired result. Transplanting one specific program that is associated with success in one country, such as the US Small Business Innovation Research (SBIR) grants, or implementing one policy change such as the Bayh–Dole Act, may not lead to the desired outcome: the system is more than the sum of its respective parts. Not only is it difficult to transplant institutional and policy interventions to a different setting, but also if the complementary and supporting policies and institutions are not in place the effort may be wasted.

The literature also suggests that the public and private entities in innovation systems co-evolve to form their own coherent logic (Wolfe and Gertler, 2006). The economic success of Silicon Valley, Route 128, and other innovative regions around the world has prompted scholars to examine the early genesis of industrial clusters in order to examine regularities in how regional innovation systems emerge and transform local economies (see, for example, Braunerhjelm and Feldman, 2006).

A number of places around the world are searching for a competitive advantage as a means to create economic growth. Unfortunately, many of the policy prescriptions are rather generic and easily replicated. For a jurisdiction to gain an advantage over other localities requires that it differentiate itself by the virtue of capabilities that are not easily replicated: jurisdictional advantage could be established and maintained by implementing policies that enhance unique and location-specific capabilities (Feldman and Martin, 2004, 2005). In contrast to the more passive term locational advantage, the use of the term jurisdiction denotes a legal and political decision-making authority. There is an older tradition in political economy that defines government as the mechanism for collective action (Locke, 1967). Like firms, governments are socially constructed entities that can raise funds, organize resources, and continue on in perpetuity to achieve some objective defined by shareholders. Government, especially in democracies, has a mandate to promote the citizen's agenda, which is without doubt more complicated than the firm's objective of maximizing shareholder value or profits. Just as corporations think strategically about assessing both their capabilities and competitive strengths, jurisdictions may mobilize resources and coordinate shareholders to achieve some intended outcome. Thus, policies, programs, and incentives may be constructed and managed to promote a coherent activity set that benefits local citizens and local industry, and promotes economic growth.

There is no consensus in the literature regarding the optimum scale and scope of government intervention (Mowery, 1995). There is also an active debate about what types of projects government should fund and at what level, especially as innovation results in highly skewed outcomes with many failures and a small number of significant successes (Scherer and Harhoff, 2000). Some government policies are predicated on the notion that the market is the best mechanism to regulate and enhance economic performance, and that the only necessary condition for public intervention is market failure. Under this view the emphasis is on innovation policy measures that address systemic conditions such as basic research and education, and possibly includes initiatives that foster entrepreneurship (Lundvall and Borras, 2005). Systemic innovation policies are not only geared to prevent classic market failure, but also failures in the wider institutional and social frameworks that affect innovation and technological change (Edquist, 2005). Other government policies are proactive and design science, technology, and innovation policies that target specific sectors, industries, or places. Singapore and Taiwan, among other East Asian countries, may be considered examples where active policy intervention resulted in substantial economic growth (Masuyama, Vanderbrink and Yue, 1997; Furman *et al.*,

1998). Most notable is the highly focused public policy that has successfully produced a semiconductor industry in Singapore (Mathews, 1999). In other cases, innovation policy is oriented towards redistributive goals targeting underrepresented regions and groups. Examples would be the National Science Foundation's Experimental Program to Stimulate Competitive Research (Hauger, 2004), South Africa's National Advisory Council on Innovation, and current policy reform in Israel that aims to develop capacity in science and technology and provide access to underrepresented constituencies.

Overall, governments, at the federal, state or provincial, and local level, define a system of institutions that set the stage for subsequent private sector activity. Most importantly, public institutions, at their best, form coherent systems that promote entrepreneurship, innovation, and technical change. Certainly, when policies are not aligned or when the incentives are missing, innovation and economic growth suffers (Orsenigo, 2001). More specifically, government contributes directly to innovation and technological change through the funding of research, the provision of R&D tax credits that encourage private firms to invest in R&D, and the procurement of technologically sophisticated products to satisfy the public mission. When government is not effective, diminished by lack of funding, apathy, or captured by specific interests, newer types of public entities emerge that provide institutions, governance, and resources that affect innovation and technological change. These topics are the focus of the next section.

THE CONTRIBUTION OF PUBLIC ENTITIES TO THE SUPPLY OF IDEAS

Public entities contribute to the supply of ideas through the funding of research and development activities and the performance of research. As expected, private firms are the largest providers of R&D funding, totaling about 200 billion dollars in the US in 2004 (National Science Board, 2006, pp. 4–10, table 4.1). Most of this funding is for in-house R&D but an increased share is for strategic alliances involving external partners. Universities and government labs are important external partners that provide access to complementary knowledge that may extend both the exploratory capability as well as the capacity of the firm to exploit commercial opportunity (Leonard-Barton, 1995).

Private R&D funding is typically oriented towards activities that will be rewarded by the market. In contrast, government funds basic research that asks fundamental questions, without direct concern about practical applications, and is more experimental and theoretical. Applied research focuses on specific applications with a direct concern for using the results. Applied R&D may advance the findings of basic research towards some commercial object. Basic research funded by public entities is typically conceptualized at the earliest stage of knowledge creation and upstream from firms' more applied R&D. Yet, in practice, basic research may have practical implications for current commercial products and the most fruitful innovation may be at the intersection of fundamental science and practical questions (Stokes, 1997).

Economists tend to focus on market failure as the justification for government funding of research (see Martin and Scott, 2000, for a review). There are at least three reasons why private firms may not pursue promising commercial opportunities that government may address (Feldman and Kelley, 2006). First, although a technology may be promising, it may require fundamental or basic research that is far removed from the market. Although the traditional boundaries between basic and applied research appear less relevant, private companies may be unwilling to develop the required knowledge if there is a perceived lack of appropriability of the resulting profits. Knowledge in this case is a public good most appropriately provided by the public sector. Second, new technologies are increasingly complex and firms may not have the capabilities required to develop a new technology fully. Although the required knowledge may reside in multiple organizations, the cost of establishing R&D partnerships and making them work productively is a disincentive to private investment. To the extent that government programs reduce the transaction costs of establishing R&D partnerships, private R&D is encouraged. The transfer of knowledge among firms engaged in cooperative R&D activity may further increase the public benefit of the R&D program. Paradoxically, the profit potential that motivates R&D activity by an individual firm discourages the information sharing that makes collaboration most effective between firms. For this reason collaboration with universities, government labs, and other public entities may circumvent barriers to candid collaboration. Finally, market incentives may not be sufficient to induce firms to undertake R&D for projects that are risky relative to other investments, or lack sufficient market potential, as in the case of third world diseases. An investment, though worthwhile from a social point of view may not be attractive given the hurdle rate that firms can receive from alternative investments. No firm may be willing to take the lead on developing a new technology, instead preferring the often-effective strategy of fast second.

A variety of government initiatives attempt to address these market failures through direct public funding of research and R&D subsidies that lower the cost of R&D to firms. The governments of OECD member countries funded about 30 % of R&D expenditures in 2003 (OECD, 2005, p. 24, table 14). Government mission agencies with their broad responsibility to advance specific public objectives such as national security, public health, or competitiveness concerns, offer R&D contracts to private firms to develop critical, high-risk technologies. Specifically, mandated research-funding agencies such as the US National Science Foundation (which awarded $3.8 billion in 2005) and the US National Institute of Health (which has an annual extramural research budget of about $30 billion) (National Science Board 2006, pp. 4–21) are charged with funding the best and most innovative research.

Government R&D funding is justified because of the positive benefits to the country of knowledge, which creates an expectation of an externality or knowledge spillover for which the public return exceeds the private rate of return (Griliches, 1992; Mohnen, 1996). This includes, for example, the case where an industry as a whole may benefit from the development of a high-risk, platform technology, but no one firm is willing to undertake the R&D investment due to difficulties in appropriating the resulting benefits (Arrow, 1962). A large literature estimates the rates of return to R&D investments (see Salter and Martin, 2001; McMillan and Hamilton, 2003 for a review). The consensus is that the public rate of return is significant and positive, but there is disagreement about the precise impact with estimates ranging from 10–160 %, with the majority 50–100 %. With direct government funding, the public rate of return is typically estimated to be 20–50 % (Griliches, 1995).

The role of government in funding or subsidizing private firm R&D has been controversial with the debate focusing on the extent to which government funding may displace or crowd out private firm investment. In a review of empirical studies, David, Hall, and Toole (2000) conclude that 7 out of 12 studies of the US found a net substitution effect indicating that firms that received federal R&D funds spent less of their own funds on R&D, *ceteris paribus*. The authors speculate that these results stem from firms' anticipation of follow-on R&D funding or government purchases of the technology. As a consequence, firms undertaking contract R&D for the government have less incentive to spend their own funds on developing these technologies for commercial markets. Notably, the US Department of Defense (DoD) has been the single largest government source of industrial R&D funding and is an important customer for the research it funds. In a related review, Guellec and van Pottelsberghe (2003) conclude that the importance of defense spending is a major reason for the negative effect of government research on business expenditures.

Although there is some indication of dual use for DoD funding (Alic, 1993), much research is not transferable to the private sector and as defense projects become more specialized there are questions about the magnitude of the multiplier when compared to other R&D projects. Defense R&D projects may be adapted to commercial products, and this was the case with computer software, however other products are developed with a considerable time lag because private R&D investment is required to move closer to the market (Mowery and Simcoe, 2002). Certainly, defense infrastructure investment is credited with creating economic development in the Southern US (Markusen, 1991).

The conclusion in the literature is that the effectiveness of government funding is a function of the program design including incentives provided and actual implementation (Feldman and Kelley, 2006). For example, Wallsten (2000) found evidence of an effect from the Small Business Innovation Research (SBIR) Program that shares some of the features related to substitution, perhaps related to the provision of follow-on funding. Archibald and Finifter (2000) conclude that some SBIR awardees focus on providing a government service while others use the funds to develop a technology and move into commercial markets. To the extent that government funds research for its own purposes we would expect to see focused benefit.

Government procurement potentially plays a significant role in technology development as a sophisticated lead user capable of making large purchases, that can define product specifications and standards, and help establish markets for new technologies (Edquist *et al.*, 2000). Certainly, this was the case in semiconductors. In the US, large demand for components for weapons systems provided design and manufacturing experience that subsequently lowered costs and benefited private companies. Similarly, in Finland, public technology procurement, mainly through the state operated Posts and Telecommunications, played a major role in the establishment of a strong mobile telecommunications industry, which has emerged as a world-leader in this technology segment (Palmberg, 2000). Government procurement may also help to promote uniformity and interoperability, as was the case of the TCP/IP standard, which allowed diverse sets of users to communicate over the Internet regardless of which software applications they used in the background. Principally government has to find a balance between procurement policies and the provision of incentives that encourage innovation. Another suggestion is the privatization of government services, however, this potentially creates related problems of transparency, access, and a potential for limited extension to other private sector activities.

Government R&D programs may address the information problems of private investors in assessing the potential scientific and commercial value of high-risk R&D. If a government program has a rigorous evaluation process, it may provide a certification that the technology is both scientifically sound and promising, and then government funding may provide incentives for further private investment. Lerner (1999) concludes that firms participating in the SBIR program grew significantly faster than a matched set of firms and were more likely to attract subsequent venture capital financing. Feldman and Kelley (2006) find that recipients of a competitively awarded government R&D grant were more likely to receive follow-on funding from the private sector than firms that did not receive an award, even after controlling for an independent assessment of the quality of the project.

Increasingly, government programs are structured as public–private partnerships that attempt to provide incentives for private R&D, facilitate the formation of consortia, and address gaps in the commercialization process (see Link, 2006, for a review). Increasingly, these programs are designed to eliminate the features associated with the government substitution effect through what Trajtenberg (2002) defines as manifest neutrality – the focus is on industry-defined research problems and the development of technology with commercial application as part of the process. The emphasis is on correcting market failures and augmenting the capabilities of private firms. Notable American programs of this type are the Advanced Technology Program, the Manufacturing Extension Partnership, and the Experimental Program to Stimulate Competitive Technology. There has been a good deal of political controversy surrounding these programs associated with the charge of interfering with markets, picking winners, and providing corporate welfare (Malecki, 1997). These criticisms have engendered sophisticated, long-term, and intensive evaluation efforts mandated in the US by the Government Performance and Results Act (GRPA) in 1993, yet there is little consensus on how effective these policies have been (Radin, 1998).

In the absence of a market mechanism to allocate resources, research projects are awarded funding on the basis of a competitive peer review process that is aimed at evaluating quality. One alternative is to consider research as a club good, with a well-defined epistemic community. Interested actors will know each other and act as an interest group to lobby for government funding or as insiders to secure private funding. Swann (2003) concludes that public finance of research through peer review is preferable because a club will not advocate a research program that might destroy its existing technological competence. In an economy with complex inter-sectoral science–technology relationships, an open community with a diverse and fluid set of innovators appears preferable.

Large infrastructure projects may be awarded on a political basis, in what is often referred to as pork barrel. Research allocation on the basis of political cronyism does not achieve either efficiency or equity and creates welfare loss to the economy (Cohen and Noll, 1991). Thus we have one of the paradoxes of government funding: this type of funding can accrue great benefits to society but only when awards are made on the basis of merit, which may be difficult to judge when political interests come to bear. Similar to other public entities, universities are no exception; they are in fact actively involved in this form of funding competition. De Figueiredo and Silverman (2006) find that universities have caught on to the potential of securing funding through alternative means rather than just relying on the merits of scientific peer reviews. Universities increasingly seek Congressional appropriations or earmarked funds through vigorous lobbying efforts, and although this is not a novel approach, empirical evidence suggests that the returns of this type of rent-seeking heavily depend on the political representation of the university, rather than peer-reviewed competitive funding reviews.

Government procurement plays a significant role in technology development as a sophisticated lead user capable of making large purchases that can define product specifications and standards and help to create commercial markets (Edquist, Hommen, and Tsipouri, 2000). Government mission agencies such as the US Department of Defense and Department of Health and Human Services have focused research agendas that develop new products to serve their mandates and in the process create things of commercial interest. For example, many biotechnology advances in trauma care, environmental remediation, and vaccines were developed from the DoD SBIR program and subsequently purchased by the government, only to migrate to general commercial usage (Feldman, 2001b).

Another problem with the market is that economic adjustments are not instantaneous and there are always winners and losers in the wake of the disruptive changes wrought by innovation and technological change. Glaeser (2005) argues that the city of Boston has been able to restructure itself due to the high quality of the local labor force. Increasingly there is a realization that social policy is important to economic development. This is the historical justification for public support for education and is certainly salient in the knowledge economy.

The contribution of more local levels of government

The importance of regional economies, as fundamental units of social life and policymaking, is widely acknowledged in the literature (Storper, 1995, 1997). More recently, the quest to explain the sources of innovation and technological change has shifted the geographic scope of analysis even further down the sub-national scale, and now a substantial body of the literature attempts to emphasize the importance of cities and localities as primary spaces of knowledge and innovation producing sites (Crevoisier, 1999; Scott *et al.*, 2001). A variety of empirical studies demonstrate that innovation and technological change heavily depend on such aspects as creativity (Florida, 2002) or the embeddedness of certain innovative actors in the regional context (Gertler, Wolfe, and Garkut, 2000). The realization that sub-national places compete for investment, migrants, and tourists, as well as media attention (Malecki, 2004), adds to the complexity of innovation and economic development studies, which in turn makes it very difficult for public policymakers to create and implement relevant public policies to assist the innovation process, and subsequently generate economic growth and sustainability in a particular jurisdiction (Tödtling and Trippl, 2005).

As economic growth has become recognized as a local process, sub-national or state science and technology programs have become more prevalent. More local levels of government typically have stronger relationships with the companies and industries located in their jurisdiction (Osborne, 1988; Kingsley and Melkers, 1999). National governments have funded local competitions such as the German BioRegio as a means to encourage local initiatives targeted towards knowledge-based economic development (Dohse, 2000). In turn, local governments also attempt to leverage national technology programs, increasing the chances that firms may submit success-ful applications and provide matching funds with their own budgets (Feldman and Kelley, 2003). State programs also support the commercialization of technologies, especially for startup companies, because entrepreneurship is now understood to be localized with most new startups located in the region where the entrepreneur was previously employed.

State and local government are typically responsible for providing infrastructure, which is funded through property or income taxes. The tradeoff is how tax rates translate into tangible benefits to that firm's value. The empirical literature on variation in state tax rates concerning outcome measures, such as new company formation rates and employment growth, is mixed (see Bartik, 1991, for a review). There is recent empirical evidence that specific state policy instruments such as R&D tax credits are able to induce greater industry investment (Wu, 2005). States are also important providers of infrastructure, which is demonstrated to have positive effects on economic growth (Haughwout, 2002; Nijkamp and Poot, 2004).

State governments in the US are noted to have moved away from an industrial recruitment focus, beginning to institutionalize state science and technology pol-icy and agencies during the 1990s (Plosila, 2004). Increasingly, with the passage of Proposition 71 California's authorized $3 billion for stem cell research, wealthy states, which engage in science policy. Interestingly, the rhetoric of the Proposi-tion 71 discussion focuses on the economic development potential that might result from the investment, indicating a belief that the local area would be able to capture the benefits (Holden, 2004).

THE CONTRIBUTIONS OF THE NONPROFIT SECTOR

The nonprofit sector is a set of institutions and organizations that are neither government nor business. There is no agreement on what to even call this phe-nomenon: the third sector, the independent sector, the philanthropic sector, the voluntary sector, nongovernmental organizations (NGOs), or civil society organ-izations. Typically these organizations have special tax status that recognizes their civic orientation[2]. The only accepted fact is that this is a growing sector of the

---

[2]For example, in the US these organizations are governed by Section 510(c) of the tax code and there are more than 25 subcategories. For example, hospitals and private universities are one type of nonprofit, foundations are another, and professional organizations yet another.

economy that is increasingly important for innovation and technical change, but is not very well understood. As government retrenches, this sector has become more important (Weisbrod, 1997, 1998).

Foundations are one of the most complex components of the nonprofit sector. There are more than 100 000 foundations in the United States (National Center for Charitable Statistics, 2006) Private foundations usually have a single source of funding from an individual, a family, or a business, and use income from investments to make grants to other nonprofit organizations. The Sloan Foundation, The Gates Foundation, and the Robert Wood Johnson Foundation are well known examples of foundations that fund research.

There are a variety of other nonprofit entities to consider. Community foundations pool the resources of many donors and focus their grant-making activities on a particular city or region. The Cleveland Foundation and the New York Community Trust are examples of community foundations. While local governments focus on primary and secondary education, it is increasingly common for local community foundations to fund science and technology projects and focus on economic development and thereby influence local systems of innovation. Government agencies such as the Centers for Disease Control or the National Institutes of Health have established foundations that accept charitable contributions from the public to augment the budget allocations that they receive from Congress. In addition, charities and nonprofit organizations such as the National Cancer Foundation and American Cancer Society raise significant amounts of money that are dedicated to research. Almost $3 billion of health related research grants were awarded by such organizations in 2003 (Foundation Center, 2005). Although these amounts may be relatively small, they can be used as leverage to raise other funds and may focus researchers to look at specific diseases.

There are important implications of these efforts, which suggest a new model for funding science and defining technological opportunity. First, foundations are able to give monies to priorities that their trustees define. They are not subject to the same scrutiny and requirements for peer review employed by government agencies. As a result more radical ideas, such as the case in Judah Folksman's early work on angiogenesis, may move forward (Cooke, 2001). Toepler and Feldman (2003) find that academic scientists use foundation money to explore risky topics, which have been passed over by government agencies, and that foundation funding allows these individuals to advance their ideas to the point where subsequent government funding may be secured. On the more negative side, while democratically-elected governments are accountable to their citizens, the accountability of foundations is to their donors and boards of directors and not subject to the same transparency.

Also relevant for innovation are a series of professional, trade associations and other organizations that promote the business or professional interests of a community, an industry, or a profession generally qualifying for tax-exemption. Although contributions to these organizations are not tax-deductible, membership dues may be deductible as business expenses. These organizations provide a forum for the dissemination of information, an efficient vehicle for enforcing professional standards, and a community of common interests around an industry. They also preserve tacit knowledge, establish standards of practice, and provide a forum for open discussion.

The literature focuses on social capital, and certainly social capital affects human interaction and sense of community, but the network literature focuses on interrelationships and information flow between individuals and does not have much to say about outcomes or individual's motivations for organizing. Perhaps the term civic capital would be more appropriate and could capture the objective that motivates individuals when they engage in activity that has a goal of advancing the public good.

When we think about community we often think locally and define community based on spatial proximity. However, people who have common experiences develop shared meanings, a shared language, and act in their common interest – that is, they exhibit epistemic proximity (Steinmueller, 2000; Breschi and Lissoni, 2001; Boschma, 2005). Certainly these types of relationships and the intensity of them are increasing in the Internet era, and sometimes they form specific innovation communities that are frequently initiated by lead-users rather than private enterprises (von Hippel, 2005).

The Contribution of Universities

Universities are public entities that contribute to technological advance through the production and dissemination of knowledge as well as through the education of students. Salter and Martin (2001) find that the literature describes six ways in which universities influence innovation and technological change:

- increasing the stock of knowledge;
- training skilled graduates;
- creating new instrumentation and methodologies;
- facilitating the formation of problem solving networks;
- increasing the capacity for problem solving;
- creating new firms.

Yet this conceptualization reduces universities to a simple factor of production and ignores the fact that universities have long been places of contemplation and exploration, unfettered inquiry, free expression, and public discourse. Gertler and Vinodrai (2005) argue that universities are a creative force in the economy, foster tolerance and diversity, and create humane capital in the form of people who are better citizens and members of society.

The link between scientific research, technological innovation, and economic growth was demonstrated empirically by Mansfield (1972), Rosenberg (1974), Sveikauskas (1981), and Adams (1990). Sorenson and Fleming (2004) find that science is specifically relevant to complex inventions: public science helps to delineate the search space and increases the efficiency of the invention process.

The historical conceptualization of innovation, the linear model, places universities at the earliest stage of knowledge creation (Rothaermel and Deeds, 2004). Yet, in practice, university research involves a rich mix of scientific discovery, clinical trials, beta testing, and prototype development, and industry linkages to university-based research are demonstrated to be complementary to firms' R&D strategies (Bercovitz and Feldman, 2006). Cohen, Nelson, and Walsh (2002) find that more than one-third of industrial R&D managers use university research as an input. In a survey of R&D managers, Mansfield (1998) found that, in the absence of academic research, approximately 14 % of new product introductions in seven US industries would not have been developed without substantial time delay. Beise and Stahl (1999) arrive at similar results for industrial innovations in Germany. The importance of such linkages varies considerably among industry sectors; generally, however, university-industry partnerships are more important in sectors where science plays a major role as is the case in the biotechnology and information technology fields. The Yale and Carnegie Mellon Surveys of R&D labs have tended to emphasize industry differences, noting that pharmaceutical firms spend the greatest percentage of sales on R&D and tend to use university research disproportionately (Klevorick *et al.*, 1995; Cohen, Nelson, and Walsh, 2002).

Of course, once knowledge is created in universities there is the need to transfer that knowledge to the private sector. The conventional wisdom is that university technology transfer is a contact sport that involves active and ongoing participation (Thursby and Thursby, 2002). Although the traditional norms of open science favor publication, recently, governments have experimented with a variety of mechanisms to provide incentives for academics to become more entrepreneurial and to engage more with industry. Bercovitz and Feldman (2006) argue that promoting technology transfer is a three-step process: first, it requires changes in the legal system clarifying the ownership of academic discoveries; second, organizational changes, such as the establishment of a university technology transfer office, are needed to encourage and support interaction with industry; and finally, individual academics need to change their behavior and adopt new social norms that favor commercial activities. Although universities are frequently seen as the new engines of innovation and economic development (Feller, 1990; Miner *et al.*, 2001), there are many counterfactual examples of prominent research universities that have not been able to succeed at commercial activity, and yet their contribution to innovation is still profound (Feldman and Desrochers, 2004). Basic science and unfettered inquiry provide longer-term benefits to economic welfare and the current focus on more immediate quantitative outcomes forces attention to those metrics. Moreover, one of the most important ways that universities transfer technology is though the education of students and the wide dissemination of research results. There is a larger positive question about what the most appropriate role for universities should be in the economy and whether the current emphasis on partnering with industry may be to the detriment of longer-term economic growth (Nelson, 2001).

THE CONTRIBUTION OF GOVERNMENT LABORATORIES

Government laboratories are considered a key component of most national science and innovation systems (see Crow and Bozeman, 1998, for a review). Established with the goal of advancing science and securing economic and national defense interests, government-owned laboratories may be government-operated or contracted to outside operators (Cox, Gummett, and Barker, 2001).

The engagement of government laboratories with industry has a long-standing history. The foundations for national research institutions were laid out in the

19th and early 20th centuries, especially in the pre- and post-World War Two period when European and North American governments increasingly set up government laboratories to promote large scale R&D programs (Heim, 1988). For example, the National Institute of Standards and Technology (NIST), the United States federal government's first physical science research laboratory, has been collaborating with industry since 1905. Mission oriented assignments, such as the Manhattan Project in the US, or substantial scientific projects, such as the nuclear energy and space programs, which demanded capital expenditures, facilities, and human resources that exceeded the capabilities or resources of private sector research organizations, led to the establishment of many new government-owned laboratories, as well as the expansion of existing ones (Leslie, 1993). In addition to scale, national security issues, in particular those associated with defense-related R&D and mission and regulatory requirements, which demand that agencies such as the Food and Drug Administration carry out a certain amount of R&D to fulfill their mandate and ensure the impartiality and fairness in the market, are other rationales that explain the need for national laboratories (National Science Board, 2006, pp. 4–22). The contribution of government laboratories to innovation and technological progress is widely recognized (Packard Report, 1983). However, despite the magnitude of public funding and the potential impact on economic development, the study of national labs has attracted little academic scrutiny (Jaffe and Lerner, 2001).

More recently national laboratories have been subject to drastic changes in legislation and regulatory framework concerning technology and skill transfers in order to support civilian industry (Rood, 2000). In the US, a series of technology transfer related legislation in the 1980s was enacted to provide better access to federally-funded R&D. In particular the Stevenson-Wydler Technology Innovation Act, which required the installation of technology transfer offices in federal laboratories, and the Federal Technology Transfer Act, which allowed federal and defense laboratory directors to enter into cooperative research and development agreements (CRADAs) with private partners, appear to have contributed considerably to an increase in industrial patents and company-financed R&D (Adams et al., 2003). In addition, the National Cooperative Research Act that eased antitrust criteria for research consortia of companies, led to further cooperative research between the public and private sector. One important example is the SEMANTECH (SEmiconductor MANufacturing TECHnology) consortium initiated in 1986 with the aim of strengthening the US semiconductor industry, which at that time was rapidly losing ground to other national economies (Irwin and Klenow, 1996). This industry–government cooperation is just one instance of how competitive R&D consortia are established, and it is efficient in restructuring an industry that is losing competitiveness (Grindley, Mowery, and Silverman, 1994; Browning, Beyer, and Shetler, 1995).

The political, economic, and technological changes that have occurred over the past few decades have also initiated a reassessment process, which has led to a radical restructuring of the regulatory framework of national laboratories in many countries (Lawton Smith, 1997). This has resulted in an increased level of awareness concerning the technology and skill transfer functions, and their impact on the utilization and exploitation of national scientific and technological resources (Bozeman, 2000).

Some of these interrelated trends and series of events include the end of the Cold War, which consequently resulted in R&D funding cutbacks for military research facilities. The military-industrial complex, which in some countries has been instrumental in the development and advancement of whole industries in the past, had to be reorganized towards the commercial market. This included the application of dual uses for its technologies and the promotion of its products to a multitude of customers rather than only to the Defense Department. Kelley and Watkins (1995) find that the vast majority of defense contractors have dual-use capabilities, making products for commercial (nongovernment) customers as well. Similarly, Kelley and Cook (1998) show that the technical support and information-sharing norms of the defense contractors' network provide a productivity benefit that is captured in the commercial (nongovernment) side of their businesses.

Increased international competition due to globalization is another reason why national science and technology (S&T), and in particular government laboratories, have become the focus of S&T policy initiatives in the past decades (Rood, 2000). High-technology sectors, which are knowledge intensive and complex in their struc-ture, conduct more R&D than traditional industries and pay higher wages. This makes them the driver of the modern economy. Although national laboratories still play a significant role in this economic structure, their role has changed sig-nificantly (Cohen and Noll, 1996). Basic research funding is now often substituted with applied research funding and the commercialization of science becomes the focal point. Rather than undertaking individual research tasks, laboratories are now embedded in a system of collaboration between public and private sector inno-vation systems (Branscomb, 1993). CRADAs are one of several technology-based industry-government collaboration tools available in the US. Other types of collab-oration include patent licensing, technical assistance, materials and other technical standards development, and the use of instrumentation or other equipment. In addition, as federal funding for basic research has decreased, funding for national technology programs, such as technology development funds or technical assistance programs, have been increasing (Rood, 2000).

Different models and institutional practices exist with regards to the extent and application of government laboratories for securing national competitiveness and for supporting industry in various countries. For example, in Germany a distinct network of laboratories has separated basic science, which is carried out in Max Planck Institutes, and applied research, which is conducted at the Fraunhofer Laboratories and is aimed at supporting industry (Keck, 1993).

CONCLUSIONS

What then is the role of public entities? Government provides a system of insti-tutions that regulate the functioning of markets, provide infrastructure, protect property rights, and allow firms to engage in contracts for scarce resources. As emerging economies, such as India and China, embrace capitalism and promote entrepreneurship it will be interesting to see how their institutions and policies evolve. The tensions in the policy tradeoff between efficiency and equity are intensified when there are increasing returns to agglomeration economies. Collectively, state and federal programs can offer a framework of supporting public and private services available to firms for technological innovation and economic development.

As a thought experiment, consider a computer game that simulates innovation. The goal is to find an idea for a new product and take that idea to market. The winner is the player who makes the largest profits – simple enough. Where are public entities in this game? First, government defines the rules of the game, affecting everything from the supply of ideas to the demand for final products, the legal and regulatory frameworks that determine the functioning of market, and the ultimate accountings of what are profits and how these will be allocated. Nonprofit organizations, such as universities, government labs, and research consortia organizations, have a role in determining scientific opportunity and the rate of diffusion of innovation. Public entities, increasingly including philanthropic foundations, may fund research and help create product markets, especially when private efforts fail, as in the case of tropical diseases. Firms may voluntarily join together to form professional organizations that advance their common interests through setting standards, lobbying for resources, or simply disseminating information and best practices. These efforts, either informally in social networks or epistemic communities or more formally, organized as voluntary membership organizations that are afforded a government subsidy through special tax status, provide civic capital that may be defined as public entities. The reality stands in stark contrast to the romantic image of the solo entrepreneur guided by the invisible hand.

The role of public entities in innovation and technological change is certainly significant and important. A large literature evaluates the effect of federal, state, and local government programs in promoting innovation (Georghiou and Roessner, 2000; Klette, Møen, and Griliches, 2000; Roper, Hewitt-Dundas, and Love, 2004). Although rigorous empirical evaluations exist, many evaluations of government programs are politically motivated and funded or conducted internally by the agency that is being analyzed. Many of these efforts provide little more than thinly veiled public relations campaigns or alternatively are part of ideological attacks or campaigns to cut funding.

There are substantial problems evaluating government programs. It takes several years to get a program organized and publicized, evaluate award recipients, and begin to see results. Often programs become identified with one political administration and just as the program is starting to function, another administration may come along with their own signature program. Evaluations of the effect of government programs are subject to the inherent complexity of factors affecting economic growth such as macroeconomic conditions and international trade. It is difficult to find an appropriate control group to provide meaningful comparison (Brown *et al.*, 1995). In addition, the impact of specific programs may not be as important as the array of government macroeconomic, regulatory, and other policies that influence firms' decisions to invest in innovation and new technologies. The larger systemic effects associated with government may overwhelm the specific effects associated with any one government program. Difficulties in evaluating research programs in particular are intensified when we consider public programs because of inter-organizational transfers; lack of the metrics to measure research performance; lack of metrics to identify and measure the spillover from the funded projects; the need to track the long-term impact of government funding; and a selective bias arising from the fact that evaluations are typically conducted *ex post.*

Evaluations of government programs tend to ignore this complex web of funding sources, technology development programs, business assistance services, and incentives available to firms; and we have a limited understanding of how firms combine these different funding sources to develop new technologies (Kingsley and Melkers, 1999). Given the demands of justifying government programs, evaluations understandably focus on the effectiveness of specific agency activities in assisting client firms. However, from a policy perspective this ignores the larger environment of technology programs and services that firms may rely on in their technology and business development. Indeed, there are myriad problems in evaluating government programs because of the long time horizons, the circuitous route that technology takes when it moves from discovery to invention, and the fact that, in the absence of market logic, it is difficult to discern costs and benefits. In addition, this is coupled with the fact that government is typically left doing the tasks in the economy that cannot be privatized. Government research policy focuses on building capacity, augmenting human capital, providing incentives, and lowering risk for the private sector. These outcomes are not directly comparable to the economic productivity models used to evaluate private sector activity.

Yet, we may ask whether the focus on program evaluation may distract us from considering the most substantial contributions of government programs that relate to the unpredictable nature of scientific discovery. Government policies designed around other concerns have had significant impact on innovation in the private sector. For example, large US government defense expenditures are credited with playing a decisive role in the development of the Internet even though this was not their intended outcome (Mowery and Simcoe, 2002). Microwave technology was largely developed through federal funding during the Second World War (Leslie, 1993). The intention was to perfect the radar system to promote national defense. However, the commercial applications were significant and changed the nature of competition in the transportation and communications industries.

There is a need for a new and more contextual, flexible, and nuanced approach to the role of the public entities and the assessment of its impacts. More research is needed on the role of public entities, such as how voluntary membership organizations contribute to technological advance by facilitating networking and the advancement of common goals such as standard setting or by lobbying for collective goods that aid private firms.

REFERENCES

Adams, J.D. (1990). Fundamental stocks of knowledge and productivity growth. *Journal of Political Economy*, 98(4), 673–702.

Adams, J.D, Chiang, E.P., and Jensen, J.L. (2003). The influence of federal laboratory R&D on industrial research. *Review of Economics and Statistics*, 85(4), 1003–20.

Aharonson, B.S., Baum, J.A.C., and Feldman, M.P. (2007). Desperately seeking spillovers? Increasing returns, industrial organization and the location of new entrants in geographic and technological space. *Journal of Industrial and Corporate Change*, 16(1), 89–130.

Albert, M. (1993). *Capitalism against capitalism*. London: Whurr.

Alic, J.A. (1993). Technical knowledge and technology diffusion: new issues for US government policy. *Technology Analysis & Strategic Management*, 5(4), 369–83.

Amable, B., Barré, R., and Boyer, R. (1997). *Les systémes d'innovation a l'ére de la globalization*, Paris: Economica.

Archibald, R.B., and Finifter, D.H. (2000). Evaluation of the Department of Defense Small Business Innovation Research Program and the Fast Track Initiative: a balanced approach. In C.W. Wessner (ed.), *The Small Business Innovation Research Program: an assessment of the Department of Defense Fast Track Initiative*, Washington, DC: National Academy Press, 219–40.

Arrow, K.J. (1962). Economic welfare and the allocation of resources for invention. In R.R. Nelson (ed.), *The Rate and Direction of Inventive Activity*, Princeton, NJ: Princeton University Press, 609–26.

Bartik, T.J. (1991). *Who benefits from state and local economic development policies?* Kalamazoo, MI: Upjohn Institute for Employment Research.

Baumol, W.J. (2002). *The free-market innovation machine: analyzing the growth miracle of capitalism*. Princeton, NJ: Princeton University Press.

Beise, M., and Stahl, H. (1999). Public research and industrial innovations in Germany. *Research Policy*, 28(4), 397–422.

Bercovitz, J., and Feldman, M.P. (2006). Entrepreneurial universities and technology transfer: a conceptual framework for understanding knowledge-based economic development. *Journal of Technology Transfer*, 31(1), 175–88.

Berger, S. (2005). *How we compete: what companies around the world are doing to make it in today's global economy*. New York: Currency Doubleday.

Berman, E.M. (1997). Cooperative research and development agreements. In Y.S. Lee (ed.), *Technology Transfer and Public policy*, Westport, CT: Quorum Books, 159–71.

Boschma, R.A. (2005). Proximity and innovation: a critical assessment. *Regional Studies*, 39(1), 61–74.

Bozeman, B. (2000). Technology transfer and public policy: a review of research and theory. *Research Policy*, 29(4–5), 627–55.

Bozeman, B., and Crow, M. (1991). Technology transfer from U.S. government and university R&D laboratories. *Technovation*, 11(4), 231–46.

Bozeman, B., and Rogers, J. (2002). A churn model of scientific knowledge value: Internet researchers as a knowledge value collective. *Research Policy*, 31(5), 769–94.

Branscomb, L.M. (1993). National laboratories; the search for new missions and structures. In L.M. Branscomb (ed.), *Empowering Technology: Implementing a US Strategy*, Cambridge, MA: MIT.

Braunerhjelm, P., and Feldman, M.P. (eds) (2006). *Cluster genesis: the origins and emergence of technology-based economic development*. Oxford: Oxford University Press.

Breschi, S., and Lissoni, F. (2001). Localised knowledge spillovers vs. innovative milieux: knowledge tacitness reconsidered. *Papers in Regional Science*, 80(3), 255–73.

Breschi, S., and Malerba, F. (1997). Sectoral innovation systems: technological regimes, Schumpeterian dynamics, and spatial boundaries. In C. Edquist (ed.), *Systems of Innovation: Technologies, Institutions and Organizations*, London: Pinter, 130–56.

Brown, M.A., Curlee, T.R., and Elliott S.R. (1995). Evaluating technology innovation programs: the use of comparison groups to identify impacts. *Research Policy*, 24(5), 669–84.

Browning, L.D., Beyer, J.M., and Shetler, J.C. (1995). Building cooperation in a competitive industry: SEMATECH and the semiconductor industry. *Academy of Management Journal*, 38(1), 113–51.

Carlsson, B., and Jacobsson, S. (1997). Diversity creation and technological systems: a technology policy perspective. In C. Edquist (ed.), *Systems of Innovation: Technologies, Institutions and Organizations*, London: Pinter, 266–94.

Cohen, W.M., Nelson, R.R., and Walsh, J.P. (2002). Links and impacts: the influence of public research on industrial R&D. *Management Science*, 48(1), 1–23.

Cohen, L.R., and Noll, R.G. (eds) (1991). *The technology pork barrel*. Washington, DC: Brookings Institution Press.

Cohen, L.R., and Noll R.G. (1996). The future of the national laboratories. *Proceedings of the National Academy of Sciences of the United States of America*, 93(23), 12678–85.

Cooke, P., and Morgan, K. (1998). *The associational economy: firms, regions, and innovation*. Oxford: Oxford University Press.

Cooke, R. (2001). *Dr. Folkman's war: angiogenesis and the struggle to defeat cancer*. New York: Random House.

Cox, D., Gummett, P., and Barker, K. (eds) (2001). *Government laboratories: transition and transformation*. Amsterdam: IOS Press.

Crevoisier, O. (1999). Innovation and the city. In E. Malecki and P. Oinas (eds), *Making Connections: Technological Learning and Regional Economic Change*, Aldershot, UK: Ashgate, 61–78.

Crow, M., and Bozeman, B. (1998). *Limited by design: R&D laboratories in the U.S. national innovation system*. New York: Columbia University Press.

David, P.A., Hall, B.H., and Toole, A.A. (2000). Is public R&D a complement or substitute for private R&D? A review of the econometric evidence., *Research Policy*, 29(4–5), 497–529.

De Figueiredo J.M., and Silverman B.S. (2006). Academic earmarks and the returns to lobbying. *Journal of Law and Economics*, 49(2), 597–625.

De Soto, H. (2000). *The mystery of capital: why capitalism triumphs in the West and fails everywhere else*. New York: Basic Books

Dohse, D. (2000). Technology policy and the regions – the case of the BioRegio contest. *Research Policy*, 29(9), 1111–33.

Edquist, C. (2005). Systems of innovation: perspectives and challenges. In J. Fagerberg, D.C. Mowery, and R.R. Nelson (eds), *The Oxford Handbook of Innovation*, Oxford: Oxford University Press, 181–208.

Edquist, C., Hommen, L., and Tsipouri, L. (eds) (2000). *Public technology procurement and innovation*. Boston, MA: Kluwer Academic.

Edquist, C., and Johnson, B. (1997). Institutions and organizations in systems of organization. In C. Edquist (ed.), *Systems of Innovation: Technologies, Institutions and Organizations*, London: Pinter.

Etzkowitz, H. (2003). Innovation in innovation: the Triple Helix of university-industry-government relations. *Social Science Information*, 42(3), 293–337.

Etzkowitz, H., and Leydesdorff, L. (2000). The dynamics of innovation: from National Systems and 'Mode 2' to a Triple Helix of university-industry-government relations. *Research Policy*, 29(2), 109–23.

Feldman, M.P. (1994). *The geography of innovation*. Boston, MA: Kluwer Academic.

Feldman, M.P. (2001a). The entrepreneurial event revisited: firm formation in a regional context, *Industrial and Corporate Change.* 10(4), 861–91.

Feldman, M.P. (2001b). Role of the Department of Defense in building biotech expertise. In C.W. Wessner (ed.), *The Small Business Innovation Research Program: An Assessment of the Department of Defense Fast Track Initiative,* Washington, DC: National Academy Press, 251–74.

Feldman, M.P., and Bercovitz, J. (2005). Creating a cluster while building a firm: entrepreneurs and the formation of industrial clusters. *Regional Studies,* 39(1), 129–41.

Feldman, M.P., and Desrochers, P. (2004). Truth for its own sake: academic culture and technology transfer at Johns Hopkins University. *Minerva,* 42(2), 105–26.

Feldman, M.P., and Kelley, M.R. (2002). How states augment the capabilities of technology-pioneering firms. *Growth and Change,* 33(2), 173–95.

Feldman, M.P., and Kelley, M.R. (2003). Leveraging research and development: assessing the impact of the U.S. Advanced Technology Program. *Small Business Economics,* 20(2), 153–63

Feldman, M.P., and Kelley, M.R. (2006). The ex ante assessment of knowledge spillovers: government R&D policy, economic incentives and private firm behavior., *Research Policy,* 35, (10), 1509–21.

Feldman, M.P., and Martin, R. (2004). Jurisdictional advantage. In A.B. Jaffe, J. Lerner and S. Stern (eds), *NBER Innovation Policy and the Economy,* Volume 5, Cambridge, MA: MIT Press, 57–85.

Feldman, M.P., and Martin, R. (2005). Constructing jurisdictional advantage. *Research Policy,* 34(8), 1235–49.

Feldman, M.P., and Romanelli, E. (2006). Organizational legacy and the internal dynamics of clusters: the US human bio-therapeutics industry, 1976–2002. In P. Braunerhjelm and M.P. Feldman (eds), *Cluster Genesis: The Origins and Emergence of Technology-based Economic Development,* Oxford: Oxford University Press.

Feller, I. (1990). Universities as engines of R&D-based economic growth: they think they can. *Research Policy,* 19(4), 335–48.

Florida, R. (2002). *The rise of the creative class: and how it's transforming work, leisure, community, and everyday life.* New York: Basic Books.

Forbes.com (2006). *Special Report: Best Places for Business and Careers.* K. Badenhausen (ed.), New York, viewed 28 May 2008, http://www.forbes.com/lists/2006/05/03/06bestplaces_best-places-for-business_land.html.

Foundation Center (2005). *Distribution of Foundations Grants by Subject Category, circa 2003.* The Foundation Center, viewed 10 July 2006, http://foundationcenter.org/findfunders/statistics/pdf/04_fund_sub/2003/10_03.pdf.

Freeman, C. (1987). *Technology policy and economic performance: lessons from Japan.* London: Pinter.

Furman, J., Stiglitz, J.E., Bosworth, B.P., and Radelet S. (1998). Economic crises: evidence and insights from East Asia. *Brookings Papers on Economic Activity,* 2, 1–135.

Georghiou, L., and Roessner, D. (2000). Evaluating technology programs: tools and methods, *Research Policy.* 29(4–5), 657–78.

Gertler, M.S., and Vinodrai T. (2005). Anchors of creativity: how do public universities create competitive and cohesive communities? In F. Iacobucci and C. Tuohy (eds), *Taking Public Universities Seriously,* Toronto: University of Toronto Press, 293–315.

Gertler, M.S., Wolfe, D.A., and Garkut, D. (2000). No place like home? The embeddedness of innovation in a regional economy. *Review of International Political Economy,* 7(4), 688–718.

Gilson, R.J. (1999). The legal infrastructure of high technology industrial districts: Silicon Valley, Route 128, and covenants not to compete. *New York University Law Review,* 74(3), 575–629.

Glaeser, E.L. (2005). Reinventing Boston: 1630–2003. *Journal of Economic Geography,* 5(2), 119–53.

Goldfarb, A. (2006). The (teaching) role of universities in the diffusion of the internet. *International Journal of Industrial Organization*, 24(2), 203–25.

Greenstein, S. (2007). Innovation and the evolution of internet access in the United States. In W. Aspray and P. Ceruzzi (eds), *The Commercialization of the Internet and its Impact on American Business*, Cambridge, MA: MIT Press.

Griliches, Z. (1992). The search for R&D spillovers. *Scandinavian Journal of Economics*, 94, S29–S47.

Griliches, Z. (1995). R&D and productivity: econometric results and measurement issues. In P. Stoneman (ed.), *Handbook of the Economics of Innovation and Technological Change*, Oxford: Blackwell, 52–89.

Grindley, P., Mowery, D.C., and Silverman, B. (1994). SEMATECH and collaborative research: lessons in the design of high-technology consortia. *Journal of Policy Analysis and Management*, 13(4), 723–58.

Grossman, G.M., and Helpman, E. (1992). *Innovation and growth in the global economy*. Cambridge, MA: MIT Press.

Guellec, D., and van Pottelsberghe de la Potterie, B. (2003). The impact of public R&D expenditure on business R&D. *Economics of Innovation and New Technology*, 12(3), 225–43.

Hall, P.A., and Soskice, D.W. (2001). An introduction to varieties of capitalism. In P.A. Hall and D.W. Soskice (eds), *Varieties of Capitalism: The Institutional Foundations of Comparative Advantage*, Oxford: Oxford University Press, 1–68.

Ham, R.M., and Mowery, D.C. (1998). Improving the effectiveness of public-private R&D collaboration: case studies at a US weapons laboratory. *Research Policy*, 26(6), 661–75.

Hauger, J.S. (2004). From best science toward economic development: the evolution of NFS's Experimental Program to Stimulate Competitive Research (EPSCoR). *Economic Development Quarterly*, 18(2), 97–112.

Haughwout, A.F. (2002). Public infrastructure investments, productivity and welfare in fixed geographic areas. *Journal of Public Economics*, 83(3), 405–28.

Heim, C. (1988). Government research establishments, state capacity and distribution of industry policy in Britain. *Regional Studies*, 22(5), 375–86.

Holden, C. (2004). U.S. science policy – California's proposition 71 launches stem cell gold rush, *Science*. 306(5699), p. 1111.

Internet Society (2006). Viewed 10 July 2006, http://www.isoc.org/index.shtml.

Irwin, D.A., and Klenow, P.J. (1996). Sematech: purpose and performance. *Proceedings of the National Academy of Sciences of the United States of America*, 93(23), 12739–42.

Jaffe, A.B, and Lerner, J. (2001). Reinventing public R&D: patent policy and the commercialization of national laboratory technologies. *The Rand Journal of Economics*, 32(1), 167–98.

Jones, C.I. (2002). *Introduction to economic growth*. New York: W.W. Norton.

Kahn R.E. (1994). The role of government in the evolution of the internet. *Communications of the ACM*, 37(8), 15–9.

Keck, O. (1993). The national system for technical innovation in Germany. In R.R. Nelson (ed.), *National Innovation Systems: A Comparative Analysis*, Oxford: Oxford University Press, 115–57.

Kelley, M.R., and Cook C.R. (1998). The institutional context and manufacturing performance: the case of the U.S. defense industrial network. *NBER Working Papers*, 6460, National Bureau of Economic Research, Inc.

Kelley, M.R., and Watkins, T.A. (1995). In from the cold: prospects for conversion of the defense industrial base. *Science*, 268(5210), 525–32.

Kingsley, G., and Melkers, J. (1999). Value mapping social capital outcomes in state research and development programs. *Research Evaluation*, 3(8), 165–75.

Klein, P.G., and Luu, H. (2003). Politics and productivity. *Economic Inquiry*, 41(3), 433–47.

Klette, J., Møen, J., and Griliches, Z. (2000). Do subsidies to commercial R&D reduce market failures? Microeconometric evaluation studies. *Research Policy*, 29(4–5), 471–95.

Klevorick, A.K., Levin, R.C., Nelson, R.R., and Winter, S.G. (1995). On the sources and significance of interindustry differences in technological opportunities. *Research Policy*, 24(2), 185–205.

Langlois, R.N., and Mowery D.C. (1996). The federal government role in the development of the US software industry. In D.C. Mowery (ed.), *The International Computer Software Industry: A Comparative Study of Industry Evolution and Structure*, New York: Oxford University Press, 53–85.

La Porta, R., Lopez-de-Silanes, F., Shleifer, A., and Vishny, R. (1999). The quality of government. *Journal of Law, Economics and Organization*, 15(1), 222–79.

Lawton Smith, H. (1997). Regulatory change and skill transfer: the case of national laboratories in the UK, France and Belgium. *Regional Studies*, 31(1), 41–54.

Leonard-Barton, D. (1995). *Wellsprings of knowledge: building and sustaining the sources of innovation.* Boston, MA: Harvard Business School Press.

Lerner, J. (1999). The government as venture capitalist: the long-run impact of the SBIR Program. *Journal of Business*, 72(3), 285–318.

Leslie, S.W. (1993). *The Cold War and American science: the military-industrial-academic complex at MIT and Stanford.* New York: Columbia University Press, New York.

Link, A.N. (2006). *Public/private partnerships: innovation strategies and policy alternatives.* New York: Springer.

Lipsey, R.G., Bekar, C., and Carlaw, K.I. (1998). What requires explanation. In E. Helpman (ed.), *General Purpose Technologies and Economic Growth*, Cambridge, MA: MIT Press, 15–54.

Locke, J. (1967). *Two treatises of government*, P. Laslett (ed.), Cambridge: Cambridge University Press.

Lundvall, B-Å. (ed.) (1992). *National Innovation Systems: towards a theory of innovation and interactive learning.* London: Pinter.

Lundvall, B-Å., and Borras, S. (2005). Science, technology, and innovation policy. In J. Fagerberg, D.C. Mowery, and R.R. Nelson (eds), *The Oxford Handbook of Innovation*, Oxford: Oxford University Press, 599–631.

Malecki, E. (1997). *Technology and economic development: the dynamics of local, regional and national competitiveness*, 2nd edition. London: Addison Wesley Longman.

Malecki, E. (2004). Jockeying for position: what it means and why it matters to regional development policy when places compete. *Regional Studies*, 38(9), 1101–20.

Mankiw, N.G., Phelps, E.S., and Romer, P.M. (1995). The growth of nations. *Brookings Papers on Economic Activity*, 1, 275–326.

Mansfield, E. (1972). Contribution of R&D to economic growth in the United States. *Science*, 175(4021), 477–86.

Mansfield, E. (1998). Academic research and industrial innovation: an update of empirical findings. *Research Policy*, 26(7–8), 773–76.

Markusen, A. (1991). *The rise of the gunbelt: the military remapping of industrial America.* Oxford: Oxford University Press.

Marshall, A. (1920). *Principles of economics.* London: Macmillan.

Martin, S., and Scott, J.T. (2000). The nature of innovation market failure and the design of public support for private innovation. *Research Policy*, 29(4–5), 437–47.

Masuyama, S., Vanderbrink, D., and Yue C.S. (1997). *Industrial policies in East Asia.* Tokyo: Nornura Research Institute.

Mathews, J.A. (1999). A silicon island of the East: creating a semiconductor industry in Singapore. *California Management Review*, 41(2), 55–78.

McMillan, G.S., and Hamilton, R.D., III (2003). The impact of publicly funded basic research: an integrative extension of Martin and Salter. *IEEE Transactions on Engineering Management*, 50(2), 184–91.

Miner, A.S., Eesley, D.T., Devaughn, M., and Rura-Polley, T. (2001). The magic beanstalk vision: commercializing university inventions and research. In C. Bird Schoonhoven and E. Romanelli (eds), *The Entrepreneurship Dynamic: Origins of Entrepreneurship and the Evolution of Industries*, Stanford, CA: Stanford University Press, 109–146.

Mohnen, P. (1996). R&D externalities and productivity growth. *STI Review*, 18, 39–66.

Mowery, D.C. (1995). The practice of technology policy. In P. Stoneman (ed.), *Handbook of the Economics of Innovation and Technological Change*, Oxford: Blackwell, 513–57.

Mowery D.C., and Simcoe, T. (2002). Is the Internet a US invention? An economic and technological history of computer networking. *Research Policy*, 31(8–9), 1369–87.

National Center for Charitable Statistics (2006). *The Urban Institute, National Center for Charitable Statistics, Business Master File 01/06, NCC Quick Facts*, Washington, DC, (viewed 10 July 2006), http://nccsdataweb.urban.org/NCCS/files/quickFacts.htm.

National Science Board (2006). *Science and engineering indicators 2006*, (two volumes). Arlington, VA: National Science Foundation (volume 1, NSB 06-01; volume 2, NSB 06-01A).

Nelson, R.R. (ed.) (1993). *National Innovation Systems: a comparative analysis*. New York: Oxford University Press.

Nelson, R.R. (2001). Observations on the post-Bayh–Dole rise of patenting at American universities. *Journal of Technology Transfer*, 26(1–2), 13–9.

Nelson, R.R., and Winter, S.G. (1982). *An evolutionary theory of economic change*. Cambridge, MA: Harvard University Press.

Nijkamp, P., and Poot, J. (2004). Meta-analysis of the effect of fiscal policies on long-run growth. *European Journal of Political Economy*, 20(1), 91–124.

North, D.C. (1984). Transaction costs, institutions, and economic history. *Journal of Institutional and Theoretical Economics*, 140(1), 7–17.

North, D.C. (2005). *Understanding the process of economic change*. Princeton, NJ: Princeton University Press.

OECD (2005). *Main science and technology indicators*. Paris: OECD.

Orsenigo, L. (2001). The (failed) development of a biotechnology cluster: the case of Lombardy. *Small Business Economics*, 17(1–2), 77–92.

Osborne, D. (1988). *Laboratories of democracy*. Boston, MA: Harvard Business School Press.

Packard Report (1983). Federal Laboratory Review Panel, *Report of the White House Science Council*. Washington, DC: Office of Science and Technology Policy.

Palmberg, C. (2000). Industrial transformation through public technology procurement? The case of Nokia and the Finnish telecommunications industry. In C. Edquist, L. Hommen, and L. Tsipouri (eds), *Public Technology Procurement and Innovation*, Boston, MA: Kluwer, 167–96.

Plosila, W.H. (2004). State Science- and technology-based economic development policy: history, trends and developments, and future directions. *Economic Development Quarterly*, 18(2), 113–26.

Porter, M.E. (1990). *The competitive advantage of nations*. New York: Free Press.

Pyke, F., Beccattini, G., and Sengenberger, W. (eds) (1990). *Industrial districts and inter-firm co-operation in Italy*. Geneva: International Institute for Labour Studies.

Radin, B.A. (1998). The Government Performance and Results Act (GPRA): hydra-headed monster or flexible management tool? *Public Administration Review*, 58(4), 307–16.

Rogers, J.D., and Kingsley, G. (2004). Denying public value: the role of the public sector in accounts of the development of the internet. *Journal of Public Administration Research and Theory*, 14(3), 371–93.

Romer, P.M. (1990). Endogenous technological change. *Journal of Political Economy*, 98(5), part 2, S71–S102.

Romer, P.M. (1996). Why, indeed, in America? Theory, history, and the origins of modern economic growth. *American Economic Review*, 86(2), 202–6.

Rood, S.A. (2000). *Government laboratory technology transfer*. Aldershot, UK: Ashgate.

Roper, S., Hewitt-Dundas, N., and Love, J.H. (2004). An ex ante evaluation framework for the regional benefits of publicly supported R&D projects. *Research Policy*, 33(3), 487–509.

Rosenberg, N. (1974). Science, innovation and economic growth. *Economic Journal*, 84, 90–108.

Rosenberg, N., and Birdzell, L.E. (1986). *How the West grew rich: the economic transformation of the industrial world*. New York: Basic Books.

Rosenthal, S.S., and Strange, W.C. (2003). Geography, industrial organization, and agglomeration. *The Review of Economics and Statistics*, 85(2), 377–93.

Rothaermel, F., and Deeds, D. (2004). Exploration and exploitation alliances in biotechnology: a system of new product development. *Strategic Management Journal*, 25(3), 201–21.

Salter, A.J., and Martin, B.R. (2001). The economic benefits of publicly funded basic research: a critical review. *Research Policy*, 30(3), 509–32.

Sargent, A.J. (1899). *The economic policy of Colbert*. London: Longmans, Green & Co.

Saxenian, A. (1994). *Regional advantage culture and competition in Silicon Valley and Route 128*. Cambridge, MA: Harvard University Press.

Scherer, F.M., and Harhoff, D. (2000). Technology policy for a world of skew-distributed outcomes. *Research Policy*, 29(4–5), 559–66.

Scotchmer, S. (2004). *Innovation and incentives*. Cambridge, MA: MIT Press.

Scott, A.J. (1988). *New industrial spaces*. London: Pergamon.

Scott, A.J., Agnew, J., Soja, E.W., and Storper, M. (2001). Global city-regions. In A.J. Scott (ed.), *Global City-Regions: Trends, Theory, Policy*, Oxford: Oxford University Press, 11–30.

Smith, A. (1776), (1937), *The wealth of nations*. New York: Random House.

Solow, R.M. (1957). Technical change and the aggregate production function. *Review of Economics and Statistics*, 39(3), 312–20.

Sorenson, O., and Fleming, L. (2004). Science and the diffusion of knowledge. *Research Policy*, 33(10), 1615–34.

Sorenson, O., and Stuart, T.E. (2001). Syndication networks and the spatial distribution of venture capital investments. *American Journal of Sociology*, 106(6), 1546–88.

Steinmueller, W.E. (2000). Will new information and communication technologies improve the 'codification' of knowledge? *Industrial and Corporate Change*, 9(2), 361–76.

Stokes, D.E. (1997). *Pasteur's quadrant: basic science and technological innovation*. Washington, DC: Brookings Institution Press.

Storper, M. (1995). The resurgence of regional economies, ten years later: the region as a nexus of untraded interdependencies. *European Urban and Regional Studies*, 2(3), 191–22.

Storper, M. (1997). *The regional world: territorial development in a global economy*. London: Guilford Press.

Stuart, T.E., and Sorenson, O. (2003). Liquidity events and the geographic distribution of entrepreneurial activity. *Administrative Science Quarterly*, 48(2), 175–201.

Sveikauskas, L. (1981). Technological inputs and multifactor productivity growth. *Review of Economics and Statistics*, 63(2), 275–82.

Swann, P. (2003). Funding basic research: when is public finance preferable to attainable club good solutions? In A. Geuna, A. Salter, and W. Steinmueller (eds), *Science and Innovation: Rethinking the Rationales for Funding and Governance*. Cheltenham, UK: Edward Elgar, 335–59

Temple, J. (1999). The new growth evidence. *Journal of Economic Literature*, 37(1), 112–56.

Thursby, J.G., and Thursby, M.C. (2002). Who is selling the ivory tower? Sources of growth in university licensing. *Management Science*, 48(1), 90–104.

Tödtling, F., and Trippl, M. (2005). One size fits all? Towards a differentiated regional innovation policy approach. *Research Policy*, 34(8), 1203–19.

Toepler, S., and Feldman, M.P. (2003). Philanthropic foundations and the innovation function: evidence from a survey of university researchers. mimeo. George Mason University and University of Toronto.

Trajtenberg, M. (2002). Government support for commercial R&D: lessons from the Israeli experience. In A.B. Jaffe, J. Lerner, and S. Stern (eds), *NBER Innovation Policy and the Economy*, Volume 2, Cambridge, MA: MIT Press, 79–134.

von Hippel, E. (2005). *Democratizing innovation*. Cambridge, MA: MIT Press.

Wallsten, S.J. (2000). The effects of government-industry R&D programs on private R&D: the case of the small business innovation research program. *The RAND Journal of Economics*, 31(1), 82–100.

Weisbrod, B.A. (1997). The future of the nonprofit sector: its entwining with private enterprise and government. *Journal of Policy Analysis and Management*, 16(4), 541–55.

Weisbrod, B.A. (ed.) (1998). *To profit or not to profit: the commercial transformation of the nonprofit sector*. New York: Cambridge University Press.

Westwick, P.J. (2003). *The national labs: science in an American system, 1947–1974*. Cambridge, MA: Harvard University Press.

Wolfe, D.A., and Gertler, M.S. (2006). Local antecedents and trigger events: policy implications of path dependence for cluster formation. In P. Braunerhjelm and M.P. Feldman (eds), *Cluster Genesis: The Origins and Emergence of Technology-based Economic Development*, Oxford: Oxford University Press.

World Economic Forum (2005) *Global competitiveness report 2005–2006*. New York: Palgrave Macmillan.

Wu, Y. (2005). The effects of state R&D tax credits in stimulating private R&D expenditure: a cross-state empirical analysis. *Journal of Policy Analysis and Management*, 24(4), 785–805.

Index

Note: Page numbers in italics refer to tables and figures

Handbook of Technology and Innovation Management. Edited by Scott Shane
© 2008 John Wiley & Sons, Ltd

— regain
— spur or hinder